BRITISH ART TREASURES
FROM RUSSIAN IMPERIAL COLLECTIONS
IN THE HERMITAGE

BRITISH ART TREASURES
FROM RUSSIAN IMPERIAL COLLECTIONS
IN THE HERMITAGE

Edited by Brian Allen and Larissa Dukelskaya

PUBLISHED FOR THE YALE CENTER FOR BRITISH ART
THE TOLEDO MUSEUM OF ART
THE SAINT LOUIS ART MUSEUM
THE STATE HERMITAGE MUSEUM
and the
PAUL MELLON CENTRE FOR STUDIES IN BRITISH ART
by
YALE UNIVERSITY PRESS
NEW HAVEN & LONDON

This catalogue was first published on the occasion of the exhibition
British Art Treasures from Russian Imperial Collections in the Hermitage
organised by the Yale Center for British Art, New Haven, Connecticut

Yale Center for British Art, New Haven, Connecticut
5 October 1996–5 January 1997

The Toledo Museum of Art, Toledo, Ohio
13th February–11 May 1997

The Saint Louis Art Museum, Saint Louis, Missouri
27 June – 7 September 1997

The State Hermitage Museum, St Petersburg, Russian Federation
Winter 1997–1998

This exhibition and its national tour are made possible by Ford Motor Company.

Additional support is provided by a grant from the National Endowment for the Arts,
a Federal Agency, and an indemnity from the Federal Council on the Arts and Humanities

Translated from the Russian by Catherine Phillips

Translated from the English by Marina Maydanyuk, Alexander Chernoglazov,
Elizaveta Renne and Marsha Karp

Editorial Coordinator Robert Williams

Catalogue design by Derek Birdsall RDI

Typeset in Monotype Walbaum at Omnific

Printed in Hong Kong

ISBN   0 300 06946–4 (cloth)

         0 300 06956 –1 (paper)

Library of Congress Catalog Card no. 96–60986

Cover illustration: Joseph Wright of Derby, *Firework Display at the Castel Sant. Angelo in
Rome (La Girandola)*, 1774–5 (cat. 18)

CONTENTS

COMMITTEE OF HONOUR

H.E. Sir John Kerr
The British Ambassador to the United States of America

H.E. Yuli Vorontsov
The Ambassador of the Russian Federation
to the United States of America

Richard C. Levin
President of Yale University

Paul Mellon K.B.E.

Peter J. Pestillo
Executive Vice-President, Corporate Relations
Ford Motor Company

Ford Motor Company is pleased to bring *British Art Treasures from Russian Imperial Collections in the Hermitage* to the United States.

This is the first time that many of these masterpieces of fine and decorative arts have been out of the Hermitage since Catherine the Great and other Russian rulers collected them in the eighteenth and early nineteenth centuries. The arts speak a universal language which transcends national barriers and unifies people in broader understanding. Ford Motor Company, a global manufacturer of automobiles and trucks, wishes to increase this international dialogue through its ongoing support of the arts. We hope that you enjoy this unique collection of British masterpieces which combines many talents and traditions of the past to help global understanding in the future.

Peter J. Pestillo
Executive Vice President, Corporate Relations
Ford Motor Company

THE HERMITAGE AND BRITISH ART

It is generally assumed that the second language of the Russian nobility was unfailingly French. This is not quite the case. A love for the language more than simply a knowledge of English and Britain itself was widespread in Russia at least as early as the reign of Peter the Great, who not only studied shipbuilding in England but also, according to legend, left a daughter behind him. While Tolstoy's novel *War and Peace* opens with French conversation in a Moscow salon, the high-society characters of *Anna Karenina* are more like Englishmen, with their passion for the races, their use of English words and anglicized nicknames. The language spoken by the last Emperor of Russia and his wife in the intimacy of their private apartments was English, and one of the windows of the Winter Palace still bears the inscription, scratched on the glass with a diamond ring: 'Nicky [Nicholas II] looking at the Hussars'.

The higher echelons of Russian society, despite serious conflicts between the two great powers, always included a considerable Anglophile contingent, for whom the British way of life was the ideal. From one such family came Vladimir Nabokov, who was to become a master of sparkling prose in both the Russian and English languages. The cultural links between the two countries were abundant and productive. they have found their incarnation both in larger literary masterpieces and finer details of culture, such as some peculiarities and allusions in Pushkin's *Eugene Onegin*.

I have conducted British guests around the Hermitage many times, and it is always a pleasure to show them – tucked away in different corners of the museum – our remarkable British works of art, now an inalienable part of our culture and history. It was in England that Anna Ioannovna's silver-gilt throne – henceforward to be used by all Russian Emperors – was made. James Cox's mechanical Peacock clock was brought to St Petersburg from England and it still stands, providing entertainment for both adults and children alike in the Pavilion Hall of the Winter Palace. The outstanding examples of English silver, such as the famous Jerningham wine-cooler by Charles Kandler (cat. 60) and the Oranienbaum Service, which now adorn the Armorial Hall and many other rooms, include masterpieces from which copies were taken by the Victoria and Albert Museum in London. Some of the best works of Josiah Wedgwood, including pieces from the celebrated Green Frog service (see cats. 74–93) decorate cases in the different Imperial apartments. The Hermitage also has an extremely rare collection of engraved gems from Britain (see cats. 131–42)

Walking through the Hermitage's Treasury we can admire precious snuffboxes (cats. 121 and 122) and pocket watches (cats. 114–19) made by British craftsmen who in some cases lived in St Petersburg. Many of the museum rooms contain remarkable English table clocks. In the 1812 Gallery, a monument to victory over Napoleon (see Fig. 17), hangs – opposite a portrait of Kutozov and the entrance to the Great Throne Room – a portrait of the Duke of Wellington. The portraits of Russian military leaders were painted by the outstanding English portraitist George Dawe.

The collection of British art in the Hermitage, which forms the basis of this exhibition, is not of great size compared, for instance, with the Dutch, French or Italian departments, but it contains, for example, masterpieces by Wright of Derby, including his superb *Iron Forge* (cat. 19). For Catherine II, Joshua Reynolds painted his *Infant Hercules Strangling the Serpents* (Fig. 36), destined to become not simply one of the stars of our picture gallery, but also a famous symbol of the young Russia, gaining strength and emerging onto a world stage.

The Hermitage collections contain several marvellous canvases by Angelica Kauffman (see fig. 19), one of the first two women to be honoured with membership of the Royal Academy of Arts in London, and enough pieces by the Scottish painter Christina Robertson (see figs. 93–5) to form a separate exhibition, shown in Edinburgh in August–September 1996.

Like Robertson, many British artists worked not only for St Petersburg, but actually in the city itself. Among these was Robert Ker Porter, whose surviving works in St Petersburg include not only large portraits and battle scenes, but also a remarkable album with drawings of ancient Persian monuments. The drawings were made during his famous romantic journey – albeit with the dubious purpose of espionage – from St Petersburg to Persia. The materials he gathered played a vital role in the study of ancient Iranian art and to a certain extent in the significance acquired by Achemaenid and Sassanid monuments in Russian Oriental studies.

All these objects were to exert great influence on the development of Russian art, becoming a characteristic part of what is sometimes called Petersburg culture. We cannot ignore here the significance for Russian culture (and for the development of the Hermitage) of the purchase of a number of famous collections from England – above all the Walpole paintings (see pp. 46–55) and the Lyde-Brown collection of antiquities.

Several centuries of direct Russian acquaintance with English art has led to the mutual enrichment of the two nations. The comparatively few Russian pieces in British collections have also made their small contribution to this process. One symbol of this is the huge Russian malachite vase which survived the terrible fire at Windsor in 1992. Similarly, soldiers rescued George Dawe's paintings from the 1812 Gallery during the fire which in 1837 totally laid waste the Winter Palace.

Art is fragile, and yet it has a magical inner strength in the face of the vicissitudes of fate, continuing to bring pleasure and to inform us of the achievements of our ancestors. This exhibition, the work of British and Russian scholars is just one more example of this and I would like to take this opportunity to offer them my thanks. I hope that visitors to the exhibition will share my sense of gratitude.

Mikhail Piotrovsky
Director, State Hermitage Museum

DIRECTOR'S FOREWORD

It was a stroke of genius to create an exhibition of British art from the State Hermitage Museum in St Petersburg. Such great treasures and so little known beyond a small circle of specialists and the fortunate visitor to the Hermitage deserve a broader international airing. Thus we owe a fundamental debt of gratitude to Professor Mikhail Piotrovsky, director of the State Hermitage Museum, and to Duncan Robinson, director of the Fitzwilliam Museum in Cambridge and former director of the Yale Center for British Art.

As co-curators of the exhibition, Brian Allen and Larissa Dukelskaya took this insight and have turned it into a rich and satisfying exhibition. The memorable image and the distinctive object alike vie for our attention. We thank and congratulate both of them for their great labours and the necessary depths of stamina required to see this major undertaking to a successful conclusion.

International enterprises of this kind depend on patrons with global vision. How fortunate we are to have Ford Motor Company as a generous supporter of this exhibition and its national tour. We are doubly fortunate to have Mabel Brandon, Director of Corporate Programming at Ford Motor Company, as the enthusiastic and sensitive interlocutor between the company and the American art museums participating in this exhibition. Fred Schroeder of Reniscow Schroeder Associates Inc. has given wise and helpful counsel at critical junctures during the organization of the exhibition.

The National Endowment for the Arts, a federal agency, provided early and crucial support to this project, again underscoring the value and importance of this agency.

Many distinguished authorities have contributed to the catalogue, and we thank them on behalf of the common reader and the scholarly community. We are particularly grateful to John Russell for his interest in the exhibition from the beginning and his contribution to the catalogue.

When the Yale Center for British Art was opened in 1977, through the munificence and enterprise of Paul Mellon, part of its brief was to rekindle interest in British art among the art audience of North America. We are thus particularly grateful that The Toledo Museum of Art and The Saint Louis Art Museum, two art museums of the front rank in collections and scholarship, should be our fellow exhibitors of *British Art Treasures from Russian Imperial Collections in the Hermitage*. To their distinguished directors, David Steadman and James Burke respectively, I express my warm appreciation for their participation.

Lastly, an exhibition of this kind places many different kinds of demands on the staff of an institution the size of the Yale Center for British Art. To all my colleagues can I extend a warm sense of gratitude for their wholehearted and enthusiastic participation in the execution of this exhibition.

Patrick McCaughey
Director, Yale Center for British Art

EDITORS' ACKNOWLEDGEMENTS

In planning an exhibition as wide-ranging and ambitious as this we have inevitably incurred debts from sources too numerous to acknowledge in full. We would like to thank all those individuals who have offered assistance over the past two years, but a number merit a special acknowledgement.

Duncan Robinson, former Director of the Yale Center for British Art and now Director of the Fitzwilliam Museum at Cambridge, encouraged this project from its inception, and without his support the exhibition would never have come to fruition. At every stage in the planning Professor Mikhail Piotrovsky, Director of the State Hermitage Museum was unfailingly cooperative, and his whole-hearted enthusiasm for this venture, not to mention his personal charm, has sustained us through some uncertain moments. We would also like to thank his Deputy Director, Dr Vladimir Matveyev, for considerable help with many practical matters.

Our colleagues in St Petersburg, New Haven and London have contributed in numerous ways. At the Hermitage we would especially like to thank Elizaveta Renne, Curator of English and Scandinavian Painting, who played a major part in the project from the outset. We must also thank the many Hermitage curators who either offered advice or contributed to the catalogue with essays or entries on individual objects, and their names are listed separately on page 11.

A special acknowledgement must be made to Professor Anthony Cross of the University of Cambridge, who for thirty years has made the study of Anglo-Russian cultural relations his own and who has contributed two important essays to this catalogue. The essays by the other British scholars have ensured that this is a thoroughly international venture and we thank them for their important contributions.

We can hardly adequately express our gratitude to Catherine Phillips. To describe her as this catalogue's translator would certainly not do justice to the vital role she has played in acting as our go-between from her base in St Petersburg. It is not an exaggeration to state that without her willingness to translate at great speed, to organize photography and to soothe jangling nerves this catalogue might never have been completed in both its English and Russian editions. She was assisted in translating into Russian by Marina Maydanyuk, Alexander Chernoglazov, Masha Karp and Elizaveta Renne.

At the Yale Center for British Art we would like to thank the Director, Patrick McCaughey and many of his colleagues. Constance Clement, Acting-Director at an important point in the exhibition's development, offered much help and encouragement. Beth Miller, Assistant Director for Development was actively involved at every stage. Timothy Goodhue, Registrar, was his usual unflappable and efficient self, and Patrick Noon, Scott Wilcox, Elisabeth Fairman, Theresa Fairbanks, Rick Johnson, Julie Lavorgna and Lorelei Watson all made important contributions. At the Paul Mellon Centre in London, Elizabeth Powis, Kasha Jenkinson, Emma Scrase, Amanda Robinson, Douglas Smith and John Ingamells have all helped.

Numerous other friends and colleagues have helped in various ways, especially Michael Snodin and Richard Edgcumbe at the Victoria & Albert Museum, Antony Griffiths, Keeper of Prints and Drawings at the British Museum, John Nicoll of Yale University Press, and Larry Nichols and Davira Taragin at the Toledo Museum of Art. A special thanks must be made to our editorial coordinator Robert Williams who laboured tirelessly for many weeks. His calmness under pressure and quiet confidence that this catalogue could be produced in an uncomfortably short time was immensely reassuring to us both at difficult moments. Last, but by no means least, we must thank Derek Birdsall, the designer of the catalogue and his colleagues Martin Lee and John Morgan. All worked under considerable pressure to ensure that the catalogue was produced on schedule in this handsome form. It has been a privilege and a pleasure to work with them.

Brian Allen and *Larissa Dukelskaya*
London and St Petersburg, July 1996

CONTRIBUTORS TO THE CATALOGUE

Brian Allen (BA) is Director of Studies, Paul Mellon Centre
for Studies in British Art

Alan Bird is an independent art historian

Anthony Cross is Professor of Slavonic Studies at
Cambridge University

Larissa Dukelskaya (LD) is Curator of English Prints at the
Hermitage

Natalya Gritsay (NG) is Head of the Department of Old Master
Paintings and Curator of Flemish 17th- and 18th-century
Paintings at the Hermitage

Yulia Kagan (YU.K) is Curator of Western European and Russian
Engraved Gems in the Hermitage

Asya Kantor-Gukovskaya (AK-G) is Curator of 19th-century
Western European Drawings at the Hermitage

Yelena Karchova (YE.K) is Curator of German and English Sculpture
at the Hermitage

Miliza Korshunova (MK) is Curator of Western European
Architectural Drawings at the Hermitage

Tatanya Kosaurova (TK) is Curator of Embroideries at the
Hermitage

Olga Kostyuk (OK) is Curator of the Special Collection (Jewelry)
at the Hermitage

Aleksey Larionov (AL) is Curator of North European Drawings at
the Hermitage

Lydia Liackhova (LL) is Curator of English, Scandinavian and
Italian Porcelain and Ceramics at the Hermitage

Marina Lopato (ML) is Head of the Department of Precious
Metals and Stones and Curator of Western European Precious
Metals at the Hermitage

Natalya Mavrodina (NM) is Curator of Coloured Stones at the
Hermitage

Andrew Moore is Keeper of Art at Norwich Castle Museum,
Norwich

Martin Postle is Director of the University of Delaware's
London Programme

Tamara Rappe (TR) is Chief Curator of Western European Art
and Curator of Western European Furniture at the Hermitage

Elizaveta Renne (ER) is Curator of English and Scandinavian
Painting at the Hermitage

Yevgeniya Shchukina (YE.shch.) is Keeper of Russian and Western
European Medals at the Hermitage

TABLE OF HISTORICAL EVENTS
1703–1855

1703 Peter the Great founds St Petersburg

1707 Act of Union between England and Scotland passed

1709 Peter the Great defeats Charles XII of Sweden at Poltava

1713–14 Peace treaties of Utrecht end the War of the Spanish Succession between Britain, her allies and the French

1714 Death of Queen Anne. Accession of George I, Elector of Hanover to the throne of Great Britain and Ireland. Russia overruns Finland

1715 Jacobite rebellion aimed at overthrowing Hanoverian succession in Britain fails

1721 Peace of Nystad. Peter the Great obtains Baltic Provinces from Sweden. Sir Robert Walpole appointed First Lord of the Treasury (Prime Minister)

1722 Russian expansion in the Caspian Provinces of Persia

1724 Treaty of Stockholm between Russia and Sweden. Treaty of Constantinople between Russia and Turkey

1725 Death of Peter the Great. Accession of Catherine I

1727 Death of Catherine I of Russia and George I of England. Succession of Peter II of Russia and George II of England

1730 Death of Peter II and accession of Anna.

1733–35 War of the Polish Succession. French ousted from Poland

1735 Russo-Turkish War begins

1739 War of Jenkins' Ear: Anglo-Spanish naval war. Treaty of Belgrade between Russia and Turkey ends Russo-Turkish War

1740 Death of Anna and accession of Ivan VI. War of the Austrian Succession begins

1741 Ivan VI overthrown and succession of Elizabeth. Russo-Swedish War begins

1742 Fall of Sir Robert Walpole

1743 Russia obtains South Finland from Sweden by Treaty of Abo

1745 Second Jacobite Rebellion begins in Britain (rebels defeated at Culloden in April 1746)

1748 Peace of Aix-la-Chapelle concludes War of Austrian Succession

1756 Seven Years War begins

1757 Russia enters Seven Years War against Prussia. Batttle of Plassey: British vistory over Bengal

1759 Capture of Quebec: British victory over the French in Canada

1760 Death of George II and succession of George III

1762 Peace between Russia and Prussia. Death of Elizabeth and accession and assassination of Peter III. His wife Catherine becomes Empress. Manifesto of the Emancipation of the Russian Nobility, liberating them from compulsory service to the state

1763 Peace of Paris concludes the Seven Years War

1764 Stanlislaus Poniatowski, the protégé of Russia, elected King of Poland

1768 Russian invasion of Poland. Stanislaus Poniatowski forced to sign Polish–Russian Treaty, whereby Russia guaranteed the Polish constitution 'for all time to come'

1770 Turkish fleet defeated at Chesme

1771 Russian completes conquest of the Crimea

1772 First partition of Poland, Russia takes lands east of Dvina and Dnieper

1773 Boston Tea Party. American colonists protest against the East India Company's monopoly of tea exports to America

1774 Russians defeat Turks at Battle of Shumla followed by Treaty of Kuchuk Kainardzhi by which Turkey cedes the Crimea to Russia

1776 Declaration of American Independence

1778 Britain declares War on France

1781 Austro-Russian Alliance against Turkey. Surrender at Yorktown: Franco-American victory over British troops

1783 Peace of Versailles between Britain, France, Spain and USA recognizes independence of American colonies

1787 Catherine II visits the Crimea, where she is joined by Joseph II, Emperor of Austria. Austria and Russia declare war on Turkey

1788 Sweden declares war on Russia

1789 French Revolution begins. Austrian and Russian troops defeat Turks at Focshani and at Rimnik

1790 Treaty of Verala ends Swedish-Russian war, Russia acquiring part of Finland

1792 Russia obtains North Black Sea coast by Treaty of Jassy which ends war with Turkey. Russia invades Poland

1793 Second partition of Poland, Russia taking Lithuania and West Ukraine. Britain enters the war against France

1794 Alliance of St Petersburg of Britain, Russia and Austria against France. Russia suppresses Koscinszko's rising in Warsaw

1795 Third partition of Poland, by which Russia takes the area between Galicia and the River Dvina

1796 Death of Catherine the Great and succession of Emperor Paul. Spain declares war on Britain

1797 Paul I limits Russian peasants' work for their landlords to three days a week and decrees succession to property by strict seniority

1799 Napoleon comes to power in France

1801 Act of Union between England and Ireland comes into force Death of Tsar Paul and succession of Alexander I, who annexes Georgia

1802 Treaty of Amiens ends the French Revolutionary War

1803 Napoleonic War begins

1805 By Treaty of St Petersburg, Britain and Russia agree to form a European League for the liberation of the northern German states. Lord Nelson's victory over French and Spanish fleets at the Battle of Trafalgar. Russia defeated at Austerlitz

1807 Russia defeated at Eylau. Napoleon meets Tsar Alexander and Frederick William II and by Treaty of Tilsit Russia agrees to establishment of Duchy of Warsaw, recognizes confederation of Rhine and agrees to close all ports to British ships. Alexander I agrees to coerce Denmark, Sweden and Portugal into joining alliance against Britain, and is given a free hand in Finland

1808 The Spanish Peninsular War begins

1809 Russia defeats Turkey at Brailoff and subsequently at Silestria

1811 Russians take Bucharest and capture Turkish army

1812 Secret Treaty of Abo by which Sweden agrees to aid Russia. By the Alliance of Orebro Britain joins with Sweden and Russia. Russia defeated at Smolensk and Borodino. Napoleon marches on Moscow only to begin retreat on 19 October

1813 Treaty of Teplitz confirms Reichenbach agreement uniting Russia, Prussia and Austria against France. Napoleon defeated at Leipzig

1814 Congress of Vienna by which Russia made large territorial gains

1815 Napoleon defeated at Battle of Waterloo

1820 Death of George III and accession of Prince Regent as George IV

1825 Death of tsar Alexander I and accession of Nicholas I

1826 St Petersburg Protocol between Britain and Russia supporting complete autonomy for Greece under Turkish suzerainty. Russia declares war against Persia

1827 Russia defeats Persian forces and takes Erivan in Armenia

1829 Treaty of Adrianople ends Russo-Turkish war and Sultan Mahmud II recognizes London protocol that guarantees territory of Greece while tsar Nicholas obtains land south of Caucasus

1830 Greece is declared independent at London Conference under the protection of Russia, Britain and France. Death of George IV and accession of William IV

1832 Great Reform Bill passed through British Parliament, enlarging the franchise and restructuring representation of Parliament

1837 Death of William IV and accession of Victoria

1838 Britain's First Afghan War, to prevent increased influence of Russia, which constitutes a threat to the British position in India

1839 Chartist riots in England

1840 Russia, Britain, Prussia and Austria form Quadruple Alliance in support of Turkey, and by the Treaty of London offer Mehemet Ali Egypt as hereditary possession, and southern Syria for life, provided he gives up Crete and northern Syria. He refuses in the hope of French aid but finally accepts in 1841. Afghan forces surrender to Britain

1842 Second Afghan War ends with British proclamation of victory

1844 Tsar Nicholas I visits London and suggests partition of Ottoman Empire

1846 Austrian and Russian troops occupy Cracow

1847 Poland made a Russian province

1848 Revolutions in Europe

1849 Russian advance into Persia

1852 Russia obtains territory at mouth of River Amur and continues expansion into coastal area of Pacific

1853 Tsar Nicholas I orders occupation of Danubian Principalities. Turkey declares War on Russia. Turkish fleet destroyed by Russia off Sinope

1854 Crimea War begins. Britain and France conclude alliance with Turkey against Russia. British victory over Russia at Alma, Balaclava and Inkerman

1855 Death of tsar Nicholas I. Succeeded by Alexander II. Russia capitulates at Sebastopol

THE ROMANOV DYNASTY

Mikhail Romanov	1613–1645
Alexis	1645–1676
Fyodor III	1676–1682
(Regency of tsarevna Sophia	1682–1689)
(Ivan V, co-tsar 1682–96) Peter I	1682–1725
Catherine I	1725–1727
Peter II	1727–1730
Anna	1730–1740
Ivan VI	1740–1741
Elizabeth	1741–1762
Peter III	1762
Catherine II (the Great)	1762–1796
Paul I	1796–1801
Alexander I	1801–1825
Nicholas I	1825–1855
Alexander II	1855–1881
Alexander III	1881–1894
Nicholas II	1894–1917

BRITISH MONARCHS, 1603–1901

James I	1603–1625
Charles I	1625–1649
Charles II	1660–1685
James II	1685–1688
William III and Mary II	1689–1702
Anne	1702–1714
George I	1714–1727
George II	1727–1760
George III	1760–1820
George IV	1820–1830
William IV	1830–1837
Victoria	1837–1901

INTRODUCTION

John Russell

As every visitor knows, the State Hermitage Museum in St Petersburg is a perpetual astonishment. It is a museum, as its name indicates, but it is also a palace. The coexistence of the two results in a pandemonium of sensations of every kind. Multiplicity mates with abundance, and between them they produce an informational overload that leaves us dazzled and dazed, but none the less eager for more.

The Hermitage is, however, not the kind of museum in which an architect of genius has created sublime spaces that allow the art to speak for itself. For that, we must go to Louis Kahn's Yale Center for British Art in New Haven, where this exhibition originates.

The Hermitage speaks, on the contrary, for a succession of people who bought in bulk, went on to build in bulk, and trusted that all would end happily. There would be great art and vivacious architecture, but there would also be living spaces, ceremonial spaces, spaces for colossal entertainments, and offices that command some of the world's finest metropolitan views.

What we find in the four interconnected buildings that make up the Hermitage is therefore somewhat akin to a tournament in which architecture, decoration, high art and multifarious monuments of antiquity strive with one another to catch and hold our attention. The Hermitage also has an enclosed hanging garden, a theatre (designed in 1785 by Giacomo Quarenghi, and lately put back into full working order), and a church.

Fig. 1: The Winter Palace from the River Neva. Designed by the Italian architect Rastrelli and built in 1754–62, the Palace now houses the State Hermitage Museum. Photo: Brian Allen

First-time visitors who go there in search of what they regard as 'the old Russia' are often astonished to find how many of the state rooms in the Hermitage date essentially from the 1840s and early 1850s, having been rebuilt after the fire of 1837. Nor did the architects concerned with its reconstruction – Stasov, Briullov and Stakenschneider – go in for understatement.

But, this notwithstanding, 'the old Russia' is still very much there in the Hermitage. This is principally due to Peter the Great's fiat that every 'ancient and curious object' that was found in the provinces of Russia should be bought at the Treasury's expense and forwarded for his personal inspection. Within three years (1715–18) 200 gold pieces from the 6th century BC were on their way to St Petersburg from Tobolsk in Siberia. Peter the Great passed them on, one and all, and they are now in the Hermitage.

The variety of the finds reflects the immensity and variety of the terrain to be worked over. In 1912 more than 650 gold objects from the Pereshchepina Treasure were found near Poltava. In 1959 an 8th –9th-century woman's shoe was excavated in Ladoga. And there are untold amazements in the antiquities that were dug up in the Pazyryk Burial Mounds in the High Altai from 1929 onwards. Chestnut-coloured sacrificial horses were found, complete with their harnesses, masks and leather cushions. There were fragments of felt hanging with coloured appliqués from the 5th century BC, and from the same period little figures of swans made from coloured felt and stuffed with deer hair. There is, in short, a huge substructure of old Russian material, and it is the business of the Hermitage to study and preserve it.

There has always been a British presence of one kind or another in St Petersburg. Peter the Great never forgot the London dockyards that he had visited in his youth, and he was always delighted to have news of them. In 1785, an Englishman, Sir Joshua Reynolds, was called on by Catherine the Great to celebrate the greatness of Russia by painting for her an intractable subject of his own choosing – *The Infant Hercules Strangling the Serpents* (fig. 36). Huge and effortful it was too, and the product of more than two years' work. It is likely that with his intense though outwardly decorous eye for beautiful young women, Reynolds had more fun painting its companion in the Hermitage, *Cupid Untying the Zone of Venus* (cat. 13)

Later, when Alexander I wanted to commemorate the 300 and more Russian generals who had driven Napoleon back to France, he commissioned identical-sized portraits of every one of them (cats. 23, 24), together with majestic state portraits of Wellington, Kutuzov and Barclay de Tolly, from an English painter, George Dawe, whom he had happened to meet in Aachen. Dawe proved himself a true foot-soldier of his profession, though not every British visitor goes the full stretch of his achievement in the Hermitage.

There was also a distinctive and miscellaneous British colony in St Petersburg. There was from early on the Trollopean to-and-fro of doctor and clergyman, Embassy secretary and distinguished visitor. There were also many British residents – importers, exporters and shipbuilders, above all – and often they did memorably well. In a fashionable neighbourhood of the city, on the left bank of the river Neva, and just two blocks away from the Admiralty, there was the Angliskaya Naberezhnaya or English Quay. This was a prime location, over which stately houses presided, and the English Church was just around the corner.

By 1830, when mechanics and tradesmen in large numbers had hung up their shingles in the city, British names abounded. This was especially the case with the many skilled craftsmen who had been attracted by the craving for high-level luxuries for which the city was becoming famous.

All this thickened the plot of life in St Petersburg, but it did not promote the interests of British art in the capital. French art in the 18th century had a very effective lobby with a hot-line to the Winter Palace, where every word from Diderot and Baron Grimm was welcome. But although Britain in the 18th century was not short of grandees who doubled as connoisseurs, the marketing of British painting and sculpture abroad was not one of their concerns.

On the other hand, as is made clear in this catalogue, the British presence was very strong in architecture, in town planning, in landscape gardening and in the building of the sturdy, hard-wearing iron bridges that can be found all over St Petersburg. There were also individual feats of almost maniacal fancy, like the Peacock Clock by James Cox (fig. 15), purchased from Potemkin's heirs by Catherine the Great.

The only British artist who might have hoped – had he stayed in Russia – for a regular entrée to the tsar's palace was Alexander Cozens, who was taken to St Petersburg soon after his birth in 1717. At one time he was rumoured to have been a natural son of Peter the Great. His father was in fact a British shipbuilder who did great service to the Russian navy. This can only have recommended him to Peter the Great. The fact that Alexander Cozens's great-nephew became a general in the Russian army would not have done him any harm either.

The full extent of Alexander Cozens's acquaintance with Peter the Great may now never be discovered. But at least one letter from his intimate friend William Beckford, the owner of Fonthill and the author of *Vathek*, may be relevant. Beckford referred to the funeral of Peter the Great in 1725, when Alexander Cozens had 'kissed his pale hand'. He also wrote of 'Your early years, when every month was marked by some great spectacle or splendid feast, when you still retain a memory of the gilded halls and bright lights of a long train of nobles led by the Empress'. This may of course have been no more than flirtatious teasing on Beckford's part.

For the reasons just touched on, neither the size nor the quality of the British contribution to the Hermitage collections can be evident to the casual visitor. This exhibition marks the first time that it has ever been seen together in anything approaching its full variety. There are aspects of the British collections that call for privileged access. A case in point is that of the 200 or so cameos and intaglios that were commissioned by Catherine the Great over a ten-year period from William and Charles Brown (see cats. 13-3, 135-6, 138-42). The brothers Brown were champion achievers in their field, though we must regret that the animal paintings of George Stubbs exist only in this medium (see cat. 133).

Among other examples of British art that normally lead an almost covert existence is the album by Alexander Cozens that is in the present exhibition (cat. 30). Access to this is normally and necessarily by special request only. Kept in seclusion, likewise, are the British mezzotint engravings that, when seen, astound by their freshness. To have lain so quietly for close on 200 years is a rare event; and it has kept their blacks – sumptuous beyond even the dreams of Georges Seurat in his drawings – intact and pristine.

There is also at least one instance of an unpredictable passion for British art. Sergei Shchukin is by now famous the world over for his patronage of Matisse and Picasso. It is thanks above all to him that a visit to the Hermitage is now mandatory for students of their development. Less well known, and not always visible, is an enormous tapestry, which measures eight by twelve feet, which is also from the Shchukin collection. It is after Edward Burne-Jones, on the subject of *The Adoration of the Magi*, and it was executed by William Morris & Co. at Merton Abbey in Surrey. It might seem that Shchukin in making this purchase was completely off track. But the facts are, first, that Picasso in his youth was rather taken with Burne-Jones and, second, that at least one of the figures in the Burne-Jones tapestry is very close to the subject-matter of Picasso's *Two Sisters* of 1902, which is also in the Hermitage.

Finally, it needs to be said that the role of the Hermitage in St Petersburg is to be a city within the city. It offers us almost everything that we can want in a foreign city – except, perhaps, that we can't spend the night there. For generations, and in spite of political pressures of every kind, it has been, in terms of civilization, the first house in Russia. It owes this title to the fact that it is a sophisticated amalgam of scholarship, intellectual hospitality and enlightened connoisseurship. This is part of what the present director, Mikhail Piotrovsky, has in mind when he says that the Hermitage is 'a museum not just for Russia, but for the whole world'.

It also stands for a continuity of feeling that affects everyone who has ever worked there. This was made clear in 1989, when the Hermitage marked its 225th anniversary. There were formal commemorations of every kind, to which dignitaries from all over had been invited. But the then director, Boris Piotrovsky, had also invited every living person who had ever worked in the Hermitage to come along and bring their families to a party that was for them alone. The resulting scene would have delighted Peter the Great, who liked nothing better than a party in which the stuffed shirt had no place. The guests came in their hundreds. Every face was aglow with pride and delight. They knew that the Hermitage was a place unlike anywhere else, and they stood taller for being, or having been, a part of it. They also felt, I think, that the Hermitage had come through our tumultuous century more or less intact.

Fig. 2: The New Hermitage completed to the designs of Leo von Klenze in 1851. Photo: Brian Allen

CULTURAL RELATIONS BETWEEN BRITAIN AND RUSSIA IN THE EIGHTEENTH CENTURY

Anthony Cross

Fig. 3: Sir Godfrey Kneller, *Peter the Great.*
Oil on canvas, 95 × 57 ¼ in. (241.3 × 145.4 cm).
The Royal Collection © Her Majesty Queen
Elizabeth II. Painted during the Tsar's visit to
William III in 1698. Peter stayed at John
Evelyn's house at Deptford.

In one of the very few first-hand British accounts of Russia not only written but also published in the 17th century, Samuel Collins, who was physician to tsar Aleksei Mikhailovich in the 1660s, contemptuously dismissed the Russians as 'wholly devoted to their own ignorance' and look[ing] upon learning as a Monster, and fear[ing] it no less than a Ship of Wildfire'.[1] It was a verdict echoed by John Milton, writing a few years later in his *Brief History of Muscovia* (1682) that the Russians 'have no learning, nor will suffer it to be among them'.[2] Interestingly, however, Milton compiled his work on the basis of 16th-century British sources, pre-eminently Giles Fletcher's *Of the Russe Commonwealth*, first published in 1591 and appearing again in 1643 and 1657. In Fletcher we read: 'As themselves are void of all manner of learning, so are they wary to keep out all means that might bring any in',[3] the 'they' being the clergy and a particular target of British scorn. In 1716, in what was to become one of the most influential and best-known accounts of the new Russia of Peter the Great, John Perry, an engineer recruited into Russian service during the tsar's momentous visit to London in 1698, copied those very words (and many more) from Fletcher and gave them as his own considered opinion.[4] That writers indulged in outrageous plagiarism is not as such the issue; it is rather that frequently by such plagiarism were myths created and perpetuated. The myth of the 'rude and barbarous kingdom' that was Russia, or rather Muscovy, was thus carried into the 18th century and maintained thereafter to the degree that it served both the interests of Britain and its perception of Peter as the great enlightener of a backward country.

From the beginning there were in the judgements of the British about Russia almost inevitable comparisons in favour of British ways and institutions. Fletcher, for example, widening his attack against the Russian clergy to include their 'images [icons] and superstitions', had a Russian confide that 'God had given unto England light today and might give it tomorrow to them'. Perry emphasized at every turn Peter's 'great Affection … of England in general, and what he observed here', his acknowledgement of the excellence of 'the English way of Building' ships, and even his moves to 'reform the Fashion of their Cloaths, according to the English Manner'.[5] As the century wore on and Russia was seen to make strides towards Enlightenment (as the British were prepared to understand it), the element of superiority and condescension never waned. Even when praise was seemingly generously bestowed, it was undercut by British self-satisfaction. Anthony Brough, passionately defending commercial ties with Russia in 1789 at a time of particular political tension between the two countries, did not fail to emphasize Britain's civilizing role: 'There is no nation in the records of history that has so rapidly risen from a state of darkness and barbarism, to a great height of splendour and civilization, as the Russians have done during this century. The causes of this rapid and wonderful change have been many; but I would venture to affirm, that her intercourse with Great-Britain has been the greatest.'[6] In the light of such attitudes it is not difficult to understand that the British generally felt that they had little to learn from Russia, that in terms of culture, science or technical expertise it was essentially a one-way traffic. The Anglomania that was characteristic for many European countries in the 18th century and made its way to Russia only served to bolster British prejudice in this regard; indeed, many contemporary Russians would not have demurred, however differently they might have argued the reasons. Nevertheless, a growing awareness in Britain of Russian potential and attainments in many fields was also to have its cultural dimension, not least in literature.

II

The British literary response to Russia, the emergence of a 'Russian theme' in English literature, goes back to the 16th century, when George Turberville, secretary to Sir Thomas Randolph's embassy in 1568–9, penned three verse epistles in which he outdid even Fletcher in his condemnation of a 'people passing rude to vices vile inclin'd', and Shakespeare responded to visiting Russian embassies with a masque of Muscovites in *Love's Labours Lost*.[7] Mention of things Russian was relatively common in the plays and poems of Elizabethan England, and by the end of the 17th century there had been at least one play (by John Fletcher, nephew of Giles) and one short prose work set in Russia and concerned with the events of the Time of Troubles. The short reign of the False Dimitrii, who had overthrown Boris Godunov, was in fact the theme of the first English work in the 18th century to be devoted to a Russian subject, Mrs Mary Pix's five-act tragedy *The Czar of Muscovy* (1701), but the tsar mentioned in the play's prologue was Peter I.

Peter, greeted on his arrival in London three years earlier by 'A Congratulatory Poem, to the High and Mighty Czar of Muscovy', was to become a hero of epic poetry, tragedy, comedy, and eventually of the novel and of tales for children, at no time near to the reality of his character or his Russia.[8] While enjoying a special relationship with Britain because of his visit, he was always larger than life, the stuff of anecdote and legend. Histories of his reign, even when written by men who had been in his Russia, were virtual hagiographies and, as was suggested earlier, served the aesthetic *chiaroscuro* of an enlightener at battle with the forces of darkness. A handsome knight in shining armour and cape was how he appeared on the full-length portrait painted by Sir Godfrey Kneller at the behest of William III in 1698 (fig. 3).[9] It was an image that Peter himself promoted in Russia, consciously introducing Western ceremonies and symbols to emphasize his break with the past. In Britain, the Petrine cult reached a peak in his lifetime in Aaron Hill's long panegyric *The Northern Star*, published in 1718 and not only appearing in a fifth edition by 1739 but also earning a gold medal for its author from the hero himself.

Hill, in seeking to suggest that Peter was ever anxious to promote 'thy love of art's soft charms',[10] was in line with the British emphasis on the tsar as an enlightener. In May 1714 there had appeared in London a short-lived journal that in its four issues idealized the new Petrine man. The editor-narrator passed on his alleged conversations with one Plescou, 'a Muscovite, who, having enjoyed a noble

Encouragement from his Prince, has employed it in travelling through the most civilized Countries, where he has filled his Mind with the most Valuable Parts of Knowledge, but especially with that of Mankind'.[11] It was, incidentally, in that same year of 1714 that the Royal Society elected to honorary membership one of Peter's closest associates, Prince Aleksandr Menshikov; in communicating the Society's decision, its President, Sir Isaac Newton, mentioned that 'it had for some time become known to the Royal Society that the Tsar, your Emperor, was promoting the arts and sciences in his dominions, and that he was especially assisted by your personal ministration, not only in administering the affairs of war and peace, but also in propagating literature and science'.[12] Before the end of Peter's reign there had appeared in English works attempts to give some detail of what he had accomplished in these areas, although literature, understood as *belles-lettres*, was not high in his list of priorities. Perry, for instance, drew attention to the tsar's establishment of the School of Mathematics and Navigation in Moscow (under a professor from Aberdeen and two graduates from Christ's Hospital whom Peter had recruited in London) and to the new printing-presses and translations of books on useful subjects. Perhaps the most significant publication of these years was *The Present State of Russia* (1722–3), a translation from the German of Friedrich Weber, the Hanoverian Resident in Russia. Weber provided details of advances in Russian cultural life, mentioning the new Assemblies (begun in 1719), new schools and their curricula, the existence of libraries and other collections, and recent translations from European authors; most importantly, he gave the first solid information about the growth of St Petersburg, complete with a plan of the city.

Weber contended that 'at Present Petersburg may with Reason be looked upon as a Wonder of the World, considering its magnificent Palaces, sixty odd thousand Houses, and the short time that was employed in the building of it'.[13] It was a capital city, however, towards the construction and embellishment of which the British made virtually no contribution during Peter's reign or subsequently, although British architects and gardeners were, much later, to work on Imperial estates outside Petersburg. The British whom Peter invited to Russia were pre-eminently naval officers, shipbuilders and all manner of skilled craftsmen and specialists, and the young Russians he dispatched to Britain went to acquire similar skills. When Petersburg was made, first the capital (in 1712), then the trading centre (in 1723) of the empire, it attracted a British community, at the heart of which were merchants of the Russia Company, which was to grow considerably down the century and exert a powerful cultural influence, most noticeably in the reign of Catherine II. St Petersburg was also to fulfil Menshikov's prediction, cited by Weber, that it 'should become another Venice, to see which Foreigners would travel thither purely out of Curiosity'.[14] By the end of the century Russia, and particularly St Petersburg, formed with the Scandinavian countries and Poland part of what became known as the 'Northern Tour', a somewhat exotic variant on the Grand Tour and one which was to attract increasing numbers of British visitors, a few of whom were to

Fig. 4: *Peter the Great*, Frontispiece to John Motley's *History of the Life and Reign of Czar Peter the Great* (1739).

publish travel accounts that spread some knowledge and awareness of Russia among the British public.

III

The cult of Peter in Britain did not end with his death and easily survived the rupture in formal diplomatic links between the two countries that had occurred earlier in 1720 and continued until 1731. During the subsequent reigns of Anna and Elizabeth, there appeared in Britain – and the list is not exhaustive – John Motley's enormously successful *History of the Life and Reign of the Czar Peter the Great* (fig. 4), which attracted 600 subscribers, including members of the royal family, for its first edition in 1739 and followed with a second edition in 1740; John Banks's *History of the Life and Reign of the Czar Peter the Great*, which enjoyed three editions between 1740 and 1755; and W. H. Dilworth's *The Father of His Country; or, The History of the Life and Glorious Exploits of Peter the Great* (1758 and 1760). These were all derivative compilations, yet made greater impact than Alexander Gordon's *History of Peter the Great, Emperor of Russia* (1755) based on the author's own experiences in Russian service but published in distant Aberdeen.

This virtual apotheosis of Peter coincided with a period of improved relations between Britain and Russia, when a momentous first Commercial Agreement (1734), ensuring Britain the status of 'most favoured nation', was signed and there emerged the idea of 'natural allies'. Anna and Elizabeth, however, made little impact on the British imagination and it was above all commercial interests that loomed large in two of the few more general accounts of contemporary Russia to appear. The creation of a Russian Academy of Sciences, opened only after Peter's death and staffed initially with foreign professors, brought more direct contacts with the Royal Society and similar British bodies interested in the sciences, natural history and exploration in particular, but cultural ties were virtually non-existent. Fewer British subjects were entering Russian service, but they included a skilled instrument-maker in Benjamin Scott (d. 1751), who was to work for the Academy, repairing after the fire of 1747 the great globe of Gottorp, acquired by Peter in 1713, and Scott's son, also called Benjamin, who was to produce a number of coins and medals for the Russian mint, including his last known work, a medal commemorating the death of the empress Elizabeth.[15] Even fewer Russians had the opportunity to visit Britain other than as members of the London embassy and church, although the young Antiokh Kantemir (1708–44), poet, philosopher and ambassador between 1732 and 1738, created a very favourable impression at the Court of St James's, was active in literary circles, and became a firm Anglophile. He was, however, never to return to Russia, where it was said of the Empress, not without malice, that she lived out her life 'unaware that Great Britain was an island'.[16] Given the existence of only one newspaper and very few presses, publishing very few books, her subjects also had little access to printed sources to help develop any sense of Britain and its culture. However, the last years of her reign saw the founding of

Moscow University (1755) and of the Academy of Arts in St Petersburg (1757), as well as an unprecedented surge in literary activity in both cities, expressed in salons, journals and book publishing. Four literary journals appeared between 1759 and 1761 and included many translations from English moral weeklies such as *The Spectator*; of only seven translations of English works published in book form in the first five decades of the century (and none translated directly from the original), five appeared after 1757, headed by a famous version (via French) of Alexander Pope's verse *Essay on Man* by the appropriately named Nikolai Popovskii.

IV

It was during these years that the Grand-Duchess Ekaterina Alekseevna turned her attention to the English language. In a letter of March 1757 to her friend and confidant, the British ambassador Sir Charles Hanbury-Williams, she wrote that 'Je commence à comprendre assez l'anglais et je l'étudie trois heures par jour'. Her study of the language never progressed very far, but she was to betray the predilection for the British which she expressed in a further letter on the ambassador's departure from Russia later that year: 'Je regarde la nation anglaise comme celle, dont l'alliance est la plus naturelle et la plus utile à Russie'.[17] Coming to the throne five years later as Catherine II, she was to recognize that for the British, who 'toujours sont marchands',[18] 'the natural' might appear synonymous with 'the commercial', and she was to prove an astute and formidable rival rather than a submissive ally in her negotiations with the British government. Catherine, the German princess on the Russian throne (fig. 5), inherited Peter I's desire to make Russia a great power, to improve and increase both the army and navy and to seek further territorial gains; she followed him in looking to the West, and particularly to Britain, for the expertise and inspiration that would help to make such designs possible. Unlike Peter and her predecessors as empress, she also looked to Britain with admiration for its cultural traditions and achievements. It was an admiration nurtured by her reading of the French *philosophes* and articulated in many ways throughout her reign.

While responsibility for all the manifestations that Anglophilia – or in its more virulent form, Anglomania – produced can scarcely be attributed to the Empress alone, the significance of Imperial example and taste was not to be underestimated, as Jane, Lady Cathcart, writing to a friend in February 1769, clearly recognized: 'Her Majesty was pleased to say something extremely flattering to the nation to me the other night and upon all occasions shews the highest opinion of it, and desires all her people should think the same – and, by the bye, her hint is sufficient for that purpose'.[19] At the same time, the favouring of Britain was not at the exclusion of France or Italy, which remained the most potent cultural influences, except in the significant area of garden design. Britain, nevertheless, created demand by the excellence of what it produced and commanded respect by its institutions and way of life, particularly of its most affluent and distinguished

Fig. 5: Walker after Shibanov, *Catherine the Great*. 15 ¼ × 11 in. (38.8 × 28 cm). Published 1 November 1787. The Trustees of the British Museum.

aristocrats, who provided role models for their Russian counterparts. During Catherine's reign Britain attracted Russians in unprecedented numbers. The aristocracy and gentry, freed from the obligations of state service by a decree of Peter III in 1762, embarked on their versions of the Grand Tour, which frequently included an excursion across the English Channel; and in their number were travellers, such as Nikita Demidov, Princess Catherine Dashkova (fig. 39), Nikolai Karamzin and Petr Makarov, who were to publish before the end of the century the first tourist accounts of Britain, thereby contributing to the spread of its appeal for their fellow countrymen. Britain was also increasingly the destination for young Russians, sent officially to serve, as in Peter's time, in the British navy, but also to observe and practise the famed methods of British agriculture, to attend classes, and in some cases gain degrees at Oxford or Cambridge, Glasgow or Edinburgh, to become apprenticed to leading craftsmen and specialists, and to learn the ways of gardening, engraving, even distilling.[20]

Britain received, but it also exported. Lady Cathcart and her husband, Charles, 9th Baron Cathcart, the British ambassador (fig. 6), had arrived in St Petersburg in August 1768, shortly before Dr Thomas Dimsdale, whose brilliant success in inoculating the Empress and her son against smallpox was not among the least significant factors in her favouring 'Britain, that island of wisdom, courage, and virtue', as it was described at the thanksgiving service for her recovery in December.[21] Cathcart easily added to his role of diplomatic representative activities nowadays associated with the cultural and commercial attachés and gratefully exploited by British manufacturers and craftsmen.

Matthew Boulton of the great manufactory at Soho, Birmingham, whose partner John Fothergill had visited St Petersburg in 1767 to gain a Russian market, was hailing Cathcart the following year as ready 'to promote every usefull and laudable Art and every branch of the Commerce of your Country' and their ormolu in particular.[22] Cathcart was successful in getting the Empress to buy a consignment of vases in 1772. On hearing the order for Boulton's vases, the potter Josiah Wedgwood suggested, however, that 'the Russians must have Etruscan and Grecian Vases about the 19th Century. I fear they will not be ripe for them much sooner, unless our good friend William Hamilton should go Ambassador thither and prepare a hot bed to bring these Northern plants to maturity before their *natural* time'.[23] He had obviously forgotten that Lady Cathcart was in fact Sir William's sister; and she had already had the opportunity of introducing the empress to her brother's *Collection of Etruscan, Greek, and Roman Antiquities* (4 vols, 1767, 1770 and 1776). On 16 January 1769 she wrote to Sir William: *I believe I told you we were repairing & new furnishing these Objects are pretty near accomplished & you will be please to hear that our Dining Room is painted from y^r Etruscan Collection. My lord presided over it himself & the German Artist that Executed it, in Figures as large as the life, has succeeded surprisingly well, you can't think how much my L^d had this at heart. I was much afraid it w^d not succeed, but it really has. The Russian nobility here*

Fig. 6: Sir Joshua Reynolds, *9th Lord Cathcart*, 1753–4. Oil on canvas, 50 × 40 in. (127 × 101.6 cm). © Manchester City Art Galleries.

reported it Charming to the Empress, who will I flatter myself see it herself in the Course of the winter in the Mean while she has the Book. We are unluckily possessed as yet but of one Vol.[24]

Wedgwood himself had reason to be grateful to the Cathcarts, for it was precisely during Cathcart's embassy and with the encouragement of 'our good Patroness', as he called Lady Cathcart, that he began his trade with Russia, initiated by the so-called Husk service, reaching a notable peak with the Green Frog service, but continuing to the end of Catherine's reign, when he was supplying quantities of Jasper ware (see cats. 104–9).[25] Working with a number of British merchant houses, initially Porter & Jackson and later Capper & Co., Wedgwood exported a considerable quantity of his cream ware, which became fashionable among the Russian gentry. The Revd William Coxe, passing into Russia from Poland in 1778, was surprised to find at the posthouse 'English strong beer and no less pleased to see our supper served in dishes of Wedgewood's ware'; a day later, entertained by a gentleman in Smolensk, he noted that 'the table was neatly set out, the dinner excellent, and served up in English cream-coloured ware'.[26]

The commissioning of the Green Frog service (cats. 74–92), broached already in 1770 but finally agreed in 1773 through the Russian consul in London, Alexander Baxter, was a prestige order, one that brought Wedgwood and his partner Bentley little financial profit but enormously enhanced their reputation both in Britain and on the Continent. Wedgwood and Bentley were hard put to assemble enough views for the service and were obliged to commission many new ones, while astutely aiming to flatter past patrons and prospective future ones by arranging for views of their country seats to be represented on the service. A place was inevitably found for a 'View of Shaw Park, Lord Cathcart's country seat in Scotland'. Among the many artists whose work was used was Paul Sandby, who specifically underlined the importance of the Green Frog service for British topographical art, when between 1778 and 1781 he issued his *The Virtuosi's Museum*, comprising 108 plates of views he had drawn throughout Britain: *In the choice of our subjects … we follow an illustrious example. The renowned Empress of Russia … has paid the highest compliment to the genius and taste of this country; by procuring, at an immense expence, views of all the noblemen and gentlemen's seats, and of every delightful spot throughout the kingdom, drawn on the spot, and painted upon setts of china dishes and plates. If these views appear so enchanting in the eyes of this Princess, surely it must afford the highest satisfaction to Britons themselves, to have in their possession complete representations of them on a better plan for preservation, and on much easier terms.*[27]

It is not known whether Catherine herself acquired Sandby's publication, but by the time of its appearance she had gathered more than enough engravings and books of plates for her to have become well acquainted with the views of British castles, monuments, bridges, estates and 'every delightful spot throughout the kingdom'.

It was Longford Castle in Wiltshire, one of 200 or so castles depicted on the Green Frog service, that provided Iurii Felten with the

basic design for the palace on the Petersburg – Tsarskoye Selo road that was to house the service and was initially named Kekerekeksinen (deriving from the Finnish word meaning 'frog marsh') and called by Catherine 'La Grenouillère'. It was the famous garden of Stowe, represented no less than forty-eight times on the service and the subject of some sixteen engravings she acquired in 1776, that she sought above all to re-create or emulate at Tsarskoye Selo. The order for the Green Frog service was made at a time when, as she wrote to Voltaire, 'l'anglomanie domine ma plantomanie', and her enthusiasm for the English landscape garden was channelled into producing (but never publishing) a textbook of 'Principes pour former le jardin dans le goût anglois', based on Latapie's French version of Thomas Whately's influential *Observations on Modern Gardening*.[28] Catherine's book was clearly intended to spread the vogue for the English landscape style among her courtiers, but many of them were travelling on their Grand Tours and were bringing back reports of the gardens and estates they had seen throughout Britain. Some, like Princess Dashkova or Prince Aleksandr Kurakin, were subsequently to spend much time and money on improving their estates far removed from the Peterhof road. An amusing comment from a British gardener, dating from 1780, brings together the new Russian passion for the English garden and Latapie's Whately, which apparently exerted its influence, the non-appearance of Catherine's work notwithstanding: *Till of late Years the Taste of Gardening among the Great was confined to fruits but the Nobles who have been in England are so much tempted with the English pleasure gardens that they are cried up here much more beautiful than perhaps they have appeared to your or my Eye. Mr Whateley's Observations on modern Gardening translated into French perhaps has not a little contributed to this opinion. This has set them all Gardening mad. Any of the Nobility will give £100 per Ann for an English Gardener. I have been applied to for more than one but we few who are already here are not desirous of seeing any more arrive lest one scabby sheep spoil the whole flock.*[29]

The Empress, who never had the opportunity to see for herself the gardens of Great Britain but had the authority and finances, inevitably led the way both in the recruitment of British gardeners and in the dispatch of her own gardeners and architects to Britain 'to observe the art of gardening in the English manner, to take plans and to improve their knowledge by practical experience'.[30]

Catherine turned her attentions to Tsarskoye Selo from the earliest days of her reign, and by the end of the 1760s was instructing Vasiliy Neyelov, who had been employed at the palace since the 1740s, to introduce more natural features in the landscaping of the grounds. She decided, however, that he should also spend some time in England 'in order to visit all the notable gardens and, having seen them, to lay out similar ones here'.[31] After his return in the summer of 1771 Neyelov began to embellish the park at Tsarskoye with a series of impressive pavilions and bridges, including one closely modelled on the famous Palladian bridge at Wilton (figs. 63–4), and to continue landscaping the grounds, but now in collaboration with a newly recruited head gardener, Johann Busch, or John Bush (c. 1730–95), a Hanoverian

Fig. 7: James Walker, *Prince Potemkin Tauride*.
Mezzotint, 15 ¼ × 11 ⅛ (38.8 × 28.2 cm).
Published 1 January 1792.
The Trustees of the British Museum.

Fig. 8: James Meader, *The English Garden at
Peterhof*. Watercolour, 23 ¾ × 16 ⅛ in.
(60.5 × 41 cm). State Hermitage Museum.

Fig. 9: James Meader, *The English Garden at
Peterhof*. Watercolour, 23 ¾ × 16 ³⁄₁₆
(60.3 × 41.1 cm). State Hermitage Museum

who had owned a celebrated nursery garden at Hackney. Bush had
been preceded in Russia by the Scot Charles Sparrow two years
earlier, who was to work at Gatchina, the estate some fifteen miles
south-east of Tsarskoye Selo that Catherine had presented to her
lover Grigorii Orlov soon after she came to the throne (fig. 60). Both
Bush and Sparrow remained in Russia for many years, and by the
time Bush returned to London in 1789 many other British gardeners
were at work on estates in and around the capital and in Moscow.

Within the capital itself, William Gould (1735–1812) who was to be
hailed by Joseph Loudon as the Capability Brown of Russia and by
another British visitor as its Humphry Repton, also worked for an
Imperial favourite, the all-powerful Prince Potemkin (fig. 7), transforming the flat and featureless land surrounding the Taurida Palace
into a landscape garden that impressed even the most blasé of British
tourists.[32] The Palace's Russian architect Ivan Starov and Gould
worked in close harmony; a similar creative collaboration was forged
between James Meader, whom Catherine had invited into her service
in 1779, and the great Italian architect Giacomo Quarenghi, who had
arrived the following year. Meader, who had worked for the Duke of
Northumberland at Syon House near London and was author of *The
Planter's Guide: or, Pleasure Gardener's Companion* (1779), was given
the task of creating for Catherine what became known as the English
Park above and beyond the Baroque palace and formal gardens at
Peter the Great's beloved Peterhof. Meader selected the site on the
west bank of the main lake where Quarenghi was to build his English
Palace. Sadly, World War II left nothing of either park or palace for
posterity, but Meader's letter-book provides a spirited account of his
plans and projects and his watercolours capture something of the
garden's early charm (figs. 8–9).[33] During the same period, a third
such partnership of gardener and architect was established at
Tsarskoye Selo, where Charles Cameron (1746–1812) arrived in 1779
to work with Bush (and soon after married Bush's daughter). The
Palladianism of Quarenghi's English Palace at Peterhof in a landscape garden worthy of Capability Brown was paralleled at Tsarskoye
Selo in Cameron's triumphant Colonnade (in the 19th century known
fittingly as the Cameron Gallery) and in the way it harmoniously
merged with the garden around the Great Pond (fig. 69), much closer
in style and intent to the emblematic gardens of Stowe or Rousham in
England and to which Cameron was to add to the monuments and
bridges already built by Neyelov. It was to be at nearby Pavlovsk,
however, which the Empress had given to her son Paul and his wife,
that Cameron took on from the beginning the roles of both architect
and landscape designer to achieve his most poetic monument, seen at
its best across the River Slavianka (fig. 52).[34]

Cameron was the only British architect invited as such to Russia by
Catherine; but from the ranks of skilled Scottish workmen that he insisted on bringing to Tsarskoye Selo in 1784 in order to produce
building work of a high standard came two men who achieved great
prominence as architects in subsequent reigns. Adam Menelaws
(1749–1831) soon left Cameron to work with Nikolai L'vov
(1751–1803), the remarkable Russian architect, inventor, landscape

Veüe du *PORTIQUE* et du *PONT* attenant le *Parc* des *Daim, dans le* JARDIN-*anglois à* PETERHOFF   1782

Veüe du *CHAUMIERE, et du* PONT à *pierre-petrifie, de là* Cascade; *dans le* Jardin-*anglois à* PETERHOFF   1782

designer and man of letters, on various building projects, including the cathedral at the monastery of Boris and Gleb near Torzhok. Through his association with L'vov, Menelaws became acquainted with members of St Petersburg's leading cultural and intellectual circles, including poets and artists, one of whom, Vasilii Borovikovskii, painted the delightful portrait miniatures of Menelaws and his wife now in the Russian Museum. It was only after the death of L'vov in 1803 that Menelaws embarked on a further 25 years of prodigious independent activity, both as architect and as landscape designer at Tsarskoye Selo and Peterhof.[35] During the same period the most powerful voice in Russian town planning was that of William Hastie (1755–1832), who had worked for six years for Cameron at Tsarskoye Selo but by 1794 so impressed Catherine with an album of architectural drawings that she took him into her service as an architect. At the end of her reign he had become chief architect to the Governor of the Ekaterinoslav and Taurida regions, working on the restoration of the Khan's palace at Bakhchisarai. It was, however, as a designer of iron bridges in St Petersburg that he achieved wide recognition in the first decade of the new century, beginning in 1806 with the Police Bridge on Nevskii Prospekt at the point where it crosses the Moika. His long and illustrious career as town-planner began in 1808, when he was appointed chief architect at Tsarskoye Selo: his plan is still essentially preserved in the central layout of the modern town of Pushkin.[36]

British gardeners and architects made a very positive contribution to the imperial and aristocratic estates around St Petersburg and Moscow; British painters, whom Catherine began to attract into her service in the late 1770s, made considerably less impact.

The handful of British artists known to have worked in Russia arrived from England with little or no reputation, with the exception of Richard Brompton (1734–83), who had been President of The Society of Artists and had painted a number of portraits including one of the Prince of Wales and his brother Prince Frederick and, most notably, of the Earl of Chatham. He was said to have been rescued from a London debtors' prison in 1779 by the intervention of the Empress, while the British ambassador in St Petersburg, Sir James Harris, declared that he had 'got him a good berth, six hundred a year salary, paid bonds for his extraordinary work, & leave to paint *en ville*.'[37] In July 1780 Brompton was officially appointed painter to the Imperial court but lived to enjoy the distinction a mere two and a half years, leaving his widow with considerable new debts and the Empress with a number of portraits of herself and of the young Grand-Dukes Alexander and Constantine. Brompton's best-known painting from these years which delighted the Empress was a heavily allegorical portrayal of the realization of her 'Greek Project', with her little grandsons in the starring roles of a future Alexander the Great, cutting the Gordian knot, and of a Constantine the Great (fig. 23). Better testimony to the skill of a painter whom Jeremy Bentham called 'a harum-scarum ingenious sort of an artist' and evidence of his painting *en ville* are portraits of two members of the aristocracy, Countess A. V. Branitskaia and Prince A. B. Kurakin.[38]

One of Brompton's portraits of Catherine was not from life but a variation on an earlier half-length original by Roslin; an engraving after it by Charles Ruotte, described as 'from an original in Brumpton', appeared in Coxe's *Travels* in 1784 and subsequent editions. A further portrait after Roslin of the Empress was painted by the Scot Edward Francis Cunningham (1742–?95) and is known only by the engraving made by Charles Townley and published in Berlin in 1786. Cunningham, who, like Brompton, was a former pupil of Anton Rafael Mengs, was so much associated with Italy that he was often described as Italian and was better known by the name of Francesco Calze. He seems to have gone to Russia in the suite of the notorious Duchess of Kingston in either 1777 or 1779. Virtually nothing is known of his career in Russia except that supplied by an interesting passage in a letter by the illustrator Daniel Chodowiecki from Berlin, where Cunningham had settled after leaving Russia in 1783: 'I recently saw a family portrait he had begun in Russia and has brought with him to finish here. The figures are full-length, the father, mother, and two children are one third natural size. The drawing is not bad, the composition unremarkable, the colouring untrue and harsh, his hand heavy and rough.'[39]

There is some evidence that Brompton was recommended to the Russian court by Dr Dimsdale; it was certainly Dimsdale who recommended the little-known George Carter (1737–94), who had also exhibited in London at the Royal Academy and the Society of Artists in the 1770s. Carter may well have travelled out to Russia with Brompton but was already on his way back a year later (to paint Dimsdale and his son), with 5,000 roubles and a gold medal from Catherine but apparently still dissatisfied: 'Mr Carter doubtless is convinced of his own merit; but everybody here, even all the english with one voice pronounce him to be more enterprizing, than skillful; and his pencil inferior by many degrees to the Majestic Subject'.[40] His painting of the Empress has not survived, or it remains unidentified in some Russian collection.

If Cunningham and Carter left virtually no trace of their sojourns in Russia, a folder in green morocco, bearing the title 'Voyage de la Crimée fait par Sa Majesté Impériale de Toutes les Russies 1787' and preserved in the Department of Drawings in the Hermitage, is a unique and virtually unknown reminder of an even more shadowy artist. It contains or contained 26 watercolours of places and scenes from Catherine's journey to see her newly acquired territories in 'New Russia', and as such provides an exciting pictorial accompaniment to the official descriptions of the visit and descriptions by participants such as the Prince de Ligne (figs. 10, 11). The first in the series is signed 'Hadfield 1787' and the last 'Hadfield – 1787 St Petersburg'. This is the sole indication of an artist, who, given the lack of any other evidence, might be identified as William Hadfield, the brother of Maria Cosway (*née* Hadfield), who died by the Black Sea sometime before 1810.[41] The watercolours of another British artist did become comparatively widely known through their publication as a series of engravings. Joseph Hearn, who also arrived in Russia in 1787, produced six scenes of St Petersburg that were engraved in

Fig. 11: William Hadfield, *The Baths at Bachessarai*, from an album of drawings entitled 'Voyage de la Crimée'. Watercolour, 23 5/16 × 17 3/8 in. (59.2 × 44.2 cm). State Hermitage Museum.

1789–90 by Thomas Malton in London and were on sale in both capitals (fig. 12).[42] There is, however, no record of Hearn's subsequent work, although he was in Russia through the 1790s. A witness at his wedding in 1793 was James Walker (?1758–after 1823), the best-known British artist working in Russia at the end of the century, but as an engraver not as a painter. It was in engraving that the most significant and productive artistic interchange between the two countries took place.

Walker was appointed Imperial engraver in 1785, the same year as Gavriil Ivanovich Skorodumov (1755–92). During the 1760s the Imperial Academy of Arts sent its outstanding graduates to study architecture, painting, and sculpture in Paris and Rome, but in 1773 Skorodumov and the painter Mikhail Ivanovich Bel'skii (1753–94) were dispatched to London and enrolled for classes in the schools of the recently established Royal Academy, at the same time, incidentally, as Thomas Rowlandson, who is said to have produced a sketch of the young Russians and other students at a life-class. Skorodumov was enthusiastic about the opportunities England offered him, not least the cosmopolitanism of London:

The best engravers are to be found in London, namely F. Bartolozzi in the historical genre, Wollett for landscapes as well as Vivares and several other skilful masters in their field of art whose work is found in every country. In painting Mr Loutherbourg is the best painter of landscape and battle scenes in Europe and Mrs Angelica Kauffmann is an extremely skilled woman in the historical genre. The best English artists are the famous portrait painter Sir Joshua Reynolds, Mr West, Mr Mortimer, N. Dance, and Cipriani. Here the arts flourish and artists are highly esteemed and greatly encouraged.[43]

Fig. 12: Thomas Malton the Elder after Joseph Hearn, *View of the Academy of Arts in St Petersburg from Vasilevskii Island.* Aquatint, 13 ⅜ × 12 ⁹⁄₁₆ in. (34 × 32 cm). State Hermitage Museum.
The English artist Joseph Hearn lived in St Petersburg for several years and drew a series of views of the city. The Academy of Arts, shown here, was built to the designs of architects Vallin de la Motte and Kokorinov in 1764–8.

Skorodumov's own work was to be closely linked with that of Francesco Bartolozzi and Angelica Kauffman. On becoming Bartolozzi's pupil in 1773, Skorodumov learnt from him the art of stipple engraving and followed him by concentrating on Kauffman's work: approximately half of the 50 or so engravings he produced during his nine years in England were after her and included such subjects as *Cupid's Revenge*, *The Discovery of Achilles by Ulysses* (fig. 13), and a series of four plates entitled *Justice*, *Temperance*, *Fortitude* and *Prudence*, which he dedicated to Catherine. Skorodumov became fashionable, particularly with Russian visitors on the Grand Tour such as Princess Dashkova, but it was with some reluctance that he returned to Russia in 1782 to become Keeper of Engravings in the Hermitage and Imperial engraver. His career did

not prosper; he took to drink and finished comparatively little in the last decade of his short life.[44]

Skorodumov did not establish a tradition of Russian artists going to England to study. Bel'skii soon left for Paris, but one of the foremost Russian painters of the time, Anton Ivanovich Losenko (1737–73), and the outstanding sculptor Fedot Ivanovich Shubin (1740–1805) paid brief visits to London in the course of their journeys home from Rome in 1769 and 1773 respectively. It had been in Rome that the Duke of Gloucester had admired Shubin's work and ordered marble copies of the busts of Aleksei and Fedor Orlov;[45] and it is important to stress Rome's importance, rather than London's, as the focus of Anglo-Russian artistic contacts from the 1760s through to the 1780s. It was there that British and Russian artists met, studied, exchanged

Angelica Kauffman, Pinxit.   John Boydell excudit 1782.   Scorodomoff, Sculpsit.

Ulysses *having by Craft discover'd* Achilles, *under his Disguise of a Virgin, among the Daughters of King* Lycomedes, *where he had been secreted in his adult Age by his Mother* Thetis, *to avoid the Fate foretold by the Oracle to attend him at* Troy; *persuades him to go with him and have the Glory of taking that City.* Deidamia, *one of the King's Daughters, being with Child by* Achilles, *puts him in Mind of her Condition.*

From the Original Picture in the Possession of his Excellency Count de Panin.

Size of the Picture   Published, May 1st 1782, by John Boydell, Engraver, in Cheapside London.

views and mingled with the British and Russian tourists who bought, commissioned, and issued invitations.[46]

All the British artists mentioned had spent time in Rome, as had, of course, Charles Cameron, but not Walker, who had been a pupil of Valentine Green in London and had gained a reputation for his portrait plates. In Russia he was contracted to teach the art of mezzotint engraving to a small number of students of his own at the Academy of Arts, of which he became a full Academician in 1794. Two years earlier, he had produced the first set of engravings to be made from paintings the Empress had acquired for her Hermitage gallery: two folders, containing a total of twelve engravings, were published in London as *A Collection of Prints from the Most Celebrated Pictures in the Gallery of Her Imperial Majesty Catherine the Second*. Walker's eminence in Russia, however, was due principally to the quality of his mezzotint engravings after portraits of members of the Russian Imperial family and aristocracy (fig. 79). He was to remain in Russia for seventeen years before returning to England in 1802 with his stepson John Augustus Atkinson (1775–84), whose own talent as a painter had developed over the previous decade. In London in 1803–4 they published *A Picturesque Representation of the Manners, Customs, and Amusements of the Russians*. The 100 coloured etchings are without a doubt the most impressive production by a British artist working in 18th-century Russia and, as vivid and in many respects unique evocations of Russian types, traditions and scenes of everyday life, are far more significant than the better-known work of Le Prince. The artist, however, was not Walker but Atkinson (cat. 51). Walker was responsible for the descriptions accompanying the plates that marked his debut as an author, which he continued at the end of his life by publishing anonymously his *Paramythia; or, Mental Pastimes*. This was a collection of anecdotes mainly dating from his time in Russia and revealing the depth of his admiration for Catherine and her 'bounty and encouragement to living men of talents; not exclusively to those she personally knew, or that visited her empire, but throughout the enlightened world'.[47]

The last anecdote in *Paramythia* is devoted to one such 'man of talents', Sir Joshua Reynolds, from whom Catherine had commissioned a painting on a subject of his choosing, and her somewhat mixed reaction to *The Infant Hercules* on its arrival in 1789 and to the implication that 'her empire was still in its leading strings'.[48] The commission to Reynolds was apparently in response to Lord Carysfort's comment during his visit to the Hermitage in 1785 that the English school was not well represented in the Empress's collection (see pp. 36–45).[49] The observation was essentially true, and pointed to a general lack of Russian response to English painting, reflected perhaps in the advertisements of a London art dealer, bringing with him for sale in the Russian capital in 1788 'an exceptional collection of paintings by the most famous Italian, Netherlands, Dutch, and French artists' but nothing by the British.[50] Catherine, however, did possess a few paintings by British painters, including several contemporary ones. Four huge canvases, depicting the great Russian naval victory over the Turks at Chesme Bay in 1770, were a gift from the London marine artist Richard Paton (1717–91) and had hung in her Hermitage gallery until their transfer in 1779 to the Great Palace at Peterhof (fig. 14).[51] Portraits of George III and of Queen Charlotte by George Dance and of George, Prince of Wales, and his brother Henry Frederick by Benjamin West were received in 1773 and 1778 respectively and placed in the gallery of European royals in the Chesmenskii Palace (figs. 20–22), while the Hermitage received three paintings by Joseph Wright of Derby, beginning with *The Iron Forge* in 1773 and two landscapes in 1779 (cats. 18,19). The

Fig. 13: Gavriil Skorodumov after Angelica Kauffman, *Achilles Discovered by Ulysses*. Stipple engraving, 13 ¹/₁₆ × 15 ⁵/₈ in. (33.2 × 39.6 cm). Published 1 May 1782. The Trustees of the British Museum.

Fig. 14: P. C. Canot after Richard Paton, *The Imperial Russian Fleet commanded by Count Alexis Orlov defeating the Turkish Fleet and obliging it to retire into Chesme Bay on 5 July 1770*. Engraving, 19 ⁷/₈ × 26 ⁷/₈ in. (50.5 × 68.3 cm). The Trustees of the British Museum. Paton's four large canvases depicting the great naval victories over Turkey at Chesme Bay now hang in the Throne Room of the Great Palace at Peterhof.

Fig. 15: The 'Peacock' clock made by the London clockmaker James Cox which now stands in the Pavilion Hall of the State Hermitage Museum. Photo: Brian Allen

year 1779 was also the one in which the Walpole collection arrived from Houghton, which included a few paintings by British artists of an earlier age.

The acquisition of the Walpole collection (see Andrew Moore's essay 'The Houghton Sale') was one of Catherine's most spectacular purchases and evidence of her collectomania in the major key. Her ambassadors and agents throughout Europe were instructed to be on the lookout for collections that would enhance the Hermitage. Britain, itself the home of numerous great collectors and countless cultural kleptomaniacs, was to prove a happy hunting-ground. In 1771 she had purchased the Blackwood collection and in 1779 that of Robert Udny.[52] Her interests were not confined to paintings, however. She was a magpie, but a discriminating one. She declined to purchase a collection of medals formed by Lord Pembroke or a library offered by Lady Diane Beauclerk, but in 1788 she captured the famous collection of classical sculpture formed by Lyde Browne of Wimbledon near London.[53] In 1791 her first piece of contemporary sculpture, a marble bust of her hero Charles James Fox by Joseph Nollekens (cat. 54) was placed in the Hermitage, while a bronze copy was set up between busts of Demosthenes and Cicero in her Colonnade at Tsarskoye Selo, until Fox's sympathies for Revolutionary France and divided Poland soon led her to oust it![54] The Empress indulged her love of 'pierres gravées' by acquiring the collection of the British antiquary James Byres in Rome in 1780 and that of Lord Algernon Percy in 1785, the same year her ambassador in London selected for her the best pieces from the Duchess of Portland's collection.[55] Of much greater significance was her patronage in the 1780s of British masters working in London. In 1782 James Tassie, the Scottish portrait medallionist and reproducer of gemstones (see figs. 119–124, 130–31), dispatched the full range of his work in a specially prepared 200-drawer cabinet, and over the next decade provided many thousand more items, while the gemstone artists William and Charles Brown (from whose work Tassie had included casts) worked almost exclusively to fulfil orders from Catherine during the last decade of her life (see cats. 131–3, 135–6, 138–42).[56]

The Empress was also a great admirer of British horological prowess. Although she – and Potemkin – rejected an elaborate and expensive sidereal clock that Boulton had sent to St Petersburg because 'it did not strike the hours, nor play any tunes',[57] Potemkin was to acquire several pieces by the London watchmaker James Cox, including the exotic 'Peacock' clock (fig. 15), which was originally in the Taurida Palace and is now in the Hermitage, while Catherine appointed Richard Hyman (1737–1818) Imperial watchmaker in 1777. Hyman, incidentally, was to enjoy a long and varied career in Russian service, producing not only exquisite pocket watches (see cat. 116) and table clocks, inventing various machines, which earned him awards from the Russian Academy of Sciences and the Society for the Encouragement of Arts, Manufactures and Commerce in London, but, most conspicuously, creating the standard linear measure (the *arshin*) adopted for the Russian empire in 1807.[58]

Among the cameos of famous historical figures the Browns created for Catherine was one of Shakespeare (see cat. 102). A genuine admiration for Shakespeare and for English literature in general formed part of Catherine's Anglophilia and, indeed, spurred her to emulation. She read and liked novels by Fielding (particularly *Joseph Andrews*), Richardson and Sterne. Sterne's *Tristram Shandy*, which she read first in French and then in a preferred German version, caught her imagination and was mentioned many times in her correspondence over a number of years. She had a passionate love of the theatre. Anxious to improve standards in the Imperial companies, she had sent abroad in 1765 one of her outstanding actors, Ivan Dmitrevskii (1733–1821), 'to see the English and French theatres' and to improve his art by watching David Garrick.[59] She also supported financially a travelling company of English actors in St Petersburg in 1770–72 and was present at performances (in English) of John Home's *Douglas* and Nicholas Rowe's *Jane Shore*, but not, as far as is known, of *Othello* on 7 January 1772, the first performance in any language of a play by Shakespeare in Russia.[60] As playwright, she not only produced a version of Sheridan's *School for Scandal*, but in the 1780s, when she was reading Shakespeare in the German translation by Eschenburg, she wrote 'a free and weak imitation' of *The Merry Wives of Windsor*, in which Falstaff became a frenchified fop by the name of Polkadov, a variant on *Timon of Athens*, and two pageants from Russian history, which she described as 'ces imitations de Schakespeare [qui] sont très commodes, parce que n'étant ni comédies, ni tragédies et n'ayant règles que celle du tact du supportable pour le spectateur'.[61]

The enthusiasm for English literature, characteristic of European Anglomania in general, gained momentum in Russia in the last two decades of the century.[62] *Julius Caesar* and *Richard III* were the only plays by Shakespeare to be published (both in 1787), but Shakespeare was increasingly the name to drop. The English novel enjoyed enormous popularity both through its leading practitioners, among whom Fielding was the most renowned and the most translated, and many lesser-known figures, frequently female, such as Frances Burney, Elizabeth Inchbald and Elizabeth Bonhote. English poetry, of which the Empress made no mention, was greatly admired. Milton and Pope both continued to be much translated, but more in tune with the pre-Romantic mood of the last decades were the songs of Macpherson's mythical bard Ossian, the verse descriptions of nature in James Thomson's *The Seasons* and Graveyard poetry, relished above all in Edward Young's *The Complaint, or Night-Thoughts on Life, Death and Immortality*. Translations from English poetry and prose, particularly from journals and newspapers such as *The Spectator*, were published in a rapidly expanding range of Russian literary journals. At the same time there were relatively few translations made directly from English originals, and when they were it was mostly carried out by Russians who had studied or lived in Britain. The majority of direct translations were of practical books on medical, horticultural or sporting subjects, and Young's *Night-Thoughts* and Sterne's *Sentimental Journey* were exceptions in the field of literature. The perils of the intermediary language, be it

German or, worse, French, were well caught in a typically trenchant denunciation by Edward Daniel Clarke, a Cambridge don travelling in Paul I's Russia: *When a Russian nobleman reads, which is very rare, it is commonly a novel; either some licentious trash in French, or some English romance translated into that language ... when they attempt to translate Tom Jones, the Vicar of Wakefield, or any of those inimitable original pictures of English manners, the effect is ridiculous beyond description. Squire Western becomes a French Philosopher, and Goldsmith's Primrose a* Fleur de Lis.[63]

Russian knowledge of the English language increased significantly during Catherine's reign and a number of grammars and dictionaries were produced to aid the process. The same could not be said of England, where an almost useless *Commercial Dictionary, in the English and Russian Languages* (1800) was the only published evidence of British acknowledgement of a need to study a language that a British ambassador had, purely impressionistically, described as 'concise, nervous, musical and flowing', and would-be scholars were obliged to seek out Jean-Baptiste Charpentier's *Elémens de la langue russe* (1768 and later editions).[64] British awareness of Russian literature and culture was also retarded, but by comparison with the first two-thirds of the century the last decades brought a veritable flood of travel accounts, histories and 'present states', and contributions to journals that contained a fair number of nuggets among the dross.

The British public received very contradictory signals about the state of Russian enlightenment from works published in the first decade of Catherine's reign. An account of a Russian expedition to Siberia and Kamchata convinced the *Critical Review* in 1764 that 'every country is accessible to humanity, arts, and sciences', but within a few years a translation of the abbé Chappe d'Auteroche's *Voyage en Sibérie* (1768) informed the public that the twin oppressors of Russia – climate and despotism – had conspired so successfully that 'not one Russian has appeared in the course of more than sixty years, whose name deserves to be recorded in the history of the Arts and Sciences'.[65] Chappe's book provoked an infuriated Catherine to write a rebuttal that also made its way into English in 1772 as *The Antidote* but without the section in which she gave the names and extolled the achievements of Russian men of letters. It was only in 1784 that British readers were presented with what was to be the fullest and most influential survey of Russian literature and learning to appear in the 18th century. The Revd William Coxe (1747–1828), who had acted as travelling tutor to the young Lord Herbert on a visit to Russia in 1778, devoted the whole of chapter Eight of the second volume of his *Travels in Poland, Russia, Sweden, and Denmark* to 'a review of the lives and works of a few of the most eminent writers, who have contributed to polish and refine the language, and to diffuse a taste for science among their countrymen'.[66] Coxe's work (enlarged after a second visit to Russia in 1784) proved enormously popular and was in its sixth edition by 1803. It encouraged a new awareness of Russian cultural progress and made more familiar the names of certain historians and writers. *The New and General Biographical Dictionary*, for example, included only a biography of Peter I in its first edition of

1761–7; in its second edition of 1784 there were added those of Kantemir, Kheraskov, Khilkov, Lomonosov, Sumarokov, Shcherbatov, Prokopovich, Tatishchev, and Volkov – all extracted from Coxe.

The 'bear-leader' accompanying young aristocratic cubs, as exemplified by Coxe and Clarke, was an increasingly common phenomenon in St Petersburg; more typical representatives of the flourishing British resident community were the chaplain of the English church and the doctor in Russian service, whose interests ranged frequently much wider than the strictly pastoral and medical. The reverends John Glen King (1732–87) and William Tooke (1744–1820) were the chaplains for much of Catherine's reign, while the Scot Dr Matthew Guthrie (1743–1807) served for over 30 years as physician to the Noble Land Cadet Corps. All three (and Coxe as well) were Fellows of the Royal Society and of many other learned bodies in Britain and Russia and testify to the lively scholarly and scientific contacts between the two countries, to the dissemination of information about Russian discoveries, antiquities, geology and natural history through the medium of papers published in *Philosophical Transactions*, *Proceedings* and *Commentaries*. Tooke and Guthrie, and to a lesser extent King, went beyond the confines of the scientific audience in their publishing activity, reaching and informing a more

general public through their contributions to widely read journals and their books.

King's *The Rites and Ceremonies of the Greek Church, in Russia*, published in 1772, became the standard work on doctrine and liturgy until well into the 19th century and revealed the author's erudition – and the continuing British blindness to icons: *Though religion was the cause which called forth such excellency and perfection in painting and sculpture in popish countries, and in all countries where these works were consecrated to the services and the temples of the Deities; yet the same cause has not been so lucky in Russia: on the contrary these are the wretched daubings that can be conceived, some of them notwithstanding are said to be the works of angels.*[67]

Tooke's reputation rested not on original works but, as he would have wished it, on the translation and judicious arrangement of other men's researches. Beginning with *Russia: or, A Compleat Historical Account of All the Nations which Compose that Empire* (1780–83, from the German of Georgi), he produced after his final return from Russia in 1792 a series of weighty compilations, including *The Life of Catharine II* (1798 and many subsequent, enlarged editions) and his influential *View of the Russian Empire, during the Reign of Catharine the Second, and to the Close of the Present Century* (1799). In the course of another of his translations, Tooke produced the first metric versions of Russian poems, albeit via German, to appear in English.[68] Guthrie, too, could claim a similarly modest niche as a translator of the first Russian literary work to appear in English book form – a totally undeserving little allegorical tale by the Empress Catherine herself, *Ivan Czarowitz, or the Rose without Prickles that Stings Not* (1799). Earlier that year it appeared in the literary journal *The Bee*, to which Guthrie, under the pseudonym Arcticus, made some 50 contributions, mostly dealing with Russian history, folklore and ethnography, and he emerged as a significant, if largely unsung, pioneer in the dissemination of information about Russia in Britain.[69]

V

The reign of Catherine had witnessed cultural interchange between Britain and Russia on an unprecedented scale against a background of political tension and confrontation. In the years following her death, through the short reign (1796–1801) of Paul I (fig. 16)and the first half of Alexander I's, political relations went through a rapid sequence of highs and lows, the lows exemplified in Paul's renewal in 1800 of the Armed Neutrality, first instituted by Catherine in 1780, and Alexander's Tilsit treaty with Napoleon in 1807, and the highs, most notably in the euphoria of 1812, the subsequent entry of the Russians into Paris and the visit of Alexander and his suite to London in 1814, when the Russian ambassador wrote of 'l'enthousiasme qu'on a ici pour les Russes; généraux, officiers, soldats, nobles, bourgeois et peuple, tous sont estimés, admirés, et loués'.[70] The Russian theme achieved a new prominence as British poets, dramatists and journalists seized their pens to laud the tsar and his warriors, not least his Cossack general Platov, but timing was all: a grandiose poetic epistle

Son Altesse Imperiale
PAUL PETROVITCH,
GRAND DUC
de Russie, &c&c&c
Dedié a Son Altesse Imperiale
MADAME LA GRANDE DUCHESSE,
Par Son tres Humble et tres Obeissant Serviteur
Published as the Act directs 22.d April 1781

eulogizing Paul, *The Sovereign*, was a disaster when it appeared in 1800, and *The Alexandriad* (1805), subtitled 'an humble attempt to enumerate in rhyme some of those acts which distinguish the reign of the Emperor Alexander', did not anticipate that Austerlitz and Tilsit would be among them.

The ambassador had not included artists and writers among the categories of Russians receiving British acclaim, but efforts were being made to introduce both the names of writers and their works to the Russian public from the beginning of the 19th century, not least those by William Tooke. In 1803–4 there appeared a volume of translations of short stories by Karamzin, the leading contemporary Russian writer, followed by his *Letters of A Russian Traveller*: both works were widely, if not always favourably, reviewed. In 1806 there was published what the translator himself called a 'literary novelty – a Russian tragedy, in a British dress', A. P. Sumarokov's *Demetrius, the Impostor*. In the wake of the Russian euphoria of 1812–14, a former British chaplain in Moscow, Benjamin Bereford, sought to interest British readers in his *The Russian Troubadour, Or a Collection of Ukranian* [sic], *and Other National Melodies* (London, 1816), but it made no impact. The role of 'introducing' Russian poetry was reserved for John Bowring, producing in 1821 and 1823 the two volumes of his *Specimens of the Russian Poets*, which received long and enthusiastic notices in numerous journals from reviewers who had discovered that, 'in a country which, until the days of Peter the Great, had never made its voice heard among the dynasties of Europe, there had grown up, almost with the suddenness of an exhalation, a poetical literature betraying no marks of its barbaric origins; possessing, in fact, the very qualities which are most commonly found associated with a long-established literature'.[71]

Similar discoveries were not, however, forthcoming about Russian painting or sculpture, although in 1801 Prince Hoare, the Secretary for Foreign Correspondence at the Royal Academy, had approached his opposite number in Russia with a view to establishing regular contacts between the two academies, and he published the following year *Extracts from a Correspondence*, which gave details of the Russian Academy's activities.[72] It was, however, only in 1830 that the Russian Academy of Arts was to send its first student since Skorodumov to London, the engraver F. I. Iordan, whose teacher in St Petersburg, N. I. Utkin, had himself been briefly in London in the suite of Alexander I and had met the leading engraver Abraham Raimbach, with whom Iordan was to study.[73]

During the same period British artists enjoyed mixed fortunes in Russia. Walker and Atkinson returned home in 1802, but Walker was to be followed as Imperial engraver by Joseph Saunders (1773–1845). Saunders seems to have arrived in St Petersburg in 1794 and in 1800 became an Academician of the Academy of Arts, submitting two engravings, one of which was after a painting in the Hermitage. He was to make a major contribution to the two volumes of *La Galerie de l'Hermitage* (1805), producing 48 of the 75 engravings after paintings as well as portrait engravings of Catherine II and Alexander I. Saunders created a particular niche for himself as an engraver of

Fig. 16: Gavriil Skorodumov, *Emperor Paul I*. Stipple engraving, 11 ⅝ × 8 ⅝ in. (29.4 × 21.8 cm). The Trustees of the British Museum.

Fig. 17: Edward Hau, *The Gallery of 1812* (The War Gallery). Watercolour, white lead, 17 ¼ × 12 ³⁄₁₆ (43.8 × 31 cm.) 1862. State Hermitage Museum.

Fig. 18: Thomas Wright after George Dawe,
Alexander I. Engraving, 28 5/16 × 18 1/16 in.
(72.5 × 45.8 cm).
The Trustees of the British Museum.

vignettes for literary and scholarly works, as well as of family crests for the Heraldry Office. In 1809 he became Professor of Engraving at the University of Vilnius, but virtually nothing is known of this final period of his life.[74] The only known painter to seek his fortune in Paul's Russia was Edward Miles (1752–1828), whose reputation in Britain was for miniatures after portraits by Reynolds. He found brief favour with the Empress Maria Fyodorovna, who described his talent as 'bien agréable' on seeing his portrait of her eldest daughter, but by 1798 another courtier suggested that 'le peintre Miles va son petit train. Ce n'est pas un grand talent, et nous avons icy Ritt [August-Christian Ritt, another miniaturist] qui vaut mieux que lui'.[75] He nevertheless remained in Russia until about 1807, when he departed for Philadelphia. It was shortly before that time that William Allan (1782–1850) arrived in St Petersburg. He is best known for the studies of Bakshirs and other native peoples of the empire he exhibited in London and Edinburgh in 1815, the year following his return to Britain (see cats. 25, 26).[76] It was, however, George Dawe (1781–1829) who occupied an exceptional position among British artists in Alexander I's Russia. Introduced to the tsar in 1818 at Aachen, he was invited to create the War of 1812 Gallery for the Winter Palace (fig. 17). Over the years 1819–29 Dawe completed 329 portraits of Russian generals as well as full-length studies of Wellington, Barclay de Tolly and Kutuzov, many of which were engraved by his brother Henry (1790–1848) and his brother-in-law Thomas Wright (1792–1849; see fig. 18). It was George Dawe who met and drew Pushkin in 1828 and to whom the poet dedicated his 'Why is your wondrous pencil / Drawing my negroid profile?'.[77]

It was also in 1828 that in his book *St Petersburg* A. B. Granville, an Anglo-Italian doctor who had been employed in Russia, wrote that 'the name of Alexander Pouschkine, the Byron of Russia, is probably familiar to most English readers'.[78] The opposite was true, but Pushkin and his contemporaries knew, really knew, Byron. The Anglomania that is generally considered to have reached a new highpoint during Alexander's reign was sustained above all by a widespread enthusiasm for English literature and culture. While the first years of the century saw the vogue of Ann Radcliffe and the Gothic novel, it was Walter Scott, initially as poet, then as novelist, and Byron who overwhelmed the Russian imagination and were translated and endlessly imitated.

Byron's 'new and polished nation / Whose names lack nothing but pronunciation' had come very near to Britain in the 120 or so years since Peter I had descended on an unsuspecting London; Britain in its turn had also learnt much about its now formidable ally, but in some ways it still had the more to learn.

1. Collins 1671, p 2.

2. Milton 1682, p. 21.

3. Berry and Crummey 1968, p. 214.

4. Perry 1716, p. 209.

5. Berry and Crummey 1968, p. 229; Perry 1716, pp. 164–5, 198.

6. Brough 1789, p. 45.

7. See Cross 1985.

8. See Cross 1996b, pp. 3–10.

9. The well-known engraving by John Smith was from an engraving by Petrus Schenk from an earlier half-length study of Peter that Kneller made in Utrecht in 1697. See Ernst 1965, p. 425. There is also a half-length engraving (1698) by William Faithorne from Kneller's second portrait.

10. Hill 1744, III, p. 186.

11. The *Muscovite*, no. 1 (Wednesday 5 May 1714), p. 1.

12. Original in Latin, quoted in Radovskiy 1961, pp. 6, 8.

13. Weber 1723, I, p. 4.

14. *Ibid.*, p. 190.

15. Sivers 1927, pp. 157–78.

16. Shcherbatov 1969, p. 194.

17. *Perepiska velikoy knyagini Yekateriny Alekseyevny i angliyskogo posla sera Charl'za G. Uill'yamsa 1756 / 1757 gg.* (Moscow, 1909), pp. 332, 339.

18. *Sbornik Imperatorskogo Russkogo istoricheskogo obshchestva*, 19 (St Petersburg, 1876), p. 124.

19. Graham 1927, pp. 12–13.

20. See Cross 1980.

21. Richardson 1784, p. 36.

22. City of Birmingham Reference Libraries, Matthew Boulton Papers, Letter Book E, fol. 236.

23. Finer and Savage 1965, p. 120.

24. Auchindoune, Cawdor, Nairne, Cathcart Papers, Folio I, no. 43, fols. 1v–2.

25. Finer and Savage 1965, pp. 105–6, 144–61, 299–300.

26. Coxe 1802, I, pp. 253–4, 264.

27. Herrmann 1986, p. 47.

28. Besterman 1990, pp. 21–9.

29. Peterburgskoye otdeleniye Arkhiva Rossiyskoy Akademii nauk, Razriad iv, op. 1, delo 999, fols. 27v–28.

30. Arkhiv vneshnei politiki Rossii, Moscow, Fond Londonskaia missiia, op. 36/1, delo 261, fol. 85.

31. *Ibid.*, delo 296, fol. 22.

32. Loudon 1834, p. 265; Porter 1809, p. 58.

33. See Glezer 1979.

34. See Shvidkovskiy 1986, pp. 163–214.

35. On Menelaws, see Andreyev 1977, pp. 58–59; Cross 1991a, pp. 7–19; Shvidkovsky 1992, pp. 36–41.

36. On Hastie, see Korshunova 1974, pp. 14–21; Schmidt 1970, pp. 226–43; Shvidkovsky 1991, pp. 69–78.

37. Herbert 1950, p. 111.

38. *Sbornik Imp. Russkogo istoricheskogo obshchestva*, 23 (1878), p. 206; Sprigge 1968, II, p. 512. See generally, Renne 1987, pp. 56–62.

39. *Briefe Daniel Chodowieki's an Anton Graff* (Berlin and Leipzig, 1921), quoted in Ettinger 1922, p. 25.

40. Barkway House, Barkway, Essex, Dimsdale Collection, A/39.

41. State Hermitage, St Petersburg, Department of Drawings, inv. nos. 3815–39. The only previous mention of the watercolours is by Timofeev 1974, p. 76. See the letter from W. Hadfield to O. Humphry, n.d.; Humphry MSS, Royal Academy, London, HU/2/34.

42. *Sankt-Peterburgskiye vedomosti*, 98 (1790), 1600; Guildhall Library, London, MS II, 192B, fols. 137, 144, 208.

43. Quoted in Trubnikov 1916, p. 81.

44. See in more detail Nekrasova 1954; Komelova 1974, pp. 36–57; Cross 1980, pp. 212–17. Mention should be made here of Filiter Stepanov (?1745–?97), apparently the runaway servant of a Russian aristocrat, who also studied engraving at the Royal Academy, married an English painter, and produced two sons and a daughter who became prolific artists. See Cross 1980, pp. 217–19.

45. Malinovskii 1990, I, p. 91; Lazareva 1965, pp. 24, 26–7.

46. See, for instance, Andreyeva 1991, pp. 9–12.

47. *Paramythia* has been reprinted in Cross 1993; see p. 104. My introduction (pp. 1–25) provides the most detailed account of his and Atkinson's careers in Russia.

48. *Ibid.*, pp. 146–7.

49. Carysfort also conveyed to Reynolds an order from Potemkin, resulting in *The Continence of Scipio*. See Hilles 1970, pp. 267–77.

50. *Sankt-Peterburgskiye vedomosti*, 69 (29 August 1788), p. 1214.

51. The gold medal with which Catherine rewarded Paton is now in the British Museum. See Cross 1986, pp. 31–7.

52. Levinson-Lessing 1986, pp. 87–9, 266–7.

53. Herbert 1950, p. 22; Levinson-Lessing 1986, p. 107; Gorbunova 1974, pp. 460–67.

54. Ilchester 1937, pp. 117–18; Parkinson 1971, p. 78.

55. Fitzlyon 1958, p. 22; *Sbornik Imp. Russkogo istoricheskogo obshchestva*, 23, pp. 328–9, 384, 387, 412; Archive of Prince Vorontsov 1870, 13, p. 102.

56. Kagan 1973b, pp. 82–96; Hartley 1994, pp. 21–4; Etkind 1965b, pp. 421–4; Kagan 1976, pp. 5–18.

57. Goodison 1974, pp. 96–100, 119–23.

58. Dukelskaya 1983, pp. 29–32; Swann 1968, pp. 47–59.

59. Poroshin 1881, p. 383.

60. See Cross 1976, pp. 49–56.

61. *Sbornik Imp. Russkogo istoricheskogo obshchestva*, pp. 383–4. See Cross 1994, pp. 13–19.

62. See, among numerous works by the following author, Levin 1994a; Levin 1994b, pp. 143–67; Levin 1994c, pp. xxv–xxxix.

63. Clarke 1810, I p. 72.

64. *Critical Review*, 17 (February 1764), p. 81.

65. Auteroche 1770, p. 320.

66. Coxe 1784, II, p. 184.

67. King 1772, p. 33.

68. See Cross 1969a, pp. 106–15.

69. See Cross 1969b, pp. 62–76. On Catherine, see Cross 1970, pp. 85–99.

70. Archive of Prince Vorontsov 1880, 17, p. 254.

71. *Edinburgh Review*, 53 (January 1831), pp. 323–4. On the reception of Russian literature in Britain at the beginning of the 19th century, see Cross 1975a, pp. 449–62; Alekseyev 1982.

72. Hoare 1802.

73. 'Zapiski Fyodora Ivanovicha Iordana', *Russkaya starina*, 70 (May 1891), pp. 316–37; (June 1891), pp. 548–57; Verizhnikova 1986, pp. 71–86.

74. Rovinskii 1895, II, pp. 867–78.

75. Archive of Prince Vorontsov 1883, 27, p. 340; 22, p. 77. See on Miles, Foskett 1972, I, pp. 406–7.

76. Krol' 1961b, pp. 389–92.

77. Glinka and Pomarnatskiy 1963в, pp. 9–10, 82–3.

78. Granville 1828, II, p. 244.

BRITISH PAINTINGS IN THE HERMITAGE
AND CATHERINE THE GREAT

Larissa Dukelskaya

Russian interest in British painting did not begin until Catherine II's reign (1762–96). It was at this time that the most important paintings and examples of applied art were acquired, that the basis for the Hermitage prints collection was laid, that the palaces, garden temples and other works by British (mainly Scottish) architects were built, and that English-style landscape gardens and parks were made. Anglomania is perhaps too strong a word to apply to the late 18th century in Russia, but British culture was increasingly attracting Russian interest, and it was in this context that British paintings, almost unknown even to the most informed Russian collectors before this, began to be acquired. Catherine collected fast and furiously, and works by British artists had a special place in her acquisitions both for the Hermitage and for the royal palaces near St Petersburg. These works lie somewhat outside the main areas of collecting, occupying a relatively modest place in the vast museum. Indeed, an unrepresentative selection of British art from the 16th century to the 18th is characteristic of most European museums even today, for British art was long without recognition on the Continent and not generally sought after. The famous collections acquired for the Hermitage in the second half of the 18th century from sources in Berlin, Paris, Vienna and Geneva contained no British paintings, and Russia was to be one of the few countries, if not the only one, in the 18th century to acquire works by contemporary British painters.

In 1773 Catherine ordered the purchase of *The Iron Forge Viewed from Without* (cat. 19) by Joseph Wright of Derby, at that time an almost unknown artist on the Continent. On 12 February 1774 Wright informed his brother that 'the Empress of Russia has taken ye picture of the Iron Forge'.[1] Wright's was the first identifiably British picture acquired for the Hermitage collection, for the *Ordeal by Fire* (cat. 5) by Sir Peter Lely that entered the museum sometime between 1763 and 1783 was for many years attributed to the Italian Giovanni Antonio Lellio. In 1779 a pair of large works by Wright was purchased, the *Firework Display at the Castel S. Angelo (La Girandola)* (cat. 18) and *An Eruption of Mt Vesuvius with the Procession of St Januarius's Head* (Pushkin Museum of Fine Arts, Moscow). 'It is astonishing', wrote the leading modern scholar of the artist's work, Benedict Nicolson, 'to consider that the only ripple Wright ever stirred up on the European continent was in remote St Petersburg, before he was forty and before he had achieved comparable success in his own country town'.[2]

But we should note that Catherine was far from indifferent to the works she was offered by contemporary artists. She turned down Wright's *Hermit Studying Anatomy* and she also rejected the suggestion by her sculptor Etienne Falconet that she invite Philippe de Loutherbourg to Russia: 'M. Loutherbourg … m'écrit de Londres et me prie de recommander son talent à Votre Majesté Impériale. Il peint les batailles, les marines, les paysages, et il desire beaucoup d'être honoré de quelques ouvrages pour Votre Majesté', wrote Falconet to Catherine on 2 December 1773.[3] This was followed (7 December) by a reply in the negative: 'A vous dire la vérité, je ne me soucie point des ouvrages de Loutherbourg ci cette fantasie me prend, je lui en ferais parler par mon ministre à Londres'.[4]

Among the first paintings to find their way into Catherine's possession was a work by Angelica Kauffman, one of only two women accorded the honour of founder-membership (1768) of the Royal Academy of Arts in London. It was presented to the Empress by Princess Dashkova on her return to St Petersburg after her first trip abroad (1769–72), during which she visited England. As she recalls in her diaries: 'Major-General Prince Potemkin arrived from the army telling of a complete victory over the Turks and of their agreement to the conclusion of a peace …. Due to my illness I was unable to congratulate the Empress personally on this most excellent victory of Russian arms, but I wrote to her and sent a wondrous picture by Angelica Kauffmann depicting a beauteous Greek woman …. The work of this wonderful artist and charming woman was not yet known in Russia. The picture gave her Majesty great pleasure.'[5] The gift was probably made in 1774 (Potemkin returned to St Petersburg on 4 February), the year of the conclusion of the Treaty of Kuchuk-Kainardji with Turkey.

Between 1785 and 1797 Kauffman's '*Greek Woman*' (untraced) was joined by three small works by her, *The Parting of Abelard and Heloise*, inspired by Alexander Pope's poem 'Eloisa to Abelard', and two linked with Laurence Sterne's *A Sentimental Journey through France and Italy* (1768): *A Monk at Calais* and *Mad Maria* (all in the Hermitage).[6] These works, sensitive responses to Sterne's chapters on 'The Snuff-box: Calais' and 'Maria: Moulines', were quite in keeping with the sentimentalist tenor to be found in Russian literature of the period. The popularity of Kauffman's works in Russia can be illustrated by Gavriil Derzhavin's poem of 1795, 'On Angelica Kauffmann', which praises the power of her brush, describing her as the 'friend of the Muses'.[7] And in the author's commentary we find an explanation: 'This is a description of a portrait of the author's second wife and is addressed to Kauffmann for this painter usually painted long, slender figures with Greek faces'.[8]

Fig. 19: Angelica Kauffman, *Scene from Sterne's 'Maria'. Oil on canvas*, 25 × 25 ¾ in. (63.5 × 65.5 cm). State Hermitage Museum.

Kauffman's popularity was no doubt in large measure due to the prints made after her paintings, in particular by Francesco Bartolozzi and his Russian pupil Gavriil Skorodumov, whose works include a stipple engraving of *Mad Maria*.[9] By the 1780s the Hermitage already had six volumes of Bartolozzi's prints, many examples of which were also owned by Count Shuvalov. Both collections even included etchings by Kauffman herself.

It should be noted that Russian interest in British art – and in the last quarter of the 18th century not only paintings but also numerous prints, engraved gems, ceramics by Wedgwood, sculptures by Nollekens and so forth were purchased for the Hermitage, the Winter Palace and suburban palaces – was not a passing whim of the Empress, spoiled by her successful acquisition of world-famous collections, but was closely tied to her interest in British culture as a whole, in particular literature. Among the first stimuli for Catherine's personal interest may have been her conversations with the English envoy, Sir George Macartney, who loved poetry, the theatre and art in general.[10] Macartney was acquainted with Sterne, with whom he corresponded while in Russia. The Empress's circle included a large number of outstanding people from vastly differing British social groups – diplomats, scholars, physicians, military officers, architects, bankers and industrialists. 'It is said', noted an English lady who visited Petersburg, 'the Empress is very partial to the English, and I really am of that Opinion from her having so many English in her Service. Her physician Dr Rogerson, and the Governor of Cronstadt, Sir S. or Admiral Grieg, who has the care of all the Ships. The Governor of Rega, Gen[era]l Browne, the two Women that brought up the young Princes. Mr Bush her Gardener, Mr Brumpton, Painter, Mr Campbell [i.e. Cameron], Architect, Mr Hynam her Watchmaker are all English'.[11] In addition to the British, however, there were also Russians in the circles attached to the Empress who were familiar with British culture and could, like Dashkova, provide her with information, particularly on literature. One such was the poet Vasily Petrov (1736–99), who spent two years in Britain (1772–4) and

was on his return appointed the Empress's librarian.[12] Petrov was familiar with a wide range of 17th- and 18th-century English poetry in the original. Evidence of Catherine's knowledge of contemporary English literature is to be found scattered through her letters to Baron Grimm, where she often mentions Sterne's *The Life and Opinions of Tristram Shandy*. In a letter dated 16 April 1779, for example, she notes 'Je trouvé une grande analogie entre sa tête et la mienne…',[13] and as if to sum up her interest in the novel, writes on 18 July to say 'Tristam Schendy …. L'excellent chef d'oeuvre'.[14] Catherine also mentions Fielding's *Joseph Andrews*,[15] and in a note (11 August 1787) to her Secretary of State, A. V. Khrapovitsky, we learn of her interest in Richard Brinsley Sheridan: 'Please seek out one who could translate into German this English comedy', whereupon Khrapovitsky scribbled down 'Die Lasterschule' – *The School for Scandal*.[16] On 4 October 1787 Khrapovitsy noted that he had 'Brought the translation from the English into German of Mr Sheridan's comedy, called 'Die Lasterschule'. It was said that 200 roubles is expensive for a translation, but then the comedy was praised and is very funny.'[17] Two years later (7 September) he 'purchased and presented "la Clarisse de Richardson"'. Twice it was asked for: 'She read Clarissa' (11 October); 30 October: 'Returned me 10 volumes of Clarissa: il falloit avoir les temps pour la lire' (30 October).[18]

Catherine's familiarity with English literature extended her knowledge of, and interest in, British culture generally. The information she regularly received from her ambassadors in London, in particular A. S. Musin-Pushkin and Count Semyon Vorontsov, helped to keep her up to date concerning the sales of works of art, an area of interest in which her Consul in London, Alexander Baxter, seems also to have played a significant role. Although works by contemporary British painters were acquired on a lesser scale than those by French or German artists, the diplomatic channels connecting St Petersburg to London continued to serve both political and acquisitive ends.

In 1778 Nathaniel Dance, another founder-member of London's Royal Academy, made copies of two of his own full-length portraits, *George III* and *Queen Charlotte*, while Benjamin West, the leading history painter and future president of the Academy, copied his own full-length double portrait *The Prince of Wales with his brother Prince Frederick* – three works whose originals were painted for the British royal family. The copies were intended for Catherine,[19] or more precisely for her portrait gallery of contemporary European rulers in the Chesme Palace near St Petersburg, itself a propagandist assertion of the legitimacy of her rule and of her rightful place in the great 'family' of European monarchs despite unquenchable rumours that she had in fact arranged the assassination of her husband, Peter III, in 1762 in order to seize the throne for herself. The British ambassador, Sir James Harris, visited the gallery, and when writing to his father (3 June 1779) to explain his good relationship with Catherine mentioned that 'a few days ago [Catherine] carried me with only two of her courtiers to a country palace where she has placed the portraits of all the crowned heads of Europe. We discussed much on their several merits; and still more on the great demerits of the modern portrait-

Fig. 20: Nathaniel Dance, *King George III, 1773*. Oil on canvas, 94 ⅞ × 58 in. (241 × 148.5 cm). State Hermitage Museum.

Fig. 21: Nathaniel Dance, *Queen Charlotte, 1773*. Oil on canvas, 94 ½ × 57 ⅞ in. (240 × 147 cm). State Hermitage Museum.

Fig. 22: Benjamin West, *George, Prince of Wales, and Prince Frederick, later Duke of York 1778*. Oil on canvas, 94 ¾ × 64 ⅜ in. (240.5 × 166 cm). State Hermitage Museum. These three Royal portraits were displayed in the Chesme Palace in St Petersburg in Catherine II's reign.

painters, since in the whole collection, except one of our two eldest Princes done by West, there is not a single picture that has either design, colour, or composition.'[20] A later visitor, Georgi in 1794, paid particular attention to the portraits, noting that those 'of each court, the Austrian, English, Prussian and such like, are grouped together'.[21] After the order was given for the Chesme Palace to be turned into a home for war invalids in 1830, the portraits were moved to the English Palace at Peterhof and from there to the Hermitage in 1931.

Portraits of politicians Catherine purchased include works by Richard Brompton (?1734–83), who arrived in Russia c.1780.[22] The London artist Joseph Farington (1747–1821) explains in his *Diary* how this came about: 'His wife went to Russia & Carried with Her a picture which He had painted of the great Lord Chatham & some other works, and exhibited them to the Empress Catherine, and represented that the Artist was confined in prison in England for debts of £600 or £1000. The Empress ordered the debts to be paid & that He shd. come to Russia upon an establishment viz: to be pd. £600 a year & for His works. He went and resided there a few years & died there.'[23] Soon after his arrival Brompton became court painter, and in 1781 on Catherine's orders he undertook a double portrait of Grand-Dukes Alexander and Konstantine, her two eldest grandsons. This work, of which Brompton made several copies, is replete with allegorical details concerning Catherine's policies in the East and victories won in the Russo–Turkish War of 1768–74. In 1782 he completed a portrait of the Empress herself (cat. 15), for she was more than satisfied by the works of this somewhat mediocre artist, who had a talent for adapting not so much to the aesthetic taste of the times as to her requirements regarding portraits of the Imperial family. It was perhaps because of these that Catherine praised his work in so fulsome a manner in a letter to Grimm of 24 May 1781: 'Brompton, peintre anglais, établi ici et qui a beaucoup de talent; il a peint mes deux petits-fils, et c'est un tableau charmant .... Ce tableau dans ma galerie n'est pas de figure par les Van Dyck.'[24]

Similar, wholly official, commissions include four large works by the marine painter Richard Paton (1717–91), depictions of sea battles at Chesme in the Aegean in late June 1770 when Russia's navy annihilated the Turkish fleet. These were begun in England in 1771, as we can read in the *Memoirs* of Thomas Jones: 'The remainder of this month, assisted Mr Paton in some large Pictures of the defeat of the Turkish fleet – for the Empress of Russia – Mortimer painted the figures',[25] and they were completed in 1774. Georgi reports seeing them in the Hermitage ('The destruction of the Turkish fleet by the Russian on 4 pictures'[26]), although later they were transferred to the palace at Peterhof.

The year 1779 was of course one of the great moments in the history of collecting in Russia. According to the leading Russian art historian V. F. Levinson-Lessing, it 'was marked by one of the greatest events in the life of the Hermitage, the purchase in England of the famous gallery of Lord Walpole. It was of as great importance for the make-up of the Hermitage collections as the Crozat collection, and its sale was just such a sensation in England as the sale of the Crozat

Fig. 23: Richard Brompton, *Grand-Dukes Alexander Pavlovich and Constantine Pavlovich, 1781*. Oil on canvas, 82 ¾ × 57 ¾ in. (210 × 146.5 cm). State Hermitage Museum.

gallery had been seven years earlier in Paris.'[27] Apart from enriching the Hermitage with canvases by leading European painters of the 17th century and, to a lesser extent, of the 16th, it also supplied the museum with various British works dating from the late 16th century to the early 18th.

The sale by George Walpole, 3rd Earl of Orford, of the magnificent collection put together by his grandfather Sir Robert Walpole and displayed at the family home, Houghton Hall in Norfolk, was a dramatic event that was perceived very differently on the banks of the Thames and the Neva. Elsewhere in this volume, in his essay on 'The Houghton Sale', Andrew Moore details the strong opposition there was in England, for by the autumn of 1778 rumours were abroad that the Earl was considering a private sale to the Empress, though it was only agreed between the two parties during the following year. Catherine, meanwhile, was busy dreaming of the arrival of the collection in St Petersburg, as we learn from her letter to Baron Grimm of 5 February 1779: 'savez-vous que je suis en marché avec le comte d'Orforth pour toutes les peintures qui ont appartenu à feu son père [sic] Robert Walpole? Voyez un peu comme les allouettes viennent donner dans mes filets.'[28] In a dispatch to Catherine from Musin-Pushkin in London regarding the purchase is a record of the extraordinary value attached to the collection, confirmed by all specialists, and it is also noted that Lord Orford 'prend la liberté de la déposer toute, ou en partie aux pieds de Votre Majesté Impériale…'.[29] On 13 February 1779, 'with regard to materials on the pictures being sold by Lord Orford a personal Highest Order has been given to the Plenipotentiary Minister Musin-Pushkin' and the purchase was confirmed, followed by listings and valuations and decisions about means of payment and transportation. On 12 April Catherine wrote to Grimm: 'Pour les Walpole et les Udney,[30] ils ne sont plus à avoir, parce que votre très humble servante à déjà mis la patte dessus et qu'elle ne les lêchera pas plus qu'un chat une souris'.[31]

Meanwhile, in London a drama was unfolding, and Musin-Pushkin wrote to Catherine to explain his concern: 'Your humble servant must inform Your Imperial Majesty that the greater part of the nobility here expresses alike general dissatisfaction and dismay at the release of the pictures from this land, and are drawing up different plans to keep them here: in the defeat of all these merely vain plans, much is being achieved through the Lord Orford's honest desire that they would best be united with the gallery of Your Imperial Highness than to sell them to Parliament and even worse broken in parts by sale to individuals.'[32] All this of course came to nothing. Two years earlier John Wilkes, the journalist and MP, had addressed Parliament in an attempt to persuade it to buy the collection for the nation, but to no avail.[33] For the Earl of Orford's uncle, Horace Walpole, however, who had compiled a catalogue of his father's collection entitled *Aedes Walpolianae*,[34] and who cherished the memory of his parent, the Houghton sale was the source of incredible emotional stress. His torment at its loss was exacerbated in that the purchaser was the hated Catherine II, whom he described in one of his letters as a 'philosophic tyrant'. On 1 February 1779 he told

Lady Ossory: 'The pictures at Houghton, I hear, and I fear, are sold – what can I say? I do not like even to think on it. It is the most signal mortification to my idolatry for my father's memory, that it could receive. It is stripping the temple of his glory and of his affection ….I must never cast a thought towards Norfolk more.'[35] Walpole's letters to his numerous correspondents, particularly those close to him, and the replies, are filled with bitter regrets and concern at the loss of this unique and 'noble' collection, of the indifference of both King and Parliament to the Britain's art treasures. But despite all the protests the collection was sold, the pictures placed in 50 boxes 'by one most expert in the packing of pictures' and loaded onto two ships[36] that then set sail for St Petersburg escorted by a special convoy. The pictures were gone. On 1 March 1780 Catherine wrote to Grimm: 'les Walpole se portent au mieux et ont passé l'hiver, entassés dans ma galerie'.[37] On 24 August M. Corberon, the French chargé d'affaires in Russia, reported that he had seen 'l'Ermitage de l'impératrice et la superb collection de tableaux qu'elle à achetee en Angleterre …. Elle est placee dans la galerie de tableaux aux palais, mais mal en ordre, n'y ayant pas assez de place.'[38]

The loss of the collection was still provoking a response in visitors to Houghton Hall in 1781: 'At Houghton we proposed again seeing Lord Orford's, a seat once so famed for the most capital collection of pictures in England, lately purchased by the Empress of Russia. We had most fortunately seen them in the year 1756 ….' Tis really melancholy to see the hangings disrob'd of those beautiful ornaments, and only one picture now there, a portrait of the Empress herself, which she made my Lord a present of … it rather gives one pain to see the person who must deprive every one who now visits Houghton of the entertainment given to them by these pictures, and their going out of the kingdom makes it still worse.'[39]

On arrival at St Petersburg the pictures were added to E. Munich's manuscript catalogue,[40] and a little later Walpole's *Aedes Walpolianae* was translated into Russian (Hermitage Archive Fund 1, op. VI–A, no. 146). Works by British artists formed only a small part of the vast Walpole collection, in which were numerous paintings by famous Italian, Dutch and Flemish masters, among them several by Van Dyck painted in England (cats. 1–3). But there were examples by William Dobson (cat. 4), Sir Godfrey Kneller (cats. 6–8) and John Wootton (cat. 9), plus the mid-16th-century anonymous portrait *Edward VI* (fig. 24), then attributed to Hans Holbein.[41] In addition to these works, the appendix to the main inventory – 'Additional paintings without increase in price' – included 'A hound, Old Vaik' [Wyck], 'Field Hunt, Wootton', 'Portrait of King William III', 'Gotfrey-Neller [sic], 'Portrait of King George I', 'Hishpanic [sic] poet', 'Gotfrid-Kneller', 'Archbishop Laub [Laud], main culprit in the sad fate of King I [sic], copy from Vandalak' [Van Dyck], 'Lord Wharton, Vandyck', and a portrait of Sir Robert Walpole.[42] But while the small study by Jan Wyck remained in the Hermitage, the canvases by Wootton and Kneller were dispatched to the palace at Gatchina,[43] also the new home for Jean-Baptiste van Loo's portrait of Sir Robert (transferred to the Hermitage in 1920). As for the portrait of the

Fig. 24: Unknown artist, *Edward VI*.
Oil on canvas, 19 ⅞ × 14 in. (50.5 × 35.6 cm).
State Hermitage Museum.

Spanish poet Juan Carreras, this was sold on the command of Nicholas I,[44] and eventually returned to Sir Robert's descendants at Houghton Hall in 1974.

Catherine continued to collect British works after her acquisition of the Walpole collection. Thomas Jones's *Landscape with Dido and Aeneas (Storm)* (cat. 11), which the Welsh artist himself considered his best work, plus the engraving from it that the engraver's widow dedicated to Catherine, entered the Hermitage no later than 1786 and then passed to the private collection of Grigorii Potemkin, which was kept in his apartments in the Winter Palace. The high-point of the history of collecting British art in the 18th century came with the acquisition of large subject pictures by Sir Joshua Reynolds, an event that the artist himself perceived as one of the most important episodes of his career. In 1785 Catherine announced that she wanted a work by Reynolds, who was then President of the Royal Academy, a desire stimulated by her meeting with Lord Carysfort in St Petersburg in December of that year.[45] The *Kamer-Fuhrer Journal*, which recorded all those given official invitations to court, includes the following entry for 4 December: 'To the theatre the following Ministers were invited …. 2. The English Fitz Herbert ….14. Milord Kirnsfort'.[46] Just three days later Carysfort wrote to Reynolds in London, informing him that the Empress and Prince Potemkin wished to commission a painting for which he should himself select the subject.[47] It should be noted that this commission was arranged through Potemkin, with whom he must have been on good terms, for after Carysfort's return to England he presented the Prince in 1788 with a copy by Reynolds of one of the artist's own works then in the Carysfort collection, *Cupid Untying the Zone of Venus* (cat. 13).

This was neither the first nor the last commission that Reynolds received from the Russian aristocracy. In his account ledgers the artist noted: 'July. 1782. Princess Gagarin, Prince and Child. Sent to Russia. 157. 10. February 1787. Mr Baxter, for a picture painted for Prince de Yusapoff, one of the Chamberlains of H.I.M., and her Ambassador at the Court of Turin – 52.10.'[48] Receiving a commission from one of the most powerful and enlightened crowned heads of Europe was a great honour for Reynolds and raised his prestige even higher in the eyes of the public. He was extremely flattered that he was sought for not as a portraitist but as a history painter. The commission was widely discussed – in the British press, in conversation among the artist's friends and admirers, and in numerous letters. In January 1786 Reynolds began mulling over his choice of subject: 'at the present he is undetermind what to chuse', wrote his niece Mary Palmer to her cousin in Calcutta,[49] but by February, after hearing suggestions of various themes taken from Russian and English history from Edmund Burke, Samuel Johnson, Hannah More, Horace Walpole and others, Reynolds decided to go his own way and chose the description of the young Hercules throttling serpents as described in Pindar's first Nemean Ode, despite all efforts to persuade him otherwise. In a letter to Potemkin of 8 August 1789, written to accompany the picture, he expressed his concern that the subject was unknown in Russia and gave a long explanation of it.[50] He need not have, for the Ode was known both to Catherine and Potemkin. In a letter to Grimm of 2 February 1780, she mentioned 'odes Pindariennes que le pr. Potemkin se faisait traduire à Moscou et dont il raffolait, parsque M. Pindar traitait avec une facilité ettonnante dix matières à la fois'.[51]

On completing his vast canvas (almost 10 x 10 feet) titled *The Infant Hercules Strangling the Serpents* in the spring of 1788, James Northcote noted that Reynolds had said that 'there were ten pictures under it, some better, some worse'.[52] Those who saw it that spring exhibited in the place of honour at the Royal Academy were divided,[53] but he was more praised than criticized. Henry Fuseli noted several defects but called it 'a work which may properly be called the triumph of professional execution … the pathos of the subject is in its colour, the colour agitates the eyes, the hearts, that scorn the frigid actors …. Such is the work … we must pronounce it, formed on principles, not sufficiently understood even in this country of arts.'[54] Horace Walpole, however, who had seen *The Infant Hercules* prior to completion in the artist's studio, thought otherwise, as he told Lady Ossory: 'I called at Sir Joshua's, while he was at Ampthill, and saw his Hercules for Russia; I did not at all admire it: the principal babe put me in mind of what I read so often, but have not seen, the monstrous craws …. Blind Tiresias is staring with horror at the terrible spectacle. If Sir Joshua is satisfied with his own departed pictures, it is more than the possessors or posterity will be…'.[55]

The following year at the Royal Academy Reynolds showed another picture destined for Russia, *The Continence of Scipio* commissioned by Prince Potemkin (cat. 12). *The Friendship* set sail for St Petersburg with both works aboard plus two copies of Reynolds's *Discourses*, one each for Catherine and Potemkin. And in a long letter to Potemkin of 4 August 1789, the artist requested the Empress's permission to dedicate the second volume of his *Discourses* to her.

It was about this time that Catherine expressed her desire to invite a leading British portraitist to St Petersburg, and negotiations conducted through Semyon Vorontsov, then ambassador in London, went on through 1789 and 1790. Vorontsov turned to Reynolds for advice, and two names were suggested, Thomas Lawrence and John Hoppner, but in the end no agreement was reached.[56] In St Petersburg meanwhile, Catherine seems to have been more enthusiastic about the artist's *Discourses* than she was about *The Infant Hercules*, as is indicated in a letter she sent on 5 March 1790 to Count Semyon Vorontsov in London, along with a snuffbox decorated with gems and a portrait cameo of the Empress surrounded with diamonds, intended for the artist:[57] 'J'ai lu, je puis dire avec avidité, les discours prononces à l'académie royale de peinture de Londres par mr Reynolds, que cet illustre artiste m'a envoyes avec son grand tableau; dans l'un et l'autres de ses ouvrages l'on reconnait la marche d'un génie distingué. Je vous recommande de l'en remercier.'[58] A flattered Reynolds immediately sent her a letter of thanks,[59] though his friends were divided over its contents, some finding it too complimentary and overstuffed with declarations of gratitude, others reckoning it an elegant epistle.

Soon after its arrival in St Petersburg, Catherine and her court, together with the French painter Gabriel-François Doyen and the engraver James Walker, took a close look *The Infant Hercules*. According to Walker, 'when she came with her courtiers, Doyen and myself were present. Her majesty spoke to me of the great talents of Sir J. R., whom she admired, not only as a painter, but as an author; and gave me a copy of his excellent discourses to the Royal Academy, which she had read and caused to be translated, for the use of the students in her Imperial Academy of Arts. The picture was not so much admired as it ought to have been. The style was new to them, and his mode of loaded colouring not understood; in short, it was too voluptuous for their taste; for, however exquisite his feeling may be, his undecided drawing, and his distribution of effect, light, and shadow, are certainly not in the severe classic style of N. Poussin.'[60] None the less, the picture was exhibited in the Hermitage and in 1792 were added two pictures by Reynolds from Potemkin's collection (cats. 12,13). In 1794 Georgi, in his description of the Hermitage, mentioned three pictures by Reynolds, although he did not give the titles.[61] But at the beginning of the next century *The Infant Hercules* was apparently removed, as John Carr discovered on his visit to the Hermitage: 'I searched in vain for Sir Joshua Reynolds's celebrated Infant Hercules, purchased by the late Empress for the Hermitage. Upon enquiry I found that it had been removed into a private appartment below and was seldom shewn.'[62] In the 1820s George Dawe attempted to acquire it in lieu of payment for his portrait of Grand-Duchess Maria Pavlovna done in 1822.[63] There was active correspondence between different high-ranking court officials as to whether the request from this highly respected painter should be granted, but Labensky, keeper of the Hermitage picture gallery and author of the second manuscript catalogue of the paintings in 1797, was opposed to the idea. He wrote two reports showing the error of such a deal, which would have meant the loss of one of the Hermitage's masterpieces, for which 'the Empress Catherine paid quite a high price'. In his last report to the Ober-Hofmarshal, Labensky wrote: *Subject mythological: this picture, the work of Reynolds, one of the most famous British artists, of whom even now England is proud …. This picture was commissioned from Reynolds by the Empress Catherine II and is considered in England to be amongst the first of his works, it was kept in the Imperial Hermitage in a room which now houses the Malmaison collection and suffered greatly from cracking not by the passing of time but from the artist's excessive use of varnish mixed with paint, a reason why many of his works suffer. This picture may be* [illegible] *placed, according to its merit – in the old gallery, moreover in that the restoration of it has been successfully completed …*

I must say in addition that the frame to this picture must be regilded and the carving amended, which will cost 365 roubles … [64]

His request was granted and in 1838 *The Infant Hercules* was given a worthy place in the Hermitage's gallery XXIV alongside paintings by Rubens, Ostade, Maratta, Chardin and Veronese.[65] Since then the work has only left the gallery once, in 1986 for an exhibition devoted to Reynolds held in Paris and London.

Reynolds's reputation in Russia was not limited purely to his paintings and their fate, for his *Discourses* made a great impression on Catherine, and in a note to her Secretary of State, Khrapovitsky, we read: 'Le 6 de janvier 1790. Faîtes imprimer en Russe la traduction de Tatischef, des Discours de Reynolds.'[66] Tatishchev's translation of the first seven *Discourses* did indeed appear that year in St Petersburg.[67] Reynolds died in London in 1792 without carrying out his promise of sending the Empress the second volume, and Catherine herself died in 1796. The following year Edward Malone, a publisher and writer and one of the artist's executors, published Reynolds's writings in two volumes, in connection with which he approached Lady Inchiquin, formerly Mary Palmer, reminding her that her uncle, Sir Joshua, had thought to dedicate the second volume to Catherine, who had gained much pleasure from reading the first one. (Catherine had indeed enclosed a note in the snuffbox presented in 1790 that read 'Pour le Chevalier Reynolds en temoignage du contentement que j'ai ressentie à la lecture de ses excellens discours sur la peinture.'[68]) 'Would it not therefore', wrote Malone, 'in return for the favours and patronage shown by her, be right to send this set to her son, the present Emperor?'[69] Expressing full agreement, Lady Inchiquin sent Paul I two volumes of Reynolds's works bound in red leather with gold stamping on the spine,[70] and a letter in which it was explained that 'La Comtess Inchiquin, nièce et héritière de M. Reynolds, pénétrée de la plus vive reconaissance pour les bontes dont feue L'Impératrice à honore Son Oncle, et du plus profond respect pour Paul I, se fait un devoir de mettre aux pieds de Sa Majesté Impériale, toutes les oeuvres de M. Reynolds, qu'on vient de publier.'[71] The gift seems to have been graciously received, as Farington noted in his *Diary* for 1–2 December 1798: 'Lady Inchiquin shewed me a letter written in French in the name of the Emperor of Russia by one of His Ministers … expressing His high sense of Sir Joshua's merits, and as a testimony of the consideration in which His Imperial Majesty holds the memory of Sir Joshua, desires she will accept a memorial in remembrance of it. This letter was dated July 14th, 1798 – and is accompanied by a Diamond Star…'.[72]

This polite exchange of gifts marks the end of British art collecting in Russia in the 18th century, though during the reign of Catherine's grandsons, Alexander I and his younger brother Nicholas I, a new stage in the course of artistic and cultural links between Russia and Britain began. In our own century, in 1912, portraits by Thomas Gainsborough (cat. 10), George Romney, John Hoppner (cat. 16) and early works by John Opie and Henry Raeburn were acquired by the Hermitage, the bequest of the famous Petersburg collector Aleksey Khitrovo.[73] The gift was widely reported in the press, and the newspaper *Rech*' [Speech] for 27 November informed the public that 'in one of the as yet closed rooms of the Hermitage exhibited on easels is a series of portraits by famous English artists of the second half of the 18th century …. We feel that these portraits represent one of the most valuable acquisitions by the Hermitage in recent years not only because of the need to add to the department but because in themselves they are now great artistic rarities.'

1. Bemrose 1885, p. 30.
2. Nicolson 1968, I, p. 107.
3. SbRIO 1876, XVII, p. 210.
4. *Ibid.*, p. 212.
5. Dashkova 1987, p. 110.
6. The Hermitage now has 12 works by Kauffman. In addition to those already mentioned there is one further work from her English period, *Hector Summoning Paris to Battle* (115; inv. no. 6472).
7. Derzhavin 1987, p. 32.
8. *Ibid.*, p. 410.
9. Skorodumov (1755–92), an engraver, miniaturist and painter, studied at the Academy of Arts, St Petersburg; from 1773 to 1782 he lived in England, where he worked under Francesco Bartolozzi. In St Petersburg in 1785 he was made an Academician, being appointed engraver to the Cabinet of Her Majesty and Curator of Prints at the Hermitage.
10. Alekseyev 1982, p. 121.
11. Cross 1989, p. 77.
12. Alekseyev 1982, pp. 111–12.
13. SbRIO 1878, XXIII, pp. 135–6.
14. *Ibid.*, p. 153.
15. *Ibid.*, p. 208.
16. 'Sobstvennoruchnyye pis'ma i zapiski imperatritsy Yekateriny II-y k A. V. Khrapovitskomu. 1783–1793' [Letters and Notes in her Own Hand from the Empress Catherine II to A. V. Khrapovitsky. 1783–1793], Russkiy Arkhiv (Moscow, 1872), 10th year, p. 2072, no. 34.
17. *Pamyatnyye zapiski A. V. Khrapovitskogo, stats-sekretarya imperatritsy Yekateriny II* [Notes of A. V. Khrapovitsky, Secretary of State to the Empress Catherine II] (Moscow, 1862), p. 41; reprinted 1990.
18. Ibid., pp. 205–10.
19. Lord Cathcart, English Ambassador in Russia from 1768 to 1771, wrote to George III that Catherine has asked the Russian Ambassador in Britain, Musin-Pushkin, to get her full-length portraits of the King, Queen, Prince of Wales and Prince Frederick. See *The Correspondence of King George III*, ed. Sir John Fortescue (London, 1927), II, pp. 452–3. Whether the portraits by Dance were paid for by Catherine or presented by the King is unknown. As regards West's portrait of the Princes, his Account Book includes the following: '12. His R.H. the Prince of Wales and Prince Frederic (Duke of York) in one picture whole length …. 210. 13. A second picture of Ditto, for Empress of Russia, sent by His Majesty … 210. See Gold 1820, II, p. 208. See also Dukelskaya and Renne 1990, nos. 12, 13, 106.
20. Harris 1844, pp. 198–9.
21. Georgi 1794, III, p. 65.
22. Renne 1987.
23. Farington 1978–84, VI, p. 2244.
24. SbRIO 1878, XXIII, p. 206.
25. Jones 1946–8, p. 24.
26. Georgi 1794, pt. 11, p. 480.
27. Levinson-Lessing 1986, p. 87.
28. SbRIO 1878, XXIII, p. 126.
29. 'Depeshi poslannika pri Velikobritanskom dvore Musina-Pushkina o pokupke gallerei Val'pol' [Despatches from the Ambassador to the British Court Musin-Pushkin on the Purchase of the Walpole Gallery], SbRIO 1876, XVII, p. 395 (later Despatches…).
30. Robert Udny had put together collections in London specially for sale, and he occasionally sold individual pieces. One of these collections was acquired by Catherine. His brother, John Udny, was Consul in Venice and Livorno, and himself had a collection of paintings. See: Levinson-Lessing 1986, p. 266, no. 88.
31. SbRIO 1878, XXIII, p. 136.
32. Despatches…, SbRIO 1876, XVII, p. 397.
33. William Cobbett, *The Parliamentary History of England from the Early Period to the Year 1803* (London, 1814), XIX, p. 188–90.
34. *Aedes Walpolianae, or a Description of the Collection of Pictures at Houghton Hall in Norfolk, the Seat of the Right Honourable Sir Robert Walpole, Earl of*

Orford (1st edn 1747; 2nd edn 1752, considerably amended; 3rd edn 1767, which is merely a reprint of the 2nd edn). The Hermitage Library has in its rare books section the editions of 1752 and 1767 with annotations in pencil of the prices of the works.

35. Walpole 1937–83, XXXIII, p. 86.

36. The false rumours that the ship bearing the pictures had sunk was apparently based on the fact that the *Nathalie*, which had set sail from Russia to England in order to collect the pictures did indeed sink off Germany en route there. Extract from a Despatch from Sir James Harris to Lord Viscount Weymouth: 'Petersburg, 7th, 18th August 1779. My Lord, the Empress having permitted my sister to return home on board a Russian frigate … the frigate was lost'; in Harris 1844, I, p. 243.

37. SbRIO 1878, XXIII, p. 175.

38. *Un diplomate français à la cour de Catherine II 1775–1780. Journal intime du Chevalier de Corberon, chargé d'affaires de France en Russie* (Paris, 1901), II, p. 296.

39. Mrs Philip Lybbe Powys, *Passages from the Diaries* (London, New York and Bombay, 1896), pp. 212–13.

40. E. Munich, 'Catalogue raisonné des tableaux qui se trouvent dans les galeries et Cabinets du Palais Imperial à St Petersburg', compiled at the request of Catherine between 1773 and 1783. Now in the Hermitage Archive Fund 1, op. VI-A, no. 85. Count Johann Ernst Munich, the son of a Field-Marshal, received a broad education. For some time he carried out various diplomatic tasks and then occupied several high state posts. In 1782 he was elected Honorary Amateur of the Academy of Arts.

41. The portrait of Edward VI is a reduced copy of a well-known three-quarters-length at Windsor Castle. The copy was made just after the legs (below the knee) on the Windsor portrait were being extended (they were later removed). Dukelskaya and Renne 1990, no. 93.

42. Despatches…, SbRIO 1876, XVII, p. 400.

43. Trubnikov 1914. This article reproduces all the pictures. Their fate is unknown. Gatchina Palace, built 1766–77 to a design by Antonio Rinaldi and surrounded by an English Park, was in 1783 given to the heir to the throne, the future Paul I, on the Empress's orders, and became his favourite residence.

44. Wrangel 1913, p. 151, no. 983.

45. John Joshua Proby, 2nd Baron Carysfort (1751–1828). After the first mention of his name in the *Kamer-Fuhrer Journal* for 4 December 1785, he is mentioned as among the guests on 14 December 1785 ('Milord Carnsfort') and on 17 June 1786 ('Milord Carisdorf'). His forthcoming departure is mentioned on three occasions in the *Sankt-Peterburgskiye vedomosti* [Saint Petersburg Gazette] in 1786, on 17, 21 and 24 April. His address in St Petersburg is given as no. 246 by Galerny Court, in the English district.

46. *Kamer-Fuhrer Journal* (1785), pp. 736–7.

47. Trubnikov 1913, p. 40.

48. Cotton 1856.

49. Hilles 1970, p. 269.

50. *Ibid.*, pp. 271–2

51. SbRIO 1878, XXIII, p. 172.

52. Northcote 1813–15, p. 219.

53. London 1986, no. 140; Dukelskaya and Renne 1990, no. 73.

54. *The Analytical Review, or History of Literature, Domestic and Foreign, on an Enlarged Plan* (May–August 1788), I, pp. 218–9, no. 167, 'Hercules by Sir Joshua Reynolds, RA'.

55. Walpole 1937–83, XXXIII, pp. 571–2.

56. Krol' 1960; Hilles 1970, p. 274.

57. Such snuffboxes were a sign of Catherine's particular goodwill, and were also presented, for instance, to Lord Chesterfield in 1779 'in return for some compliments he paid her to her ambassador [Musin-Pushkin]' (Walpole 1937–83, XXIII, p. 376), and to the British Ambassador Fitzherbert in 1789 'as a sign of Her Majesty's most excellent goodwill to him' (Archive of Prince Vorontsov 1870, XIII, p. 159, no. 108). In 1793 'Lord Granville was presented with … a snuffbox with a portrait of Her Majesty' (A. V. Khrapovitsky: *Pamyatnyye zapiski…*, 1862, p. 284).

58. Archive of Prince Vorontsov 1888, XXVIII, p. 113, no. 22.

59. Hilles 1929, pp. 205–6.

60. Cross 1993, p. 146.

61. Georgi 1794, pt II, p. 480. There is a description of Catherine's personal cabinet in the Winter Palace, made by Labensky in 1797, the year after her death. This mentions, among other pictures, 'No. 1: Josue Reynolds Le Contenance de Scipion; No. 39 Josue Reynolds Une Couleuvre dans l'herbe', with a detailed description: 'Catalogue raisonné des Tableaux qui se trouvent dans les Cabinets et Galeries de Sa Majesté l'Impératrice fait en 1797 par … François Labensky' (Hermitage Archive Fund 1, op. VI-A, no. 143).

62. Carr 1805, pp. 364–5.

63. Trubnikov 1912b.

64. Hermitage Archive Fund 1, op. 2 (1835), yed. khr. 36.

65. Livret 1838, p. 259, no. 47.

66. *Dnevnik A. V. Khrapovitskogo s 18 yanvarya 1782 po 17 sentyabrya 1793 goda* [Diary of A. V. Khrapovitsky from 18 January 1782 to 17 September 1793] (Moscow, 1901), p. 380, no. 122.

67. Ivan Ivanovich Tatishchev (1743–1802), in 1764 attached to the Collegium of Foreign Affairs, from 1769 to the embassy in London. From 1775 to 1779 he served once more in the Collegium of Foreign Affairs, and was then appointed Moscow Post Director. Author of a number of historical works and numerous translations. He also wrote a description of the pictures of the Battle of Chesme by Paton. *Russkiy biograficheskiy slovar* [Russian Biographical Dictionary], vol. *Suvorova-Tkachova* (St Petersburg, 1912), p. 350.

68. Hilles 1970, p. 267.

69. *Ibid.*, p. 273 n. 11.

70. The copy sent to Paul I is probably that now in the Russian National Library in St Petersburg (16.28.2.19/1–2), *The Works of Sir Joshua Reynolds, Knt. Late President of the Royal Academy: Containing his Discourses, Idlers, A Journey to Flandres and Holland (now first published) and his Commentary on du Fresnoy's Art of Painting.* London, printed for T. Cadell, Jun. and W. Davies, in the Strand. MDCCXCVII, 2 vols. This would seem to have been one of the specially printed editions of the kind Lady Inchiquin presented to the Royal Academy, though the Academy example is neither bound in red leather nor is there gold stamping on the edges and down the spine. It measures 12 x 8½ ins. The first volume has a label with the name of the binder, H. Walter.

71. Bodleian Library, MSS Malone 41, fol. 14. Published in Hilles 1970, p. 273.

72. Farington 1978–84, III, p. 1100.

73. Aleksey Zakharovich Khitrovo (1848–1919), Master of the Hunt at the Imperial Court. He collected Russian painting of the 17th and 18th centuries, French 18th-century applied art and English portraits, all of which he kept in his house on Sergiyev Street in St Petersburg. In his memoirs, Alexandre Benois wrote of Khitrovo: 'his apartments were full of wonderful French furniture, bronzes, porcelain, from the walls looked down portraits by Hoppner, Gainsborough, Romney, Raeburn and Lawrence, which he gave to the Hermitage …. Did Aleksey Zakharovich himself actually have any understanding of art? Judging by the fact that alongside these marvellous works he put up with a revolting portrait of two boys, which he thought to be an original by Reynolds [now Pushkin Museum of Fine Arts, Moscow, attributed to an unknown English artist of the mid-18th century, inv. no. 1302], we can doubt it.' (A. N. Benois: *Moi vospominaniya* [My Reminiscences] (Moscow, 1980), IV–V, pp. 450–52. See also Ye. Renne, 'Khitrovo i yego vklad v sobraniye angliyskoy zhivopisi v Ermitazhe' [Khitrovo and his Contribution to the Collection of English Painting in the Hermitage], *Problemy razvitiya zarubezhnogo iskusstva* [Questions in the Development of Foreign Art] (St Petersburg, 1993), pt 2.

THE HOUGHTON SALE

Andrew Moore

Fig. 25: J. G. Eccardt and John Wootton, *Sir Robert and Lady Walpole*. Oil on canvas, 19 ⅞ × 44 ¼ in. (50.5 × 102.4 cm). Courtesy of the Lewis Walpole Library, Yale University. Eccardt's portraits of Walpole and his wife Catherine Shorter are based on earlier portraits by Zincke. The hounds and the view of Houghton were painted by Wootton. Next to Sir Robert on the table is the purse of the Chancellor of the Exchequer leaning against busts of kings George I and II, to whom he was Prime Minister. The splendid frame is the work of the celebrated wood-carver Grinling Gibbons.

Prior to its redevelopment in the mid-19th century, many British visitors to the State Hermitage Museum at St Petersburg knew of the Houghton collection displayed there, but found it difficult to identify individual items. This was the collection, formerly at Houghton Hall, Norfolk, that had been amassed early in the 18th century by Britain's first prime minister, Sir Robert Walpole, and sold by his descendants in 1779. The Revd R. Lister Venables, for example, was at the Hermitage in 1839; he found the lack of a catalogue a real hindrance.[1] The fact that admittance was only by ticket was also a deterrent to foreign visitors: 'these are given indeed without difficulty, yet even this little obstacle is sufficient to keep numbers away'.[2] In the summer of 1870 the young art critic J. Beavington Atkinson embarked on a 5,000-mile round trip to explore the great art galleries and museums of Russia, and his description of the Hermitage is one of the most informed made by an art-loving British tourist. He knew well – via the writings of Horace Walpole – the story of the sale of the Walpole collection, and commented then that 'under the amazing rise of prices it were hazardous to estimate its present monetary worth'. Of the 198 Houghton pictures at the Hermitage, Atkinson pointed out that just five were of the English School. As for the portraits by Sir Anthony van Dyck (see cats. 1–3), he commented: 'It is a calamity that por-

traits, essentially English, should ever have left our shores. It is hard for an Englishman to see exiled in a foreign gallery, Charles I and Henrietta his wife, Archbishop Laud, Inigo Jones &c.'[3]

To gain a true impression of the impact of the collection amassed by Sir Robert Walpole (1676–1745) as it was originally hung at Houghton Hall, the best source is undoubtedly the *Aedes Walpolianae* of 1747 (cat. 50) written by Sir Robert's third son, Horace (1717–97). Horace Walpole records, and often describes, almost the entirety of his father's collection at a time when it was first housed under one roof. Horace's estimation of the collection amply supports the one that the antiquary George Vertue made in 1739: 'Houghton Hall Sr Robert Walpole's fine and rare collections of Paintings statues Busts &c the most considerable now of any in England' (fig. 29).[4] Sir Robert's collection had grown through the gifts and agency of friends, family and diplomats as well as by purchase at London auctions. Jacob Jordaens's *Self-portrait with Parents, Brothers and Sisters* (inv. no 484) came, for example, from the Duke of Portland's collection and was an important early purchase. Horace records four major acquisitions from the collection of the sculptor Grinling Gibbons, notably Luca Giordano's *The Cyclops at their Forge* (fig. 26).

Undoubtedly Sir Robert's greatest prize was the acquisition in 1725 of Lord Wharton's collection of portraits by Van Dyck and Sir Peter Lely. These included not only Wharton family portraits but those of notable 17th-century figures too, for example *William Laud, Archbishop of Canterbury* (fig. 27), a significant version of one of Van Dyck's most striking likenesses, although a studio production. Even so, two of Sir Robert's most important Van Dycks were not acquired via the Wharton sale: *The Rest on the Flight into Egypt* was purchased through the agency of the artist Charles Jervas, while the portrait *Henry Danvers* (cat. 3) was a present from Sir Joseph Danvers. Since

Fig. 26: John Murphy after Luca Giordano, *The Cyclops at their Forge*. Mezzotint, 19 ⅞ × 13 ⅞ in. (50.6 × 35.3 cm). Published 1 January 1788. Plate 66 in vol. II of *The Houghton Gallery*. Yale Center for British Art, Paul Mellon Collection.

Fig. 27: Studio of Sir Anthony van Dyck, *William Laud, Archbishop of Canterbury*, c. 1638. Oil on canvas, 48 × 36 ¾ in. (122 × 93.5 cm). State Hermitage Museum, formerly hung in the Drawing-room at Houghton Hall.

Van Dyck shows Danvers in his Garter robes, this was an especially appropriate and flattering gift, an acknowledgement of the fact that Sir Robert was himself the first commoner to have been made a Knight of the Garter since the Restoration of Charles II back in 1660.

Although this essay concentrates on the sale to Catherine the Great of the collection of paintings put together for display at Houghton by Sir Robert Walpole (created 1st Earl of Orford in 1742), the dispersal of the collection was by no means limited to the private sale to Catherine of the finest Old Master paintings. Just as Sir Robert had been busy enlarging his collection for nearly 30 years, it took a similar period for his sons and one grandson to cope with the consequences of his death in 1745. Horace Walpole (fig. 28) spent most of his own life lamenting his father's failure to secure Houghton from debt. Soon after Sir Robert's death he explained to Horace Mann: 'his debts, with his legacies which are trifling, amount to fifty thousand pounds. His estate, a nominal eight thousand a year, much mortgaged ....If he had not so overdone it, he might have left such an estate to his family, as might have secured the glory of [Houghton] for many years: another such debt must expose it to sale!'[5] Horace's assessment of his father was not to change. In 1745 he felt that Sir Robert's 'fondness for Houghton, has endangered Houghton'.[6] In 1783 he told Thomas Pownall that his father 'had made Houghton much too magnificent for the moderate estate which he left to support it ... his fondness for

his paternal seat, and his boundless generosity were too expensive for his fortune'.[7]

Among the first attempts to make the Walpole estate solvent seems to have been the sale of paintings in 1748 determined on by Horace's eldest brother, the second Sir Robert (and 2nd Earl of Orford), which was organized in London by the auctioneer Christopher Cock. On 4 May the antiquary William Stukeley recorded a sale that is known through the survival of just one copy of the catalogue: 'Dr [Edward] Milward carried me to Cock's auction room where there is a most magnificent show of paintings to be sold by auction ... they are the pictures of Sir Robert Walpole, under the fictitious name of Mr Robert Bragge. I have seen 'em at Sir Robert's house. Thus, fares it with power and grandeur ...'.[8] The sale took place on 5–6 May and consisted of 125 lots, of which 60 were sold for a total of £851 11s.[9] A second sale was held that year with no attempt at pseudonymity. It is known only through a manuscript transcription, now in the National Art Library in London, made by Richard Houlditch.[10] Although we know nothing of the buyers at the 'Bragge' sale, the Houlditch manuscript does record the buyers at the second sale. These included familiar figures who had themselves acted as Sir Robert's agents or sold paintings to him, among them Robert Bragge and John Ellys. Relatives and friends also made purchases: Horace Walpole, Sir Paul Methuen and Sir Thomas Robinson were all successful bidders.

In 1751 the second Sir Robert died, leaving his son George to inherit the estate and the title Earl of Orford. The 2nd Earl left little to his son besides debts, which included his own in addition to those of the first Sir Robert. 'I think his son the most ruined young man in England', Horace Walpole commented.[11] A third sale of the first Sir Robert's pictures, together with pictures belonging to the second, took place at Langford's auction room in London's Covent Garden on 13–14 June 1751: 'The genuine collection of Italian, Dutch, and Flemish pictures of ... the Earls of Orford ... brought from the Exchequer and Richmond Park'.[12] Horace became increasingly involved in attempting to sort out the family fortunes, becoming the most informed of the family almost despite himself. The first Sir Robert's legacy was very different from the one envisaged by those that had warbled the chorus reputedly sung to honour the Walpole line at the celebrated Houghton Congresses, the Norfolk hunt gatherings organized by the first Sir Robert:

May Houghton long flourish to give us delight
May its masters be all great and good as the Knight;
May a race long succeed, like the place without faults,
That may tread in his paths, and keep full the vaults.[13]

George Walpole, 3rd Earl of Orford (1730–91) has long been remembered – mainly through the letters of his uncle Horace – as the 'mad Earl', although R. W. Ketton-Cremer provides a more rounded pen portrait in an essay published in *A Norfolk Gallery* (1948). Horace's friend John Chute met George when the latter was a young man; Chute was 'quite astonished at his sense and cleverness'.[14]

George, none the less, turned into a spendthrift character, happiest in the role of country squire, succeeding John Hobart, 1st Earl of Buckinghamshire, as Lord Lieutenant of Norfolk in 1757. He also played a leading part in raising and organizing the Norfolk Militia at the outbreak of the Seven Years War in 1756. Two major bouts of mental illness in 1773 and in 1777–8 were readily labelled, for want of a more informed prognosis, as insanity.

The possible sale of the Houghton paintings was evidently on the family agenda throughout the years following the second Sir Robert's death. In March 1754 Horace learned of the death of Margaret Tuckfield, the mother of Horace's sister-in-law Margaret, Countess of Orford (widow of the second Sir Robert): 'My Lord Orford's [i.e., George's] grandmother is dead too; and after her husband's death [which came in 1767] ... has left everything to her grandson ... and the Houghton pictures may still be saved'.[15] It is the case, though, that even Horace for a time believed that the sale of the Houghton paintings was the only possible course of action if the family debts were to be paid off. He was impressed at the way the art market was raising significant sale prices at auction in 1758, telling Horace Mann: 'I want to paint my coat and sell it off my back – there never was such a season – I am mad [i.e., keen] to have the Houghton pictures sold now; what injury to the creditors to have them postponed, till half of these vast estates are spent, and the other half grown ten years older'.[16] Mann responded encouragingly: 'I think you would be in the right to profit

of the season to sell the Houghton pictures. If they cost 100,000, by the proportion which Sir Luke Schaub's sold for and the emulation of the rich bidders, one should hope to get three times that sum for them. The present possessor does not seem to value them, and in a generation or two his heirs may get them again for half their first cost!'[17] Horace later chose to overlook his assessment at that time. The question of the Houghton pictures arose once more in the summer of 1773. John Manners (1730–92), an illegitimate son of Lord William Manners (1697–1772), told Horace that he proposed to seize the Houghton pictures, which he had heard were worth £60,000, in exchange for the £9,000 he had lent George, the 3rd Earl: 'the vulture's throat panted for them all – what a scene is opened! Houghton will be a rookery of harpies – I doubt there are worse scenes to follow, and black transactions!'[18]

Fig. 28: J. G. Eccardt, *Horace Walpole, 4th Earl of Orford*, 1754. Oil on canvas, 15 ½ × 12 ½ in. (39.4 × 31.8 cm). By courtesy of the National Portrait Gallery, London

Fig. 29: The west front of Houghton Hall, Norfolk. Houghton was begun for Sir Robert Walpole in 1722 to the designs of Colen Campbell and completed in 1735. The towers were designed by James Gibbs and the interiors of the house by William Kent. Photo: Brian Allen

Fig. 30: Dedication page from volume I of *A Set of Prints Engraved after the Most Capital Paintings in the Collection of her Imperial Majesty the Empress of Russia, Lately in the Possession of the Earl of Orford at Houghton Hall in Norfolk* (commonly known as *The Houghton Gallery*; see cat. 51). Yale Center for British Art, Paul Mellon Collection.

That summer Horace was impelled to visit Houghton (fig. 29). On returning to his home, Strawberry Hill near London, he wrote a long letter to his sister-in-law Lady Ossory recounting something of his feelings. Fond as he was of Houghton, he was horrified to see the condition into which George had allowed it to fall. He had found it 'half a ruin, though the pictures, the glorious pictures, and furniture are in general admirably well preserved. All the rest is destruction and desolation! The two great staircases exposed to all weathers, every room in the wings rotting with wet; the ceiling of the gallery in danger ...'. On that visit Horace had occasionally 'stole from the steward and lawyer I carried with me, to peep at a room full of painters, who ... are making drawings from the whole collection, which Boydell is going to engrave ...' (fig. 30).[19] It does appear to be the case that the publishing project dreamed up by John Boydell (1719–1804) to engrave the finest of the Houghton pictures was intimately connected with the plans to sell the collection, even though the interest of the Empress Catherine was to be at least five years into the future. Boydell himself must have been aware of the developing discussions to sell the paintings. Horace, meanwhile, evidently regarded the project in a positive light.

Horace was still interested in the idea of selling the Houghton pictures when the merchant and banker Sir George Colebrooke (1729–1809) sold his paintings by auction in April 1774. In response to the Colebrooke sale, Horace's mental arithmetic led him to value the Houghton pictures at £200,000.[20] It was three years later, on 28 April 1777, that John Wilkes, then Member of Parliament for Middlesex, gave a speech in the House of Commons answering Sir Grey Cooper's motion 'that the petition of the trustees of the British Museum, together with the general state of accounts ... be referred to a committee of supply'. Wilkes advocated acquiring the Houghton pictures, 'one of the first collections in Europe'.

Thus a matter of family concern formally became one of national importance. In Parliament Wilkes proposed that the Houghton pictures be purchased by the nation as the basis for a National Gallery, to be housed in a purpose-built museum within the grounds of the British Museum: *The British Museum, possesses few valuable paintings, yet we are anxious to have an English School of painters. If we expect to rival the Italian, the Flemish, or even the French school, our artists must have before their eyes the finished works of the greatest masters. Such an opportunity, if I am rightly informed, will soon present itself. I understand that an application is intended to parliament, that one of the first collections in Europe, that at Houghton, made by Sir Robert Walpole, of acknowledged superiority to most in Italy and scarcely inferior even to the Duke of Orléans's in the Palais Royal at Paris, may be sold by the family. I hope it will not be dispersed, but purchased by parliament, and added to the British Museum. I wish, Sir, the eye of painting as fully gratified, as the ear of music is in this island, which at last bids fair to become a favourite abode of the polite arts. A noble gallery ought to be built in the spacious garden of the British Museum for the reception of that invaluable treasure.*

Horace Mann wrote to Horace Walpole of his approval of the proposal and asked 'was it a thought of his own, or suggested to him by anybody?'[21] It is unlikely that Horace Walpole suggested the idea to Wilkes; although they were acquainted, Walpole 'saw no wit' in Wilkes.[22] By the spring of 1777 the question of the family pictures was quite evidently subject to rumour and debate in the capital.

By the autumn of the following year a deal had been struck between George, 3rd Earl, and his two uncles, Horace and Sir Edward Walpole, whereby both brothers renounced their claim to the inheritance of Houghton. In return Horace was secured £4,000 plus interest and his London townhouse at Arlington Street, worth £3,000. Almost immediately George set about the sale of the Houghton pictures, contracting James Christie to value the collection. On 18 December 1778 Horace wrote to Mann in Florence: 'The mad master has sent his final demand of forty-five thousand pounds to the Empress of Russia'.[23] Mann was understandably puzzled by his friend's apparently sudden rejection of the idea of the sale: 'I thought you had formerly advised Lord Orford to sell his pictures. I am sorry he should do it, if you disapprove … but the sum for which he has offered them to the Empress of Russia seems to be vastly inferior to what I had always heard them valued at. I wonder that the King does not purchase them. One should be tempted in some cases almost to wish that there was authority lodged in some hand to prevent such mad owners from dissipating their patrimony and injuring their descendants.'[24] Horace explained his change of attitude in the following terms: *It is very true, I did desire the pictures should be sold, as I preferred his paying his grandfather's and father's debts to false splendour – but this is not the case now. As he is not legally obliged, he does not think of acquitting his father's debts; and as he has compounded his – grandfather's unsatisfied debts for fifteen thousand pounds, he does not want forty thousand. In short, I am persuaded that the villainous crew about him, knowing they could not make away clandestinely with the collection in case of his death, prefer money, which they can easily appropriate to themselves …*[25]

Horace had in fact acted honourably throughout his dealings with his nephew. It was a great sadness to him that now the sale was at hand the market was not what it had been five years previously.

There was a further delay when, as Horace records, Giovanni Battista Cipriani (1727–85) was called in to give a second opinion concerning the valuation. Cipriani was an historical and decorative painter who had recently completed a decorative scheme (now at the Philadelphia Museum of Art, McFadden Bequest) for Shelburne (later Lansdowne) House in London. An Academician himself, Cipriani appears to have turned to the Royal Academy's future president, Benjamin West (1738–1820), for help with the task. It is unclear as to why precisely these two had become involved, but we do know that both artists had connections with George, 3rd Earl. One of West's pupils was Joseph Farington, whose meticulous watercolour copies of the Walpole family portraits (private collection) are still at Houghton. Farington had been copying paintings on behalf of John Boydell since at least the autumn of 1774, and could well have added his recommendation of West to that of Cipriani.

Cipriani himself proved to be a favourite with the 3rd Earl. Once

the sale of the Houghton pictures was finally complete, George commissioned Cipriani to paint a series of three vast decorative canvases in the Neoclassical style. These works, *Philoctetes on Lemnos* (1781), *Castor and Pollux* (1783) and *Oedipus on Colonus* (undated) were hung by the 3rd Earl in Houghton's cavernously empty Saloon alongside the full-length portrait of Catherine the Great by Roslin that he received as a gift from the Empress in 1780.

It appears that James Christie, West and Cipriani must have conferred to agree the final valuation of £40,555. A list of pictures showing this total value, once in West's possession, is now in the W. S. Lewis Library, Farmington, Connecticut. The correspondence between Christie and the 3rd Earl's agent, Carlos Cony, makes it clear that certain pictures were not finally included in the valuation, and a number of draft lists, notably those in Cambridge University Library, the Fitzwilliam Museum and the British Library, show differences.[26] The collection sold to Catherine did not include the family portraits or the statues. According to an inscription (9 November 1824) in a grangerized copy of the *Aedes Walpolianae* in Cambridge University Library, 'Mr Christie's catalogue' recorded that the collection was 'purchased by her Imperial Majesty at said valuation, £40,500 witness the signature of the Russian Ambassador'. The inscription also recorded that 'Mr [Philip Joseph] Tassaert – Spring Gardens assisted Mr James Christie in valuing those paintings'.

It is not certain at precisely what point the interest of the Empress Catherine was aroused. The idea of conducting a private sale with her was evidently in the air in the autumn of 1778. On 12 November the coin collector and antiquary Matthew Duane (1701–85) wrote to Carlos Cony from Lincoln's Inn in London: 'I met at Bath, the Reverend Dr Arnold King, who transacts business for The Empress of Russia; he assured me that the Empress has expressly signified to him lately that she cannot buy any pictures, medals &c'.[27] The following April Horace Walpole received the inaccurate message that the pictures had indeed been sold: 'I have been told today that they are actually sold to the Czarina – *sic transit!* – mortifying enough, were not everything transitory!'[28]

In *The Gentleman's Magazine* of 31 July 1779 it was reported that the paintings had been 'viewed by the Russian Ambassador, who sent over a list of one hundred of them to the Empress which are valued at £40,525'. In fact George, 3rd Earl, had discussed the matter with the Ambassador himself in November 1778, and it was this meeting that caused him to appoint James Christie to value the pictures at Houghton.[29] Catherine's ambassador to the Court of St James at this period was Aleksei Semonovich Musin-Pushkin (1732–1817). He and his wife Ekaterina were familiar Anglophiles at Court over a fourteen-year period. The negotiations with the 3rd Earl were among the last Musin-Pushkin undertook on behalf of the Empress before being recalled in 1779. The outbreak of the American War for Independence in 1775–6 and Britain's subsequent strained relations with France led in turn to diplomatic complications between Britain and Russia. The Houghton sale was secured just in time from Catherine's point of view, and it was time for Musin-Pushkin to be replaced by a new ambassador, Ivan Matveyevich Simolin (1720–99).

It was during the 1770s that Catherine had succeeded in acquiring some major European collections thanks to the diligence of her ambassadors and her own insatiable desire to collect on a grand scale. She can be seen to have regarded art collecting virtually as a matter of state policy, recognizing the ability of major collections to consolidate and enhance the authority and international prestige of her empire. Her commission of a special pavilion to house the collection of 225 pictures bought in 1764 from the Berlin merchant Johann Ernst Gotskowski (1710–75) enabled her to set about acquiring not simply individual works but entire collections. She did not rely simply on her own taste but on that of a panoply of advisers, most notably Diderot, Baron Friedrich-Melchior Grimm, and her ambassador to Paris and later The Hague, Prince Golitsyn. She also corresponded with Voltaire and invited numerous artists to work in St Petersburg. Among the most notable of the collections she acquired were those of Count Heinrich von Bruhl in 1769, prime minister under Augustus III, King of Poland and Elector of Saxony. It must have seemed to her most appropriate to negotiate for another prime-ministerial collection ten years later.

News of the imminent Walpole sale reached Josiah Wedgwood, who 'lamented the approaching fate of the Houghton collection of paintings' in a letter to Thomas Bentley of 18 September 1779. He drew bleak inference from the news: 'Everything shows we have past our meridian, and we have only to pray that our decline may be gentle, and free from those sudden shocks which tear up empires by the roots, and make the most dreadfull havock amongst the wretched inhabitants. Russia is sacking our palaces and museums, France and Spain are conquering our outposts, and braving us to our very doors at home ...'.[30] Horace had in fact made one last attempt to save the Houghton pictures by appealing directly to the King through his cousin Francis Seymour Conway, 1st Earl of Hertford, then serving as Lord Chamberlain, who sent on a letter to Windsor Castle on behalf of Horace, but to no avail.[31] Horace finally acknowledged the completion of the sale in a letter to Horace Mann of 4 August 1779: 'The sum stipulated is forty or forty five thousand pounds, I neither know nor care which ...'.[32] One further irony was to come ten years later when a fire gutted the picture gallery at Houghton: 'One of the wings of Houghton ... is burnt down .... As the gallery is burnt, the glorious pictures have escaped – or are rescued, to be consumed in a wooden palace on the first revolution at Petersburg'.[33]

The sale of the Houghton paintings continued to provide material for the national press. On 14–16 December 1779 the *Whitehall Evening Post* reported: 'The celebrated Houghton collection of pictures, late the property of Lord Orford ... are totally lost at sea; the *Natalia*, the ship in which they were carrying to Russia, having foundered'. When William Cole heard this news he wrote to Horace: 'I hope and wish that the news we had in all our papers, that the Houghton Collection of pictures are at the bottom of the sea, is false. Good God! what a destruction! I am shocked when I think of it'. The rumour was also reported in *The London Chronicle* (11–14 December). Mann gave a more measured response in his letter to Horace of 3 January 1780: 'In the last newspaper I read an article that the ship with the Houghton pictures was cast away. This I believe I

Fig. 31: John Sell Cotman, *Lee Shore, with the Wreck of the Houghton Pictures, Books &c., sold to the Empress Catherine of Russia*, 1838. Pencil and watercolour with bodycolour and gum arabic, 26 ¾ × 35 ½ in. (68 × 90.2 cm). Fitzwilliam Museum, Cambridge.

Fig. 32: Peter Paul Rubens, *The Apotheosis of King James I*. Oil on canvas, 35 ¼ × 36 ¾ in. (89.7 × 55.3 cm). 1632–3. State Hermitage Museum. A sketch for the central oval on the ceiling of the Whitehall Banqueting House in London.

can contradict by the authority of a Russian officer who told me a fortnight ago that they were arrived safe at Petersbergh.' The rumour had only days previously been denied in the *Whitehall Evening Post* (25–26 December), where it was stated that 'the master of the ship … saw them safely unpacked in the Empress's palace'.

Four years after, the dust had still not entirely settled on the affair. The letter that 'C.D.' wrote to the editors of *The European Magazine* in February 1782 employed arguments that remain in force today concerning issues of cultural heritage: *The removal of the Houghton Collection of Pictures to Russia is, perhaps, one of the most striking instances that can be produced of the decline of the empire of Great Britain, and the advancement of our powerful ally in the North. The riches of a nation have generally been estimated according as it abounds in works of art, and so careful of these treasures have some states been, that, knowing their value and importance, they have prohibited the sending them out of their dominions.*

In 1824 the dealer William Buchanan believed the loss to the nation's artistic heritage was surpassed only by the dispersal through the Commonwealth sales of the collections of Charles I.

The story of the sale was to live on in the national memory. In 1838 John Sell Cotman painted an inventive resurrection of the rumour that the pictures had been lost at sea. His watercolour, which he titled *Lee Shore, with the Wreck of the Houghton pictures, books, &c., sold to the Empress Catharine of Russia, including the gorgeous landscape of the Wagoner by Rubens* (fig. 31), survives today as a nightmare scenario for any curator proposing a loan exhibition.

The question arises as to how important the Walpole collection was to the growing museum at the Hermitage. Sir Robert's collection was the quintessential collection of the early 18th-century Englishman of taste. Rich in works by Dutch and, more particularly, Flemish artists, it was also well representative of the French and Italian schools. It included a number of masterpieces and many full-scale works that continue to enhance the rooms of the Hermitage today, most notably major works by Parmigianino, Rembrandt, Rubens (fig. 32), Van Dyck, Maratti, Poussin, Salvator Rosa, Giordano, Guido Reni and Snyders. The arrival of the Houghton collection at St Petersburg marked the end of an important phase in the development of the Hermitage's. The first Sir Robert's pictures effectively consolidated the Empress's collections, and even included a few paintings by English masters, such as William Dobson's *Abraham van der Doort* (cat. 4), John Wootton's *Hounds* (cat. 9) and Sir Godfrey Kneller's *Grinling Gibbons* and *John Locke* (cats. 6, 7).

It is not entirely clear just how much the Empress did pay for the Houghton collection. Although West and Cipriani confirmed a valuation of £40,455 for those pictures that were sold, William Cole recorded in his copy of the *Aedes Walpolianae* that the Empress paid only £36,000, a figure roughly consistent with that given by Sir Robert's modern biographer, J. H. Plumb.[54] Gerald Reitlinger, in *The Economics of Taste: The Rise and Fall of the Picture Market, 1760–1960* cites the Houghton sale as a perfect cross-section of picture values in the mid-18th century. The Empress is recorded as having spent

£150,000 in total on the six collections she purchased between 1764 and 1779; this includes Houghton's, which was by far the largest acquisition of an individual picture collection. Cole's copy of the valuation lists a total of 181 pictures. Among the highest valuations placed by West and Cipriani, and also by James Christie's colleague Philip Tassaert, were those for Guido Reni's *Doctors of the Church* at £3,500, Van Dyck's *Holy Family* (inv. no. 539) at £1,600 and Rubens's *Mary Magdalen Washing the Feet of Christ* (inv. no. 479), also at £1,600. These were high values for the period, but they were also high-quality works that carried significant provenances.

Although Catherine undoubtedly did purchase the collection at a bargain price, this was rather through lack of a realistic competitor on the market than through any undervaluing of the works themselves by West and his colleagues. Horace Walpole finally did consider the collection overvalued by the time it came to be sold,[35] and the prices do seem to bear him out for the period in question. Although the Van

Dyck full-lengths were only valued at £200 each or less, this was still twice what Sir Robert had paid for them. The French classicists were valued highly, presumably based on the French market rather than on the London sale-rooms of the time. Poussin's *Moses Striking the Rock* (inv. no. 1177) and *The Holy Family* (inv. no. 1213) were priced at £900 and £800 respectively. It is the case that the lists of values invariably reflect not only a recognition of the most important works but also the vagaries of taste.[36] Sir Robert's belief in Carlo Maratti, while fully justified in the case of the painter's *Clement IX*, was not to stand up to the taste of the late 18th century. Artists' reputations continued to fluctuate, as do critical judgements of individual works. Nevertheless, it is sobering that Sir Robert's two flowerpieces by Jan van Huysum, for instance, were valued at £1,200 for the pair (fig. 33), while the superb Rembrandt, *Abraham's Sacrifice* (fig. 34), was considered to be worth just £300.

The Empress had achieved an undoubted coup. When her adviser Baron Grimm informed her at one stage that he had heard the Houghton collection was no longer available, Catherine is reported to have replied: 'The Walpole pictures are no longer to be had, for the simple reason that your humble servant has already got her claws on them, and will no more let them go than a cat would a mouse.'[37]

By 1781, however, her collecting zeal had moderated and she wrote to Grimm: 'I renew my resolution to buy nothing more, not a picture, nothing ...'.[38] But her change of heart had come too late for Houghton.

The scale and magnificence of the art collection amassed by Britain's first prime minister can still be judged beyond the galleries of the State Hermitage Museum through the plates of the remarkable publication that was the brainchild of the engraver John Boydell, who secured his reputation as a printseller and publisher of nationalistic art projects (notably *The Shakespeare Gallery*, 1786). His project known as *The Houghton Gallery* was a particularly jingoistic concept, the only one of Boydell's many publishing ventures devoted to a single collection. In the prospectus published on 25 March 1775 to accompany the first portfolio of prints, Boydell stated that 'The Proprietor exerts his utmost Care to have the Work performed in a Manner which shall render it an Honour to our Country, a faithful Imitation of the Originals from which it is taken, and a Credit to every Artist employed in it'. Boydell ensured that the majority of the plates were of the highest quality.[39]

The 162 prints that represent the most splendid works (excluding family portraits) in the collection were published, usually ten at a

time, between 1774 and 1788. In 1788 they were gathered into two folio volumes, each prefaced by a text catalogue based on Horace Walpole's *Aedes Walpolianae* (1747). A total of 45 engravers contributed plates to *The Houghton Gallery*, most notably Richard Earlom (1743–1822), J. B. Michel (1748–1804) and Valentine Green (1739–1813). Volume I consists of an engraved frontispiece, title-page and dedication page, followed by 28 'plans, elevations, perspective views, chimney pieces, ceilings &c' of Houghton Hall (first published by Isaac Ware) and 60 (numbered) prints after paintings in the collection. Volume II contains an engraved frontispiece and title-page and 69 prints after paintings. The 129 prints after the paintings comprise 60 mezzotints, 54 line engravings and 15 stipple engravings. In his prospectus Boydell promised that 'no more than Four Hundred complete sets shall be printed'. The final publication in 1788 of the whole set in two volumes serves as a breathtaking reminder of a collection of paintings that represented a significant coup for Catherine not only as a patron of the arts but also as a zealous collector. The quality of Sir Robert Walpole's collection and the scale of Catherine's prize continue to inform the displays of the Hermitage today.

1. Venables 1839, p 17.
2. Kohl 1844, p. 110.
3. Atkinson 1986, p. 40.
4. Vertue 1929–50, XVIII (1929–30), p. 6.
5. Walpole 1937–83, XIX, p. 32 (15 April 1745).
6. *Ibid.*
7. Walpole 1937–83, XLII, p. 81 (27 October 1783).
8. Stukeley 1882–7, III, p. 5.
9. Oxford Bodleian Library, Johnson D 762.
10. Houlditch MSS 86.00.1849, London, National Art Library (Victoria & Albert Museum). Two volumes of sale catalogues of the principal collections of pictures (170 in total), sold by auction in England 1711–59, the majority with MS additions giving prices and names of purchasers. The source of information concerning acquisitions by Sir Robert Walpole for his picture collection.
11. Walpole 1937–83, XX, p. 238 (1 April 1751, to Horace Mann).
12. *The Daily Advertiser* (13 June 1751).
13. Ketton-Cremer 1948, p. 165.
14. *Ibid.*, p. 166.
15. Walpole 1937–83, XX, p. 418 (28 March 1754, to Mann).
16. *Ibid.*, XXI, p. 200 (10 May 1758).
17. *Ibid.*, XXI, p. 208 (3 June 1758).
18. *Ibid.*, XXXII, p. 121 (11 June 1773, to Lady Ossery).
19. *Ibid.*, XXXII, pp. 140–42.
20. *Ibid.*, XXIII, p. 569 (1 May 1774, to Mann).
21. *Ibid.*, XXIV, p. 304 (16 May 1777).
22. *Ibid.*, X, p. 180 (16 October 1765, to George Montagu).
23. *Ibid.*, XXIV, p. 427.
24. *Ibid.*, XXIV, p. 434 (16 January 1779).
25. *Ibid.*, XXIV, p. 441 (11 February 1779, to Mann).
26. Moore 1996, nos. 20, 73.
27. Norfolk Record Office, BL VI b.
28. Walpole 1937–83, II, p. 158 (23 April 1779, to W. Cole).
29. C. Cony to J. Christie (26 November 1778), Norfolk Record Office, BL VI b.
30. Savage 1965, p. 239.
31. Walpole 1937–83, XXXIX, p. 337 (2 August 1779, Lord Hertford to HW).
32. *Ibid.*, XXIV, p. 502 (4 August 1779, to Mann).
33. *Ibid.*, XXXIV, pp. 87–8 (12 December 1789, to Lady Ossery).
34. Plumb 1972, II, p. 87.
35. Walpole 1937–83, II, p. 168–70 (12 July 1779, to W. Cole).
36. Published in *The Gentleman's Magazine* and also in Chambers 1829, pp 520–39, with small variations to Cole's list.
37. Descargues 1961, p. 42.
38. Waliszewskl 1894, p. 137.
39. Rubinstein 1991.

Fig. 33: Richard Earlom (drawn by Joseph Farington) after Jan van Huysum, *A Flower Piece*. Mezzotint, 21 ⅞ × 16 ½ in. (55.7 × 41.9 cm). Published 25 June 1778. Plate 59 in vol. I of *The Houghton Gallery*. Yale Center for British Art, Paul Mellon Collection. The original painting hung in the Cabinet at Houghton.

Fig. 34: J. C. Murphy after Rembrandt, *Abraham's Sacrifice*. Mezzotint, 19 ¹¹⁄₁₆ × 13 ⅞ in. (50 × 35.2 cm). Published 1 September 1781. Plate 33 in vol. II of *The Houghton Gallery*. Yale Center for British Art, Paul Mellon Collection.

Fig. 35: James Watson after J. B. van Loo, *Sir Robert Walpole*. Mezzotint, 19 ¾ × 13 ¾ in. (50 × 35 cm). Published 1 January 1788. Frontispiece to vol. II of *The Houghton Gallery*. Yale Center for British Art, Paul Mellon Collection.

SIR JOSHUA REYNOLDS AND THE COURT
OF CATHERINE THE GREAT

Martin Postle

On 8 December 1785 John Joshua Proby, 2nd Baron (later 1st Earl) of Carysfort (1752–1828), wrote to Sir Joshua Reynolds with news of the most prestigious commission of his career. Lord Carysfort, who was then visiting the Imperial Russian court, informed Reynolds that the Empress Catherine II wished him to paint a history painting for her, the size and subject-matter of which was to be left entirely to the artist's discretion. In addition, Reynolds was requested to carry out a similar commission for Prince Grigorii Aleksandrovich Potemkin.[1] For the Empress Reynolds painted *The Infant Hercules Strangling the Serpents* (fig. 36). Prince Potemkin received *The Continence of Scipio* (cat. 12). A third picture, a version of Reynolds's *A Nymph and Cupid* (cat. 13), was also presented to Potemkin by Carysfort.

In 1970 Frederick Hilles made available to an English-speaking audience hitherto inaccessible documents in Russian periodicals relating to Reynolds's various commissions for the Empress Catherine and Prince Potemkin.[2] Since that time further research has been carried out on Reynolds's relations with his Continental clientele, and the role that history painting played in his own *oeuvre*.[3] In 1986 *The Infant Hercules* was exhibited to audiences in Paris and London for the first time since its export to Russia in 1789. Now, with the present exhibition, *The Continence of Scipio* and *A Nymph and Cupid* are also to be shown outside Russia. The exhibition of these works, together with recent advances in Reynolds scholarship, provides a timely opportunity to review Reynolds's professional relationship with, and his commissions for, the court of Catherine the Great.

By the early 1780s Reynolds had reached the peak of his career. He commanded large sums for his portraits, which, through the medium of the mezzotint, had also reached audiences on the Continent. His lectures, published as the *Discourses on Art*, were available in French, German and Italian editions – a copy even finding its way into the hands of Marie Antoinette.[4] In the *Discourses* Reynolds boasted of the vigour of the native British school of art, which, untramelled by the constraints imposed by tradition, had 'nothing to unlearn' and could look with a detached and dispassionate eye on the art of the past. As a result he was confident enough, by the 1780s, to redirect his audience's attention from the mecca of Italy towards the virtues of the Northern European tradition in Western art. And while he continued to promote respect for the twin pillars of Italian art – Michelangelo and Raphael – it was the Flemish artist Sir Peter Paul Rubens who captured his heart and imagination in the last decade of his career (fig. 37).

In 1781 Reynolds made a pilgrimage to Flanders, a journey that was in part a confirmation of the conversion he was undergoing. 'Those who cannot see the extraordinary merit of this great painter', he concluded at the end of the visit, 'have a narrow conception of the variety of art, or are led away by the affectation of approving nothing but what comes from the Italian School'.[5] The commission from Catherine II in December 1785 could not have come at a more opportune moment. Reynolds had affirmed Britain as the new spiritual home of the arts. He had 'rehabilitated' Rubens as the leader of the Northern European school. Now, fittingly, he himself was to create a major work of his own for Catherine the Great, the 'Semiramis of the North'.

Reynolds was a genuinely cosmopolitan figure. He had travelled extensively in Italy and France from 1749 to 1752, had made further visits to Paris in 1768 and 1771, as well as the visits to Flanders, the

Fig. 36: Sir Joshua Reynolds, *The Infant Hercules Strangling the Serpents*. Oil on canvas, 119 ¼ × 116 ⅞ in. (303 × 297 cm). Exhibited at the Royal Academy in London in 1788. State Hermitage Museum.

Fig. 37: John Browne (drawn by Joseph Farington) after Rubens, *The Waggoner*. Line engraving, 19 1/16 × 24 in. (48.4 × 61 cm). Published 30 September 1776. From vol. I of *The Houghton Gallery*. Yale Center for British Art, Paul Mellon Collection.

Netherlands and Germany in 1781 and Flanders again in 1785. Many of his closest friends, including James Boswell and the musicologist and composer Charles Burney, were seasoned European travellers. His clients too were principally drawn from the Georgian 'jet-set' – those members of the landed aristocracy who had made the Grand Tour and were *au fait* with Continental art and culture. Quite the most influential advocates for Reynolds's art on the Continent were those friends who were actively engaged in business in foreign courts. Here Reynolds was extremely well connected, being on intimate terms with Thomas Robinson, 2nd Baron Grantham (ambassador in 1771–9 to the court at Madrid), John Sackville, 3rd Duke of Dorset (ambassador in 1783–9 to the court of Louis XV), and Lord Carysfort, who attended the Imperial Russian court in 1784. He also courted the representatives of foreign embassies in England. Indeed, the French ambassador, Comte d'Adhémar, who had purchased work from Reynolds, told him on his departure for France in 1785 that he would endeavour to persuade Marie Antoinette to commission him to paint her portrait.[6] Nothing came of the idea. However, the very possibility of such a commission demonstrates that Reynolds was more than willing by the mid-1780s to offer his services to royal patrons abroad.

By the early 1780s Reynolds's desire to gain the favour of foreign courts was no doubt heightened by the ingrained animosity that existed between himself and the court of George III. The King, who

regarded Reynolds as 'poison in his sight', turned instead to the American artist Benjamin West and to Thomas Gainsborough, who by the 1780s was Reynolds's principal rival as a portrait painter. Reynolds did not as a rule seek the friendship of his fellow artists in England. He had, however, continued to maintain links with several Continental artists, including the French sculptor Etienne-Maurice Falconet, with whom he appears to have been in regular correspondence by the 1770s, and who had worked in St Petersburg from 1766 to 1778 on his monumental equestrian statue of Peter the Great.

While Reynolds had no direct experience of Russia, during the early 1780s he made the acquaintance of several prominent Russians in London. They included Prince Serge Gagarin, whose family portrait he painted in 1784, and Count Semyon Vorontsov, Russian ambassador in London from 1785 to 1806 (see cat. 20). Indeed, in the spring of 1790, when Catherine was searching for an English portrait painter to work at her court, she asked Vorontsov to discuss the matter with Reynolds, which he did on several occasions. Reynolds suggested his young favourite, Thomas Lawrence (see cats. 20,21), although Lawrence declined the invitation.[7]

The most important Russian contact secured by Reynolds during this period was, however, not Vorontsov but his half-sister Princess Catherine Dashkova, whom Reynolds evidently met for the first time during the summer of 1780.[8] Princess Dashkova, by now a widow in her mid-forties, was a talented amateur musician and painter. She had also travelled widely throughout Europe, collecting a wide circle of admirers, including Diderot and Voltaire. In Edinburgh, where her son was studying for a Master of Arts degree, she had also met two of Reynolds's Scottish friends, the moral philosopher and economist Adam Smith and the historian William Robertson. In 1782 Princess Dashkova returned to Russia. The following year, on 21 October, Catherine, in a conscious act of reconciliation, appointed her as first President of the St Petersburg Academy of Arts and Sciences.

Princess Dashkova did not forgot Reynolds, and on at least one occasion they corresponded. Her letter reveals a warm friendship with Reynolds and his niece, Mary Palmer: 'I am', she told him, 'as steady in friendship as I am difficult in forming it, and that in the confined circle of those I believe and call my friends, my worthy Sir Joshua holds a distinguished place'. Although Reynolds's letter to her is lost, it appears that he had written to congratulate the Princess on her new appointment, enclosing a copy of his *Discourses*.[9]

According to a postscript to the Princess's letter, he had also begged one favour: that she should send him a 'Calmuck girl' – presumably to act as a servant in his household. (The 'Calmucks', or Kamchadals, were the native inhabitants of Kamchatka in eastern Siberia.) Unfortunately, the Princess was unable to comply with Reynolds's request owing, she said, to a similar 'experiment' elsewhere in which the girl had died of smallpox – a disease that at the time was wiping out a large proportion of the Kamchadal population.[10] On a more positive note she intimated that a Russian edition of the *Discourses* would be forthcoming, telling Reynolds: 'When you shall appear in our language, I shall take care that you appear in a garb not intirely unbecoming to you'.[11] The first seven of Reynolds's *Discourses*, based on the English octavo edition of 1778, were eventually published in a Russian edition in 1790, although Reynolds probably never knew of its existence.[12]

In Princess Dashkova Reynolds had a loyal ally at the Russian court. However, it was Lord Carysfort who persuaded the Empress Catherine to add the name of Reynolds to her list of British artists whose works she was acquiring. Reynolds had known Carysfort since at least 1765, when as a thirteen-year-old he and his sister had sat to Reynolds for a portrait.[13] Since that time the two had become firm friends. Carysfort was also Reynolds's patron, purchasing family portraits and several fancy pictures, including *A Nymph and Cupid*, exhibited by Reynolds at the Royal Academy in 1784.[14] Following the death of his first wife in November 1783 and his failure to gain a seat in Parliament the following year, Carysfort left England. He had reached St Petersburg by December 1784, travelling by way of the court of Frederick II at Potsdam.[15] He was evidently in Russia until the autumn of 1787.[16] The nature of his mission remains unclear, although there is evidence to suggest that he was involved in securing information on Russia's military capabilities.[17] In any event, we know that he had access to the highest levels of the Imperial court through his friendship with the British envoy, Alleyne Fitzherbert.

As Lord Carysfort would have noted, Catherine II already owned several paintings by Reynolds's contemporaries – West (fig. 22) and Joseph Wright (cats. 18–19). He duly persuaded the Empress that her collection would not be complete without at least one work by Sir Joshua. In December 1785 Carysfort wrote to Reynolds, giving him news of the commission from Catherine and Prince Potemkin. The artist was at first uncertain about the choice of subject for the commission.[18] Initially he contemplated an English historical episode involving Elizabeth I visiting her army at Tilbury dockyard in 1588 as it prepared to repel the Spanish Armada – a theme that would not only form a direct comparison between the great English Queen of the past and the present Russian Empress, but recall Peter the Great's own visit to the same dockyard.[19] In a similar vein Horace Walpole suggested that Reynolds should depict Peter the Great inspecting the dockyard at Deptford, 'which he thought would include something honourable to both nations'.[20] However, by the end of January, *The English Chronicle* (26–28 January) was able to report that Reynolds had decided on 'a young Hercules strangling the serpents', although it 'wished that a subject from the *Russian* history had employed his genius'. It is uncertain quite why Reynolds chose the story of the infant Hercules (which is recounted in the first of Pindar's Nemean Odes), although the subject had been exhibited as an oil painting the previous year at the Paris salon by Jean-Hugues Taraval.[21] It is also possible that he recalled the iconography employed by Falconet in his equestrian statue of Peter the Great, which has the tsar's horse crushing a writhing serpent under its hoof as a symbol of Imperial might.[22]

Reynolds's English contemporaries were clearly perplexed by his choice of subject.[23] By the 1780s, accompanied by a rising tide of patriotic pride, historical subject-matter that related to the nation's

Fig. 38: Caroline Watson after Sir Joshua Reynolds, *Their Excellencies Prince Serge and Princess Barbra Gagarin, with Prince Nicholas their Son*. Stipple engraving, 6 ¼ × 4 ⅞ in. (15.9 × 12.3 cm). 1777. The Trustees of the British Museum.

Fig. 39: Alexei Agapievich Osipov after Nikolai Ivanovich Tonchi, *Princess Catherine Romanovna Dashkova in Exile*. Coloured engraving, 19 ⅞ × 14 in. (50.6 × 35.5 cm). The State Hermitage Museum.

КНЯГИНЯ ЕКАТЕРИНА РОМАНОВНА ДАШКАВА

history and character was increasingly in vogue.[24] Reynolds's commission, as contemporaries were keenly aware, reflected not only on the artist but on the nation as a whole. Yet while popular opinion poured scorn on his chosen subject-matter, Reynolds continued to put his faith in the supremacy of 'poetic' truth over dry historical fact. Classical mythology may have been anathema to an English lay audience but to Reynolds it remained the touchstone of high art and the true *lingua franca* of the international artistic community. Indeed, only a few years earlier, in one of the Notes appended to William Mason's translation (1783) of C. A. Dufresnoy's *De arte graphica* of 1668, Reynolds had written that 'as the Painter speaks to the eye, a story in which fine feeling and curious sentiment is predominant, rather than palpable situation, gross interest, and distinct passion, is not suited to his purpose'.[25]

Reynolds devoted more time and effort on *The Infant Hercules Strangling the Serpents* than any other painting in his entire career, labouring over it between portrait commissions from February 1786 until the spring of 1788, when it was exhibited at the Royal Academy.[26] The picture proved problematic for several reasons. First, his ongoing portrait commitments meant that Reynolds could only

work on it sporadically. Second, Reynolds was quite inexperienced in dealing with groups of figures that were not conceived primarily as portraits. Further, despite his familiarity with Rubens's practice of making preparatory oil sketches, Reynolds did not follow this tried and tested method of work. Instead he began by concentrating on the figure of the infant Hercules, the only figure for which there are related pen-and-ink and oil studies.[27] The final problem that faced Reynolds was his decision to illustrate successive episodes from Pindar's verse narrative in one painting, incorporating the strangling of the serpents by Hercules and Amphitryon's subsequent arrival. As he later told Prince Potemkin, it was the first time that the entire subject had been painted in accordance with Pindar's text.[28]

Despite his faltering progress on the commission Reynolds continued to allow visitors into his picture gallery, the painting receiving more intense press coverage than had any other recent British painting.[29] Collectively, these reports reveal that Reynolds did not have any clear plan in mind before he began the work. More significantly, they show the extent to which the subject of the picture was overshadowed by Reynolds's obsession with form – the manipulation of colour and tone, which in his view were the principal aims of the painter.[30] By the spring of 1787 the work appeared to be progressing quite well, *The Morning Herald* for 11 April describing the painting as 'an extensive work consisting of thirteen figures'. Three months later *The World* (3 July) reported that 'all that few months since appeared upon the canvas, has been obliterated; and the story is told anew'. When it was eventually ready for exhibition in 1788, Reynolds candidly admitted that there were 'ten pictures under it, some better, some worse'.[31]

Reynolds appears to have painted his principal commission for Prince Potemkin, *The Continence of Scipio* (cat. 12), rather more rapidly. The painting depicted Scipio Africanus handing back a captive Carthaginian woman to her fiancé, and was clearly intended to advert to Potemkin's honour and self-discipline as a military leader. (Although, as Frederick Hilles has observed, 'whatever Potemkin's virtues may have been, continence was surely not one of them'.[32]) The textual sources for the painting were the chronicles of Livy and Valerius Maximus, a story that, as Reynolds later told Potemkin, was too well known to require a description.[33] Reynolds was familiar with the historical account of the story. He was also aware of at least two earlier (17th-century) paintings of the episode, one by Van Dyck (Oxford, Christ Church), the other by Nicolas Poussin. Indeed Poussin's *Continence of Scipio*, at one time part of the Walpole collection at Houghton, had been acquired from there only a few years earlier, in 1779, by the Empress Catherine – a factor that may have influenced Reynolds's decision to address the theme.[34] Even so, the subject had remained popular with artists in both England and France during the 18th century.[35]

As with *The Infant Hercules*, Reynolds permitted inspections of *The Continence of Scipio* before it was exhibited publicly. Among those who saw it was the amateur artist and critic William Young Ottley (1771–1836). Ottley, who could not then have been more than eighteen, told Reynolds that it reminded him of Parmigianino. 'Sir Joshua', he noted later, 'seemed angry, for it was stolen from that painter'.[36] Reynolds's *Continence of Scipio* does share strong stylistic affinities with Parmigianino, especially in the Mannerist elongation of the figures. However, the painting as a whole does not appear to have been based on Parmigianino, but rather resembles a version of the same subject by Jean-François de Troy (fig. 40), one of four large paintings executed in 1728 for Samuel Bernard's gallery in the rue Notre-Dame des Victoires, Paris. The prominent location of De Troy's picture in the 18th century, together with the close compositional similarities between the two works (not least in the attitude and attire of the figure of Scipio and the attendant figures behind), suggest that Reynolds had studied De Troy's picture prior to formulating his own work.

On a theoretical level, the work against which Reynolds may have measured his own achievement in *The Continence of Scipio* was Charles Lebrun's *The Queens of Persia at the Feet of Alexander* (fig. 41), commissioned by Louis XIV in 1660 and completed the following year. Known familiarly as '*The Tent of Darius*', Lebrun's painting (which Reynolds would have known via Jean Audran's engraving) had achieved a paradigmatic status through André Félibien's treatise of 1663 on the work, which was translated (1703) by William Parsons as *The Tent of Darius Explain'd*. Reynolds had discussed both Lebrun's painting (which he deeply admired) and Félibien's *Treatise* in his 'Eighth Discourse', delivered in 1778, as well as making substantial annotations to his own copy of the translation by Parsons.[37] His sole criticism was reserved for Lebrun's sober use of colour, because of which, 'the whole picture has a heavy air, and by no means

answers the expectation raised by the Print'.[38] Reynolds set out his own views on the matter earlier in the same 'Discourse': 'It ought, in my opinion, to be indispensably observed, that the masses of light in a picture be always of a warm mellow colour, yellow, red, or a yellowish-white; and that the blue, the grey, or the green colours be kept almost entirely out of these masses, and be used only to support and set off these warm colours; and for this purpose, a small proportion of cold colours will be sufficient.'[39] These dicta were scrupulously observed in *The Continence of Scipio*.

Fig. 40: Jean-François de Troy, *The Continence of Scipio*. Oil on canvas, 270 × 204 cm. Signed and dated 'DE TROY 1728'. Musée des Beaux-Arts, Neuchâtel.

Fig. 41: Charles Audran after Charles LeBrun, *The Queens of Persia at the Feet of Alexander*. Line engraving. The Trustees of the British Museum.

Fig. 42: Sir Joshua Reynolds, *A Nymph and Cupid*. Oil on canvas, 50 × 40 in. (127 × 101.6 cm). Sir John Soane's Museum, London.

Fig. 43: Sir Joshua Reynolds, *Girl Lounging in a Chair*. Pen and brown ink, 7 9/16 × 5 3/4 in. (19.2 × 14.6 cm). Private Collection (on loan to the Royal Academy of Arts, London).

Fig. 44: Sir Joshua Reynolds, *Venus*. Oil on canvas, 48 7/8 × 39 in. (124.2 × 99 cm). Exhibited at the Royal Academy exhibition in 1785. Robert and Jane Rosenblum.

Fig. 45: J. R. Smith after Sir Joshua Reynolds, *A Bacchante*. Mezzotint, 15 × 11 in. (38 × 27.9 cm). Published 6 September 1784. Private Collection.

Reynolds's one other commission for the Imperial Russian court was a version of a painting he had already exhibited at the Royal Academy in 1784 with the title *A Nymph and Cupid* and which he sold to Lord Carysfort, apparently for 200 guineas.[40] According to Reynolds's sales ledger, the version painted for Prince Potemkin (cat. 13) was also bought by Carysfort, who paid 100 guineas for it in June 1788.[41] Carysfort may, in turn, have presented it as a gift to Potemkin.[42] A third 'prime' version, retained by Reynolds, was purchased in 1821 by Sir John Soane (fig. 42).[43] *A Nymph and Cupid* was among Reynolds's most popular subject pictures, being reproduced as a stipple engraving in 1787 by John Raphael Smith, and extensively copied by Reynolds's acolytes well into the 19th century.[44]

Although *A Nymph and Cupid* was the title by which Reynolds exhibited the painting at the Royal Academy in 1784, it was also known as 'Love Untying the Zone of Beauty' and, more popularly, as 'Snake in the Grass' (the title inscribed on Smith's engraving), owing to the presence of a serpent in the foreground of certain versions (although not in the version presented to Potemkin). Reynolds himself called it 'the half-consenting', a reference to the coy attitude of the figure.[45] *A Nymph and Cupid* presents an overt depiction of sexuality. Even so, a formal link between the picture and Reynolds's 'fancy pictures' in-

volving children exists via the attitude of the female figure in the composition, which is partly derived from an earlier pen-and-ink sketch (fig. 43) of a much younger girl (one of his nieces perhaps) shown shielding herself bashfully from the eyes of the artist.[46]

A Nymph and Cupid was painted for pleasure, and to appeal to a specific group of cosmopolitan clients who appreciated its comparatively *risqué* subject-matter. Indeed, in terms of its market, a close parallel may be drawn between *A Nymph and Cupid* and *Venus* (fig. 44), which Reynolds exhibited at the Royal Academy in 1785, and which one reviewer described as 'a picture of temptation from her auburn lock to her painted toe'.[47] As with his *Nymph and Cupid* Reynolds retained the prime version of *Venus* (which he displayed prominently at the entrance to his picture gallery). The Duke of Dorset, who was at that time the ambassador to France, purchased a replica – or possibly even two versions – for export to Paris. And while the identity of the French buyers has never satisfactorily been established, one, according to contemporary newspaper accounts, was Louis XVI.[48] *Venus* was exactly the same size as *A Nymph and Cupid*. And since it was on the back page of his sitter-book for 1784 that Reynolds had referred to *A Nymph and Cupid* as 'the half-consenting', *Venus* was presumably the 'fully consenting' version, the two paintings (which are identical in size) possibly having been conceived as pendants, and painted for the delectation of Reynolds's courtly clientele.

When *A Nymph and Cupid* was shown at the Royal Academy, Horace Walpole described it as 'bad and gross'. He also identified Reynolds's model as one 'Miss Wilson', suggesting that he recognized her features at least, if not her form.[49] The identity of 'Miss Wilson' remains a mystery, although she may have been a courtesan or, less probably, an actress. More recently it has been suggested that Reynolds's 'nymph' was Emma Hart, erstwhile lover of the Honourable Charles Greville, and the future wife of Sir William Hamilton and notorious mistress of Admiral, Lord Nelson.[50] It is true that Emma was sitting to Reynolds around that time and was the model for *A Bacchante* (fig. 45), which Reynolds also exhibited at the Royal Academy in 1784.[51] It is also true that Reynolds's 'nymph' bears more than a passing resemblance to her (at the time it was also scurrilously rumoured that Emma had modelled naked at the Royal Academy).[52] However, even if Reynolds had used Emma as his model (or any other young woman known to his public), he ensured, through the coquettish gesture of the hand half-covering the face, that the public should be kept guessing as to her true identity.

A Nymph and Cupid was a deliberate tease, aimed at amusing the more worldly members of Reynolds's public and the private collectors who purchased replicas. *The Infant Hercules*, on the other hand, was entirely serious in intention, a visible sign of Reynolds's attention to the highest branch of art and a paradigm of the aims and ambitions of the British school of art. The importance of the painting as

an object of national pride was indicated by the placing of *The Infant Hercules*, over the chimneypiece in the Great Room at the Royal Academy exhibition of 1788 (fig. 46). The position was apparently chosen by Reynolds himself, not least because it was the first picture one would see on entering the room.[53] Although the painting has since darkened with age, its surface scarred by cracks and stained by bitumen, one can still understand why its richly impasted surface impressed Reynolds's fellow artist William Hodges, who memorably remarked that 'it looked as if it had been boiled in brandy'.[54] Fellow artists were intrigued by *The Infant Hercules*. Henry Fuseli, whose literary background equipped him uniquely among artists in Britain to function as an art critic of some distinction, wrote a fascinating review of it, in which he stated that the 'pathos of the subject' lay not in the narrative, but in the colour. Indeed, Fuseli believed the true value of the work could only be appreciated by viewing it in abstract terms: *The light and shade of the picture is balanced by two distinct masses. To him, who with a half-shut eye contemplates its effect, an illuminated torrent seems to wind between two darksome rocks from the top, and to lose itself in the lower parts of the picture.... Such is the work, which, if we may judge from the impressions it made during its exhibition, we must pronounce it, formed on principles, not sufficiently understood even in this country of the arts.*[55]

Fuseli, like Reynolds, believed in the supremacy of form over fable and shared his suspicion over the current popularity of modern-life history painting, which he regarded as faddish. It was not, however, an approach calculated to appeal to the layman, and newspaper critics were largely hostile to Reynolds's picture.[56]

In 1789 *The Continence of Scipio* was also shown to the British public at the Royal Academy. Compared to *The Infant Hercules*, reaction was quite favourable. It was, stated 'Candidus' of *The Public Advertiser* (30 April), 'worthy of the pencil of the President of the Royal Academy; and that, however the invidious and spiteful may rail, it is such as will adorn the cabinet of some future *connoisseur*'. However, the same critic also queried the cramped nature of the composition: 'The canvas is perhaps too small for the design, and the figures are, consequently, thrown together too closely.'[57] Less politely, *The Morning Post* (6 May) put forward the amusing – and visually plausible – suggestion that the 'man who is supposed to be praying, appears to be putting the tent in proper order'. It remained to be seen whether the compositional shortcomings of *The Continence of Scipio* or the principles on which *The Infant Hercules* was grounded would find a more sympathetic audience in Imperial Russia.

In November 1788, before it was shipped to Russia, *The Infant Hercules* was sent to be engraved at John Boydell's premises in Hampstead (although the resulting engraving by Charles Howard Hodges was not published until after Reynolds's death in 1793).[58] In August 1789 the painting, together with the *The Continence of Scipio*, was exported to St Petersburg under the care of Richard Sutherland, 'banker to her Imperial Majesty'.[59] Shortly before the pictures left England, Reynolds wrote to Prince Potemkin, informing him of their imminent arrival. With the letter he enclosed a description of *The*

Fig. 46: Pietro Martini after J. H. Ramberg, *The Royal Academy Exhibition 1788*. Line engraving, 14 ⅝ × 20 in. (35.6 × 50.8 cm). This detail shows Reynolds's *The Infant Hercules* on the west wall of the Great Room of Somerset House. Private Collection.

Fig. 47: C. H. Hodges after Sir Joshua Reynolds, *The Infant Hercules Strangling the Serpents*. Mezzotint, 25 ⅝ × 23 ⁷⁄₁₆ in. (65 × 59.5 cm). Published 1793. State Hermitage Museum.

Infant Hercules for the Empress as well as several editions of his collected *Discourses* in English, French and Italian, offering to dedicate a further projected volume of later *Discourses* to the Empress.[60] Uncharacteristically, Reynolds also took the opportunity to apologize for the shortcomings of Potemkin's picture (for which the Prince had apparently paid 500 guineas[61]), stating that he had been compelled to paint it on a smaller canvas than he had originally intended.[62] As has been suggested, Reynolds was probably prompted not merely by his own misgivings about the cramped composition of *The Continence of Scipio* but by similar criticism that had appeared in the British press.

We do not know whether Prince Potemkin, who died in 1791, admired *The Continence of Scipio*. However, a graphic account of the reception of *The Infant Hercules* was provided by the English engraver James Walker, whose print of it was published in January 1792 (fig. 76). Walker was present in the Russian court when Catherine inspected the painting in the Hermitage. He recalled with acute embarrassment that it 'was not so much admired as it ought to have been. The style was new to them, and his mode of loaded colouring not understood; in short, it was too voluptuous for their taste'.[63] To make matters worse, the French artist Gabriel-François Doyen, who was also in attendance, delighted in amusing the assembled company with a stream of sarcastic banter: 'Superbe tableau, Magnifique, Grand effet, Beau colori, Plein d'expression'. 'Then', stated Walker, 'after some little hesitation, he added with emphasis, "Renversez le, c'est toujours un beau tableau". I could have strangled him. In short, turn it topsy-turvy, it is always a fine picture.'[64] The criticism – based on the 'abstract' nature of the work – was ironically not dissimilar to that proffered in London by Fuseli. There was a further twist. Doyen, or so Reynolds had imagined, was among his closest French allies in the French Academy, the two artists having sworn a vow of eternal friendship some 40 years earlier in Rome.[65]

Whatever her personal feelings about *The Infant Hercules*, in March 1790 the Empress sent Reynolds a letter of gratitude via her ambassador in London, Count Vorontsov, together with a gold snuffbox with her own portrait medallion set in diamonds (although it was left to Reynolds's executors to collect the actual payment for *The Infant Hercules* and *Scipio*.[66]) The letter, written in French, was published in English by various London newspapers the following month.[67] According to the letter, both the *Discourses* and the painting revealed 'a most elevated genius'. Reynolds, in return, replied to thank her for the gift of the snuffbox and the opportunity to 'sollicit the patronage of a Sovereign to whom all the Poets, Philosophers, & Artists of the time have done homage & whose approbation has been courted by all the Geniuses of her Age'.[68]

1. Extracts from Lord Carysfort's letter are printed (in Russian) by Trubnikov 1913, p. 40. See also Hilles 1970, p. 269 and n. 6.
2. See Hilles 1970, n. 1.
3. See London 1986; Postle 1995.
4. See Hilles 1936, pp. 67 and 294.
5. Malone 1819, II, p. 427.
6. According to Northcote, the story was related by Reynolds himself. See Northcote 1818, II, p. 265.
7. Lord Carysfort also recommended John Hoppner, although nothing came of it. Correspondence relating to Reynolds and Vorontsov is printed in A. Krol' 1960, pp. 42–4. See also Hilles 1970, p. 274. Semyon (Simon) Vorontsov and Count Mikhail Vorontsov, were both painted by Lawrence in England (see cats. 20, 21).
8. Reynolds made the following memoranda of meetings with Princess Dashkova in his sitter book for 1780: 15 June, '5 Princess Desceau'; 22 June, 'Princess Desceau'; 7 July, '9 Princess Desceau', and later the same day (possibly in a different hand), '8 Princess Daschkaw'.
9. The letter is reproduced in Cotton 1859, pp. 71–2.
10. For a contemporary account of the Kamchadals, written in 1787 by the Frenchman, Jean de Lesseps, see Cross 1971, pp. 235–41. Lesseps noted (p. 239): 'The precocity of the girls is astonishing, and seems not at all to be affected by the coldness of the climate'.
11. Cotton 1859, p. 72.
12. The translation was by Ivan Tatishchev, 'Departmental Councillor', and was printed in St. Petersburg at the Printing Office of the School of Mines. See Hilles 1970, pp. 274–5.
13. My principal source of information on Reynolds's relations with Lord Carysfort is Nigel Aston's unpublished MS essay, 'Lord Carysfort and Sir Joshua Reynolds: the Patron as Friend'.
14. Reynolds recorded the sales of the first two paintings to Lord Carysfort in his account ledgers: 'June 8, 1774. Lord Carisfort, for Mrs Hartley and Bacchus. Frame paid 52 10 0 / Do. for a Strawberry Girl 52 10 0'. See Cormack 1968–70, p. 148. See also Graves and Conin 1899–1901, I, p. 444, III, pp. 1210–11, 1213–14; Postle 1995, pp. 13, 36–9, 42, 206 (*A Nymph with a Young Bacchus*); pp. 79–85, 206, 322 (*A Strawberry Girl*); pp. 198–9, 225, 322 (*A Nymph and Cupid*).
15. Lord Carysfort's permit from Frederick II to enter Prussia is dated 13 July 1784, British Library, Add. MSS 33610, fol. 6. For his arrival in St Petersburg see his letter to Sir Robert Keith, British Envoy in Vienna, dated 3 December 1784, British Library, *Hardwicke Papers*, Add. MSS 35533, fol. 54.
16. On 11 December 1786 Thomas Orde told the Duke of Rutland, that Lord Carysfort would return to England for the ensuing parliamentary session. See *Historical Manuscript Commission. Fourteenth Report, Appendix, Part I. The Manuscripts of his Grace the Duke of Rutland, K.G., preserved at Belvoir Castle* (London, 1894), III, p. 361. He was apparently still out of the country the following August, although he was apparently planning to return imminently. See Lord Buckingham to W. W. Grenville, 9 September 1787, *Historical Manuscript Commission. Thirteenth Report, Appendix, Part III. The Manuscripts of J. B. Fortescue, Esq., preserved at Dropmore* (London, 1892), I, p. 281.
17. See *H.M.C. Dropmore*, I, p. 281.
18. See the letter from Theophila Palmer to William Johnson, in Leslie and Taylor 1865, II, p. 482.
19. Northcote 1818, II, p. 214. It has been suggested that Reynolds rejected the idea of Elizabeth I's visit to Tilbury because the it had been burlesqued in Sheridan's *The Critic* of 1779. See Tinker 1938, p. 65.
20. Hannah More (10 May 1786), in Roberts 1834, II, p. 21. See also Walpole 1937–83, XXXI, p. 243.
21. Rosenblum 1986, p. 51, fig. 38.
22. Although Reynolds had not seen the statue he would have known it through Falconet's autobiography, which he owned. See Falconet 1781, VI, p. 202f.
23. Hannah More was evidently reflecting general opinion, when she told her sister that Walpole's idea about Peter the Great at Deptford was 'much more worthy of the pencil of the artist than nonsensical Hercules'. See Roberts 1834, II, p. 16.
24. See Postle 1995, pp. 208–9.
25. Quoted in Malone 1819, III, p. 104.

26. Reynolds's first recorded appointment with a model relating to *The Infant Hercules* was on Sunday 12 February 1786, when he noted in his pocket book 'Boy for Hercules'. (It was not 12 January, as stated by Hilles 1970, p. 269.)

27. See Postle 1995, pp. 211–12.

28. Reynolds to Potemkin (4 August, 1789). Hilles 1970, p. 271. See also Trubnikov 1913, p. 41; Postle 1995, pp. 212–13. The version (in French) printed in Hilles 1970 was transcribed from the original letter, and differs slightly in spelling and punctuation from the text originally published in Trubnikov 1913.

29. For press reports on *The Infant Hercules* see Postle 1995, p. 213ff. Evidence suggests that when Reynolds was not at work on paintings in his studio, they were hung in the custom-built picture gallery in his house. It was here, rather than in his own studio, that visitors would have inspected *The Infant Hercules*.

30. See Postle 1995, pp. 213–18.

31. Northcote 1818, II, p. 219.

32. Hilles 1970, p. 271.

33. *Ibid.*

34. *Ibid.*

35. Benjamin West had exhibited the subject at the Society of Artists in 1766, while, in 1789, the same year that Reynolds showed his version of the subject at the Royal Academy, Nicholas-Guy Brenet (1728–92) exhibited his version of *The Continence of Scipio* at the Paris Salon.

36. Haydon 1960–63, IV, p. 100.

37. See Postle 1995, pp. 227–8.

38. Reynolds 1975, p. 158.

39. *Ibid.*

40. There is no record of the purchase in Reynolds's sales ledger. The price of 200 guineas is cited in an appendix (unpaginated) to Northcote 1813–15. See also Northcote 1818, II, p. 350.

41. 'June 14, 1788 Lord Carisfort, for the Nymph, to be sent to Prince Potemkin 105 0 0'. See Cormack 1968–70, p. 149.

42. See Dukelskaya and Renne 1990, cat. 72.

43. Sold by the estate of the Marchioness of Thomond (Reynolds's niece), 19 May, 1821, lot 74, for £535 10s to Sir John Soane, RA. See Graves and Cronin 1899–1901, III, p. 1211; Postle 1995, pp. 199–200. A fourth full-scale version was also painted as a gift for Reynolds's friend Henry Hope. See Northcote 1813, appendix (unpaginated). Although it appears to have been painted entirely by a pupil of Reynolds there is no reason to believe (as it has been stated) that this, or similar studio copies, were painted by James Northcote, who had left Reynolds's studio nearly ten years earlier.

44. See Graves and Cronin 1899–1901, III, p. 1211.

45. Reynolds's reference to the painting is contained in the back of his sitter-book for 1784 among a list of the paintings he intended to exhibit at the Royal Academy that year.

46. See Herrmann 1968, p. 65, fig. 14.

47. *The Public Advertiser* (5 April 1785).

48. See Postle 1995, pp. 203–4.

49. Walpole identified Reynolds's model as Miss Wilson in his copy of the Royal Academy exhibition catalogue. The model's name does not appear in Reynolds's sitter-book in 1784. (A 'Miss Jones', whose address Reynolds gives as No. 4 Cross Court, Bow Street, Covent Garden, and who sat to him twice in November and December 1784, was probably a model - although there is no way of knowing whether she was linked to *A Nymph and Cupid*.)

50. See Krol' 1939, p. 28; Lisenkov 1964, p. 149.

51. See Graves and Cronin 1899–1901, II, pp. 425–6.

52. See Angelo 1904, II, p. 184. Angelo states, on the authority of James Northcote, that the rumour was 'entirely void of truth'.

53. See Northcote 1818, II, p. 218.

54. *Ibid.*

55. *Analytical Review* (May–August 1788), I, p. 218.

56. See Postle 1995, p. 219.

57. 'Candidus', *The Public Advertiser* (30 April 1789).

58. See Postle 1995, pp. 221–2. Hodges's engraving (fig. 47) was published on 25 March 1793 by J. & J. Boydell at the Shakespeare Gallery, Pall Mall, 90 Cheapside. See Van der Feltz 1982, p. 302, cat. 602.

59. In his letter to Potemkin of 4 August 1789 Reynolds stated: 'Ces deux ouvrages … sont adresses à Monsieur Sutherland, et viennent d'être portes à bord du navire le Friendship qui doit incessamment mettre à la voile pour St Petersburg'. See Trubnikov 1913, pp. 40–41, also Hilles 1970, p. 270.

60. As a second volume was not produced during Reynolds's lifetime it was not necessary to reply to Reynolds's offer. See Hilles 1970, p. 273 and n. 11.

61. Malone 1819, I, p. lxiv, stated that Potemkin paid 500 guineas for *The Continence of Scipio*. There is no record of the transaction in Reynolds's accounts ledger, although Graves and Cronin 1899–1901, III, p. 1139, state that the entry was probably recorded on the missing page of the relevant ledger.

62. Reynolds's letter to Potemkin is reprinted in Hilles 1970, p. 271. In relation to Reynolds's comments on the cramped composition of the present picture it is worth noting that while *The Infant Hercules* measures 119 x 117 ins., *The Continence of Scipio* measures only 94 x 65 ins., only slightly larger than the canvas used by Reynolds for his standard full-length portraits (which measure around 94 x 57 ins.).

63. Cross 1993, p. 146.

64. *Ibid.*, p. 147.

65. See Leslie and Taylor 1865, I, p. 55 and pp. 414–15. A note inside Reynolds's 1782 sitter-book reads 'a copy of a Paper I gave to Mr. Doyen to bye [*sic*] those Pictures at the Abbe Renoux at St Sulpice'.

66. According to the text of her original letter Catherine had presented Reynolds with the snuffbox 'as a testimony of the great satisfaction the perusal of his Discourses' had given her, rather than for the paintings. However, she later mis-remembered that the snuffbox had been in lieu of payment – a point contested by Reynolds's executors. See Hilles 1970, pp. 276–7.

67. The letter is dated 4 March 1790. It is reproduced in full in Archive of Prince Vorontsov 1883, XXVIII, p. 113; Trubnikov 1913, p. 49f; and in part in Hilles 1970, p. 273, and n. 12. The English version appeared in *The London Chronicle* (8–10 April 1790); *The English Chronicle and Universal Evening Post* (8–10 April 1790); *The Diary* (12 April 1790); *The Whitehall Evening Post* (10–13 April 1790). It was also reprinted in Northcote 1818, II, p. 217.

68. Reprinted in Hilles 1929, pp. 205–6; Hilles 1970, pp. 275–6.

SCOTTISH ARCHITECTS IN IMPERIAL RUSSIA AND THEIR DRAWINGS IN THE HERMITAGE

Miliza Korshunova

In the late 18th century, three Scottish architects discovered that Russia offered real opportunities for them to put into practice their knowledge and skills – Charles Cameron (1745–1812), William Hastie (1755–1832) and Adam Menelaws (1749–1831), and architectural drawings by all three can be found in the Hermitage. Thanks to the particularly elegant and widely admired structures Cameron designed for the Imperial palaces and grounds at Tsarskoye Selo and Pavlovsk he is the best known, but the lack of information readily available on his background has in the past led many Russians to imagine him as a somewhat glamourous *émigré* figure, and even as a Jacobite aristocrat.[1] As we now know, much of that fantastic, almost wholly bogus, persona was invented by Cameron himself, for recently Professor Dmitry Shvidkovsky has been piecing together every fact available on Cameron, delving deeply into both Russian and foreign archives as well as re-examining all the published literature. Shvidkovsky has solved many hitherto vexing puzzles, and the result is that at last we have a coherent and detailed account of Cameron's background and early years as well as his architectural achievements in Russia.[2]

According to his birth certificate, Cameron was born on 1 July 1745,[3] and was actually the son of a London builder, albeit one of Scottish origin. He had some training in London as a carpenter, then as an engraver, and he also gained his earliest knowledge about architecture while there, after which he continued his studies in the 1760s in Italy, devoting his time wholly to classical architecture and its remains, as did many of his generation. Even so, although Cameron was certainly in Rome in 1768, opinion differs as to the length of time he spent abroad.[4] Apparently while there he attached himself to the Scots *émigrés* grouped around the Young Pretender, Charles Edward Stuart, a number of whom had been involved in the failed Jacobite rebellion of 1745. The result of Cameron's stay in Italy was *The Baths of the Romans explained and illustrated* (1772), a careful series of measurements that corrected those undertaken by the Renaissance architect Andrea Palladio (1508–80).[5] A copy of Cameron's rare publication, which is illustrated with a number of engravings, is in the Hermitage library, a library that in fact was largely assembled by Catherine II herself.

The circumstances that led Cameron to depart for St Petersburg are not wholly clear. There are no letters of recommendation; no contracts inviting him to Russia have been found. It appears that he somehow learned of Catherine's desire to build a villa in 'the Roman style', a project originally accepted by the French architect Charles-Louis Clérisseau in 1773 but which Clérisseau was afterwards unable to carry out. Cameron was soon hurrying to Russia in the hope of being able to put to use his knowledge of the Antique. At the same time, of course, like all his contemporaries flocking to Russia he was not uninterested in the great financial rewards that might be obtained from the richest ruler in Europe. On 25 October 1779 he was taken into service at the Imperial court, perhaps partly on the basis of *The Baths of the Romans*, the proof to the Russian court of his erudition.

Cameron's ideas regarding the recreation of an Antique villa with all the necessary furnishings for everyday use impressed the Empress. She was also particularly attracted to things British, which was perhaps part of the reason for her patronage of a foreign architect, moreover an architect that hitherto seems never to have actually built anything. He was soon put in charge of all the building works at her favourite residence, Tsarskoye Selo. During this early phase Cameron had no competitors in Russia, although in January 1780 Giacomo Quarenghi (1744–1817) and Giacomo Trombara (1746–1812) both entered the service of the Russian court. Unlike Cameron, who was responsible for realizing Catherine's personal architectural fantasies, they received state commissions, but soon the equally talented but far more unctuous Quarenghi was beginning to oust Cameron as favourite. Prior to that, however, Catherine was boasting to Voltaire that 'A present, je me suis emparée de mister Cameron, écossais de nation, jacobite de profession, grand dessinateur, nourri d'antiquités, connu par un livre sur les bains anciens; nous faconnons avec lui un jardin en terrace avec bains dessous, galéries dessus; cela sera du beau.'[6] She was referring to Cameron's creation of a whole complex, the so-called Cold Baths at Tsarskoye Selo, which united her personal baths, a pavilion for rest and relaxation (the Agate rooms), a hanging garden and a promenade gallery flanked by colonnades, later known as the Cameron Gallery. And although the Empress liked to be involved in all the details of design and construction, she had total confidence in his artistic taste.

The construction of the Cold Baths began in the spring of 1780 and it was not finished until 1787. It was sited close to the Catherine Palace built by Bartolomeo Rastrelli in the Late Baroque style in the 1750s. The ground floor housed the bathing-room and Russian steam-baths. Above it was a pavilion of austere design. Two rooms, at the insistence of the Empress, were finished in coloured stones, mainly variegated jasper from the Urals. Since at that time the many different kinds of jasper were known as agates, the whole building afterwards became known as the Agate Pavilion. Its main façade is a half-rotunda facing the hanging garden, of which the colonnaded promenade gallery forms a continuation.

The promenade gallery, recalling an antique temple, rises over Tsarskoye Selo's parkland. It gave shade from the sun and protection from bad weather, and it was also home to numerous portraits of ancient Greek philosophers, poets and Roman emperors. Catherine liked to walk along this gallery, from which she could step out to the colonnade to gaze across the surrounding landscape. Later, in 1792, at the request of the ageing Empress, Cameron added a limestone *pente douce*, a gentle ramp supported by a series of descending arches that descended from the hanging garden to the park.

In the 1780s Cameron also worked on interior decorations for the Catherine Palace, designing the Empress's private rooms and those of the heir to the throne, Grand-Duke Paul Petrovich, and his wife, Maria Fyodorovna. Unlike Rastrelli's interiors, which were richly decorated with gilded carving and had vast ceilings, Cameron's novel living accommodation was a model of elegant refinement in which Antique motifs were played up and arabesques blended with garlands of stylized plants and stucco compositions in low relief.

While still busy at Tsarskoye Selo, Cameron was put in charge of designing a country residence for Grand-Duke Paul in the village of Pavlovskoye (now Pavlovsk), which had been presented to the Grand-Duke on the birth in 1777 of his first son, the future Alexander I. Work at Pavlovsk began on 25 May 1782, a palace very different to

Fig. 48: The Main Hall of the Agate Pavilion in the Cameron Gallery at the Catherine Palace at Tsarskoye Selo, 1780–85. The columns of grey-pink Karelia marble are the work of Alexei Kochetov. Photo courtesy of Hazar Publishing.

Fig. 49: F. I. Alexeyev, *The Cameron Gallery and the Private Garden*, 1823. Oil on canvas, 32 ¼ × 45 ¼ in. (82 × 115 cm). State Hermitage Museum.

that at Tsarskoye Selo, being of the country estate type, with a central block, semicircular colonnades and lateral pavilions. The scheme was Palladian in spirit, one that had been widely utilized in England for much of the 18th century and which in turn gave rise to many imitations in Russia. The surrounding woods were turned by Cameron into an English landscape garden, with small structures forming compositional accents: a Temple of Friendship, the Apollo Colonnade, the Cold Baths, an aviary, and the Pavilion of the Three Graces.

Although during his feverish career under Catherine, Cameron basked in the Empress's approval, following her death in 1796 he came to know the bitter experience of disfavour, for he was neglected by Paul I and his consort Maria. Several years of inactivity in a kind of wilderness followed, yet for Cameron there seemed to be no point in returning to an England where his name meant little. Only in 1802 did the situation improve. Following Alexander I's accession in 1801, he was assigned the position of architect to the Admiralty, a post in which he served until his retirement in 1805.

Cameron's ideas were captured perfectly in his office drawings, the greater part of which are today in the Hermitage. The story of how they came to be there is itself an intriguing one, for after the architect's death in St Petersburg in 1812, his widow, the daughter of the Imperial gardener John Bush, had travelled to England, taking her husband's entire archive with her.

On 12 May 1820, however, a serious fire broke out in the Catherine Palace, and that part of the Palace which included Cameron's interiors was destroyed. Two years later (on 11 April) the Minister of the Imperial Court, Prince Pyotr Mikhaylovich Volkonsky, who was then drawing up plans for its reconstruction, found himself obliged to contact Count Khristofor Liven, the Russian ambassador in London: 'We now discover that in order to redecorate the burned interiors of the Tsarskoye Selo palace we must have those drawings from which the rooms — particularly the ceilings — of the said palace were reworked during the time of the court architect Cameron, thus … would it not be possible, through your mediation, kind sir, to acquire from the heirs … all the drawings he left behind, which relate to the decoration of the walls and ceilings …'.[7] Count Liven was able to respond on 11 July with the welcome news that, 'under a different name, in order to avoid the demand of too high a sum', he had seen the heir, a Mr Cameron, who had agreed to a sale. Having sorted through 'a somewhat numerous collection of all kinds of plans and drawings by the said architect … selected everything that answered to the description of Your Highness, comprising 114 sheets. Mr Cameron at first demanded for this selection £200, but finally agreed to the sum of £105.'[8] On 3 August 1822 Prince Volkonsky confirmed receipt of Cameron's drawings.[9]

We can only speculate about Count Liven's qualifications in architectural matters and about the artistic criteria that guided him when selecting the drawings. To judge from his letter, some of Cameron's 'plans and drawings' still remained with Cameron's heir after Liven's departure, and these perhaps should be sought in England. The sheets that Liven acquired for the Russian court were used in the reconstruction of the Tsarskoye Selo palace, and were used a second time for the

Fig. 50: A. Y. Martynov, *The Balconies of the Cameron Gallery, the Terasse des Miroirs, the Pandous Ramp and the Zubov Wing*, c. 1810. Watercolour on paper, 14 9/16 × 18 1/8 in. (37 × 46 cm). State Hermitage Museum.

Fig. 51: Giacomo Quaranghi, *The Apollo Colonnade and Cascade at Pavlovsk*, c. 1800. Watercolour, 8 3/16 × 11 7/8 in. (20.8 × 30.3 cm). State Hermitage Museum.

Fig. 52: The Palace at Pavlovsk designed by Charles Cameron. © Francesco Venturi / KEA.

Fig. 53: Charles Cameron, *Design for a Ceiling,*
with the author's signature. Watercolour.
State Hermitage Museum.

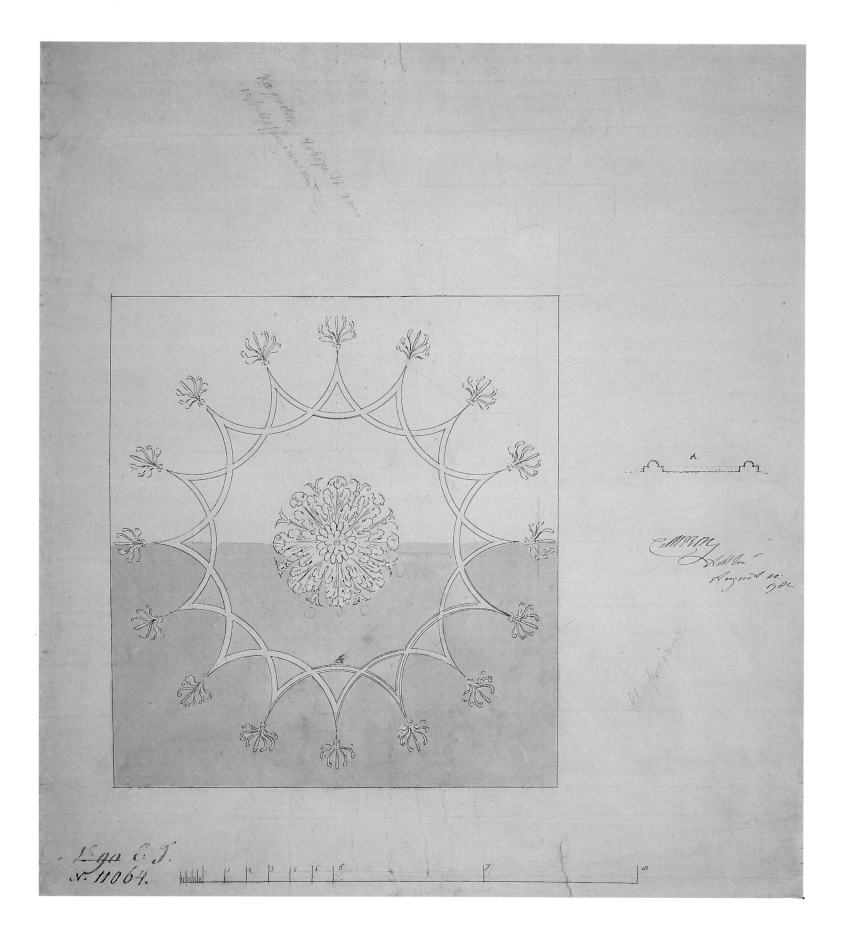

same purpose after the palace was almost destroyed during the Second World War.

The drawings that returned to Russia are various. Some can be linked to specific rooms in the Palace and to the Agate Pavilion (see cats. 33–46), though others cannot. They are also by different hands. Of 114 sheets, two have been attributed to Yuri Velten, who also worked at Tsarskoye Selo in the 1770s and 1780s.[10] Of the rest, very few are by Cameron himself, the greater part having been produced in his office, presumably by assistants. They tend to be records of finished appearances rather than preliminary designs. It is possible that they were copies from the architect's own designs and were used as working drawings during construction, as is suggested by the fact that some of them bear relevant notes and scribbles. Cameron's original drawings in the 1764 album,[11] and a few in the Hermitage and Pavlovsk Palace collections, give us a very clear idea of the architect's own graphic style. Spurning pen and ink, he worked with brush and watercolour, producing compositions of elegant colouring that precisely reproduce the outline of objects but which give no sense of volume, making the drawings appear very flat. Only one of Cameron's drawings in the Hermitage, a design for an ornamental stuccoed ceiling, is signed by him (fig. 53).

Although the majority of drawings in the Cameron archive are somewhat weak in execution, they convey the rich fantasy and colourful variety of the architect's decorative compositions. The inscriptions on the scales at the bottom of these drawings are in Russian, which suggests that his assistants were themselves Russians. The refined details of the decorative elements in the interiors, and the use of a variety of artistic expression, suggest none the less that some of the draughtsmen were from a different school. In fact Cameron brought in a large number of Scottish craftsmen to speed up construction at Tsarskoye Selo as well as to ensure some independence from the vagaries of local craftsmen. The Scots were settled in sixteen houses built of timber on stone foundations belonging to the Treasury, erected to a design by Cameron himself, in the newly founded town of Sofiya, which abutted the southern edge of the Tsarskoye Selo complex. These buildings can be seen in a drawing by Giacomo Quarenghi of the Sophia Cathedral, also designed by Cameron (Museum of the History of St Petersburg, A–I–526a). Among the Scots who arrived to work under Cameron were William Hastie and Adam Menelaws.

Compared to Cameron's legacy, Hastie's work in Russia is less brilliant, but it is far from mediocre. Catherine also played a direct role in Hastie's fate, since it has recently been possible to establish that he arrived in 1784 with a group of craftsmen invited from Scotland by the Empress to help Cameron.[12] On 21 January 1784, the *Edinburgh Evening News* had published an announcement offering work in Russia to those in the building trades.[13] The advertisement was answered by 73 men, who signed contracts for three years and set off for Russia by sea, many of them travelling with their wives and children. On 23 May of that year they arrived at Kronstadt, the Russian capital's port, where they were met by Cameron, who did much to help them establish themselves.[14] Because of the urgent nature of the work at Tsarskoye Selo, it was simpler and more reliable for Cameron to work with his fellow countrymen, among whom were representatives of every trade: masons, plasterers, blacksmiths, vault-builders, bricklayers, journeymen and so forth.[15]

Hastie, then 29 years old, had trained as a stonemason. His varied interests, undoubted talent and the favourable conditions helped the young Scot to climb from the position of artisan to that of a recognized architect and engineer. We cannot fully unravel all the twists and turns of his career, but we do have the main facts. The year 1794 marked a turning point: on 4 September the Empress told the literary critic and connoisseur of the arts Friedrich Melchior Grimm, for many years her correspondent: 'J'ai tous les ouvrages des frères Adams. Ce Hastie, architecte dont vous me parlez, je l'ai pris à mon service; c'est un sujet très recommandable: il a fait des choses charmantes.'[16] Unfortunately the published letters of Grimm do not contain the document that must have served as a recommendation and which greatly influenced Hastie's subsequent career.

It was evidently at this time that Hastie was presented to the Empress, a suggestion supported by material in the Hermitage. First we have two notes accompanying drawings, and second, Hastie's drawings themselves. An album of 57 drawings has, on the title-page, the inscription: 'This book was presented by Candidate of Architecture Hastie at Tsarskoye Selo 1794.'[17] The second text is directly linked with the first: 'I am sending you with this for the library of Her Imperial Majesty two plans, a façade and cross-section(?) made to the set programme by Candidate of Architecture Hastie, to be put with the book presented by him [...]. 20 August 1794.' If we put together Catherine's letter to Grimm, and the date of the second text, we can conclude that the drawings in the Hermitage collection are the very ones that the Empress looked at and which resulted in her approving estimate of his abilities.[18]

In accordance with the 'set programme', Hastie presented a design for a country house on four sheets: plans of the first floor, a plan of the second floor of the main building, an elevation and a cross-section through the central axis of the main building (cats. 47, 48). All the drawings are signed. The estate complex consists of a main building and four wings placed at equal distances from it connected by colonnades, on two sides enclosing in a semi-circle the immediate territory of the main block. The division of volumes, the emphatic centrality and the wide use of classical orders determine the proportional relationship of all the parts of the building in a way characteristic of 18th-century Palladianism. Hastie's design is not a particularly original work, and would seem to have been influenced by the British architect James Paine, indicating that he must have been familiar with Paine's published drawings.[19] The closest analogy in Russia for this kind of country house was the palace at Pavlovsk, built by Hastie's master, Cameron.

The common elements in the work of Hastie and Cameron lie mainly in the principles of planning, which became known in the Russian specialist literature as the English estate system. This scheme was developed by Ivan Starov in his construction of the Tauride Palace in St Petersburg (1783–6), by Giacomo Quarenghi at the Lyalichi estate in the Ukraine (1780s) and Nikolai L'vov at Polyustrovo, near Petersburg, as well as in the Znamenskoye-Rayok estate in Tver' province (1780s). Hastie's drawings are professionally and very carefully executed, and are marked by great subtlety in both the drawing and use of wash.

Of no less interest is Hastie's album of drawings mentioned above. This includes proposed designs for the area around the palace at Tsarskoye Selo: façades, mainly for residential buildings, as well as palaces and garden pavilions. The greater part of the designs are in a classicizing style, although several sheets show some similarity with 18th-century Gothic structures.[20] The drawings are in pen and ink, some of them tinted with watercolour, and it is more than likely that Hastie developed his skills in Cameron's office. Hastie's *chiaroscuro* modelling of architectural forms is very expressive, although the manner is somewhat laboured, and he was less successful in his depiction of sculptural details on the elevations. The Hermitage also has another fifteen varied pieces by Hastie, who appears to have been copying engravings of famous buildings in Paris by leading French architects, including the Hôtel de Salme (by Pierre Rousseau), the Hôtel Guimard (C.-N. Ledoux) and the Théâtre de l'Odéon (J.-M. Peyre and Charles de Wailly).

Hastie's career was further advanced by Catherine's favourite, Prince Pavel Zubov, who was appointed Governor of Yekaterinoslav and Tauris (the Crimea), and on 5 July 1795 he invited Hastie to serve as architect of the province, a post Hastie accepted and occupied until 3 June 1799.[21] In 1798 Hastie supplied volumetric drawings of the Bakchisarai Palace in the Crimea in connection with major repair works being undertaken in the dilapidated building. These drawings are important in that they capture the appearance of the palace and give us some idea of the lost interiors. Hastie has also bequeathed us an album of drawings and measurements of a number of other sites in the Crimea.[22] According to his service record, in 1801 Hastie – along with his fellow countryman Charles Gascoign – was also working on the construction of a building for the Kolpino Factory near St Petersburg, which was to be one of the largest enterprises in the country.

In 1804 Hastie was appointed to the Office of Waterways, run by Count N. P. Rumyantsev who, according to his contemporaries, 'patronized people of talent and learning'.[23] It was at this time that Hastie proved himself to be a talented bridge-builder. He was the first in Russia, apparently not without some help from Gascoign, to develop a technique for making cast-iron parts for broad-span bridges, which he put to good use on the main roads of St Petersburg. He designed several bridges to replace the wooden ones across the River Moika. The opening of the first of these on 14 November 1806, the Police Bridge on Nevskii Prospekt (see cat. 52), became a city-wide holiday and was marked with a great celebration. This was followed by the Red, Blue, Yellow (or Kiss) bridges and others.

The success in building these iron bridges, and the wide public recognition that followed as they became significant elements in the ornamentation of the Russian capital, made Hastie one of the leading masters of his time in Russia. Soon after this he returned to architectural practice, and in the next phase of his life was active in town planning and construction. In 1808, on the orders of Alexander I, the provincial town of Tsarskoye Selo was founded, on the basis of the settlement that had grown up around the palaces there, and the town of

Fig. 54: Adam Menelaws, *Landscape in the Aleksandrovsky Park at Tsarskoye Selo*, after 1828. Watercolour over pencil, 14 × 19 ⅞ in. (35.5 × 50.5 cm). State Hermitage Museum.

Fig. 55: Adam Menelaws, *Design for a Farm in the Aleksandrovsky Park at Tsarskoye Selo*, 1818. Watercolour, pen and ink and wash, 23 ⅝ × 37 ¾ in. (60 × 96 cm). State Hermitage Museum.

Sofiya. The already inhabited area, however, formed only a small part of the new-planned town. Hastie was appointed its architect, and his suggestion that it be built on a strict regular scheme was adopted; it continues to influence the layout of the town today. The architect developed designs for new buildings in Tsarskoye Selo,[24] determined the direction and width of the streets, the administrative centre, and the height of the buildings, which are still to be seen in the old part of the town.

From 1810 Hastie was in control of town building in Russia according to plans approved by the state's Construction Committee. The need to improve and give some order to the construction of towns that arose at this time had made it necessary to draw up model plans. Hastie was also involved in the drawing up of two parts of the *Collection of Façades approved by His Imperial Highness for private buildings in towns of the Russian Empire*, published in 1809 in an edition of 200 copies and sent out to the different provinces. In 1813 he produced a plan for the reconstruction of Moscow, laid waste by the fire of 1812 after its brief occupation by Napoleon's army. This plan was never executed, but many of Hastie's suggestions were used by the architects S. S. Cassarino and Osip Bove when they produced their final plan for Moscow in 1818.

Hastie continued as town architect at Tsarskoye Selo until his death on 4 June 1832; he was buried at Tsarskoye Selo, in the Kazan Cemetery for those not of the Orthodox faith.[25]

The career of another member of the Scottish colony in Sofiya, Adam Menelaws, is also of interest, for his reputation has fared badly in comparison with that of his Russian colleagues,[26] and is therefore in need of more objective assessment.[27] According to the 'Bulletin of Workers', Menelaws was 35 years old when he arrived in Russia, and

was a 'master of free crafts'.[28] In the first year he worked in Cameron's team, but the following year he was attached to the famous Russian architect Nikolai Aleksandrovich L'vov (1751–1803), initially on the construction of the Cathedral of St Joseph at Mogilyov and then on the Monastery of SS Boris and Gleb at Torzhok. A man of varied interests and great erudition, L'vov was also a great patriot and a proponent of charcoal and turf as a cheap source of energy for heating. He was the first to develop a school of construction using *terre pisé* (rammed earth). In all his undertakings L'vov's mainstay was Menelaws, who looked on L'vov as his teacher and patron. With the death of L'vov in December 1803, the first period of Menelaws's active and varied career came to an end. In the following February Menelaws requested that he be relieved from his duties in the service of the state, and although there were a number of offers of well-paid posts as architect in the Saratov and Mogilyov provinces, in Moscow and in the capital, he insisted on resigning, and this took effect in August 1806.[29]

Henceforward, Menelaws preferred to carry out private commissions. His main patron and client was to be Count Aleksey Kirillovich Razumovsky (1748–1822), for whom he designed buildings in Moscow and the Ukraine.[30] In 1814 Razumovsky, then Minister of Education, and A. N. Olenin, President of the Academy of Arts, recommended Menelaws to the Construction Committee attached to the Ministry of Internal Affairs. In May 1817 work began on the reconstruction of the former Menagerie at Tsarskoye Selo, on land immediately abutting the Alexander Palace, in the new landscape park. Work on planning and improvement were the responsibility of Menelaws.[31] Over the course of twenty years he created a romantic ensemble in the English Gothic style, in keeping with the taste and

mood of the era. His idea was to transform the area, planting thousands of trees and bushes and decorating the park with pavilions, gates, bridges, cascades and ponds.[32] A large number of Menelaws's designs linked with this ensemble are in the Hermitage. It is possible that the artist Ivan Alekseyevich Ivanov (1781–1848) may have been involved in the execution of some of them since the two met while working together under L'vov. Over the years, working with Russian masters, Menelaws acquired a reasonably good knowledge of the Russian language, and many of his drawings and documents linked with construction have his characteristic signature and inscriptions in Russian, albeit with grammatical mistakes.[33] In the centre of the park Menelaws rebuilt the dilapidated Baroque Monbijou Pavilion, erected in the 1740s to a design by Savva Chevakinsky and Francesco Rastrelli. In 1819 he transformed it into something clearly comparable to Shrubs Hill, a Gothic castle in England. After its later remodelling the building became known as the Arsenal, and it was there that Nicholas I kept his rich collection of weapons (now in the Hermitage).

Near the Alexander Palace a 'medieval' complex grew up, including the so-called White Tower (1821–7), a five-storey, square tower with lancet windows that reached 37.8 metres. Eight iron sculptures of knights by Vasily Demut-Malinovsky were set on the terrace, in the niches in the walls. This Knights' Tower, as it came to be known, was guarded by cast-iron lions. Near the Tower were gates with small round towers and a bridge over a moat. This building also has its English precedent in Carisbrooke Castle on the Isle of Wight.

The Knights' Tower was intended for games and entertainment for the heir to the throne, Grand-Duke Alexander Nikolayevich, the future Alexander II, for at the beginning of each summer the Imperial family usually left St Petersburg for Tsarskoye Selo and settled in the Alexander Palace. The park also had a chapel, the Sainte-Chapelle, suggesting a medieval ruin; its stained-glass lancet windows, and the azure vault straining upwards with its gilded stars, recalled a Gothic church. Inside the chapel, on a granite pedestal, stood a white marble Crucifixion executed in 1824 by the German sculptor Johann Danneker (1758–1841).[34] This romantic ensemble in the Alexander Park was the backdrop on 23 May 1842 for one of the most grandiose court celebrations of Nicholas I's reign. This masquerade was painted by Horace Vernet in his Carousel at Tsarskoye Selo (carousel being the name for a French tourney).

The most important household building was the farm running along the northern edge of the Alexander Park. This large complex of buildings with Gothic decorative elements on the façades was erected between 1818 and 1822 and included cow-stalls, a barn for sheep, a dairy for cheesemaking (see fig. 55), a dovecote, an aviary, and a barn for hay and feedstuffs, while cottages were also built for those employed there.

Between 1827 and 1832 the Egyptian Gates designed by Menelaws were erected at the entry into Tsarskoye Selo from St Petersburg (completed after his death; see fig. 56).[35] This late work reflects a number of new elements that began to make their appearance in the

Fig. 56: The Egyptian Gates at Tsarskoye Selo (1827–32) designed by Adam Menelaws. Photo courtesy of Jeremy Howard.

19th century. The gates were decorated with reliefs, partial copies of genuine Egyptian antiquities of which outline drawings were made by Ivan Ivanov.

While he was working on the Alexander Park, Menelaws also received a private commission from Nicholas I, and from 1826 he was in charge of the creation of an estate complex at Peterhof, to the east of the famous palace.[36] This estate was a present from Nicholas to his wife Alexandra Fyodorovna, and was named Alexandria in her honour. The main building was a small palace in the style of rural English buildings in the pseudo-Gothic style, and by analogy was thus called the Cottage (fig. 101). The Cottage, with its landscaped park and small farm (soon also turned into a palace), was intended to be an idyllic retreat for the Imperial family, far from the bustle of the court.[37] This private estate was given a symbolic coat of arms: on a blue shield a knight's sword in a wreath of white roses, with the device 'For faith, the tsar and loyalty'. This motif was included in the decoration on the façade of the palace and on many everyday objects used at Alexandria.

Menelaws was undoubtedly proud of his achievement, as we can judge from the memoirs of his contemporary, the Anglo-Italian Augustus Bozzi Granville, who visited St Petersburg in 1827 and left the following impressions: 'Our steps shall first be directed to Tzarsco-celo the Windsor, or St Cloud of the Imperial family of Russia; and in visiting that celebrated spot, we shall have the benefit of the architect's company, M. Menelas, a gentleman from Edinburgh, who has been resident in Russia upwards of forty years; worked with his countryman, the late Mr Cameron, another eminent architect; and has been filling for many years the office of Imperial Architect, attached to the palaces of Tzarsco-celo and Peterhoff. We assuredly cannot have a better or more obliging Cicerone...'. Later they went to Peterhof: 'The first object to which M. Menelas, the architect, directed our attention, was an exceedingly pretty and picturesque cottage, built by himself, in which the Gothic style predominates. The reigning Empress, to whom ostentation and pomp are equally uncongenial, erected this simple yet tasteful structure, where she may enjoy the real comforts and pleasures of a rural retreat. The external design is at once light and elegant; it rises in the centre of a hillock which overlooks the Gulf, the intervening ground being gently sloped towards a very large flower-garden.'[38]

The works of these three Scottish architects form a significant part of the palace ensembles in the environs of St Petersburg, and to this day their buildings and interiors continue to attract the interest of numerous visitors.

1. Grabar 1911, III, pp. 361–85; Lansere 1924, pp. 9–20; Loukomski 1943; Taleporovsky 1939.
2. Shvidkovsky 1996.
3. Shvidkovsky 1994a, pp. 52–4.
4. Rae 1971; Salmon 1993.
5. The full title of this work is *The Baths of the Romans explained and illustrated, with the Restorations of Palladio corrected and improved* (London, 1772), with identical texts in English and French.
6. Cited in Voronov and Khodasevich 1982, p. 6.
7. Arkhiv vneshnikh Snosheniy [Archive of Foreign Relations] Fund I, razryad 1–26, d. 36, 1882, fols. 1, 2.
8. *Ibid.*, fol. 3.
9. *Ibid.*, fol. 5.
10. Korshunova 1976, pp. 313–14 and p. 317 n. 38.
11. Library of the St Petersburg State University of Transport, inv. no. 4891.
12. Korshunova 1974, pp.14–21; Korshunova 1977, pp. 132–43.
13. Rice 1967, p. 245; Edinburgh–Glasgow–London 1967–8.
14. Rice, in Edinburgh–Glasgow–London 1967–8, pp. 19–21.
15. RGADA Fund 14, d. 52, ch. III, fol. 256: 'Vedomost' o nakhodyashchikhsya pri proizvodstve pri Sele Tsarskom kazyonnykh rabot pribyvshikh iz Anglii 1784 goda v Rossiyu Aglinskikh raznykh khudozhestv masterakh i masterovykh lyudyakh zhitel'stvo imeyushchikh v gorode Sofii, s pokazaniyem ikh imyan i familiy ravno zhyon i detey i o protchem chto prinadlezhit k formulyarnomu spisku' [Bulletin of the state workers present at the works at Tsarskoye Selo, arrived from England 1784 to Russia, English masters of various arts and skilled people, living in the town of Sofiya, with a list of their names and surnames, also that of their wives and children and other things relative to the service record].
16. Réau 1932, p. 61.
17. Hermitage inv. no. OP 3125–80.
18. Hermitage inv. no. OP 23295–8.
19. James Paine, *Plans, Elevations and Sections of Noblemen and Gentlemen's Houses...*, I (London, 1767, 2nd edn 1783), II (London, 1783).
20. Tait 1971, p. 166.
21. RGIA Fund 1286, op. 2, d. 123, 1819, fols. 8–10 (the architect's record of service).
22. Russian National Library, St Petersburg, Manuscript department, Fund 500, OCPK.P.XIII, no. 6.
23. Zhikharev 1955, p. 281.
24. Moscow Academy of Arts, Album 1–B–15.
25. Mikhaylovich 1912, I, p. 59.
26. Fomin 1911, pp. 2, 38.
27. Andreyev 1977. This article lists the most valuable archive documents, although Andreyev treated them somewhat freely, tendentiously reducing Menelaws's role in favour of those of his Russian colleagues. See also Shvidkovsky 1994b, p. 33, and Andreyev 1991a.
28. Judging from Menelaws's age as given in the 'Bulletin' of 1784, his year of birth was 1749, although Andreyev 1977, p. 57 reckoned it to be 1756.
29. RGIA Fund 1286, op. 1, d. 266, 1804, fols. 6, 12, 17, 32, 45v.
30. RGIA Fund 1285, op. 8, d. 637, 1813, fols. 9, 10. The nature of Menelaws's work for Razumovsky has yet to be properly studied.
31. RGIA Fund 487, op. 6, d. 2254, 1817–21, fols. 4, 7.
32. RGIA Fund 519, op. 1, d. 354, 1817, fols. 1, 7.
33. Hermitage inv. nos. OP 12964, 12968, 12919, 12922, 12925 etc.
34. This statue was acquired by the Dowager Empress Maria Fyodorovna and presented to Alexander I in 1824. It is now in the Hermitage.
35. Catherine Palace, Tsarskoye Selo, inv. no. ED–730, a design for the Egyptian Gates signed by Menelaws.
36. All-Union Academy of Architecture, Moscow, p. I–1738, 5949 (now transferred to the Shchusev Museum of Architecture). Plans of Alexandria.
37. RGIA Fund 485, op. 3, d. 306, 1828. Plans and elevations of the Farm Palace, copied from Menelaws's drawings.
38. Granville 1828, II, pp. 487, 507.

BRITISH GARDENERS
AND THE VOGUE OF THE ENGLISH GARDEN
IN LATE-EIGHTEENTH-CENTURY RUSSIA

Anthony Cross

Fig. 57: S. P. Galaktionov after S. F. Schedrin, *View of the Palace of Monplaisir at Peterhof*, 1805. Etching, 28 ½ × 36 ⅞ in (72.3 × 93.7 cm). State Hermitage Museum.

In his recent examination of the myths and ceremonies surrounding the Russian monarchy, Richard Wortman highlights the nobility's particular nearness to the ruler and the degree to which they 'participated in court ceremonies and celebrations and adopted their sovereign's notions of rule, as well as his literary, artistic, and architectural tastes'.[1] He could well have added the ruler's tastes in gardens to the list, particularly with respect to 18th-century Russia's most powerful monarchs, Peter I and Catherine II. Over the last few years the Russian garden historians A. P. Vergunov and V. A. Gorokhov have emphasized that 'it is difficult to overestimate Peter I's personal contribution to the creation of palace and park ensembles in the first decades of the 18th century', while Academician D. S. Likhachev has concluded that 'the art of gardening in Peter's reign bore the strongly distinctive imprint of Peter's personal tastes, Peter's energy and Peter's subordination of everything initiated by him to a single reformist plan'.[2] Similar recognition has not, however, been accorded to Catherine II, although as patroness, connoisseur and arbiter of taste, she surpassed even Peter, and her knowledge of garden design was extensive and influential.

The pervasive influence on Peter's tastes in gardens was Dutch Baroque rather than French Classicism. Already in some measure acquainted with the style from gardens in the Foreign Quarter in Moscow, he was able during the Grand Embassy of 1697–8 to visit gardens in the United Provinces of the Dutch Republic, notably Het Loo and Honselaarsdijk, and in England, Kensington and Hampton Court palaces, although he is best remembered for the scant respect he accorded John Evelyn's Sayes Court at Deptford near London. Following the foundation of St Petersburg in 1703 and, particularly, after the victory at Poltava in 1709, which brought a sense of permanence to Russia's hold on the Baltic, the tsar was to order the laying-out of gardens in accord with his tastes both in the new capital, notably the Summer Garden, and along the Gulf of Finland on his estates at Strel'na and Peterhof. Peter sent Russian apprentices to the United Provinces to learn about gardening, and ordered from there plants, trees and books; his favourite among the many gardeners and specialists in areas of garden design, such as hydraulics, that he recruited from abroad was the Dutchman Jan Roosen. It was the comparatively modest dimensions of the Dutch garden, the presence of canals and water features, the use of flowers, the profusion of statues and what he termed 'meaningful objects', the non-dominance of the house or palace, frequently shielded or obscured by trees, and its position at an angle to the main axis of the garden's geometric paths and beds that had an especial appeal for Peter.

Peterhof has frequently been called Peter's Versailles, which it is, if understood not as imitation but as emulation, as a statement of Peter's own ideal layout, embodying his vision of Russia as a maritime power. He was, of course, deeply interested in the *roi soleil* and his symbols of power; he possessed books about the gardens at Versailles by 1706, purchased a model of them in 1711, and recruited into his service in 1716 Jean-Baptiste Le Blond, architect and pupil of Le Nôtre. It was, however, Marly, the Trianon and Saint-Cloud that attracted him more than Versailles when he made his visit to France in 1717. Peter's preferred palaces within Peterhof were Monplaisir on a site he chose by the sea (fig. 57), Marly and the Hermitage rather than the Grand Palace itself, positioned above the famous cascades and the Samson Fountain.[3]

Formality and regularity in garden design were, none the less, the order of the day in Peter's time, as they were to be in the ensuing decades, when first his niece Anna Ioannovna and then his daughter Elizabeth occupied the throne. The scale was, however, grander, the influence more obviously French than Dutch; the palace or main house was given greater prominence and sought to command unending perspectives in its park in the manner of Vaux-le-Vicomte or Versailles. It was Elizabeth's architect Rastrelli who enlarged the Grand Palace at Peterhof and built the Catherine Palace at Tsarskoye Selo, both of which had their impressive formal gardens. Existing imperial residences and gardens were re-planned and extended, but new complexes were also being constructed for a widening circle of affluent aristocrats on estates around St Petersburg, Moscow (Kuskovo and Arkhangel'skoe) and in the provinces. Great formal gardens continued to be laid out into the 1770s, while in other parts of some estates new trends and tastes were accommodated.[4] Such was the case at Oranienbaum, where Peter's favourite, Prince Menshikov, had his imposing palace (built by Giovanni Maria Fontana and Gottfried Schädel in 1710–27) on a terrace overlooking the Gulf of Finland (fig. 58).

Fig. 58: Oranienbaum. Colour lithograph by C. Shulz. Private Collection, Paris. © Francesco Venturi / KEA.

In the 1740s and 1750s Oranienbaum became the summer residence of Grand-Duke Peter Petrovich, the future Peter III, and his young wife, the future Catherine II. It was with Oranienbaum that Catherine associated her first attempts at 'gardening', writing in her memoirs that 'it was at this time [1755] that I took a fancy to form a garden at Oranienbaum …. I began then to plan and plant, and as this was my first whim in the constructive line, my plans assumed very grand proportions.'[5] These plans were quickly abandoned, but it was in the upper park of Oranienbaum, known thereafter as 'the Empress's own *dacha*' and at some distance from the sea, that the Italian architect Antonio Rinaldi was to build for her from 1762 the Chinese Palace (long known, incidentally, as 'the little Dutch house', like Monplaisir; see fig. 59). The Palace faced both to the north and south formal gardens, but to the west Rinaldi laid out the 'new garden', a mixture of both formal and picturesque elements, incorporating winding paths, a multitude of pavilions and other structures, many with Chinese motifs, and a 'water labyrinth' of streams, islands and wooden bridges.[6] Catherine, however, was to spend little time at Oranienbaum; it was Tsarskoye Selo, where, soon after her accession, she moved rapidly to stop the clipping of hedges and shrubs,[7] that became the focus of her desire to restore 'nature' to the gardens of Russia.

Unlike Peter, Catherine never left Russia. Without the opportunity to see for herself the gardens of Britain, she became, nevertheless, in the words of a British ambassador, 'a great adept' of gardening in the English style,[8] reading the authorities and seeing what they described on the engravings she ordered in large numbers and on the pieces of the Green Frog service prepared by Josiah Wedgwood and Bentley (cats. 74–92). Unlike Peter, who had looked to the Dutch Republic both as a place of instruction for his Russian gardeners and as a source

of experts to recruit (although mention might be made of a virtually unknown British gardener by the name of Denis Brockett in their number), Catherine sent her Russians to Britain and recruited from there a steady stream of professional gardeners in the 1770s. There were, however, Russians of a somewhat different status who from the beginning of Catherine's reign began to enjoy the opportunities she lacked to visit the gardens and estates of 'blessed Albion'.

It was the near coincidence in time of an edict promulgated in 1762, during the short reign of Catherine's husband, the unfortunate Peter III, giving the Russian nobility new freedom of movement, and of a period of peace in Europe following the end of the Seven Years War in 1763 that was to launch Russians on their version of the Grand Tour.[9] Although the majority visited Germany, France and Italy, there were many who braved the crossing of the Channel. London and its social life beckoned, but if there were those who once in the capital went no further, others took the fashionable west road to Bath, while a few more adventurous souls went north – to the Midlands, to Yorkshire and, very occasionally, to Scotland. Russian aristocratic tourists of the 1770s and 1780s in particular had the opportunity to see for themselves the great English houses and estates and had the means and often the wish to imitate what they saw on their return to Russia. Russians saw Kew and Hampton Court, Richmond and Twickenham, Strawberry Hill and Windsor, Painshill and Claremont, and, further afield, Wilton, Longleat, Blenheim, The Leasowes, Stowe, Hagley, Clumber, Thoresby, Studley Royal, Chatsworth, Harewood – the list is endless. From their letters and diaries we can see how impressed almost all the visitors were by both the novelty and the beauty of what they encountered.

As early as 1764 Ivan Shuvalov, the favourite of the Empress Elizabeth, a moving spirit behind the founding of the Moscow

Fig. 59: The Chinese Pavilion at Oranienbaum designed by the Italian architect Antonio Rinaldi for Catherine II. Its name derives from the Chinese wallpapers used to decorate the interiors. © Francesco Venturi / KEA.

University and the first President of the Russian Academy of Arts, wrote from England that 'the gardens are beautiful, in a taste completely distinct from all others. When I return, I will give you an idea of how you can lay one out at Kimora [an estate of his correspondent, Count M. L. Vorontsov, on the Volga in Tver province]: the whole art is about being close to nature. I think that is the best way'.[10] Youngest brother of Catherine's first official favourite and Director of the Academy of Sciences, Vladimir Orlov opined a few years later that 'in their design the attempt is made to imitate nature and conceal the work that is necessary and frequently greater than in regular gardens; in these gardens everything is spread around – here a wood, here a shrubbery, here flowers, here a pond'.[11] The young Aleksandr Kurakin, later to be known as 'le prince superbe', arriving in England in 1771 after a spell at the University of Leiden, was to pen 'quelques réflexions sur le goût des Anglais quant au jardinage'.[12] He himself was never to be fully weaned from his love of French regularity, using 'bizarre' and 'étrange' to describe English taste, which arose from the wish to do things differently from other nations, but admitted that 'Lorsque l'on parcourt ces promenades, on est frappé sans contredit de la nouveauté du spectacle. A chaque pas, la scène varie. Tout est contraste'. He concurred, moreover, with Orlov in that 'on trouve dans ces campagnes tout ce que la nature aidée par l'art peut offrir de plus agréable, et ce qui est un effet de l'art y paraît être celui de la nature' and rightly discerned the great costs involved in creating these landscapes, despite English assurances to the contrary. Far more ardent in his praise of the English style of gardening was the young (anonymous) nobleman who exclaimed in 1783 'voyez ce que peut l'homme, dont la génie libre ne connaît pas les entraves du despotisme et de la tyrannie! Il embellit de mille façons la nature, quelquefois même ingrate, et jouit ainsi de son existence'. With such sentiments it is not surprising that he spent three hours walking around Stowe in Buckinghamshire, 'ce superbe parc'.[13]

A particularly notable, not to say, loud voice in the Russian chorus was that of Princess Catherine Dashkova, participant in the court revolution that put Catherine on the throne, future Director of the Academy of Sciences and first President (from 1783) of the Russian Academy (fig. 39). Dashkova first descended on England in October 1770 and included in her month's stay a fortnight's tour that would take in not only Portsmouth, Southampton, Salisbury, Bath and Oxford but also a number of estates, including Claremont, Painshill, Longleat and Wilton. Five years later, back in Russia, Dashkova published the account of her tour, suggesting in her introduction that 'English gardens are worthy of being described by a writer of epics'.[14] Remarkable, nevertheless, is her own detailed description of Painshill in Surrey and her delight and astonishment at the ever-changing scenes and the intricacies of the famous grotto, where 'the sun, penetrating through specially contrived cracks, was so blinding that our eyes could scarce bear it. All the walls are covered with, or rather composed of, precious crystals and fossils, such as all types of coral, amethyst, topaz and amber which had been assembled so cleverly that nature itself would have been deceived'. On the basis of her experiences she argued that 'art is so concealed that their gardens seem well-chosen purely natural places'.[15] In 1776 Dashkova returned to Britain to place her son at Edinburgh University. Towards the end of August in the following year she and her family made a two-week tour through the Scottish Highlands. Unlike her journal of the tour to the West of England, her unique account of the Highlands was regrettably not published for the edification of her compatriots, for it contains interesting and not consistently flattering descriptions of Scottish estates, including those of Lord Kames at Blair Drummond, of the Duke of Atholl at Dunkeld and of Lord Breadalbane at Taymouth Castle.[16] Her reaction to Painshill is an anticipation of her now pronounced enthusiasm for the Picturesque, the Romantic and the Sublime, found both in landscaped estates and, more often, in untouched nature. She writes, for instance, of Blair Drummond: 'L'on découvre par-ci, par-là, des ruines d'anciens Châteaux qui je suppose dans les tems plus reculés, ont été aussi utiles, qu'ils sont necessaires maintenant pour rendre le paysage romanesque, ajoutez à cela une belle rivière qui en serpentant souvent, semble retourner sur ses pas, et vous aurez le tableau complet'.[17]

The edict of 1762 had given the Russian nobility the freedom not only to travel but also to retire to their estates. There began the true efflorescence of Russian estate culture.[18] Travellers such as Orlov, Kurakin and Princess Dashkova were subsequently to spend much time and money on improving their estates and 'cultivating their gardens' after the English model. Forgetting both his resistance to the English style and his remarks about the enormous costs involved, Kurakin during a long period of exile from the court in the 1780s turned his modest Borisglebskoe in distant Saratov province into the imposing Nadezhdino, complete with an English garden, some three miles in circumference. From his house he had views over lawns and lake and distant forests, but his delight was in nearer pleasure gardens, through which paths wound their way, revealing temples (built after prints of English pavilions) and other structures, all labelled in a way that recalls Shenstone's Leasowes. 'J'ai donné des noms à ces temples et à tous les chemins grands et petits de ce délceux jardin. Sur chaque chemin, on trouvera plusieurs poteaux avec des écriteaux qui apprendront son nom, afin que tous les passants puissent s'imprégner incontinent d'idées et de sensations qui y soient analogues'.[19]

On her estate at Troiskoe to the south of Moscow in Kaluga province Princess Dashkova also spent years of exile under Paul, finding comfort in her last years with a young Irish companion, Martha Wilmot, whose letters highlight the Princess's 'English tastes', particularly with respect to gardens. It is Martha's sister Catherine, however, who writes of the 'winding walk among the birch trees [which] is a favourite one of the Princess because of its leading to the Monument of Granite erected on a Mount and dedicated to the remembrance of the day Catherine ascended the throne!' She adds that 'behind it is scoop'd a Hermit's Cell furnish'd with moss & rocky seats out of which You plunge into the depth of a wood!'[20] On her travels to Scotland Dashkova had sought out noted hermitages at both Dunkeld – where she was overcome by the sublimity of the setting but dismayed by the wretchedness of the building – and at Taymouth Castle, where, by contrast, both setting and the 'charmante retraite', complete with mossy walls and deerskin-covered furniture, delighted her, leaving her to regret only the absence of the 'rent-a-hermit'.[21]

The Revd William Coxe, travelling tutor to the young Lord Herbert, visited several estates around Moscow at the end of the 1770s, and reflected after a visit to Count Petr Panin's Mikhalkovo that 'we could not avoid feeling extreme satisfaction that the English style of gardening had penetrated even into these distant regions. The English taste, indeed, can display itself in this country to great advantage, where the parks are extensive, and the verdure, during the hot summer, uncommonly beautiful. Most of the Russian nobles have gardeners of our nation, and resign themselves implicitly to their direction.'[22] Princess Dashkova, who had recommended herself to her brother, Count Aleksandr Vorontsov, as 'your English gardener',[23]

seems not to have employed a foreign professional. Vladimir Orlov was among those who did, at his estate of Otrada in Moscow province near Serpukhov. Orlov began with the declared intention of creating an estate worthy of an English lord and a large park was laid out by the River Lopasnia with a series of interconnecting lakes and numerous garden structures. He even brought in nightingales and attempted, without success, to breed deer. His chief gardener was named Piterman, seemingly a Dutchman or German, but in 1787 Orlov invited the Scot Francis Reid to produce an overall plan for the grounds.[24]

Since 1784 Reid had worked at the empress's estate at Tsaritsyno near Moscow, where he was responsible for the grounds, and lived there until his death in 1798, although building work on the palace designed by the ill-starred Vasilii Bazhenov came to an abrupt end after the Empress's visit in 1785.[25] Reid also carried out private commissions for such as Count Sheremetev at his Ostankino estate, and he was one of the considerable number of British gardeners active in and

around Moscow from the 1780s until way into the following century. It was, however, in and around St Petersburg some two decades earlier than Catherine had initiated the vogue for both the English garden and British gardeners.

As far as I can establish, the first British gardener to be recruited was Charles Sparrow, a Scot, like so many of his successors, who arrived in 1769 after Catherine had instructed her ambassador in London to pay the £350 he demanded because he was bringing his brother with him![26] It was almost certainly Sparrow who was the subject of the following assessment of his talents, penned by a certain Frederick Roberts of Chiswick: 'At the request of Count Czernichew [the Russian ambassador in London] I procured a Man qualified in an extraordinary Manner for Gardening, in all its Branches; he also understood Botany, Agriculture, the designing, surveying & laying-out of Pleasure-Grounds, in the present English Taste, with rural Architecture &c.'[27] Sparrow began work at Gatchina, an estate that the Empress had given to her lover Grigorii Orlov in 1762, and over the next decade he landscaped the lake and grounds and made the extensive plantings that were to enthuse one of his fellow-countrymen, who wrote of 'the beautiful garden; and surely among all the fine things of this delightful summer residence, the noble plantations are the most conspicuous, and draw most attention'.[28] Catherine herself took great interest in the development of Gatchina (fig. 60), flattered that Orlov recognized 'mon mérite jardinier'.[29] It was, however, Tsarskoye Selo that inevitably and increasingly absorbed her.

Catherine's earnest desire to enlist British expertise is clearly reflected in the flurry of letters between St Petersburg and the Russian ambassador in London over the period 1770–71. Among English gardeners wishing to serve the 'great patroness of the north' was Thomas Cloase from Hampton Court, on whose behalf no less a figure than Capability Brown himself wrote on 20 October 1770 to say 'that he thought him a Person very fit for the Place he [Cloase] wishes to undertake, being a perfect Master of the Kitchen Garden, Hotwalls, Stoves and Greenhouses. If he should meet with his Excellencys approbation, Mr Brown will be happy to give him any assistance in Plans, or other things, that may be of use to her Imperial Majesty or him.'[30] In the event Cloase did not go and there was no follow-up to Brown's offer, which was as real in this case as his alleged collaboration with a later English gardener, William Gould, is apocryphal.[31] The man who did arrive was to be called by Catherine 'mon jardinier anglaise', but it was in German that he conversed with her, for he was by origin from Hanover. Johann Busch, or John Bush (*c.* 1730–95), who had settled in England in 1744 and subsequently ran a successful nursery garden in Hackney, seems to have had no formal training or experience as a landscape gardener – but neither had Capability Brown or many others when they made the transition. The original intention was to send Bush to lay out the gardens at Kolomenskoe, the Imperial residence on the Moscow River, where a new palace for Catherine was being built from 1768, but instead he went first to Oranienbaum for a few months, and possibly also assisted Sparrow at Gatchina, before settling at Tsarskoye Selo.[32] Bush was soon to lay out

'some pleasure ground' at nearby Pulkove (the site of the future observatory and one of the few hills in the environs of St Petersburg), where according to the Court journal, in May 1774 Catherine and her suite 'walked in the English garden and after inspecting everything, sat on the grass on a knoll and ate a cold repast'.[33] His energies thereafter until his retirement and return to England in 1789 were to be concentrated on the English Garden at Tsarskoye Selo, where he worked in apparently amicable collaboration with the Russian architect and designer Ilya Neyelov (1722–82).

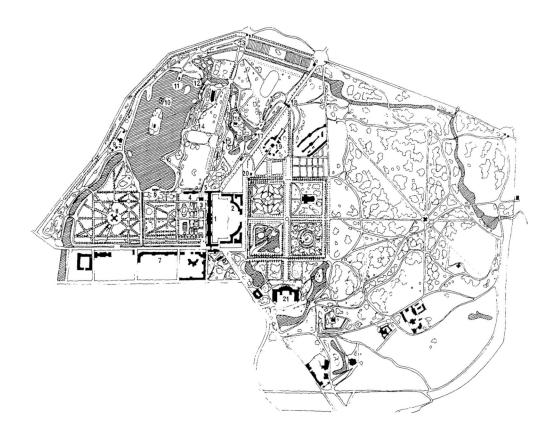

Fig. 62: Plan of the grounds at Tsarskoye Selo.

1. Catherine Palace
2. Circumference
3. Agate Pavilion
4. Cameron Gallery
5. Ramp
6. Grotto
7. Large Orangery
8. Hermitage
9. Admiralty and Aviary
10. Rostral or Chesme Column
11. Turkish Bath
12. Palladian Bridge
13. Tower Ruin
14. Milkmaid Fountain
15. Monument to Lanskoy
16. Concert Hall
17. Creaking Pavilion Alexandrovsky Park
18. Bolshoi Kapriz
19. Chinese Village
20. Cross Bridge
21. Alexandrovsky Palace

Fig. 63: The Marble or Palladian Bridge in the grounds at Tsarskoye Selo designed by Ilya Neyelov and completed in 1774. © Francesco Venturi / KEA.

Neyelov had worked at Tsarskoye Selo since 1744 and had been faced under Catherine with new challenges. It was around 1768 that she issued instructions for an English garden to be created on waste land to the west of the Great Pond. Neyelov attempted to effect the necessary changes to paths and ponds and ground elevations to produce a more 'natural' look, but the Empress decided to send him and his younger son Petr to England 'in order to visit all the notable gardens and, having seen them, to lay out similar ones here'.[34] Returning after six months in the summer of 1771, Neyelov, who was more architect than gardener, spent the remaining decade of his life embellishing the park of Tsarskoye Selo with a whole series of buildings and bridges, often modelled closely on English examples he had personally seen on his travels or studies in design books. It is not known precisely which gardens Neyelov visited but he had ample time to see all the estates in London and its environs and he certainly went as far from the capital as Oxford. His most famous construction was the Siberian or Marble Bridge (fig. 63), his version of the Palladian bridge he had probably seen at Wilton in Wiltshire, or else a close copy of it at Stowe (fig. 64), but of which he had already produced a model before his journey.[35] Neyelov's contribution to the architectural embellishment of Tsarskoye Selo's English garden was equalled a few years later by Charles Cameron, who built for Catherine not only the colonnade or gallery that later became known by his name but also many monuments, pavilions and bridges. Both Neyelov and Cameron catered for Catherine's love of the Gothic and the Chinese, particularly in the building of the Chinese Village (fig. 65), for which a pagoda, based on that of Kew, was included in the model but never erected.[36]

Fig. 65: The Chinese Pavilion in the grounds at Tsarskoye Selo designed by Ilya Neyelov. © Francesco Venturi / KEA.

Fig. 64: *The Palladian Bridge*, from Benton Seeley's *A Description of the Gardens ... at Stowe*, a guidebook first issued in 1744.

The beauty that Tsarskoye Selo achieved in the last decades of the 18th century is well caught in the watercolours of Russian artists such as Semen Shchedrin (fig. 60), Mikhail Ivanov, Vasilii Petrov and Andreii Sergeiev, while Bush himself left a plan of the gardens, framed by illustrations of many of the buildings and monuments and dedicated to the Empress, on his retirement in 1789.[37] An English visitor's reaction in 1781 was that 'the Gardens are laid out in the English Taste and are very prettily diversified with Lawns, Gravel Walks and Wood, a very fine large piece of Water is near the centre with an Island which has a building on it'.[38] It is elsewhere suggested that the Russians 'had no idea of Gravel walks till those of England were so much extolled & Bush & Sparrow came to this Country & set the example by introducing them; the beauty firmness & superior lustre of gravel being visible to every eye has made the great one [i.e. Catherine] gravel mad'.[39]

That observation is found in a letter of 22 October 1780, written by a third 'English' gardener recruited by Catherine. James Meader was in fact another Scot who had been employed until the previous year by the Duke of Northumberland at Syon Park near London and had published *The Planter's Guide; or, Pleasure Gardener's Companion* (1779). It is Meader's letter-book, covering the period 1779 to 1787, that provides the most vivid and lively account of the creation of an 'English garden'. Meader was set to work at Peterhof, Peter the Great's beloved palace on the Gulf of Finland. It was not, however, the existing gardens with their famous fountains and cascades that were to be changed (although he was quick to substitute gravel for sand along existing paths), for, as Meader himself writes, 'the spot allotted to me is a park though great part thereof is full of fine Trees.

Here are fine pieces of Water which want but little help to make them elegant, with a vale where I propose to form a magnificent Cascade & in these affairs I am under no restraint either to extent of land or water; the bounds are only limited by the Gulf of Finland'.[40] Unlimited also were the financial and human resources at his disposal. Meader was to create what became known as the English Park and on a site within it, which he recommended, the Italian architect Giacomo Quarenghi was to build the – no longer standing – English Palace (fig. 66). Catherine, whose dislike of Peterhof was as strong as her love of Tsarskoye Selo, was, none the less, very interested in Meader's progress and made several visits there in the early years, walking in the grounds and resting in the sumptuously appointed so-called Birch Cottage that Quarenghi built for her in 1780. The cottage is depicted on one of four watercolours painted by Meader himself in 1782; others show a cascade as well as several of the extraordinary bridges that included 'a most remarkable Bridge with petrified Moss & roots; ... also four curious wooden Bridges of an original construction'.[41] A project obsessing Meader over a number of years was a grotto to surpass the one built by Joseph Lane at Painshill in the 1760s (and described by Princess Dashkova). Although he obtained with some difficulty a sample of the Derbyshire spar of which the Empress approved, it is not certain that he ever received sufficient supplies to complete the task. In December 1784 he was still waiting, and there is no further reference to the grotto in his letters or in any other source. His overall success, however, in transforming the site into a garden of variety and beauty is attested by several visitors, including Andrew Swinton, author of a travel account published in 1792, who wrote of 'a very beautiful spot; and when the natural flat-

Fig. 66: K. K. Schulz after J. J. Meier,
The English Palace at Peterhof (now destroyed).
Lithograph, 14 ¹¹⁄₁₆ × 15 ¾ in. (37.3 × 40 cm),
c. 1850. State Hermitage Museum.

ness of the ground is considered, it is amazing what art and taste have been exerted in finishing it. Here are winding rivulets, cascades dashing over moss-clad rocks, antique bridges, temples, ruins, and cottages amazing.'[42]

A final example to illustrate that there were truly English gardeners among the influential 'English' gardeners active in Catherine's Russia is William Gould (1735–1812), who hailed from Ormskirk in Lancashire and had worked for Richard Wilbraham-Bootle at Lathom House in the same county before departing for St Petersburg in 1776. Gould also exemplifies the gardener working not for Catherine but for one of the aristocracy, albeit Orlov's successor as the Empress's favourite, Prince Grigorii Potemkin. It was for the design and realization of the Taurida Garden adjoining the Taurida Palace in St Petersburg that Gould earned his reputation. He brought the charms of the English garden within the precincts of the capital itself, showing, according to one of his 19th-century English successors, 'great judgement in forming the ponds, out of which he got sufficient materials to make the agreeable variety of swells and declivities'.[43] After his patron's death in 1791, Gould was appointed Imperial gardener by Catherine, who was more than content for him to bring to perfection the Tauride gardens, where a small Palladian villa was built for him in 1793 by the Russian architect Fedor Volkov and where, a year later, he was visited by Edward Wilbraham-Bootle, the son of his former employer, who found him completing an 'Ah Ah and iron railing to encompass the whole building'. We are fortunate in having three oil paintings by the Dane Benjamin Pattersen that show the palace and gardens as they were in the 1790s: like the watercolours of Tsarskoye Selo and Peterhof, they too are held in the Hermitage, and only rarely are they on public display.[44]

Sparrow, Bush, Meader and Gould are but four of a long list of British gardeners active in Russia from 1769 until well into Alexander's reign. Bush was succeeded at Tsarskoye Selo in 1789 by his son Joseph, who was replaced in 1810 by Charles Manners; Gould was followed at the Tauride Gardens by Martin Call; Sparrow's work at Gatchina was eventually continued by Charles Hackett, when the estate passed to the Grand Duke Paul in the 1790s. At Tsaritsyno, as we have seen, there was Francis Reid, and several more gardeners could be named, working not only in Moscow province, but at Krichev (a Potemkin estate in Belorussia), on estates in the Ukraine, elsewhere near St Petersburg, and, indeed, for the colourful Duchess of Kingston on her estate overlooking the Baltic.[45] And it would be remiss not to include in the list yet two more Scots whose emergence as landscape gardeners resulted from their work as architects, designing garden pavilions and other structures: Charles Cameron at Pavlovsk (figs. 52, 67); and in the early 19th century, Adam Menelaws in the Alexander Park at Tsarskoye Selo and at Alexandria within the territory of Peterhof (figs. 54, 55).[46]

There occurs in Meader's long letter of 22 October 1780, devoted to 'the state Gardening is in this Country', the following passage: 'Till of late Years the taste of Gardening among the Great was confined to fruits but the Nobles who have been in England are so much enrap-

Fig. 67: Plan of part of the park at Pavlovsk.

1. Palace
2. Temple of Friendship
3. Apollo Colonnade
4. Pavilion of the Three Graces
5. Aviary
6. Great Stone Staircase
7. Theatre Gate
8. Dairy
9. Monument to the Parents
10. Mausoleum of the Emperor Paul

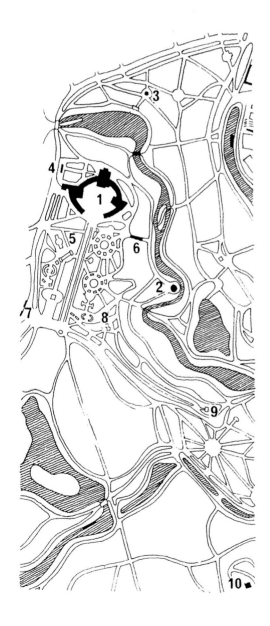

Fig. 68: View of the gardens at Pavlovsk looking towards the Temple of Friendship. © Francesco Venturi / KEA.

Fig. 69: A. Bugreyev, *The Centaur Bridge and Apollo Pavilion at Pavlovsk*. Watercolour, c. 1803. © Francesco Venturi / KEA

tured with the English pleasure gardens that they are cried up here much more beautiful than perhaps they have appeared to your or my Eye. Mr Whately's Observations on modern Gardening translated into French perhaps has not a little contributed to this opinion. This has set them all Gardening mad.'[47] Meader may well have remembered the Empress's particular enthusiasm for Whately, but his observation was acute and widely applicable. In August 1771 Horace Walpole, who was in Paris at the time of the publication of François de Paule Latapie's version of Thomas Whately's *Observations on Modern Gardening* (1770) under the title *L'Art de former les jardins modernes, ou l'art des jardins anglois*, wrote of the French that 'they have translated Mr Whateley's book, and the Lord knows what barbarism is going to be laid at our door. This new *Anglomanie* will literally be *mad English*.'[48] Both Walpole and Meader are emphasizing the 'madness', to which Catherine in her famous effusion of 1772 to Voltaire about the charms of the 'English garden' was also to allude: *J'aime à la folie présentement les jardins à l'anglaise, les lignes courbs, les pentes douces, les étangs en form de lacs, les archipels en terre ferme, et j'ai un profound mépris pour les lignes droites, les allées jumelles. Je hais les fontaines qui donnent la torture à l'eau pour lui faire prendre un cours contraire à sa nature: les statues sont reléguées dans les galeries, les vestibules, etc.; en un mot, l'anglomanie domine ma plantomanie.*[49]

This was written at a time of her intensive study of sources, visual and literary, and her particular absorption in Whateley's *Observations* in Latapie's translation. Anxious for the work to appear in Russian, Catherine was not prepared simply to hand it to a translator, preferring instead to edit the French text herself in order to increase its usefulness in the Russian context. A translation was in fact never published, for reasons that remain unclear. What we have is a manuscript in Catherine's hand that bears the title 'Principes pour former le jardin dans le gout anglois' and a dedication (original in Russian) that reads as follows: 'To the owners of estates bordering the sea and lying along the Peterhof road this book is presented by one who has seen their natural attractions and capabilities, so that they should be further improved according to the principles herein prescribed'.[50] Catherine was clearly intending the work to be a manual for, in the first instance, the owners of estates along the Peterhof road, and by implication, for estate owners throughout the empire.[51]

Latapie had appended to Whately's text a detailed description of Stowe, together with a plan. As Peter Hayden has shown,[52] the resemblances between Stowe and Tsarskoye Selo go beyond mere coincidence, not least with regard to garden architecture and its profusion. Meader during his initial stay of five weeks at Tsarskoye Selo in 1779 remarked on the great variety of buildings interspersed with cascades and other devices; indeed, 'the fault is their being too numerous, but the Empress is very fond of Buildings', while, amusingly, a Russian visitor to Stowe in 1786 was to note that with its numerous buildings in the garden, 'Stowe is very like Tsarskoye Selo and does not please me at all'.[53] Catherine's knowledge of the gardens and buildings of Stowe came, of course, not only from Latapie. There

were no less than 48 views of Stowe on the famous Frog service she ordered from Wedgwood in 1770 and received four years later; and in a large consignment of engravings that were sent to her from London in 1776 there were another sixteen views.[54]

The Russian Whately was thus never published. Whately continued to be read in French, and the Russian gentry undoubtedly read French versions of any other English source as well as works of European popularizers. Little appeared in Russian, however, to further the cause of the English garden. The first work chronologically dates from 1771 and was a version of 'Of the Art of Laying Out Gardens Among the Chinese' from Sir William Chambers's *Designs of Chinese Buildings, Furniture, Dresses, Machines, and Utensils* (London, 1757). Although the Russian version was translated directly from the English, a French translation appeared in Latapie's extensive Introduction to Whately's *Observations*, 'pour fournir une preuve complètte de la parfaite ressemblance des jardins Anglois avec les jardins Chinois' that Catherine with her love of Chinoiserie also espoused.[55] In 1776 there appeared a work that was also translated directly from English and bore a promising title. The anonymous *Opyt o raspolozhenii sadov* was in fact a version of the equally anonymous *Essay on Design in Gardening*, published in London in 1768 and republished only in 1796 in an augmented edition that now bore the name of its author, George Mason. Sadly, any use the work might have had in acquainting Russian readers with new concepts of garden design as well as with descriptions of famous English gardens was virtually neutralized by the ineptness of the translation.[56]

The English cause was much better served by the publication in the previous year of Princess Dashkova's account, mentioned above, of her journey of 1770. This had appeared in a journal, and it was in journals that over the next decade the most valuable information was passed on to Russian readers. However, both in the journals and in the books that began to appear in the 1790s it was frequently through a German filter that the English garden was largely perceived.

Foremost among the German champions of the English garden was C.C.L. Hirschfeld, whose *Theorie der Gartenkunst*, originally published in Leipzig in 1775, became even more influential after its translation into French in 1779.[57] Hirschfeld's work occasioned a veritable revolution in the views of Andrei Bolotov, an agronomist and garden addict from the middle gentry, who abandoned French regularity to preach in his widely read *Ekonomicheskii magazin* (1780–89) the delights of the English garden, or, as he increasingly was wont to call it, the natural or new-type garden. Bolotov published over 80 articles, many of them translated or adapted from Hirschfeld, in which he touched on every aspect of garden design and architecture. Hirschfeld also influenced the writings of Nikolai L'vov, poet, scholar, architect and much else. It is interesting that while Latapie in the influential introduction to his translation of Whately had contrasted the aims of Andre Le Nôtre and William Kent, L'vov aimed for a reconciliation, which was to become a feature of many of the great Russian estates. In his proposals for laying out the grounds of Prince Bezborodko's estate on the edge of Moscow, he wrote: *What a task the garden designer has set himself! To resolve it, he believes it possible to reconcile the teachings of the two opposing artists Kent and Le Nôtre, to reanimate the cold monotony of the latter, who in pursuit of magnificence enslaved nature beneath the straight line, with the lively and varied beauties of the reformer of the English garden, and to encompass within one picture the formal and the pleasure garden.*[58]

Both L'vov and Bolotov were able to practise their ideas on their own estates an on the estates of those affluent enough to commission their services. Bolotov's work at Bogoroditsk, an estate near Tula given by Catherine to Count Aleksei Bobrinskoe, her bastard son by Grigorii Orlov, is particularly notable and its contemporary appearance is caught in a series of Bolotov's own watercolours.[59]

Fig. 70: A. Bugreyev, *The Gardens at Pavlovsk*. Watercolour, early 19th century. © Francesco Venturi / KEA.

Hirschfeld did not appear in Russian translation in book form, but there were amidst a plethora of gardening dictionaries, encyclopaedias and manuals two further publications of German origin that deserve particular mention for the plans they provide for the layout of gardens in the English style as well for their illustrations of garden architecture. In 1796, the last year of Catherine's reign, Ludwig Christian Mansa produced an album of seven hand-coloured plans under the title *Plany dlia razpolozheniia i razvedeniia aglinskikh sadov* ('Plans for the Laying Out and Cultivation of English Gardens'). A second augmented edition appeared in 1798 and in the following year there was published a *Sobranie novykh myslei dlia ukrasheniia sadov i dach', vo vkuse angliskom, gotticheskom, kitaiskom: dlia upotrebleniia liubitelei anglinskish sadov i pomeshchikov, zhelaiushchkh ukrashat' svoi dachi* ('Collection of New Ideas for the Adornment of Gardens and Estates in the English, Gothic and Chinese Styles: For the Benefit of Lovers of English Gardens and Landowners Wishing to Adorn Their Estates'). This represents a Russian edition of the first 26 folders, each containing ten drawings

with explanatory texts in Russian, German and French, of Johann Grohmann's *Ideenmagazin für Liebhaber von Gärten...* (Leipzig, 1797). As the titles of both works make clear, Russian landowners were being encouraged to follow the English fashion and were being given the designs to imitate.

The publication of Grohmann occurred in the reign of the Emperor Paul, whose tastes in gardening, in keeping with his passion for military drill and parades, inclined more to the regular and geometric, although he possessed in Pavlovsk as fine an example of a landscape garden in the English style that Russia could exhibit and in Maria Fedorovna, a Marie-Antoinette of an Empress who was also a passionate plantswoman. The English influence, however, continued strong into the reign of Alexander I, and British gardeners, as we have seen, remained much in evidence. At the same time, these influences are to be seen in the context of the views of Bolotov and others who during Catherine's reign had sought to emphasize the Russianness of Russian gardens, even if this was essentially to recognize the 'capabilities' and particularities of topography and climate and flora and to follow the sound advice of Hirschfeld, who had upbraided the French for too close imitation of the English.[60]

1. Wortman 1995, I, p. 406.
2. Vergunov and Gorokov 1989, p. 43; Likhachev 1982, p.158.
3. See Likhachev 1982, pp.121–42.
4. Vergunov and Gorokov 1989, p. 65ff.
5. *Memoirs* 1859, p. 228.
6. Raskin 1981, pp. 36–8.
7. Balog 1972, p.16.
8. Harris 1844, I, p. 231.
9. See chapter of Cross 1980.
10. Archive of Prince Vorontsov 1872, VI, p. 304.
11. Orlov-Davydov 1878, II, pp. 64–7.
12. *Arkhiv knyazya F. A. Kurakina* (Saratov 1894), V, pp. 395–6.
13. Russian State Library, Moscow, Manuscript Room, Fond183, Inostrannaya literatura, shiffr no. 1673, fols. 27v, 77v.
14. 'Puteshestviye odnoy rossiyskoy znatnoi gospozhi, po nekotorym aglinskim provintsiyam', *Opyt trudov Vol'nogo rossiyskogo sobraniya pri Moskovshom universitete* (Moscow, 1775), II, p.106.
15. *Ibid.*, p.113.
16. Dashkova 1995, pp. 239–53.
17. *Ibid.*, p. 243.
18. See Roosevelt 1995, a recent and wide-ranging study.
19. Golombievskiy 1911, p.17.
20. Wilmot 1934, p. 209.
21. Dashkova 1995, pp. 245–6.
22. Coxe 1802, pp. 312–13.
23. Archive of Prince Vorontsov 1881, XX1, p. 410.
24. *Biographicheskii ocherk grafa Vladimira Grigor'evicha Orlova*, I, pp. 2–3. (Reid is not identified by name.)
25. Mikhailov 1990, pp.104–9.
26. *Russkiy archiv* (1871), pp.1327,1335.
27. Arkhiv vneshney politiki Rossii, Moscow, Fond Londonskaia missiia, op. 36/1, delo 283, fol. 21.
28. Guthrie 1792, p.156. See also John, 2nd Lord Henniker, 'A northern tour in the years 1775 and 1776 through Copenhagen and Petersburg to the River Swirr joining the lakes of Onega and Ladoga in a series of letters', Cambridge University Library, Add. MSS 8720, fol.146.
29. *Sbornik imperatorskogo russkogo istoricheskogo obshchestva* (St Petersburg, 1874), XIII, p. 238.
30. Archiv vneshney politiki Rossii, op. 36/1, delo 261, fol. 56.
31. See the note by Peter Hayden in *The Garden*, 108 (1983), p. 78.
32. Archiv vneshney politiki Rossii, op. 36/1, delo 261, fol. 4 (a letter from Catherine's secretary Ivan Elagin to the Russian ambassador in London, 6 April (O.S.) 1771).
33. Walther 1877, I, p. 431; British Library, Add. MSS 31,192, fols. 88–88v; *Kamer-fur'erskii tseremonial'nyi zhurnal 1774 goda* (St Petersburg, 1864), pp. 252–3.
34. Archiv vneshney politiki Rossii, opis' 36/1, delo 296, fol. 22.
35. Stepanenko 1994, p. 36. On Neyelov in England see Cross 1980, pp. 219–21.
36. Petrov 1969, p.131, n.117. Catherine had ordered a model 'of the Chinese building' from her ambassador in London in 1772; a little earlier she had asked for a recent book on Kew, most probably Sir William Chambers's *Plans, Elevations, Sections, and Perspective Views of the Gardens and Buildings at Kew in Surrey* (1763), which of course included a plan of the pagoda (see Archiv vneshney politiki Rossii, op. 36/1, delo 261, fol. 69).
37. For the watercolours, see Printseva 1988, pls. 1–3,13–14. For the plan, drawn by Bush's son Joseph and engraved in London by Tobias Müller, see Cross 1989, between pp. 54 and 55.
38. Cross 1989, p. 54.
39. Peterburgskoye otdeleniye Arkhiva Rossiyskoy Akademii nauk, Razriad IV, op. I, delo 999, fols. 26–26v.
40. *Ibid.*, fols. 4–4v. (The letter-book was presented to the Soviet authorities in 1942 by H. M. Cos, who had previously published extracts from it in his 'An English Gardener at the Russian Court, 1779-87', *New Flora and Silva*, II (1939), pp.103–112.)
41. *Ibid.*, fol. 41v. Black-and-white reproductions of the watercolours are in Glezer 1979. Mme Glezer's work also contains further information about Meader, supplementing his letter book; see pp.19–23 in particular.
42. Swinton 1792, p. 414.
43. Call 1827, p. 388.
44. Parkinson 1971, p. 226. Excellent reproductions are in Komelova 1978, pls. 107–12.
45. For greater detail on all the British gardeners, see chapter 7 of Cross 1996a.
46. See Cross 1991a, pp. 7–19.
47. Petersburgskoe otdelenie Arkhiva, Razriad IV, op. I, delo 999, fols. 27v–28.
48. Walpole 1937–83, XXXV, p.126.
49. Besterman 1953–65, LXXXII, p.130.
50. Rossiiskii gosudarstvennyi arkhiv drevnikh aktov, Moscow, Fond 10, op.1, ed. khr. 383, fols.1, 2.
51. For a detailed study, see Cross 1990, pp. 21–9.
52. Hayden 1991, 21–7.
53. Petersburgskoye otdeleniye Archiva, Razriad IV, opis' I, delo 999, fol.1v.; 'Zhurnal puteshestviia V. N. Zinov'eva po Germanii, Italii, Frantsii i Anglii v 1784–1788 gg.', *Russkaya starina* [Russian Days of Old], XXIII (1878), p. 429.
54. See Cross 1991b, pp. 21–2.
55. *L'Art de former les jardins modernes, ou l'art des jardins anglois* (Paris, 1771), pp. ix–xxiii.
56. See Cross 1974, pp. 25–9.
57. See Parshall 1993, pp.125–71.
58. 'Kakim obrazom dolzhno by bylo raspolozhit' sad knyazya Bezborodki v Moskve', in L'vov 1994, p. 316.
59. Colour reproductions of six of Bolotov's watercolours are in Vergunov and Gorokov 1989, between pp. 224 and 225. There is little in English about either Bolotov or L'vov, but see, most recently, Hughes 1988, pp. 289–300 and Roosevelt 1994, pp. 79–92.
60. Adams 1979, pp.112–13.

JAMES WALKER:
A BRITISH ENGRAVER IN ST PETERSBURG

Alan Bird

Fig. 71: James Walker after George Romney,
Frances Woodley. Mezzotint, 24 ¼ × 15 ¹⁄₁₆ in.
(61.5 × 38.3 cm). Published 12 December 1788.
The Trustees of the British Museum.

In the second half of the 18th century it was universally acknowledged that British engravers, especially those who had mastered the technique of mezzotint, were the finest in Europe. Exports of prints of all kinds rose quickly until the French Revolution and subsequent wars put an end to the trade, much to the dismay of its many workers.[1] But in Britain itself there were changes in fashion; above all there was a craze for coloured prints that led to experiments in many mediums and which was not satisfied until the advent of coloured photographic reproduction at the end of the last century. By the end of the 18th century, stipple engravings and aquatints, especially as exemplified in the decorative prints of Francesco Bartolozzi and the many artists associated with him, had swept all before them, so that the subtle greys and blacks of the mezzotint had begun to seem rather old-fashioned.

In the hostile economic climate that existed at the end of the 18th century and the first decades of the 19th it was natural that artists – engravers among them – should look to countries where their skills might be better appreciated, both aesthetically and financially. One such artist was James Walker, who lived in Russia for some eighteen years, initially serving under Catherine the Great and then under her successors. For an artist of his eminence very little is known about him. It has been stated that he was the son of a captain in the merchant navy and to have been born about 1758, but he himself says nothing about this. His parents must have had financial resources because he was apprenticed on 28 January 1773 to Valentine Green, the most distinguished mezzotint engraver of his day, for the sum of £50, a very considerable amount of money for that time.[2] By the age of 21, when he would have served his time, Walker had already made mezzotint engravings of quality. By the time of his departure for Russia in 1784 he had made some 30 plates, mostly issued on his own initiative, publishing them from four different addresses and establishing himself as the foremost engraver of the day. He made prints after works by leading portrait painters, notably George Romney (1734–1802), for whom he seems to have had a particular sympathy (fig, 71), and also genre and theatrical scenes, occasionally carried out in the new and fashionable technique of stipple but for the most part exploiting the rich tones of the mezzotint. Surprisingly, perhaps, Walker does not seem to have involved himself with the Royal Academy, despite the fact that Green, his master, was an Associate Engraver, perhaps because he refused to accept the lowly status begrudgingly accorded to practitioners of his craft. His relations with the Society of Artists must have been happier because in 1783 he exhibited four mezzotints at their exhibition: *Faith* after Daniel Gardner, *The Village Doctress* and *Hobnelia, or The Spell* after James Northcote, and a portrait of a lady, perhaps after Romney. During his eighteen years residence in St Petersburg (1784–1802) he seems to have visited Britain several times, probably to keep his name before the public by publishing prints or to maintain professional contacts.

Quite how and why James Walker made his way to Russia cannot be determined: it seems unlikely that he went simply as a speculative venture. He may have been commended to the Empress Catherine by her ambassador in London, or quite possibly by another artist. There are indications that he had made gestures to ingratiate himself with the Russian court. On 1 September 1783, Harrison & Co. published *Catherine II. Empress of Russia. Engraved by Mr Walker, from a Painting in the Possession of his Excellency the Russian Ambassador*. While this may simply have been a commission given by Ivan Simolin, Catherine's representative in London, to an engraver whose work was highly esteemed among connoisseurs, it may have been a venture undertaken by Walker and the publishers hoping to profit from British interest in all things Russian; it certainly points to the fact that Walker was already making influential contacts. He evidently worked from a portrait of the Empress by the Danish artist Vergilius Eriksen, given by her to Thomas, Baron Dimsdale, one of the many gifts she gave the physician who on two separate occasions successfully innoculated the Imperial family against the dreaded smallpox.[3] The following year, on 1 April, Harrison & Co. published another engraving by Walker, also on a Russian theme, but this time allegedly after a work by one of the Metz family, depicting a team of horses pulling a sledge on which is mounted a large box-like structure, a room in itself, and entitled *The Empress of Russia's Travelling Equipage*. Within a few months Walker was in Russia itself and in a position to verify the accuracy of this representation. At the age of 24, a leading member of his profession, of good family, married with a baby daughter, probably speaking French and, as he says of himself, tall and well-built, he was doubtless quite acceptable at a court ruled by an Empress who, as was notorious, was far from averse to the company of outstanding young men.

Walker's arrival in Russia coincided with a particularly difficult time in Anglo-Russian relations that lasted for almost the entire length of his stay in there. However much of an Anglophile she professed to be – and there can be no doubt that she both admired and respected Britain – Catherine had no intention of letting sentiment overrule the interests of the country of which she was sovereign. She saw that the American War for Independence had not only shattered British complacency, it had created an opportunity to extend Russian trade and challenge British maritime supremacy. She was far from averse to stirring up trouble for the major European powers in their colonial empires, and thus, for instance, she encouraged the Venezuelan patriot Francesco de Miranda, then struggling to free South America from Spanish and Portuguese domination. By a series of alliances she sought to oppose British power, especially on the high seas. On his accession, her son Paul I joined in an alliance with Austria and Britain but soon reversed his policy and the old enmity with Britain reasserted itself. It was only with the advent to the throne of Alexander I in 1801 that a sincere and friendly relationship was established.

Alexander's grandmother, the Empress Catherine, had not limited her foreign policy to diplomacy and to military and naval operations aimed at territorial expansion in the Crimea and the establishment of Russian power in the Baltic, but equally importantly had engaged in a campaign of cultural aggression intended to create an image in Europe of Russia as a civilized and liberal state in which under her generous and philanthropic patronage the arts flourished as nowhere else in the West. To this end she corresponded with leading savants of the time, gave full rein to her mania for collecting works of all kinds, and hired artists to portray the leading figures of her court and printmakers who could mass-reproduce those images as well as supply images of St Petersburg, the festivals and theatrical events of her court and the wonders of her art collections, all for dissemination abroad in glorification of her reign. A character such as James Walker suited her plans admirably.

Since no contract between Walker and the Imperial court appears to have survived, the exact nature of the services required of him are unknown, but they doubtless included teaching his engraving techniques to young Russian artists at the Imperial Academy of Arts, although the most obvious and immediate duty would be to translate into mezzotint some of the works in her collection of pictures housed in the Hermitage. Among her major acquisitions was that of the Houghton collection in 1779, when George Walpole, 3rd Earl of Orford, sold to her for more than £40,000 the collection of Old Master paintings that his grandfather, Sir Robert, had put together (see Andrew Moore's essay, 'The Houghton Sale'). So proud was she of this purchase (which was widely deplored in Britain, the Government declaring, as is customarily the case, that it had no funds with which to buy the collection and keep it in the country), that she dispatched a frigate of the Russian navy to London to convey the pictures safely to St Petersburg. Walker was to produce two folders of engravings of several of the major paintings, dedicated, as one might expect, to Catherine (fig. 72).

Throughout the years of his employment at the Russian court, well placed to be an observer of great events and policies, several of them aimed against his native land, Walker must frequently have felt himself to be in an unenviable, even precarious position. As we shall see, unlike most artists he was not, however, a political innocent.

By the time of his departure from Russia in 1802, Walker had served under three sovereigns: Catherine II, whose reign ended in 1796; Paul I, who was assassinated in 1801; and Alexander I, who had connived in his own father's murder. For Catherine, Walker appears to have had the greatest respect, relating several anecdotes that displayed her constant presence of mind and generosity of spirit. On one occasion she asked Walker about an amusement called cricket of which she had heard, and wondered if it would not be a good means of exercise for her grandsons Alexander and Constantine.[4] Another time, walking through her hothouses followed by a train of courtiers, with a meaningful nod of the head she told John Bush, her gardener, to keep an eye on them and on the ripe fruit growing there. The few anecdotes or 'scraps' that Walker relates concerning her son, the future tsar Paul, serve only to highlight the paranoia and fits of madness that increasingly were to terrify his subjects. All who had worked for Catherine were anathema in the eyes of her son: thus the great architect Charles Cameron was dismissed from Imperial service, while many others, including Walker, must have feared for

TO THE

EMPRESS OF RUSSIA:

THIS COLLECTION

OF

ENGRAVINGS,

Executed under Her Imperial Patronage,

IS,

By Her gracious Permiffion,

Moft humbly Dedicated;

By Her Imperial Majefty's

Moft devoted, and grateful Servant,

JAMES WALKER.

CATHERINE II.
IMPERATRICE de toutes les RUSSIES,
d'après une pierre gravée à S.t Petersbourg en 1789.
par Son Alteffe Impériale MARIE FŒDOROWNA
Grande Ducheffe de toutes les Ruffies.

their lives. Of Alexander I, whose advent to the throne came as a tremendous relief and who awarded him a pension, Walker has nothing to say.

There was no means of escape from close observation by the court and the police, for at the time of Walker's arrival – and it is almost impossible to appreciate the fact today – St Petersburg was a small place, no larger than an unassuming English country town. It was barely 80 years old, and having arisen from a barren marsh had not a single building dating from before 1700. (Writing in 1827, Dr Granville exclaimed that it was entirely a city of palaces![5]) What is certain is that in what was comparatively a small city Walker must have known and frequently encountered almost every British resident or visitor there, whether in the services held in the church attached to the Factory of the Russia Company or in its lending library situated in rooms above the church itself, or at the many clubs set up at the time or in the community at large. Generally the British lived either on the English Quay or in the surrounding district until the straight streets called The Lines, partly because of their having been built on filled-in canals on Vasilyevsky Island, became fashionable and wealthy merchants moved there. When the Neva and the Baltic were free of ice, numerous visiting ships, some of them British, were tied up at the embankments; Walker delighted in the characters among their crews, perhaps because seamen had been part of his childhood world. He could hold his own in the city's society (he tells us that he was for his whole time in St Petersburg the member of a social club that included men of all ranks and nationalities and of which he was three times director), especially with his position at court, where Catherine's appreciation of his character and abilities must have been widely noted.

It seems that his appointment was initially as Engraver to Her Imperial Majesty, although this can by no means have been a full-time appointment. After the presentation of an engraving of Guido Reni's *Simeon Bearing the Infant Cross*, a painting from the Houghton collection, lost from the Hermitage in the 1850s, he was made an Associate Member of the Academy of Arts on 30 December 1786.[6] Eight years later, on 12 September 1794, he became a full Academician, and a Counsellor almost immediately after. Teaching at the Academy was included among his various duties.[7]

Although Walker describes himself as being in various places with the court, at both the summer palace at Tsarskoye Selo and the Winter Palace in St Petersburg itself, his principal duties probably lay in the Hermitage galleries, possibly as some kind of superintendent of the Collection to which Catherine was continually adding. There are records of two occasions when he showed foreign visitors the pictures kept there, notably William Petty, 2nd Baron Wycombe, and captains Bentinck, Hawkins and Markham,[8] and also Francesco de Miranda, who at Walker's home watched him engraving the portrait after Shebanov of Dmitriev-Mamontov and, later, at the Hermitage, at work on the plate after Murillo's *Flight into Egypt*.[9]

During his eighteen years residence in Russia Walker produced fewer engravings than might have been expected, especially bearing in mind the productive years between 1780 and 1784. It appears that he was free to accept commissions for other patrons, because he relates that Count Alexander Andreyevich Bezborodko proposed that Walker should supervise the engraving of the paintings in his collection by Russian, English, French and Italian artists, and that after paying for the expenses entailed in wages, printing, paper, etc., and giving the Count 100 copies of the work to be entitled *Gallerie de Besborodke* for distribution to the courts of Europe, the copyright would lapse to Walker, who would, as a result, gain a small fortune and European fame. Unfortunately, the project, suggested in the greatest secrecy, fell by the wayside when the Count died.

Walker would have had little difficulty in selling his prints in the Russian capital. *The Sankt-Petersburgskiye Vedomosti* regularly published advertisements of drawings, paintings and engravings for sale. In 1779, five years before Walker took up his post, it announced that Signor Rospini had arrived in the city and was selling a collection of English, Roman and French engravings, including many architectural decorations, and works on English gardens. The Hermitage acquired prints from Rospini through the bookseller Weitbrecht and the antiquary Klostermann, whose shop at 69 Nevskii Prospekt regularly sold prints by artists resident in the city. In 1793 the same newspaper announced the sale of 2,000 British prints and also a collection of pictures by celebrated contemporary English painters (together with a collection of old pictures by various painters) to be sold next to the Smirnov residence on the fifth line of the embankment, house 35, Vasilyevsky Island.[10]

Walker made some 40 engravings during his Russian years, from which a selection was issued in two sets as *A Collection of Prints, from the Most Celebrated Pictures in the Gallery of Her Imperial Majesty Catherine the Second*. Excluding the two identical frontispiece sheets carrying dedications to the Empress with a stipple vignette of her cameo portrait (fig. 73) against a blue ground and dated 1 January 1792 (as are all the other prints unless otherwise noted), there are thirteen sheets divided between the two folders: *Catherine II* after Shibanov (published 1 May 1789); *Potemkin* after Lampi; *The Infant Hercules* after Reynolds; *Arise and Take … (The Flight into Egypt)* after Murillo; *The Holy Family* after Batoni; *A Russian Peasant* after Eriksen; *Conversation Piece* after Verkolje (dated 1 July 1789); *The Card-players* after Rombouts; *Peter Denies Christ* after Moise Valentin; *Hannah Instructing Samuel* after Rembrandt; and *Young Woman* and *Boy with a Flute*, both after Greuze and printed on the one sheet (dated 20 November 1785).

In 1792, on one of Walker's periodic returns to London, he took out the Freedom of the Russia Company so that he could import 'sundry Pictures and Copper-Plate Engravings from Russia'.[11] The identity of the 'sundry Pictures' cannot now be determined, but the 'Copper-Plate Engravings' must have included the two folders of prints listed above that were issued through the book- and printsellers R. Blamire and William Hodges at the price of three and a half guineas. He had prepared well in advance for this visit: most of the prints were issued with letterpress in both English and French.[12]

Fig. 72: Dedication page from *A Collection of Prints, from the Most Celebrated Pictures in the Gallery of Her Imperial Majesty Catherine II … by James Walker*, London, 1792. The Trustees of the British Museum.

Fig. 73: Portrait vignette of Catherine II. Engraving, 7 × 5 ¼ in. (17.7 × 13.5 cm). Detail of Figure 72.

Fig. 74: James Walker after Pompeo Batoni, *The Holy Family*. Mezzotint, 23 ¾ × 15 in. (60.5 × 38.2 cm). Published 1 January 1792. The Trustees of the British Museum.

Catherine cannot have raised objections to Walker taking the prints out of Russia, perhaps calculating that they would advance her reputation as a liberal promoter of the arts and also advertise the triumphs of her collections. It must be said that the claim made in the subtitle to *A Collection of Prints* is not reflected in the contents, since neither Shibanov's *Catherine II in Travelling Costume* (fig. 5) nor Lampi's *Potemkin* nor Eriksen's *Russian Peasants* (fig. 75), fine pictures as they were, could be counted among the masterpieces 'in the Gallery': rather, they are an assortment of miscellaneous prints, reflecting Walker's extraordinary skill as an engraver. There was no-one else of his quality working in Europe, and although it has often been stated that he was at his best making mezzotints after Romney's portraits of women, several of the Hermitage prints, notably the *Hannah Instructing Samuel* after Rembrandt (fig. 77), are unequalled in their graduations of blacks and greys and in the sympathy he brought to his transcriptions of the paintings. There cannot have been many of these prints in circulation because it was rarely possible to pull more than 200 mezzotints from any one plate. A number would have been reserved for the Empress, who would have retained sets for presentation to visiting dignitaries, while Walker was left free to sell sets and individual prints. It is known, for instance, that his engraving of Reynolds's *Infant Hercules* (fig. 76) was on sale in Klostermann's shop.[15] In fact, the manner in which prints were distributed suggests a degree of financial adventurism on the part of Walker, who was as astute as Catherine herself, capitalizing on her almost mythical renown as a patron of the arts.

Despite his jovial, open nature, Walker displayed a strong sense of his own abilities; and the uniqueness of his position at court, where, as he wrote himself, he passed many years of his life 'in the very bosom of a splendid court, almost daily honoured by the confidence and conversation of a truly great and amiable sovereign', may have resulted in a slightly excessive superiority, which might explain the fact that he rarely mentions other artists either in Britain or St Petersburg.[14] And there were certainly many other foreign, and Russian, artists employed in the city at the time of his residence, some of them British, including Edward Miles, miniature painter to Queen Charlotte and the Duchess of York, who went there in 1797, the Irishman Thomas Snagge, who made a miniature of the Empress Catherine, and Joseph Hearn, almost certainly a brother-in-law of Walker, who drew views of the city that were engraved in London by Thomas Malton.[15] During Walker's own time in St Petersburg, no other British engravers were there, but after his departure a number arrived, notably Henry Dawe, brother of the celebrated portraitist, and their brother-in-law Thomas Wright, a fine miniature painter and equally fine engraver whose prints are treasured in Russia today.[16] Before them, in 1805 and 1808, came the two Vendramini brothers, Giovanni and Francesco, who had earlier settled in London as pupils of Bartolozzi.[17] Walker makes no mention of the numerous Scandinavian, French, German and Italian artists working in Russia as portraitists, decorators or architects. Nor does he refer to the trio of brilliant Russian portraitists – Rokotov, Borovikovsky and Levitsky, of whose existence he was certainly aware because he engraved mezzotints after portraits by the last two, Rokotov's subtle, non-linear style being unsuited for reproductive engraving of any kind.

The one artist who is mentioned by Walker and who was a colleague of his both at the Hermitage and the Academy was Gabriel-François Doyen, who arrived in Russia in December 1791 as a teacher at the Academy on a yearly salary of 1,200 roubles, becoming a professor of painting in 1801 with some of the leading artists of the next generation, such as Kiprensky, Varnek and Tropinin, among his pupils. In 1794 he was made a court painter. Doyen, too, officiated at the Hermitage, presumably in much the same capacity as Walker, and they shared the same studio there. A man of incredible energy and inventiveness, Doyen was aged about 65 when he first met Walker, and remained in Russia until his death in 1806.[18]

What is most remarkable of all is that Walker does not mention another of his colleagues in the Hermitage, the engraver Gavriil Ivanovich Skorodumov who had studied in London with his fellow Russian Mikhail Ivanovich Belsky at the schools of the Royal Academy from 1773 on a pension awarded by the Academy of Arts in St Petersburg. Skorodumov's career in London is linked to that of Bartolozzi and more particularly with Angelica Kauffman, with whom he had a close association, engraving over 25 plates after her paintings, usually in stipple (fig. 13).[19] Catherine the Great invited him to work for her; and in September 1782, two years before Walker arrived, he was back in the Russian capital on a salary of 1,200 roubles a year and 600 roubles for housing for himself and his English wife, herself a talented artist, with the title of Imperial Engraver and the sinecure of curator of the engravings in Catherine's collections in the Hermitage and elsewhere. Two years later, in July 1785, he became an Academician. Unlike Walker, he is supposed to have disliked working in the Hermitage, where he was expected to wear the uniform of an Academician in anticipation of visits by the Empress; and he is said to have produced work of little consequence except for some excellent miniatures and a print depicting the death of Potemkin. It is worth noting that whatever Skorodumov's grievances, he was paid exactly the same salary as Doyen, a famous and far greater artist, and probably Walker too. At the same time it has to be said that by working so closely, and successfully, with Kauffman (his engraving after her portrait of Countess Protasova and her nieces was published on 1 January 1792), Skorodumov would have appeared to have been in the vanguard of fashionable European artistic taste compared to Walker, whose work would have seemed decidedly conservative, particularly to Paul I and his wife, who had met and commissioned work from Kauffman.[20]

From the end of Catherine's reign to his departure from Russia in 1802, Walker forsook reproductive prints of works by Old Masters in favour of portraits of outstanding Russians of his day, perhaps because the latter had the greater sale, although it is difficult to understand how his mezzotint of the dramatist A. P. Sumarokov after A. P. Losenko, published in London in 1792, could have appealed to the British public. Altogether Walker produced some 39 engravings of

Fig. 75: James Walker after Vergilius Eriksen, *Russian Peasants*. Mezzotint, 23 ¾ × 16 ⅞ in. (60.3 × 43 cm). Published 1 January 1792. The Trustees of the British Museum. The elderly woman, shown here with her children, was 108 years old.

Fig. 76: James Walker after Sir Joshua Reynolds, *The Infant Hercules Strangling the Serpents*. Mezzotint, 26 × 23 in. (66 × 58.4 cm). Published 1 January 1792. Yale Center for British Art, Paul Mellon Collection. Walker's engraving appeared just weeks before Reynolds's death and a year earlier than Hodges's print (Figure 47).

Fig. 77: James Walker after Rembrandt, *Hannah Instructing Samuel*. Mezzotint, 20 × 14 ⅛ in. (50.7 × 35.8 cm). The Trustees of the British Museum.

Fig. 78: John Augustus Atkinson, *A Panoramic View of St Petersburg* from *Four Panoramic Views of St Petersburg*, c. 1802. Coloured aquatint, 15 × 30 in. (38.1 × 76.2 cm). Yale Center for British Art, Paul Mellon Collection (see cat. 53).

Based on drawings done from the Observatory of the Academy of Sciences. The fortress of St Peter and St Paul can be seen in the distance.

Russian rulers, their consorts and families and the distinguished men and women of the age, helping to establish, as Catherine had no doubt wished when appointing him, that Russia had been transformed from a backward and barbaric state into a liberal and enlightened one, and St Petersburg into one of Europe's great social and cultural centres.

Walker is said to have suffered a great misfortune on the voyage home from Russia when all his 24 copper-plates, comprising four executed before he left England and twenty engraved in Russia, were washed overboard during a storm off Yarmouth. Twenty years later he seems to have said farewell to his career as a printmaker when his remaining stock, which comprised ten prints from the Hermitage folders, a few from three of his early engravings after Romney, and a number of his Russian portraits, was sold in London at Sotheby's on 29 November 1822. In addition, the sale included plates after John Augustus Atkinson's paintings of *Cleobis and Biton* and *The Death of Lord Nelson* and twelve copper-plates, one of them by him and Atkinson of the Empress Elizabeth Alekseyevna, said never to have been published, possibly a trade puff to increase their value at auction. This was also said to be the case for *Ariosto*, *William Jackson* and *Arthur Shakespeare*, whereas, in fact, all three had been issued by Hurst & Robinson in 1819. Nevertheless, Walker's production was intermittent in the extreme, and only two other engravings are known: a mezzotint after *The Entombment of Our Saviour* by Spada, then in the collection of Sir Samuel Young, dedicated to Alexander I and published in 1816; and a print that may, however, have been issued earlier: *Rough Joe: A Cottager* after William Owen, published by

PANORAMIC VIEW OF S.ᵗ PETERSBURG *Dedicated by permission* TO HIS IMPERIAL MAJESTY ALEXANDER 1.ˢᵗ

VUE PANORAMIQUE DE S.ᵗ PETERSBOURG *Dédiée avec permission* A SA MAJESTE IMPERIALE ALEXANDRE 1.ᵉʳ

W. M. Cooke on 10 February 1825, also with a dedication to Alexander. This may have been an attempt to help Owen, who was then living in the direst poverty.

An artist to whom Walker does refer – evidently a relative of his – was J. A. Atkinson, who was born in London in 1775 and died there in 1830. Taken to Russia by Walker in 1784 when he was about eight or nine years old, he showed precocious artistic talent and attracted the attention of the Empress. Atkinson's skill as a draughtsman and his appreciation of the passing hour both complement and contrast with Walker's breadth, gravity and sensitivity to the great masters of painting. Atkinson's art has all the gifts of spontaneity, exuberance and delight in the never-ending variety of the human scene.

During his time in St Petersburg Atkinson made a number of drawings of the city, taken from the observatory of the Academy of Sciences, which he reproduced as four coloured acquatints entitled *Four Panoramic Views of St Petersburg* (fig. 78, cat. 53), published by Boydell. The preface has an uncoloured print of Falconet's equestrian statue of Peter the Great, Catherine's magnificent tribute to her powerful predecessor, which, for better or worse, had become a symbol of the city. Atkinson may also have made preparatory sketches for later use of a portrait of the young Empress Elizabeth Alekseyevna and two of the Emperor, one of which was engraved by Edward Scriven, Engraver to the Princess of Wales, for *A Picturesque Representation* … and the other, of the Emperor full-length, engraved by Walker and published by Boydell on 1 September 1814, presumably to capitalize on Alexander I's visit to London in June 1814. Three months after Alexander had succeeded to the throne in 1801, Walker had himself engraved a bust-portrait of him after G. Kügelchen, which he and W. Brown published at Green Street, Grosvenor Square, London, on 1 June (fig. 79).

There are only two references, both extremely brief, to Walker and Atkinson after their return from Russia. The first is in Joseph Farington's *Diary* for 5 April 1803: *Walker, who was formerly a pupil of Val Green came in accompanied by a young man, his son in law named Atkinson. They have long resided at Petersburgh. Atkinson studies painting.*[21]

There is nothing in the *Diary* regarding Walker's reputation as a superb mezzotint engraver, nor does Farington seem to have been aware of Atkinson's early successes, though he is twice mentioned in later entries, once when Atkinson had submitted designs for the Duke of Wellington's shield, and again when Atkinson visits Paris with A. W. Devis to collect material for a painting of the Battle of Waterloo.

James Walker, however, was a man of many parts; and on at least two occasions he turned his hand to literature. Sometime around 1816 he put together a reflective collection of illustrative anecdotes published as *Paramythia* in 1821. Most of what is known about Walker's life in Russia is in this volume. It reveals, in turn, his humour, his happy and phlegmatic attitude to life around him, and the distinct pride he had in his attainments and his position at the Russian court: 'I have myself resided in palaces and in large houses; have at one time kept carriages and servants; and at another lived in one room, with a

sprat hot from the gridiron.'[22] This philosophical acceptance of life's ups and downs apart, Walker makes a surprising confession – that if he were to state what he thought was the truest source of human happiness he would say, without hesitation – successful endeavours![23]

In the Preface to *Paramythia* Walker begs the reviewers to treat him as handsomely as they did some years past when *Russian Costumes* was published. He is referring here to *A Picturesque Representation of the Manners, Customs, and Amusements of the Russians, in one hundred coloured plates; with an accurate explanation of each plate in English and French*. The book, dedicated to Alexander I, was issued in three volumes: the prints in the first volume are dated 1 May 1803, those in the second 1 February 1804, and the third 2 July 1804. Originally published in London by Walker and Atkinson themselves (at '8 Conway Street, Fitzroy Square'), and by John and Josiah Boydell ('Pall Mall & Cheapside'), it was reissued in 1812, again in three volumes, by James Carpenter and Joseph Booker. The different dates on the plates in the original volumes are probably due to the custom at that time of publishing the prints in monthly or periodic parts that were later bound up and reissued in volume form. The first edition was priced at fifteen guineas.[24]

A Picturesque Representation was perhaps the first work to give the British public a true impression of the life of ordinary Russians as well as of their appearance and customs; in that sense, in addition to demonstrating that Walker and Atkinson must have been observing both urban and rural ways of life in Russia, it has an importance in its own right as an ethnographical report on a land that hitherto had been described in terms that were sensational rather than accurate (figs. 80, 81 and cat. 51). As Walker must have been aware, 'domestic exercise', so-called, was included in the curriculum of the Academy of Arts in the latter part of the 18th century; and several artists, Shibanov, Tonkov, M. M. Ivanov and Skorodumov among them, depicted scenes of peasant life. Foreign artists, too, had interested themselves in Russian life and manners, one of the most observant being Jean-Baptiste Le Prince, who from 1764 issued ten volumes of engravings of costumes and customs. In 1777 Vergilius Eriksen had painted an aged peasant woman and her family that Walker engraved

Drawn and Etched by John Augustus Atkinson

Village council.

Published as the Act directs, May 1st, 1803, by J. A. Atkinson, and Jd. Walker, No. 8, Conway Street, Fitzroy Square, and Messrs. John & Josiah Boydell, Pall Mall, & Cheapside, London.

for his folder dedicated to the Empress Catherine (fig. 75).[25]

Apart from his contribution to this charming and informative book of splendid lively engravings by Atkinson, Walker, as has been noted, seems to have produced comparatively little after his return home. However, the first decades of the 19th century saw a tremendous interest in books on foreign costumes and manners, either hand-tinted or in aquatint, many of them published by W. Miller. Taking advantage of this taste for volumes of aquatints, while also promoting Atkinson's ready skill with the pen, and further encouraged by the success of the three volumes on Russian life, Walker may have set up as a publisher. Thus in 1807 there appeared *A Picturesque Representation of the Naval, Military, and Miscellaneous Costumes of Great Britain*, each of the 33 coloured plates carrying the imprint 'London Published Jany 1, 1807, by William Miller 49 Albemarle Street & James Walker N. 8 Conway Street, Fitzroy Square' and 'Drawn & Etched by J. A. Atkinson'.[26] Also extant are several additional plates on military subjects that may have been intended for further volumes: Atkinson's favourite subjects after all, though he is

Figs. 80, 81: John Augustus Atkinson, *Village Council* and *Katcheli*, plates 29 and 31 of *A Picturesque Representation of the Manners, Customs, and Amusements of the Russians* (see cat. 51). Coloured soft-ground etching, 19 × 27 ¼ in. (48.3 × 69.2 cm). Published 1 May 1803. Yale Center for British Art, Paul Mellon Collection.

The text of this volume, written by Atkinson's uncle James Walker, describes the peace meeting (Figure 80) thus: '*the oldest man generally presides, and is distinguished from the rest by a white wand fresh cut from the hedge, and stripped of its bark. He always takes his place close by a new-laid cow's dung, and sticks the lower point of his wand into it.*' Figure 81 depicts the swings ('Katcheli'), '*with booths of strolling players, tumblers, and exhibitions of wild beasts, around which, the court, nobility, gentry, &c. &c. driving in their dress carriages and gay liveries, form a great part of the amusement of Easter-week.*'

Katcheli

sometimes mistakenly referred to as a 'battle-painter', were actually sketches of military life, including minor skirmishes.[27]

The second mention of James Walker is rather more extraordinary than at first appears. Arthur Young, a well-known writer on agricultural topics, whose son Arthur and daughter-in-law Jane had moved to Russia in order to manage an estate there, recorded in his Diary a visit to the London town-house of Augustus Fitzroy, 3rd Duke of Grafton, on 15 February 1806: *In the evening Walker, an engraver, who has been twenty years at St. Petersburg, and who brought letters from Jane some time ago, called. He gives but a bad account of Russia, and it is from every authority a very bad country to live in, in every respect that should make a country desirable, except the people being very good tempered and very ingenious.*[28]

Evidently, Walker had access to at least one of the grand houses in the capital; and he must already have known Young, since he had 'brought letters from Jane some time ago'. This reference means either that four years ago, on Walker's return, he had brought letters for Young, or that more recently Walker had again visited Russia itself, bringing back letters with him, as, in fact, people still do today in order to circumvent the tardy postal system. In addition, *A Picturesque Representation…of Great Britain* was advertised as being sold by Mr Alici in St Petersburg and by Riss & Saucer in Moscow, so it is not inconceivable that Walker had been to Russia to make arrangements for its sale there. Here it is perhaps apposite to give in full the only extant letter by Walker, which dates from the last year or so of Catherine's reign. It was sent from his lodgings at 2 New Street, Brighton, on the Sussex coast to William Eaton, a British agent attached to the Embassy in St Petersburg but who was then in London at 100 High Street, Marylebone:

Dear Sir,

The Empresses Plans are so Grand her Schemes so deeply laid and has them so much at heart, that with the very favourable circumstances of the Times I believe she will succeed in almost all of them – In the arrangements with the French as they are mutually so distant as not to interfere with each other, an accommodation will easily be arranged between them – to which their Mutual Enmity to us will contribute – I have delayed writing to you in hopes of sending you some particulars more accurate than the following – The Empress is not to acknowledge the Republic but Spain will guarantee the Performance of the Various Articles – of the Treaty The Empress is not to be disturbed in obtaining ye Possession of Constantinople – The Crimea is to be a free Port. & the French to have a free trade to the Ports in the Crimea & the Black Sea – the Spaniards are to permit the Russians to trade to Manilla for what they want at their settlements in Kamtschatka – The French to have Alexandria Cyprus Candia & Poros & and as the Sugar Cane is produced in Candia as well Egypt & the Coast of Barbary it is conceived that this will compleat the Sum of our Political Misery – I am yours very sincerely J Walker
do not part with this.

Walker must have asked Eaton not to part with the letter because public knowledge of it would certainly have meant the end of his own career at the Russian court.[29] It would be interesting to have the 'particulars' he intended to send. What we do have reveals that Walker was somehow involved in espionage relating to Russia's foreign policy; further, that he had no illusions about Catherine and her ministers where a warring Britain and France were concerned. Was Walker employed by the British Government in some capacity while nominally in the employ of the Empress? Was he in the confidence of Count Semyon Vorontsov, Russian Ambassador to the Court of St James's from 1785 (see cat. 20), or Count Bezborodko in Russia, both privy to Catherine's deepest schemes, who may have used Walker for some – now inexplicable – purpose?

The last reference to Walker comes in a document drawn up by Atkinson on 10 August 1823, which was later to serve as a draft will. In it Atkinson bequeathed to Walker the sum of £100 plus six drawings to be selected by Walker as a token of his regard, while the pictures in Atkinson's possession were to be at Walker's disposal and any claims Atkinson had on him were to be cancelled.[30]

Atkinson died on 25 March 1830 at 48 London Street, Fitzroy Square, which he shared with Marianne Richardson, Walker's only surviving child, with whom Atkinson had grown up and whom he looked on as his sister. He was 57 years old. Energetic and resourceful, he had never ceased working, producing a variety of drawings, watercolours and prints, intermittently on Russian themes. He was a master of the decisive line, sometimes brilliant in the vigour and liveliness of his drawing, clear and untroubled in his compositions, and confident in his powers of selection and omission.

Perhaps, despite Walker's efforts to keep his name before the British public, both his and Atkinson's reputations suffered from their long absence in Russia. The fact remains that Walker was a great engraver with a 'rich simplicity in the handling of tones' and a 'fine intuition as to the pictorial essentials' as well as a 'happy instinct for the sufficing touches'; while Atkinson's depictions of military subjects and the joys and miseries of life in both Britain and Russia placed him among the foremost graphic artists of his day.[31]

All writers on cultural relations between Britain and Russia in the 18th century are necessarily indebted to Anthony Cross, whose many publications have immeasurably enriched this field of knowledge. In particular, I am obliged throughout this essay to his edition of *Paramythia* (in Cross 1993), which he was the first person to identify as having been written by James Walker.

1. See Frankau 1902.
2. Maxted 1983.
3. This portrait now only exists in copies. See Houffe 1989, pp. 78–81.
4. Cross 1975b, p. 60.
5. Granville 1828, p. 34.
6. Vsevolozhskaya 1981, p. 283.
7. The only named pupil of Walker was Ivan Selivanov; see Flekel 1983, pp. 12–13.
8. Le Blond 1912, II, pp. 117–18.
9. *Archivio de General Miranda, Viajes* (Caracas, 1929), II, p. 379.
10. Dukelskaya 1979, p. 8. See also Bruk 1990, p. 253.
11. Court Records of the Russia Company, MS 11, 741/8, fol. 344, Guildhall Library, London.
12. Alexander 1995, pp. 412–14.
13. Dukelskaya 1979, p. 9.
14. Cross 1993, p. 28.
15. Bird 1974, pp. 17–22.
16. Saprikina 1980, pp. 116–29.
17. There is a collection of items engraved by G. Vendramini in the Heber Mardon Collection of Napoleana held in the Central Library, Exeter, Devon. See also *Otechestvennya voyna 1812 goda*, Lenin State History Museum (Moscow, n.d.).
18. *Dictionnaire de biographie française* (Paris, 1967).
19. See Alexander 1992, pp. 141–78.
20. See Karev 1989, pp. 102–12.
21. Farington 1978–84, VI, p. 2005.
22. Cross 1993, p. 90.
23. *Ibid.* Walker and his family seem to have been rather vague about their precise relationships. *Harleian Society Publication*, LI (1921), p. 82 records 'James Walker esq, bachelor married Mary Hearn, spinster, by licence on 17 February 1781 at St mary le Bone parish church, Middlesex.' A daughter, Mary Ann, was born the following year. The records of the English Church attached to the Russia Company Factory in St Petersburg show the birth of a son, Charles James, and a daughter, Catherine, in 1786 and 1791 respectively, both of whom died in infancy. Walker refers to Atkinson as his son-in-law, but Atkinson himself acknowledges a half-brother, Thomas Atkinson, which suggests that his mother had died and that his father afterwards remarried. Walker's daughter Mary Ann married Warwick Calmedy Richardson at St Pancras Old Church, London, on 10 August 1809, had a son, Calmedy Charles, in 1817, but in a document dated 1830 was to describe herself as a widow.
24. Abbey 1972, I, p. 223; and Tooley 1935, pp. 59–61.
25. Bruk 1990, pp. 143–4. Eriksen made two versions of this picture, one in pastels, now in the Tretyakov Gallery, Moscow, the other in oils, now in the the Russian Museum, St Petersburg. It has also had several titles, among them 'A hundred-and-eight-year-old peasant woman and her family'. It is significant as one of the first depictions of ordinary Russians painted by a foreign artist.
26. Abbey 1972, p. 221; Tooley 1935, p. 59.
27. *Index to British Military Costume Prints*, Army Museums Ogilby Trust (London, 1972).
28. Young 1898, p. 426.
29. Melville Castle MSS, GD 51/Sec. 1/508, Scottish Record Office, Edinburgh. Here published by kind permission of Viscount Melville.
30. Prob. 11/1769 30, Public Record Office, London.
31. Salamani 1910, p. 32.
   There are collections of prints by Walker in the British Museum (including the folder of Hermitage prints), in the Victoria and Albert Museum, and in the Royal Collection at Windsor Castle. The Hermitage and the Russian Museum, St Petersburg, have collections of Walker's prints, as do several other Russian museums and libraries. The Austrian State Library, Vienna, also has a collection of works by Walker and Atkinson. The major publications listing prints by Walker are Chaloner Smith 1878–83, IV, part 1; Russell 1926, II; and Rovinskii 1895.

BRITISH ARTISTS IN RUSSIA IN THE FIRST HALF OF THE NINETEENTH CENTURY

Elizaveta Renne

That a field so ample, should hitherto have been so little trodden, is certainly surprising, while, for many years back, we have been inundated with tours through Greece, picturesque journeys through Italy and Switzerland, and most other known countries, while Russia, whether viewed in point of scenery, character, costume, nay even antiquities, at least as interesting as any of them, remains, excepting a few desultory unimportant attempts, untouched. To remedy, in some sort, this deficiency, is the particular object of the present work.

With these words James Walker (*c.* 1758–after 1823) and J. A. Atkinson (1775–1831) prefaced their marvellous three-volume publication of coloured etchings, *A Picturesque Representation of the Manners, Customs, and Amusements of the Russians* (see figs. 80, 81 and cat. 51). Atkinson was in effect the first British artist to capture such a variety of features of Russian life and culture.[1] His joint project with Walker, who wrote the explanatory text, was to initiate a whole series of British illustrated books devoted to Russia.

The first half of the 19th century saw contacts of every kind between Britain and Russia – trade, art, literature, science and education. Even the occasional coolings off in political relations could not dampen the strong mutual interest that had first manifested itself in the 16th century, was given added stimulus during the reign of Peter the Great, and blossomed luxuriously under Catherine the Great. With Catherine on the throne, Russia became the home and workplace of numerous Englishmen, and even more Scots, among them merchants, military officers, physicians, architects, artists, gardeners and missionaries. They included leading specialists, such as Dr John Rogerson (1741–1823) and Admiral Samuel Grieg (1735–88), the architect Charles Cameron (1745–1812) and the merchant John Venning (1766–1858) as well as Charles Gascoign (1739–1806), the former director of the Carron casting factory who reorganized the production of cast iron in Russia, and his colleague Charles Baird (1766–1843), the founder of a mechanical casting factory in St Petersburg and shipyards. Many lived in Russia for long periods, in some instances passing the remainder of their lives in St Peterburg or elsewhere, their children and relatives in turn inheriting the businesses, and they frequently brought with them assistants, craftsmen and contractors from abroad. By the beginning of the 19th century the large British colony in St Petersburg enjoyed a high reputation. The new arrivals usually settled around Galernaya Quay (renamed the English Quay at the end of the 18th century), along the Krykov Canal – where one of the avenues became known as English Prospekt, and on Vasilyevsky Island, nearer to the Neva and the sea. On the banks of the Neva and along Galernaya Street stood the houses of leading merchants, the English Inn, the English Church, and from 1770 the new-founded English Club, although the Club was moved to the Blue Bridge at the beginning of the 19th century. Robert Harrison, who left a fascinating record of his stay in Russia from 1844 to 1853, wrote that 'The liveliest part of the town is the neighbourhood of the Mole, or mercantile harbour, where you seem to meet none but Englishmen, and to hear only our native language, a very delightful change to one who has been long among a strange people. English inscriptions over shop doors abound, "Grog", and "Porter sold here", being of frequent occurrence. The English Vice-Consul is one of the most important personages in the place, and the English Church one of the handsomest edifices.'[2]

From the first decades of the 19th century, the notable figures of St Petersburg and Moscow included not only the British merchants resident in Russia but also British tourists. The journal *Syn Otechestva* Son of the Fatherland noted that 'in the winter period in Moscow 1815' the travellers in town were 'largely Englishmen',[3] and this was to lead to the publication of a number of postal lists and guides to Russia.[4] In addition to the foreign tourists who visited the big cities, there were those who undertook to cross the vast open spaces of the country, from north to south and from west to east. In the 1820s, for instance, John Dundas Cochrane (1780–1825) travelled through the European and Asian parts of Russia, eventually reaching Kamchatka, having crossed the whole of Siberia on foot.[5]

Fig. 82: Sir Robert Ker Porter, *Senate Square, St Petersburg with the Equestrian Statue of Peter the Great by Falconet*. Pen and wash, 7 ½ × 9 ½ in. (19.1 × 24.1 cm). Private Collection.

Fig. 83: W. O. Burgess after G. H. Harlow, *Sir Robert Ker Porter*. Mezzotint, 18 ½ × 12 ⅞ in. (46.9 × 32.6 cm). The Trustees of the British Museum.

Thus Atkinson's illustrations heralded a foreign interest in Russia that increased as the years passed, and they went some way towards filling the gap in available information on a country seen by many as a highly exotic one. This attention to Russia was also marked by the stream of literature that poured from the London presses, for it seems that almost everyone who visited the country sought to publish impressions, reminiscences, travel diaries or collections of letters that ranged from slim volumes to quite weighty ones. Of course, these publications vary greatly in terms of content and value, but many do contain intriguing and out of the way information concerning the manners and customs of Russians, their culture and art. Such books, however, were rarely illustrated. A few visiting artists made views of towns, street scenes, national pastimes and such like, anything that caught their attention or seemed unusual, and sought to convey their impressions to an intrigued public. The drawings that were published helped broaden the wider perception of Russia, most importantly those by Robert Ker Porter, F. F. Larpent (1776–1845), A. G. Vickers (1810–1845) and G. F. Atkinson.[6]

But artists came to Russia not merely to capture Russian life and manners or architectural monuments for their fellow Britons. Some stayed on, found work, received commissions, painted portraits, created history and genre paintings. Although some of them have entered the annals of the history of Russian culture, we have little biographical information about them and it is often difficult to reconstruct their careers.

Of J. A. Atkinson's early years we know, for instance, only that he arrived in St Petersburg as a small boy with his adoptive father, the engraver James Walker (see Alan Bird's essay on Walker). In addition to the enchantingly spontaneous drawings for *A Picturesque Representation…*, which were taken from the life and successfully convey some idea of reality, at the very end of the 1790s and in the early 1800s Atkinson also made a number of portraits. Two survive, *Paul I* (Pavlovsk Palace Museum) and *A. Z. Khitrovo* (Kuskovo Museum Estate, near Moscow), while others – *Alexander Suvorov, Alexander I* and *D. V. Sol'tau* – can be judged only from prints made after the lost originals by Walker and I. K. Mayr. What they tell us is that Atkinson was only modestly talented as a portraitist. He was also commissioned by Paul I to paint two vast canvases (19½ × 13 feet, untraced) to decorate the Emperor's new palace in St Petersburg, the Mikhail Castle, on the subjects of Dmitry Donskoy's victory at Kulikovo Field and the Baptism of Rus' by Grand-Duke Vladimir. A. Kotsebu, in his description of the completed Fortress and its decoration, mentioned 'both pictures by the English painter Atkinson, who has a marvellous use of the brush but often errs in his drawing'.[7] The only known genre oil painting by Atkinson is *Sledging from the Hills* (1792; Russian Museum, St Petersburg), which lacks the charming lightness to be found in the drawings and watercolours.

Robert Ker Porter (1777–1842), an artist whose interests ranged from history and archaeology to diplomacy, geography, military affairs, literature and art, and whose eventful life has been covered in numerous publications (see fig. 83),[8] was also honoured with a commission from the Russian emperor. We should note, however, that Porter's commission to paint three large canvases for the Main Hall of the Admiralty Collegium was a considered one. Alexander I must have heard reports of this painter, whose vast battle scenes and history paintings had impressed his contemporaries. Porter's most famous panorama first shown in London, *The Storming of Seringapatam* (1800), was 128 feet long and contained 700 life-size figures; women swooned when they saw the violent details so naturalistically depicted. Two other paintings by Porter may have been well-known in Russia – Suvorov's *Defeat of the French at the Passage of Mont St Gothard*, and *Prince Bagration Leading on the Cossacks* (both 1804) – if not in the original, as was suggested by Ancketill,[9] then at least from the engravings by Giovanni Vendramini that appeared in January 1805 (fig. 84). The fact that Porter arrived in Russia bearing letters of recommendation from Semyon Vorontsov, the Russian ambassador in London, was also significant. One of these was addressed to Admiral P. V. Chichagov (1767–1849),[10] whose passion for all things British, which included law and order, had at times given cause for criticism. In any case, at this time Chichagov was directly linked to the Admiralty Collegium and his name is mentioned in connection with the transferral of Porter's pictures to the Main Hall (completed in 1809) from the Hermitage, where they were stored temporarily while the central part of the Admiralty was undergoing repairs.[11] In the centre of this Main Hall, a velvet baldacchino rose up above a portrait of Peter the Great, founder of the Russian fleet and the Admiralty. The present location of this painting is unknown, but Porter described it in detail in his *Travelling Sketches in Russia and Sweden: A large full length portrait of the immortal Peter is to be placed at the upper end of this State apartment, under a rich canopy of crimson velvet and gold, draperied in regal style, and surmounted with every insignia of the imperial dignity. I am now painting on this picture. It is ten feet by seven and a half. I represent my illustrious subject surrounded by naval and military trophies. He rests his right hand upon an anchor also holding in the same charts of the Caspian and Black Seas, on the waves of which he was anxious to see the fleets he was then projecting …. At his feet lie the colours of his great northern rival, whose fortune he made stoop in the dreadful day of Pultowa; and over his head waves the imperial flag of his marine. The background is a view of Cronstadt; with fleets of men of war and merchant ships, to show the progress of arms and commerce under his cherishing auspices.'[12]

Two more pictures heralded the glory of Peter's naval victories, *Peter's Victory Against the Turks at Azov on the Don*, and *The Capture of Swedish Counter-Admiral Ehrenshceid* (Central Naval Museum, St Petersburg), which once hung in the Admiralty to either side of the portrait of Peter himself but were transferred in the 19th century to the Museum of the Cadet Corps and were then lost for many years. When they were rediscovered in 1981,[13] they were attributed to another artist, Richard Paton (1716–91), who had produced for Catherine II paintings depicting the Battle of Chesme (formerly Great Palace, Peterhof). The two works produced for the Admiralty are now the only known paintings by Porter in Russia, although M. D. Ancketill has suggested that a portrait of Lord Nelson, presented to Alexander I, and *The Founding of the Port of Kronstadt by Peter the Great*, may have survived.[14] If so, they have yet to be found.

Porter's career will no doubt continue to be of interest to scholars of several disciplines. There is, for instance, much that is intriguing in his journey of 1817–20 from St Petersburg to Persia, the latter one of the regions of conflict between Russian and British political interests. Thanks to assistance from the then Director of the Imperial Library and President of the Academy of Arts, A. N. Olenin, a cousin of Porter's wife,[15] this trip took on something of the nature of an official scholarly expedition. Its results and their significance for the study of history, archaeology, ancient writing and art of the Achaemenid and Sasanian eras have been discussed in detail by R. Barnett, with some additional material supplied by N. Vasil'yeva.[16] Porter was interested not only in the beauty of the Caucasian landscape, so poetically described in his *Travels in Georgia, Persia, Armenia, Ancient Babylonia etc.*,[17] or the architecture he depicted in detailed drawings. He concentrated his attention on Russia's strengthening position in the areas around the Persian border and her increasing influence on Persia's government. His detailed analysis of the situation was not, for obvious reasons, included in the book, but was recorded in a secret note to some unidentified but influential person, a note recently unearthed in the Bodleian Library:[18] *Much of the time intended for my general tour was passed at Teheran the capital of Persia, and Azerbijan, the Province governed by Abbas Mirza, the heir apparent to the throne …. Whilst at these courts … I had many opportunities of becoming intimately acquainted not only with the political relations existing between Persia and ourselves, but of knowing the private sentiments of the King and the Prince on the subject: – while from the particular circumstances that connected me with the Great adjacent Northern Empire* [Russia], *I had similar advantages in learning more of its views in that quarter, than are likely to fall in the way of most diplomatic agents. But the nature of these advantages, compels me to say, that what I communicate is in the strictest confidence respecting the channel whence it flows.*[19]

Porter goes on to give a detailed picture of the locations of Russian military and trading settlements, the routes taken by the trading caravans, the political and business relations between Russia and Persia as a whole, and what advantages all these would bring Russia in the near future, to the detriment of British interests, if Britain failed to take steps immediately.

On his return to St Petersburg, Porter presented Alexander I with five objects from the collection he had put together in the East and he also dedicated to him the French edition of his book. Olenin was highly impressed by the 'difficult, daring and in all ways useful undertaking of travelling through Southern Persia, solely for the sake of learning and the arts',[20] and noted that Porter's works were worthy of reward. Having no suspicions regarding Porter's secret activities, Alexander I gave him a signet ring bearing his own monogram. Back in Britain Porter's writings, art and diplomatic skills (he became Sir Robert in 1813) were also appreciated. His talent for observation and for precise analyses and clear presentation of his impressions must have played no small role in his appointment as Consul in Caracas, where his duties included drawing up highly detailed reports on events in Venezuela.

Porter's aims and abilities as an artist can be judged from the reminiscences of his contemporaries, his own writings, engravings after his works, the numerous drawings of uneven artistic quality, and the few canvases that survive. The rarity of his paintings today makes the

Fig. 84: J. Vendramini after Robert Ker Porter, *Prince Bagration Leading the Cossacks.* Engraving. Copied from a photograph of the original print in the Department of Prints and Drawings at the British Museum.
The Trustees of the British Museum.

two in Russia of particular interest. They are examples of those brightly coloured, restless, overloaded compositions in the rather tedious academic style that was so typical of the late 18th century and early 19th. None the less, they both represent the sum of much hard work and an extensive knowledge of details relating to events of a different era, events of great importance to his contemporaries and here presented in an epic manner. Looking at these pictures it becomes clear that Porter himself, as an individual, arouses greater curiosity than the fruits of his labours as an artist.

The Scot William Allan (1782–1850) was another painter who spent a considerable time in Russia before establishing himself in Edinburgh. There, in December 1816, towards the end of his tour of Europe, Grand-Duke Nikolay Pavlovich (fig. 85) visited Allan's studio, 'the most picturesque painting-room … in Europe'.[21] Having returned to Scotland in 1814 after a long journey through the southern regions of Russia – the Crimea, Caucasus and the Caspian steppes – Allan put all his trophies on display in his studio on Princes Street, and the 'Turkish scimitars, Circassian bows and quivers, hauberks of twisted mail from Caucasus, daggers, dirks, javelins and all manner of unweildy [sic] fowling-pieces – Georgian, Armenian, and Tartar … helmets of all kinds and sizes … shawls, turbans, and saddle-cloths',[22] gave the room an unusual, exotic appearance, while the artist himself, dressed in a Circassian coat that harmonized with the interior, pre-

sented his works to visitors (fig. 86). Allan's studio and the subjects of his paintings on scenes from the life of the Circassians, Tartars and Bashkirs, among whom he had spent some considerable time, were in keeping with the romantic mood of a generation that avidly read Byron's *The Bride of Abydos* and Thomas Moore's *Lalla Rookh*, and were highly popular. During his visit to the studio, the Grand-Duke spent some time talking to Allan in Russian and French, allowing the artist to sketch in pencil a portrait of the future emperor, Nicholas II (private collection, Scotland). The Grand-Duke was very taken with the pictures, in which he praised most highly the precision of the details, and of those offered to his attention he picked out three – *Haslan Gheray Conducting Alkazia across the Kuban* (Makhachkala Art Museum, Daghestan), *Bashkirs Conducting Convicts to Siberia* (cat. 25) and the painting now known as *Frontier Guards* (cat. 26). All three were kept until 1918 in Nicholas's study in his favourite Petersburg residence, the Anichkov Palace.

Allan, a history, genre and portrait painter, became President of the Royal Scottish Academy in 1836, and was made a baronet in 1842. But when he had decided to seek fame and fortune abroad in 1805 and set off for Russia, he was an obscure young artist: 'Russia suggested itself as a country where an opening for his talents might be expected, and as one abounding in stirring and novel subjects for his pencil.'[23] On his arrival in St Petersburg, thanks to protection of the physician-

in-ordinary Sir Alexander Crichton, also a Scot by birth, he received several commissions for portraits, although these are lost.[24] It seems possible that Allan's Petersburg acquaintances included people linked with Scottish missions, those who sought to spread Christianity to the Muslim tribes of the Caucasus, Crimea and Caspian Steppes. One such mission, for instance, was founded in 1802 in the Northern Caucasus at Karass, not far from Pyatigorsk, between Stavropol and Vladikavkaz. Of course the artist visited those places where he would find his compatriots and where he could observe the scenes that were later to fill his paintings – *Captive Circassian Women, A Circassian Chief Selling to a Turkish Pasha Captives of a Native Tribe Taken in War, Tartar Robbers Dividing Spoil* (fig. 87), paintings he was to show at the Royal Academy in London between 1815 and 1817.

Allan spent some time living at Tul'chin in the Ukraine with Prince Feliks Pototsky, on his well-known Sofiyevka estate near Uman'[25] It is likely to have been there that he painted *Jewish Wedding, Don Cossacks Conveying French Prisoners to a Russian Camp, A Cossack Dancing and Playing the Theorban to a Family-group Before a Cottage Door*, and *The Raising of Lazarus* (seen in 1826 by J. Webster[26]), and his *Self-portrait in Circassian Dress*, shown in 1814 at the Edinburgh Exhibition Society (no. 42), where it was indicated that the work was produced at Toulizen (?Tul'chin) in 1813.

Fig. 85: Sir William Allan, *Grand-Duke Nikolay Pavlovich*. Pencil, 8 ⅞ × 6 ⅞ in. (22.5 × 17.5 cm). Signed and dated *W. Allan fecit. 1816*. Scottish Private Collection. Photo courtesy of Tom Scott, Edinburgh.

Fig. 86: William Nicholson, *Sir William Allan in Circassian Dress*, 1818. Oil on canvas, 36 × 28 ⅛ in. (91.4 × 71.4 cm). Scottish National Portrait Gallery.

Fig. 87: Sir Willian Allan, *Tartar Robbers Dividing Spoil*, 1817. Oil on canvas, 25 ¼ × 20 ½ in. (64.2 × 52 cm). Tate Gallery, London.

Fig. 88: Sir William Allan, *Mohammed Ali Bey*. Oil on canvas, 14 ½ × 10 ¾ in. (36 × 27.5 cm). Sold by Sotheby's, 4 November 1987 (lot 352).

Fig. 89: George Dawe, *Tsar Nicholas I.*
Watercolour, 7 × 5 ¼ in. (17.8 × 13.3 cm).
The Trustees of the British Museum.

Fig. 90: J. Bennet and Thomas Wright after
A. Martynov, *Alexander I Visiting Dawe's
Studio.* Engraving. State Hermitage Museum.

Allan also visited Odessa, where he was warmly received by the Governor-General, the Duc de Richelieu, to whom he presented a view of Odessa. 'I should desire Odessa would be so fine in reality as you have represented it in this delightful drawing', the Governor noted in thanks.[27]

Allan spent eight years in Russia on his first visit, leaving St Petersburg in 1814. The second visit was made in 1844, when Nicholas I (fig. 89) commissioned from him *Peter the Great Teaching his Subjects Shipbuilding.* Allan began the work in St Petersburg but then begged to be allowed to finish it in London, where it was shown at the Royal Academy in 1845. The painting was then dispatched to St Petersburg, as the artist informed the Minister of the Court, Prince P. M. Volkonsky, in a letter in which he also mentioned the price as £250. On 3 January 1846 the Hermitage curator F. Labensky answered a request from the Chancellory of the Ministry of the Palace for information regarding the location of the picture, stating that he 'saw it in 1844 in unfinished state … but that nothing is known to him as to where it is now'.[28] The canvas was never found, but then judging by what we know of it, it was not to be counted among the artist's successes. In 1845 *The Athenaeum* criticized the picture as 'characterless, feeble, and unworthy of a place of distinction'.[29]

Allan is also attributed with the authorship of a portrait of Mohammed Ali Bey (fig. 88) or, as he became known after converting to Christianity and joining the Russian service, Alexander Kazimovich Kazim-Bek,[30] professor of oriental languages at Kazan university, and from 1849 at St Petersburg's. Despite A.D.H. Bivar's opinion that the portrait could not have been painted by Allan on his first visit to Russia, i.e. before 1814, Bivar sees no reason why the artist could not have met the future professor during his travels across the south of Russia, through the mountains of the Caucasus or in the Caspian region, and have painted his portrait then. At any rate, an engraving after the portrait was published as early as 1836.[31]

It is interesting to note that it was roughly around the time when Allan was drawing his picturesque inhabitants of the Bashkirian and Kirghiz steppes and the Caucasian hills that similar themes attracted the attention of another Romantic artist, A. O. Orlovsky (1777–1832), who although of Polish origin spent most of his life in Russia but also travelled extensively in Europe, living in England for some time. His paintings of 1807–9, Circassian, Bashkir, Cossack and Bivouac subjects, reflected his interest in exotic and ethnographical details, precisely reproducing typical traits of these freedom-loving peoples living by the laws of the steppes and hills. This coincidence in the choice of subjects may be more than merely the product of the Romantic mood common to the whole of Russian art at that period. Orlovsky was very sensitive to changing fashions, and one gets the impression that he looked at Russian life with the eyes of a foreigner, selecting his subjects so as to be saleable both in Russia and abroad. Later, in the 1820s, Orlovsky was to scrutinize closely the work of another British artist working in Russia, George Dawe (1781–1829).

During Dawe's time in St Petersburg (1819–28), both he and his works aroused great interest in the Russian literary and artistic worlds. No Russian artist at this time was deemed worthy of so much close attention from clients, colleagues and the press, or enjoyed such great popularity and gave rise to such conflicting opinions among the public. Initial awareness of him was of course brought about by the commission that first brought him to the Russian capital, for Alexander I (fig. 90) had invited him to undertake a grandiose and unusual project, the creation of a gallery of portraits of over 300 generals, participants in the Patriotic War against Napoleon of 1812 and the foreign campaigns of 1813–14 that ended Napoleon's run of victories in Europe. The gallery was to be a monument to the glory of the Russian army. Between June and November 1826, the architect Carlo Rossi designed a special room for the paintings in the Winter Palace, near the Throne Room.[32] Great importance was attached to the construction of the gallery and thus we can understand why, despite the admiration for Dawe's talents in Russian publications devoted to his work,[33] starting with articles in the 1820s, Russian portraitists felt injured that they had not the chance 'of passing onto their heirs the appearance of the Russian generals'. Why was it, then, that Dawe was so fortunate as to receive this commission?

During the Congress of Aachen in the autumn of 1818, and perhaps earlier, when Dawe painted Alexander's portrait in 1817,[34] the Russian emperor was able to see for himself Dawe's ability to

work at great speed while achieving a remarkable likeness. Dawe was already acclaimed for his success in genre and history painting, 'few in number, though of undoubted excellence',[35] but was best known for his portraits. He arrived at Aachen in the suite of the Duke of Kent, and the Congress was attended by many potential clients. Here, as Lawrence wrote, Dawe 'prowled' and 'crept' in search of the most influential connections. At Aachen he painted the portraits of Lord Hill, General Alava and several Russian citizens accompanying Alexander I. He managed to win the tsar's favour and received the enviable invitation to work at St Petersburg, which resulted in extensive patronage by members of the Russian court.

Dawe was an untiring worker, painting in Russia not only the portraits for the 1812 Gallery in the Winter Palace but also portraits of all the members of the royal family (some of them several times), from Alexander I and the Dowager Empress Maria Fyodorovna right down to the future Alexander II, then still a boy. He also received a vast number of private commissions from every quarter. His popularity reached even greater heights after his exhibition at the Petersburg Academy of Arts in September 1820, which included not only his recent works but also past successes, among them full-length portraits of Princess Charlotte, the Duke of Kent and the actress Miss O'Neil. In his spacious studio in the Shepeleve House, on the site of which

now stands the New Hermitage, visitors could see other works brought from Britain, such as *Young Shepherd Caught by the Storm* and *Mother Rescuing her Child from the Eagle's Nest*, all captured in the well-known engraving by J. Bennet and Thomas Wright after A. Martynov's celebrated drawing of 1826, *Alexander I Visiting Dawe's Studio*. Dawe's works undoubtedly influenced Russian artists, and not only portrait painters. His *Mother Rescuing her Child from the Eagle's Nest*, recently identified by G. B. Andreyeva (now in the Peterhof Palace Museum) gave rise to similar works by A. Orlovsky and M. Markov I, who used the same subject in 1828 and 1833 respectively.[36]

From 1822, Dawe had two assistants, Vasily Golike and Alexander Polyakov, who helped him with the portraits of Alexander I and later Nicholas I that were required for various government bodies. It was at this time that Dawe was given a monopoly over prints made after his portraits of generals. He brought in relatives for this purpose – his brother Henry Dawe (1790–1848) and his brother-in-law, Thomas Wright (1782–1849).[37] *Otechestvennyye zapiski* [Notes from the Fatherland] announced that the engravings after the portraits in the 1812 Gallery were to appear in a separate publication containing between 75 and 100 portraits, the price of which was to be, 'on the best Indian paper, 1000, and other copies 600 roubles'.[38] In 1824 the same journal described the work of Henry Dawe and Thomas Wright exhibited in the Academy of Arts in St Petersburg: 'engraved from the portraits of the famed Dawe … portraits of Russian generals and

several grandees, very like [see fig. 91]. Henry Dawe wished to give the engraving that originality which marks the painted portraits by his brother. They seem to be drawn in ink and with a daring hand. The portraits of Thomas Wright are more lovely.'[39]

George Dawe's 'originality' both delighted and disturbed the critics. All were startled by his ability to convey a likeness, to the extent that the 'faces seemed to emerge from the frames'. The viewers were amazed by his painting technique: 'the mechanical work of his hand is of a very special nature: broad brushstrokes, daring, fast, but too fast, even coarse [*heurté*], he does not lay the paint, but throws it …'.[40] They perceived it as carelessness and imperfection. The artist was accused of errors in perspective, the use of strange, sharp lighting, theatricality, bright colouring and a mannered style, but all these deficiencies could not detract from the main point, that Dawe's portraits, for all their unusual expressiveness, remained true to life and preserved an unconstrained lightness of execution.

The strong impression created by Dawe's works, his energy, at times giving rise to scandalous rumours of abuse of his assistant Polyakov, whose labour he exploited mercilessly, the thirst for profit of which he was accused, particularly by the more patriotically inclined critics, all contributed to the fact that his name appeared only too frequently in the press. Influenced by his portraits of the generals, Fyodor Glinka, a leading publicist, decided to publish 'A Collection of Poetic Inscriptions to Portraits of Russian Generals, painted by the brush of Mr Dawe on the highest command', although this was actually reduced to several poems published in *Severnaya pchela* [Northern Bee]. Dawe was enshrined in Russian literature: Pushkin dedicated to him the poem 'To Dawe ESQ' and wrote 'The General', inspired by the portrait of Barclay de Tolly in the Gallery of 1812, while Nikolay Gogol's tale 'The Portrait' is suffused with the image of the British portrait painter.

While on the subject of portrait painters in early 19th-century Russia, one cannot omit mention of another artist whose fate there is a total mystery. James Saxon (1767–1840)[41] is almost as little known in his own country – where his name is associated mainly with one of the numerous portraits of Sir Walter Scott – as in Russia. He may have visited Russia on several occasions, for *Sankt-Petrburgskiye vedemosti* [St Petersburg Gazette] mentioned his departure at least twice, in 1805 and 1819.[42] There is no precise information as to how long he spent in Russia and what he achieved there. His portraits *John Rogers* (fig. 92) and *James Leighton*,[43] the latter known only from an engraving by Grigory Yanov, reveal him to have been a skilful artist, although of course not so brilliant as Lawrence, or as capable as Dawe.

In 1839 at an exhibition at the Petersburg Academy of Arts, the visitors' attention was drawn to a portrait entitled *A Woman Playing the Organ*, executed with an 'animated, powerful' brush, as the reviewer from the journal *Biblioteka dlya chteniya* [Library for Reading] put it, adding 'How much feeling, thought, nature! How easy and natural it all is, how alien to effort and strain! What superb colouring! And who would have thought all this is the work of a weak female hand! … It is immediately clear that Miss Robertson is English, that she has been educated in the traditions of the most sublime portrait painting, that she studied the mastery of her brush in the land of Reynolds and Lawrence.'[44] Such rapture over the work of Christina Robertson (1796–1854) now seems greatly exaggerated,[45] but tells us much of the taste of the reign of Nicholas I. The critic was ready to place a portrait by an artist of modest talent alongside the works of Rembrandt, without fear of reproach. He preferred it to all the other portraits at the exhibition, and this opinion was supported by members of the Russian aristocracy, who thronged to pose for Robertson between 1840 and 1844 and again between 1849 and 1854. Her work perfectly suited the tastes of the Russian court, where members of the royal family made up the majority of her clients. Robertson was principally a miniaturist and was able to paint very fine depictions of faces. She could convey the texture of satin, velvet and lace, making the image so convincing that it was bound to please the public (fig. 93). Most of her portraits were of women, and she was willing to undertake the most outrageous flattery. It is hard to believe that the portrait of T. V. Yusupova, painted not long before the Princess's death in 1841, shows a woman of 74 years old. In 1841 Robertson exhibited full-length portraits of the Empress Alexandra Fyodorovna (see fig. 95) and three of her daughters at the Academy of Arts, after which she was elected Honorary Free Associate of the Academy. Count M. Buturlin recalled his impressions of the exhibition and of Robertson's works: 'Of the

Fig. 91: George Dawe, *George Dawe with Vasily Golicke and his Family*. Oil on canvas, 35 × 36 ¼ in. (89 × 92 cm). Russian State Museum, St Petersburg.

Fig. 92: James Saxon, *John Rogers (1739–1811)*, c. 1800. Oil on canvas, 29 ⅛ × 25 ³⁄₁₆ in. (74 × 64 cm). State Hermitage Museum. The sitter was a British physician invited to Russia in 1774 and who served in the Black Sea Fleet. In 1805 he was appointed General-Headquarters Physician to the Ministry of the Navy.

Fig. 93: Christina Robertson, *Self-portrait*. Miniature on ivory, 7 ⅛ × 5 ³⁄₁₆ in. (18.1 × 13.2 cm). Victoria & Albert Museum, London.

Empress Aleksandra Fyodorovna, who looks all of her 40 years, the flattering brush of the British lady made a twenty-year-old beauty…'.[46] Along with Horace Vernet (1789–1863), Joseph-Désiré Court (1797–1865) and Karl von Steuben (1788–1856), she was the most popular and highly-paid portraitist in the capital. Her clients included the Yusupovs, the Baryatinskys, the Orlov-Davydovs, Shuvalovs, Sheremetyevs, Belosel'skys and Bobrinskys, the very cream of the Russian aristocracy. Her works, mostly small and intimate (fig. 94), decorated studies and private apartments of the owners of the largest mansions and were intended to be admired by one's nearest and dearest. It is possible that this is why an art once so popular was gradually forgotten both in Britain, where her works are to be found almost solely in private collections, and in Russia, where together with the remaining property of their former owners they were nationalized after the Revolution and are to be found in the least-known or most far-flung museums. She died in St Petersburg, far from her homeland, at the height of the Crimean War and therefore at the time of the worst possible relations between Britain and Russia.

The Crimean War and the resulting readjustment in the political and economic situation in Russia put an end to further efforts by British painters to move in on the Russian art world. And yet even though the names of those few British artists who had spent some time in Russia during the first half of the 19th century are known, remarkably few details of their lives are available. Reconstructing their careers is like doing a jigsaw puzzle, piecing together the whole from small, irregularly shaped fragments. At present we have the general outlines and some details, but many other details have been lost along the way, and until they can be found the picture will remain incomplete.

Fig. 94: Christina Robertson, *Grand-Duchesses Olga Nikolayevna and Alexandra Nikolayevna at a Harpsichord*. Oil on canvas, 14 ⅜ × 10 ⅝ in. Signed and dated 1840. (36.5 × 29.5 cm). State Hermitage Museum. The sitters were daughters of tsar Nicholas I.

Fig. 95: Edward Hau, *The Rotunda of the Winter Palace*, 1862. Watercolour, white lead, 16 ⅜ × 12 ¾ in. (41.5 × 32.5 cm). State Hermitage Museum. In the background can be seen G. Bottmann's *Nicholas I in Cossack Uniform* and Christina Robertson's full-length portrait of *Alexandra Fyodorovna*.

1. J. A. Atkinson and J. Walker, *A Picturesque Representation of the Manners, Customs, and Amusements of the Russians in one hundred coloured plates* (London, 1803–4). He was not, however, the first Briton to capture the beauties of St Petersburg. More than ten years earlier Thomas Malton had published several engravings with views of the city after the drawings of the little-known artist Joseph Hearn (see fig. 12).

2. Harrison 1855, pp. 41–2.

3. *Syn Otechestva* (1815), no. 8, p. 92.

4. For example, *Post-Guide through Russia … translated into English from the last Imperial Ukase*, by J. Tournier, 2nd edn (London, 1812); F. Coghlan, *A Guide to St Petersburg and Moscow* (London, 1836).

5. Alekseyev 1982, pp. 576, 639.

6. R. Ker Porter, *Travelling Sketches in Russia and Sweden, during the years 1805, 1806, 1807, 1808*, 2 vols. (London, 1807–9); F. S. Larpent, *Private Journals*, 3 vols. (London, 1853); L. Ritchie, *A Journey to St Petersburg and Moscow through Courland and Livonia, with twenty-five splendid engravings by the first artists after drawings by A. G. Vickers* (London, 1836); G. F. Atkinson, *Pictures from the North in Pen and Pencil, Sketched During a Summer Ramble* (London, 1848).

7. A. Kotsebu: 'Kratkoye opisaniye imperatorskogo Mikhaylovskogo dvortsa 1801 goda' [A short description of the Imperial Mikhail Palace 1801], *Russkiy Arkhiv* [Russian Archive] (Moscow, 1871), pp. 975–6.

8. See T. Seccombe, 'Robert Ker Porter', *Dictionary of National Biography*, XLVI (London, 1896), pp. 190–2; Armstrong 1962; W. Dupouy, *Sir Robert Ker Porter's Caracas Diary 1825–1842* (Caracas, 1969); Barnett 1972; Ancketill 1978); Renne 1985; Vasil'yeva 1995; N. Vasil'yeva, 'About the History of Sir Robert Ker Porter's Album with his Sketches of Sasanian Monuments', *Archaeologische Mitteilungen aus Iran*, 27 (forthcoming), pp. 81–90; MS monograph on Porter by M. D. Ancketill in St Anthony's College, Oxford.

9. Ancketill 1978, p. 7. If Porter took these pictures with him and exhibited them in St Petersburg and Moscow, there should have been some reaction in the press and memoirs of contemporaries, for this would have been a notable event.

10. P. V. Chichagov had an English wife (Elizabeth Proby), as did another Russian admiral, N. S. Mordvinov (Henrietta Cobley).

11. S. F. Ogorodnikov: 'Model'-kamera vposledstvii Morskoy muzey imeni imp. Petra Velikogo. Isoricheskiy ocherk. 1709–1909' [Model Chamber, later the Peter the Great Naval Museum. Historical Outline. 1709–1909] (St Petersburg, 1909), p. 24.

12. Porter, *Travelling Sketches*, II, pp. 8, 9.

13. Renne 1985.

14. Ancketill 1978.

15. Porter married Princess M. F. Shcherbatova in February 1812.

16. Barnett 1972; Vasil'yeva, *op. cit.*

17. R. Ker Porter, *Travels in Georgia, Persia, Armenia, Ancient Babylonia during the years 1817, 1818, 1819, 1820, 1823* (London, 1821–2).

18. 'Notes by Sir R. Ker Porter chiefly on military colonies in Russia and the situation in Persia in 1820', Bodleian Library, MS Eng.his.c.409. This document, discovered in 1994 by E. Renne, is currently being prepared for publication.

19. *Ibid.*, p. 32.

20. Vasil'yeva, *op. cit.*, pp. 81–90.

21. Lockhart 1819, II, p. 116.

22. *Ibid.*

23. Anon., 'Sir William Allan', *Art Journal* (1849), p. 108.

24. We know only a male portrait (Hermitage inv. no. 6871), ascribed to Allan on the basis of similarity to a pencil drawing also in the Hermitage (inv. no. 43428) with the inscription 'William Allan 1814.' on the reverse.

25. At any rate, his drawings with views of the Schlotterbeck garden were used as the basis for engravings in S. Trembecki's book of poems, *Zofiowka* (Vienna, 1815).

26. Webster 1830, p. 39.

27. Cited in Bivar 1994, p. 292.

28. Hermitage Archive, op. 2, 1846, d. 56/9, fol. 19.

29. *Athenaeum* (1845), p. 466.

30. Sotheby's, London, 4 November 1987, lot 352.

31. Revd Dr R. Ross, 'The Persian Convert', *The Keepsake and a Missionary Annual* (1836). See Bivar 1994.

32. After the fire that tore through the Winter Palace in December 1837, the gallery was rebuilt with some changes to a design by V. Stasov. All the portraits had been saved from the burning palace.

33. Above all this relates to articles and journals and the newspapers in the 1820s, such as *Otechestvennyy zapiskit* [Notes from the Fatherland], *Syn Otechestva* [Son of the Fatherland], *Moskovskiy vestnik* [Moscow Herald] and *Severnaya pchela* [Northern Bee]. See also Makarov 1940; Glinka and Pomarnatskiy 1981; Andreyeva 1989; Ye. P. Renne, 'Voyennaya galereya Zimnego dvortsa' [The Military Gallery of 1812], in Dukelskaya and Renne 1990, pp. 185–7; Andreeva 1993; Andreyeva 1995.

34. Portrait of Alexander I, signed by Dawe and dated 1817 (Royal Collection, Windsor Castle). The details surrounding its production are unknown.

35. *Arnold's Library of Fine Arts*, I (1831), p. 10.

36. See Andreyeva 1995.

37. After Dawe's death, Wright, who had arrived in Russia to deal with the artist's effects, finished three half-length portraits and a portrait of Grand-Duke Constantine Pavlovich, all begun by Dawe himself, and produced a portrait of A. B. Fok (Dukelskaya and Renne 1990, p. 186 and nn. 143, 276, 340, 351, 411).

38. *Otechestvennyye zapiski*, pt. 12 (1822), p. 413.

39. *Ibid*, pt. 206 (1824), p. 311.

40. 'Akademiya khudozhestv' [Academy of Art], *Syn Otechestva* [Son of the Fatherland] (1820), pt. 64, no. 40, p. 299.

41. These dates are quoted in Bird 1974, p. 19.

42. *Sankt-Petrburgskiye vedemosti* (1805), nos. 36, 64; (1819), no. 50.

43. For further information see Krol' 1961b, pp. 383–94.

44. *Biblioteka dlya cheteniya*, XXXVII (1839), pt III, pp. 53–4.

45. On Robertson see Bird 1977; Renne 1995.

46. M. D. Buturlin, 'Zapiski' [Notes], *Russkiy Arkhiv* [Russian archive] (Moscow, 1901), book 3, p. 451.

WEDGWOOD'S GREEN FROG SERVICE
AND THE IMPERIAL COURT

Lydia Liackhova

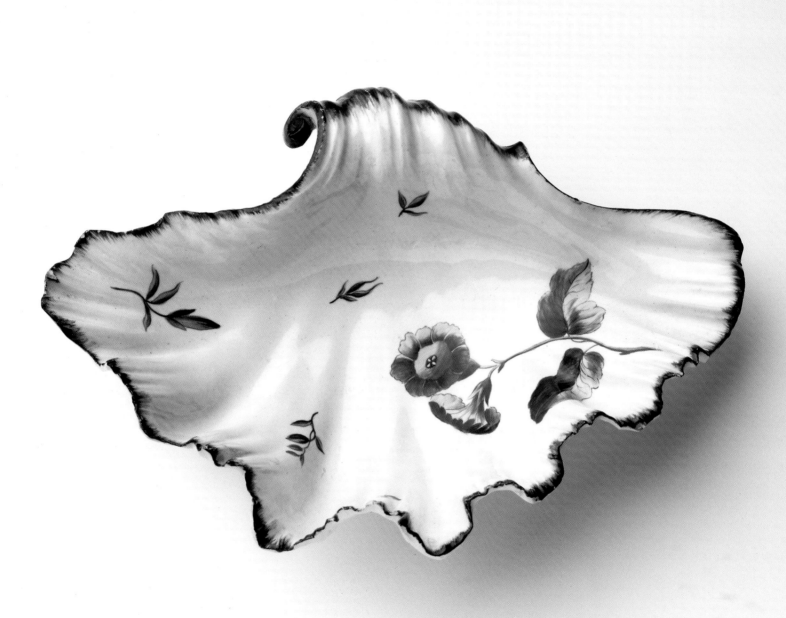

Fig. 96: Shell dish, *c.* 1770. Queen's ware, enamelled in purple with sprays of flowers. Wedgwood. Width, 7 ⅞ in. (19.9 cm), Victoria & Albert Museum, London, Gift of Miss Lily Antrobus. This dish is identical to those in the Husk service ordered in 1770 by Catherine the Great. Part of the service survives at the Great Palace at Peterhof.

In 1766 the second Anglo-Russian trading agreement was signed. It was to run for twenty years and resulted in a flood of British goods onto the Russian market, as this advertisement in the *Sankt-Peterburgskiye vedomosti* [St Petersburg Gazette] for 3 June 1774 suggests: 'On the Admiralty Side in the stone trading rows at stall 39 there is for sale a set of English straw-coloured crockery, smooth and painted, available complete or separately ...'. Ceramics in fact made up a large part of British exports to the Continent: 'When travelling from Paris to St Petersburg, from Amsterdam to the farthest point of Sweden, from Denmark to the southern extremity of France, one is served at every inn from English earthenware', noted Faujais de Saint-Fond in *Voyage en Angleterre*.[1] In Russia, English ceramics were to be found not only at inns and in the homes of state officials, but also at the court of the Empress Catherine.

On 20 September 1769 the firm of Wedgwood sent the first examples of its goods to the Russian court. Wedgwood enjoyed the patronage of Lady Jane Cathcart, wife of the English ambassador to Russia in 1768–71, Charles, Lord Cathcart (fig. 6), and sister of the famous collector of antiquities, the English ambassador in Naples, Sir William Hamilton. His familiarity with Hamilton's collection of Antique vases strongly influenced Wedgwood's Neoclassical taste. Lady Cathcart, meanwhile, enjoyed a high position at court, being the first foreign woman to have the honour of receiving the Empress in her own home. The first lot of goods sent to Russia by Wedgwood included examples of various wares produced by the firm: items of the fine English faïence that Wedgwood perfected and which in 1766 became known as Queen's ware in honour of the patronage of the Britain's Queen Charlotte, and his own pride and joy – 'Etruscan vases' of black basaltes ware. The material used for the latter recalled the noble hue of Antique black-lacquer vases. The red-figure painting on the Wedgwood vases reinforced the similarity with Antique art. In letters dated 28 January and 8 February 1770, Lady Cathcart informed Wedgwood of the receipt of all the goods he had sent and expressed her satisfaction that one of the vases repeated an Antique original from her brother's collection, but she also expressed some doubts about the possible success of the firm in Russia: 'I rather am inclined to think their taste this way is very confined & that the useful is all they will ever commission'.[2] Eight months later, however, on 5 October, Lady Cathcart wrote again, stating that Wedgwood's initiatives for that year had been very successful and that 'her Im. Majesty has kept all the Vases & the Dejeune you sent to me, as samples & that they were much liked'.[3]

None the less, Catherine's first order – given in 1770 – was for utilitarian pieces, albeit quite imposing: a table service (including both dinner and dessert services) for 24 persons. This is known in the literature as the Husk service, as the pieces have on them, in addition to large lilac flowers, garlands of small lilac-coloured husks, opened up like tulips. The Husk service, which was made of Queen's ware, was delivered to Russia in the autumn of 1770 (on 4 November Catherine signed the decree confirming that payment should be made in full), and was placed in the service stores of the Winter Palace.[4] Ordering a large service from Wedgwood was a notable event: for the first time a service was ordered for the Russian court not of porcelain, but of faïence, albeit Queen's ware, and it was also the first time that Catherine had turned to an English ceramics firm. Even so, on this occasion she had not shown any great originality or initiative as a client.

The situation was radically different in 1773: Wedgwood was given the largest and most complicated commission ever to be received by an English ceramics firm – the famous Green Frog service. The idea was wholly Catherine's own. The commission was for a large service for 50 persons, and it was completed in 1774. The 944 pieces displayed no less than 1,222 handpainted landscape views of Britain, none of which appeared more than once. 'We have attempted on the different pieces to give a true and picturesque idea of the beauties of this country, both natural and artificial', wrote Wedgwood's partner, Thomas Bentley, in his foreword to the manuscript catalogue of views compiled in French for their client.[5]

The commission had been passed to Wedgwood verbally, via Alexander Baxter, the Russian consul in London, and through Wedgwood's letters to Bentley we can see how difficult a task he had been set. Wedgwood had no hesitation in selecting forms for the items and also had no doubts as to how to draw up a system for their decoration: 'I suppose it must be painted upon the Royal Pattern & there must be a border upon the rims of the dishes & plates &c of some kind, & the building &c in the middle only,' he wrote on 23 March 1773.[6] Questions of form and decoration were left wholly to the professional talents of the Wedgwood firm, the client having only made demands regarding the subjects of the paintings on the service. And it was this that worried Wedgwood: 'Why all the Gardens in England will scarcely furnish subjects sufficient for this sett, every piece having a different subject', he wrote to Bentley.[7] On 29 March he again expressed his doubts to his partner: 'Do you think the subjects must all be from real views and real Buildings .... As to our being confin'd to Gothique Buildings only, why there are not enough I am perswaded in Great Britain to furnish subjects for this service.'[8] To judge from Wedgwood's letters, Catherine's commission specified that the landscapes should not repeat one another, that they should be topographically correct, and that particular attention be paid to the depiction of parks, gardens and Gothic buildings. There was undoubtedly much emphasis placed on the Gothic style: on 3 April Wedgwood asked Bentley: 'What do you think of the Etruscan, long pointed border, the same as Ld. Stormonts Desert, I think it is nearly as much Gothic as Etruscan.'[9] Even the borders on the objects had to be Gothic.

Since the service was intended for a Gothic-style castle, which was what Catherine wanted her new palace to be, we should not be suprised by this. Designed by the architect Yuri Velten, and built 1774–7, the palace was sited in an uninhabited area, overgrown with trees and bushes, south of St Petersburg on the Moscow road to Tsarskoye Selo. The Finnish name for the area was Kekerekeksinen (or in Russian Kekeriki), which means a frog marsh. This title was also given to the new Palace, which led to the service ordered for it having

Fig. 97: Plan of the first floor of the Chesme Palace, St Petersburg. Until 1780 the Palace was called Kekerekeksinen ('frog marsh'), or, by Catherine herself, La Grenouillière.

Fig. 98: Plans of Longford Castle, Wiltshire, from *Vitruvius Britannicus*, V (1771).

Fig. 99: Sir Joshua Reynolds, *James Harris, 1st Earl of Malmesbury*. Oil on canvas, 49 ½ × 40 in. (125.7 × 101.6 cm). Shown at the Royal Academy exhibition in 1785. Private Collection. Lord Malmesbury was Ambassador to Russia in 1778–83.

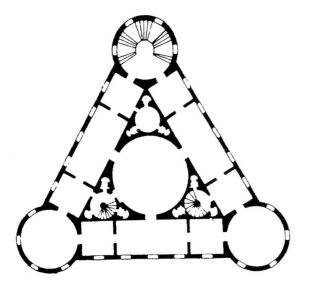

the unusual emblem of a green frog in a shield. The Kekerekeksinen Palace indeed created the impression of a medieval castle: built on a triangular plan very like the English late-16th-century Longford Castle, Wiltshire (fig. 98), and having towers at the angles and lancet windows, it was surrounded by a moat (which also served to drain the swampy land) and earth ramparts (fig. 97). As in any family castle belonging to the European aristocracy, with its portrait gallery showing pictures of ancestors, Kekerekeksinen Palace had portrait bas-reliefs of the Grand-Dukes and tsars from Ryurik to Elizabeth Petrovna, plus portraits of all the ruling European monarchs of the time with their families (including the British royal family: see figs. 20–22), which, as it were, reinforced Catherine II's right to be counted among them.

The palace-cum-castle of Kekerekeksinen was one of the first examples of Gothic revival architecture to be built in or near St Petersburg, and without doubt it is the most important. The fashion for Gothic had reached Russia via Britain, where the Gothic style had continued almost without interruption, despite the Palladian and more recent Greek Revival movements. It certainly explains why a service with views of Britain – and especially Gothic ruins – was ordered for Kekerekeksinen. In the 18th century, furniture and services were usually transported from palace to palace as the court moved around; but the Green Frog Service differed in that it was conceived as an integral part of Kekerekeksinen's ensemble. Its amusing emblem was to remind everyone of that fact.

Large official dinners meant that additional tableware was brought to the Palace. The *Kamer-Fuhrer* ceremonial journal, a record of the day-to-day life of the Empress and her court, details the dinner that was given there on 24 June 1780 in the central round hall.

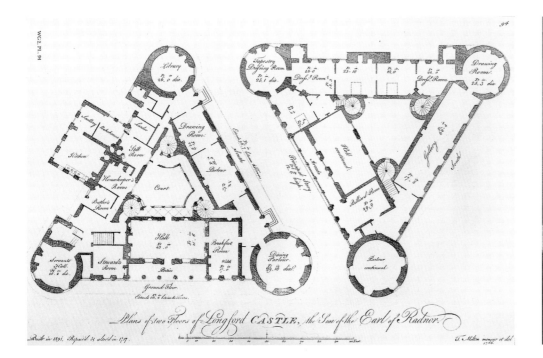

The tables were laid with 'a faïence service, kept in the Palace, and beneath were plates from the same service … at the same table was carved crystal tableware, from the Hermitage.'[10] Other tableware was also used at Kekerekeksinen, and in the *Kamer-Fuhrer Journal* for 6 June 1777 we learn that 'the table was served with a faïence service. The confiture service was new, gilded. The crystal service ordinary.'[11] The confiture service (for fruits and berries boiled in sugar) and the ordinary crystal service were clearly not so inseparably linked with the Gothic palace as was the Green Frog service.

Catherine never lived in the Kekerekeksinen Palace: it was built as a place for her to stop over on the journey between the capital's Winter Palace and Tsarskoye Selo (although it was sometimes also used for grand court ceremonies). She herself called it La Grenouillière, preferring the French version of the name, rather than the Finnish, which was difficult to pronounce, or the Russian, which had a clumsy sound. During her short visits to it the Green Frog service was not used, since Wedgwood's famous creation was kept more to be admired than regularly used. The British ambassador to Russia in 1778–83, James Harris, later 1st Earl of Malmesbury (fig. 99), wrote to his father on 3 June 1779 to boast that: *I have the good fortune to have made myself not disagreeable to the Empress. She notices me much more than any of my colleagues; more, indeed, I believe, than any stranger is used to. She admits me to all her parties of cards, and a few days ago carried me with only two of her courtiers to a country palace, where she has placed the portraits of all the crowned heads of Europe. We discoursed much of their several merits; and still more on the great demerits of the modern portrait-painters …. She calls this place la Grenouillière; and it was for it that Wedgwood made, some years ago, a very remarkable service of his ware, on which a green frog was painted. It represented the different country-houses and gardens in England. This also, we were shown; and this led us to a conversation on English gardening, in which the Empress is a great adept.*[12]

According to the *Kamer-Fuhrer Journal*, Catherine's trip to the Kekerekeksinen Palace with Harris had taken place on 20 May. The Empress stopped there as usual en route to Tsarskoye Selo. Little is recorded in the journal of how she spent her time there: 'On arrival at the said palace she deigned, both with those in her suite and with the accompanying persons, to take coffee, and continued at the palace over an hour.'[13] The Green Frog service in this case was presented to the high-ranking visitors as a typical 'cabinet' service. Although the Empress 'took coffee' (as she did on several other trips there in the spring and summer of that year), some other crockery must have been used, since coffee cups were not part of the Wedgwood service.

Harris was certainly not wrong to think that the Empress was well disposed towards him, for he was regularly honoured with a 'private audience' with Catherine. Earlier that year (10 March) on behalf of King George III she had awarded Harris the Order of the Bath, while her own personal mark of approval was the gift of 'a sword with a golden hilt, studded with diamonds'.[14] Harris's daughter, born the following year, was named Catherine in honour of the Empress, who became her godmother.[15] The Empress's warmth for the ambassador

was not by chance: his father was the famous linguist James Harris senior, who had just completed the first critical study in English on Russian literature, *Some Account of Literature in Russia, and of its Progress Towards being Civilised* (London, 1780). The new Russian books that formed the material for this analysis were dispatched by the son to the father, having been selected personally by the Empress and Prince Potemkin, the latter a close acquaintance of Smith.[16] These were in fact translations into Greek (the elder Harris knew no Russian) of several Russian odes praising the Empress and Potemkin as admirers of ancient classical culture, and of some Latin treatises by professors at Moscow University and St Petersburg's Academy of Sciences. Catherine never missed an opportunity to present herself as an enlightened European monarch.

A similar desire led to the commission by Catherine – who had never visited Britain – for a service decorated with views of that country. She perceived Britain as a land of democratic freedoms, while France continued to suffer under despotic rule. Catherine wished to demonstrate her commitment to liberalism both to her subjects and the rest of Europe. Undoubtedly the exhibition (from 1 June 1774) in London of the completed Green Frog service prior to its dispatch to Russia could only have been organized with Catherine's agreement, for it was in itself part of her broader programme of propaganda. A similar exhibition had been held in Berlin two years earlier, when the public was shown a state dessert service made at the Berlin porcelain manufactory on the orders of the Prussian King Friedrich II as a present for Catherine. The porcelain sculpture that formed the table decorations of this service (which included a figure of the Empress enthroned) and the battle scenes depicted on the plates were intended to glorify her enlightened rule and Russian military successes against the Turks. The Wedgwood commission and its exhibition in London was effectively a diplomatic riposte to the Prussian monarch.

Wedgwood knew of the diplomatic reverberations of the commission: 'I suppose this service is order'd upon the idea of the two services getting up by the King of Prussia …. One with all the battles between the Russians & the Turks, drawn under his Majestys inspection & intended as a present you know to the Empress – & the other with all the remarkable views & landskips in his Dominions, for his own use', he wrote to Bentley on 23 March 1773.[17] Catherine's little trick worked. The exhibition of the Green Frog service in London was visited by Queen Charlotte and her brother, the Duke of Mecklenburg-Strelitz. The role of the high-ranking client as author of the idea for this unusual project was not veiled. One visitor wrote to her daughter: 'The Empress's directions were all from herself. She chose the Colours, order'd the views to be confin'd to this Island, & to contain all that could be of Gothic Remains, of Natural Views, & of Improved Scenes and Ornaments in Parks & Gardens Which they [Wedgwood and Bentley] say are what she wants to collect & imitate.'[18]

Wedgwood and Bentley, without false modesty, reckoned that the images they supplied on the Green Frog service would be a successful substitute for Catherine for first-hand impressions: 'The principal subjects are: the ruins, the most remarkable buildings, parks, gardens, and other natural curiosities which distinguish Great Britain, and mostly attract the attention of tourists. Though we have purposely omitted to represent the most modern buildings, considering them unpicturesque, there will be found nevertheless specimens of architecture of all ages and styles, from the most ancient to our present day; from rural cottages and farms, to the most superb palaces; and from the huts of the Hebrides to the masterpieces of the best known English architects', wrote Bentley in the foreword to the catalogue of views.[19]

It was not an everyday need that had prompted Catherine to order the unusual service, but politics and diplomacy, a love for English parks and the desire to piece together a little England within her remote, make-believe Gothic castle. Empty for most of the time, Kekerekeksinen Palace (which from 1780 was known as Chesme Palace) was listed as 'a castle for entertainments' in the description of St Petersburg and its surroundings published in 1794.[20] It was also described in a short story by the Empress, who had some literary talent, as a place where amazing events took place. From her own pen came the unfinished 'The Chesme Palace: Conversation between Portraits and Medallions': 'The old soldier, doing his rounds at the Chesme Palace, heard a noise within. He pricked up his ears, and to his great amazement discovered that the portraits and medallions within were talking among themselves ...'.[21] And whatever the subject of the conversation was between the crowned heads of Europe and their ministers and generals, the Green Frog service formed a most fitting background.

Court life did, however, occasionally disturb the calm of the Palace, as the records in the *Kamer-Fuhrer Journals* of dinners given there indicate. On 6 June 1777, for instance, the Empress set off from Tsarskoye Selo to her new-built Palace to lay the foundation stone for the church there, also designed by Yuri Velten (fig. 100). From St Petersburg came the Swedish King Gustav III, travelling as the Duke of Gotland, and his suite. After the blessing of the site where the church – dedicated to St John the Baptist – was to be built, a service was held. Then everyone entered the Palace, where 'all the rooms were sprinkled with holy water'. A state dinner of 36 places followed, served on the Wedgwood service.[22]

Three years later, on 24 June, the day of St John the Baptist, the church was consecrated, a ceremony attended by Paul Petrovich with his wife and the Austrian Emperor Josef II, who, as 'Count Falkenstein', was visiting the capital incognito. An artillery salute followed. Returning to the Palace, the visitors stopped to converse in the 'Russian portrait room', after which came a state dinner 'for 56 places with music for wind instruments whilst at table'. Six tables were served in all, on 'a faïence service kept in the palace'.[23] It was on this day that Catherine gave the Palace its new name – Chesme – in honour of the Russian fleet's victory over the Turks at Chesme Bay in the Aegean in June 1770.

The following year Catherine organized a state dinner in the Palace after prayers in memory of the Chesme victory.[24] Once again

there were six tables (this time circular ones, according to the *Journal*) arranged in the circular hall and set for 53 diners. There was music on wind instruments, and 'the said tables were served with two courses on the faïence service'. On 24 June in both 1782 and 1783 Catherine again briefly stopped there, but gave no official dinners and rested only briefly after prayers in the church before returning to Tsarskoye Selo, where she spent her summers. In 1784, while marking the anniversary of the victory over the Turks, she did not visit Chesme Palace at all, and in general the prayers held in honour of the victory were from then on taken in the church at Tsarskoye Selo. Chesme Palace began a new phase in its history when sittings of the Council of Knights of the Order of St George, founded by Catherine in 1783, were established there.

Although the building had ceased to be an official place of residence of the Russian court it continued to be a place of entertainment, and on 18 February 1791 a 'procession of sledges' was organized there to mark Shrovetide.[25] Four rooms of the Palace were used to set four tables for 105 places for a dinner at which the Empress, Paul Petrovich and his wife and two eldest sons were present. The tables 'were served on the Chesme faïence service', for it is in the *Kamer-Fuhrer Journal* for that year that the Green Frog service is first called the 'Chesme service'. After lunch, around four o'clock, the elegant gathering returned to St Petersburg.

An even more luxurious Shrovetide procession took place on 10 February 1795.[26] First on large town sledges, then on 'small toboggans', Catherine and her grandchildren (Grand-Duke Alexander with his wife, Grand-Duke Constantine, Grand-Duchesses Alexandra, Yelena and Maria), and a large suite arrived at Chesme Palace. The tables were set out in various rooms with 112 places, and once again those at table 'were served on the Chesme faïence service'. After dinner the royal family and their guests returned to St Petersburg on sledges.

The number of people that attended these special dinners held at the Palace is remarkable. As we know, the Green Frog service was intended for only 50 persons. But the situation is clarified by documents in the archives that reveal that additional pieces were made in St Petersburg at the Imperial Porcelain Manufactory. These pieces were not copies of the original Wedgwood objects but, judging by the documents, were made in the same style, albeit with some significant differences, which might explain why they were never included in the various inventories of the service. In the record of 'How many different porcelain pieces were brought to the rooms of your Imperial Highness in 1793 from 1 January to 1 May', we read: 'Chesme service deep plates, painted with views of English gardens, edges decorated with gold' – 37 altogether at a cost of 592 roubles.[27] The additions to the Wedgwood service are mentioned in special records 'on the tableware kept at the Imperial Porcelain Manufactory, made as part of the service ordered for the Chesme Palace. Painted with English views of gardens and the edges decorated with gold'.[28] The list of objects includes an oval tureen with a cover and heads, 'to be placed under this an oval platter of the 2nd kind', an oval sauce-boat 'of the 2nd kind with a lid', an oval sauce-boat with platter, a sugar-bowl with platter and spoon, a large ice-cream bowl 'of three parts, 2nd kind', a monteith, 'oval with heads', a wine-cooler with heads, an openwork basket with platter and 38 table plates. The list of additions mentions items whose forms distinctly differ from similar ones in the Wedgwood service – the tureen, monteith and wine-cooler 'with heads' (probably decorative handles in the form of female heads). In addition, the pieces made at the Imperial Porcelain Manufactory had a gilded edge and the white Imperial porcelain had a very different tone to the cream Queen's ware. The collections in the Hermitage and the Peterhof Palace include examples of Russian porcelain from Catherine's era (and a similar group from the time of Paul I) with monochrome landscapes and a gilded edge that were undoubtedly in-fluenced by the Green Frog service.[29] The handles of the monteith and the wine-cooler are both in the form of female heads. Unfortunately, despite these coincidences, it is impossible to state with absolute certainty that these were the pieces made as additions to the famous service. Even so, it is still of interest that the Wedgwood faïence had such a notable influence on the style of Russian porcelain.

Additions were also made to the above-mentioned Husk service.[30] These were produced in the first half of the 19th century at the Pokochin, Otto and Ginter factories, and at a fourth, unknown, factory that marked its goods with the Russian character 'theta'. In 1858 a large group of additions was delivered by the Imperial Porcelain Manufactory.

Lady Cathcart's fear of introducing the Wedgwood ceramics to the court of Catherine II back in 1770 – that Russians might not like 'all sorts of Gilding & Colouring' – was to prove unfounded.[31] Taste in Russia was catching up fast, taking as its guide Neoclassical, particu-larly British Neoclassical, art. One order of 1775 is typical: 'design'd for one of the first Ministers of the Empress of Russia. A compleat Service Earthenware for 18 persons, to be of a higher yellow than the former sent & quite even in the very newest & neatest Taste, quite plain, without any gold on or pictures.'[32] The cream colour of the faïence was perceived to be its main merit. At the end of the 18th century the export of Wedgwood faïence to Russia had reached an unprecedented scale. For instance, in August 1789 alone, the firm sent to Russia 18,449 faïence objects.[33]

At the end of the 1780s Wedgwood undertook another large com-mission for the Russian court, plaques that were supplied to adorn Catherine's bedroom in the Great Palace at Tsarskoye Selo (the int-erior, designed by the architect Charles Cameron, was destroyed during World War II). A guide to Tsarskoye Selo, published in 1911, informs us that: *All the walls and the ceiling were finished in glass plaques of milky colour with massive decorations of gilded bronze, into which in places are set porcelain medallions of different forms and sizes, the work of the English firm Wedgwood. Between the windows is Phaeton, produced between 1770 and 1780 by the famous draughtsman who drew horses, the Englishman Stubbs. Over the doors are plaques with Apollo and the Nine Muses by a contemporary of Flaxman's. Over the alcove is a Sacrifice to Bacchus by the same artist. Over the fireplace and opposite it is Dancing Hours by the said Flaxman and, again by him, Bacchanalian scenes. The subjects in the round medallions have not been fully indentified. Around the fireplace itself are fifteen round medallions, apparently by the same artist: Hercules and Theseus, Medea, Diomedes, Philosopher, Diana, Ganymede, Vestal Virgin, Aesculepius, Abundance, Sacrifice, Philosopher reading, Muses.*[34]

Fig. 100: The church at Chesme Palace, built 1777–80 to commemorate the naval victory over the Turks at Chesme Bay in 1770. Photo: Brian Allen

While far from correct in the titles supplied and somewhat imprecise in terms of attribution and dating, this description does give us a clear idea of the scale of the project, which is first mentioned in a letter from Benjamin Hawksford dated 25 July 1786: 'I am at present endeavouring to introduce some of the basreliefs for a new Room filling up at Tarsko & I hope I shall succeed in it.'[35] Among Wedgwood's papers at Keele University, however, there are a number of letters with requests for the delivery of Wedgwood plaques signed by Peter Capper.[36] Alison Kelly also mentions a London merchant known as 'N' (possibly George Neunberg of Cornhill), who purchased a large number of plaques at the sale of Wedgwood products in 1781 and might have supplied them to the Russian court.[37] But it is still unclear when or through whom the Wedgwood plaques reached Tsarskoye Selo.

Wedgwood's ceramic masterpieces at the Russian court suffered all the vicissitudes of fate, and there are some curious incidents in their history. For instance, on 31 October 1777, the *Sankt-Petrburgskiye vedomosti* reported: 'Stolen last week from the house at Kekerekeksinen, from the straw-coloured and painted faïence service, were 85 flat plates, two openwork baskets, eight small bowls with lids for ice-cream, with a frog of green colour depicted on each item.' It is now impossible to discover if all the objects listed were recovered by the police, but it certainly seems that most of them were returned to their owner.

After Catherine's death in 1796 Chesme Palace gradually fell into desuetude, and the Green Frog service kept there was not often seen. One of the last foreign nobles to visit the Palace was the overthrown Polish monarch Stanislaw Poniatowski, who had been invited to St Petersburg by Paul I. In his diary Poniatowski mentions the visit he made in 1797: he evidently found Chesme Palace 'strange', but he described the service in some detail (noting that it was then kept on the lower floor of the two-storey palace).[38] At the beginning of the 19th century there still seemed to be some interest in Wedgwood's famous service, and in 1818 Grand-Duke Mikhail Pavlovich, during his visit to England, ordered from Chamberlain's factory at Worcester a porcelain service decorated with views of Britain. The Grand-Duke must have recalled the Green Frog service made for his grandmother.

By this date of course the court rarely visited Chesme Palace, and in 1827–8 the young girls of the Elizabeth Institute were housed there while the Institute's own home was undergoing renovation. It was seen by Nicholas I, his wife Alexandra Fyodorovna and the Dowager Empress Maria Fyodorovna, and on 21 April 1830 Nicholas ordered that the Palace be converted to house war invalids. On 25 August he ordered that 'Two chandeliers, the table service and portraits of rulers in the rooms of the said Palace should be sent to Peterhof to Major-General Eykhen I, so that the service and portraits can be placed in the English Palace.'[39] Built by Giacomo Quarenghi in 1794, the English Palace, in the English Park at Peterhof (laid out by the Scot James Meader), thus became the new, *English*, home for the Wedgwood service (figs. 8, 9).

The Husk service had started its travels even earlier. The greater part was transferred from the Winter Palace to the New Palace (later the Alexander Palace; built by Quarenghi in 1796) in 1819. The service was accompanied by instructions that it be used only 'for the highest tables during visits by the Imperial family'.[40] In 1831 the remaining pieces were sent to the New Palace, and in 1841 the whole lot was transferred to the Peterhof Palace Administration, 'for use at Monplaisir for visiting persons and on occasions when the tsar should

Fig. 101: J. Meyer, *The Gothic Cottage in the Park at Peterhof*. Coloured lithograph. Private Collection. © Francesco Venturi / KEA.

be present'.[41] At this time the Husk service took its new name from its new home, and became known as the Monplaisir service.

In 1879 the heir to the Russian throne, the future Alexander III, personally picked out for himself a representative selection of pieces from both the Green Frog and Husk services.[42] To these were added some rare early pieces from the St Petersburg Imperial Porcelain Manufactory. The list of items selected included around 100 pieces, and these were placed in the Cottage at Peterhof, where Alexander was living. The Cottage had been built in 1829 by Adam Menelaws in the then popular Gothic Revival style, along the lines of an English country house (fig. 101). Archive documents state that 'These belongings His Imperial Majesty wishes to place in one of the rooms of the Cottage Palace on specially designed what-nots, and until then he has ordered them to be kept in store together with the tableware belonging to the Cottage Palace.'[43]

Even by the end of the 19th century the famous Wedgwood services had not been wholly forgotten. In 1885 an 'Inventory of Objects of largely Artistic Significance' compiled by V. D. Grigorovich was published, describing all the main sights of the Peterhof palaces, including both services,[44] and in 1899 the Chancellory of the Ministry of the Imperial Court received a letter from Bernet Goldney, keeper of Canterbury Museum in England, requesting information on whether the famous Green Frog service had survived. From the official reply from the Administration of the Hofmarshal's Department in St Petersburg, dated 6 July 1899, we learn that 'The Administration on the order of His Highness Hofmarshal Count Benckendorf has the honour to inform you that the table service called Grenouillière is kept in the stores of the English Palace in Peterhof, while part is at Alexandria [a park at Peterhof] in the Cottage. Although this service is of no particular interest in artistic terms, it is of undoubted rare historical significance …'.[45]

The Green Frog service again drew public attention in 1909 in connection with preparations for the Wedgwood jubilee exhibition in London, held to mark the firm's 150th anniversary. Thirty-four pieces were sent to England, and in 1912 the service was once more a star attraction at the exhibition of Wedgwood products held in the Academy of Arts in St Petersburg 'under the patronage of Her Imperial Majesty Grand-Duchess Maria Pavlovna', who was president of the Academy.[46] It was after this exhibition that the greater part of the service, that in the English Palace, was transferred to the Imperial Hermitage. The order directing the removal of the service to the Hermitage particularly stated that 'Some pieces of the said service are in Alexandria, in the Cottage, where in the summer Her Majesty Empress Maria Fyodorovna [widow of Alexander III and mother of the reigning tsar, Nicholas II] lives in summer; these pieces cannot be released for the Imperial Hermitage.'[47] In 1921 these objects were reunited with the rest in the Hermitage. The Husk service, meanwhile, remained at Peterhof, occupying its deserved place in the White Dining-room of the Great Palace, where it is the pride of the museum.

1. Cited in Blake Roberts 1986, p. 77.
2. Cited in Blake Roberts 1995, p. 214.
3. *Ibid.*
4. Vernova 1995b, p. 150; Vernova 1995a.
5. Cited in Williamson 1909, p. 61.
6. Cited in Williamson 1909, p. 8. The 'Royal Pattern' was the design of the service Wedgwood made for George III.
7. *Ibid.*
8. *Ibid.*, p. 10.
9. Cited in Hayden 1985, p. 20.
10. *Kamer-Fuhrer Journal* 1780, p. 473.
11. *Ibid.*, 1777, p. 401.
12. Harris 1844, pp. 198–9.
13. *Kamer-Fuhrer Journal* 1779, pp. 226–8.
14. *Ibid.*, p. 103.
15. Cross 1992, no. 29, p. 20.
16. Alekseyev 1982, pp. 126–7.
17. Cited in Williamson 1909, p. 8.
18. Cited in Raeburn 1995, p. 136.
19. Cited in Williamson 1909, p. 61.
20. Georgi 1794, p. 682.
21. Cited in Russian archive 1907, p. 516.
22. *Kamer Fuhrer Journal* 1777, pp. 398–402.
23. *Ibid.*, 1780, pp. 469–77.
24. *Ibid.*, 1781, pp. 348–51.
25. *Ibid.*, 1791, pp. 146–55.
26. *Ibid.*, 1795, pp. 163–75.
27. RGIA Fund 468, op. 37, d. 1, fol. 5; published in Liackhova 1995, pp. 210–11.
28. *Ibid.*, fol. 144. This document was uncovered by R. R. Gafifullin.
29. Kudriavtseva 1994, nos. 94–8; *La porcellane Imperiale Russe* 1993, pp. 24–5; *An Imperial Fascination* 1991, pp. 37–8.
30. Vernova 1995b, pp. 149–51; Vernova 1995a.
31. Cited in Reilly 1992, p. 102.
32. Cited in Blake Roberts 1995, p. 217.
33. Blake Roberts 1986, p. 81.
34. Vil'chkovsky 1992, pp. 124–5.
35. Cited in Blake Roberts 1995, p. 220.
36. *Ibid.*, pp. 220–21.
37. Kelly 1965, p. 103.
38. Goryainov 1908, pp. 602–3.
39. RGIA Fund 470, op. 2/106/540, d. 44, fol. 9; published in Liackhova 1995, p. 211.
40. Cited in Vernova 1995a; Vernova 1995b, pp. 149–51.
41. *Ibid.* (both).
42. Liackhova 1995, pp. 211–12.
43. RGIA Fund 469, op. 9, d. 2608, fol. 6; published in Liackhova 1995, p. 212.
44. Peterhof inventory 1885.
45. RGIA Fund 472, op. 43/472/2421, d. 145, fol. 11; published in Liackhova 1995, p. 212.
46. RGIA Fund 789, op. 13, d. 47, fol. 253; published in Liackhova 1992, p. 21.
47. RGIA Fund 472, op. 49, d. 1146, fol. 5; published in Liackhova 1995, p. 212.

Marina Lopato

Fig. 102: Silver-gilt ewers, made by Ann
Tanqueray, *c.* 1725–6, from the English service of
Catherine I. Sold through Antikvariat in 1932.

The collection of English silver in the Hermitage comprises around 200 pieces, the greater part of which, and those of the highest quality, date from the 18th century. This collection is perhaps better known both to specialists and connoisseurs than is any other part of the Hermitage's silver. A number of items first became better known to the outside world back in 1881 after a 'List of Objects Selected from Museums and Private Collections in Russia' appeared, 'of which copies [of the objects] have been made in electrotype by Messrs. Elkington & Co of Birmingham and London'. Only the previous year Wilfrid Joseph Cripps, a well-known silver specialist, and Alfred Maskell had visited Russia with the aim of discovering outstanding works by English silversmiths.[1] After visiting the Armoury in Moscow, Maskell and his assistants spent several months undertaking research in the Imperial Hermitage. Since then, E. A. Jones's *The Old English Plate of the Emperor of Russia* (1909) and scholarly articles published in the 1950s by N. M. Penzer and Charles Oman have made all scholars of the subject very aware the holdings at St Petersburg.[2]

In what way does the Hermitage's collection of 18th-century English silver deserve such close attention? It is without exaggeration one of the world's unique collections, for almost every object is a masterpiece. This comparatively small collection includes four monumental wine-coolers, that by Charles Kandler having no equal anywhere (cat. 60). Almost all the other objects formed part of one of six different services and were made by leading English craftsmen. The greater part belonged to the Imperial family. Less clear, however, is who commissioned these services, or when and by whom they were delivered to the court. At the beginning of this century the keeper of the Gallery of *objets de vertù* at the Imperial Hermitage, Baron Foelkersam, undertook a thorough study of the archives of the Ministry of the Court and the Ministry of Foreign Affairs. He sought documents relating to the English silver, but was unable to discover anything of great significance. Later, part of the archives relating to the 18th century were moved to Moscow, during which process the numbers of the funds and files were changed, making it extremely difficult even to check the existing information.

The love Russian tsars and princes had for luxury items is well-known. Almost all the foreigners who visited Russia in the 16th century and early 17th wrote of the numerous gold and silver vessels to be found in the homes of princely families, and of their rich banqueting tables, where gold and silver vessels set with precious stones were laid out, on occasions for up to 200 guests. Almost all this wealth was destroyed during the bloody disturbances connected with the struggle for the throne known as the Time of Troubles (1584–1613). Towards the end of the 17th century, however, the state coffers began to fill again, trading and diplomatic links were extended, and, as can be seen from the collection still in the Armoury, palace treasuries once more gleamed with their former magnificence.

Everything changed under Peter the Great. First, this youthful reformer quit 'long-bearded' Moscow, dominated by boyars, and began to build a new Russia in a new place. On the banks of the Neva a totally new way of life was to be formed. As for his own court, it was

Fig. 103: Basin and cup, made by Samuel Margas, *c.* 1725–6, from the English service of Catherine I. Sold through Antikvariat in 1932.

perfectly in keeping with the tsar's own unpretentious lifestyle, and thus there was no real court, in terms of ceremonies, rituals and hierarchies. Peter surrounded himself with a somewhat motley, multi-lingual crowd, which reflected the nature of the town new-built on the swamps. Instead of festive receptions and decorous banquets he organized endless feasts, humorous masquerades and assemblies; women were obliged to attend, and dancing went on until dawn. The new lifestyle, the new customs that were developing brought with them changes in dress, furniture and everyday objects. European goods began to flood into the new capital as foreign merchants sought to move in on the new market. As early as the end of 1703, the year in which the city was founded, the first Dutch ship, carrying wine and salt, arrived under the command of Captain Wybes. According to other sources, in the same year St Petersburg was visited by three merchant vessels – two Dutch and one English – carrying not only wine and salt but Dutch and English cloth, furniture, clocks and tin pots, snuffboxes and table silver.

If Peter's personal lifestyle was somewhat austere, the same could not be said for those of his courtiers – grandees such as Prince Menshikov, or Villem Mons, who later became Catherine I's favourite. By the 1720s the Petersburg nobility was acquiring wealth at a great rate. Inventories of property of the time list numerous gems, gold snuffboxes, silver vessels, clocks and watches and European apparel richly embellished with precious stones. The short list of clothes that belonged to Mons just prior his execution, for example, includes 22 camisoles and caftans alone, sewn with gold and silver. In 1723, for services to the Empress, Praskovya Fyodorovna (the widow of Peter's half-brother, tsar Ivan V), Mons had been presented with 2,000 roubles, land near Strelna and a silver service.[3] And since Peter's heirs did not share his simplicity of habits, they restored the former luxury of the court, but now in the European spirit.

The extensive correspondence that survives between one of Peter's associates, Field-Marshal Fyodor Apraksin, and his foreign agents allows us to see how purchases abroad of artistic and household goods, 'such as would be fitting to persons of high rank', were made. As a result of his status, his intimacy with the tsar and his active role in Peter's reforms, Apraksin adapted his own lifestyle to the latest fashions, thus encouraging their introduction into Russian society as a whole. He ordered 'haberdashery' from Hamburg, furniture and table linen from Holland, and 'cloths of the new fashion' from England. Silver services decorated with his arms were ordered for him in Berlin and London.

The leading figure in this trend, however, was probably Peter's favourite, Prince Menshikov. A remarkably talented statesman, but one who was easy to bribe, he possessed vast wealth and had a fine eye for the arts. His house in Kronstadt and his 'pleasure' palace at Oranienbaum (figs. 58), both near St Petersburg, plus his palace on Vasilyevsky Island in the city itself, all amazed visitors with their luxury and were more imperial than the palaces of the tsar himself. The French traveller A. de la Mottre noted that 'the emperor and empress and Menshikov, these three persons seemed to be one and

were inseparable. I could add that Peter I always imitated a subject, and Alexander Menshikov a sovereign, in that he [Peter I] left to him all the luxury, majesty and roses of the crown, leaving himself nothing except cares and thorns.'[4] Menshikov's palaces were filled with the works of art he ordered and purchased abroad through his agents. We know that after he was exiled to Siberia, his household included three silver services alone, 'each with 24 dozen plates, spoons, knives and forks. The first was made in London, the second in Augsburg, the third in Hamburg. In addition, Menshikov ordered himself a silver service in Paris in 1727,[5] and sent 35,500 *yefimki* for it.'[6] In describing the palace on Vasilyevsky Island, De la Mottre noted: *everything was in keeping with the majesty of the palace itself; there were numerous silver services of all possible types and forms. I was still in Petersburg when the Prince received from England a new service at a cost of £6,000. That which the Prince already had was worth far more both in terms of weight and in true value, but the fine work of this new service was incomparably higher than the others in its art and price. Some said that the Prince acquired it as a gift for the Empress, others that she had ordered it as a gift for the Prince, and the latter is most likely, for as soon as the service came into his hands the Empress arrived at the palace to look at it and take dinner with the Prince. The Empress was served on this service; she remained there until after midnight.*[7]

According to a document in the archives, De la Mottre was referring to an event that took place on 23 September 1726, and which is described in Menshikov's own 'Daily Notes': Catherine arrived at his palace after five o'clock and 'entered the room to look at the service newly brought from England and then went into the Walnut Room, where she deigned to enjoy herself'.[8] Two days earlier, on 21 September, an 'English' service was received in the service stores of the Imperial palace from the Main Palace Chancellory.[9] Thus two services arrived at St Petersburg from London at exactly the same moment.

Susan Hare has published a document from the London Goldsmith's Company in which we learn that in August 1726 one Robert Dingley dispatched to Russia by ship a large amount of silver, mainly objects by the Huguenot jewellers Nicolas Clausen, Peze Pilleau, Isaac Ribouleau, Simon Pantin, Augustine Courtauld, Joseph Barbut, Abraham Buteux, and (almost half of the whole lot) Paul de Lamerie.[10] Possibly among these objects were the services for Menshikov and Catherine. It is of course tempting to suggest that the marvellous wine fountain of 1720 by Paul de Lamerie (cat. 58), the punchbowl of 1710 by Gabriel Sleath and the wine-cooler of 1712 by Lewis Mettayer listed in the inventories of the Winter Palace from the mid-18th century formed part of this shipment.[11] As regards the service for Catherine, the 'Accounting Extract for Service Duties for the Receipt and Allocation of Gold and Silver Services etc. for the past years 1734 to 1753' has a list of items from the English service (see the Appendix to this essay).[12]

After 1760, worn-out items in this service were either put aside as surplus to requirements or melted down.[13] Thus by the 1920s only fourteen pieces remained: the gilded two-handled cup by Paul

Crespin; two ewers by Ann Tanqueray; two smaller ewers by the same person; three tankards by William Fleming; a finger-bowl with a ewer by Samuel Margas; two octagonal platters on four legs; two similar platters with fancy edges, one by Isaac Ribouleau, the second apparently made in Russia; and last, an ungilded soup tureen by Simon Pantin I. In 1933 seven pieces were sold abroad through the Soviet foreign trading organization Antikvariat, while one dish was transferred to the Russian Museum, so that the Hermitage now has only six pieces from the service. To judge from the surviving objects and from photographs, the service originally comprised varied pieces in different styles, although all of course corresponding to the same high standard. Later, suppliers were to seek as far as possible to maintain some stylistic unity, an example of this being a service that belonged to I. E. Biron, Duke of Courland (fig. 104).

Fig. 104: The silver Toilet Set of I. E. Biron, Duke of Courland, made by William Gould, Paul de Lamerie, Simon Pantin the Younger, Augustine Courtauld, George Greenhill Jones and Edward Vincent, 1719–38. State Hermitage Museum.

Nevertheless, during the first half of the 18th century, foreign suppliers assembled services from unrelated pieces, apparently because high-ranking Russian clients who sought to create an impression demanded exclusively expensive and unusual pieces, and in large quantities, and these could not be produced in a short time. The wine-cooler with the arms of the Duke of Scarsdale of 1726 by Paul de Lamerie formed part of just such a heterogeneous service,[14] in this case one of the so-called Augsburg services ordered for Biron, a favourite of the Empress Anna Ioannovna. Although the service was made in Germany, it included a plat-de-ménage of 1724 by the Parisian master Claude Ballin II and the wine-cooler. In 1740, after Biron's arrest, these objects were confiscated and joined others in the Imperial palace, where they were included in the 'Second new service'.

It was during the reign (1730–40) of Peter the Great's niece Anna Ioannovna that the famous Jerningham – Kandler wine-cooler (cat. 60) came into existence. Thanks to the work of British scholars, the history of how this piece came to be made is well known.[15] In 1730 the banker and jeweller Henry Jerningham sought to create a wine-cooler that would in its grandeur outstrip everything that had gone before. The engraver and antiquary George Vertue was commissioned to produce the design, and the sculptor John Michael Rysbrack made the wax models for the handles in the form of a bacchant and bacchante. The silverwork was undertaken by Charles Kandler, assisted by others. According to Penzer, an inscription on the back of a surviving drawing explains that the creator sought to make it slightly larger than any others (at least an inch), and to the highest standard by the best hands possible. The work was finished in 1734 and presented to the public. Despite the general admiration for the piece, however, no one could afford to purchase it. In 1735 Jerningham presented a petition to Parliament, in which he requested that they decide the fate of: *a Silver Cistern, that has been acknowledged, by all Persons of Skill, who have seen the same, to excel whatever of the Kind has been attempted in this Kingdom; and has manifested, that the Sculptors and Artificers of Great Britain are not inferior to those of other Nations; but that, after an Expence of several Thousand Pounds upon the Workmanship alone, exclusive of the Weight in Silver, and after great Variety of Hazards in the Furnace, and Four Years Application in raising and adorning the Model, the said Cistern remains on the Hands of the Petitioner; and, the same being of so great Value, there appears no Hopes of disposing thereof to any private Purchaser.*

As a result it was decided that the wine-cooler should be the prize in a special lottery, part of the proceeds from which would go to the construction of a new bridge, Westminster, over the river Thames. In 1736 a medal (designed by Gravelot and cut by John Sigismund Tanner) with a portrait of Queen Caroline – Jerningham's patron in this matter – was issued to mark the lottery. The prize was won the following year by William Battine, a landowner from East Marden in Sussex. We do not know how the wine-cooler reached Russia, but in 1740 it was in the apartments of the regent, Anna Leopoldovna, and in 1741 entered the Treasury.[16]

The circumstances surrounding the making of this wine-cooler would seem to be extraordinary, for it is difficult to imagine that an experienced banker and silversmith should undertake so grandiose and expensive a work without prior agreement with an exceptionally wealthy client. As it happens, the widowed Duchess of Courland, Anna Ioannovna (1693–1740), unexpectedly became Empress of Russia in 1730. After fourteen years in the remote province of Mitavo, forgotten by almost everyone, she was suddenly elevated to a position she could not have imagined in her wildest dreams. Transformed into the powerful ruler of a vast empire, she sought to consolidate her position through a demonstration of her power and wealth. This included the acquisition of vastly expensive objects for the palace to symbolize her regal status. It was during these years that she and her favourite, Biron, commissioned abroad items of great value that are still to be seen in the Hermitage. They include the golden toilet service by the Augsburg craftsman Johann Ludwig Biller (for many years this was thought to be English work), the silver throne by the London silversmith Nicholas Clausen, the above-mentioned Augsburg service, Courland's Riga service, and – made a little later – the toilet service ordered for him from Edward Vincent, Paul de Lamerie and other London masters. It is possible that the Jerningham–Kandler wine-cooler falls into the same category. I suspect that in 1730 Russian representatives ordered this exceptionally expensive piece, but that on completion, for some reason or other, the Russian side would not complete the purchase, and only a few years later were the Russian representatives able to come to a deal with Mr Battine.

The history of relations between Anna Ioannovna and Biron, despite the vast literature on the subject, is still not wholly clear. We do know that during the first years of her reign neither she nor her favourite showed any interest in state affairs, spending all their time on personal matters. It would seem that Biron managed to gain power over Anna Ioannovna thanks to his incredible adaptability. 'One of the unclarified questions in the history of Biron is his finances, from the sources of his wealth to its true scale', wrote the Latvian scholar I. Lantsmanis.[17] Documents relating to the confiscation of Biron's property in 1741, the year after he fell from favour, list a quite astonishing number of pieces of furniture, silver, porcelain, textiles, clothing and so on, all far beyond any real need, even if we allow that they would have been divided between several residences. In 1734 Biron spent 37,000 reichsthalers buying up land in Silesia, Courland and Lifland. However, since initially he lacked the funds to do this, what was the source of his wealth? 'We must allow', argues Lantsmanis, 'that the main source of his wealth was Imperial presents: in this connection it is usual to mention the golden chalice presented to him on 14 February 1740, which contained a paper promising him half a million roubles.'[18] Contemporaries suspected Biron of financial machinations conducted through his banker, the court commissar Isaak Liebman. At his trial in 1741 Biron was accused of the appropriation of monies and other valuables from the state treasury, although this was not proved.

Since Isaak Liebman supplied the court with a number of items of silver, including the Augsburg services and objects that joined the Second New Service, perhaps he was involved in the commissioning of the Jerningham–Kandler wine-cooler? As mentioned above, in 1734 Biron was financially overstretched regarding his land purchases, and help was provided from some quarter. Also, it was with Liebman's help that the toilet service mentioned above was acquired, with its pieces by William Gould (1719 and 1736), Paul de Lamerie (1720), Peter Archambo (1723), Simon Pantin the Younger (1731), Augustine Courtauld (1734), George Greenhill Jones (1735) and Edward Vincent (1738).[19] All the pieces have Biron's ducal arms engraved on them. As early as 1734 the Polish monarch Augustus III secretly offered the throne of Courland to Biron, but he was only able to occupy it in 1737, after the death of Duke Ferdinand, when he was elected to the post by the Courland nobility. It was probably in connection with this event that the toilet service was ordered, the arms announcing the owner's new rank. There are, in fact, two kinds of arms on the objects: in abbreviated form, without the frame, where there is less space, and – by different engravers – set in a detailed frame. In both cases, however, there are a number of errors, which suggests that the arms were not engraved by local masters.

Fig. 105: Silver platters from the Tula (left) and Yaroslavl (right) Governors' Services made by Robert Jones and John Schofield, 1776–7. State Hermitage Museum.

According to one of Biron's descendants, a Mr Wulffius, the toilet service was in Biron's possession until June 1741, when it was confiscated while he was journeying to his place of exile in Siberia, and returned to St Petersburg. In 1742 all Biron's silver, including this toilet service, was transferred to Moscow. In 1759 the Empress Elizabeth Petrovna presented the service and other objects formerly in Biron's possession to his daughter, as a dowry on the occasion of her marriage to Alexander Cherkasov. In the 19th century it belonged to Biron's niece, Countess N. Sollogub, who in her turn brought it as part of her dowry to the Wulffius home. Later in the same century it was kept at their Selnava estate in Latvia, until it was sold by the family early in the 20th century.[20] In 1904 it was the property of Count M. G. Mecklenburg-Strelitz,[21] from whom it passed to Countess Yelena Georgiyevna of Saxon-Altenburg. In 1922 it entered the Hermitage.

Unfortunately, lack of documentation means that we cannot so well trace the history of other pieces of English silver that reached Russia. All we can confirm is that they arrived in St Petersburg in large quantities. In addition to direct commissions made abroad, aristocrats and wealthy citizens of St Petersburg were able to purchase silver at auctions, the number of which increased every year. Advertisements for these auctions, however, do not always record the place where the silver had been made, although with regard to furniture, clocks, mirrors and table services it was often stressed that they were of English origin, as we can see from adverts in the Sankt-Peterburgskiye vedomosti (St Petersburg Gazette):

2 December 1736: 'at the Imperial Post Office are to be sold various goods at public auction. Superb English cabinets and chairs, silver vessels, and other objects'.
7 October 1740: 'there shall be sold at public auction for cash various household goods, that is chairs, tables, stands, English cabinets, silver vessels'.
10 January 1746: 'there shall be sold … silver goods … English mirrors'.
14 February 1749: 'on the 16th of this month … at public auction shall be sold the goods of the late Mr Severne and Mr Velngs, consisting of English linens and such like, and on the 17th … silver vessels'.
20 September 1756: 'In the wooden trading court at stall nos. 61 and 67 of the St Petersburg merchant Semyon Zaytsev are on sale imported objects in the new style: English cabinets of mahogany, tables, mirrors, commodes, caskets and platters, silver table-knives in cases, Saxony porcelain'.
11 November 1757: 'in the house of the auctioneer Kenke is to be sold … a silver plat-de-ménage weighing around 20 pounds'.
18 February 1765: 'by the Galerny yard in the home of His Highness Field-Marshal General Count Pyotr Semyonovich Saltykov, where are also for sale various pieces of English furniture … pictures, various objects of English silver, a new English table service, an English wall-clock and similar'.

1 July 1765: 'in the Auction Room by the Galerny yard are for sale … various pieces of English furniture … mirrors, gold snuffboxes, clocks, porcelain and silver vessels'.
6 September 1765: 'on the order of the office of the State Collegium of Justice at a public auction in the Auction room shall be sold … also an English silver plat-de-ménage'.

In the 1770s the number of auctions, and the number of objects offered for sale, grew rapidly, but their descriptions grew more brief. During the first three months of 1774, for instance, there were three announcements relating to the sale of silver plats-de-ménage. Perhaps one of these was the Hermitage's magnificent plat-de-ménage of 1741 by Augustine Courtauld (cat. 63), which entered the collection of the Princes Yusupov, or that by Paul de Lamerie, later the property of Count A. A. Bobinsky.[22] Thus, while the Danish envoy, Just Juel, could write in 1710 that in St Petersburg 'there is nothing to say of beautiful goods: in this regard it is impossible to find anything worthwhile',[23] by the middle of the century the trade in imported goods was increasing rapidly, and the St Petersburg aristocracy could acquire expensive objects not only through suppliers and agents abroad but also in their own city.

Two dessert services from the reign of Elizabeth Petrovna were still to be found in the Winter Palace at the beginning of our own century – the Oranienbaum and Pleshcheyev services. They both received their names after 1762, when on the orders of Catherine II all silver belonging to the state and then held in different locations was brought to the Winter Palace, where it was assayed and handed over to the Court Office. The Oranienbaum service came, as its name suggests, from the palace of that name, while the Pleshcheyev service was delivered to the palace by Lieutenant Grigory Pleshcheyev. Foelkersam listed 82 pieces in the Pleshcheyev service, including a table decoration of 1745 by Samuel Wood and William Cripps (cat. 64). Better known are two coffee-pots, a teapot and a shaving-bowl dating from 1757–8 made by Samuel Courtauld and a tea container of the same period by Peter Gillois. It also included a hand-mirror and three plain beakers by Samuel Courtauld, six sets of cutlery, five boxes with London hallmarks for 1757–9, several pieces of Augsburg production and many items either without hallmarks or with St Petersburg marks for 1764.[24] The Oranienbaum service, in the Chinoiserie style, now consists of six pieces by the London craftsmen Nicholas Sprimont (tea-kettle, 1750; cat. 65), Fuller White (coffee-pot, 1756; teapot, 1757; slop basin, 1758) and Thomas Heming (sugar-bowl, 1750).[25] This service would seem to have been in use as late as the 1840s, and nineteen objects – the work of Petersburg craftsmen – were added to it.

It was perhaps during the reign of Elizabeth Petrovna that the gilded mirror by Charles Kandler was commissioned (cat. 59). This is topped with the Imperial crown and was traditionally thought to have belonged to Peter III. Grimwade dates a very similar version of the hallmark to 1751.[26] This also affects the dating of a gold and diamond toilet set mentioned in the archives of the Ministry of the

Court as having been brought from England by ship in 1754, ordered by the English Consul-General and Resident, Jacob Wolf. This set, according to Foelkersam, was temporarily given to Baron Cherkasov.[27]

The 1770s were marked by further large imports of English silver, including the Governors' or Viceroys' services. In 1775 Russia was divided up into eleven provinces, thus reviving those reforms in local government begun by Peter I. The new reforms began in 1775 with the 'opening up' of the Tver province and ended in 1796 with the setting up of Vilno province, and in all 40 provinces came into existence. At the same time Catherine decided to supply all the governors with silver services in order for them to be able to entertain with the dignity befitting their position. This also meant that if the Empress decided to visit the provinces, there would be no need for the staff accompanying her to take services with them.

The first services sent to the local governors were ordered in England. The expense books of the Ministry of the Court for 1774 include the following: '19 December to Baron Frideriks to be transferred to England for two silver table services ordered there, 50,000 roubles'. And in the margin: 'on the verbal order of Her Imperial Majesty, conveyed through State Councillor Olsuf'yev'. Then: '11 May 1775, to the 50,000 sent in December … 30,000'. On 5 June, 'another 20,000'. A little later payment was made 'for the transferral from Moscow to St Petersburg of the first part of the two services', and in October 'payment for fur coats for officers in the troop accompanying the last part of the English silver services – 42 roubles, 32 kopeks'. Finally, on 10 December payment was made 'to Baron Frideriks additional to the 100,000 given in 1774 and 1775 … for final payment, 25,000 roubles'.[28]

Foelkersam cites a copy of a letter from the head of the Court Office, Privy Councillor A. V. Olsuf'yev, to the Hofmarshal, Grigorii Nikitich Orlov, dated 14 November 1775: 'Her Imperial Majesty saw fit to order me to give the silver table service made in England to the Court Office, in the department of your Highness'. The following day came an order from the Court Office to receive the service itself: 'Register of the silver service made in England. 8 terrines, 8 stands to them, 16 trays, 102 varied dishes, 48 stands for hot water, 94 lids for dishes, 8 sauce-boats and 8 stands to them, 8 spoons to them, 6 mazarines, 8 soup-spoons, 24 sauce-spoons, 6 fishknives, 12 dozen plates, 12 dozen knife-and-fork handles, 12 dozen forks, 10 dozen spoons, 7 dozen sweet knives with silver blades, 7 dozen forks, 7 dozen spoons, 4 stands and to them 8 crystal cruet-pots with silver handles, 8 sugar-bowls 8 spoons to them, 4 mustard-pots 4 spoons to them, 24 salt-cellars 24 spoons to them, 4 hotplates with lamps, 2 coffee-pots, 2 milk-jugs, 2 platters with mahogany and green baize below, 22 varied platters, 8 monteiths, 8 bottle-servers, 44 nameplates for bottles to identify wines, 16 triple large candlesticks, 80 single large candlesticks. A total weight of 45 poods 21 pounds 93 zolotniki.'[29] In December 1775 the service was sent to the Tver governor's office, and on 29 February 1776 Lieutenant-General Governor Yakov Sivers informed the Court Office that it had been received.

As we see from the 'Book of Internal Expenses' for 1774, however,

Fig. 106: The Queen's Cup made by Robert Garrard from the design and model by Edmund Cotterill. Silver, partly gilded. A copy of the cup made for Ascot Races in 1844. State Hermitage Museum.

there were two English services. We know that before the Revolution the service stores of the Winter Palace had eleven dishes from the so-called Volynsk service, ten with English hallmarks for 1774, and on two the year stamp for 1775.[30] This would seem to be indentifiable with the second service, imported in 1775.

In the register of personal decrees of Her Imperial Majesty for 1777, Baron Frideriks is again given money 'for transfer to England for two silver services made there, 128,653 roubles', and on 4 April another 20,653 roubles were paid.[31] In June 'for the last two silver table services made there, in addition to the 5,653 roubles already given, another 23,000 roubles'.[32] The services would seem to have arrived a month earlier, in May, when customs payment was made 'for two silver services ordered from England 6,240 roubles, 88.5 kopeks'.[33] It is worth noting that at the same time money was given to Baron Frideriks 'for transfer to England, for the silver table service ordered there, an advance of 20,000 roubles'.[34] Payments were made in July (13,000 roubles, 1,420 roubles), September (12,000 roubles), November (11,827 roubles) and, finally, in December 'to the Port Customs tax for the silver table service ordered from England in 1777, 2,756 roubles 34.75 kopeks'.[35]

The decree setting up the viceroyships for which the services were intended survives in the archives. In a note of 4 October 1777 addressed to Olsuf'yev, the Empress writes: 'Adam Vasil'yevich for the setting up of Tula province give from the Cabinet to Lieutenant-General Krechetnikov, 6,000 roubles. Catherine',[36] and 24 September issue was made 'to State Councillor Mel'gunov, on the opening of the Yaroslavl viceroyship, 6,000 roubles'.[37] Thus two further services, Yaroslavl and Tula (fig. 105), were added to the Tver and Volynsk services. The question remains open with regard to a fifth English service, ordered in haste and made within six months. Up to now we had known, thanks to Foelkersam, only of three English services, and he described the Yaroslavl and Tver services as one, which he named the Yaroslavl. Before the Revolution the Winter Palace had eight round platters and three dish lids by Robert Jones and John Schofield, the remaining objects being made later in St Petersburg. At the present time the Hermitage has only one platter from the Yaroslavl service.[38] At the beginning of the 20th century the remains of the Tula service consisted of eight oval dishes and nine round platters by Jones and Schofield, one round platter by J. Carter and 38 candlesticks by Thomas Heming. There are now five platters by Schofield and Jones and two Heming candlesticks.[39] Nothing remains of the Volynsk and Tver services. In 1797 all the services were returned to St Petersburg from the provinces on the orders of Paul I, who had a tendency to countermand his mother's orders and who was in need of silver for his new palace in the city.

Catherine's reign was marked by one further event of relevance to the history of the Hermitage's English silver, the arrival in St Petersburg of the notorious Elizabeth Chudleigh, the so-called Duchess of Kingston, thanks to whom the Hermitage now has some outstanding pieces. Chudleigh (1720–88) came from an old Dorset family and at the age of eighteen was appointed as a maid-of-honour to the Princess of Wales. Beautiful, energetic, with a lively, sharp wit, she had many love affairs in her somewhat wild youth. Her complicated relations with her husband, Augustus Hervey, later 3rd Earl of Bristol, whom she married in 1744, ended in separation. In 1769, having insisted under oath that her marriage to Hervey had not been legally performed, she married the incredibly wealthy Evelyn Pierrepont, 2nd Duke of Kingston. The Duke died in 1773, leaving everything to her, whereupon his relatives immediately contested the will and began criminal proceedings, accusing her of bigamy. After a lengthy trial before the House of Lords, which was reported in newspapers throughout Europe, she was found guilty, but not painfully punished. She then left for the Continent, and travelled to Russia in order to satisfy her curiosity regarding the Empress Catherine. The 'Duchess', as Chudleigh insisted she still was (in law, as Hervey's wife she was in fact the Countess of Bristol), first sent Catherine a number of excellent pictures from the collection of the late Duke of Kingston, which entailed lengthy correspondence between the Russian embassy in London and the Empress. In 1777 the Duchess herself arrived in St Petersburg aboard her private yacht and was soon graciously received by Catherine, on whose orders she was given one of the best houses in the capital. Local society received the Duchess well, and soon she expressed a desire to become a lady in waiting to Catherine. To make herself eligible she acquired property in the form of a house on the river Fontanka, an estate in Estland (Estonia) and several pieces of land near St Petersburg. But Catherine rejected her request for a court appointment and soon after (28 January 1785) the disappointed Duchess quit the country for France, returning in 1779–80 and 1784–5, when she stayed at Count Vorontsov's house next to the Obukhov Bridge.

It is possible that Catherine's coolness was the result of the Duchess's friendship with Prince Radziwill, a member of the camp opposing the Empress that had supported Princess Tarakanova (the Princess claimed to be the daughter of Empress Elizabeth and hence rightful heir to the throne). It is also possible that rumours had reached Catherine from London regarding the notorious court-case there, particularly in view of the fact that the English ambassador at St Petersburg remained noticeably aloof whenever the Duchess was present. Following the death of the Duchess in Paris in 1788, the property she had taken to Russia found its way into the hands of General Garnovsky, one of the most audacious swindlers of the time, who had managed to make himself legal agent to both Potemkin and the Duchess. Garnovsky removed all her property from the Estonian estate (called, perhaps suprisingly, plain Chudleigh) and appropriated it along with everything that was left in St Petersburg. As a result, part of his property was confiscated and part sold during the reign of Paul I.

The superb wine-cooler of 1699 by Philip Rollos, with the arms of the Duke of Kingston (cat. 56), and two silver vases of 1770 by Andrew Fogelberg (cat. 68) were acquired from the Duchess by Catherine II and presented to Prince Potemkin. In the inventory of his property, acquired for the treasury after his death, we find: 'Silver, presented by Her Imperial Majesty to the late Prince Grigory Alexandrovich: two vases with covers and copper spigots on two pedestals of varied foreign woods, covered in silver, with a weight of 1 pood 24 pounds 48 zolotniki. Large punchbowl of 6 poods 36 pounds 48 zolotniki. For which on assessment was paid by the Cabinet 28,942 roubles. And 700 given to his Highness to have them cleaned. In total 29,642 roubles.'[40] The wine-cooler, incorrectly described as a punchbowl, is mentioned by T. P. Kir'yak in his description of the famous party given by Prince Potemkin in the Tauride Palace on 28 April 1791 to celebrate the taking of Ismail: 'On both days there were simply repetitions of quadrilles and small balls such as were usually held on such occasions, i.e. those when the table might be laid for 180 and never less than for 100; on which the fish soup alone cost over 1,000 roubles, and was served in a vast seven- or eight-pood silver bowl: two people stood and served the whole table, and when they had finished there was enough left for the same number of guests.'[41] According to M. I. Pylyayev, on the first day, when Catherine honoured Potemkin with her presence, 3,000 people were in attendance. The Palace was decorated so as to seem like a magical recreation of a tale from the *Thousand and One Nights*: 'The platform on which the Empress was to sit was covered with a precious Persian silk carpet, and similar platforms stood along the walls, on each of them a huge vase of white Carrara marble on a pedestal of grey marble; suspended above the vases were two chandeliers of black crystal with musical clocks set inside. The chandeliers cost Potemkin 42,000 roubles (he bought them from the Duchess of Kingston, née Miss Chudleigh).'[42] The same author adds: 'In the room before the hall was a table on which stood a silver soup tureen of great size, and to the sides of it two vases, also large, brought from the estate of the Duchess of Kingston.'[43] This must refer to the Rollos wine-cooler and the two Fogelberg vases.

Pylyayev also mentions the Kingston wine-cooler in an unexpected context, describing the travels of Russian grandees: 'Potemkin also did not stint himself on food during his travels and consumed with great appetite both the most expensive viands, such as fish soup at 1,300 roubles from a silver bath of 7 to 8 poods weight, as well as the most simple cakes and biscuits …'.[44] It is difficult to imagine now a journey across the whole of Russia with a silver wine-cooler weighing 112 kg! But Potemkin had many whimsical habits. For instance, 'during his travels, an English gardener and his assistants travelled ahead of him, and with incredible speed cut a garden in the English style on that place where the Prince was to stop, even if only for a day …. If the Prince stayed there longer than one day, the wilting plants were replaced with fresh ones, often brought from afar.'[45]

Undoubtedly many of the rich inhabitants of St Petersburg owned silver services, toilet sets and individual objects, but it is difficult today to assess the extent of their wealth on the basis of the few unconnected pieces that survive. But *Sankt-Petrburgskiye vedemosti* continued to publish its announcements, as it did on 29 April 1794: 'On Sadovaya Street in the Turchaninov House, no. 79, is for sale an English silver Lady's toilet service, with everything belonging to it,

Fig. 107: Stand for vase. From the service of Grand-Duchess Yekaterina Mikhaylovna (granddaughter of Emperor Paul I) made by Hunt & Roskell, 1850–51. State Hermitage Museum.

two silver soup tureens with two dishes, five silver dishes and a large silver platter. The butler, Linkrot, will supply further information about them.' After the Revolution all private collections were confiscated, and in 1919 a Museums Fund was set up to allocate art objects to state museums. English silver was to be found among the pieces that entered the Hermitage from the palaces of the Princes Yusupov, of Countess Shuvalova, Count Stroganov and Prince Golitsyn. Odd pieces also came from the collections of counts Bobrinsky, Rudanovsky and Dolgorukov. Of all these post-Revolutionary acquisitions, one worthy of special note is the epergne (table-centre) by Thomas Pitts (1790) from the Yusupov collection, whose arms are in the medallions in the openwork bowls.[46] This epergne is an exact copy of a work of 1778 by Pitts, now in the Victoria and Albert Museum.[47]

The works in the Adam style from the last two decades of the 18th century, all by John Robins, entered the Hermitage from the collections of the Yusupovs,[48] Count Bobrinsky,[49] and Princess Shakhovskaya.[50] The decoration is characteristic of Robins's work, with a predominance of precise geometrical lines and masses, and abundant curves. The most expressive of these pieces is the samovar formerly belonging to Princess Shakhovskaya, in which Rococo echoes can be discerned in the gently rounded lines.

In the 19th century the Imperial court and Petersburg aristocracy continued to order and purchase silver directly from England, although little of this has survived: when objects were transferred from royal and private collections to the Hermitage in the 1920s, many pieces ended up being sold at auctions in St Petersburg, in Moscow and abroad. As a result the Hermitage has many leftovers from what were once large tea and coffee services, cutlery sets as well as odd items, such as the tankard of 1812 with the arms of the Counts Orlov,[51] a monteith of 1837, the work of Robert Garrard, and a large tankard of 1841 by Robert Hennell from the Yusupov collection, plus a teapot with the arms of the Yusupovs of 1850, the work of Hunt and Roskell,[52] teaspoons of 1847 with the monogram 'DD' from the Dolgoruky collection.[53] Also from the Dolgoruky collection came three knives of 1847 by Hunt and Roskell and a fork of 1850 by George Angell.[54] More important pieces came in 1925 from the house-museum of Countess Yelizaveta Shuvalova, above all the marvellous Paul de Lamerie dish of 1726 with the arms of the Stroganovs (cat. 57) and a tankard of 1776 by Charles Wright with a marvellous mixture of different styles (cat. 69). No less original, but in a totally different style, is the prize cup of 1831 by Paul Storr (cat. 70). Also notable are a travelling nécessaire of 1874 by George Angell,[55] a travelling flask of white glass with a silver cup and stopper of 1875,[56] and pieces of a gilded tea service of 1875 by Hunt and Roskell, consisting of a kettle, teapot and milk-jug.[57] The gilded platter of 1843 by George Hunt, with the joint arms of the Vorontsovs, Dashkovs and Shuvalovs, came (in 1918) from the famous Petersburg collector F. F. Uteman.[58]

As regards the Imperial court, pieces by leading London silversmiths and jewellers were continually being acquired throughout the 19th century. Most often these came from the firms Mortimer and Hunt, or Hunt and Roskell, and also from Garrard, mainly in the 1840s and 1850s. This would seem to have been a new phase of that Anglomania so sharply felt back in the 1770s and 1780s, and marked by close contacts between the Russian court and leading English firms. There were two large orders in this period, for a large table service, known as the London service, and the service of Grand-Duchess Yekaterina Mikhaylovna. These orders would seem to have been prompted by Nicholas I's visit to London with his suite at the beginning of June 1844. As *The Illustrated London News* noted, Nicholas visited the workshops and showrooms of Mortimer and Hunt, Hunt and Roskell, and Garrard's, the royal jewellers, and was much impressed by their work.

Foelkersam devoted several pages to the London service in his *Inventories of the Silver of the Court of His Imperial Highness*,[59] but stated that no trace of it remained. Thanks to a 'Journal on the London Service', however, kept in the 19th century in the Gothic Cottage at Peterhof (fig. 101) and now in the Hermitage archives, we can follow the story of its commission and identify some of the surviving pieces. The London service was intended for 50 persons (some sources say for 40) and consisted of around 1,680 pieces. Among these were seven sculptural groups, candelabra, epergnes, salt-cellars in the form of sculptural compositions, girandoles, ewers etc. Glass, crystal, porcelain, stands for the sculptures and a number of other elements were added in St Petersburg – in the English Shop of Nichols and Plinke, at the Sazikov manufactory and at the Imperial Porcelain and Glass manufactories. The 'Journal' opens on 8 June 1844: 'Order in the English Shop, for the three silver groups brought from London and the two also to be brought from there, pedestals to the select design …'. The description of the first of these groups corresponds to one in the Hermitage: 'A knight on a horse, with a cup in his hands, a figure standing before the knight (weight 29 pounds 35 zolotniki).[60] This group was the work of the firm of Robert Garrard (cat. 72), designed and modelled by Edmund Cotterill, whose appointment as head of the team of designers in 1831 proved to be important for the success of the firm. Contemporaries said of Cotterill that 'he introduced in his work a lively sense of the plastic nature of silver', bringing out the texture of nature both living and dead. Forms for his works were often made by Edward Lorenzo Percy and by William Spencer, a passionate admirer of the Tudor style who made stylish use of cartouches.

The Hermitage has another piece by Garrard, a copy of the Queen's Cup,[61] made for Ascot in 1844 to a design and model by Cotterill (fig. 106). This appeared in Petersburg in the same year: clearly the original appealed to Nicholas I, as it had to the correspondent of *The Illustrated London News*, who noted that this 'marvellous cup' was widely admired on its appearance at the Ascot racecourse.[62]

To return to the London service, another group in the Hermitage, the *Hunter*,[63] came from the same source. This was made by Hunt and Roskell, with E. N. Baily (R.A.) in 1847, again as the Queen's Cup for races held at Ascot. This group was a replacement for another piece originally intended to be included in the service, *Mazeppa*,

mentioned in archival documents for 1844. Taken from a picture by Horace Vernet, *Mazeppa*, or a copy, was shown at the Great Exhibition in 1851.

London firms made prizes from 1844 for the Ascot races, held every year in July, and the Russian emperor also commissioned prizes on subjects from Russian history. They included the *Bronze Horseman*, a shield showing the history of the reign of Peter I, and a group with St George (1846), a copy of which was also in the London service. This was designed by Frank Howard and modelled by Alfred Brown under Baily's guidance, and was described as 'incredibly vivid, treated with great originality and exceptionally skilfully', and as 'elegant and decorative'.

In 1850–51 a large service was ordered from England, from Hunt and Roskell, probably for the marriage of Grand-Duchess Yekaterina Mikhaylovna (granddaughter of Paul I).[64] This then passed to Duchess Yelena Georgiyevna of Saxon-Altenburg. Judging by the surviving pieces, it was a large set that included table, tea and dessert services. The most characteristic pieces are stands for vases (the glass bowls are not extant) in the form of tall vines, forming a ring at the top to hold the vase, and with cast figures of women and children on the foot (fig. 107). The combination of naturalism in the vegetable motifs and the Salon-like affectation of the figures is typical of Victorian art. The Imperial palaces yet contained other services by English craftsmen. We know, for example, that there were services by Rundell, Bridge and Rundell, and by Paul Storr dating to 1816, as well as a Garrard's service of 1845 for the yacht *Queen Victoria*, a service by E. C. Brown of 1867 and another of 1891 by Heath and Middleton.[65] And in addition to their own purchases and commissions, the Imperial family also received gifts from England on numerous occasions. One superb example of this is a gold box with a porcelain plaque presented to Alexander II by the Lord Mayor of London in 1874 on the occasion of the marriage of the tsar's daughter Grand-Duchess Maria Alexandrovna to Queen Victoria's son Alfred, Duke of Edinburgh,[66] the box having been made in the Tudor style by the firm of I. Benson (fig. 108).

As this essay has sought to illustrate, English silver was therefore to be widely found in the palaces and private houses of St Petersburg and elsewhere, a situation largely due to the close trading and cultural links there were between Russia and England, the relatively frequent trips made by Russians to England, and the active role played by English shops in the Russian capital.[67]

APPENDIX

English Silver (RGIA Fund 469, op. 9, yed. khr. 656: information from the Service Stores on the gold and silver gilded services there in 1759):

fol. 3v: Silver services (English service received in 1726, on the 21st day of September from the main palace chancellory):

Silver gilded vessels
1 lavabo with plate
2 cups with covers
4 ewers
3 tankards with handles without covers
14 platters
14 fluted cups without lids
24 silver knife handles, gilded
24 triple strainers, gilded
23 spoons, gilded
Weight of gilded vessels 3 poods 37 pounds 74 1/4 zolotniki.
To the same service ungilded vessels:
43 dishes including 2 pieces by Palm* as an addition to this service
24 covers for dishes
4 stands for dishes
89 plates including 61 pieces by Palm as an addition to this service
3 cups with covers
2 fluted cups with a grille on hotplates
4 fluted cups with a grille on hotplates

fol. 4v:
1 (?)cup by Palm
2 pyramids each on four legs with handles and on each 5 large bowls and 4 small
2 candelabra with seven pipes
10 candelabra with twelve double branches
14 single candelabra including 4 made additionally by Palm
12 salt-cellars on three legs
4 salt-cellars octagonal on 4 legs and three divisions within gilded with double lids
4 sugar-bowls with lids
4 pepper-pots with lids
4 mustard-pots with lids
4 mustard spoons including 1 by Palm

fol. 5:
4 snuffers on stands
4 fluted tazzas on elongated saucers
4 cups in which to stand baskets for drink
4 fluted cups on which to put sweets
8 vorschneider spoons
6 double stands for crystal ewers
2 pyramids on four legs (?) on which to warm plates
2 hotplates to warm food with burners and covers
2 strainers with handles to put lemon in (?)
2 openwork baskets with handles

fol. 5v:
2 platters including 1 by Palm made in addition
1 small silver table on an oak board
1 pyramidal body and with it 8 handles and 8 inserts plus 4 candelabra branches with candle-holders and screwed-on handles
1 dish with pyramidal body on 4 legs
2 handles with openwork dishes on which to put a sugar-bowl, pepper-pot and mustard-pot
4 fluted bowls which can be screwed onto candelabra [*illegible word*] 4 handles
24 silver dessert knives with chased handles
24 spoons of the same kind
25 forks of the same kind, 1 by Palm

fol. 6:
24 dessert knives with iron blades
23 dessert spoons
23 forks of the same kind
46 table knives with iron blades, 4 by Palm

43 table spoons, 25 by Palm
46 triple table forks, 7 by Palm
8 spoons for eating bone marrow
4 vorschneider knives, 1 of which gilded
4 vorschneider forks, 1 of which gilded
Weight of ungilded vessels 25 poods 20 pounds 41.25 zolotniki.
Altogether in one service both of gilded and ungilded a weight of 29 poods 18 pounds 19.5 zolotniki.
* Probably the jeweller Carl Gustave Palm (b. 1725 in Revel), who was registered in the guild in 1752 and who worked at court.

1. Cripps 1886; Maskell 1884.
2. Jones 1909; Penzer 1958; Oman 1959.
3. Semevsky 1884, p. 123.
4. De la Mottre 1991, p. 235.
5. Was this perhaps the service that included two plats-de-ménage by Claude Ballin II, now in the Hermitage?
6. De la Mottre 1991, p. 250 n. 100. I would like to thank N. V. Kalyazina for providing this information, uncovered by her and I. V. Saverkina in the archives of RGADA (Fund. 11, ch. 6, fol. 110).
7. *Ibid.*, p. 237.
8. *Ibid.*, p. 250.
9. RGIA Fund. 469, op. 9, yed. khr. 656, fol. 3v.
10. In Lamerie 1990, pp. 10–11.
11. Hermitage inv. nos. 7022, 7023.
12. RGIA Fund 469, op. 9, yed. khr. 656, fols. 3v–6.
13. Foelkersam published his list of the English service from a different document in the archives. See Foelkersam 1907, II, pp. 8–11.
14. Hermitage inv. no. 7040.
15. The fullest study of the creation of the wine-cooler is Penzer 1956.
16. The 'Inventory of Various Silver and Gilded Objects in the Stores of the Winter Palace' for 1859 includes the following list with regarding to the wine-cooler: 'Transfer: Large 90 fineness with chased figures, with plates and wheels, copper and iron screws, wight 13 poods, 24 pounds, 13 zolotniki, inside along the edge a vine. Number of objects, 506. Received in 1741 from the Court Office' (RGIA Fund 469, op. 13, d. 447, fol. 17v).
17. Lantsmanis 1992, p. 19.
18. *Ibid.* In 1730 the income for the Russian state budget was 8 million roubles.
19. Hermitage inv. nos. 13764–83.
20. Lantsmanis 1992, no. 116, p. 130.
21. *Al'bom Istoricheskoy vystavki predmetov iskusstva 1904 g. v S.-Peterburge* [Album of the Historical Exhibition of Art Objects held in 1904, in St Petersburg], text by Adrian Prakhov (St Petersburg, 1907), p. 144, drawing 55 on p. 143. Prakhov mistakenly indicates that the toilet service had belonged to the Emperor Peter III and identified the arms as those of Golstein.
22. State History Museum, Moscow; Lamerie 1990, no, 40, pp. 80–81.
23. *Zapiski Yusta Yulya, datskogo poslannika pri Petre Velikom* [The Writings of Just Juel, Danish Envoy under Peter the Great] (Moscow, 1900), p. 268.
24. Hermitage inv. nos. 7042–124. It must be this service that Foelkersam described as the 'Toilet service of Elizabeth Petrovna by Samuel Courtauld' (Foelkersam 1907, I, p. 9). The Winter Palace also had a writing set of 1730 by Augustine Courtauld: 'A stand … gilded on four legs, with two projecting drawers, and accessories to it' (Foelkersam 1907, II, pp. 526–7).
25. Hermitage inv. nos. 7125–49.
26. Grimwade 1976, no. 186a.
27. Foelkersam 1907, I, p. 17.
28. RGIA Fund 468, op. 1, yed. khr. 3889, fols. 9, 11, 16, 24, 186.
29. Foelkersam 1907, II, pp. 248–50.
30. *Ibid.*, pp. 257–8.
31. RGIA Fund 468, op. 1, yed. khr. 3892, fol. 4.
32. *Ibid.*, fol. 115.
33. *Ibid.*, fol. 119.
34. *Ibid.* I would like to thank Mrs L. Voronikchina for drawing my attention to these documents.
35. *Ibid.*, fol. 14v.
36. *Ibid.*, fol. 145.
37. *Ibid.*, fol. 152v.
38. Hermitage inv. no. 7158.
39. Hermitage inv. nos. 7150–57.
40. Potemkin 1891, p. 31.
41. 'Potyomkinskiy prazdnik 1791g' [Potemkin's celebration of 1791], *Russkiy Arkhiv* [Russian archive] (1867), p. 679.
42. Pylyayev 1889, p. 310.
43. *Ibid.*, pp. 312, 314.
44. *Ibid.*, p. 200.
45. *Ibid.*, p. 200. Reference would seem to be made to Potemkin's chief gardener, William Gould of Lancashire, creator of 'immediate gardens', which he built along the route taken by Catherine II during her journey to the Crimea in 1787.
46. Hermitage inv. no. 13449.
47. Schroder 1988, p. 226.
48. Cream jug, 1802, Hermitage inv. no. 13596; two-handled cup with cover, 1804, inv. no. 13362.
49. Coffee-pot, 1801, Hermitage inv. no. 13976.
50. Samovar 1786; Hermitage inv. no. 13760.
51. Hermitage inv. no. 7527.
52. Hermitage inv. nos. PO 4420, 13363, 13365.
53. Hermitage inv. nos. 14035–7.
54. Hermitage inv. nos.14030–33.
55. Hermitage inv. nos.13608–12.
56. Hermitage inv. nos. 13585.
57. Hermitage inv. nos: kettle, 13978; teapot, 14001; milk-jug, 13979.
58. Hermitage inv. no. 11695.
59. Foelkersam 1907, II, pp. 180–201.
60. Hermitage Archives, 'Journal on the London Service', 1844–8, fol. 1v.
61. Hermitage inv. no. 7933.
62. *The Illustrated London News* (1844), pp. 369, 370.
63. Hermitage inv. no. 7673.
64. Hermitage inv. nos. 14002–29; 14042–4; 13188–91.
65. Foelkersam 1907, II, pp. 718, 721.
66. Inv. no. 2.
67. The most important of these was the English Shop on Nevsky Prospekt, near the Admiralty, which was first mentioned in 1786, when it was owned by Goy and Bellis. From 1804 to the end of the 1840s it belonged to Constantine Nichols and Wilhelm Plinke, and from then to 1880 by Robert Cahoun.

ENGRAVED GEMS IN BRITAIN: THE RUSSIAN PERSPECTIVE

Yulia Kagan

Fig. 109: *Victory Writing on a Shield*. Carnelian intaglio, 2nd century. ¹⁵⁄₁₆ in. (2.28 cm). Lullingstone Villa, Kent.
Photo courtesy of English Heritage.

The earliest-known examples of English engraved gems date from the 13th century, although the art has been practised, if intermittently, in Britain since Roman times.[1] The high level of English carving achieved in the 16th century laid the basis for a tradition that maintained its importance even during the upheavals of the 17th century, so that by the 18th numerous craftsmen were producing many hundreds of high-quality works, craftsmen whose fame in some cases was to reach far beyond Britain. Yet despite this, until quite recently anyone interested in the history of English engraved gems was hindered by the dearth of published work on the subject, a situation quite unlike that for French or Italian Renaissance gems and their craftsmen. A brief list of engravers active in England and incomplete tallies of their works were all that was available, and even the catalogues and articles written by British authors that did provide some details on the formation of English collections and the making of individual works failed to identify what it was that distinguished the English school from schools elsewhere. The situation has only begun to improve in the last twenty years: Gertrud Seidmann has published a number of articles, including a major one on the work of Nathaniel Marchant (she is presently working on Edward Burch);[2] Diane Scarisbrick has written extensively on various aspects of gem collecting and their links with jewelry;[3] and Shirley Bury has examined the use of cameos in English royal orders.[4] In addition there is now a mass of literature on James Tassie and on Wedgwood's cameos. But these studies cannot be put together to give us an overall picture, limited as they are to accounting for discrete moments in the history of English cameos and intaglios.

To arrive at any understanding of an art form of the past depends to a large measure on having access to a variety of extant examples of that art. This truism explains why English engraved gems have until recently attracted little attention, for museums in Britain contain very few examples of work by either native gem-engravers or those foreign masters who worked in Britain. Suffice it to say that the British Museum's post-Classical gem collection prior to its partial destruction by bombing in 1941 included only 50 or so items attributed to the English school. Today the Museum has around 1,500 examples from various schools, while Windsor Castle and the Victoria and Albert Museum have even less. The same is true of the Fitzwilliam Museum, Cambridge.

Inevitably, over the centuries many English engraved gems disappeared into Continental collections, either as gifts or through sales. Elizabeth I, for example, presented an engraved portrait of herself to one of her most earnest suitors, the future Swedish king Erik XIV, and in the list of gifts sent by her to tsar Fyodor Ioannovich in 1598 (but which did not arrive until after his death), we find a 'golden button, in it a stone, and on the stone is engraved the physiognomy of the Queen' (this work is thought to have inspired a Russian-made gold donative bearing the image of Boris Godunov). Similar stones figure in contemporary documents relating to the court of Navarre, the collection of the Holy Roman Emperor Matthias (1557–1619) and the French royal collection. Other gems left England in the 1640s and

1650s as a result of the sales of the collection of Charles I and the confiscation of property belonging to his Royalist supporters. During the 18th century English gem-cutters received commissions from abroad and also worked at foreign courts; England's early initiative in the mass-production of works of art for a world market inevitably included all kinds of 'gem-works'; and foreign tourists returned home from England with an English seal or a small box of casts as a souvenir (in the Victorian era it was usually with a fashionable brooch set with a shell cameo).

Despite this dispersal, Continental museums contain only a few English examples, although we know that they were highly regarded by connoisseurs. The Polish monarch Stanislaw II (1732–98) owned some, for example, as did his nephew Stanislaw Poniatowski, the famous collector Philipp von Stosch, the artist Jakob Philipp Hackert (1737–1807) and many others. Jacques Guay (1711–93), gem-cutter to the French court, on his resignation recommended the Englishman Nathaniel Marchant as his replacement. Goethe, who owned casts taken from Marchant's gems, praised them highly, and among the intaglio seals he used (Goethe maintained the tradition of proving his signature with a seal) there were at least two English works, impressions of which can be seen on his extant letters. Even today, numerous pieces are still in private collections in England and abroad, and when rare portrait cameos of the Tudors and Stuarts or intaglios signed by 18th-century English masters appear at auction, the interest shown in them reflects the respect with which they were regarded in the past.

In the light of the fact that museums both in Britain and on the Continent hold so few examples, that the Hermitage's collection of western European engraved gems includes 300 cameos and intaglios of English work (or which can be attributed to the English school with some confidence) is significant. This is the largest collection of its type in the world, having been put together over many years, although the last quarter of the 18th century was the most intensive period of acquisition. The collections acquired by the Hermitage that formerly belonged to the Duc d'Orléans, Saint-Moryce and Jean-Baptiste Casanova include important gem-engraved portraits of Elizabeth I and cameos by Thomas Rawlins and Thomas Simon. During the same period, a unique collection of works by the leading London gem-cutters William and Charles Brown – 200 pieces in all, almost half of their joint output (the British Museum and the Victoria and Albert Museum together have only a dozen or so signed gems by the Brown brothers) – was put together in the Museum. In the 19th century, English engraved gems arrived with the collections of Jean-Baptiste Mallia and the Russian diplomat D. P. Tatishchev from Vienna, the Petersburg collections of L. A. Perovsky and V. I. Myatlev, and after 1917 from the nationalized collection of the Princes Yusupov. The Hermitage continues its acquisitions policy through purchases, gifts and bequests. As a result it has works by no less than fifteen English masters, and it also has a good number of anonymous English pieces. The collection of reproduction casts by James Tassie (as far as is known, the only collection to have survived in full, complete with its systematic arrangement) is particularly important, reproducing

almost 1,500 English engraved gems. The Hermitage also has a series of casts made in Italy by Tommaso Cades in the first quarter of the 19th century taken from gems made in England at the very end of the 18th century and the beginning of the 19th.

Clearly, anyone studying the history of English engraved gems cannot ignore the collections at the Hermitage, even though the inevitably piecemeal process of acquiring items means that the Museum cannot alone present a complete history. There are, for example, almost no medieval examples (but perhaps the state of contemporary knowledge is insufficient for distinguishing English from Continental work); the Renaissance pieces, with rare exceptions, all date from the end of the 16th century; and there are hardly any examples of characteristic English heraldic seals. In addition, however extensive is the Hermitage's collection of pieces by 18th-century English masters in comparison with other museums, it is still only a fraction of what once existed. None the less, the Hermitage's English engraved gems, through being concentrated in one complex, allow us to begin assessing the peculiar individuality of the English school and its place in the history of the subject.

Engraved gems were introduced to the British Isles in the middle of the first century BC at the time of Julius Caesar's campaigns, and began to be circulated in some numbers a century later, following the conquest that added Southern Britain to the Roman empire. The gems were used in London and elsewhere as seals and amulets, for personal adornment and as phalerae, and many examples of Mediterranean origin have been recovered by archaeologists at various sites. In addition to those of obvious Roman origin, intaglios made in a crude, barbaric style – presumably for local chieftains who sought to emulate Roman habits – have been found, which led J. Toynbee to propose that these must have been produced within Britain. A characteristic example found in 1959 is a cornelian intaglio with a single-winged Nike writing on a shield with her right hand (fig. 109); presumably its engraver had failed to realize that an intaglio seal pressed into wax produces a mirror image of the image engraved![5]

Antique gems were highly valued in England in Anglo-Saxon times (as they were on the Continent), by which era most pagan works of art had been lost or destroyed. The Anglo-Saxons used them to ornament tombs (for example, Edward the Confessor's), for brooches and pendants, to decorate reliquaries, prayer-book bindings, staffs and crosses, although the iconoclasm of the Reformation was to lead to the destruction of much of it. By the time of the Norman invasion in 1066, the role of engraved gem amulets was growing, and this was reflected in lapidaries – books in Latin or Old English on the magical properties of stones, including engraved stones. These included recommendations regarding to whom and in what circumstances the depiction of one or other of the gods from the Roman pantheon would bring health, wealth, victory, etc. The magical power of stones was linked to all kinds of astrological theories, and indeed 'the great popularity of the lapidary is one of the curious aspects of English medieval literature'.[6]

The impressions made by Antique intaglios can be found on various historical documents (charters, deeds, contracts), for prior to the papal ban of 1194 they were used as seals by clerics as well as by secular rulers and officials, the pagan gods or Roman emperors depicted on them being reinterpreted, in accordance with Christian symbolism, as saints. Undoubtedly, the appreciation of engraved stones in medieval times in part was due to the high value then put on materials not easily destroyed: the 'imperishability' of such stones, their almost perfect preservation, gleaming surfaces and transparency were in keeping with an aesthetics of metaphysical beauty. 'Medieval' work implies that gems were ornamented with Christian subjects, but the German medievalist H. Wentzel has shown that carved gems of this period actually preserved classical motifs in their imagery that had already been lost from the iconography of other arts.[7] Around 1200, imitations of ancient gems having profile or three-quarter busts began to appear in England. This pseudo-Antique style of depiction, which is indissolubly linked with cameos, came in its turn to be reproduced in other materials, such as clay and plaster. Thus Wentzel explained their presence on two medallions on a retable from Westminster Abbey made c. 1270 (fig. 110). As we can see from the *Noli me tangere* cameo in the British Museum (fig. 111), the Gothic style is also present in the art of this period, featuring broken folds of drapery, unstable poses, disproportionate figures, deep

carving and an overall air of *non finito*, all of which link this piece with similar small-scale sculpture of the time. Both Antique and Gothic tendencies were to continue into the 15th century (fig. 112).

The earliest craftsmen whose names we know from documents relating to payments for work are from the 14th and 15th centuries, and include Richard of Grimsby, mentioned in 1351, and John Esmond and John Domgood (1410s–20s). An intriguing item (now in the Victoria and Albert Museum) from the medieval era began as a spinel intaglio of French work bearing a portrait of Charles V and dating to the second half of the 14th century (the height of the art of gem-engraving in France) but which afterwards was set into a signet that had been made in England. On the whole the 15th century in England is marked by a general decline in both quality and quantity. Overshadowed for 30 years of that century by the dynastic Wars of the Roses (1455–85), so expensive an art as the engraving of hard stones, moreover an art that was largely dependent on support from wealthy clients, could not but be detrimentally affected.

The powerful influence of the Italian Renaissance was not felt in England until the 16th century. The term 'agate-stone' or simply 'agate' entered the language – in addition to its main meaning – as equivalents to a cameo. Classical motifs on Antique gems were once more recognized for what they really were, although English gem-engraving ignored mythological themes, at first following the main

Fig. 110: Medallions with profiles. Details of the altar at Westminster Abbey, c. 1270. Photo courtesy of the Warburg Institute, University of London.

Fig. 111: *Noli me tangere*. Onyx cameo, 13th century. The Trustees of the British Museum.

trend in court art, the cult of the portrait. Under Henry VIII a standard type of official portrait cameo was established, combining traits of Italian Renaissance engraved portraits, the revived tradition of Roman imperial gems and the portrait genre in English painting. Portraiture tended to be used as dynastic propaganda, and the iconographical peculiarities of Tudor engraved portraits, often using the intaglio relievato technique (such that the relief rises above the sunk ground no higher than the edge around the cameo), always charged these pieces with political meaning. In doing so it tied each of them to a particular moment in British history, thus allowing us to date them with some precision. For instance, cameos with separate and joint *en face* portraits of Henry VIII and Prince Edward (fig. 113) were part of the cult of the reigning monarch and his future male heir, and thus must have been made between 1539/40 and 1544, at the end of which a new Act of Succession restored the right of Henry's two daughters, Mary and Elizabeth, to succeed to the throne. Deriving, although not directly, from the works of Hans Holbein the Younger, these cameos convey not merely the outer features but also the spirit of the Holbein masterpieces – a heaviness that never becomes gloomy, a decorativeness that does not prevent us from concentrating on the faces; and a flatness that is combined with the finest modelling of forms. The accounts of the court of Henry VIII do mention a gem-cutter by name, Richard Atsill, and although he is not referred to in subsequent

records, engraved royal portraits continued to be made during Mary I's reign. In fact, when Mary's death in 1558 interrupted work on what was to have been another engraved portrait of her, it was later taken up again and reworked as a portrait of her successor, Elizabeth (Munt- en Penningkabinet der Rijksuniversiteit, Leiden).

Portrait cameos of Elizabeth I make up a very considerable, and important, part of surviving Tudor engraved gems (fig. 114). Numerous museums and private collections around the world have several dozen such works (engraved in three-layer, or more rarely two-layer, sardonyx, measuring between one and six centimetres in height), a far higher number than are to found bearing the image of any other monarch, although even this is only a small percentage of what must once have existed. References to the 'phisnamy', 'image', 'picture', 'head' and 'profile head of Queene Elizabeth' engraved on stone are repeatedly to be found in inventories of valuables and wardrobes, wills and letters, and painted portraits and processions often feature individuals wearing a signet ring, clasp, brooch or pendant ornamented in this way. These precious gifts or awards were a sign of the highest favour, and during state ceremonies in the presence of the Queen cameo portraits were worn by Knights of the Order of the Garter along with the Order's insignia. Cameos, like painted miniatures, contributed to and reflected the fervent cult of England's Virgin Queen.

Fig. 112: Impression of a seal. Red jasper and heliotrope, 14th century. The Trustees of the British Museum.

Fig. 113: Richard Atsill, *Henry VIII and Prince Edward*. Cameo, height 2 ¼ in. (5.7 cm). The Royal Collection, © Her Majesty Queen Elizabeth II.

In these portraits Elizabeth is usually shown in profile, in ceremonial dress decorated with embroidery and precious jewels and wearing chains of jewellery around her neck, among which we can easily identify pieces known to have belonged to her. On her head she wears a crown, diadem or cap tipped back to reveal her shaven forehead. Although this is a clear stereotypal form of presentation, the cameos do not simply copy one another, for what seems on first glance to be just another – as a sign of the highest favour – unchanging mask is in fact one in a subtly nuanced series. An unusual example is the cameo in which her bared neck is adorned simply with a string of pearls, while a twisted lock of hair falls down her back. The face is that of a young woman, but this should not mislead us: the cameo belongs to a group of late portraits of the Queen (*c.* 1600), of a type classified by Roy Strong in his catalogue of portraits of Elizabeth as 'the Hilliard mask of youth'.[8]

The question of the authorship of these cameos remains open. Italian, English and, more likely, French craftsmen have been suggested (see cat. 127), but whichever of these might one day be confirmed, the sheer quantity of examples – far exceeding the powers of a single gem-cutter – indicates that they must have been produced by a busy court workshop set up expressly to undertake such work. The period during which they were produced is also much broader than the one generally accepted (1580–85): the earliest examples appeared in the 1560s, while the very latest were made around 1600. If we compare this large group of cameos with paintings, miniatures, medals, coins and engravings showing portrait types that are more or less precisely dated, then the cameos too can be dated. One example of this is the image on a cameo of the Virgin Queen with a sieve (as the Vestal Virgin Tuccia) that is also to be seen in a painting dated 1580 now in the Pinacoteca Nazionale, Siena.

A cameo from the collection of the dukes of Devonshire depicting Henry VIII and his children – of which there used to be several replicas and even lead casts – should also be dated to the reign of Elizabeth, rather than to that of Henry (died 1547) as previously thought (fig. 115). An iconographical analysis reveals that it is a mechanical combination of standard portrait types taken from several periods, a combination that could not have been found earlier than 1570–75 or later than 1587, the year in which Mary, Queen of Scots, was executed and armed conflict with Spain began, after which the inclusion in a group portrait of the deceased Catholic fanatic Mary I (Philip II of Spain's second wife) would have been unacceptable in a Protestant England at war. The cameo was intended to assert the continuity of the Tudor dynastic line – Henry, Edward, Mary, Elizabeth – and the legitimacy of Elizabeth's own rule, a legitimacy that was repeatedly challenged abroad, and thus it should perhaps be recatalogued as 'Elizabeth I and her Predecessors'. For this reason, Horace Walpole's suggestion that the Elizabethan miniaturist and medallist Nicholas Hilliard (*c.* 1547– 1619) may have been involved in its production,[9] a suggestion once derided for its apparent anachronism, is worth reconsidering. Dating Tudor cameos more accurately, from the first portraits of Henry to late Elizabethan pieces, enables us to begin tracing out the line of development English Renaissance engraved gems took, from flat, frontal depictions to profile images with higher relief, closer to the Mannerist portrait formula.

The tradition of the Tudor intaglio-seal has its roots in the 15th century, when seals bearing coats of arms and heraldic images were introduced. The seal-cutter John de Mayne worked for Henry VIII, while Jacob Thronus, who made seals for Mary I, is sometimes even identified with the famous Jacopo da Trezzo, who had arrived in England before 1554, the year Mary had married Philip of Spain. A

Fig. 114: *The Barbor Jewel*, 1586. Onyx cameo of Elizabeth I made for Richard Barbor. Victoria & Albert Museum, London.

Fig. 115: *Elizabeth I and her Predecessors*, 1575/87. Cameo, sardonyx. The Duke of Devonshire, Chatsworth.

new technique appeared during the Elizabethan era, in which the seal was engraved in rock crystal and the carved side laid on foil tinted with one of the colours that formed part of the coat of arms. These objects were not very durable, for the colour soon faded. Of those that have survived intact, a set of seven is of particular interest: it was made for Thomas Gresham, the founder (in 1570) of London's trading centre, the Royal Exchange, and the individual items bear the coats of arms of his partners (portrait seals, like portrait cameos, remained almost solely a royal prerogative until the mid-17th century).

One type of the gem-cutter's art peculiar to England comprises cameos with a depiction of St George. The statutes of the Order of the Garter for 1522 made its insignia more complex and at the same time the so-called 'Great George' – a rich pendant with a figure of the Saint on horseback battling the dragon *en ronde bosse*, the wearing of which was permitted only during ceremonies of the Order – was joined by the 'Lesser George' (cat. 128), a medallion showing the Order's patron on an enamel miniature or cameo (in which case the device of the Order was engraved on the stone itself or on the precious setting). Although the number of Knights of the Order was strictly limited, each new member ordered himself such an insignia in a setting of his choice. The production of these cameos almost disappeared in the mid-16th century as a result of Reformist iconoclasm, but was afterwards revived, although they were used in the reigns of Mary and Elizabeth for opposing ideological ends. Elizabeth shown wearing the insignia of the Order, in a number of cases on a cameo, represents a particular type of painted portrait of 1575 to 1580, known as the Garter Portraits. When her death in 1603 put an end to the flood of royal portraits, almost the full potential of gem production was directed towards the production of the 'Lesser Georges'. It is worth noting that this and certain other Orders continued to have their insignias made in this way right up to the late 19th century, among them the Order of the Bath, the Order of St Patrick, and the Star of India (with a portrait cameo of Queen Victoria).

The considerable number of 17th-century engraved gems, generally not of a very high quality and somewhat reduced in size, suggests that not all of them were used as Order insignia, but rather perhaps had some wider purpose for Royalists during the Civil Wars, serving as a kind of political badge. None the less, despite differences in quality, each is unique in its way. In England they were – and are – appreciated as historical relics. Although after the death of a Knight of the Order the symbol, like other insignia, remained unused and should have been returned to the Order's administrators, it was often kept by the family and either passed down or sold, but even as part of a private or museum collection was often surrounded by legends (there are a whole string of pieces that it is claimed belonged to Charles I at the time of his execution).

In England, collecting engraved gems did not become popular until c. 1600, some 200 years after the fashion had been established on the Continent. The most important early example was the royal collection. In 1609 James I purchased for Prince Henry a large number of engraved gems left in Delft following the death of the Antwerp antiquary Abracham de Gorley. After Henry's sudden death three years later the collection passed to his brother, the future Charles I, who made several major additions to it both before and after his accession in 1625, but who also put as much effort into selling off some of the pieces. Many of the pieces he chose to keep were scattered as a result of the Civil Wars and only a small part was recovered after the Restoration, including a cameo depicting Henry VIII and Edward, which had been absent for 30 years. Under Charles II the royal collection was kept at Whitehall Palace, but it is now very difficult to identify the Whitehall pieces among those that make up the present Royal Collection kept at Windsor Castle.

At the same time as Charles was building up his collection, his favourite, George Villiers, 1st Duke of Buckingham (1592–1628), and Thomas Howard, 2nd Earl of Arundel (1590–1642), were both putting their own together. The greater part of Buckingham's came from the private collection of Peter Paul Rubens, which the artist sold to him, although not in its entirety, in 1626. Buckingham, however, was assassinated soon after, and in 1649 the collection was confiscated by Parliament and sold, one of the purchasers being Gaston d'Orléans, brother of Louis XIII. Arundel had acquired the gem collection of the Italian antiquary Pietro Stephanoni in 1627, and in 1636 added to it the famous Venetian cabinet of engraved gems formerly belonging to Daniel Nys, the adroit merchant who had helped Charles I to buy the bulk of the Gonzaga collection of pictures in Mantua (Charles turned down the Gonzaga gems). The Dutch artist Hendrik van der Borcht, resident in Frankfurt but a frequent traveller to Italy, helped Arundel to further enlarge his collection. Among the Earl's gems were many Antique examples, including such masterpieces as Felix's intaglio with *Odysseus and Diomedes with a Palladium* (Ashmolean Museum, Oxford) and the cameo with the *Marriage of Cupid and Psyche* by Tryphon (Museum of Fine Arts, Boston). Eventually, in 1762, much of what Arundel had put together became the property of George Spencer, 4th Duke of Marlborough, and remained with the family until it was split up in 1875.

The example of Arundel, whose passion for art was such that his purchases ranged from modern portraits to classical sculpture, shows better than any other that in England collecting engraved gems was a significant aspect of collecting Antique art in general. Michaelis stressed that the early steps taken to transfer classical marbles from Italy and elsewhere to Britain – and Arundel was in the forefront here – were closely linked with an awakening love for engraved gems.[10] And even then this enthusiasm did not reach only to the fringes of the court, for there were also smaller private cabinets of gems in existence in the 17th century, for instance that of the artist John Michael Wright (1617–94). One amazing find was made during construction work near St Paul's Cathedral in London in 1912: the remains of a 17th-century jeweller's shop (possibly a victim of the Great Fire of 1666) that contained numerous engraved gems of a sort clearly aimed at the tastes and purses of the rising merchant class.

English portrait gems underwent radical changes in the 17th century. Whereas earlier there had been a dependence on painted portraits, now the art of gem-engraving began to move closer to the work of medallists, and by the 1630s both spheres had merged. In the 1630s the medallist's art also took a great step forward thanks to the arrival in London of the Frenchman Nicolas Briot (1579–1646), and although he himself had little to do with gem-engraving, two of his pupils, Thomas Rawlins and Thomas Simon, leading medallists of their time, were also renowned gem-engravers. They were to find themselves on opposing sides during the Civil Wars, a circumstance reflected in the nature of their works. Rawlins, an ardent Royalist, worked through to the end in the Baroque tradition (following the Restoration he returned to England from enforced exile in Paris), while Simon, in his portraits of Oliver Cromwell on engraved gems, coins and medals, produced the first English examples of the classical style in art (fig. 116).

There are seals with the arms of the Stuarts, including diamond examples (Francis Walwin, for instance, engraved such a seal for Henrietta Maria), but the Revolution of the 1640s broadened the social range of clients for engraved gems. Simon is attributed with portrait seals of Cromwell's associate Algernon Sidney, the leader of the Levellers, John Lilburne, the Archbishop of Canterbury, William Laud (see fig. 27), and of the artist's close friends. Simon later worked for Charles II, although he had competition not only from Rawlins but from the medallist and gem engraver Jean Roettier, who was invited over from Antwerp in 1662. Later, the gem- and seal-engraver Christian Reisen of Trondheim arrived in London after spending two years in Aberdeen.

At the end of the 17th century, seals with ciphers, monograms and emblems were used for private purposes; from France came the fashion for gems with 'devices'; and thanks to Antique intaglios and pastes from Italy, English engravers began to produce intaglios with classicized heads and busts. These anticipated the next stage in the history of English gem-engraving, for in the early 18th century, Classicism, coming together with the enlightened ideas of the Age of Reason, made itself increasingly felt in artistic theory and practice. The new tendencies, replacing the Restoration era's conception of gems as items of luxury, soon had their effect on the production of engraved gems and their ownership, and of course on collecting. The import of large quantities of Antique pieces to England, on a scale not seen anywhere else in Europe, included many examples of engraved gems, which became more popular than any other art form thanks to their accessibility, precious materials, good state of preservation and easy transportability, plus of course their attractiveness and rich repertory of subjects that answered the most refined and varied tastes.

Fig. 116: Thomas Simon, *Oliver Cromwell*, 1659. Cameo, sardonyx. 1 × ¾ in. (2.4 × 2 cm). State Hermitage Museum.

Fig. 117: Lorenz Natter, *The Triumph of Britannia*. Pencil, pen and ink, 1754. Design for the obverse of a two-sided cameo. State Hermitage Museum.

Fig. 118: Lorenz Natter, *Algernon Sidney*. Pencil, pen and ink, 1754. Design for the reverse of a two-sided cameo. State Hermitage Museum.

In 1719 the Roman Nicolas Francesco Haym, a musician by profession, arrived in London with the intention – alas unrealized – of publishing 'The Museum of Gems', the second part of his *Tesoro Britannico* (part One was devoted to medals). Later, Johann Lorenz Natter (1705–63) also failed to get into print his 'Museum Britannicum', in which he had intended to present the broad panorama of English collecting in that sphere. Despite this apparent lack of interest in England, P. J. Mariette, who refers to no less than fourteen gem collections in England in his *Traité des pierres gravées* (Paris, 1750), could not restrain himself from marvelling 'car il n'y a certainement aucun endroit, ou l'on fasse paroître autant d'amour pour les Gravures antiques', though even he reckoned that the low prices then being asked for gems signalled a declining interest in them.[11] The new collections being put together in the 18th century followed the example of Englishmen based in Italy – the Consul in Venice, Joseph Smith, the Envoy in Naples, William Hamilton, and the antiquary James Byres, who for many years lived in Rome. Some took shape within the 'encyclopaedic' cabinets that belonged to the London physicians Richard Mead and Hans Sloane, as well as those of John Wright, John Kemp, Henry Howard, 4th Earl of Carlisle (now in the British Museum), the Marquess of Rockingham, Philip Dormer Stanhope, 4th Earl of Chesterfield (part of which was later acquired by Viscount Duncannon, later Earl of Bessborough), and the dukes of Devonshire (still at Chatsworth today); a third group, somewhat later, formed part of collections of antiquities, such as those of Charles Townley, Richard Payne Knight and Sir Richard Worsley. Sloane's, we know, was transferred to the British Museum following its foundation in 1753, and in 1772 Hamilton's collection arrived there, while in 1762 George III acquired Joseph Smith's *dactiliothèque*, for although the King had little understanding of engraved gems he did not want to be left behind by monarchs elsewhere in Europe.

This period was also the one in which patrons appeared who were interested not merely in collecting Antique gems but actively sought to commission contemporary works. In the first decades of the 18th century there were almost no native gem-cutters in England, and thus there was heavy dependence on foreign masters. Johann Rudolf Ochs, for instance, made several trips to England from Switzerland before settling there; another Swiss artist was the miniaturist, gem- and seal-engraver George Michael Moser; the Norwegian Karl Christian Reisen settled in England with his father Christian Reisen, and trained two assistants, the Englishman Claus Smart and the Scot Christopher Seaton. This effectively marked the beginning of a national school.

At that time English engraved gems tended to be small, modest, inexpensive intaglio-seals devoid of rich settings; they were the first stage in the establishment of the new style. Purchasers of these works were more concerned with content than artistic worth, and the search for the ideal tended towards a correlation between the subject and the status and intellectual interests of the patron or purchaser. Themes formerly unknown in the sphere of gem production gradually made their appearance, the classical repertory broadened and the character of portrait gems began to change: instead of portraits of monarchs we increasingly encounter those of celebrated figures, for example Shakespeare, Milton and Newton, at first portrayed with a strong Baroque element (*en face* or in a three-quarters view) but in time overtaken by profile busts. After these came portraits of Inigo Jones, John Locke, Alexander Pope and others. The status of the engraver himself also underwent a radical change: no longer a court artist, he was freed from the limitations imposed by patronage. Thus the free craftsman made his appearance, either working to commission or making pieces for sale in his own shop. But these were as yet just the first symptoms of a situation that was not to be fully established until the second half of the century.

Such was the situation when, in 1739, J. L. Natter decided to settle in England. Born in Germany, this famous medallist, engraver and theoretician of gem-engraving had trained in Switzerland and studied in Italy. Although he afterwards travelled to various parts of northern Europe to carry out commissions, Natter always returned to his family in London, the city in which he was to spend some seventeen years, more than half his career. The engraved gems, mostly portraits, that he made in England reveal both Baroque and classicizing tendencies, characteristic of the time. Portraits *à l'antique*, free copies from Antique gems alongside complex allegorical pieces, are to be found in Natter's work alongside those in which his sitters are bewigged. In those of Sir Robert Walpole, which mark the height of Natter's work as a medallist and engraver, we see the most harmonious combination of these conflicting stylistic elements. He published *A Treatise on the Ancient Methode of engraving on precious Stones compared with the Modern* in London in 1754, although, as mentioned above, his 'Museum Britannicum' never appeared, Natter lacking the necessary means to allow him to carry the idea through to its conclusion. But in 1761 he did manage to publish a catalogue of the Bessborough collection, which effectively served as an auction catalogue when the collection was sold to the Duke of Marlborough.

Prints depicting gems, however, which it was hoped would acquaint the public with items in private hands, were particularly widely found in England at this time. Put together by the collectors themselves – antiquaries, connoisseurs, artists, engravers – they continued to appear right up to the invention of photography in the 19th century, but it was in the second half of the 18th century that this means of reproduction, in England as on the Continent, began to replace the serial production of casts from engraved gems and imitations in ceramics, glass or paste.

In the 1760s a fresh wave of classicism from Rome made itself felt in the world of gem-engraving, moving over as it then was from hand craftsmanship to mechanical reproduction and thus able to mass-produce objects reflecting popular taste. The most widespread manifestation of this taste included the Classical cameo, which in turn dictated the production of other pieces stimulated by the cult of Antiquity, such as cameo-like plaques, portrait medallions, insets for jewelry, ceramics and furniture, everything that was generally described in Britain under the general title of 'gem-works'. According to Clifford Smith, 'in the latter part of the century England occupied a unique position with regard to the production of objects of this kind, which were eagerly sought for throughout the whole of the Continent'.[12]

The possible originator of 'gem-works' in England may have been Domenico Bartoli of Livorno. In 1764 he moved to London where, according to Aldini in 1785, 'he created marvellous pieces in scaliola [plaster] and paste'.[13] Although Aldini reports that Bartoli achieved some success, we know nothing else about him, and the standard examples of 'gem-works' remain the ceramic imitations made by Josiah Wedgwood. Through the letters to Wedgwood written by his partner, Thomas Bentley, we can trace the development of the firm's production step by step. 'Intaglios' were made largely in basaltes ware, while the perfection of the necessary paste and technology led Wedgwood in 1775 to produce works in the newly invented jasper ware, with an elegant range of colours for the ground, decorated with the finest white relief.

The first pages of Wedgwood's catalogues of his products were always given over to his 'cameos' and 'intaglios'. But however much he advertised these ceramic gems as being as close as was possible to the originals, they could not, for technical reasons, be regarded as facsimiles. Recognizing this, he moved from the direct reproduction of engraved gems to modelling, and brought in the best sculptor-modellers of the time. Thus his 'cameos' are the result not of a literal translation of the language of engraved gems into the language of ceramics, rather they are an artistic pretence, like the translation of a poem from one language into another. Some of the gems Wedgwood produced at his Etruria Factory were widely used in the decoration of both luxury items and everyday objects. Sheraton, and Chippendale too in his Neoclassical period, both set them into pieces of their furniture, while the Adam brothers and their followers used them in fireplaces and panels. Laid out symmetrically on pieces of Bristol glass and set into severe frames, Wedgwood's cameos became the favourite wall decoration in the houses of both the aristocracy and wealthier members of the middle classes.

Wedgwood's products gave rise to many imitations: similar pieces were produced by Humphrey Palmer, Jean Voyez, John Turner and Josiah Spode. The manufactories run by Eleanor Coade and James Hennig, which specialized in items made from artificial stone, also adopted the fashion, and even the ormolu products of Matthew Boulton and John Fothergill included oval and round 'cameo' medallions. The last interesting phenomenon in this trend was 'sulphides', or porcelain-like reliefs set into crystal plaques. The technique, invented in Bohemia, was first used by the Ridgway brothers, Job and George, in 1792, working in partnership with James Abington, but it was more fully utilized by Apsley Pellatt.

The greatest success in the actual reproduction of engraved cameos – series of casts and 'facsimiles' in a special glass paste – was enjoyed

Fig. 119: *The Speaker of Parliament ([?]Charles James Fox)*, a cast by James Tassie from an unknown Gem engraver 1⅜ × 1¹⁄₁₆ in. (3.6 × 2.8 cm). State Hermitage Museum.

Fig. 120: *Caricature*, a cast by James Tassie. State Hermitage Museum.

Fig. 121: *Hot-Air Balloon*, a cast by James Tassie from an unknown Gem engraver, 1¹⁄₁₆ × 1⅜ in. (4.3 × 13.3 cm). State Hermitage Museum.

by the London workshop of the Scot James Tassie, who supplied Wedgwood with the first models for his 'cameos'. By 1775, when Wedgwood invented his jasper ware, Tassie had already offered the public over 3,000 casts, reaching the scale of the largest series issued on the Continent. It was Tassie who was approached in 1781 by Catherine the Great, who wished to add to her fast-growing collection of engraved gems a 'pan-European' collection of casts (figs. 119–24). Her commission contributed greatly to the growth of his workshop and its production, and ten years later, when the author of the famous *Adventures of Baron Münchausen*, Rudolf Erich Raspe, compiled his catalogue of Tassie's casts, there were already almost 16,000 different kinds. Unlike others working on similar series, who generally followed Antique models, Tassie was particularly keen on contacts with modern engravers, and above all with his fellow countrymen. His agents regularly visited London workshops to take casts or forms of new-engraved pieces. The so-called 'tassies' that resulted are uniquely English in style.

In the 18th century the art of gem-engraving reached unheard of proportions, aided by the unceasing stream of coloured minerals from the colonies, while in London, Brighton and other towns there were stone-polishing workshops that undertook the first, rough work on stones, making the work of the engraver even easier. Prepared stones were also imported from Idar-Oberstein in Germany, the European centre for the working of such stones. In less than twenty years the price of engraved gems increased four or five times from a starting price of 20 to 25 guineas apiece, and remained at this high level for some considerable time. As J. Reitlinger has noted, 'the collector … might well have bought Carolingian ivories and 15th-century tapestries for a few pounds apiece. But he would certainly have bought spurious Graeco-Roman cameos and intaglios (the work of signor Pistrucci) for anything up to 100 guineas each …'.[14]

Since it became accepted practice in the 18th century to sign works, we know the names of around 50 craftsmen; other sources double this number. While in earlier times the court and the aristocracy had sought to employ skilled individuals from abroad, the new bourgeoisie supported native practitioners. As one specialist in the period has noted, 'the neoclassic phase of European art is the last period in which the medallist and gem engraver ranked as a major rather than a secondary artist',[15] and this is confirmed in England by the fact that native masters now participated in important public exhibitions, and the leading engravers of 'gems and seals' won prizes in artistic competitions.

Fig. 122: *Going to the Hunt*, a cast by
James Tassie from an unknown Gem engraver
1 11/16 × 1 3/8 in. (4.3 × 3.4 cm).
State Hermitage Museum.

Fig. 123: *The Shipwreck*, a cast by James Tassie.
State Hermitage Museum.

Fig. 124: *The Apotheosis of David Garrick*
(after the painting by George Carter),
a cast of an intaglio by James Tassie.
State Hermitage Museum.

The large number of people who were actively engaged in gem-engraving at this time confirms that an English school was then thriving. Its early stage of development (1750s–1760s) is linked with the names of Robert Bateman Wray, Richard Yeo (fig. 125), John Kirk and John Frewin. These men were both engravers and medallists, and in their work they remained faithful to the portrait genre they inherited. The second phase (1770–1800) marked the peak of the national school. This was the time of the best work by the engraver to the British and Polish kings, Edward Burch (fig. 128), and his famous pupil Nathaniel Marchant (cats. 134, 137). The former, in his long career, always aimed to 'animate' Antiquity in traditional forms of academic sculpture, while the latter, who was based in Italy for sixteen years, moved on to a new stage of Neoclassicism and made his own contribution to the formation of an international style. The most notable proponents of this English school of gem-engraving, who worked for many years for foreign clients and thus were little known in their native land, were the brothers William and Charles Brown (cats. 131–135–6, 138–42). After them come a number of secondary masters: Richard Dean, William Barnett (figs. 130–31), George Bemfleet, William Lane, John Milton, Thomas and William Pawnell, William Harris (fig. 126) and, at the end of the century, J. B. Varley, Thomas Bragg, Robert Priddle (fig. 127), William Whitley, Gibbon and a few engravers such as John Logan, the James Wicksteads (elder and younger), George Brown, George Macquestion, John Madden, William Berry, and others who worked in Ireland and Scotland. We also have numerous works by unidentified craftsmen that allow us to see the full range of the English school.

There are many examples of gem-engravers who turned directly to English paintings, prints and sculpture for imagery, not least hunting scenes and pedigree dogs, and the development of the portrait genre can also be traced in gem-engraving over the decades. In widening the accepted parameters of subject-matter, engraved gems reflected the broad interest there then was for literature, the theatre, social life and politics. English engraved gems of this period portray sailing ships and hot-air balloons, shipwrecks and fires, politicking orators, pugilists, even women shown outside cottages feeding their hens. There are also gems symbolizing Fortune, Victory, Friendship, Hope, and the Age of Sentimentalism gave birth to a fashion for mourning cameos with emblems of the *memento mori* type, with urns and doleful apophthegms. Under the influence of topical satirical prints, they even began to reflect English humour and caricatures.

English gem-engravers also developed their own peculiar approach to the Antique. This was most fully represented in gems where the Antique theme served as a pretext for the creation of detailed multi-layer compositions, full of movement, figures, landscapes and the play of light and shade. This manner, which was first seen in the works of Burch and which is later characteristic of the Browns in the 1770s and 1780s, was the opposite of the statue-like pieces typical of Marchant.

With the new century came the last, critical, phase. The new generation of engravers – Thomas Brown, Brett, Rafael Clint, Thomas Flavell, John Nicholson and the William Warners (father and son) – inherited the high level of professionalism of the late-18th-century masters, but no longer displayed their variety of style or their freedom in the use of Classical and contemporary artistic forms. They replaced them by coldness, the 'salon' style and a search for outward beauty. The traditional portrait genre became increasingly representational. The polarization of society once again made engraved gems the privilege of the few. Their demands, initially the response to the new Empire-style fashion for gems, and then to post-Empire modifications in classical taste in jewelry (the 'archaeological' trend – Castellani and Giuliano – and other manifestations of eclecticism) were now satisfied by foreign cameo masters with Benedetto Pestrucci at the head, to whom English craftsmen were once again forced to cede their previously dominant position.

Fig. 125: Richard Yeo, *Diana with an Arrow*. Intaglio, cornelian, sard. cast, *c.* 1760. State Hermitage Museum.

Fig. 126: William Harris, *Bust of a Woman with a Veil*. Intaglio, cornelian, sard. cast, late 18th century. State Hermitage Museum.

Fig. 127: Robert Priddle, *Leda and the Swan*. Cornelian, sard. cast, late 18th century. State Hermitage Museum

Fig. 128: Edward Burch *Sacrifice to Minerva*. Intaglio, chalcedony, cast, before 1769. State Hermitage Museum.

1. See M. Henig, *Corpus of Roman Engraved Gemstones from British Sites*, British Archaeological Reports 8/1, II (1974), an important early contribution to recent research on the history of engraved gems.
2. See Seidmann 1981, 1983–4, 1984–5, and 1987.
3. See Scarisbrick 1977, 1978, 1979a and b, 1980, 1981, 1985, 1986, 1987 and 1994.
4. Bury 1979. See also Bury 1978.
5. J. Toynbee, *Art in Britain under the Romans* (Oxford, 1964), p. 85.
6. Evans 1951, p. xi. See also Evans and Studer 1924, and Evans and Serjeanston 1933.
7. H. Wentzel, 'Die vier Kameen in Aachener Domschatz und die Französische Gemmenschneidekunst des 13. Jahrh.', *Zeitschrift für Kunstwissenschaft*, VIII/1 (1954), pp. 4–5; Wentzel, 'Mittelalterliche Gemmen in der Sammlungen Italiens', *Mitteilungen des kunsthistorischen Instituts in Florenz*, VII/3–4 (1956), p. 244.

8. See Roy Strong, *Portraits of Queen Elizabeth I* (Oxford, 1963), pp. 94–7.
9. Walpole 1862, II, pp. 108, 183.
10. A. Michaelis, *Ancient Marbles in Great Britain* (Cambridge, 1882), p. 6.
11. P. J. Mariette, *Traité des pierres gravées* (Paris, 1750), I, p. 336.
12. H. Clifford Smith, *Jewellery* (London, 1908), p. 315.
13. G. A. Aldini, *Instituzioni Glittografiche* (Cesena, 1785), p. 339.
14. Reitlinger 1962–70, II, p. 15.
15. G. Vermeuil, *European Art and the Classical Past* (Cambridge, MA, 1964), p. 149.

Fig. 129: William Woollett after Benjamin West, *The Death of General Wolfe*. Engraving, 16⅞ × 23 5/16 in. (42.9 × 59.2 cm). Published 1 January 1776. The Trustees of the British Museum.

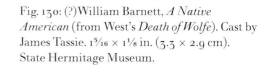

Fig. 130: (?)William Barnett, *A Native American* (from West's *Death of Wolfe*). Cast by James Tassie. 1 5/16 × 1⅛ in. (3.3 × 2.9 cm). State Hermitage Museum.

Fig. 131: (?)William Barnett, *The Death of General Wolfe* (from West's *Death of Wolfe*). Cast by James Tassie. State Hermitage Museum.

1

Sir Anthony van Dyck (1599–1641)

SIR THOMAS WHARTON, 1639

Oil on canvas, 85½ × 50½ in. 217 × 128.3 cm
Inscribed (from the time of the first owner) at
bottom left: *P. Sr. Ant. Vandike*; and
right: *Sr. Thomas Wharton brother to Philip
now Lord Wharton / 1639 about ye age of 25*
Inv. no. 547

Provenance: Collection of Philip, 4th Lord
Wharton, Winchendon, Buckinghamshire;
acquired from his heirs in 1725 by Sir Robert
Walpole, later 1st Earl of Orford; kept in
London, then at his estate, Houghton Hall,
Norfolk; sold by his grandson George, 3rd Earl
of Orford, in 1779; acquired by Catherine II
for the Hermitage as part of the Walpole
Collection.

Literature: Vertue I, 1929–30, p. 109; Vertue II,
1931–32, p. 99; Vertue III, 1933–34, pp. 12, 44;
Walpole 1752, p. 72; SbRIO, XVII, 1876 p. 400;
Smith 1829–42, III, p. 187, no. 640; IX, p. 339,
No. 89; Cust 1900, pp. 123, 286, no. 225; Somov
1902, p. 181; Glück 1931, pl. 468; Cat. 1958, II,
p. 60; Varshavskaya 1963, pp. 123–4, no. 18;
Larsen 1980, no. 865; Cat. 1981, p. 40; Millar
1994, no. 9.

Sir Thomas Wharton (1615–84), younger son
of Sir Thomas Wharton of Aske (1587–1622)
and Philadelphia Carey (d. 1654), brother of
Philip, 4th Lord Wharton (1613–96), was a
well-known courtier. He served in the army
in Ireland for over twenty years and devoted
much of his time to acts of charity.

In this portrait Wharton wears the Order
of the Bath, which he received in 1635. The
sign of the Order – a cross surrounded by three
crowns, in the middle of the cross a sceptre
with a rose and thistle – hangs on the red
ribbon thrown across his right shoulder. The
metal breastplate is also part of the uniform
of the Order. The portrait presents us with an
elegant and somewhat romantic image, with
Wharton standing in front of a rocky cavern,
beyond which is a bluish-grey cloudy sky.

This portrait (engraved by Valentine Green
in 1775) is one of a group of works
commissioned from Van Dyck between 1637
and 1639 by Philip, Lord Wharton, Thomas's
brother, and intended for a purpose-built
gallery in Lord Wharton's new house on his
estate at Winchendon, Buckinghamshire.
According to George Vertue (Vertue I, 1929–30,
p. 109), by the time of the sale of Wharton's
collection, the gallery included eighteen
portraits by Van Dyck (six half-length and
twelve full-length), eleven of the latter being
acquired in 1725 by Sir Robert Walpole.
Wharton's portrait is superbly painted,
although the background and costume may
have been carried out by assistants
(Varshavskaya 1963, p. 124). With its fine,
enamel-like surface, characteristic of the
entire group of Van Dycks from Wharton's
collection, the style is entirely consistent with
the inscribed date, 1639. The inscriptions were
probably added at Winchendon, as similar ones
are to be found only on the pictures that came
from the Wharton collection. NG

2

Sir Anthony van Dyck (1599–1641)

ELIZABETH AND PHILADELPHIA WHARTON,
(?)1640

Oil on canvas, 63¾ × 51³⁄₁₆ in. 162 × 130 cm
Inscribed (from the time of the first owner)
at bottom right: *P. Sr. Ant. Vandike*; and
left: *Philadelphia Wharton and Elizabeth
Wharton ye only daughters of Philip now Lord
Wharton by Elizabeth his first wife, 1640 about
ye age of 4 and 5*
Inv. no. 533

Provenance: collection of Philip, 4th Lord
Wharton, Winchendon, Buckinghamshire;
acquired from his heirs in 1725 by Sir Robert
Walpole, later 1st Earl of Orford; kept in
London, then at his estate, Houghton Hall,
Norfolk; sold by his grandson, George, 3rd Earl
of Orford, in 1779; acquired by Catherine II for
the Hermitage as part of the Walpole
collection.

Exhibitions: 1982 London, no. 56;
1987 New Delhi, no. 32; 1992 Tobu, no. 32.

Literature: Vertue I, 1929–30 pp. 29, 109;
Vertue III, 1933–34, p. 12; Walpole 1752, p. 51;
Smith 1829–42, III, p. 187, no. 642; IX, p. 393,
no. 90; Waagen 1864, p. 152; Cust 1900, pp. 123,
272, no. 48; Somov 1902, p. 182; Glück 1931,
pl. 486; Cat. 1958, II, p. 60; Varshavskaya 1963,
pp. 124–5, no. 19; Larsen 1980, no. 977;
Cat. 1981, p. 40; Millar 1994, no. 14.

Elizabeth and Philadelphia Wharton were the
daughters of Philip, 4th Lord Wharton, by his
first wife, Elizabeth, daughter of Sir Rowland
Wandesford, whom he married in 1632.
Elizabeth married Robert Bertie, later 3rd Earl
of Lindsey, in 1659, and died in 1669. We know
nothing of the fate of Philadelphia, her
younger sister, who may well have died while
still a child.

Despite the inscriptions on the picture and
the engraving after it by Pieter van Gunst,
doubt has arisen as to the identification of the
sitters. Cust (1900), basing his ideas on the
official version that Lord Wharton had only
one daughter, Elizabeth, by his first marriage,
suggested that the girls were Philip's cousins,
Philadelphia (b. 1631) and Elizabeth (b. 1632),
daughters of his mother's brother, Thomas
Carey. This idea was reiterated in the
Hermitage catalogues of 1902 to 1958.
As Varshavskaya has noted, however
(Varshavskaya 1963), there is insufficient
evidence to question the correctness of the
inscription, which was added during Lord
Wharton's own lifetime (see cat. 1). We know
that Wharton married three times and
fathered fifteen children, of whom six died in
childhood. Of Wharton's children from his
second marriage, there were four 'with other
issue'. The last daughter from this marriage
was also called Philadelphia, and it is possible
that she was named after her deceased sister.

This double portrait is one of Van Dyck's
most appealing images of children. The figures
were undoubtedly painted by the artist
himself. There are *pentimenti* in the outlines of
the dress, and the dry, somewhat schematically
painted, background (particularly the
landscape) clearly indicates the involvement
of assistants.

The portrait was engraved by Pieter van
Gunst with the inscription 'P. van Gunst sc.
Philadelphia and Elizabeth Wharton the only
daughters of Philip Lord Wharton by
Elizabeth his first Lady. Ant. V. Dyck. 1640.
Ex Museo Serenissimi Domini de Wharton'.
To judge from the final phrase, the engraving
would seem to have been made after Lord
Wharton's death in 1696. NG

Philadelphia Wharton and Elizabeth
Wharton ye onely daughters of Philip
now Lord Wharton by Elizabeth his
first wife, 1640 about ye age of 4 & 3

3

Sir Anthony van Dyck (1599–1641)

HENRY DANVERS, EARL OF DANBY, late 1630s

Oil on canvas, 87¾ × 51⅜ in. 223 × 130.6 cm
Inv. no. 545

Provenance: Bequeathed by the Earl's nephew, John Danvers, and presented by his son, Sir Joseph Danvers, to Sir Robert Walpole; collection of Sir Robert Walpole, later 1st Earl of Orford, at London, then at his estate, Houghton Hall, Norfolk; sold by his grandson, George, 3rd Earl of Orford, in 1779; acquired by Catherine II for the Hermitage as part of the Walpole Collection.

Exhibition: 1982 London, no. 20.

Literature: Walpole 1752, p. 72; Schnitzler 1828, p. 103; Smith 1829–42, III, p. 188, no. 647; IX, p. 394, no. 92; Labensky 1838, p. 350; Waagen 1864, p. 151; Cust 1900, pp. 124, 273, no. 61; Hind 1923, p. 68; Glück 1931, pl. 247; Varshavskaya 1963, p. 127, no. 24; Larsen 1980, no. 934; Millar 1982, p. 62, no. 20.

Henry Danvers, Earl of Danby (1573–1644), took part in military campaigns in Ireland, the Southern Netherlands and France, in one of which he appears to have received a slight wound (in this portrait there is a scar by his left eye, covered with a black patch). In 1621 he founded the first botanical garden in England, for which he presented Oxford University with a parcel of land in the city and a sum of money. In November 1633 he was made a Knight of the Order of the Garter.

Danvers is depicted full-length in the red and white robes of the Order, wearing a blue cloak with a white lining. Beside him, on the table on which he rests his right hand, lies the hat of a Knight of the Order. The pink and light-blue tones of the clothing, shining in a soft light, combine in the portrait with the black and gold drapery of the background and the tablecloth of the same material. This portrait is among Van Dyck's best works of his English period. It is the only one of his portraits of a Knight of the Order in which the subject is depicted full-length. The fluid, almost sketch-like manner of the painting suggests a date close to the end of the 1630s.

A preparatory drawing (three-quarters-length) is in the British Museum, London (Vey 1962, no. 212). There are copies of the finished work in the Stamford Collection at Dunham Massey, Greater Manchester, and at Wentworth Castle, Yorkshire; a third, showing some alterations, was sold at Christie's, London, 22 November 1974 (lot 105). The portrait was engraved by Valentine Green in 1775. NG

4

William Dobson (1611–1646)

ABRAHAM VAN DER DOORT, late 1630s

Oil on canvas, 17¾ × 15 in. 45 × 38 cm
Inv. no. 2103

Provenance: Jonathan Richardson collection,
London; collection of Sir Robert Walpole, later
1st Earl of Orford, at Downing Street, London,
then at his estate, Houghton Hall, Norfolk; sold
by his grandson George, 3rd Earl of Orford, in
1779; acquired by Catherine II for the
Hermitage as part of the Walpole Collection.

Exhibitions: 1956 Moscow, p. 27; 1983 Moscow.

Literature: Walpole 1752, p. 66; Georgi 1794,
pt. 2, p. 501; Fiorillo 1808, V, p. 369; Livret
1838, p. 446, no. 12; Walpole 1862, I, p. 269; II,
p. 353; Waagen 1864, p. 277; Faré 1866, pp. 5-6,
no. 1387; Holmes and Milner 1911, XIX, p. 163;
Collins Baker 1912, I, p. 99; II, p. 116; Vertue II,
1931-2, p. 77; Vertue IV, 1935-6, p. 14; Vertue
VI, 1948-50, p. 175; Millar 1958-60, p. xvi;
Millar 1963, text vol. p. 114; Piper 1963, pp.
357-8; English Art 1979, no. 20; Rogers 1983,
p. 9, fig. 1; Dukelskaya and Renne 1990, no. 48.

Abraham van der Doort (*c.* 1575/80–1640) was
a medallist, Keeper of pictures and antiquities
to Charles I, and the author of the first
catalogue of the royal pictures. Dobson's
portrait of him is first mentioned by George
Vertue in his Notebooks of 1721–31: 'Ab. Vander
Doort keeper of K. Charles Museum pictures.
his head in poses of Mr. Richardson painter
painted by Dobson. - <sold to Sr. R.bt.
Walpole.>' (Vertue II, 1931–2). The second
mention comes in the fourth Notebook, which
dates to 1731–6: 'a year Salary graunted by K.
Charles.I. an.o 1625 to ... Vanderdoort. of forty
pounds a year. as his Majesties modeller and
embosser for medals. & keeper of his Cabinett
of medals & other Curiosities. - <his picture a
head at Mr Richardsons ye painter>' (Vertue
IV, 1935–6). In both of these notes Vertue
unhesitatingly identifies the sitter for this
picture as Van der Doort and the artist as
Dobson.

This portrait should be dated to the very end
of the 1630s, when Van der Doort's life and
career were blighted, mainly because he was
unable to find when required a miniature of
particular value that the King had entrusted to
him. The thought that he had possibly lost the
object became so unbearable that the Keeper
committed suicide. His troubled state of mind,
disturbed gaze and sense of self-absorption
were keenly felt by the artist, who was clearly
not indifferent to Van der Doort's fate, for it
was thanks to him that Dobson was able to
examine Charles I's extraordinary collection of
paintings. There is a certain intimacy in this
early portrait by Dobson, managed in a soft
painterly style; its psychological tension and
free execution make it one of his best works.
The last lines of an epigram by James Elsum
devoted to the artist's portrait known as *Old
Stone and his Son* (Rogers 1983, no. 3) can
equally well be applied to this work:

Here you see Nature thoro' understood,
A portrait not like Paint, but Flesh and Blood,
And not to praise Dobson below his Merit,
This Flesh and Blood is quickend with a Spirit.
(Vertue II, 1931–2, p. 16)

It was the tragic nature of this portrait that
was highly praised by Millar in his
introduction to the publication of Van der
Doort's catalogue: 'If the portrait in the
Hermitage ... attributed to William Dobson,
is really a portrait of van der Doort, we can
perhaps see in this drawn and harassed face the
care that gradually overwhelmed him and
finally drove him to suicide in the summer of
1640' (Millar 1958–60, p. xvi).

According to the manuscript catalogue now
in the Pierpont Morgan Library, New York, by
1736 Van der Doort's portrait was in Robert
Walpole's London collection: 'A catalogue of
the right Honble Sir Robert Walpoles'
Collection of Pictures - 1736': 'Downing Street,
Westminster. In the parlour ... Dobson ...'.
The presence of the portrait in Walpole's
London house is confirmed by another
inventory of his collection, made by Vertue in
1739: 'Pictures of Sir. R. Walpole, at his House
near the Treasury, Whitehall ... in the Closet
a man's head. Vdr Doort. Dobson' (Vertue VI,
1948–50). After the picture was transferred
to Houghton Hall, however, Horace Walpole
mistakenly described this work by Dobson as
a 'portrait of the artist's father' in his *Aedes
Walpolianae*, and it was under this title that it
was engraved in 1776 by Valentine Green.
Walpole corrected his own mistake in his
Anecdotes (first published 1780): 'There is an
admirable head of Vanderdort, by Dobson, at
Houghton .... In the *Aedes Walpolianae*, I have
called this Dobson's father, as it was then
believed; but I find by various notes in Vertue's
MSS. that it was bought of Richardson the
painter, and is certainly the portrait of
Vanderdort' (Walpole 1862). In his essay on
Dobson in the second volume of the *Anecdotes*,
Walpole again identified the portrait correctly
(Walpole 1862).

A copy of the portrait is in the National
Portrait Gallery, London (no. 1569). Close to
the Hermitage portrait is a 'Portrait of a man;
a so-called portrait of Abrahan van der Dort',
painted in Dobson's style and now in the Royal
Collection, St James's Palace (Millar 1963,
pl. 114, no. 206). LD

282.

5

Sir Peter Lely (1618–1680)

ORDEAL BY FIRE, *c.* 1650

Oil on canvas, 45½ × 61⅔ in. 115.5 × 156.5 cm
On the pedestal at left, a half-erased
inscription, the first letter of which is: *L*
Inv. no. 2219

Provenance: entered the Hermitage between
1763 and 1783; in the 19th century kept in the
Tauride Palace, St Petersburg, then in
Gatchina Palace; returned to the Hermitage
in 1925.

Literature: Cat. 1773, I, no. 214; Wrangel 1913,
p. 102, no. 310; Krol' 1969, p. 65; Cat. 1981,
p. 243; English Art 1979, nos. 43–4; Dukelskaya
and Renne 1990, no. 58.

E. Munich's manuscript catalogue (see Cat.
1773) provides the following description of
this work: 'Ce Tableau n'a rien qui le mette au
dessus du mediocre. On y lit: peint a Rome en
1629'. This inscription has not been found on
the painting. In his catalogue Munich
attributed the painting to Giovanni Antonio
Lellio (Lelli; 1580–1640), and under this name
it was added to the list of works put up for sale
in 1854 on the orders of Nicholas I (Wrangel
1913), but it remained unsold.

The first suggestion of a connection with
Peter Lely was made by the Hermitage keeper
James Shmidt (Krol' 1969). This attribution is
supported by a comparison with a number of
multi-figure compositions on mythological and
biblical themes produced by Lely at the end of
the 1640s and in the 1650s: *Susanna and the
Elders* (City Art Gallery, Birmingham), the
Satyr and Nymph (destroyed 1941) and *The
Music Concert* (Courtauld Institute Galleries,
Lee Collection). The female figures and their
clothing in these works are close to those in
the Hermitage canvas, while the faces of the
Elders in the *Susanna* recall those of the
'oriental' figures here. It is very likely that this
work dates to the period in Lely's career
described by Richard Graham in 1695.
According to Graham, on his arrival in London
in the early 1640s Lely 'pursu'd the natural
bent of his Genius in Landscapes with small
Figures, and Historical compositions; but
finding the practice of Painting after the Life
generally more encourag'd, he apply'd himself
to Portraits' (cited in Millar 1978–9, p. 9). This
suggests a date for the Hermitage canvas of the
late 1640s or early 1650s, since after that Lely
painted only portraits.

The subject of the picture was originally
identified by Munich (Cat. 1773) as
'L'Imperatrice Cunnegonde, femme de
l'Empereur Henri Second, se justifiant par
l'epreuve du feu', and this remained the
accepted interpretation until 1969. But the
scene, in which a young woman stands
resolutely on glowing coals before an oriental
potentate, and in the background we see a
statue of Themis, is totally out of keeping with
the legend of St Cunegonde's trial by fire in
1040 following an accusation of adultery.
Her usual attribute is a model of Bamberg
Cathedral, which she founded together with
her husband in 1017, or the burning
ploughshare on which she was tortured.

We know of only one 17th-century painting
of this subject, *St Cunigonde Before Henry II*
(*c.* 1666) by I. Schonfeld for the altar of
Bamberg Cathedral, and the composition and
treatment of the subject have absolutely
nothing in common with Lely's painting. It
is possible that Lely borrowed the subject for
his picture from some literary source. But
although A. Krol' expressed her doubts about
the subject really being that of the Judgment
of Cunigonde (Cat. 1981), she retained the
traditional title. LD

Literature: Walpole 1752, p. 48; Locke 1768, IV, p. 632; Livret 1838, p. 344, no. 18; Waagen 1864, p. 277; Faré 1866, pp. 7,8, no. 1388; Williamson 1904, p. 15; Krol' 1961a, pp. 9, 80; Ernst 1965, p. 426; Stewart 1978, p. 219; Locke 1979–82, VI, pp. 503, 506; VII, p. 574; English Art 1979, no. 45; Stewart 1983, p. 115, no. 440, pl. 54d; Dukelskaya 1987, pp. 13–15; Dukelskaya and Renne 1990, no. 52.

Portraits of the philosopher John Locke (1632–1704) can be found in many private collections as well as at the Royal Society, Christ Church in Oxford, and Hampton Court Palace. But of particular importance are two portraits by Kneller, this one of 1697 and the other of 1704.

The Hermitage portrait shows Locke without a wig, in informal attire, unlike earlier ones painted by John Greenhill (1672-6), Verelst (1689) and Michael Dahl (1696). The most important difference is the great emphasis on the sitter's inner state: the nervous, expressive face is unfettered by the usual social conventions As Vertue wrote, Kneller, in his best portraits, 'chose the most agreeable Turn of a Face always adding to it a Mien and Grace; suitable to the Character, and peculiar to the Person he represented' (Vertue II, 1931–2, p. 123).

In 1691 Locke settled at Oates, the Essex estate of his close friend and talented student Dameris Masham. His health was failing and he sought to associate only with a close circle of friends, and rarely travelled to London. Locke's words, addressed to his Dublin friend William Molyneux in a letter of 4 August 1697, captures the mood of the Hermitage portrait: 'My age and health demand a retreat from bustle and business, and the pursuit of some inquirires I have in my thoughts, makes it more desirable than any of those rewards, which publick employments tempt people with' (Locke 1979–82, V, p. 677). In summing up his life, Locke wrote his own epitaph: 'Stay traveller: near this place lies John Locke. If you ask what sort of man he was the answer is that he was contented with his modest lot. Bred a scholar, he used his studies to devote himself to truth alone. This you may learn from his writings' (Locke 1927, p. 71).

We do not know for whom Kneller painted the portrait, the back of which the artist signed and dated. This work was long kept in his studio, as we learn from a letter dated 1 November 1698 from Locke's secretary, Sylvester Brounover, to his patron at Oates: 'Mr. Molineux's picture is not finish'd, nor is yours any further than you saw at the last sitting ...'

6

Sir Godfrey Kneller (?1646–1723)

JOHN LOCKE, 1697

Oil on canvas (oval painted within a rectangle), 30 × 25¼ in. 76 × 64 cm
Signed and dated on the back of the original canvas by the artist: *Mr. John Locke by Sr G. Kneller. 1697* (see fig. 133)
Inv. no. 1345

Provenance: collection of Alexander Geekie, London; collection of William Geekie, London; collection of Sir Robert Walpole, later 1st Earl of Orford, at his estate, Houghton Hall, Norfolk; sold by his grandson George, 3rd Earl of Orford, in 1779; acquired by Catherine II for the Hermitage as part of the Walpole Collection.

Exhibitions: 1937–8 Leningrad, no. 71; 1956 Moscow, p. 31; 1972 Leningrad, no. 363; 1983 Moscow.

(Locke 1979–82), and in a letter of 15 November informs him that the artist promises to finish it in the near future (Locke 1979–82). The editor of Locke's letters, E. S. De Beer, suggests that the reference here was to an artist's copy from the portrait of 1697, i.e. of the picture in the Hermitage (Locke 1979–82), but it seems more likely that this portrait itself was under discussion. In 1703 the Hermitage picture was acquired by the well-known London surgeon Alexander Geekie, who wrote to Locke on 26 February 1703: 'Sir. G.–Kneller has been so kind to let me have that Picture he did of you upon some consideration …' (Locke 1979–82). Geekie's ownership is confirmed by the inscription on Vertue's engraving of 1713 (O'Donoghue 1908–25, III, p. 80, no. 16). It would seem to have been around this time that Vertue made a watercolour sketch (fig. 132) after the portrait of Locke (perhaps for an engraving), which has the inscription 'Sketched from a painting and afterwards, not long before his decease, finished up from the life by George Vertue' (sketch sold at Christie's, 20 October 1953, lot 306–3). After the Geekie's death in 1721, the portrait was in the collection of his son William (c. 1690–1767), as confirmed by the inscription on an engraving of 1738 by Vertue, 'In the Possession of the Revd Dr William Geekie'. Indeed we know that Geekie had several portraits by Kneller. The engraving was included in Thomas Birch's *The Heads of Illustrious Persons of Great Britain…* (London, 1747; O'Donoghue 1908–25, III, p. 80, no. 8). Robert Walpole would seem to have acquired the portrait of Locke from Geekie after 1739, since the catalogue of Walpole's collection in

both London and at Houghton Hall, made by Vertue in 1739 (Vertue V, 1937–8, pp. 175–80), does not mention this work.

In 1704 Kneller painted another portrait of the philosopher (Virginia Museum of Fine Arts, Richmond) at the request of Anthony Collins (1676–1729), a young friend of Locke's, which is almost identical to that of 1697 in composition, appearance and style of execution. On 11 September 1704, just six weeks before Locke's death, and concerned about the fate of this portrait, Locke wrote to Collins: 'pray get Sir Godfrey to write upon … the backside of mine, John Locke, 1704. This he did on Mr. Molyneux's and mine, the last he drew; and this is necessary to be done or else the pictures of private persons are lost in two or three generations; and so the picture loses of its value, it being not known whom it was made to represent' (Locke 1768). This inscription is indeed to be found on the Hermitage portrait. The portrait of 1704 now at Richmond was engraved in 1721 by John Smith, and on the engraving is the following: 'Johannes Locke Ob. A.D.1704. Aelat.72. Ex Autographo G. Kneller Baroti prv Ant. Collins Arm.codn Anno depicto. Fecit J. Smith, A.o 1721' (John Locke. Died 1704 at the age of 72. Painted in that year by Baronet G. Kneller for Ant. Collins Esquire …) (Smith 1884, III, p. 1190, no. 157; Hermitage inv. no. 34221).

The closest painted copies are those formerly in the collection of the Earl of Ilchester at Holland House (no. 216), and that sold at Sotheby's, 5 February 1969 (no. 60).

The portrait of 1697 was used by Jean Dacier in the making of a medal to

commemorate Locke's death in 1794 for the series of portraits of famous men (Hermitage inv. no. 10780), and in 1759 John Michael Rysbrack used it while working on a statue of the philosopher, later used by Josiah Wedgwood as the model for a portrait medallion.

In the 19th century the portrait was reproduced on a decorative porcelain vase made at the Imperial Porcelain Manufactory in St Petersburg, which the Emperor Alexander II presented to the South Kensington Museum (now Victoria and Albert Museum, inv. no. 9093–1862) after the International Exhibition of 1862 (fig. 134). LD

Fig. 132: George Vertue, *John Locke*. Watercolour. Sold Christie's, 20 October 1953 (lot 306). Photo courtesy of the National Portrait Gallery, London.

Fig. 133: Reverse of canvas with inscription, signature and date.

Fig. 134: Porcelain vase decorated with Kneller's portrait of Locke. Made at the Imperial Porcelain Manufactory in St Petersburg and presented to the Victoria & Albert Museum. Victoria & Albert Museum, London.

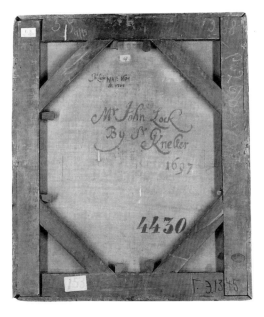

Sir Godfrey Kneller (?1646–1723)

GRINLING GIBBONS, 1680s

Oil on canvas, 49¼ × 35½ in. 125 × 90 cm
Inv. no. 1346

Provenance: collection of Sir Robert Walpole, later 1st Earl of Orford, at his estate, Houghton Hall, Norfolk; sold by his grandson George, 3rd Earl of Orford, in 1779; acquired by Catherine II for the Hermitage as part of the Walpole Collection.

Exhibitions: 1937–8 Leningrad, no. 72; 1956 Moscow, p. 31.

Literature: Walpole 1752, pp. 44–5; Fiorillo 1808, V, p. 496; Livret 1838, p. 431, no. 3; Somov 1859, p. 97; Walpole 1862, II, p. 588; Waagen 1864, p. 277; Faré 1866, pp. 8–9, no. 1389; Williamson 1904, p. 15; Trubnikov 1914, p. 91; Vertue VI, 1948–50, p. 178; Krol' 1961a, pp. 8–9, 79–80; Piper 1963, p. 137; Stewart 1965, pp. 478–9; English Art 1979, no. 46; Stewart 1983, pp. 47, 107, no. 302, p. 175, no. 79; Dukelskaya and Renne 1990, no. 51.

Grinling Gibbons (1648–1720), woodcarver and sculptor, is best known for his limewood garlands and varied decorative pieces of flowers, fruits and game. This portrait must have been painted by Kneller no later than 1690, for in that year John Smith produced a superb mezzotint after it (fig. 135). Although the portrait is unsigned, the engraving has the words 'G. Kneller pinx.' prominently placed on the pedestal with a head of Proserpine.

It was roughly at this time that John Closterman painted a portrait of Gibbons and his wife Elizabeth (lost, known only from Smith's engraving of 1691; fig. 136). But if Closterman's official portrait depicts a successful man, proud of his success and position in society, Kneller's painting shows Gibbons without any outward brilliance. This is above all a depiction of Gibbons the creative man. The artist shows him deep in thought, and distanced from worldly matters. His left hand rests on a cast from the head of Bernini's *Proserpine*, which Stewart suggests was in Kneller's studio and from which he did two drawings in the period 1700–05. Kneller may well have seen Bernini's *Pluto and Proserpine* in Rome during his stay in Italy in 1672–4 (Stewart 1983, p. 175, no. 79).

In Vertue's inventory of the collection of Robert Walpole for 1739, is the following: 'At Houghton in Norfolk the Seat of Sr. Rob.t. Walpole are these pictures viz ... on the first Floor Dining Room <over the Chimney> Gibbons the Carver 1/2 len – Kneller' (Vertue VI, 1948–50). In his *Aedes Walpolianae*, Horace Walpole picked out this work of all the pictures by Kneller in his father's collection: 'It is a Master-piece, and equal to any of Vandyke's' (Walpole 1752).

There is a version in the National Portrait Gallery, London (no. 2925); another was sold at Christie's on 23 November 1979 (lot 150). LD

Fig. 135: John Smith after Godfrey Kneller, *Grinling Gibbons*. Mezzotint, 13 ½ × 10 ⁵⁄₁₆ in. (34.2 × 26.2 cm). 1690. The Trustees of the British Museum.

Fig. 136: John Smith after John Closterman, *Mr Gibbon and Mrs Gibbon*. Mezzotint, 11 ⅞ × 13 ⅞ in. (30.2 × 35.1 cm). 1691. The Trustees of the British Museum.

1549.

Sir Godfrey Kneller (?1646–1723)

PYOTR POTEMKIN, 1682

Oil on canvas, 53⅛ × 40¾ in. 135 × 103.5 cm
On the reverse of the backing canvas is a copy
of an old inscription in black ink: *His
Excelency Peter John Potemkin Ambassador
Extraordinary from Czar of Moscovy. 1682.
GKneller pinxit.*
Inv. no. 10583

Provenance: collection of Prince Grigory
Potemkin in the Winter Palace, St Petersburg;
in the 19th century kept in the palace at
Gatchina, from where it was transferred to the
Hermitage in 1931.

Exhibitions: 1870 Petersburg, no. 31; 1905
St Petersburg, issue 5, p. 54.

Literature: Potemkin 1891, p. 54; Stewart 1983,
p. 124, no. 585; Dukelskaya and Renne 1990,
no. 50.

Fig. 137: J. Blooteling after Godfrey Kneller,
Peter John Potemkin, 1682. Mezzotint, 7 ⅜ ×
5 ⅝ in. (18.7 × 14.2 cm). The Trustees of the
British Museum.

Pyotr Ivanovich Potemkin (1617–1700), *stolnik*
and later *okolnichy* (high-ranking court
official), participated in the war against Poland
in 1654–5, was envoy to Spain and France in
1667–8, and in 1674 was in Vienna on
diplomatic business. From 1680 to 1682, under
the title Viceroy of Uglich, he was on an
ambassadorial mission to Spain, France and
lastly to England, where he stayed from 21
November 1681 to 15 February 1682. It has
been suggested that during his visit Potemkin
visited the theatre and saw Shakespeare's
The Tempest (Alekseyev 1982, p. 66).

According to John Evelyn, writing in his
Diary for 24 November 1681, Evelyn attended
'the audience of Russian Ambassador which
was before both Majesties in the Banqueting-
House: The presents were carried before them
… but nothing so splendid & exotick, as the
Ambassador…. In a word, the Russian
Ambassador still at Court behaved himself like
a Clowne, compar'd to this Civil Heaven'
(Evelyn 1955, IV, pp. 262, 269).

There is no record of any meeting between
Potemkin and Kneller, though in 1698 Kneller
was to paint a portrait of Peter I from the life
(Stewart 1983, p. 123, no. 570). Until 1792
Potemkin's portrait was in the collection of
Prince Grigory Potemkin who was not, despite
the common surname, a relative. The
catalogue of pictures in the Prince's private
apartments in the Winter Palace includes it:
'Le portrait du ci devant ambassadeur à la cour
de la grande Bretagne, le boyard Jean Pierre
Potemkin, en habillement russe; peint du
fameux Kneller a Londres' (Potemkin 1891).

The traditional attribution is confirmed
by two 17th-century engravings that give the
author of the portrait as Kneller. One of these
is a mezzotint attributed to A. Blooteling
(Chaloner Smith 1878–83, I, p. 68; Rovinskii
1886–9, III, col. 1824, no. 1); the second was
engraved by R. White (*ibid.*, no. 3). The
engravings (figs. 137, 138) repeat the
inscription on the back of the canvas, and give
the date 1682 (they also have the additional
text after the word 'Moscovy': 'to his Majesty of
Great Britain'). But it should be noted that the
engravings present a shoulder-length image
rather than the three-quarters-length
depiction of the painting, and at the bottom of
the decorative frame that in White's engraving
surrounds the image is a small cartouche with
Potemkin standing full-length in front of a
valley with low hills in the distance; he holds a
staff in his right hand. All this leads us to
suggest that Kneller may have painted several
versions of the portrait.

The authenticity of the Hermitage portrait
is also confirmed by the high quality of the
painting, with its broad, free manner. Probably
the inscription and signature on the back
(visible before it was relined and copied onto
the backing canvas) are genuine, as the ellision
of the *G* and *K*, and the straight *L* are all
characteristic of Kneller's signature. Graves
(1918–21, II, p. 98) reveals that a sale at Cock's
in London in 1741 included a 'Portrait of
Prince Potemkin', the work of Kneller, from
the collection of the Earl of Oxford.

A copy of the portrait (on the back, in
Russian, is an inscription in ink: 'Pyotr
Ivanovich Potemkin former ambassador in
London in 1682. From the Marble Palace') is
now in the Armoury in the Moscow Kremlin
(inv. no. 2018/1–2). Rovinsky (1886–9, III,
col. 1823) thought this to be the original, and
this assumption was repeated in exhibition
catalogues in 1870 and 1905. The painting is
now thought to be an 18th-century copy.

Potemkin also had his portrait painted by
Juan Carreno de Miranda (1614–85) in Madrid
(Prado, inv. no. 645) during his second
diplomatic trip, when he was received at the
Spanish court. LD

Fig. 138: R. White after Godfrey Kneller,
Peter John Potemkin. Mezzotint,
15 ¼ × 11 in. (38.8 × 28 cm).
The Trustees of the British Museum.

9

John Wootton (*c.* 1682–1764)

HOUNDS AND A MAGPIE, *c.* 1715–20

Oil on canvas, 59¾ × 50⅜ in. 152 × 128 cm
Signed, on the right: *John Wootton pinx*
Inv. no. 9781

Provenance: collection of Sir Robert Walpole, 1st Earl of Orford, Houghton Hall, Norfolk; sold by his grandson George, 3rd Earl of Orford, in 1779; acquired by Catherine II for the Hermitage as part of the Walpole Collection; in the 19th century kept in the Winter Palace, then at Gatchina Palace; returned to the Hermitage in 1958.

Literature: Walpole 1752, p. 38; Kendall 1932–3, XXI, p. 41; English Art 1979, no. 71; Mayer 1984; Dukelskaya and Renne 1990, no. 111.

According to the description that accompanied the engraving made by William Byrne after this painting, these are 'Portraits of favourite hounds, and a magpye which generally attended them at chase' (*A Set of prints after the paintings in the collection of … the Empress of Russia. Lately in the possession of the Earl of Orford. Published by John Boydell*, London, 1788, I, pl. 14). Arline Meyer dates the Hermitage picture to the second half of the 1710s, citing a letter from Humphrey Wanley to Edward Harley of 14 October 1716 in which Wanley mentions that Wootton 'talks of a journey he must soon make into Norfolk in Order to make Pictures for a whole Pack of Hounds there' (Mayer 1984, p. 80).

In the anonymous manuscript catalogue of 1736 of the collection at Houghton Hall (Pierpont Morgan Library, New York) is 'Wooton – 4″ 1 – 4″ 9 Dogs over the Chimney – the Little Breakfast Room', and the dimensions it gives in feet and inches almost perfectly match those of the Hermitage canvas. That Wootton's *Hounds and a Magpie* was hung there seems to be confirmed in the *Aedes Walpolianae* (2nd edn, 1752), in which Horace Walpole noted that Houghton's small breakfast-room has 'Over the Chimney … a very good picture of Hounds by Wootton'. At Houghton were, in fact, several pictures by the artist, and Walpole, as if summing up his work, wrote in his *Anecdotes* that Wootton 'was peculiarly qualified to please in this country – I mean, by painting horses and dogs, which he both drew and coloured with consummate skill, fire and truth' (Walpole 1862, II, p. 706).
LD

Thomas Gainsborough (1727–1788)

A WOMAN IN BLUE, *c.* 1780

Oil on canvas, 29¹⁵⁄₁₆ × 25³⁄₁₆ in. 76 × 64 cm
Inv. no. 3509

Provenance: collection of Aleksey Khitrovo,
St Petersburg; bequeathed to the Hermitage
in 1912.

Exhibitions: 1937–8 Leningrad, no. 213;
1956 Moscow, p. 14; 1972 Leningrad, no. 322;
1975–6 Washington–New York–Detroit–
Los Angeles–Houston, p. 86 (Portrait of a
Woman); 1976 San Francisco; 1976 Mexico,
no. 24; 1976 Winnipeg–Montreal, no. 24;
1983 Moscow.

Literature: Armstrong 1898, p. 198; Armstrong
1900, p. 271; Weiner 1912, pp. 22–3; Conway
1925, p. 168; Krol' 1939, p. 239; Waterhouse
1953, XXXIII, p. 120; Waterhouse 1958, p. 101;
Krol' 1961a, p. 14; English Art 1979, no. 131;
Dukelskaya and Renne 1990, no. 44.

This portrait entered the Hermitage in 1912
from the collection of the famous Petersburg
collector and Master of the Hunt at the
Imperial Court, Aleksei Z. Khitrovo, where it
was listed as a portrait of the Duchess of
Beaufort (Weiner 1912, p. 22). No documentary
evidence for this attribution has been found,
and the portrait has since been called 'The
Lady in Blue': Cat. 1981, p. 241). The name
Beaufort may have arisen because
Gainsborough's wife, Margaret Burr, was an
illegitimate daughter of the Duke of Beaufort.
There is no evidence to suggest, however, that
Gainsborough painted the portraits of any of
the Beaufort family.

A Woman in Blue should be dated to the late
1770s or early 1780s on the basis of stylistic
comparison with works known to have been
painted by Gainsborough in that period:
Mrs W. Villebois (1777; Collection of Viscount
Cowdray), *Mrs Elliot* (1778; Metropolitan
Museum of Art, New York), *Mrs Henry
Beaufoy* (1780; Huntington Art Gallery, San
Marino) and *Mrs Elliot* (1782; Frick Collection,
New York). Ellis Waterhouse (1953, p. 120)
suggested that the portrait may have been
acquired by Khitrovo from Wertheimer in
Paris around 1892.

Painted throughout in cold, silver-grey
tones, *A Woman in Blue* is executed with light,
feathery brushstrokes, and is one of the
Hermitage's finest examples of English
painting. It is perhaps best characterized by
Sir Joshua Reynolds in his fourteenth
Discourse, dedicated to the memory of
Gainsborough: 'However, it is certain, that all
those odd scratches and marks, which, on a
close examination, are so observable in
Gainsborough's pictures, and which even to
experienced painters appear rather the effect of
accident than design; this chaos, this uncouth
and shapeless appearance, by a kind of magick,
at a certain distance assumes form, and all
the parts seem to drop into their proper places;
so that we can hardly refuse acknowledging
the full effect of diligence, under the
appearance of chance and hasty negligence …
Gainsborough himself considered this
peculiarity in his manner and the power it
possesses of exciting surprise, as a beauty in his
works…' (Reynolds, 1975, pp. 257–8). LD

11

Thomas Jones (1742–1803)

LANDSCAPE WITH DIDO AND AENEAS (STORM),
1769

(before restoration)
Oil on canvas, 54⅛ × 76³⁄₁₆ in. 137.5 × 193.5 cm
Signed and dated, bottom right:
Tho: Jones pt 1769
Inv. no. 1343

Provenance: collection of Lord Grosvenor,
England; from 1772 collection of Baronet
Watson ('landscape', sold at auction at
Christie's, 24 June 1772, no. 80); collection
of Catherine II, St Petersburg; collection of
Prince Grigory Potemkin, St Petersburg; from
1792 in the Winter Palace; in 1799 transferred
to Gatchina Palace, from where it was returned
to the Hermitage no later than 1821.

Exhibitions: 1769 London, SA, no. 74;
1956 Moscow, p. 27.

Literature: Fiorillo 1808, V, p. 707; Svin'in 1981,
IV, p. 66; Schnitzler 1828, p. 81; Livret 1838,
p. 206, no. 20; Waagen 1864, p. 279; Faré 1866,
p. 13, no. 1393; Potemkin 1891, p. 43, no. 93;
Jones 1946–8, pp. 19–20; Krol' 1961a, pp. 14–15,
81; Nicolson 1968, I, p. 107; Sunderland 1985,
no. 24; English Art 1979, no. 123; Gowing 1985,
pp. 14–15; Dukelskaya and Renne 1990, no. 49.

In 1769 the Welsh artist Thomas Jones
recorded in his *Memoirs*: 'The large picture
which won the first premium in 1767, still
remained unsold the size of it – 6 feet 4 inches
by four feet 6 inches – being much too
inconvenient for the generality of Purchases.
So I was glad to accept of the proposal of a
picture-dealer, to paint a Companion of the
same size and to take 50 Guineas for the pair –
accordingly in March last I began the Picture
(a Storm) which was now finished, and in
which my friend Mortimer had introduced the
Story of Dido and Aeneas retiring to the Cave
from Virgil – This was one of the best Pictures
I ever painted and attracted much attention.'
(Jones 1951).

This picture was exhibited in 1769 (no. 74)
under the title 'A Land-storm, with the story
of Dido and Aeneas' at the Society of Artists
of Great Britain, of which Jones was an active
member. The figures were the work of John
Hamilton Mortimer (1741–79). The well-
known engraver William Woollett, another
friend of Jones's, immediately began work on
a print after the painting but was soon
interrupted by other business; according to
Jones, the half-worked plate was 'at once
thrown aside, and remained locked up and
forgotten during the remainer of his days'
(Jones 1946–8). This, however, is untrue, for
the exhibition of the Society of Artists for 1773
included no. 408, an engraving by Woollett,
'Landscape with Dido and Aeneas, from the
painting by Mr Jones' (fig. 139).

In February 1787, two years after Woollett's
death, his widow printed a fresh edition from
the plate, which now carried an additional
inscription: 'to her Imperial Majesty Catherine
II Empress of all Russia this print of Dido and
Aeneas from a picture in her valuable
collection is with Her Majesty's permission
most respectfully inscribed by Her Most
Obedient and devoted servant Elisabeth
Woollette.' (Fagan 1885, p. 54, CXVII, 5th
state; Hermitage inv. no. 141164). On the basis
of this inscription we can assume that the
painting was acquired by the Empress between
1785 (the last year of Munich's catalogue of
the collection, in which it does not figure) and
August 1786, when Woollett's widow received
permission to dedicate the print to the
Empress. It was possibly later presented to
Prince Grigory Potemkin and kept in his
personal apartments in the Winter Palace.
After Potemkin's death in 1791, the landscape
was returned once more to Catherine's
collection. Svin'in, who wrote a book on the
sites of St Petersburg, mentioned the picture in
his description of the Hermitage: 'in the
Sneyders gallery ... a storm by the
Englishman Jonson' (Svin'in 1821). LD

Fig. 139: William Woollett after Thomas Jones,
Dido and Aeneas. Engraving, 17 × 21 ⅞ in.
(45.1 × 55.7 cm). Published 1787.
State Hermitage Museum.

Sir Joshua Reynolds (1723–1792)

THE CONTINENCE OF SCIPIO, 1788

Oil on canvas, 94¼ × 65³⁄₁₆ in.
239.5 × 165.6 cm
Inv. no. 1347

Provenance: Acquired by Prince Potemkin from the artist in 1789; entered the Hermitage in 1792.

Exhibitions: 1789 London, RA, no. 165.

Literature: Northcote 1813–15, unpaginated supplement; Waagen 1864, pp. 278–9; Leslie and Taylor 1865, II, p. 538; Faré 1866, pp. 11–12, no. 1392; Potemkin 1891, p. 39, no. 1; Graves and Cronin 1899–1901, III, p. 1139; Armstrong 1900, p. 239; Williamson 1904, pp. 14–15; Trubnikov 1913, pp. 40–41; Hilles 1929, p. 149; Waterhouse 1941, p. 115; Mitchell 1942, p. 103; Krol' 1961a, pp. 10–11; Lisenkov 1964, p. 149; Hilles 1970, p. 271; English Art 1979, no. 124; Dukelskaya and Renne 1990, no. 74; Postle 1995, pp. 225–8.

Reynolds received the commission to produce two pictures, for Catherine II and for Prince Potemkin (1739–91), the latter a favourite and close adviser to the Empress and an important military figure too, through Lord Carysfort, who was in St Petersburg in 1785–6 and attended court on many occasions. In a letter to Reynolds of 8 December 1785, Carysfort informed him that he had been able to examine the collection of paintings in the Hermitage, and during a conversation with the Empress noted with regret the lack of works of the English school. 'I pride myself', wrote Carysfort, 'that it was as a result of this that Her Majesty started to take note of our artists. She entrusted me with the task of commissioning a picture from you, and since it pleases Her Majesty to give your genius complete freedom, she leaves you the choice of a subject. Prince Potemkin, who informed me of this command, at the same time requested that I commission a picture also for him, the choice of the subject for which he, like Her Imp. Majesty, leaves to you' (cited in Trubnikov 1913, in a Russian translation from the French original).

After some indecision, Reynolds painted for the Empress *The Infant Hercules Strangling the Serpents* (fig. 36), an allegory on Russia's growing strength, while for Potemkin he produced *The Continence of Scipio*. Reynolds wrote Potemkin a long letter explaining the reasons for this on 4 August 1789, when he despatched the pictures, adding: 'Le sujet est la continence de Scipion, histoire trop connue pour qu'il soit besoin de la décrire' (Trubnikov 1913; Hilles 1970).

Reynolds's selection of a subject from Livy's *History of Rome* was probably intended as a compliment to the valour and morals of Potemkin, the leader of the Russian army during the 2nd Russo-Turkish War. This choice was also a practical confirmation of the ideas which Reynolds set out in his Fourth Discourse, delivered to the Royal Academy in December 1771: 'With respect to the choice, no subject can be proper that is not generally interesting. It ought to be either some eminent instance of heroick action, or heroick suffering. There must be something either in the action, or in the object, in which men are universally concerned, and which powerfully strikes upon the publick sympathy.' (Reynolds 1975, p. 57).

In Reynolds's notebooks for 1786–8, as in his letters of that period, there is no mention of work on *Scipio*. The artist would seem to have been concentrating all his energies on the picture for Catherine, as he explained to Potemkin in the above-mentioned letter: 'J'avois intention que le tableau destine a Votre Altesse fût de la même grandeur que celui de sa Majesté Impériale; mais je trouvais tant de difficulté et d'embarras à peindre sur une aussi grande toile, que crainte de faire mal, il me fallût renoncer à mon project, et tâcher de racheter à force de soins et d'efforts la nécessité ou je me trouvais de peindre en un moindre espace' (Trubnikov 1913; Hilles 1970). We know of only one sketch for the whole composition, auctioned at Reynolds's studio sale at Greenwood's on 14 April 1796, and then again at Christie's on 17 February 1810.

In 1789 the picture was exhibited at the Royal Academy. Horace Walpole found it 'tame, crowded; Scipio cold', while the *St James's Chronicle* (27 April) reviewer noted that 'the colouring [is] remarkably chaste, equal to the finest works of the Flemish School, rich without being gay, and dark without being heavy. The composition has considerable merit, but appears rather crowded on canvas'. Later that same year the picture was dispatched to St Petersburg aboard the *Friendship*, along with *The Infant Hercules*. Potemkin paid 500 guineas for it. After his death it was acquired from his heirs for the Hermitage. During the first half of the 19th century it was unfortunately kept rolled up in store, and it was only returned to the galleries in the 1860s (Waagen 1864; Williamson 1904). LD

13

Sir Joshua Reynolds (1723–1792)

CUPID UNTYING THE ZONE OF VENUS, 1788

Oil on canvas, 50³⁄₁₆ × 39³⁄₄ in. 127.5 × 101 cm
Inv. no. 1320

Provenance: presented by Lord Carysfort to
Prince Grigorii Potemkin in 1788; entered
the Hermitage in 1792 from the Potemkin
collection, St Petersburg.

Exhibitions: 1956 Moscow, p. 33; 1973
Leningrad, no. 24; 1987 New Delhi, p. 74,
no. 65; 1988 Sydney–Melbourne.

Literature: Northcote 1813–15, unpaginated
supplement; Leslie and Taylor 1865, II, p. 538;
Potemkin 1891, p. 43, no. 106; Graves and
Cronin 1899–1901, III, p. 1212; Armstrong
1900, p. 242; Williamson 1904, p. 9; Benois
[1911], p. 185; Krol' 1939, p. 28; Krol' 1961,
pp. 11, 80; Lisenkov 1964, p. 149; Cormack
1968–70, XLII, p. 149; English Art 1979, nos.
126, 127; Dukelskaya and Renne 1990, no. 72;
Postle 1995, pp. 198–205.

This is an autograph version of Reynolds's
famous picture of 1784, painted for Lord
Carysfort and exhibited in the same year at the
Royal Academy under the title 'Nymph and
Child' (no. 177). Four years later, Reynolds
noted in his account books: 'June 14, 1788 /
Lord Carisfort, for the Nymph, to be sent to
Prince Potemkin / 105.00' (Cormack
1968–70). The copy is almost identical to the
original version, the only significant difference
from the Carysfort picture (now in the Tate) is
the absence of the snake hiding by the nymph's
elbow. Reynolds himself at first suggested
calling the picture 'Half Consenting', but it
later became known as 'A Snake in the Grass',
under which title it was engraved by John
Raphael Smith in 1787 (Frankau 1902, p. 271,
no. 326). The original was favourably reviewed
in the press, and R. Cooper dedicated an
effusive poem to it (Northcote 1813–15, p. 213),
although Horace Walpole noted in his copy
of the exhibition catalogue 'Bad and gross,
Miss Wilson' (Graves 1970, III, p. 275, no. 177).
A Miss Wilson figures in the list of Reynolds's
models for 1784 (Leslie and Taylor 1865, II,
p. 468). Some scholars have suggested that
Lady Hamilton may have been the sitter, for
Reynolds painted her twice, in 1783 and 1784:
Wood Nymph and Faun, and *Lady Hamilton as
a Bacchante*. Some common features are also to
be found with a drawing by Reynolds of Lady
Hamilton (*Apollo*, November 1979, p. 139).

As regards this copy, it is worth noting that it
was painted at the same time as the artist was
finishing his *Infant Hercules Strangling the
Serpents* for Catherine II (exhibited at the
Royal Academy in 1788, no. 167) and another
picture for Potemkin, *The Continence of Scipio*
(see cat. 12). In 1789 both large canvases were
sent to Russia, but how and when Carysfort's
present was delivered to Potemkin is unknown.
Closest of all to the Hermitage version is a
painting in Sir John Soane's Museum, acquired
in 1821 at Christie's, where it was entitled
'A Nymph and Cupidon' (fig. 42).

In Potemkin's collection the picture was
listed as 'Venus assise et joue avec Cupidon, qui
la tire par son habit' (Potemkin 1891), but after
the acquisition by the state of his collection in
1792 (on Catherine's orders), it was catalogued
at the Hermitage under the present title. LD

Benjamin West (1728–1820)

VENUS CONSOLING CUPID STUNG BY A BEE,
(?)1787

Oil on canvas, 30⁵⁄₁₆ × 25³⁄₁₆ in. 77 × 64 cm
Inv. no. 5849

Provenance: collection of the Yusupov princes,
St Petersburg; from 1920 in the Yusupov Palace
Museum, Petrograd; from 1925 in the
Hermitage.

Exhibitions: 1956 Moscow, p. 35.

Literature: Joussoupoff 1839, p. 26, no. 123;
Yusupov 1920, p. 6, no. 60; Krol' 1961a, pp. 11,
12, 80; Lisenkov 1964, pp. 183–4; Erffa and
Staley 1986, p. 233, no. 132; Dukelskaya and
Renne 1990, no. 107.

Between 1797 and 1814, West produced a
number of compositions on the subject, taken
from Anacreon's Ode XL, 'Wounded Cupid'.
The majority of these were exhibited at the
Royal Academy in 1802, 1803, 1814 and 1818.

In their study of the work of Benjamin
West, however, Erffa and Staley consider that
West painted his earliest version of the subject
in 1786, and that this is the picture in the
Hermitage. As evidence they cite the memoirs
(*Sophie in London 1786*, London, 1933) of a
German traveller, Sophie von la Roche, who
visited West's studio in London in 1786 and
saw there 'a very attractive composition from
an ode by Anacreon'. This, she said, was
intended for Catherine II. Even so, this
evidence is not wholly convincing, for the
picture is not included in the Hermitage
catalogue for 1797, or in any of the following
catalogues of the 19th or early 20th centuries.
It only entered the Hermitage in 1925. Before
then it belong to the Yusupov princes in St
Petersburg and was recorded in the 1839
catalogue of their collection: 'West, Benjamin
… Venus consolant l'Amour blessé par une
abeille' (Joussoupoff 1839, no. 123). At the
Arkhangel'skoye Museum Estate (the former
residence of the Yusupovs near Moscow) there
is a copy of West's original by a serf painter. It
is possible that the picture was purchased by
Nikolai Yusupov the elder (1750–1831) during
one of his trips abroad between made 1802 and
1810.

The Hermitage canvas is almost identical in
composition and facial type to another painting
by West of the same subject in the Nelson
–Atkins Museum, Kansas City. There are

minor differences only in the size of the canvas
(³⁄₄ in. in height, 1 ³⁄₈ in. in width), and in some
of the secondary details, such as the upper part
of the dress by Venus' locks of hair, the number
of roses, the quiver and the folds of drapery on
Cupid's arm. The most significant difference,
however, although even this is not particularly
striking, is the more severe, dry and classical
manner of execution.

This suggests that the painting exhibited at
the Royal Academy in 1802 (no. 135: 'Cupid
wounded by a bee in the finger. "Venus thus
replied, and smiled, – Dry the tears – for
shame my child"') was the Hermitage picture,
and not that now in the Nelson–Atkins
Museum (Erffa and Staley 1986, p. 234, no.
133). This latter work would seem to have been
produced using the 'method' of Miss Provis,

a minor artist who declared that she knew the
'secret' of the Venetian painting style, which
lay in the preparation of the canvas, the
mixing of the colours and their combination.
It was perhaps this canvas that Farington
mentioned in his Diary for 17–18 January 1797,
where he describes a visit to West and 'his two
pictures painted agreeable to Provis's process. –
One 'Cupid Stung by a Bee', the other portraits
of His Sons' (Farington 1978–84, III, p. 751).
But at the end of 1797 Miss Provis's 'secret' was
scandalously exposed as a fraud, and as a result
West's picture was not submitted for exhibition
at the Royal Academy either in 1797 or 1798. It
is not possible, however, to prove which of the
two identical canvases by West was shown at
the Royal Academy exhibition in 1802. LD

15

Richard Brompton (*c.* 1734–1783)

CATHERINE II, 1782

Oil on canvas (oval painted in a rectangle),
32¹¹⁄₁₆ × 27³⁄₁₆ in. 83 × 69 cm
Signed and dated by the left shoulder:
R. Brompton pinx 1782
Inv. no. 1318

Provenance: entered the Hermitage in
1918 from the Romanov Gallery of the
Winter Palace.

Exhibitions: 1870 Petersburg, p. 110, no. 392;
1905 Petersburg, issue 4, p. 39, no. 869.

Literature: Rovinsky 1886–9, II, cols 107-16;
IV, col. 627; List of Portraits 1905, p. 248,
no. 100; Cat. 1958, p. 375; Krol' 1969a,
pp. 18–19; Cat. 1981, p. 241; Renne 1987,
pp. 56–62; Malinovskii 1990, I, pp. 92, 110;
Dukelskaya and Renne 1990, no. 10.

Fig. 140: William Dickinson after Vergilius
Eriksen, *Catherine II in a Kokoshnik.*
Mezzotint, 17 ¾ × 12 ⅝ in. (45 × 32 cm).
Published 1773.
The Trustees of the British Museum.

Catherine II (1729–96) reigned from 1762 as
Empress of Russia. Born as Princess Sophie
Auguste Fredericka in Stettin, Pomerania, in
1745 Empress Elizabeth Petrovna selected her
to be the wife of her nephew, the future tsar
Peter III. On her acceptance into the Orthodox
Church, the German Princess Sophie took a
new name, that of Catherine Alexeyevna.
She seized power in 1762, which resulted in
the assassination of her husband, and became
known as Catherine II, later Catherine the
Great.

Brompton painted Catherine at the age of
53. With a small Imperial crown on her head,
she also has an ermine cloak with a large chain
and the star of the Order of St Andrew as well
as the star and ribbon of the Order of St
George, 1st Class.

In his 'Notes on the Fine Arts in Russia',
Jacob von Stahlin (see Malinovskii 1990, I,
p. 92) mentions two portraits of the Empress
by Brompton: 'A very large full-length portrait
of Her Majesty full length with various
allegorical accessories', and 'a charming half-
length portrait' that the artist painted 'for his
close friend, court apothecary M. Grevo'. The
second painting can be identified with the
work in the Hermitage. It would seem to have
been the forerunner to a large allegorical
portrait by Brompton that was left unfinished
at the artist's death. We can gain some idea of
how the large full-length portrait might have
looked from an oil painting in the Catherine
Palace, Pushkin, attributed to an unknown
artist (inv. no. 979–X; ex-Hermitage). Poor
restoration has greatly changed the appearance
of this work, but a comparison with the
Hermitage painting still reveals a strong
similarity, although it is not possible at present
to prove their relationship.

We should note that Brompton's portrait of
Catherine did not become as widely known as,
for instance, those by the Danish artist
Vergilius Eriksen (see fig. 75) or the Swede
Alexander Roslin. It was not engraved, and we
know of only one copy (Museum of Fine Arts,
Tomsk). In 1786, however, William Coxe, who
had visited Russia, published a book (Coxe
1786) containing an engraving with a portrait
of the Russian empress and the inscription:
'Bromton (sic) pinxit A. Toppfer sculpt', but the
engraving differs greatly from Brompton's
original and has more in common with the
portrait by Roslin. It is surprising that this
mistake should have occurred just a few years
after Brompton's death. ER

This work came from the collection of Aleksei Khitrovo as being a portrait of the celebrated dramatist Richard Brinsley Sheridan (1751–1816) by Hoppner. The identity of the sitter has, however, been doubted, as the portraits of Sheridan painted in the 1780s by George Russell, Thomas Gainsborough, George Romney and Joshua Reynolds (fig. 141) are very different. We should also note that the Hermitage portrait and the portrait of Sheridan by Hoppner in the Harland-Peck Collection, England (repr. *The Connoisseur*, May 1903, p. 85) are unlike, as was noticed by Weiner in his essay on the Khitrovo collection (Weiner 1912).

Richard Walker has noted that there is no documentary evidence to suggest that Hoppner at any time undertook a portrait of Sheridan, although 'this does not prevent frequent Hoppner portraits of "unknown men" being named Sheridan' (Walker 1985, I, p. 452). A comparison between the facial features here and those in an authentic portrait of Sheridan by Reynolds dated 1788–9 (exhibited at the Royal Academy in 1789, no 252), which was engraved in 1791 by G. Hall (Clifford *et al.* 1978, no. 161) only reveals that odd features, such as the nose, the eyebrows and the shape of the face, are quite close. On the basis of the costume and wig, the Hermitage sitter can be dated to the late 1780s or early 1790s, when Sheridan was depicted by Reynolds. But Sheridan was then around 40 years old, while the sitter in this picture looks considerably younger. LD

16

John Hoppner (1758–1810)

AN UNIDENTIFIED MAN, CALLED RICHARD
BRINSLEY SHERIDAN, *c.* 1790

Oil on canvas, 30⁵⁄₁₆ × 25³⁄₁₆ in. 77 × 64 cm
(the canvas has been extended, 8 cm to the right and 12 cm at the bottom)
Inv. no. 3510

Provenance: collection of Aleksey Khitrovo; bequeathed to the Hermitage in 1912.

Exhibitions: 1937–8 Leningrad, no. 281; 1956 Moscow, p. 35.

Literature: Weiner 1912, pp. 25–6; McKay and Roberts 1914, p. 47; Krol' 1939, p. 37; Krol' 1961a, pp. 13, 81; Lisenkov 1964, p. 168; English Art 1979, no. 129; Walker 1985; Dukelskaya and Renne 1990, no. 47.

Fig. 141: Sir Joshua Reynolds, *Richard Brinsley Sheridan*. Oil on canvas, 50 × 40 in. (127 × 101.6 cm). Private Collection.

17

Charles White (*d.* 1780)

FLOWERS AND BIRDS, 1772

Oil on canvas. 22⅝ × 37⅝ in. 57.5 × 95.5 cm
Signed and dated on the end of the
window-box: *C.1772 W.*
Inv. no. 3784

Provenance: collection of Nikolai Kushelev-
Bezborodko, St Petersburg; from 1862 in the
Picture Gallery of the Imperial Academy of
Arts, St Petersburg; transferred to the
Hermitage in 1922.

Literature: Kushelev-Bezborodko 1863, no. 104;
Veselovsky 1886, III, no. 75; English Art 1979,
nos. 146–7; Dukelskaya and Renne 1990,
no. 110.

The earliest critical mention of Charles White,
a painter who specialized in flowers and fruits,
dates from 1808 (Fiorillo 1808, V, p. 369), and
the information Fiorillo supplied has been
repeated since (Redgrave 1878, p. 468;
Waterhouse 1981, p. 408). This is the only work
attributed to White (on the basis of the
picture's inscription). In the 1860s it was in the
collection of the Petersburg connoisseur Count
Nikolai Aleksandrovich Kushelev-Bezborodko,
who included it in the 1863 catalogue of his
gallery (Kushelev-Bezborodko 1863, no. 104),
which he beqeathed to the Imperial Academy
of Arts.

Since there are no other works documented
as by White, his authorship of *Flowers and
Birds* remains uncertain. The inscription on
the sheet of paper, the text in the book, and the
various objects all fail to suggest any
recognizeable national characteristics, but the
broad, free manner of painting and the colours
employed are not unlike many examples of
late-18th-century English art, and the species
of birds too were all to be found in Britain. LD

18

Joseph Wright of Derby (1734–1797)

FIREWORK DISPLAY AT THE CASTEL
SANT' ANGELO IN ROME (LA GIRANDOLA),
1774–5

Oil on canvas, 64 × 83⅞ in. 162.5 × 213 cm
Inv. no. 1315

Provenance: acquired from the artist in 1779;
in 1822 in the English Palace at Peterhof;
returned to the Hermitage in 1920.

Exhibitions: 1779 London RA, no. 358;
1956 Moscow, p. 32; 1990 London, Paris and
New York, no. 106.

Literature: Bemrose 1885, pp. 35, 85, 121;
Grundy 1931, p. 13; Nicolson 1958, p. 22; Krol'
1961a, pp. 15, 81; Lisenkov 1964, p. 192;
Nicolson 1968, I, pp. 77, 81, 85, 250, 276,
279–80; II, pl. 213; English Art 1979, no. 136;
Egerton 1990, pp. 175–6, no. 106; Dukelskaya
and Renne 1990, no. 113.

Fig. 142: Joseph Wright of Derby, *The Annual
Girandola, Castel S. Angelo, Rome.* Oil on
canvas, 54 ¼ × 34 ¹⁄₁₆ in. (137.8 × 173 cm).
National Galleries and Museums on
Merseyside, Walker Art Gallery, Liverpool.

In 1774–5, during his stay in Rome, Wright
observed the festive fireworks, known as
girandolas, which were set off from the roof of
the Castel Sant'Angelo. Firework displays were
held in Rome several times a year, for example
during Holy Week and on the eve of the
festival of SS Peter and Paul, and also to
celebrate the election of a new pope. This
grandiose, colourful spectacle, with cascades
of sparks crashing down from the roof of the
castle, lighting up the night sky and the river
Tiber, made a great impression on the artist.
On 4 June 1774, Wright made a sepia and
brown wash drawing, *The Girandola from the
Castel Sant'Angelo* (Derby Museum and Art
Gallery), and there are two other drawings
(both Derby) dating from 1774–5 showing
fireworks, the castle and the bridge from
different points of view.

In the autumn of 1774 the artist set off for
Naples in order to observe the eruption of
Vesuvius. Equally impressed by this second
fiery spectacle, of which he wrote in 1776 that
'the one is the greatest effect of Nature, the
other of Art' (Nicolson 1968, I, p. 279), Wright
executed the companion paintings *La
Girandola* and *Vesuvius in Eruption* to present
the contrasts of theatrical and natural effects
of fire.

The first paired sketches (16¾ × 28 in.)
with the same titles were made by the artist in
Rome towards the end of 1774 (Nicolson 1968,
I, p. 280). Living in Rome in somewhat
constrained financial circumstances, Wright
impatiently awaited an answer from London
about the possibility of selling *Vesuvius* to
Catherine. In a letter to his sister of 4 May
1775, he explained: 'I have staid a month longer
than I intended to have an answer from Mr
Baxter, the Russian Consul, concerning the
picture I have painted of Mount Vesuvius in a
great eruption, tis the grandest effect I ever
painted. If the Empress is to have it, it must be
shipped off from Leghorn to St Petersburg and
I must wait here to see it off' (Bemrose 1885).
Alas, the painting was not sold (now Sanderson
Collection, England; Nicolson 1968, I, p. 280;
II, pl. 166).

Once back in England, Wright returned to
the theme several times between 1775 and
1779. In 1779 he showed *The Girandola, or
Grand Firework Display at the Castel
Sant'Angelo, Rome,* as no. 358 at the Royal
Academy. This formed a pair to a picture
exhibited there a year earlier (no. 357), *An
Eruption of Mount Vesuvius with the Procession
of St Januarius's Head* (now Pushkin Museum
of Fine Arts, Moscow). In a review of the
exhibition of 1779 in the *St James's Chronicle*
(29 April–1 May), the Girandola was singled
out for particular attention: 'This picture must
be seen to have any idea of its Excellence; we
have no Method of describing Mr Wright's Art
of painting Flames, Sparks and the Reflection
of Light by Fire' (Egerton 1990, p. 176).

In 1779 both pictures were acquired from
the artist for Catherine II, and on 31 December
Wright wrote to his friend and patron Daniel
Daulby: 'The Empress of Russia has taken into
Her capital collection my two pictures of
Vesuvius & the Girandola, and given me 500 gs
for them which is a good reward accompanied
with high honour' (Bemrose 1885).

There are two other known versions of the
companion pieces: the above-mentioned
sketches of 1774, *The Girandola* (City Art
Gallery, Birmingham) and *Vesuvius*
(Sanderson Collection), plus the works of
1775–6, which at the end of the 18th century
were in the collection of John Milnes of
Wakefield, England (present location
unknown; Nicolson 1968, I, pp. 159, 279).
Wright also painted two separate Girandolas
(Walker Art Gallery, Liverpool; ex-collection of
D. Daulby, present whereabouts unknown). LD

19

Joseph Wright of Derby (1734–1797)

THE IRON FORGE VIEWED FROM WITHOUT,
1773

Oil on canvas, 41⅜ × 55⅛ in. 105 × 140 cm
Signed and dated bottom right, on the
hammer: *J Wright Pinxt: 1773*
Inv. no. 1349

Provenance: acquired from the artist in 1774;
in the 19th century housed in different parts
of the Winter Palace before its return to the
Hermitage.

Exhibitions: 1773 London, SA, no. 371; 1956
Moscow, p. 32; 1990 London, no. 40; 1990 Paris,
no. 40; 1990 New York.

Literature: Georgi 1794, II, p. 481; Bemrose
1885, pp. 30, 116, 122; Benois 1921, pp. 40–41;
Conway 1925, p. 38; Gatty 1939, p. 82; Buckley
1952, p. 164; Nicolson 1954, p. 76; Nicolson 1958,
pp. 20–21; Krol' 1961a, pp. 15, 81; Lisenkov 1964,
p. 192; Nicolson 1968, I, pp. 50, 55, 107, 121, 237;
II, pl. 104; Klingender 1968, pp. 60, 61, 206;
Watson 1970, p. 14, no. 3; English Art 1979, nos.
137–8; Dukelskaya and Renne 1990, no. 112;
Egerton 1990, pp. 103–04, no. 50.

This is one of five pictures on the theme of the
iron forge painted by Wright between 1771 and
1773. He set out his ideas in his account book:
'Two men forming a bar into a horse shoe,
whence the light must proceed. An idle fellow
might stand by the anvil in a time-killing
posture, his hands in his bosom, or yawning
with his hands stretched upwards, & a little
twisting of the body. Horse shoes hanging
upon ye walls, and other necessary things
faintly seen, being remote from the light.
Out of the room shall be seen another, in wch.
a farrier may be shoeing a horse by the light
of a candle. The horse must be saddled, and a
traveller standing by. A servant may appear
with his horse in his hand, on wch. may be a
portmanteau. This may be an indication of an
accident having happened, and show some
reason for shoeing the horse by candlelight.

The moon may appear, and illumine some part of the horses, if necessary' (Bemrose 1885, p. 116)

This version, painted in 1773, brings the cycle to an end. It is closest of all to the work of 1772 formerly in the collection of Lord Romsey at Broadlands, and now in the Tate: both canvases have a similar interior and identical tools and equipment, based on a precise documentary pen drawing made in 1772 (Derby Museum and Art Gallery). Egerton suggests that in both works the model for the young woman with a child was the etching 'Woman Carrying a Child' from Salvator Rosa's *Figurine* series (Egerton 1990, p. 104, fig. 18).

The most significant difference between this work and the others is the introduction of a night landscape and the depiction of the scene from outside the forge. We know of no independent landscape compositions by Wright before 1774. It was around 1773, on the eve of his departure for Italy, that the artist painted a number of works, including the *Iron Forge*, into which he introduced enigmatic and emotionally charged landscapes: *The Hermit Studying Anatomy*, *The Old Man and Death*, *An Earth-stopper on the Banks of the Derwent*. It is possible that Wright used the same landscape motif both for the Hermitage's *Iron Forge* and the *Earth-stopper* of the same year (Derby Museum and Art Gallery).

The Hermitage's *Iron Forge* was exhibited at the Society of Artists in London in 1773. 'Very good', Horace Walpole scribbled in the margin of his copy of the catalogue. The picture was soon sold to Catherine II, for on 12 February 1774 Wright wrote to his brother from Rome: 'Nancy [their sister] tells me she has heard the Empress of Russia has taken ye

picture of the Iron Forge' (Bemrose 1885). In Wright's accounts, cited by Bemrose (1885), we find: 'Picture of an iron forge viewed from without – Empress of Russia 136'. It was perhaps because the picture left England so soon after it was painted that it was not engraved. All the other versions were engraved in mezzotint by Richard Earlom and William Pether (fig. 143).

The *Iron Forge* was the first of three works by Wright to be acquired for the Hermitage (see cat. 18), and it attracted attention even in the 1790s: 'Three pictures, and among them the best showing a forge during the dark of night', Georgi commented in his well-known description of St Petersburg (Georgi 1794). In our own century the Russian art critic, historian and artist Alexandre Benois has written that 'This picture serves as a marvellous piece of evidence of Wright's technical perfection. To this day it enraptures with the grace of its contrasts, the depth of the dark areas and the soft force of the lighting …. Wright's picture presents us with a piece of life just as it was presented directly to the author, and in this … is perhaps its greatest virtue, its elusive charm, that which ensures that it ever remains of true artistic value' (Benois 1921). LD

Fig. 143: Joseph Wright of Derby, *An Iron Forge*, 1772. Oil on canvas, 47 × 52 in. (119 × 132 cm). Tate Gallery, London.

Fig. 144: Joseph Wright of Derby, *The Blacksmith's Shop*, 1771. Oil on canvas, 50 ½ × 41 in. (128.3 × 104 cm). Yale Center for British Art, Paul Mellon Collection.

Fig. 145: William Pether after Joseph Wright of Derby, *A Farrier's Shop*. Mezzotint, 19 ¾ × 13 ¾ in. (50 × 35 cm). Yale Center for British Art, Paul Mellon Collection.

20

Sir Thomas Lawrence (1769–1830)

COUNT SEMYON VORONTSOV, *c.* 1806

Oil on canvas, 30⅛ × 25³⁄₁₆ in. 76.5 × 64 cm
Inv. no. 1363

Provenance: collection of Mikhail Semyonovich Vorontsov; acquired by Nicholas II from his heirs, M. V. Vorontsova and N. A. Stolypin, and given to the Hermitage in 1900.

Exhibitions: 1956 Moscow, p. 34 (as by Romney); 1967 London, no. 59.

Literature: Williamson 1904, no. 33; Russian Portraits 1905–9, II, p. 42; Shmidt 1908, p. 355; Benois [1911], p. 187; Weiner 1923, p. 316; Krol' 1939, pp. 33, 46; Garlick 1954, pp. 64, 71; Garlick 1962–4, pp. 204, 271; Pembroke 1968, p. 24, no. 40; English Art 1979, no. 296; Garlick 1989, p. 288, no. 846; Dukelskaya and Renne 1990, no. 53.

Count Semyon Romanovich Vorontsov (1744–1832) served as Russia's ambassador to Great Britain in 1785–96 and again in 1801–6. After his retirement he did not return to Russia but spent the rest of his life in England – at Richmond and Southampton, where he was made an honorary citizen. Combining a great love for his native land with an admiration of the British way of life and system of government, he did all he could to encourage good relations between the two countries. One of his greatest achievements was the revival in 1793 of a trading agreement between them. At the time of his retirement he was a Knight of all the Russian orders, but in Lawrence's portrait he is seen only with the star and ribbon of the most significant of these, the Order of St Andrew.

In addition to the superbly executed Hermitage portrait there are two similar depictions of Vorontsov, one in the Pembroke collection at Wilton House, Wiltshire (Pembroke 1968), the other formerly in the collection of the late Sir Michael Duff, Bt, at Vaenol (Garlick 1989). The portrait in the Pembroke collection, which Garlick considers to be the original, was bequeathed by Vorontsov to his daughter Catherine (who in 1808 married George Augustus, 11th Earl of Pembroke). The Hermitage portrait belonged to the Count's son, Mikhail (see cat. 21), from whose heirs it was acquired by Nicholas II for the Hermitage. It is possible that all three portraits of Vorontsov were commissioned at the same time, between 1805 and 1807, which probably explains the remarkably high price for a single shoulder-length portrait of 220 pounds sterling and 10 shillings, mentioned in a list of Lawrence's works of 14 February 1806 with the name of Count Vorontsov in the column 'for whom painted' (Garlick 1954). Nevertheless, Garlick (1989) considers that the price here merely indicates that Vorontsov ordered a full-length portrait from Lawrence.

At the end of the 19th century the painting belonged to the heirs of Mikhail Vorontsov and was considered by them to be the work of George Romney. It was with this attribution that it entered the Hermitage and was listed in several catalogues (1900–07, 1958), as well as contemporary exhibitions (1956 Moscow). The misattribution has persisted in more recent publications (Cross 1977, 1992) despite the fact that Shmidt (1908), Benois (1911), Weiner (1923) and Garlick (1954) were convinced that it was the work of Lawrence.

A miniature copy of this portrait by an unknown English artist is in the collection of Giorgio Mylius in Italy (G. Cagnola: 'La mostra di miniature ventaglio a Milana', *Rassegna d'Arte*, no. 5, May 1908, p. 87). There is also an anonymous lithograph, undated and with the image reversed (Krol' 1969). ER

21

Sir Thomas Lawrence (1769–1830)

COUNT MIKHAIL VORONTSOV, 1821

Oil on canvas, 56¼ × 44½ in. 143 × 113 cm
Inv. no. 5846

Provenance: collection of Prince Mikhail
Semyonovich Vorontsov, then the Vorontsov-
Dashkov family collection; entered the
Hermitage via the State Museum Fund
in 1923.

Exhibitions: 1822 London, RA, no. 35; 1905
Petersburg, issue 4, p. 71, no. 1043; 1937–8
Leningrad, issue 4, no. 236; 1956 Moscow, p. 30;
1972 Leningrad, p. 77, no. 352; 1987
Leningrad; 1987 New Delhi, p. 79, no. 70.

Literature: Archive of Prince Vorontsov 1891,
p. 72; Gower 1900, p. 169; List of Portraits 1904,
pp. 104, no. 5; Russian Portraits 1905–9, II,
no. 44; Armstrong 1913, p. 172; Krol' 1939,
pp. 43, 46; Krol' 1940, p. 165; Garlick 1954,
p. 64; Krol' 1961a, pp. 21, 22, 83; Garlick
1962–4, p. 204; Pembroke 1968, pp. 21–2,
no. 30, pl. 137; English Art 1979, no. 296;
Garlick 1989, p. 288, no. 847; Dukelskaya and
Renne 1990, no. 55.

Count (from 1853 Prince) Mikhail
Semyonovich Vorontsov (1782–1856), a leading
military figure and statesman, was Governor-
General of Novorossiysk region and
Plenipotentiary Viceroy of Bessarabia from
1823, Viceroy of the Caucasus from 1844, and a
Field-Marshal General from 1856. He spent
his childhood and youth in England, where his
father Count Semyon Vorontsov (see cat. 20)
lived for over 40 years. After his education in
England, in 1801 the young Vorontsov returned
to Russia to enter state service. From 1802 he
took part in the Russo–Turkish and
Russo–French wars, and in 1812 he was a
divisional commander in Bagration's army, and
was wounded at the Battle of Borodino. From

1815 to 1818 he commanded the Occupation
Corps in France, where he met Countess
Yelizaveta Branitskaya (see cat. 22), whom he
married in Paris on 20 April 1819. After a spell
in France the couple set off for England to visit
Vorontsov's father and his sister, Lady
Pembroke. It was then that Lawrence, the most
fashionable painter of the time, was
commissioned to paint the Hermitage portrait.

Mikhail Vorontsov is shown wearing the
uniform of a general, with the *aiguillette* of an
adjutant-general (in 1812 he was adjutant to
Alexander I), and the stars of three Russian
orders: St Alexander Nevsky, St Vladimir 1st
Class, St George 2nd Class, plus the silver
medal For the Patriotic War and a gold

Bazardjik Cross. Lawrence's portrait, in which Vorontsov is presented as a romantic, victorious hero, can be dated to July–October 1821, since we have a record in the Vorontsovs's expenses of a payment to the artist of 420 pounds sterling (Krol' 1940, p. 165), as well as a note made by Vorontsov in his diary: 'nous passames quinze jours à Londres, et c'est dans ce temps que Lorents finit mon portrait' (Archive of Prince Vorontsov 1891).

In 1822 Lawrence exhibited the picture at the Royal Academy in London, and in the following year it was engraved by Samuel William Reynolds. Before it was sent to Russia, Frank Howard made a copy for Catherine Pembroke, Mikhail Vorontsov's sister, which is now at Wilton House, Wiltshire (Pembroke 1968). Another copy was made in 1848 by Louise Descemet (Alupka Palace Museum, Crimea, inv. no. 414).

In 1823 Mikhail Vorontsov returned to Russia, and with his natural energy and experience set out to fulfil his duties as Governor-General of Novorossiysk region and Plenipotentiary Viceroy of Bessarabia. His skilful administration helped the region to flourish, not least the development of trade in the south of Russia and to the start of steam-navigation on the Black Sea. On a picturesque site on the coast, at Alupka in the Crimea, he had a house built and the grounds landscaped to designs by Edward Blore, the favourite architect of Sir Walter Scott; the estate was a match for any of the greatest English estates in its grandeur. For some time the portrait may have hung in the palace at Alupka and also in the Vorontsov Palace in Odessa, which was virtually the southern capital of Russia during Vorontsov's administration of the Novorossiysk Region. Most probably it was later, after the Prince's death, that the portrait was moved to one of the family's Petersburg residences. ER

22

George Hayter (1792–1871)

COUNTESS YELIZAVETA VORONTSOVA, 1832

Oil on canvas, 50 × 40³⁄₁₆ in. 127 × 102 cm
Signed and dated bottom left: *George Hayter. pinxit. London 1832*
Inv. no. 5856

Provenance: collection of the Vorontsov-Dashkov family St Petersburg/Petrograd; entered the Hermitage in 1920.

Exhibitions: 1905 Petersburg, issue 4, p. 32, no. 1274 (with an incorrect attribution to Reutern); 1956 Moscow, p. 35; 1987 Leningrad.

Literature: List of Portraits 1904, p. 104, no. 9; Russian Portraits 1905–9, II, p. 171 (with an incorrect attribution to Reutern); Krol' 1939, p. 47; Dukelskaya and Renne 1990, no. 46.

Yelizaveta Ksaver'yevna Vorontsova (1792–1880), Countess Branitskaya, the heiress to a vast fortune, was from 1819 wife of Count Mikhail Vorontsov (see cat. 21). She was an extremely attractive and charming woman, and drew the attention of the most famous, educated and witty men of her time, including the great Russian poet Alexander Pushkin, several of whose most famous poems are dedicated to her. A contemporary wrote that 'during her first trip abroad she married Vorontsov and immediately all the pleasures of life were at once hers and surrounded her. She was already over 30 yet she had every right to seem the youngest of all …. With her innate Polish frivolity and coquetry she wished to please, and no one could do that better than she …. She was young at heart, and young in appearance. She had not that which is called beauty: but her quick, tender glance from her pretty small eyes pierced one through; the smile of her mouth, the like of which I have never seen, seemed to call out for kisses…' (Vigel' 1892, pp. 84–5). During Vorontsov's time as Viceroy of the Caucasus, the Countess threw herself into charitable work and patronized various educational projects.

This portrait was made in 1832 during one of the trips to England made by the Vorontsovs, probably in connection with the decline of the Count's father, Semyon Vorontsov, who died in that year (see cat. 20). Not long before this Hayter had returned from Paris, where he had been successful as a painter of portraits of the nobility, and his works there included one of a good friend of Yelizaveta Vorontsova's, Sofia Stanislavovna Kiselyova, Countess Pototskaya (Hermitage inv. no. 4929). It was she, perhaps, who had recommended him.

There are two known replicas of this portrait, both by unidentified 19th-century artists. One is in the Alupka Palace Museum, Crimea, the other in the Pushkin Museum of Fine Arts, Moscow. ER

23

George Dawe (1781–1829)

ADMIRAL ALEXANDER SHISHKOV, before 1828

Oil on canvas (unfinished), 40½ × 30¾ in.
103 × 78 cm
Inv. no. 5842

Provenance: acquired in 1831 by D. I. Tolstoy
at the sale of the artist's studio in London;
entered the Hermitage in 1923 through the
State Museums Fund.

Exhibitions: 1902 Petersburg, pp. 40, 41, 48,
no. 240; 1956 Moscow, p. 28; 1972 Leningrad,
p. 73, no. 337;
1987 Sapporo–Fukuoka–Hiroshima, p. 31.

Literature: World of Art 1902, July, p. 200
(reproduced with the incorrect caption: 'N. S.
Mordvinov'); List of Portraits 1905, p. 510,
no. 15; Dukelskaya and Renne 1990, no. 31.

Fig. 146: George Dawe, *Admiral Alexander
Shishkov.* Black, white and red chalk on paper,
16 ¾ × 11 ⅞ in. (42.5 × 30.2 cm).
The Trustees of the British Museum.

Admiral Alexander Semyonovich Shishkov
(1754–1841) was a well-known public figure
and an able linguist. He had visited Britain in
1776 when a young naval officer, and in 1795
published a Naval Dictionary in three
languages – English, Russian and French. His
best-known publication was *Rassuzhdeniye o
starom i novom sloge rossiyskogo yazyka*
[Discourse on the Old and New Style of the
Russian Language] of 1803. From 1810 he was
head of the Conversation for Lovers of the
Russian Language society, which was a central
focus for literary figures who supported the
continuation of somewhat outmoded literary
forms. During the military campaigns of
1812–14, Shishkov was constantly in the suite of
the Emperor Alexander I and poured forth
manifestos, orders for the army and addresses
to the people that, according to his
contemporaries, contributed much to raising
morale in Russia. In his views and opinions
Shishkov was a conservative, and his activities
as Minister of Education (1824–8) were
characterized by himself as a battle with the
'spirit of the times', meaning the general trend
towards 'self-will and insubordination'.

Dawe's portrait of Shishkov shows the
Admiral in full uniform, with the stars of the
orders of Alexander Nevsky and St Vladimir
2nd Class, and the silver and bronze medals
awarded for the Patriotic War. But in addition
to carrying out Alexander I's grandiose plan to
paint all the Russian generals for the gallery in
the Winter Palace, Dawe also found time
during his stay in Russia (1819–29) to produce
an enormous number of portraits of the
Russian aristocracy, from members of the
Imperial family, leading statesmen and
military leaders to famous beauties. These
portraits were often large, full-length works
that amazed contemporaries with their acute
likeness, vivid characterization, daring
brushwork and fine drawing. One such is this
portrait of Admiral Shishkov, which is of
particular interest because Dawe never
completed it, hence it enables us to follow the
artists's creative processes. In the British
Museum is Dawe's drawing of the head for the
portrait (fig. 146).

This portrait was painted no later than 1827,
as this is the date of an engraving from it by
Dawe's brother-in-law, Thomas Wright
(1782–1849). By this time Shishkov was
playing a less central role in Russian public life
than hitherto, although he remained a
member of the State Council (from 1814) and
was President of the Russian Academy of
Sciences (from 1816) until his death. ER

24

George Dawe (1781–1829)

GENERAL PYOTR BAGRATION, early 1820s

Oil on canvas, 27⁹⁄₁₆ × 24⁵⁄₈ in. 70 × 62.5 cm
Inv. no. 7818

Provenance: entered the Gallery of 1812 of the
Winter Palace from the artist's workshop no
later than 1825.

Exhibitions: 1905 Petersburg, issue 4, p. 79,
no. 1080.

Literature: List of Portraits 1905, p. 241, no. 26;
Military Gallery 1912, p. 14, no. 11; Cat. 1958,
p. 395; Glinka and Pomarnatsky 1981,
pp. 77–82; Dukelskaya and Renne 1990,
no. 124.

George Dawe arrived in Russia in 1819 at the
invitation of tsar Alexander I, who wished to
create in the Winter Palace a unique
monument to the Russian army's victory in the
war against Napoleon. The gallery, designed by
Carlo Rossi, was constructed within the palace
in the second half of 1826 and hung with 336
portraits, of which 329 were shoulder-length
depictions of the generals who took part in the
War of 1812 and the foreign campaigns of
1813–14 (fig. 17). The portraits were produced
between 1819 and 1829 by Dawe and his
assistants, Wilhelm Golike and Alexander
Polyakov. The portrait of Bagration is among
the best in the gallery.

The fame of Prince Pyotr Ivanovich
Bagration (1765–1812), a descendant of
Georgia's ruling class, spread far beyond
Russia's borders: his name was known in
Britain as early as the time of the Italian and
Swiss campaigns of Count Alexander Suvorov
(1799). Bagration's boundless daring, cool head
and determination to win were his most
outstanding characteristics. It was thus, at the
height of battle, leading his soldiers, that he
was painted in 1804 by the Robert Ker Porter.
This portrait by Dawe, engraved in 1805 by
Giovanni Vendriamini, contributed to the
popularity of Russian subject-matter in
Britain, an interest that grew in proportion to
Russia's victories over Napoleon. After the
Battle of Borodino (1812) near Moscow, which
determined the outcome of the war against
Napoleon and in many ways fixed the fate of
the Napoleon himself, John Boydell published
in London a series of engraved portraits of
Russian generals and officers. Dawe
undoubtedly saw this series. Many of the
engravings designed by L. Saint-Aubin,
F. Ferrier and P. Rossi are very similar to the
portraits made for the gallery in the Winter
Palace, which were in the main painted from
the life. Dawe sometimes simply used a
successful compositional device employed by
one of his predecessors, an effective viewpoint
or turn of the head. At times, as in the case of
the portrait of Bagration, when Dawe was
unable to paint from the life (Bagration died
from wounds received at the Battle of
Borodino), he took the engraving as the basis
for his work. It is possible that he also made use
of Saint-Aubin's pencil portrait (Hermitage,
inv. no. 6143), from which the engraving had
been made. In turn, Saint-Aubin's drawing
relates to an earlier portrait of Bagration by
Salvatore Tonci (location unknown; engraved
in 1805 by Joseph Saunders; fig. 147). Despite
the fact that Dawe relied for his work on other
portraits, he managed to introduce his own
interpretation and understanding of
Bagration's personality.

The portrait was painted no later than 1823,
as the engraving of it by the artist's brother,
Henry Dawe (1790–1848), dates to that year. ER

Fig. 147: Joseph Saunders after Salvatore Tonci,
General Pyotr Bagration. Engraving.
State Hermitage Museum.

25

William Allan (1782–1850)

BASHKIRS, 1814

(before restoration)
Oil on canvas, 16¹⁵⁄₁₆ × 24¹³⁄₁₆ in. 43 × 63 cm
Signed and dated bottom right, on the stone:
William Allan Pinxit 1814
Inv. no. 9579 (companion to cat. 26)

Provenance: acquired in 1816 from the artist by
Grand-Duke Nicholas Pavlovich, and kept in
the Anichkov Palace, St Petersburg; entered
the Hermitage in 1918.

Exhibitions: 1815 London, no. 147.

Literature: Scots Magazine, LXXIX, 1817, p. 75;
Nicholson 1818, no. 5; *Edinburgh Evening
Courant*, 5 April 1845; Allan 1849, I, p. 108;
Cat. 1958, p. 391; Krol' 1961b, pp. 389–93;
Krol' 1969, p. 13; Allan 1974, p. 89; Irwin 1975,
p. 208; Cat. 1981, p. 248; English Art 1979,
no. 303; Dukelskaya and Renne 1990, no. 1;
Bivar 1994, p. 293.

Following his return to Edinburgh in 1814 after
nine years in Russia, Allan painted several
pictures depicting the life of Circassians,
Bashkirs, Tartars and Cossacks. He had
travelled widely in the Ukraine, the Caucasus,
along the banks of the Caspian Sea and the
Don and Kuban rivers, studying the life,
national characteristics, costume and customs
of the exotic peoples who inhabited the fringes
of the Russia's empire. Notes on his
observations and sketches from nature, as well
as the rich and varied collection of costumes,
weapons and everyday objects that Allan put
together during his travels, all assisted him on
his return to Scotland in the detailed recreation
of the external appearance and culture of the
little-known, but romantically perceived,
peoples he had encountered.

The Bashkirs are accurately presented in
this work, just as they looked in the early years
of the 19th century; the costumes and weapons
of the horsemen have been reproduced with
great fidelity.

Krol' (1969) identified the picture with that
shown in 1815 at the Royal Academy in London
(no. 147) under the title *Basquiers Conducting
Convicts*. On 16 December 1816 Grand-Duke
Nicholas Pavlovich (who became Emperor
Nicholas I in 1825) visited Allan's studio
during a trip to Edinburgh. The reporter for
the *Scots Magazine* (1817) described the scene:

*While in the Parliament Square, the Grand-
Duke visited the apartments of Mr William
Allan, and conversed for a considerable time in
French and Russ with that artist. He inspected
every painting minutely, and expressed his
surprise and pleasure at the correctness with
which the costume of the various tribes of
Circassians, Cossacks etc were preserved and
exhibited. Having examined Mr. Allan's
collection of the army and costumes of the
different nations inhabiting the Russian empire,
he complimented the artist on the laborious
diligence displayed in collecting such a mass of
useful materials for delineating correctly the
manners, customs, and appearance of his
countrymen. On Allan's producing the sketches
from which his pictures were composed, Prince
Nicholas displayed no small degree of taste and
discrimination in the selection of a few. He
expressed his wish that if ever Allan revisited
Russia, he would wait upon him.*

Nicholas Pavlovich's acquisition of this
particular picture is confirmed by William
Nicholson: '*Bashkirs conducting Convicts to
Siberia* was a picture which united picturesque
effect and skilful execution, the most felicitous
conception of character and expression.
This picture, along with two others equally
interesting, was purchased by the Grand-Duke
Nicholas, brother of the Emperor of Russia,
during his visit to Edinburgh' (Nicholson
1818).

All three pictures – *Bashkirs, Frontier
Guards* (see cat. 26) and *Haslan Gheray
Conducting Alkazia across the Kuban*
(transferred in 1930 from the Hermitage to the
Museum in Makhachkala, Daghestan) – were
kept in the 19th century in Nicholas I's study in
the Anichkov Palace, St Petersburg. In earlier
descriptions of the Palace, *Bashkirs Conducting
Convicts to Siberia* is called *Two Bashkirs
Talking with Three Villagers*, thus depriving it
of political content in an attempt to evade
complex questions concerning nationalism and
the treatment of minorities within the Russian
empire. ER

26

William Allan (1782–1850)

FRONTIER GUARDS, (?)1814

(before restoration)
Oil on canvas, 16⁵⁄₁₆ × 24¹³⁄₁₆ in. 43 × 63 cm
Inv. no. 6881 (companion to cat. 25)

Provenance: acquired in 1816 from the artist by
Grand-Duke Nicholas Pavlovich, and kept in
the Anichkov Palace, St Petersburg; entered
the Hermitage in 1918.

Literature: Scots Magazine, LXXIX, 1817, p. 75;
Nicholson 1818, no. 5; *Edinburgh Evening
Courant,* 5 April 1845; Allan 1849, I, p. 108;
Cat. 1958, p. 391; Krol' 1961, pp. 389–93;
Krol' 1969, p. 13; Allan 1974, p. 89; Irwin 1975,
p. 208; Cat. 1981, p. 248; English Art 1979,
no. 303; Dukelskaya and Renne 1990, no. 2;
Bivar 1994, p. 293.

In contrast to his approach in the companion
picture, *Bashkirs* (cat. 25), here Allan presents
a freer treatment of the faces, costumes,
weapons of his characters, amalgamating
various features of both the Central Asian
peoples and the Turks in such a way that no
one particular people can be identified, except
for the the Circassian on his white horse.
Although this work is undated it may well
have been painted at the same time as its
companion, which is signed and dated 1814.

Allan's works on subjects taken from his
journey in the southern regions of Russia are
often thought to be somewhat unoriginal in
composition. That of *Frontier Guards* relates to
the traditional scheme of the Adoration of the
Magi, and the young man with his hands tied
behind his back recalls Isaac in works on the
theme of Abraham's sacrifice (Irwin 1975).
But to the contemporary viewer, Allan was far
more important for the interesting content of
his art. The narrative and exotic subjects were
greatly admired by Sir Walter Scott, whose
son-in-law, John Gibson Lockhart, fully in
agreement with Scott's opinion, noted in his
correspondence (1977 edn, Letter XLVII,
p. 117): *For many years I have received no such
feast as was now afforded me; it was a feast of
pure delight – above all, it was a feast of perfect
novelty, for the scenes in which Mr Allan has
lived have rendered the subjects of his paintings
totally different, for the most part, from those of
any other artist, dead or alive; and the manner in
which he treats his subjects is scarcely less
original and peculiar. The most striking of his
pieces are all representations of human beings,
living and moving under the influence of
manners whereof we know little, but which the
little we do know of them has tended to render
eminently interesting to our imaginations.
His pencil transports us at once into the heart of
the East.* ER

27

Sir Peter Lely (1618–1680)

A KNIGHT OF THE ORDER OF THE GARTER,
mid-1660s

Black and white chalks on grey paper,
26 × 13⁵⁄₁₆ in. 66 × 33.5 cm
In the lower-left corner, the collector's mark
of the Hermitage (L.2061)
Inv. no. 5926

Provenance: collection of Count Karl Cobenzl,
Brussels (L.2858 b); entered the Hermitage in
1768.

Exhibitions: 1926 Leningrad, no. 106; 1963
Stockholm, no. 70; 1968 Leningrad–Moscow,
no. 35; 1970 Budapest, no. 64; 1975 Berlin, no.
75; 1975 Copenhagen–Aarhus, no. 43.

Literature: Lugt 1931, p. 147; Dobroklonsky
1955, p. 72, no. 273, ill. 40; Millar 1978–9, p. 84,
no. 104; English Art 1979, no. 39; Western
European Drawing 1981, no. 222.

While in the collection of Count Cobenzl and
then, for many years, in the Hermitage, this
drawing was attributed to Van Dyck and bore
the traditional title 'Portrait of the King of
England'. That it is actually by Lely and
relates to the series of figures from the
procession of Knights of the Order of the
Garter (see cat. 28) was established by Mikhail
Dobroklonsky (1926 Leningrad, no. 106).
This drawing is undoubtedly one of the best
in the series, and depicts a Knight in the full
vestments of the Order. The subject has been
identified as Charles Stuart, 3rd Duke of
Richmond and Lennox, who was raised to the
Order in 1661 (Millar 1978–9, no. 104, though
here Millar mistakenly describes him as the
4th Duke).

The Duke of Richmond was an influential
figure at the court of Charles II. Born in 1639,
he suffered persecution during the
Interregnum (his property was confiscated and
he himself was forced into exile in France),
and on his return to England he gained a
reputation as an uncompromising opponent of
all Cromwell's former associates and as an avid
seeker of profitable posts and royal gifts. He
incurred the King's wrath on several occasions
(not least in 1667 by marrying Charles's
mistress, Frances Teresa Stuart), but was
always able to win back his good favour.
The King apparently had a high opinion of
Richmond's diplomatic talents, for in 1671 he

sent him to Denmark on the delicate but important mission of winning over the Danes to an alliance in the war against Holland. The journey was, however, a fateful one for the Duke, who died suddenly at Elsinore in 1672 at the age of 33.

This drawing stands slightly apart from the others in the series. It is considerably larger and is the only one on light-grey rather than grey-blue paper. It is hard to say if this was mere chance or whether it is evidence of particular circumstances surrounding its production. It is quite possible that the Duke of Richmond did not take part in the procession of which Lely was an observer and the depiction of him in the vestments of the Order was added to the cycle later. This theory could serve to give a more precise date to the series, as in March and April of 1665 Richmond was briefly out of favour, even spending several weeks in the Tower of London. AL

28

Sir Peter Lely (1618–1680)

TWO CANONS FROM A PROCESSION OF KNIGHTS OF THE ORDER OF THE GARTER, mid-1660s

Black and white chalks on grey-blue paper, 19⁵⁄₁₆ × 14³⁄₁₆ in. 49 × 36 cm
Inscribed bottom right in lead pencil, in a later hand: *Arme Ridders*; bottom left, the stamp of the Imperial Academy of Arts, St Petersburg [Lugt 2699a] Inv. no. 14712

Provenance: from the middle of the 18th century in the Library of the Academy of Arts, St Petersburg; transferred to the Hermitage in 1924.

Exhibitions: 1926 Leningrad, no. 107; 1986 Montevideo–Buenos Aires, no. 91; 1986 Bogota, no. 13; 1987–8 Belgrade–Ljubljana–Zagreb, no. 112.

Literature: Dobroklonsky 1955, p. 73, no. 274, ill. 42; Millar 1978–9, p. 83, no. 98; English Art 1979, no. 40.

This and the following sheet are part of a series of studies of figures from a procession of Knights of the Order of the Garter. Currently we know of around 30 such drawings, sixteen in the British Museum, the rest scattered in various collections in Europe and America. Together they form a set of unique artistic significance, not simply as part of Lely's *oeuvre*, but also for their place in the history of English Baroque drawing.

The circumstances surrounding the creation of this famous series are still not entirely clear. The annual ceremonial procession of Knights of the Garter took place in the main courtyard of the Palace of Whitehall or in the courtyard of Windsor Castle on St George's Day, 23 April. This tradition, interrupted by the Civil Wars and Interregnum, was revived with even greater pomp after the Restoration in 1660. We do not know the year of the procession depicted here, but the biographies of several of the figures who have been identified allow us to place it between 1663 and 1671 (Croft-Murray and Hulton 1960, p. 410).

All the drawings in the series employ the same technique and are close in format. They depict the participants in the procession parading from right to left, singly or in pairs. The vivacity and variety of the poses suggest that Lely was using sketches made during the event itself, although the drawings must have acquired their finished state as the result of careful working up in the studio.

The purpose of the drawings is the subject of some disagreement among scholars. The dominant view is that these large format studies were made by Lely as preparatory sketches for a large decorative composition in one of the royal palaces (apparently never executed). We know that in the 1630s Charles I intended to decorate the Palace of Whitehall with a series of four tapestries on the history and ceremonial of the Order of the Garter. The project was then entrusted to Van Dyck, who produced an oil sketch of the King and Knights of the Order 'going a processioning upon St George's Day' (collection of the Duke of Rutland, Belvoir Castle). Charles II, who attached great political significance to the Order and its official ceremonies, may well have returned to his father's original idea, although once again the project did not come to fruition. Interestingly, the Van Dyck sketch was included in the posthumous sale of Lely's own collection. It was possibly given to the artist by Charles II as some form of model (Millar 1978–9, p. 81).

We have no information regarding the original location of Lely's drawings. By the mid-18th century the series had already been split up between different collections, and odd sheets are mentioned in auction catalogues in the 1740s and 1760s. For instance a group of eight sheets was sold with the collection of Charles Jervas on 24 March 1740, and an album containing sixteen sheets passed at an anonymous auction in Amsterdam on 23 March 1763. The Hermitage drawing with its two canons most probably came from this latter group.

An obligatory element in the Procession of the Order of the Garter was the presence of twelve priests or canons of the Chapel of St George. Lely depicted them on six drawings,

all of which are extant: one in the Hermitage, four in the British Museum, and one in the Crocker Art Gallery, Sacramento, California. The Hermitage sheet can be identified with numbers 16 or 25 in the catalogue of the above-mentioned Amsterdam auction. There is no documentary evidence indicating how the drawing entered the collection of the Academy of Arts, but there is reason to suggest that it came from the collection of the first director of the Academy, Count Ivan Betskoy. We know that Betskoy put together a large collection of drawings during his travels around Europe in the mid-1760s, through purchases in Holland and Paris. In 1767 his collection was acquired by Catherine II and presented to the Museum of the Academy of Arts.

The authorship of this drawing was unknown when it entered the Hermitage, and the attribution to Lely and the connection with other drawings from the series of figures from the Procession of the Order of the Garter was established by Mikhail Dobroklonsky in the mid-1920s. AL

29

Sir Peter Lely (1618–1680)

QUEEN CATHERINE OF BRAGANZA

Black and white chalks on grey-blue paper, 20¹¹⁄₁₆ × 12³⁄₁₆ in. 52.5 × 31 cm
In the lower-left corner, the collector's mark of the Hermitage (L.2061)
Inv. no. 5925

Provenance: collection of Count Cobenzl, Brussels (L.2858 b); entered the Hermitage in 1768.

Exhibitions: 1969 Leningrad–Moscow, no. 42; 1972 Prague, no. 64; 1974 Manchester, no. 4.

Literature: Dobroklonsky 1955, no. 275; English Art 1979, no. 41.

This drawing was traditionally presumed to be by Van Dyck until it was attributed to Lely by Mikhail Dobroklonsky and identified as a portrait of Catherine of Braganza. Although the features of the woman's face are conveyed only schematically, the presence of British royal regalia, combined with the dress of the Restoration period, indicate that the subject is indeed the wife of Charles II.

Catherine of Braganza (1638–1705), the daughter of the Portuguese monarch Juan IV married Charles II on 21 May 1661; her dowry included the cities of Bombay and Tangiers. Contemporaries described her as a deeply religious woman, able to bear with dignity the humiliation brought on her by her unreliable husband with his numerous mistresses. Their marriage remained childless. In 1692, seven years after the death of her husband, she returned to Portugal, where in 1704 she became Regent during the reign of her feeble-minded brother, Pedro.

As official court painter, Lely produced numerous portraits of the Queen (Beckett 1951, nos. 69–74). Dobroklonsky saw the Hermitage drawing as a detailed sketch by the artist himself for one of the numerous state portraits made by Lely and his studio, perhaps that which was in the collection of the Marquess of Bath at Longleat (Beckett 1951, no. 71), although it has not been possible to check the validity of this theory. The stylistic link between this drawing and other works by Lely is in no doubt, but the question of its precise authorship is still open to debate.

A comparison with the studies of figures in the procession of the Order of the Garter reveals that this portrait of Catherine, although close in terms of materials and technique, does not have the same freedom and confidence that mark drawings from Lely's own hand. Moreover, the drawing does not create the impression of a sketch that was made during progress on a picture. The nature of the working of light and shade, the means of depicting fabrics and draperies, and a mass of secondary details, all lead us to see here a drawing after an existing painting, not a preliminary study. It cannot be ruled out that the drawing was produced in Lely's studio by one of the numerous assistants who imitated his style. AL

Alexander Cozens (1717–1785)

STUDY OF A CLOUDY SKY, (?)1760s

Black and grey washes on yellowish toned laid paper, 4¾ × 5⅞ in. 12 × 15 cm
Inscribed in the top-left corner, in brown ink: 7
Inv. no. 41571

Provenance: collection of William Beckford, Fonthill; from 1882 Bain Collection, Paris; from (?)1890 collection of A. B. Lobanov-Rostovsky, St Petersburg; from 1897 in the library of Nicholas II in the Winter Palace, from where it entered the Drawings Cabinet of the Hermitage.

Bibliography: Oppé 1927–8, pp. 84, 92–3; Oppé 1952, p. 46; English Art 1979, pl. 162; Wilton 1980, pp. 8, 35–7; Kantor-Gukovskaya 1982, pp. 95–8; Sloan 1986, pp. 50–56, 77–83; Sloan 1995, p. 91.

This study is one of 25 sky studies mounted in an album, bound in brown calf with gold stamping around the edges and on the spine, which also bears the stamped title 'Skies'. All the studies are the same size and are executed using the same technique on paper identical to that used in the making of the album. Some sheets have part of a watermark, a fleur-de-lis over a bend-in-shield, beneath which are the letters 'GR'. The album sheets measure 11 × 9¼ in. Six of the sheets have twelve different sketches of figures, landscapes and animals by Jean Huber, some on the back of the flyleaf. On the sheet before the title-page are two women playing cards with a barely visible inscription over the right-hand figure, 'Lady Euphemie Stewart', and the signature at the bottom of the sheet, 'Huber 1785'. The first of the four sheets that follow the studies by Cozens is signed 'by J. Huber Fonthill 1785'.

All these sketches and the notes to them in the album with Cozens's views are linked to the name of William Beckford (1760–1844), the owner of Fonthill in Wiltshire. A writer and connoisseur, Beckford took drawing lessons from Cozens as a young man and was his passionate admirer. From the autumn of 1784 to July 1785 Beckford remained at Fonthill, where Lady Euphemie Stewart, a friend of his mother, was then a guest, and where Cozens was a frequent visitor. In 1785 Fonthill was visited by a Swiss artist, a friend of the Beckford family, Jean Huber (1754–1845), who had brought a picture to the Royal Academy in

London. Huber's drawings and their location on the sheets flanking Cozens's landscapes in the album indicates that the album was put together and bound no later than 1785, i.e. during Cozens's lifetime, and Beckford kept the album in his library thereafter.

For much of the 19th century few remembered Cozens; his name only came to wider notice in 1882 at the London sale of Beckford's library, where the album with views of the sky was acquired by one Mr Bain for £25 10s. The album would seem to have been sold at the Paris sale of Bain's collection held on 18–19 December 1890, and was purchased by the Russian statesman and diplomat Prince Aleksei Borisovich Lobanov-Rostovsky (1824–96), who was also a historian and bibliophile. In 1897, after his death, Lobanov-Rostovsky's collection of books, including the album with its sky studies and two others linked with the name of Cozens, were acquired by the state for the Imperial library and later entered the Hermitage drawings collection (Hermitage Archives, Fund 2, d. 204, op. XIV 'B' – Inventory of the Library of Prince A. B. Lobanov-Rostovsky, no. 1711; this number and Lobanov-Rostovsky's ex-libris can both be found on the inside of the album's cover).

Until relatively recently, the existence of the album with drawings of views was known only through drafts of letters from Cozens to the artist William Hoare (1706–99), first published by Oppé in 1928. In one of these he wrote: 'I am at present engag'd in painting a system in 35 small pictures / for a Gentleman … / I have finish'd about 6. I have form'd 3 books of specimens Ist of 25 different sorts of Skies, 2 of 26 sorts of Trees. 3 of 35 Species of Composition of Lands. Shewing these books to … a Gentleman one day, it induc'd him to give me … an order to finish so many pictures as might include all the three books…' (Oppé 1927–8, pp. 92–3). Unfortunately, the letters are not dated; when they were written, and thus when the Hermitage album with views of skies was produced, can be deduced only from indirect evidence. All the scholars – Oppé, Wilton, Sloan – agree that they should be dated to the period between 1760 and 1771. In 1771 the first publication with engravings of views of trees appeared, by now 32 rather than 26, and clearly work on the publication and on the finished album with sky studies must have taken place before then. In support of this dating we can compare a landscape with rays of sunlight piercing through the clouds dated 1771 (British Museum) with one of the studies in the Hermitage album (inv. no. 41585). This sketch may have been a model for the composition in London.

A few of the sky studies in the album are comparatively tired, which can be explained by their functional purpose. All scholars link these drawings by Cozens with his teaching activities, requiring him to provide his students with a precise practical guide for their work on landscape composition. Cozens followed the same aim in his drawings of landscapes and views of the sky that went into the 'Praed Album', named for its owner, one of Cozens's pupils. The purpose of the sky studies is particularly clearly seen when they are put alongside the artist's theoretical work of 1785, *A New Method of assisting the invention in drawing original composition of landscape*. Rule V of this treatise states that the artist should use a sky suitable to the landscape from the collection of skies, and place the greater part of the clouds on that side of the picture where the landscape is lowest in order to preserve the balance. It also gives detailed instructions for techniques to be used. It is with the preparation of his *New Method*, supplied with 20 etchings of skies, that the Hermitage album is linked. A similar link with the sky studies can be seen in the undated publication of a detailed list of landscape subjects and their components on a single sheet with the title 'The Various Species of Landscape, in Nature' (Sloan 1986, p. 54, pl. 67). AK-G

31

Sir Thomas Lawrence (1769–1830)

PRINCESS DARYA LIVEN, 1812

Pencil and red and white chalks on
primed canvas, 30⁵⁄₁₆ × 25³⁄₁₆ in. 77 × 64 cm
Inv. no. 27319

Provenance: posthumous sale of contents of the
artist's studio, Christie's, London, 18 June 1831,
lot 411, sold for 36 guineas; collection of Grand-
Duke Nikolai Mikhailovich, Mikhail Palace,
St Petersburg; entered the Hermitage in 1923.

Literature: Rovinsky 1886–9, II, col. 1197;
Gower 1900, p. 144; Nikolay Mikhaylovich
1905–09, III, no. 24; Hanoteau 1909, p. 398;
Krol' 1940, pp. 162–5, ill. 8; English Art 1979,
no. 294; Western European Drawing 1981, no.
225; Great Art Treasures 1994, II, no. 348.

Darya (Dorothea) Khristoforovna Liven
(1785–1857) was the daughter of General
Khristofor Ivanovich Benckendorf. After
the death of her mother (*née* Schilling von
Kanstadt) she was brought up at court
under the patronage of the Empress Maria
Fyodorovna, wife of Paul I. In 1800, on
graduating from the Smolny Institute for
Young Noblewomen, she married Count
Khristofor Andreyevich Liven, who was
elevated to the rank of Prince in 1826. From
1810 to 1812 Khristofor Liven was the Russian
ambassador in Berlin, and from 1812 to 1834 in
London. The diplomatic career of her husband
was highly favourable to Darya Liven's
passionate interest in politics. Her salon in
London, and later in Paris, where she settled
after the death of her sons and husband, was
visited by leading statesmen, politicans,
historians and writers. Over a number of years
she conducted an active correspondence with
Prince Metternich and Lord Grey and to the
last years of her life was friendly with François
Guizot.

The Hermitage drawing is a study for a
painted portrait in the Tate (fig. 148), which is
the same in the turn of the head and elegant
twist of the long neck, the hairstyle with its
tight curls and the expression on the face. But
the drawing differs in that it presents the
subject waist-length, rather than bust-length,
and is considerably larger. In all probability the
London canvas was originally of the same size
as the Hermitage drawing, or thereabouts, and
was only later cut down on all sides. The style
of execution of both portraits, particularly the
pencil version, is free and sketch-like.

The fact that both canvases remained in
Lawrence's studio until his death possibly
indicates an intention to correct the lower part
of the drawing, which is only given rather
peremptory treatment, and to change the
position of the clumsily bent left elbow.

As work on the oil portrait began in 1812,
when the Livens arrived in London, the
Hermitage composition should be dated to the
same year. This date is in keeping with the age
of the young woman as seen in both portraits.
The incorrect dating of the drawing to 1823
arose as a result of an engraving by William
Bromley, which precisely copies the Hermitage
composition and is signed and dated that year
(Rovinsky 1886–9, II). AK-G

Fig. 148: Sir Thomas Lawrence, *Princess Darya
Liven*, c. 1812–15. Oil on canvas, 18 ¾ × 15 ¾
in. (47.6 × 40 cm). Tate Gallery, London.

Sir Thomas Lawrence (1769–1830)

ALEXANDER I, (?)1818

Black and red chalks, 19⅝ × 13¹³⁄₁₆ in.
49.8 × 35.1 cm
Signed, with an inscription, bottom right,
by the elbow: *TL*
Inv. no. 44959

Provenance: Gatchina Palace; 1941 Pavlovsk
Palace; entered the Hermitage in 1958.

Literature: Makarov 1925, no. 4; Krol' 1940, I,
pp. 157–9, ill. 5; Garlick 1989, p. 22.

Alexander Pavlovich (1777–1825) was
Emperor of Russia from 1801. This drawing
is a study for the state portrait of him
commissioned from Lawrence by the Prince
Regent, the future George IV, as one of 24
portraits of rulers and statesmen – the victors
of Waterloo – for the Waterloo Chamber at
Windsor Castle. The Hermitage sketch may
date from 1814, when Alexander made a short
visit to London, but is more likely to have been
produced in October/November 1818, when
Lawrence was in Aachen, continuing the
Windsor portrait (Garlick 1989).

Despite the opinion (Makarov 1925, Krol'
1940) that the comparatively crude,
mechanical drawing of the uniform and pose
of the Emperor – out of keeping with the
skilful execution of the head – makes both the
oil portrait and the pencil sketch examples of
'the mass production of the artist's studio', the
rough style of the Hermitage sketch is not at
odds with the attribution to Lawrence. We
know that during the sittings for the portrait
Alexander often expressed impatience,
changing his pose, and thus, in contrast to the
careful working up of the head, to which the
artist attached the greatest importance, the
turn of the torso and the details of the uniform
are noted only summarily in the drawing.
Moreover, Alexander was so satisfied with the
painted portrait that he commissioned
Lawrence to produce a copy of it for the
dowager Empress Maria Fyodorovna. At the
end of 1822 this autograph copy was delivered
to the Hermitage. Since 1926 it has been in
Moscow, originally in the Armoury (Kremlin),
and now in the collection of the Pushkin
Museum of Fine Arts. The Hermitage drawing
was possibly used by the artist when working
on the copy, after which it entered the Imperial
collection and was kept at Pavlovsk. AK-G

33

Charles Cameron (1745–1812)

DESIGN FOR A DOOR IN THE AGATE PAVILION IN
THE COLD BATHS AT TSARSKOYE SELO, early
1780s

Pen and ink with wash and watercolour,
15⁹⁄₁₆ × 20¾ in. 39.6 × 52.7 cm
Inscribed explanatory comments in Russian
in the margins
Inv. no. OP 11046

Provenance: purchased with other papers
from Cameron's heirs in London in 1822.

Exhibitions: 1980 Moscow.

Literature: Taleporovsky 1939, no. 87;
English Art 1979, nos. 151, 153.

The Cold Baths included several buildings,
among them the Agate Pavilion, in which the
rooms were decorated with great elegance.
Cameron intended to embellish the doors with
complex inlaid arabesques made from different
kinds of wood and mother-of-pearl
incrustation. The design of the doors as
eventually carried out was considerably
simpler. MK

34

Studio of Charles Cameron

CROSS-SECTION OF THE AGATE PAVILION AND
HANGING GARDEN AT TSARSKOYE SELO, 1780

Pen and ink with wash and watercolour,
22⅞ × 37¼ in. 58.2 × 94.7 cm
Inv. no. OP 11047

Provenance: purchased with other papers
from Cameron's heirs in London in 1822.

Exhibitions: 1967
Edinburgh–Glasgow–London, no. 26.

Literature: Taleporovsky 1939, no. 58.

That unique 18th-century architectural
fantasy – the Cold Baths – included a steam-
bath on the lower floor, with above it the Agate
Pavilion, the Hanging Garden and the
promenade or 'Cameron' Gallery. Cameron
intended that it should be something like an
Antique complex. This particular design helps
us to understand the Agate Pavilion's layout
and the lower floor of the Baths, in the right-
hand part of which were the rooms with a pool
(cat. 40). MK

35

Charles Cameron (1745–1812)

DESIGN FOR THE JASPER CABINET IN THE
AGATE PAVILION, early 1780s

Pen and ink with wash and watercolour,
15¾ × 23⅝ in. 40 × 60 cm
Inv. no. OP 11012

Provenance: purchased with other papers
from Cameron's heirs in London in 1822.

Exhibitions: 1967 Edinburgh–Glasgow–
London, no. 37; 1968 London, no. 37;
1980 Moscow.

Literature: Taleporovsky 1939, no. 77;
English Art 1979, no. 152.

Among the splendours of the Agate Pavilion,
part of the Cold Baths complex at the Imperial
palace at Tsarskoye Selo (see fig. 62), is this
pavilion, which has two cabinets decorated
with plaques of natural stone. This particular
design was for the Jasper Cabinet. The mirrors
between the piers were framed by gilt-bronze
candelabra, recalling the columns that formed
part of the decoration in Pompeiian wall
paintings. At the base of the hemispherical
vault, Cameron intended to place a frieze
replicating compositions from red-figure vases.
MK

36

Charles Cameron (1745–1812)

DESIGN FOR A STAIRCASE IN THE COLD BATHS
AT TSARSKOYE SELO, early 1780s

Pen and ink with wash and watercolour,
24⅜ × 17¾ in. 62 × 45 cm
Inv. no. OP 10990

Provenance: purchased with other papers from
Cameron's heirs in London in 1822.

Exhibitions: 1967
Edinburgh–Glasgow–London, no. 24; 1980
Moscow.

Literature: Taleporovsky 1939, no. 62;
English Art 1979, no. 154.

The staircase linked the lower floor of the
Cold Baths with the upper floor, where the
Agate Pavilion and the rooms for resting after
bathing were located. This is a cantilevered
staircase of superb construction – a spiral in
which one end of each step is fixed into the
wall, leaving the other end unattached. The
upper landing in the drawing was crowned by
a vault decorated with cassone and stucco
rosettes. The strict drawing of the pilasters
framed the wall area surmounted by niches for
sculpture and relief medallions. The sculptural
decor was by Jacques Dominique Rachette. MK

37

Charles Cameron (1745–1812)

DESIGN FOR A CEILING IN THE LYONS
DRAWING-ROOM OF THE CATHERINE PALACE
AT TSARSKOYE SELO, early 1780s

Pen and ink with wash and watercolour,
18⅜ × 23⅛ in. 46.7 × 58.8 cm
Inv. no. OP 11061

Provenance: purchased with other papers from
Cameron's heirs in London in 1822.

Exhibitions: 1980 Moscow.

Literature: Taleporovsky 1939, no. 124;
English Art 1979, no. 155.

The composition for the ceiling of the Lyons
Drawing-room included numerous medallions
of different forms, recalling Antique cameos,
framed by the finest of arabesques.
The Drawing-room was one of the state rooms
in the Catherine Palace, created by Cameron to
replace Rastrelli's Baroque interior. Gold-
coloured Lyons silk decorated with birds gave
the room its name. The numerous
architectural details were of lapis-lazuli, and
gilt bronze played a major role in the interior.
MK

Charles Cameron (1745–1812)

DESIGN FOR A STOVE IN THE ARABESQUE AND
LYONS ROOMS OF THE CATHERINE PALACE AT
TSARSKOYE SELO, early 1780s

Pen and ink with wash and watercolour,
18⅞ × 13⅜ in. 48 × 34 cm
Inv. no. OP 11087

Provenance: purchased with other papers from
Cameron's heirs in London in 1822.

Exhibitions: 1967 Edinburgh–Glasgow–
London, no. 20.

Literature: Taleporovsky 1939, no. 118; English
Art 1979, no. 156.

The stove in this design was intended for the
Arabesque Drawing-room, which took its
name from the decoration of the interior,
including varied ornamental elements of
Antique origin. A similar stove was to be
installed in the Lyons Drawing-room.
Cameron intended to make this faïence stove of
complex relief in the workshop of Friedrich
Conradi, who also produced work for Giacomo
Quarenghi. The drawing itself is typical of
Cameron's personal graphic style. MK

39

Charles Cameron (1745–1812)

DESIGNS FOR URNS OR VASES(?), 1780

Pen and ink with watercolour,
22 × 19½ in. 55.8 × 49.5 cm
Inv. no. OP 11065

Provenance: purchased with other papers from
Cameron's heirs in London in 1822.

Exhibitions: 1980 Moscow.

Literature: Taleporovsky 1939, no. 19.

Although often described as stoves, it seems
more likely that Cameron was here designing
elaborate urns or vases. This sheet, found
among a large group of the architect's papers,
is notable for its skill of execution, being one of
his best drawings. In style the drawing is close
to the sketches from Cameron's album of 1764
(Library of the St Petersburg State University
of Transport, inv. no. 4891). MK

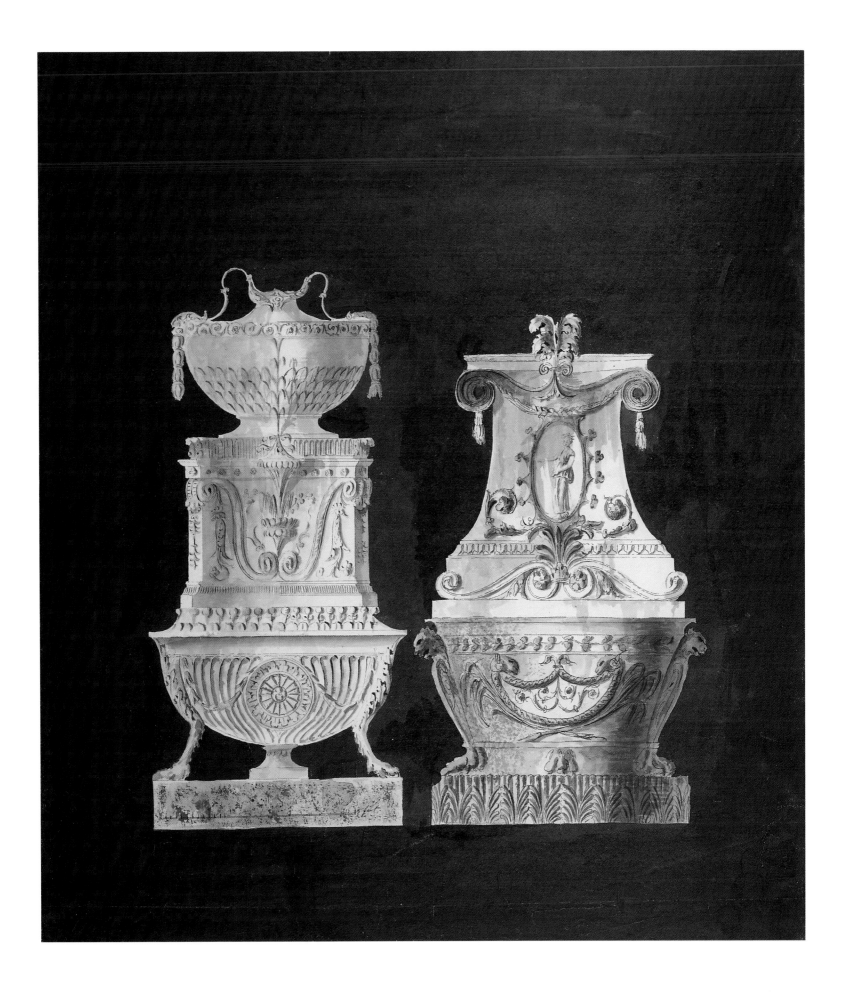

40

Studio of Charles Cameron

THE COLD BATHS AT TSARSKOYE SELO:
ELEVATION OF THE DOOR WALL, 1780

Pen and ink with wash and watercolour,
24⅝ × 25⅝ in. 62.6 × 65 cm
Inscribed in Russian (at the bottom):
*Latitudinal elevation of the Cold Bath room
under the letter D*
Inv. no. OP 11027

Provenance: purchased with other papers
from Cameron's heirs in London in 1822.

Exhibitions: 1967 Edinburgh–Glasgow–
London, no. 41; 1980 Moscow.

Literature: Taleporovsky 1939, no. 66;
Voronov and Khodasevich 1982, p. 86.

Modelled on Antique thermae, the Cold Baths
had a frigidarium in the centre of the lower
floor. According to Cameron's project, the pool
was to be covered with a luxurious baldachin
on faïence columns, the walls covered in
artificial marble and decorated with painted
ornament and gilded stucco. It was a much
simpler version that was actually built,
however, though it included decorative
sculpture of mythological subjects linked
with the watery elements. The frieze and
medallions were made by the sculptor Jacques
Domenique Rachette. MK

41

Charles Cameron (1745–1812)

ELEVATION OF THE MIRROR WALL IN THE
JASPER CABINET OF THE AGATE PAVILION AT
TSARSKOYE SELO, 1780

Pen and ink with wash and watercolour,
16½ × 26³⁄₁₆ in. 42 × 66.5 cm
Inv. no. OP 10992

Provenance: purchased with other papers
from Cameron's heirs in London in 1822.

Exhibitions: 1967 Edinburgh–Glasgow–
London, no. 34; 1980 Moscow.

Literature: Taleporovsky 1939, no. 84;
Voronov and Khodasevich 1982, p. 56.

One particular feature of the Agate Pavilion
was the presence of two cabinets or studies,
their walls covered with natural stones. The
north-eastern cabinet had plaques of different
kinds of Urals jasper. As shown in this design,
Cameron intended to use mirrors in complex
gilded bronze frames, but in the final version
he limited himself to simple gilt-bronze
reliefs. The gilt-bronze parquet added the final
touch: this was built of different kinds of wood
to a design by the architect. MK

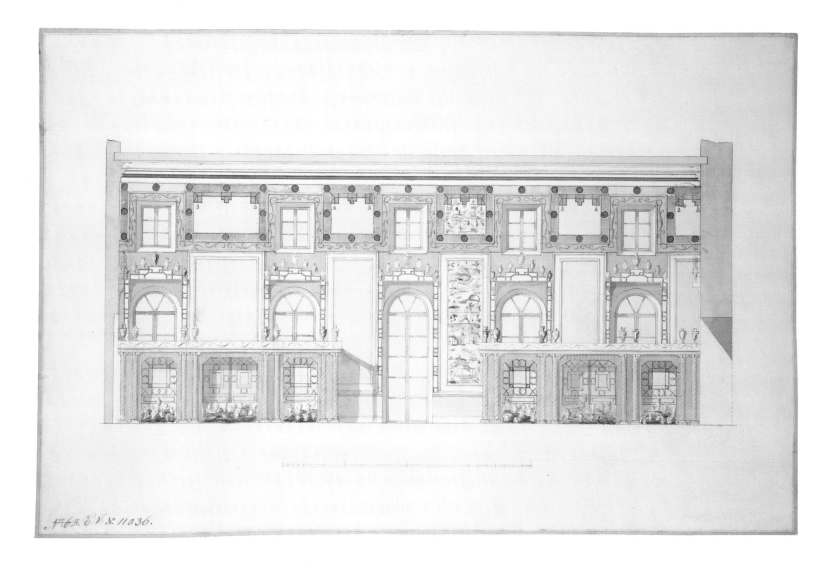

f. 62. E.V. N. 11036.

42

Charles Cameron (1745–1812)

WINDOW ELEVATION OF THE CHINESE HALL IN
THE CATHERINE PALACE, TSARSKOYE SELO,
1780s

Pen and ink with wash and watercolour,
17¾ × 27⅛ in. 45 × 69 cm
Inv. no. OP 11036

Provenance: purchased with other papers
from Cameron's heirs in London in 1822.

Exhibitions: 1967 Edinburgh–Glasgow–
London, no. 14; 1980 Moscow.

Literature: Taleporovsky 1939, no. 131.

The Chinese Hall in the Catherine Palace was
a concession to the widespread taste for oriental
art in 18th-century Europe. The large palace
collection of Chinese and Japanese porcelain,
painted lacquers and ivory and silks required
that the rooms be decorated accordingly. Thus
Cameron was requested by the Empress to
create a room in the Chinese style. He carried
out his task superbly, using real pieces of
oriental art and filling in with Chinoiserie
paintings and furniture. The Hall itself, with
its two rows of windows, formed the centre of
the intimate chambers designed by Cameron
that became known as the Zubov Wing of the
Catherine Palace (from the Empress's favourite
Platon Zubov). MK

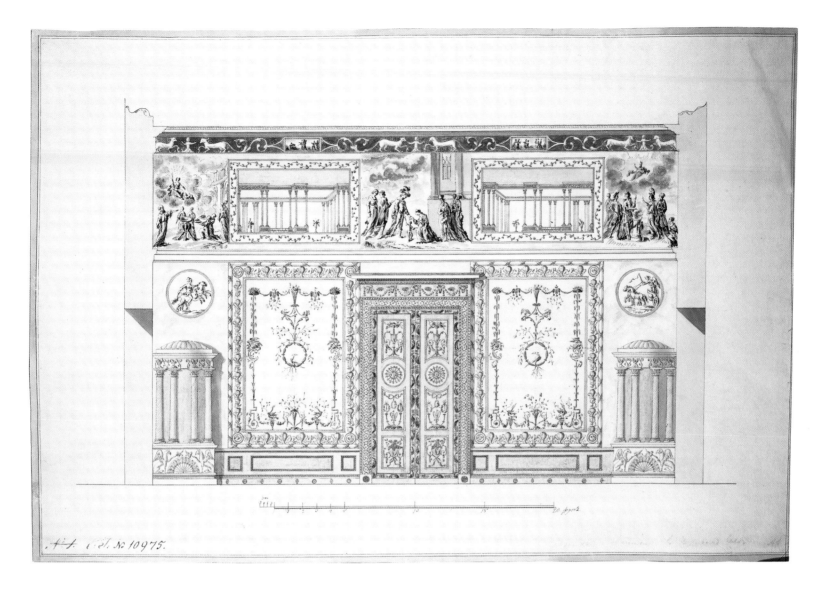

43

Charles Cameron (1745–1812)

ELEVATION OF A DOORWAY WALL, LYONS
DRAWING-ROOM, CATHERINE PALACE AT
TSARSKOYE SELO, 1780s

Pen and ink with wash and watercolour,
15¾ × 23⅝ in. 40 × 60 cm
Inv. no. OP 10975

Provenance: purchased with other papers
from Cameron's heirs in London in 1822.

Exhibitions: 1967 Edinburgh–Glasgow–
London, no. 17; 1980 Moscow.

Literature: Taleporovsky 1939, no. 123.

The Lyons Drawing-room was one of the
state rooms of the Palace, directly attached to
Catherine's private rooms, which were
designed by Cameron. The architect intended
to use Lyons silk on the walls, made to his own
design, but due to lack of time silk was used
from the manufactory of Camille de Pernaune,
designed by Philipe de Lassalles.

The golden fabric, with its peacocks, swans
and pheasants, covered the walls of the room,
and there were numerous architectural details
of lapis-lazuli. The painted frieze of the second
tier in Cameron's design was in reality replaced
by a border of light-blue silk. The room also
had faïence stoves designed by Cameron (see
cat. 38). MK

44

Charles Cameron (1745–1812)

WINDOW ELEVATION OF THE GREAT HALL OF
THE AGATE PAVILION AT TSARSKOYE SELO, 1780

Pen and ink with wash and watercolour,
15⅜ × 24¼ in. 39 × 61.5 cm
Inscribed in Russian (at bottom): *Longitudinal
elevation of the Great Hall of the Cold Bath*
Inv. no. OP 10995

Provenance: purchased with other papers from
Cameron's heirs in London in 1822.

Exhibitions: 1967 Edinburgh–Glasgow–
London, no. 31.

Literature: Taleporovsky 1939, no. 76.

This is one of the preliminary versions of the
architectural and decorative designs intended
for the Great Hall of the Agate Pavilion (see
cat. 45). MK

45

Charles Cameron (1745–1812)

FINAL DESIGN FOR THE WINDOW ELEVATION
OF THE GREAT HALL, AGATE PAVILION,
AT TSARSKOYE SELO, 1780

Pen and ink with wash and watercolour,
15⅜ × 24¼ in. 39 × 61.5 cm
Inv. no. OP 11014

Provenance: purchased with other papers
from Cameron's heirs in London in 1822.

Exhibitions: 1967 Edinburgh–Glasgow–
London, no. 32; 1980 Moscow.

Literature: Taleporovsky 1939, no. 29;
Rae 1971, no. 29.

The main room of the Agate Pavilion is
spherical, and in Cameron's design it is clearly
a recreation after Antique models. The unusual
mosaic of painted and relief insets with a
gilded frame on the vault suggests Roman
thermae. The vault rests on fluted columns
made of natural stone from Olonets.

The walls are finished in pink artificial
marble with green panels, and are decorated
with stucco reliefs and medallions of
mythological subjects. The room had eight
marble floor-lamps in the form of female
figures, holding in their hands bronze palm
and oak branches with candleholders.
The rectangular niches had, in place of the
figures on the drawing, vases of coloured stone.
MK

Plafond
pour
la première Chambre à Côté du vieu Palais

N°64. C.I.N. 11035.

46

Charles Cameron (1745–1812)

CEILING OF THE ARABESQUE ROOM IN THE
CATHERINE PALACE AT TSARSKOYE SELO, 1780s

Pen and ink with wash and watercolour,
16⅛ × 23⅝ in. 41 × 60 cm
Inscribed in French (in a later hand):
*Plafond pour la première Chambre à Côte du
Vieu Palais de Cameron Apartment*
Inv. no. OP 11035

Provenance: purchased with other papers from
Cameron's heirs in London in 1822.

Exhibitions: 1967 Edinburgh–Glasgow–
London, no. 119; 1980 Moscow.

Literature: Taleporovsky 1939, no. 119.

The Arabesque Room in the Catherine Palace,
designed by Cameron to replace Rastrelli's
Baroque interior, was named after the
arabesques decorating the walls. The ceiling,
which completed the decoration, included
various motifs from Antique art in the form of
medallions set in a rosette and surrounded by
ornamentation. In the centre of the circle is a
depiction of Venus and Cupid, with allegorical
figures in the eight other sections. MK

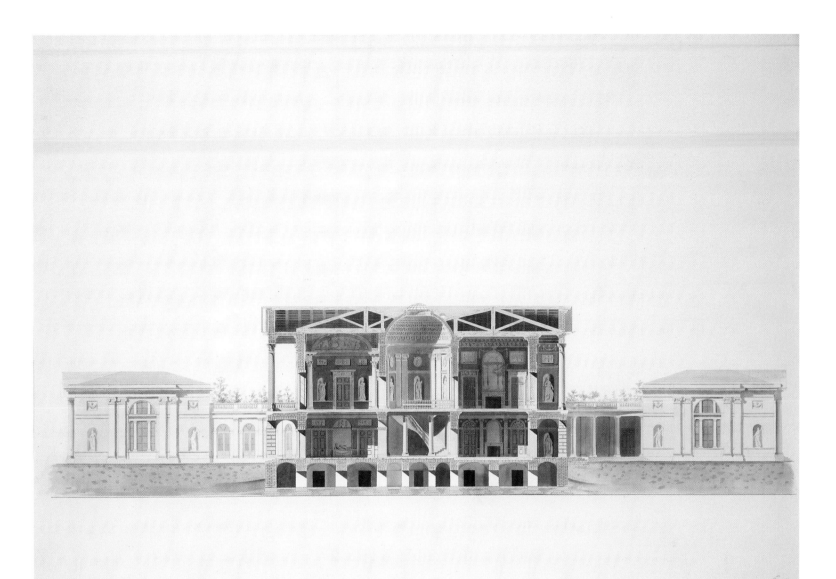

47

William Hastie (?1755–1832)

PROJECT FOR A COUNTRY HOUSE: SECTION, 1794

Pen and ink with wash, 20½ × 29 in.
52 × 73.7 cm
Signed at bottom right: *William Hastie*
Inv. no. OP 23296

Provenance: entered the Hermitage in 1794.

Literature: Korshunova 1974, pp. 14–22, ill. 13e; Korshunova 1977, pp. 132–43.

This is one of the four sheets that Hastie presented to Catherine II in 1794 (see cat. 48). This section through the central axis of the main block of the house gives some idea of the proposed interior decoration of the state rooms.
MK

48

William Hastie (?1755–1832)

PROJECT FOR A COUNTRY HOUSE: ELEVATION, 1794

Pen and ink with wash, 22¹⁄₁₆ × 55¹⁵⁄₁₆ in.
56 × 142 cm
Signed at bottom right: *William Hastie*
Inv. no. OP 23295

Provenance: entered the Hermitage in 1794.

Literature: Korshunova 1974, pp. 14–22;
Korshunova 1977, pp. 132–43;
English Art 1979, no. 149.

This project was presented to Catherine II and consisted of four sheets (OP 23296, cross-section; 23297, plan of the first floor; 23298, plan of the second floor). The building was conceived in the spirit of 18th-century Neo-Palladian structures, with a central block and four wings connected to it by galleries. The project is accompanied by a note: 'I am sending you with this to the library of Her Imperial Majesty two plans, a facade … made to the set programme by Candidate of Architecture Hastie, to be put with the book presented by him [signature illegible]. 20 August 1794.' (see p. 73).

The closest analogies in Russia are the palace at Pavlovsk (by Charles Cameron), the dacha at Polyustrovo (by Nikolai L'vov), and the Lyalichi mansion near Chernigov (by Giacomo Quarenghi). MK

49

John Boydell (1719–1804), Publisher

*A Set of Prints Engraved after the Most Capital
Paintings in the Collection of her Imperial
Majesty the Empress of Russia, lately in the
Possession of the Earl of Orford at Houghton
Hall in Norfolk*, 2 vols., London, 1788
Folio, 27¼ × 41½ in. 69 × 105 cm
Yale Center for British Art, Paul Mellon
Collection

Volume I open at frontispiece stipple engraving
by Caroline Watson after Roslin, *Catherine the
Great*
Volume II open at frontispiece mezzotint
engraving by James Watson after Van Loo,
Sir Robert Walpole, afterwards Earl of Orford

Literature: Rubinstein 1991.

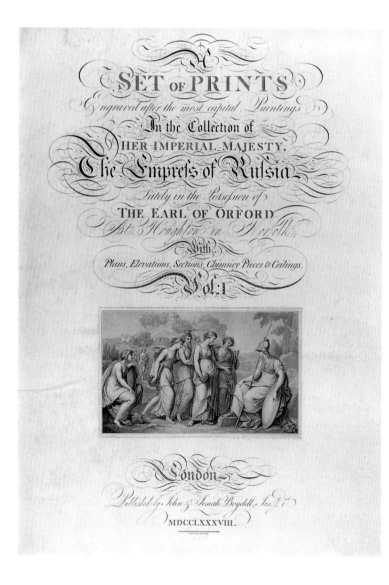

The publisher John Boydell issued the 162
prints by 45 different engravers that comprise
this collection, usually ten at a time, between
1774 and 1788, when they were gathered
together into these two splendid folio volumes,
each prefaced by a text catalogue based on
Horace Walpole's *Aedes Walpolianae* of 1747
(cat.50). As Gregory Rubinstein has
demonstrated, *The Houghton Gallery*, as these
two volumes were more commonly known, is
closely linked in both title and concept with
*A Collection of Prints Engraved after the Most
Capital Paintings in England*, which
spearheaded Boydell's attempt to counter the
Continental domination of the English market
for engravings. Both projects set the scene for
Boydell's nationalistic programme of art
patronage, the culmination of which was his
celebrated Shakespeare Gallery project in 1786.

The use of mezzotint engraving, never
particularly popular in mainland Europe,
suggests that these volumes were essentially
aimed at the domestic market, a notion
supported by Boydell's promise in the
prospectus that 'Subscribers shall have the
First Impressions' and that 'no more than Four
Hundred complete sets shall be printed'.

The increasing uncertainty in the 1770s over
the future of the Houghton collection (see
pp. 46–55) undoubtedly prompted Boydell's
initiation of the project. Once the pictures
departed for Russia, he must have encountered
great difficulties in completing his set of prints
and attempted to gather together every plate
he could find relating to the Houghton
pictures, including a number not originally
published by him. Although this led to some
inconsistencies in the quality of the plates the
overall effect remains impressive, not least due
to the contributions of the engraver Richard
Earlom. BA

50

Horace Walpole (1717–97)

ÆDES WALPOLIANÆ: or, A Description of the Collection of Pictures at Houghton-Hall in Norfolk, the seat of the right Honourable Sir Robert Walpole, Earl of Orford, London, 1747
Quarto, 11³⁄₁₆ × 8⅞ in. 28.4 × 22.7 cm
Yale Center for British Art, Paul Mellon Collection

Open at the title-page and frontispiece with an allegorical portrait of Sir Robert Walpole, engraved by Vertue after Zincke

Literature: Ketton-Cremer 1964, pp. 87–9.

This rare book – its author, Horace Walpole, variously reports having only 100 or 200 copies printed – is one of the earliest published catalogues of pictures in an English country house. Partly to alleviate the boredom of summers spent at Houghton, the nineteen-year old Walpole had compiled a manuscript catalogue of the pictures there as early as 1736, giving their sizes and the names of the artists. He may have been inspired by the first such catalogue of its kind in England, Carlo Gambarini's *Description of the Earl of Pembroke's Pictures*, which had appeared in 1731. Walpole was not pleased with the finished product, which first appeared in 1747, and corrected a number of mistakes in the second edition, published in 1752. The bulk of Sir Robert Walpole's spectacular collection was sold to Catherine the Great in 1779 and is one of the nucleus collections of the Hermitage (see pp. 46–55). BA

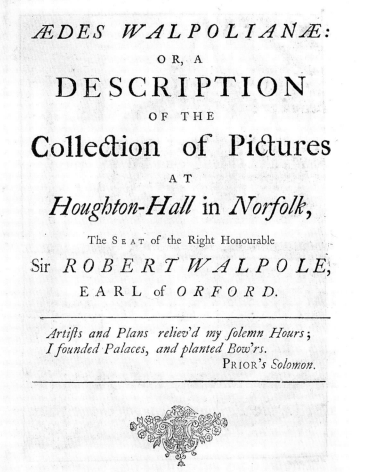

ÆDES WALPOLIANÆ:

OR, A

DESCRIPTION

OF THE

Collection of Pictures

AT

Houghton-Hall in *Norfolk,*

The SEAT of the Right Honourable

Sir *ROBERT WALPOLE,*

EARL of ORFORD.

*Artiſts and Plans reliev'd my ſolemn Hours;
I founded Palaces, and planted Bow'rs.*
PRIOR's *Solomon.*

LONDON: Printed in the Year **1747.**

John Augustus Atkinson (1775–1830)and
James Walker (*c.* 1758–after 1823)

*A Picturesque Representation of the Manners,
Customs, and Amusements of the Russians, in
one hundred coloured plates;*
*with an accurate explanation of each plate in
English and French,* London, St Petersburg and
Moscow, 1803–4
Folio, 3 vols. in one, 18¾ × 13 in. 47.6 × 33 cm
Yale Center for British Art, Paul Mellon
Collection

Open at no. 59, *Village Festival*

Literature: Abbey 1956, pp.197–9, no. 223.

This is the second of Atkinson's works to be
published after his return from St Petersburg,
the earlier one being the *Four Panoramic
Views of St Petersburg* (see cat. 53). Atkinson
had accompanied his uncle, James Walker, to
St Petersburg after Walker had been appointed
engraver to the Empress Catherine (see
pp. 92–103). Walker was only responsible for
the text of *A Picturesque Representation*: the
100 lively coloured soft-ground etchings are
entirely Atkinson's work. BA

52

Mornay and W. Balston

*A Picture of St. Petersburgh, represented in a
Collection of Twenty interesting Views of the
City, the Sledges, and the People. Taken on the
spot at twelve different months of the year: and
accompanied with an Historical and Descriptive
Account*, London, 1815
Folio, 19¼ × 13⅜ in. 48.9 × 34 cm
Yale Center for British Art, Paul Mellon Collection

Open at plate 8, *View of the Canal of the Moika,
the Bridge & the Police Establishment at
St. Petersburgh. July.*

Literature: Abbey 1956, p. 201, no. 226.

All the plates in this publication are signed
Drawn by Mornay except nos. 15, 16 and 18,
which are signed *Mornay del.* and *Clark and
Dubourgh sculp.*

The accompanying text and explanation
of the plates was supplied by W. Balston.
The iron bridge over the Moika canal designed
by William Hastie (see pp. 73–5) is one of the
better-known sites of St Petersburg. BA

VIEW OF THE CANAL OF THE MOIKA, THE BRIDGE
& THE POLICE ESTABLISHMENT AT ST PETERSBURGH.

July.

*Vue du Canal de la Moika, et du
Pont de la Police de S.ᵗ Petersbourg.*

John Augustus Atkinson (1775–1830)

Four Panoramic Views of St Petersburg, London
[*c.* 1802]

Large oblong folio, 22⅛ × 34¼ in.
56.2 × 87 cm
Yale Center for British Art, Paul Mellon
Collection

Open at the first plate, *Marble Palace.
Hermitage Theatre. Hermitage Picture
Gallery. Winter Palace.*

Literature: Abbey 1956, p.195, no. 221.

This was the first work completed by Atkinson
after his return from St Petersburg in 1802. It
consists of four large coloured aquatints 'drawn
on the spot … from the Observatory of the
Academy of Sciences', and was 'Dedicated by
permission To His Majesty Alexander 1st'. BA

PANORAMIC VIEW OF S.T PETERSBURG *Dedicated by permission* TO HIS IMPERIAL MAJESTY ALEXANDER 1.ST   VUE PANORAMIQUE DE

Marble Palace.   Hermitage Theatre.   Hermitage & Picture Gallery.   *by his much obliged humble Servant J. A. Atkinson.*   Winter Palace.
Palais de Marbre.   Theatre de l'Hermitage. Hermitage & Gallerie de Tableaux.   Palais d'Hyver.

Prise de l'Observatoire de l'Académie de Sciences par J.A. Atkinson.

SBOURG Dédiée avec permission A SA MAJESTÉ IMPERIALE ALEXANDRE 1.RE

Part of the Admiralty

Partie de L'Amirauté

par Son très devoué Serviteur J. A. Atkinson.

Planche 1.er

54

Joseph Nollekens (1737–1823)

CHARLES JAMES FOX, 1791

Marble, height 22 in. 56 cm
On the reverse: *Nollekens F.t London 1791*
Inv. no. H.ck.13

Provenance: purchased by Catherine II for the
Hermitage in 1791.

Literature: Khrapovitsky 1901, p. 218;
Troynitsky 1923b, pp. 92–4; Ettinger 1924,
p. 88; Smith 1929, p. 313; Zaretskaya, Kosareva
1960, no. 74; Zaretskaya and Kosareva 1970,
no. 91; English Art 1979, no. 135; Treasure
Houses 1985, p. 539, no. 476; Christie's,
London, 1988, no. 135.

Charles James Fox (1749–1806) was a
renowned English statesman and an
outstanding orator; he was a prominent
member and later leader of the Whig Party.
A model of portrait bust of Fox in classical
drapery was made by Nollekens in 1790, and
we know that in the following year he
exhibited a portrait of Fox at the Royal
Academy. This marble version was completed
towards the summer of 1791. In this work
Nollekens created an image of the orator
which is full of verve and energy: the face is
framed by wavy locks of hair flying up from
the sharp turn of the head to the right; the
thick brows hang low over the carefully worked
eyes; the full lips are half open as if Fox was
preparing to speak.

This bust was originally intended for Earl
Fitzwilliam, but fate took it to St Petersburg.
Catherine II's interest in Fox in the early 1790s
grew out of the political situation that had
developed during the second Russo–Turkish
war, when Russia seized lands between the
Dniester and the Danube as well as the
strategically important Ochakov Fortress.
Britain and Prussia, worried by Russia's
successes, demanded that all the lands be
returned to Turkey, threatening that they
would themselves otherwise declare war on
Russia. The British fleet prepared to depart
for the Baltic, but Fox's convincing and
eloquent speeches in Parliament forced the
Government to rethink its rash proposal.

Seeking for some tactful way of thanking
Fox for his indirect services to Russia,
Catherine ordered the acquisition in London
of a marble bust of him for her Hermitage
collection. Informed of the Empress's
passionate desire to get hold of a portrait of
Fox, Earl Fitzwilliam decided to forgo his own
version. On 8 September 1791, Catherine's
secretary, A. Khrapovitsky, noted in his diary:
'The bust of Fox has arrived and the order
given to stand it in the Hermitage and make a
bronze to be placed in the colonnade at
Tsarskoye Selo, between Demosthenes and
Cicero' (Khrapovitsky 1901). The bronze copy
was cast in St Petersburg in 1792 by Edmé
Gastecloux and set up in the colonnade of the
Cameron Gallery at Tsarskoye Selo, among the
busts of outstanding Classical figures. The
history of the acquisition of the marble by
Catherine was widely known, a fact reflected in
numerous caricatures (fig. 150).

Nollekens's *Fox* was extremely popular and
many replicas were made. In addition to those
that are similar to it, there is a version in which
Fox is depicted with short hair framing his
large, expressive head (Smith 1929, p. 304;
Whinney 1971, p. 122, no. 38). YE.K

Fig. 149: Drawn and engraved by William
Pether after Joseph Nollekens, *Charles James
Fox*. Mezzotint dedicated to Catherine the
Great. Published 1 January 1792.
State Hermitage Museum.

Fig. 150: J. Sayers, *The Patriot Exalted*.
Aquatint, 13 ⅞ × 10 ¾ in. (35.2 × 27.3 cm).
Published 15 March 1792. The Trustees of
the British Museum.
Sayers's print shows Nollekens's bust of Fox
being placed a niche in the Colonnade of the
Cameron Gallery at Tsarskoye Selo by
Catherine II to the horror of Demosthenes and
Cicero, who vacate their spaces. The Empress
later removed the bust on account of Fox's
attitude towards the French Revolution.

55

Joseph Nollekens (1737–1823)

LAUGHING CHILD, (?)before *c.* 1795

Marble, height 10⅝ in. 27 cm
On the reverse: *Nollekens. F.t*
Inv. no. H.ck.296

Provenance: Entered the Hermitage
before 1859.

Literature: English Art 1979, no. 134.

After completing his studies in England, Nollekens spent ten years in Rome (1760–70), where he copied and restored Antique marbles. On his return to London he gradually established himself as a talented portrait sculptor (his busts of Fox and Pitt are among his best-known works). He also carved statues on mythological subjects, such as *Venus Untying her Sandal* and *Diana and Minerva* (J. Paul Getty Museum, Malibu).

In the course of a long life Nollekens made many highly individual portraits. Yet common to many of his works are a particularly free and relaxed treatment of the hair, which is often depicted as careless, even untidy; the heads of the subjects are often inclined or turned sharply to one side; the eyes are carefully worked up, particularly the pupils; and drapery ends are often thrown carelessly over the breast.

Some of these characteristics are to be found in this undated small bust of a laughing child. The boy's head inclines to the left, his screwed-up eyes with their clearly marked pupils look slyly at the viewer, and the round face is framed by thick curly hair that seems to be caught in a gust of wind. The classical drapery is absent in this case, no doubt because it would have been out of place in a portrait of a mischievous child.

Interest in Nollekens's work may have been particularly acute in St Petersburg in the first half of the 1790s, when the marble bust of Fox (cat. 54) appeared in the Hermitage and a bronze copy was erected in the Cameron Gallery of the Imperial summer residence at Tsarskoye Selo. After this, however, English sculpture attracted little attention among Russian patrons, which suggests that this small bust was made and delivered to the St Petersburg no later than the mid-1790s (John Kenworthy-Browne has pointed out that Nollekens often left even his *portrait* busts undated right up to the 1790s: Treasure Houses 1985, p. 538). Ye.K

Philip Rollos I (d. *c.* 1721)

WINE-COOLER, 1699

Cast in silver, chased and engraved,
32⁵⁄₁₆ × 57²⁄₁₆ × 24 ¹³⁄₁₈ in. 82 × 145 × 63 cm
Marks: Britannia standard mark; hallmark for
London; date letter for 1699; maker's mark of
Philip Rollos I
The bottom bears the engraved arms of the
Duke of Kingston with the device: *PIE
REPONE TE*. The base and the handles have
the number 86 stamped into them, the object's
number in the silver stores of the Winter
Palace during the 18th century. Also on the
base are the engraved figures *OZ 3606*, and
3598: jo, the latter figure being scratched out
Inv. no. 7021

Provenance: to 1773 the 1st Duke of Kingston;
the Duchess of Kingston; until 1792 in the
collection of Prince Grigorii Potemkin, St
Petersburg; from 1793 in the silver stores of the
Winter Palace.

Literature: Foelkersam 1907, I, pls 10, 11,
pp. 500–04; Jones 1909, pp. xlii, 70, pl. XXXV;
Foelkersam 1913, pp. 14, 30; Troynitsky 1922,
pp. 35, 37; Troynitsky 1923a, p. 19, no. 3, pl. III;
Penzer 1957, pp. 43–4, fig. vii; Penzer 1958,
pp. 227–32; Hayward 1959, p. 36, ill. 22;
English Art 1979, nos. 55, 56.

This large vessel was used to keep wine cool just before serving at table. The obvious influence of French art can be seen in the powerful gadroons decorating the lower part, the remarkable modelling of the lions and the classical balance of the composition overall. The same decorative device and form were used by Rollos in a wine-cooler made in 1701 for George Booth, 2nd Earl of Warrington (Dunham Massey, Greater Manchester; Glanville 1987, p. 90, fig. 33). In both cases he decorated the handles with heraldic animal figures – boars or lions, borrowed from the coat of arms of the client. The arms on the Hermitage wine-cooler, executed with great skill, are engraved not on the shield on the front of the cooler, but on the base. On one of the brass plates fixed within the cooler is the following inscription: "The n^t y: of $\breve{y}$ Bras plates is 55:05"

This cooler was commissioned by Evelyn Pierrepont, Earl (later Duke) of Kingston. It was taken to Russia by his wife Elizabeth Chudleigh (see p. 132), was there acquired by Catherine II and presented to Grigorii Potemkin, after whose death it was bought for the treasury and handed over to the silver stores of the Winter Palace by Major-General V. S. Popov, Catherine's secretary from 1787 (Foelkersam 1907, II, p. 500). ML

57

Paul de Lamerie (1688–1751)

BASIN WITH THE ARMS OF BARON STROGANOV. LONDON, 1726

Cast in silver and chased, diameter 26 in. 66 cm
Marks: Britannia standard mark; hallmark for London; date letter for 1726–7; maker's mark of Paul de Lamerie
Inv. no. 13483

Provenance: collection of Countess Yelizaveta Shuvalova, St Petersburg; entered the Hermitage in 1925.

Exhibitions: 1986 Lugano, no. 5.

Literature: English Art 1979, no. 59.

In common with all the works from Lamerie's shop, this basin is notable for its elegance, beauty and expressive decoration as well as for the very high quality of the embossing and chasing. On the bottom, in the centre, is an applied embossed shield with the arms of the barons Stroganov, executed to a design by the court herald-master Count F. M. Santi (active in Russia in the 1720s). A similar basin with arms of the same design was made by Lamerie in 1723 for the Hon. George Treby (British Museum, London; Lamerie 1990, no. 25). The Hermitage basin was presumably ordered to mark the coming of age of Sergeii Grigoryevich (1707–1756), the elder son of Grigorii Stroganov. The title of baron was given to the sons of G.D. Stroganov by Peter I in 1722. ML

58

Paul de Lamerie (1688–1751)

WINE FOUNTAIN, 1720

Cast in silver, chased, height 27 9/16 in. 70 cm
Marks: Britannia standard mark; hall mark for
London; date letter for 1720–21; maker's mark
of Paul de Lamerie
Inv. no. 7025

Provenance: possibly brought to Russia in 1726
(see p. 126); in the Winter Palace from the 18th
century.

Exhibitions: 1990 London, no. 37.

Literature: Foelkersam 1907, I, pls. 17, II,
p. 376; Jones 1909, p. 84, pl. XLII; Troynitsky
1922, p. 58; Troynitsky 1923a, p. 21, no. 8,
pl. XI.

This is one of the earliest works from the
workshop of the famous English craftsman
Paul de Lamerie. The powerful, heavy form,
the massive gadroons decorating the bowl of
the fountain, and the restrained decoration, are
all also characteristic of the wine-cooler of
1699 by Philip Rollos (see cat. 56). They both
reveal the influence of the French Huguenot
style of the early 18th century. Susan Hare has
suggested that this fountain may have been
made by Paul Crespin, who worked for
Lamerie on many occasions (Lamerie 1990,
no. 37). The basic composition had already
been devised for the massive fountain made by
David Willaume in 1708 for the 5th Earl of
Meath, which was bought for the Prince of
Wales, later George II (collection of the Duke
of Brunswick; now part of the Cumberland
Plate). ML

59

Charles Frederick Kandler I (*fl.* 1720–1770s)

MIRROR WITH THE RUSSIAN IMPERIAL ARMS
AND CROWN, 1730s

Silver and mirrored glass; cast, chased, gilded
and painted, 32⁵⁄₁₆ × 20¹⁄₁₆ in. 82 × 51 cm
Marks: Britannia standard mark; date letter
indecipherable; maker's mark of Charles
Kandler I
Inv. no. 13156

Provenance: in the Russian royal household
from the mid-18th century; entered the
Hermitage in 1922 from the collection of the
Duchess of Saxon-Altenburg.

Literature: Derwis 1935, p. 36, pls. II A, B.

This two-sided mirror, which revolves on
hinges, is set into a twisted gilded frame,
richly decorated with silver flowers,
caterpillars, butterflies, snails and frogs
attached to leaves and petals, some painted in
oil. The naturalistic treatment of these details
is typical of work by Kandler, an important but
somewhat enigmatic figure. An abundance of
decorative elements is to be found in many
pieces by him, especially the well-known wine-
cooler in the Hermitage (cat. 60). The style of
his work suggests that he was of German
origin, and related to the famous modeller at
the Meissen manufactory, Johann Joachim
Kändler.

This item was restored in the 19th century.
In addition to regilding and rewelding some of
the details, the casters were added and the
mirror replaced. The painting was either
completely redone or at least retouched. At the
present time we cannot establish whose
decision it was to paint some of the decorative
details, the author's or a 19th-century owner's.
If it was part of Kandler's original concept,
were the flowers – now solely of white silver –
also painted? If so, the paint may have been
removed during the previous restoration when
the details were rewelded.

It is thought that the mirror belonged to
Peter III (it may have been a present from
Elizabeth Petrovna on the occasion of his
marriage to the future Catherine II) and was
kept in one of the palaces at Oranienbaum.
It then passed to his grandson, Grand-Duke
Mikhail Pavlovich, and from him to his
granddaughter, Duchess Yelena Georgiyevna
of Saxon-Altenburg, who kept it in her
quarters in the Mikhail Palace in St
Petersburg. ML

Charles Frederick Kandler I (*fl.* 1720–1770s)

WINE-COOLER, 1734

Cast in silver and chased, 39⅜ × 66½ × 38⅝ in.
100 × 169 × 98 cm
Marks: Britannia standard mark; hallmark for
London; date letter for 1734–5; maker's mark
of Charles Kandler I
Inv. no. 7041

Provenance: entered the Court Office of the
Winter Palace in 1741.

Exhibitions: 1956 Moscow, p. 73.

Literature: Hawkins 1885, p. 517, no. 72; Cripps
1886, pp. 230, 289; Chaffers 1899, p. 87;
Howard 1903, p. 139; Foelkersam 1907, II, pp.
263–5; Jones 1909, p. xlvii; Troynitsky 1922, p.
56; Troynitsky 1923a, p. 25, no. 27, pl. I; Penzer
1956, pp. 80–82, 111–15; Penzer 1957, p. 46;
English Art 1979, nos. 88–90; Glanville 1987,
p. 245, fig. 132; Schroder 1988, pp. 190, 297.

This remarkable wine-cooler was
commissioned by the banker and silversmith
Henry Jerningham, who made a design for it in
1730 that was engraved by George Vertue. The
wax models for the figures were undertaken by
the sculptor John Michael Rysbrack, and the
work was transferred to silver and chased by
Kandler. Once this wine-coller was completed,
however, Jerningham was unable to find a
buyer, and in 1735 he approached Parliament
with the request that it be used as a prize in a
lottery, the proceeds from which were to go
towards the building of a bridge over the
Thames at Westminster. In 1736 a medal was
issued to commemorate the lottery, designed
by Gravelot and cut by John Sigismund Tanner.
It bore a portrait of Queen Caroline, who was
Jerningham's patron for the lottery. The
winner, in 1737, was William Battine of East
Marden, Sussex. Soon after this the wine-
cooler arrived in Russia, perhaps acquired for
the Empress Anna Ioannovna. In 1741, on the
instruction of Elizabeth Petrovna, it was
declared to be state property. In 1859, in the
'Inventory of various silver and gilded objects
in the stores of the Winter Palace', the
following was noted: 'Transfer: Large 90
fineness with chased figures, with plates and
wheels copper and iron screws, weight 13
poods, 24 pounds, 13 zolotniki, inside along the
edge a vine. No. of the object 506. Received
1741 from the Court Office' (RGIA, Fund 469,
o. 13, d. 447, fol. 17v). In 1880 the applied arts
specialist Wilfred Cripps became interested in
this wine-cooler and a galvanocopy was made
for the Victoria and Albert Museum in London.

The decorative iconographic programme is
easy to decipher: the makers created a poem in
silver in honour of the god of wine, Bacchus,
linking the elements in the decoration with the
purpose of the vessel. Bacchus himself is
missing, but his companions – panthers and
goats, bacchante and fauns – are scattered
liberally throughout. The bowl of the wine-
cooler rests on the backs of four panthers
chained to each other. These non-Greek motifs
are natural to the 'alien' god Bacchus, for the
cult of Bacchus had originally been imported
from the Near East, and so panthers draw the
chariot in which the deity rides. The goats, too,
were not only his constant companions but also
the traditional sacrifice made to him. The
remarkable figures of bacchante decorating
the wine-cooler's handles form a logical
conclusion to the representational and
practical aspects of this unusual work. ML

Simon Pantin I (*c.* 1680–1728)

SOUP TUREEN, *c.* 1726

Cast in silver, chased and engraved,
11⁷⁄₁₆ × 16⅛ × 11½ in. 29 × 41 × 29.2 cm
Marks: Britannia standard mark; hall mark for
London; maker's mark of Simon Pantin I
Inv. no. 7035

Provenance: in the silver stores of the Winter
Palace from 1726.

Exhibitions: 1967 London, no. 41.

Literature: Foelkersam 1907, II, p. 7; Jones
1909, p. 78, pl. XXXIX; Troynitsky 1923a, p. 23,
no. 19, pl. V; Penzer 1958, pp. 231, 232;
Hayward 1959, p. 51, ill. 65a; Biryukova 1974,
no. 98; English Art 1979, no. 61.

This tureen formed part of the English service
ordered by Peter the Great's wife, Catherine I,
whose monogram is engraved on the body and
the cover. The service was made by the well-
known London silversmiths Simon Pantin I,
William Fleming, John Smith, Simon Margas,
Paul Crespin and Anne Tanqueray. The bowl
is decorated in high relief with rhythmic
ornament, embossing and extremely precise
engraving. This is a rare example of an early
English soup tureen. Its decoration is close to
that to be seen on a soup tureen of 1722 by Paul
de Lamerie, made to a French model (Lamerie
1990, no. 43). ML

Paul Crespin (1694–1770)

TWO-HANDLED CUP AND COVER, 1726

Cast in silver, chased and gilded, height 13⅜ in.
34 cm
Marks: Britannia standard mark; hallmark for
London; date letter for 1726–7; maker's mark of
Paul Crespin
Inv. no. 7026

Provenance: In the service stores of the Winter
Palace from 1726.

Literature: Foelkersam 1907, I, pl. 20; II, p. 3;
Jones 1909, p. 82, pl. XLI; Troynitsky 1923,
p. 22, no. 10, pl. VII.

The lower part of the body of this cup and
its high cover are decorated with two kinds
of gadroons and the powerful volutes of the
handles are 'inserted' organically into the
composition, giving the cup a particular
solemnity and elegance. It was part of the
English service (see cat. 61), ordered for the
Empress Catherine I, and thus on one side has
an engraved letter *E* (the Russian 'Ye', for
Yekaterina) set in a laurel wreath and
surmounted by an Imperial crown. On the
other side of the cup there is a similar wreath
surrounding an engraved Imperial eagle with
the Cross of St Andrew on its breast. ML

Augustus Courtauld (1685/6–1751)

CENTREPIECE (PLAT-DE-MÉNAGE), 1741

Silver and wood; cast, chased and engraved,
height 11¹³⁄₁₆ in. 30 cm
Marks: sterling standard mark; hallmark for
London; date letter for 1741–2;
maker's mark of Augustus Courtauld
Inv. no. 13429

Provenance: collection of the Princes Yusupov,
St Petersburg; from 1921 in the Yusupov Palace
Museum, Petrograd; entered the Hermitage in
1925.

Exhibitions: 1986 Lugano, no. 6.

Literature: Derwis 1935, p. 26, pl. II B; Oman
1959, p. 16, fig. 4; English Art 1979, no. 85.

This centrepiece consists of a stand on a
wooden base resting on four wheels, the body
in the form of a deep bowl with a flat dessert
dish and four small platters that screw on to
the legs. The platters can be replaced with
candleholders on saucers, turning the
centrepiece into a candlestick. The stand has
four glass flasks for vinegar and other sauces,
four silver cruet pots for pepper and sugar, as
well as four salt dishes in the form of shells.

With its high-quality embossing and
engraving, this is one of the most splendid
examples of English Rococo silver, for
Courtauld, a former apprentice to Simon
Pantin, was one of the leading craftsmen of his
day. Working in the circle of Paul de Lamerie,
Peter Harache and David Willaume, he was
undoubtedly influenced by them, particularly
in such richly decorated pieces as this one. The
idea for the central part was used by Lamerie
in a centrepiece of 1736 made for Algernon
Coote, 6th Earl of Mountrath (Lamerie 1990,
no. 87). ML

William Cripps (*fl.* 1730–1767) and
Samuel Wood (*c.* 1704–1790s)

CENTREPIECE (PLAT-DE-MÉNAGE), 1745

Silver and wood, cast, chased, and pierced,
height 11¼ in. 28.5 cm; stand 21¼ × 17⁵⁄₁₆ in.
54 × 44 cm
Marks: 1. on the body (basket): sterling
standard mark; hallmark for London; date
letter for 1745–6; maker's mark of William
Cripps; 2. on the stand: control mark for St
Petersburg; Petersburg assay-master mark of
Ivan Frolov (*fl.* 1738–79); Russian fineness
mark 86 [English equivalent 916]; 3. on the
pepperpots: sterling standard mark; hallmark
for London; date letter for 1745–6; maker's
mark of Samuel Wood

Each pot is engraved: *Pleshch. 101, Pleshch. 102,
Pleshch. 105, Pleshch. 106*
Inv. no. 7042

Provenance: in the Russian royal household
from the mid-18th century; delivered to the
Winter Palace in 1762 on the orders of the
Empress Catherine II; entered the Hermitage
after the Revolution.

Literature: Foelkersam 1907, II, p. 516;
Troynitsky 1923a, p. 26, no. 31, pl. X;
English Art 1979, no. 95.

This centrepiece consists of a stand with a
wooden base (?added later) on four legs, a fancy
basket with four candlesticks and four
pepperpots. The plat-de-ménage is in the
Rococo style, employing vegetable motifs and
garlands of flowers as decoration. Cripps was a
talented and important master of the Rococo,
while Samuel Wood specialized in making
cruet sets. According to Foelkersam, this
centrepiece formed part of the Pleshcheyev
service (see p. 130), as is indicated by the text
engraved on the cruet pots. ML

65

Nicholas Sprimont (1716–1771)

TEA-KETTLE, STAND AND BURNER, 1750

Cast in silver, chased and gilded,
height 15 9/16 in. 39.5 cm
Marks: on the kettle: sterling standard mark;
hallmark for London; date letter for 1750–51;
maker's mark of Nicholas Sprimont; control
mark for St Petersburg and the year (?)1796;
assay-master mark of Nikifor Moshchalkin
(*fl.* 1772–1800); Russian fineness mark 88
[English equivalent 916]; on the burner:
sterling standard mark; hallmark for London;
date letter for 1745–6; maker's mark of
Nicholas Sprimont
Inv. no. 7125

Provenance: in the Russian royal household
from the mid-18th century; from the end of
the 18th century (or ?1769) in the Winter
Palace.

Literature: Foelkersam 1907, I, pl. 49; II, p. 443;
Jones 1909, p. 100, pl. XLIX, no. 2; Troynitsky
1923a, p. 27, no. 33; English Art 1979, nos. 99,
100.

This kettle forms part of the Oranienbaum
service (see p. 130), of which seven items
survive, made by the London craftsmen
Nicholas Sprimont, Thomas Heming and
Fuller White in the 1750s. It received its name
because originally it was kept in the Chinese
Palace at Oranienbaum, the favourite
residence of Peter III, husband of the future
Catherine II (see figs. 58, 59).

The decoration of the kettle is unusual, with
chased scenes from Chinese life in the reserved
areas clearly borrowed from engravings. The
dragon motif dominates, and both the spout
and the burner are in dragon form. The
mascarons at the base of the leaves also have
oriental features, although executed with a
Rococo naturalism. Although at first sight the
kettle seems heavy and overloaded, its outline
too complex to be beautiful, the high quality of
the workmanship compensates for the perhaps
over-exuberant decoration. Nicholas Sprimont
had much in common with Paul de Lamerie
and Paul Crespin, the leading silversmiths of
the 18th century, and their influence is clearly
visible in his work. (It has been suggested that
Sprimont and Crespin worked closely together:
see Grimwade 1969.) ML

66

Samuel Courtauld I (1720–1765)

COFFEE-POT, 1757

Silver, wood; cast and chased, height 10¼ in.
26 cm
Marks: sterling standard mark; hallmark for
London; date letter for 1757–8; maker's mark
for Samuel Courtauld I
Inv. no. 7047

Provenance: in the Russian royal household
from the mid-18th century; from 1762 in the
Winter Palace; entered the Hermitage after
the Revolution.

Exhibitions: 1967 London, no. 47.

Literature: Foelkersam 1907, I, p. 23; II,
pp. 507–17; Troynitsky 1923a, p. 28, no. 44;
English Art 1979, no. 110.

This coffee-pot is part of the so-called
Pleshcheyev service, which arrived in Russia
during the reign of Elizabeth Petrovna (see
p. 130). This had coffee, tea and toilet articles,
the last-named without decoration. There is a
companion coffee-pot with a silver rather than
a wooden handle.

The greater part of the items from this
service were made by Samuel Courtauld and
Pierre Gillois in the Rococo style. The elegant
decoration seems to frame the form of the
object itself, in contrast with the mirror-like
undecorated service. ML

Samuel Courtauld I (1720–1765)

TEAPOT, 1757

Silver and wood; cast and chased,
height 6⅛ in. 15.5 cm
Marks: sterling standard mark; hallmark for
London; date letter for 1757–8; maker's mark
of Samuel Courtauld; Russian fineness mark
86 [English equivalent 895]
Inv. no. 7049

Provenance: in the Russian royal household
from the mid-18th century; from 1762 in the
Winter Palace; entered the Hermitage after
the Revolution.

Exhibitions: 1986 Lugano, no. 8.

Literature: Foelkersam 1907, I, p, 23; II, pp.
507–17; Troynitsky 1923a, p. 28, no. 46; pl.
XIII; Oman 1959, p. 15, ill. 5; English Art 1979,
no. 108.

This teapot forms part of the so-called
Pleshcheyev Service (see cat. 66 and p. 130).
It has a companion teapot with a silver,
rather than a wooden handle. ML

Andrew Fogelberg (*c.* 1732–1815)

VASE, 1770

Cast in silver and chased, height 34⅞ in.
88.5 cm
Marks: sterling standard mark; hallmark for
London; date letter for 1770–71; maker's mark
of Andrew Fogelberg
Inv. no. 7160

Provenance: the Duchess of Kingston in the
1780s; Prince Grigory Potemkin; 1792–7 in the
Tauride Palace, St Petersburg; in 1797 entered
the silver stores of the Winter Palace via
Colonel Delabatte (chief warden of the
palaces).

Exhibitions: 1956 Moscow, p. 75; 1967 London,
no. 99.

Literature: Foelkersam 1907, II, p. 505; Jones
1909, p. 92, pl. XLVI, no. 2; Troynitsky 1922,
p. 61; Troynitsky 1923a, p. 29, no. 59, pl. XI;
Penzer 1957, pp. 43–4; English Art 1979,
no. 180.

Fogelberg was one of the leading silversmiths
working in the Adam style in England during
the last quarter of the 18th century. The form
and decoration of the vase are both derived
from Antique models. A companion vase is also
in the Hermitage (inv. no. 7161). These two
vases would seem to have been used as wine
fountains, as they had copper spigots inserted
into them. They were acquired by Catherine II
from Elizabeth Chudleigh along with the
wine-cooler made by Rollos (cat. 56) and
presented to Prince Grigory Potemkin.

When the vases were transferred to the
Winter Palace in 1797, they were recorded as
weighing 31 pounds and 81 zolotniki, and
31 pounds and 72 zolotniki respectively
(RGIA, Fund 469, o. 13, d. 447, fol. 19v). ML

Charles Wright (d.1815)

TANKARD, 1776

Cast in silver, chased and gilded, height 21 cm,
diameter 4.¹⁵⁄₁₆ in. 12.5 cm
Marks: sterling standard mark; hallmark for
London; date letter for 1776–7; maker's mark of
Charles Wright
Inv. no. 13789

Provenance: collection of Countess Yelizaveta
Shuvalova, St Petersburg; entered the
Hermitage in 1925.

Literature: English Art 1979, no. 122.

This tankard is unusual for the period, for its
archaic form harks back to the 17th century,
while even the Chinoiserie form of decoration
was outmoded by the 1770s. Other works by
Wright reveal that he tended to combine old-
fashioned forms or decoration with the new. ML

70

Paul Storr (1771–1844)

PUNCHBOWL, 1806

Cast in silver, stamped and chased,
height 9⁹⁄₁₆ in. 24.3 cm; diameter 11¼ in.
28.6 cm
Marks: sterling standard mark; hallmark
for London; date letter for 1806–7;
maker's mark of Paul Storr
Inv. no. 7407

Provenance: purchased during a visit to
London by the heir to the throne, the future
Alexander III, 26 October 1874; kept in the
Anichkov Palace, St Petersburg, from 24
August 1878; entered the Hermitage in 1921.

Literature: Foelkersam 1907, I, pl. 18; II,
pp. 662–3; Jones 1909, p. 102, pl. L, no. 3.

This punchbowl is in a late Neoclassical style,
reminiscent of Roman art, although its stocky
proportions are consistent with the Regency
style. Storr's work is among the high-points of
English silverwork of the first half of the 19th
century. ML

Storr & Mortimer
Paul Storr (1771–1844)

PRIZE CUP, 1831

Cast in silver and chased, height 14 in. 35.5 cm;
diameter 9¼ in. 23.5 cm
Marks: sterling standard mark; hallmark for
London; date letter for 1831–2; maker's mark
of Paul Storr
Stamped on the base: *Storr & Mortimer*;
inscription along the top edge: no. *16 Published
as the Act directs by Storr & Mortimer 13 New
Bond Street London Jan. 18. 1832*
Inv. no. 14875

Provenance: collection of Countess
Yelizaveta Shuvalova, St Petersburg; entered
the Hermitage in 1925.

Exhibitions: 1986 Lugano, no. 12.

This cup by Storr, who went into partnership
with John Mortimer in 1822, is in the form of
an inverted bell-shape on a round stem. The
body is made of three combined horses' heads,
the round base with a concave stem chased
with acanthus leaves. This somewhat unusual
object was a prize cup for a horse race. Storr
combined Neoclassical elements – acanthus
leaves, a severe base – with finely and
scrupulously worked up naturalistic forms that
anticipate the style of the 1850s. ML

Robert Garrard II (1793–1881)

CENTREPIECE: KNIGHT ON HORSEBACK, 1844

Cast in silver and chased, 19¹¹⁄₁₆ × 18½ ×
13¾ in. 50 × 47 × 35 cm
Signed on the base: *R. & S. Garrard Panton St
London*
Marks: sterling standard mark; hallmark for
London; date letter for 1844–5; maker's mark
of Robert II Garrard
Inv. no. 7672

Provenance: commissioned by Nicholas I in
1844; kept in the silver stores of the Winter
Palace, then at the Cottage Palace at Peterhof;
transferred to the Hermitage in 1925.

Exhibitions: 1992 Tokyo, no. 82.

This group by Garrard was made to a design
and model by the sculptor Edmund Cotterill.
Judging by archival documents and
Foelkersam's inventory of the silver, it formed
part of the London service that was
commissioned from two English firms,
Garrard and Hunt & Roskell (before 1842
known as Mortimer & Hunt), after tsar
Nicholas I's visit to London in 1844. Of the
seven sculptural groups in the service, the first
is described in the documents as 'A Knight on a
horse, with a cup in his hands, a figure
standing before the knight'. The London
service comprised about 1,680 pieces, some of
which – mainly glass, crystal and porcelain,
plus stands for the groups – were made in St
Petersburg in the 'English shop' of Nichols &
Plinke, at the manufactory of P. Sazikov, and at
the Imperial Porcelain and Glass Manufactory.
This particular group is entirely characteristic
of work by Cotterill, Garrard's leading
designer from 1833 until 1860. ML

Matthew Boulton (1728–1809)

VASE CENSER, 1770s

Fluorite and bronze; carved, ground, polished, cast, chased and gilded, 12³⁄₁₆ × 4½ in.
31 × 11.4 cm
Inv. no. 12614

Provenance: from the 1770s in the Winter Palace.

Exhibitions: 1980 Moscow, no. 50.

Literature: Goodison 1974, pp. 48, 97, 142, pls. 117, 118.

Matthew Boulton was the owner of a well-known hardware firm in Soho, Birmingham, which was active from 1768 to 1782. His factory produced stone and bronze vases, candelabra, obelisks, clock-cases, decorative bronzes for furniture, ceramics, and marble and Derby fluorite objects. Boulton, together with his partner, John Fothergill, sold his goods (some through foreign ambassadors) in a number of European countries. Among his clients was Catherine II, to whom he was recommended by Baron F. M. Grimm. In 1771 the Russian ambassador in London, A. S. Musin-Pushkin, visited the factory with a view to purchasing some pieces for the Empress. It was then that Boulton sent vases for the Imperial court via the British ambassador in St Petersburg, Lord Cathcart. From his examination of archival material, Goodison (1974) established that at the end of 1771 Boulton also sent some tripods to St Petersburg, which were approved by the Empress. In 1772 she purchased a set of vases, and further orders were made in 1774 and 1776, for according to the Empress, Boulton's 'vases are, in all aspects, better than French ones'. Goodison suggested that a pair of vases in the Pavlovsk Palace Museum are from the group she acquired in 1771. It is possible that this vase was shipped with them, or with the next delivery that left England.

In the 1770s the English applied arts were dominated by Robert Adam, and this is reflected in the decoration of the vase censer. The form and motifs of the ornamentation are derived from Antique models, as indeed is the utilitarian function of the vase itself. In 18th-century Europe these were called pot-pourri vases, and they differ from ordinary ones in having a set of openings in the neck or, as in the present case, in the cover, enabling the scent to drift freely into the room.

In Boulton & Fothergill's 'Pattern Book I', this piece is described as a 'lyre' vase, and the dealers H. Blairman & Sons and Hotspur Ltd had similar ones made from white marble and fluorite. NM

Wedgwood:
Pieces from the Green Frog Service, 1773–4

QUEEN'S WARE, ENAMEL PAINTED

Provenance: ordered by Catherine II for the Kekerekeksinen Palace in 1773; delivered to Russia September 1774; from 1777 kept at Kekerekeksinen Palace (from 1780 known as the Chesme Palace); in 1830 moved to the English Palace at Peterhof; in 1879 a small part of the service was moved to the Cottage Palace in the Alexandria Park at Peterhof; in 1912 the pieces still in the English Palace were transferred to the Hermitage; the remaining pieces were transferred from Peterhof to the Hermitage in 1921. Pieces transferred in 1912 are inv. nos. 8443–9175; pieces transferred in 1921 are inv. nos. 20833–66.

Literature: Williamson 1909; Rotshteyn 1910; Troynitsky 1912; Filosofov 1924; Voronikhina 1962; Kelly 1980; Reilly and Savage 1980; Hayden 1985; Voronikhina 1988; Reilly 1989 I–II; Raeburn 1990; Reilly 1992; Raeburn 1992; Liackhova 1995; Raeburn 1995; Raeburn *et al.* 1995.

This service was ordered by Catherine II in 1773 through the Russian Consul in London, Alexander Baxter. It was intended for use at a wayside palace built by Yuri Velten in 1774–7 on the site of a dacha south of St Petersburg on the Moscow road. The area was known as Kekerekeksinen, the Finnish word for a frog marsh (in the 18th century it was usual to abbreviate it in Russian to Kekeriki, although Catherine used a French version of the name, Grenouillière). Hence the palace originally bore the same name and the unusual and amusing emblem of a green frog in a shield was put on each piece of the service ordered for the palace. In 1780 the building was renamed the Chesme Palace.

The service was for 50 persons and numbered 944 pieces (a 680-piece dinner service and a 264-piece dessert service). Each item was decorated with one or more topographical views of English castles, abbeys, palaces or parks. There were a total of 1,222 views, none of which were repeated (the incorrect count of 952 pieces and 1,244 views, often mentioned in the literature, is the result of an error made even while the service was in preparation: Raeburn *et al.* 1995, nos. 1–944). Josiah Wedgwood's companion, Thomas Bentley, drew up a handwritten catalogue for Catherine II in French, listing the names of all the views. The numbers of views according to his catalogue are written in brown enamel on the back of each piece. (All the known subjects for the views are listed in Raeburn *et al.*)

The greater part of the pieces from the service reproduce the so-called 'Royal Shape', which received its name after the model was used by Wedgwood in a service he made for George III. The models for some of the pieces, however – the compotiers, cream bowls and glaciers – were created specially for the Green Frog service (see Blake Roberts in Raeburn *et al.*, p. 40). The modified version of the Royal Shape as a result became known as the Catherine Shape (Reilly 1992, pp. 124, 206). The dinner service was decorated with a border of oak branches, the dessert service with a border of ivy. All the pieces were modelled and fired at the Etruria factory in Staffordshire, and decorated in Wedgwood's painting workshop at Chelsea. The service was made of then new ceramic ware that was standardized by Wedgwood through perfecting the traditional English creamware. In 1766 Wedgwood gave this material the name Queen's ware in honour of his patron Queen Charlotte.

When work on the service was nearing completion, the greater part was delivered to Portland House in London's Greek Street in order to display it to the British public before it was dispatched to Russia. The exhibition opened 1 June 1774 and was visited by Queen Charlotte herself. The service arrived in Russia in September of the same year (Hermitage Archives, Fund 1, op.5, d.32a, fol. 3, note by the head of the General Archive of the Ministry of the Imperial Court, Ober-Hofmarshal Count Paul Benckendorf), and on 8 October 1774 the order was given to make payment in full (see Voronikhina in Raeburn *et al.*, p. 13).

Today the Hermitage has 767 pieces surviving from the service. There are in addition 22 pieces outside Russia, these being items that were for one reason or another not included in the service sent by Wedgwood. One is untraced, but six are in private collections and fifteen are in museums in Britain and the United States: five in the Wedgwood Museum, Barlaston; two each in the Victoria and Albert Museum, London, and the City Museum and Art Gallery, Stoke on Trent; one each in the British Museum, Liverpool Museum, and Salisbury Museum; two in the Birmingham Museum of Art, Alabama; and one in the Brooklyn Museum, New York. LL

74

OVAL DISH DECORATED WITH A VIEW OF ETRURIA HALL, STAFFORDSHIRE
15 3/16 × 11 7/16 in. 38.5 × 29 cm

On the back: the stamped mark *WEDGWOOD*, number *1129* in brown enamel. Inv. no. 8641

Exhibitions: 1909 London; 1995 London, G.289; 1995 St Petersburg.

Literature: Williamson 1909, facing p. 8; Reilly 1989, I, p. 330; Raeburn *et al.* 1995, no. 38, view 760.

The dinner part of the service originally included 74 oval dishes of eight different sizes. The dish with the view of Josiah Wedgwood's mansion, Etruria Hall, was one of 20 dishes of 15 inches diameter. It was painted no earlier than late April or early May 1774. The artist thought responsible for the painting was James Bakewell. The Victoria and Albert Museum has another (the 21st) 15-inch dish with a view of West Wycombe (Genius of Wedgwood 1995, G.113). This view was listed in Bentley's catalogue as no. 285, a unique case, since the catalogue does not mention any other landscapes on those objects that were later excluded from the service for various reasons. The explanation seems to be quite simple: nineteen of the 15-inch dishes were decorated at quite an early stage in the work. A dish with a view of Fountains Abbey was then added (Genius of Wedgwood 1995, G.289) and only during the final stage was the dish with the view of Etruria Hall included. One of the completed oval 15-inch dishes had to be dropped, but it was of course already listed in the catalogue.

The view of Etruria Hall is listed in Bentley's catalogue under no. 1129 as 'Vue de la maison de M. Wedgwood, à Etrurie, dans le Comté de Stafford'. The Wedgwood Museum at Barlaston has a small rectangular plaque dated 1773 with polychrome painting of the same landscape composition with Etruria Hall as on the dish from the Green Frog service. The drawing from which the painting on both the dish and the plaque were taken is unknown, although tradition has it that the artist was Edward Stringer (e.g. 1974 London, no. 4). Raeburn suggested that the drawing may have been by Nicholas Dall, in whose work (particularly views of the Oakedge estate near Shugborough) we can see the same motif of a barge in the foreground, very similar to the view of Etruria Hall.

Wedgwood's mansion at Etruria was built in 1767–9 by Joseph Pickford, who was at the same time engaged on building Bank House for Wedgwood's partner, Thomas Bentley. Pickford also designed the new factory on the Etruria estate, and construction was completed in 1773. The waterway visible in the foreground of the view of Etruria on the dish is the Trent and Mersey Canal, work on which had begun 16 July 1766 and was finished in 1777.

The landscaping of the estate and the construction of the new factory were approached by Wedgwood much like the creation of a new oasis of civilization. Indeed, the perfection of the Wedgwood products would have been unattainable without a radical overhaul of all aspects of the creative

work. It was hoped that the planned classicizing works of the Etruria factory would help Wedgwood and Bentley achieve the status of heirs to the Antique ceramic tradition, and the estate with its factory would become the modern embodiment of ancient Etruria, perhaps reaching even greater perfection than the Antique models so admired in the 18th century. 'I think of making habitations for a Colony of Artists – Modellers, Carvers &c', Wedgwood wrote to Bentley on 24 March 1768 (cited in Burton 1976, p. 79). And on 23 May 1770 he mentioned his idea – never realized – for creating a professional school for painters and sculptors attached to the factory: 'A waking notion haunts me very much of late, which is beginning a regular drawing and modelling school to train up artists for ourselves … and when we wanted any hands we could draft

them out of this school. The painting upon these vases are from W. & B.'s school – so it may be said a thousand years hence' (cited in Meteyard 1875, pp. 269–70). A report of a visit to Etruria was published in *The Gentleman's Magazine* in 1794: *Here the inimitable works of Mr Wedgwood … and his magnificent house and grounds arrested my attention and speculation. The hills and valleys are here by Nature beautiful formed, but owe much to the improvement of Art. We see here a colony newly raised in a desert, where clay-built man subsists on clay. The forms into which this material are turned are innumerable, both for use and ornament. Now even the vases of ancient Etruria are outdone in this pottery* (cited in Meteyard 1866, II, p. 129). LL

75

ROUND DISH DECORATED WITH A VIEW OF
CRANBOURNE TOWER, WINDSOR GREAT PARK,
BERKSHIRE

Diameter, 13 in. 33 cm
No mark. On the back the number *514* in brown
enamel
Inv. no. 8712

Exhibitions: 1909 London; 1995 St Petersburg.

Literature: Raeburn *et al.* 1995, no. 94, view 33.

The dinner part of the Green Frog service originally included 56 round dishes of four different sizes. The dish with the view of the tower in Windsor Great Park was one of sixteen 13-inch dishes. The view is listed in Bentley's catalogue (no. 514) as 'Vue du nouveau bâtiment, sur la montagne de Shrubs, à Windsor'. The graphic source was an engraving by Pierre Charles Canot, *The New Building on Shrubs Hill*, after a drawing by Thomas Sandby, and one (no. 8) in a series titled 'Eight Views of Windsor Great Park', published in 1754 and then reissued by John Boydell on 2 March 1772.

A letter of 22 December 1909 from Francis Hamilton Wedgwood to Ober-Hofmarshal of the Russian court, Count Paul Benckendorf, allows us to identify the building shown on the dish more precisely. It relates to an exhibition of Wedgwood's ceramics in London in that year, organized in connection with the firm's 150th anniversary. In addition to the English exhibits, the show included 34 pieces from the Green Frog service brought from Russia, among them the dish with the view of the tower in Windsor Park. According to the author of the letter: *The Exhibition has been a great success in every way. Every afternoon the place is crowded with visitors who all express their delight with the kindness of the Court of Russia in allowing the ware to come to England after a lapse of 140 years, for their shape and design, but it is realised that the views are of profound interest historically. For instance, Her Majesty the Queen, and Her Royal Highness the Princess of Wales, were delighted with the view of Windsor and with no. 514 the round dish, which they identified as Cranbourne Tower in Windsor Park* (Hermitage Archives, Fund I, op. 5, d. 32a, fol. 45). LL

OBLONG DISH WITH COVER

DISH DECORATED WITH A VIEW OF LYMM CHURCH
AND RECTORY, CHESHIRE; COVER DECORATED
WITH VIEWS ON THE THAMES NEAR LONDON AND
FEATURES OF WOODSTOCK PARISH CHURCH,
OXFORDSHIRE, AND ST MARY'S CHURCH, OXFORD

33½ × 9⁷⁄₁₆ × 7¹¹⁄₁₆ in. 8.5 × 24 × 19.5 cm
On the back of the dish the stamped mark
WEDGWOOD, with the number *538* in brown
enamel (on the dish), *742, 743, 744, 745* (on the
inside of the lid)
Inv. no. 8569

Exhibitions: 1994 Kolding, no. 300; 1995
London, G.159, G.260.

Literature: Raeburn *et al.* 1995, nos. 138, 138a,
views 147, 423, 859, 687, 679.

One of eight oblong dishes with lids that
originally formed part of the dinner service.
The view on the dish (Bentley no. 538, 'Vue de
l'église et de la maison presbitériale de Lymm,
dans le Comté de Chester') is based on a
currently unknown drawing by Samuel
Stringer. The numbers of the two views of the
Thames on the lid are switched in Bentley's
catalogue: 742 relates to the view given there as
743 and vice versa. No. 742 (Bentley no. 743,
'Vue d'Erith vers la Tamise') is taken from an
engraving of 1750 by John Boydell, *A View of
Erith, Looking up the Thames* after his own
sketch and published by him in that year. This
engraving was also included in Boydell's
*Collection of One Hundred Views in England
and Wales* (1770; no. 9). No. 743 (Bentley no.
742, 'Vue sur la Tamise près du pont de Kew') is

after an engraving by Peter Paul Benazech, *A
View of Sion House and the Parts adjacent,
Taken from the road next to the Royal Garden,
at Richmond*. This was based on a drawing by
Peter Brookes and published by John Boydell
and R. Sayer on 24 January 1750. The
engraving was also included in Boydell's
Collection (no. 28). The view of the church at
Woodstock (Bentley no. 744, 'Vue de Steeple à
Oxford') is based on the engraving *A North
West View of Blenheim House and Park, in the
County of Oxford, with Woodstock in the
Distance* of 1752 by Boydell (no. 53 in his
Collection) after his own sketch. The fourth
landscape on the lid (Bentley no. 745, 'Autre
vue au même endroit [Oxford]') is also from an
engraving by Boydell, *An East Prospect of the
City of Oxford* of 1751 (no. 50 in his *Collection*),
again made after his own sketch. LL

TRIANGULAR DISH DECORATED WITH A VIEW
OF WHITTON PLACE, TWICKENHAM, LONDON

Length: 11¼ in. 28.5 cm
On the bottom the stamped mark
WEDGWOOD and the number *646* in brown
enamel
Inv. no. 8501

Exhibitions: 1995 London, G.106.

Literature: Williamson 1909, facing p. 80;
Voronikhina 1988, p. 170; Raeburn *et al.* 1995,
no. 146, view 597.

One of the eight original triangular dishes that
formed part of the dinner service. The scene
(Bentley no. 646, 'Vue du Canal et de la tour
Gothique, dans les jardins du Duc d'Argyle à
Whitton') is based on an engraving by William
Woollett, *A View of the Canal and the Gothic
Tower in the Garden of His Grace the Duke of
Argyll at Whitton*, made after his own drawing
and published in June 1757 by J. Tinney. LL

SAUCE TUREEN WITH LID, DECORATED WITH
VIEWS OF HAMPSTEAD, LONDON, AND A SPOON
WITH A VIEW OF STAINFIELD HALL AND CHURCH,
LINCOLNSHIRE

Tureen: $4^{5}/_{16} \times 5^{1}/_{8} \times 3^{15}/_{16}$ in. $11 \times 13 \times 10$ cm;
length of spoon: $6^{1}/_{2}$ in. 16.5 cm
On the back of the tureen the stamped mark
WEDGWOOD, with the numbers *492* and *493*
in brown enamel; *628* and *629* on the inside of
the lid, and *612* on the spoon
Inv. no. 8559

Exhibitions: 1995 London, G.214, G.215, G.633;
1995 St Petersburg.

Literature: Williamson 1909, facing p. XVIII;
Voronikhina 1962, ill. on p. 21; Reilly 1989, I,
pl. 332; Raeburn *et al.* 1995, nos. 163, 166a, 670,
views 533, 534, 548, 549, 58, 85, 493.

One of sixteen oval sauce tureens with lids and
spoons, of two different sizes, which formed
part of the dinner service. Both landscapes on
the sauce tureen (in Bentley's catalogue: no.
492 'Vue de la Grande Salle, à Hampstead, dans
le Comté de Middlesex'; no. 493 'Autre vue de
la même salle') are taken from a single
engraving by Jean-Baptiste-Claude Chatelain,
*A View of ye Long Room at Hampsted from the
Heath*, which formed part (pl. 4) of a series of
ten engravings by Chatelain first published by
Henry Overton and Robert Sayer as 'Vues
Diverses des Villages près de Londres'. The two
views of the lid (nos. 628, 629, both 'Autre vue
d'Hampstead') are taken from plate 3 of the
same series, *A View of Hampstead from ye
corner of Mrs Holford's Garden*. The narrow
ends of the lid show two park pavilions, but
these views have no numbers and are not listed
in Bentley's catalogue. None the less, they are
depictions of real structures, albeit set in
invented landscapes: the pavilion with the

triangular pediment is one of the Lake
Pavilions at Stowe, and the Rotunda is to be
found in the same landscape garden. The Lake
Pavilion is from the engraving *A View over the
Great Bason to the Entrance between the
Pavilions* published (pl. b) in George
Bickham's *Sixteen Perspective Views, together
with a General Plan of the Magnificent
Buildings and Gardens at Stowe, in the County
of Bucks* (1753), while the Rotunda derives
from the same publication (pl. h): *A View at the
Queen's Statue*. The view on the spoon of
Stainfield Hall (incorrectly listed in Bentley's
catalogue under no. 612 as 'Vue d'une Eglise à
Stamford') is from *The North West Prospect of
Barlings Abbey near Lincoln* (1726), an
engraving published in 1727 in volume II of
Nathaniel and Samuel Buck's *Views of Ruins of
Castles and Abbeys in England and Wales*. LL

SMALL OVAL TUREEN WITH LID

Tureen decorated with views of the Bridge at
Bedford, and Bolton Priory, North Yorkshire;
lid decorated with views of Prescot Glass
Works, Merseyside
6⅞ × 10⅞ × 7⅞ in. 17.5 × 27.75 × 20 cm
On the back the stamped mark *WEDGWOOD*,
with the numbers *772* and *773* in brown enamel
on the bottom of the tureen, and *766* and *767*
on the inside of the lid
Inv. no. 8537

Exhibitions: 1995 London, G.200, G.253.

Literature: Raeburn *et al.* 1995, nos. 194, 192a,
views 2, 982, 464, 465.

The dinner part of the Green Frog service had
four large and four small tureens with lids.
Both landscapes on this tureen were painted
from engravings by Richard Bernard Godfrey.
That of *Bedford Bridge* (Bentley no. 772, 'Vue
du pont de Bedford, dans le comté de Bedford')
is taken from Bedford Bridge, engraved 1
March 1772, made after a drawing of 1761 by
Francis Grose and published in his *Antiquities*,
I (1773). Bolton Priory (Bentley no. 773, 'Vue
du Prieuré de Bolton, à Craven, dans le Comté
d'York') is from the engraving *Bolton Priory*, in
Craven, Yorkshire dated 1 March 1773 and
based on a drawing by Paul Sandby of 1752.
This was published in Grose's *Antiquities*, IV
(1775). The landscapes on the lid (Bentley no.
766, 'Vue de l'Eglise et de le Verriere, à Prescot,
dans le Comté de Lancastre'; no. 767 'Autre vue
au même endroit [Prescot]') are derived from
an engraving by William Henry Toms of 1774,
his *South Prospect of Prescot in Lancaster*,
which Toms based on a drawing by William
Winstanley of the same year. LL

SAUCE-BOAT DECORATED WITH VIEWS OF YORK
AND LYMM RECTORY

2⁹⁄₁₆ × 8¹⁄₁₆ × 3⁹⁄₁₆ in. 6.5 × 20.5 × 9 cm
No mark. On the back the numbers *555* and *556*
in brown enamel, and the sign of a loop incised
in the paste
Inv. no. 8495

Exhibitions: 1995 London, G.160.

Literature: Raeburn *et al.* 1995, no. 175, views
1051, 148.

One of eight sauce-boats (used with stands for serving) that formed part of the dinner service. The view of York (Bentley no. 555, 'Vue eloignée d'York') is taken from an engraving by Samuel and Nathaniel Buck of 1721, *The North View of Sheriff Hutton Castle near York*, published their *Views of Ruins of Castles and Abbeys in England and Wales* of 1726 (vol. I, pl. 23), which was reissued in 1774 as *Buck's Antiquities*. The landscape with the rectory at Lymm (Bentley no. 556 'Vue auprès de Lymm, dans le Comté de Chester') is taken from an unknown drawing by Edward Stringer. LL

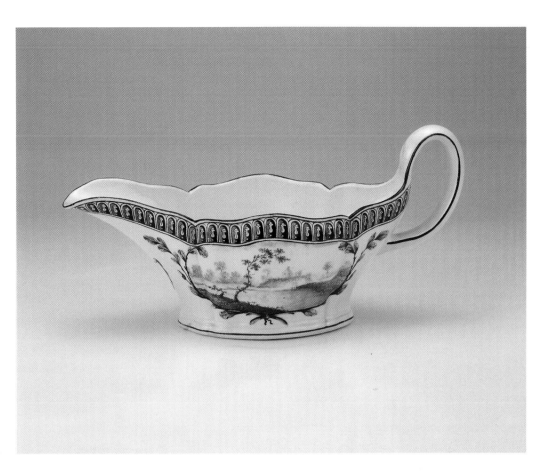

81

STAND FOR A SAUCE-BOAT, DECORATED WITH A VIEW OF THE MOSQUE IN KEW GARDENS, SURREY

8⅝ × 6½ in. 20 × 16.5 cm
On the bottom the stamped mark *WEDGWOOD* and the number *542* in brown enamel
Inv. no. 20859

Exhibitions: 1995 London, G.57; 1995 St Petersburg.

Literature: Raeburn *et al.* 1995, no. 182, view 849.

A stand for one of the eight sauce-boats from the dinner part of the service. The view of the Mosque in the royal gardens at Kew (Bentley no. 542, 'Autre vue au même endroit [Kew]') was borrowed from an engraving by Edward Rooker, *A View of the Wilderness, with the Alhambra, the Pagoda and the Mosque*, based on a drawing by William Marlow and published by William Chambers in his *Plans, Elevations, Sections and Perspective Views of the Gardens and Buildings at Kew in Surrey* (1763). Of the 29 views of Kew that were used in the Green Frog service, 27 were based on engravings in Chambers's book. LL

82

83

FLAT PLATE DECORATED WITH A VIEW OF THE
CASTLE AT FOWEY, CORNWALL

Diameter: 9½ in. 24.25 cm
No mark. On the bottom the number *38* in
brown enamel
Inv. no. 8779

Exhibitions: 1995 London, G.6.

Literature: Raeburn *et al.* 1995, no. 231,
view 173.

This is one of 288 small plates in the original
service. The landscape (Bentley no. 38, 'Vue du
Château de Fowey, dans le Cornwall') is taken
from an engraving of 1734, *The South-East
View of Fowey Castle*, published in Samuel and
Nathaniel Buck's *Views of Ruins of Castles and
Abbeys in England and Wales*, X (1735; pl. 10),
republished in 1774 as *Buck's Antiquities*. The
City Museum and Art Gallery at Stoke-on-
Trent has a plate identical to the Hermitage
one with the same number – *38* – of Bentley's
catalogue on the bottom (1995 London, G.5).
The Stoke-on-Trent plate had been damaged
during firing and thus was held back from the
service to be replaced by an undamaged one. LL

SOUP PLATE DECORATED WITH A VIEW OF A
DOLMEN NEAR CONSTANTINE, CORNWALL

Diameter: 9½ in. 24.25 cm
No mark. On the bottom the number *260* in
brown enamel
Inv. no. 8931

Exhibitions: 1995 London, G.229; 1995 St
Petersburg.

Literature: Raeburn *et al.* 1995, no. 488, view
171.

The Green Frog service originally had 120 soup
plates. The landscape shown on this one
(Bentley no. 260, 'Vue d'une monument
étonnant, appellé Tolmen, on le trou de pierre;
il consiste en un large Caillou oval, placé sur la
pointe de deux rochers naturels, dans le Comté
de Cornwall') was copied from an engraving by
James Green, *Tolmen in Constantine Parish in
Cornwall*, based on a drawing by the Revd
William Borlase and published in his
*Observations on the Antiquities Historical and
Monumental of the County of Cornwall* (1754).
LL

258

84

OVAL COVER DECORATED WITH VIEWS OF ST
BOTOLPH'S PRIORY, COLCHESTER, ESSEX, AND
CHIDDINGSTONE, KENT

13⅜ × 9⁷⁄₁₆ in. 34 × 24 cm
No mark. On the inside the numbers *667* and
674 in brown enamel, and the number *15*
scratched into the paste
Inv. no. 8448

Exhibitions: 1995 London, G.201; 1995 St
Petersburg.

Literature: Raeburn *et al.* 1995, no. 608, views
315, 401.

This is one of the 15-inch covers (hence the
number *15* scratched into the paste), of which
there were 20 for dishes of the same size,
although not all the dishes had covers: there
were 74 oval dishes of eight sizes, but only 44
covers of five different sizes.

The view of St Botolph's Priory on the lid
(Bentley no. 667 'Vue du Prieuré de St
Botolphs, à Colchester, dans le Comté d'Essex')
is after an engraving by Richard Bernard
Godfrey, *St Botolph's Priory* itself after a
drawing by Francis Grose of 1767, published in
Grose's *Antiquities*, I (1773). The view of
Chiddingstone shows the limestone cliffs that
were thought to be the site of Druidical rituals
(Bentley no. 674, 'Vue de la pierre grondante,
dans le Comté de Kent') and is based on an
engraving of 2 June 1772 by S. Sparrow, *The
Chiding Stone, Kent* after a drawing by Grose
and published in his *Antiquities*, II (1773). LL

MONTEITH DECORATED WITH VIEWS OF
MELROSE ABBEY, BORDERS, AND AUDLEY END,
ESSEX

5¾ × 12⅞ × 8⅝ in. 14.5 × 32.8 × 21.8 cm
No mark. On the insides of the vessels the
numbers *1271* and *1272* in brown enamel. On
the bottom the inscription in brown enamel:
'This Table and Dessert Service, consisting of
952 Pieces, and ornamented, in Enamel with
[…] 1244 real Views of Great-Britain, was
made at Etruria in Staffordshire and Chelsea in
Middlesex, in the years 1773 and 1774, at the
Command of that illustrious Patroness of the
Arts Catherine II, Empress of All the Russias,
by Wedgwood & Bentley.'
Inv. no. 20832

Exhibitions: 1995 London, G.293.

Literature: Filosofov 1924, p. 21; English Art
1979, no. 282; Raeburn *et al.* 1995, no. 684,
views 1197, 313.

The Green Frog dessert service originally had
four monteiths for cooling glasses. Monteiths
were filled with ice-cold water and the glasses
inverted and submerged, the stems hooked
over the scalloped edge. The view of Melrose
Abbey on this one (Bentley no. 1271, 'Vue de
l'Abbaye de Millross, en Ecosse') was taken
from a painting by George Barret the Elder,
Melrose Abbey, South Front (Collection of the
Duke of Buccleuch). Barret and Nicholas Dall
were the only artists to whom Bentley
expressed personal thanks in the foreword to
the catalogue. The iconographic source for the
view of Audley End (Bentley no. 1272 'Vue
d'Audley End, dans le Comté d'Essex') has not
been identified.

The monteith was discovered in 1922 during
an inspection of the service stores of the
Winter Palace. Inside lay a note written by the
head of household of the Hofmarshal's
department, Mily Anichkov, stating that the
monteith was brought from Denmark by
Hofmarshal Golenishchev-Kutuzov in 1892
(although it is unclear as to how it got there in
the first place). The Hermitage archives
contain an anonymous note in English, 'Some

notes on the history of the Russian Imperial
dinner service with the green frog', which
describes this find (Hermitage Archives Fund
I, op. 17, d. 41, 1922, fol. 229). The author of
this note describes the monteith as a 'flower-
stand', no doubt basing the supposition on its
description in the 'List of the Wedgwood
Service compiled by the Russian Officials,
showing which pieces of it are now in
existence', published by Williamson (1909, p.
101). This description was a precise translation
from the Russian 'stand for flowers', used by
Grigorovich in his description of the artistic
valuables of the Peterhof Palaces, which not
only provides historical information relating to
the Green Frog service, but also gives a short
list of the pieces of the service then kept in the
English Palace (Peterhof inventory 1885, p.
179). The transformation of the monteith into
a flower stand is not the only example of how
18th-century objects changed their function in
Russia at the end of the 19th century. The fruit
basket from the Green Frog service, for
instance, was listed by Grigorovich as a bread-
basket (Grigorovich 1885, p. 179). LL

ICE-PAIL DECORATED WITH VIEWS OF OLD
INVERARY CASTLE, STRATHCLYDE,
AND EDINBURGH CASTLE, LOTHIAN

6½ × 6½ in. 16.5 × 16.5 cm
No mark. On the bottom the numbers *1033*
and *1034* in brown enamel.
Inv. no. 20836

Exhibitions: 1995 London, G.246.

Literature: Voronikhikha 1962, ill. on p. 13;
Raeburn *et al.* 1995, no. 689, views 1161, 1184.

The dessert service had four ice-pails for
cooling wine bottles. The landscape with
Inverary Castle (Bentley no. 1033, 'Vue du
Vieux Inverary, en Ecosse') was taken from an
engraving by Peter Mazell, published in the
third edition of Thomas Pennant's *A Tour in
Scotland MDCCLXIX* (1774; pl. 17). The
drawing was made before 1745, as Inverary
Castle was rebuilt after this date. The view of
Edinburgh Castle (Bentley no. 1034 'Vue du
Château d'Edinbourgh, en Ecosse') was also
taken from an engraving by Mazell published
in Tennant's book (pl. 4), on this occasion from
a drawing by Moses Griffiths, *Edinburgh
Castle from Grey Friars Churchyard.* LL

ICE-CUP WITH LID, DECORATED WITH VIEWS OF
DOWNING HOUSE, CLWYD, AND MILTON ABBAS,
DORSET

2¹⁵⁄₁₆ × 2⅜ in. 7.5 × 6 cm
No mark. On the bottom the numbers *1123* and
1124 in brown enamel
Inv. no. 9164

Literature: Raeburn *et al.* 1995, no. 925, views
1109, 298.

One of the 24 ice-cups with lids that originally
formed part of the dessert service. In Bentley's
catalogue both landscapes on this ice-cup were
incorrectly named as views of Hammersmith
(Bentley no. 1123, 'Vue à Hammersmith, dans
le Comté de Middlesex'; no. 1124, 'Autre vue au
même endroit [Hammersmith]'). The graphic
source for no. 1123 was in fact part of an
engraving by Peter Mazell from a drawing by
Moses Griffiths, published as a frontispiece to
Thomas Pennant's *A Tour of Scotland
MDCCLXIX* (3rd edition, 1774). No. 1124 is
taken from Edward Rooker's *The North West
View of Milton Abbey, the Seat of the Rt Honble
Joseph Lord Milton*, an engraving published in
J. Hutchins's *History and Antiquities of Dorset*
of 1774 (II, ill. facing p. 438). LL

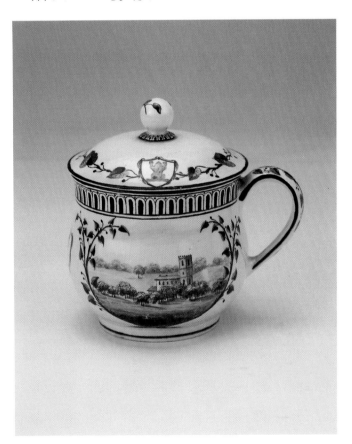

DESSERT PLATE DECORATED WITH A VIEW OF
FOUNTAINS ABBEY, NORTH YORKSHIRE

Diameter: 8⅝ in. 22 cm
No mark. On the bottom the number *806* in
brown enamel
Inv. no. 9096

Exhibitions: 1995 London, G.205.

Literature: Raeburn *et al.* 1995, no. 693, view
1001.

This is one of the original 144 dessert plates.
Bentley's catalogue incorrectly describes the
scene as 'View de l'Abbaye de Hutley, dans le
Comté de Buckingham' (no. 806), whereas it is
in fact taken from S. Sparrow's engraving
Fountains Abbey, Yorkshire (dated 1 January
1773), made after a drawing by Nicholas Dall
of 1767, that was published in Francis Grose's
Antiquities, IV (1775). LL

SQUARE COMPOTIER WITH A VIEW OF
PISTILL RHAEADR, LLANRHAEADR-YM-
MOCHNANT, CLWYD

7⅞ × 7⅞ in. 20 × 20 cm
No mark. On the bottom the number *961* in
brown enamel
Inv. no. 8597

Exhibitions: 1995 London, G.226.

Literature: Raeburn *et al.* 1995, no. 878, view
1104.

The dessert service originally had twelve
square compotiers. The iconographical source
for this composition (Bentley no. 961, 'Vue
d'une Cataracte considérable, au nord du pays
de Galles') may have been the engraving *Pistill
Rhaiadr, a great Cataract in North Wales*,
published in *The Gentleman's Magazine* for
January 1750. It is also possible that another,
unknown, engraving served as the source, for
many prints showing this famous waterfall
were produced in the 1750s. LL

CREAM BOWL WITH LID AND STAND

Cream bowl decorated with views of Weston Hall, Warwickshire, and Aysgarth Bridge, North Yorkshire; lid decorated with views of Tynemouth Priory, Northumbria, and Bamburg Castle, Northumbria; stand decorated with a view of an unidentified garden temple

6¾ × 6⅞ in. 17.25 × 17.5; diameter of the stand 8⅝ in. 22 cm

No mark. The numbers *1109* and *1110* in brown enamel (on the bottom of the bowl), *1273* and *1274* (on the inside of the lid) and *1093* (on the bottom of the stand)

Inv. nos. 8475 (cream bowl with lid); 8691 (stand)

Exhibitions: 1995 London, G.210, G.209.

Literature: Voronikhina 1988, p. 171; Raeburn *et al.* 1995, nos. 920a–b, 917c, views 978, 939, 658, 633, 1217.

This is one of the eight cream bowls and stands that originally formed part of the dessert service. The scene of Aysgarth Bridge (Bentley no. 1109, 'Vue du pont d'Ascarth dans le Comté d'York') was taken from Francis Grose's preparatory drawing of 1773 (Collection of the Society of Antiquaries) made for his *Antiquities*. On 11 July 1774, S. Sparrow finished his engraving after this drawing, which was afterwards published in Grose's *Antiquities*, IV (1775). The same scene taken from the same drawing is also to be found on a dessert plate in a set of Wedgwood pieces with polychrome painting (21 pieces extant) that were previously thought to have been trial pieces made during an early stage of work on the Green Frog service. These pieces have the same ivy borders and landscapes as the dessert part of the service, albeit here in colour, and each view has an inscription with the title beneath it, but no green frog emblem. It is now thought that Wedgwood produced the set at the end of 1774, after the completion of the Green Frog service (1995 London, G.320). On 14 August 1774, when considering the future production of faïence decorated with landscape compositions, Wedgwood wrote to Thomas Bentley: 'I think we should have a good handsome Dessert service painted in that stile' (cited in 1995 London, p. 290). On 5 November of the same year, Ben Mather, the painting workshop's head clerk at the Chelsea Decorating Studio,

told Wedgwood 'I should be glad if you will let us do Dessert Service with Landscapes in Colours …' (cited in 1995 London, D.4). The objects from this service (or set) must have been sold individually, as they all have different provenances. This would seem to have been Wedgwood's last use of the expensive decoration of faïence with landscape painting.

The source for the landscape with Weston Hall on the cream bowl (Bentley no. 1110, 'Vue de Weston, dans le comté de Warwick') has not been identified. Tynemouth Priory on the lid (Bentley no. 1273, 'Vue de la porte du Château de Tinemouth, dans le comté de Northumberland') may have been based on Grose's preparatory drawing of 1773 for his *Antiquities*, or from Richard Bernard Godfrey's engraving *The Gate of Tynemouth Castle, Northumberland* made from the same drawing and dated 12 March 1774. This was published in Grose's *Antiquities*, III (1774). The view of Bamburgh on the lid (Bentley no. 1274, 'Vue du Château du Bamborough, dans le Comté de Northumberland') may also have been taken either from Grose's preparatory drawing of 1773 or from Daniel Lerpinière's engraving made from it on 10 April 1774 and published in the same volume of Grose's *Antiquities*. The building on the stand (Bentley no. 1093 'Vue d'un temple') has not been identified, nor has the source for the painting. LL

OVAL COMPOTIER DECORATED WITH A VIEW OF
THE RUINS AND ORANGERY AT SHUGBOROUGH
PARK, STAFFORDSHIRE

12⅝ × 8⅞ in. 32 × 22.5 cm
No mark. On the bottom the number *1030* in
brown enamel
Inv. no. 8606

Exhibitions: 1995 London, G.282.

Literature: Raeburn *et al.* 1995, no. 842,
view 780.

The view of the park at Shugborough
(Bentley no. 1030, 'Autre vue au même endroit
[Shuckborough]') shown on this, one of the
eight largest oval compotiers in the dessert
service (there were 40 altogether, of five
different types), was painted after a drawing by
Nicholas Dall, *The West Front of Shugborough
with the Ruins, Orangery and Chinese House.*
This drawing was itself a preparatory sketch
for a painting by Dall (signed and dated 1768)
that remains at Shugborough (1995 London,
G.276). LL

92

LARGE COMPOTIER DECORATED WITH A VIEW
OF WESTMINSTER HALL, LONDON

12⅜ × 7⅛ in. 31.5 × 18 cm
On the bottom the stamped mark
WEDGWOOD and the number *1267* in brown
enamel
Inv. no. 8554

Exhibitions: 1995, London, G.317; 1995 St
Petersburg.

Literature: Williamson 1909, facing p. 24;
Raeburn *et al.* 1995, no. 897, view 590.

The dessert service originally included four
'large' compotiers (Wedgwood's term). The
view on this example (Bentley no. 1267, 'Vue de
la Halle de Westminster') was based on James
Green's engraving *Westminster Hall*, made
after a drawing by S. Wall, that appeared in
Robert and James Dodsley's *London and its
Environs Described* of 1761 (VI, facing p. 296).
LL

93

Derby

SOLITAIRE, *c.* 1790–95

Porcelain, overglaze painting, gilding; stand:
15¹⁄₁₆ × 10⅝ in. 38.3 × 27 cm; teapot with lid:
height 4⅛ in. 10.5 cm; sugar-bowl with lid:
height 4¼ in. 10.9 cm; cream jug: height 8¼ in.
2.1 cm; cup: height 3⅝ in. 6.7 cm; saucer:
diameter 5⅜ in. 13.7 cm
On the bottom of each piece the mark of the
Derby factory (the letter D beneath a crown) in
blue overglaze paint, and inscriptions in the
same:
on the bottom of the stand: *At Malton, Yorkshire*
on the bottom of the teapot: *Near Caernarvon in
Wales,* and *In the Isle of Wight*

inside the lid of the teapot:
Near Breadsall, Derbyshire
on the bottom of the sugar bowl:
Ulleswater, Northumberland
inside the lid of the sugar bowl:
In Dove Dale, Derbyshire
on the bottom of the cream jug:
Keswick Lake, Cumberland
on the bottom of the cup:
Near Breadsall, Derbyshire
on the bottom of the saucer:
On the Manifold, Staffordshire
Inv. nos. 19028–32

Provenance: collection of Alexander S.
Dolgoruky, St Petersburg; entered the
Hermitage in 1918.

Literature: Daydi 1957, II, pl. 128; Hoyte and
Pendred 1976, p. 71; English Art 1979, no. 197;
English Porcelain Painters 1981, no. 32;
Anderson 1986, p. 124; Twitchett 1980, pp. 45,
137, 209, 245.

The service was published by K. Butler and
R. Soloveychik and attributed to the leading
porcelain painter of the Derby manufactory,
Zachariah Boreman, a specialist in landscape
painting (English Art 1979). Boreman often
painted objects that he based on his own
picturesque drawings of the Derbyshire
countryside (Hoyte and Pendred 1976),
particularly Dovedale, a view of which is to be
seen on the lid of the sugar-bowl.
    Boreman's landscapes on porcelain were
often painted in a monochrome yellowish-

brown colour (English Porcelain Painters 1981). In the period 1783–90 he was working in a dry, somewhat schematic manner, but in 1790–95, he was following a freer and more painterly style (Anderson 1986). The Hermitage service would seem to have been produced during this later period.

A solitaire similar in technique and painting style is in the Victoria and Albert Museum (Daydi 1957). LL

94

Spode

TEAPOT WITH A LID, CREAM JUG, CUP AND SAUCER FROM A TEA SERVICE, *c.* 1800

Porcelain, overglaze painting, gilding; height of the teapot (with lid) 6⁵⁄₁₆ in. 16 cm; height of the cream jug 4⁹⁄₁₆ in. 11.5 cm; height of the cup 3⅜ in. 6 cm; diameter of the saucer 5⅜ in. 13.7 cm

On the bottom of the teapot the stamped mark *SPODE* and the number *94*; on the bottom of the cream jug the stamped mark *SPODE*

Inv. nos. 24244, 24246, 24249

Provenance: Pavlovsk Palace, later Pavlovsk Palace Museum, near St Petersburg; entered the Hermitage in 1932.

Literature: English Art 1979, no. 291; Whiter 1989, p. 126; Copeland 1993, no. 2a.

This teapot, cream jug and cup and saucer are part of a tea service in the Hermitage, now comprising eighteen pieces: two teapots (a brewing teapot, shown here, and one for hot water), a sugar-bowl and butter-dish with lids (the teapots and butter-dish also have stands), a cream jug, slop-basin with a stand, and twelve cups and saucers. Of these, however, only the brewing teapot (without its stand), the cream jug and the sugar-bowl (again not including the stand), are Spode products, bearing the factory's mark used between 1790 and 1802 (Copeland 1993, no. 2a). The other pieces, including the cup and saucer exhibited here, would seem to have been made additionally for the service in Russia itself, and have no marks. They differ from the original English pieces in the brighter tonality of the painting and more schematic approach to the depiction of landscape.

The products of the Spode manufactory were of so-called bone china, the natural colour of which differs slightly from that of traditional hard-paste porcelain used in the making of the Russian additions. Thus in the inventories of the Hermitage collection this material is mistakenly named faïence, and was published in 1979 by K. Butler and R. Soloveychik as 'stone china' (English Art 1979).

The model used in the making of the brewing teapot, cream jug and sugar-bowl was named 'Old Oval Shape', and was introduced at the Spode factory around 1800. The cup and saucer made in Russia repeat the Spode shape known as 'Bute' or 'Common Shape'. The early, rare examples of the Old Oval Shape are always found with cups of the Common Shape (Whiter 1989).

A distinguishing element in the decoration of the service is the use of stylized architectural landscapes set in roundels on an orange ground. The roundels alternate with gilded rhombuses, and everything is set on a broad horizontal lilac frieze. This motif was included in the manuscript 'Spode Pattern Book' under no. 516 and began to be used on products around 1800 (information from Robert Copeland). LL

Until 1962 all examples of small English porcelain sculpture (scent-bottles, étuis, sweet-jars, seals in the form of cupids and shepherdesses, flowers, birds and animals – known under the general title of porcelain toys) were attributed to the Chelsea manufactory. Then Arthur Lane and Robert Charleston identified a considerable group of small sculptural objects that differed from those pieces incontrovertibly produced at Chelsea not only in terms of style but also in the composition of the paste used in their production, which contained a large proportion of lead. A study of documentary sources led them to suggest that these pieces were made at another factory that was in production in 1751–4, which they called the 'Girl in a Swing Factory' because they took as the clearest evidence of the existence of a whole group of original pieces the figure of a girl in a swing. Subsequently Mallet (1965) suggested that the factory had in fact started production before 1751, and Foster (1967) divided its products into two groups. The first, showing clear signs of the influence of jewelry, was dated by Foster to 1750–54 (when production was managed by the jeweller Charles Gouyn). The other pieces were dated later, to the end of the 1750s. Foster was essentially in agreement with the leading scholar of the first quarter of the 20th century, G. E. Bryant, who had dated a number of pieces included in this last group to a relatively late period, after 1769. She none the less placed them a decade earlier. Elizabeth Adams suggested that pieces of the type attributed to the Girl in a Swing factory may have been produced between 1750 and 1754 in the same building in Chelsea which housed the business run by Nicholas Sprimont, known as the Chelsea porcelain manufactory, and suggested that they should be called 'Chelsea porcelain, Girl in a Swing type' (Adams 1987, p. 41, ills 28, 29). Recently, research by Bernard Dragesco (1993) has led to an identification of the Girl in a Swing factory with Gouyn's St James's Factory, which was in operation between 1749 and 1759. Ten years of activity (instead of the five suggested by previous scholars) was sufficient to allow for the development of the products, including stylistic changes, as well as techniques and methods of production, thus explaining the existence of the two types of products identified by Foster.

Foster (1967, p. 288, no. 18, pl. 213c) put the scent-bottle in the form of a girl and dog (cat. 95) in his second grouping of objects made at the factory, dating it to the end of the 1750s. LL

95

'Girl in a Swing'

SCENT-BOTTLE IN THE FORM OF A GIRL WITH A DOG, late 1750s

Porcelain, overglaze painting, stopper missing, height 3¹¹⁄₁₆ in. 6.8 cm
No mark. On the base the overglaze inscription in black: *Fidelle me guide*
Inv. no. 19301

Provenance: collection of the Princes Yusupov, St Petersburg; transferred to the Hermitage in 1922–3.

Exhibitions: 1991 Leningrad, no. 21.

Literature: Bryant 1925, pl. 23, no. 3; Rackham 1928–30, I, no. 245, pl. 24; Hackenbroch 1957, fig. 169, pl. 71; Lane 1961, pl. 35f; Lane, Charleston 1962; Mallet 1965; Foster 1967, pp. 284–91, pl. 213c; English Art 1979, no. 115; Adams 1987, pp. 39–42; Dragesco 1993, pp. 19–21.

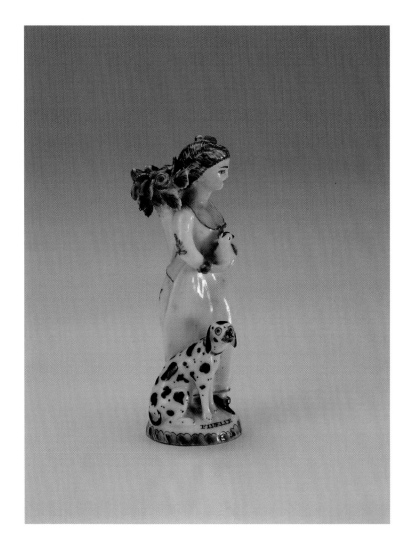

'Girl in a Swing'

SCENT-BOTTLE IN THE FORM OF VENUS AND
CUPID WITH A CLOCK, late 1750s

Porcelain, overglaze painting, height 3³⁄₁₆ in.
8 cm
No mark. On the base the overglaze inscription
in red paint: *L'HEURE DU BERGER FIDELLE*
Inv. no. 19356

Provenance: collection of Princess Maria A.
Shakhovskaya, St Petersburg; Stieglitz Museum,
St Petersburg; entered the Hermitage in 1926.

Exhibitions: 1991 Leningrad, no. 30.

Literature: Bryant 1925, pl. 19, no. 2; Rackham
1928–30, I, no. 298; Hackenbroch 1957, fig. 137,
pl. 66; Foster 1967, p. 288, no. 11, pl. 213a.

This scent-bottle on the theme of love and passing
time is another example of Girl in a Swing porcelain,
dated to the end of the 1750s (Foster 1967). LL

'Girl in a Swing'

ÉTUI WITH THE FIGURE OF A PUTTO, late 1750s

Porcelain, overglaze painting, height 4⁹⁄₁₆ in.
11.5 cm
No mark
Inv. no. 19394

Provenance: collection of the Princes Yusupov,
St Petersburg; entered the Hermitage in
1922–3.

Exhibitions: 1991 Leningrad, no. 39.

Literature: Bryant 1925, pl. 22, no. 3; Rackham
1928–30, I, no. 262; Foster 1967, p. 288, no. 3;
Adams 1987, p. 41, ill. 29.

This étui (a small case in which a woman could
keep her personal domestic items) belongs to
that group of Girl in a Swing products that
Foster has dated to the end of the 1750s. LL

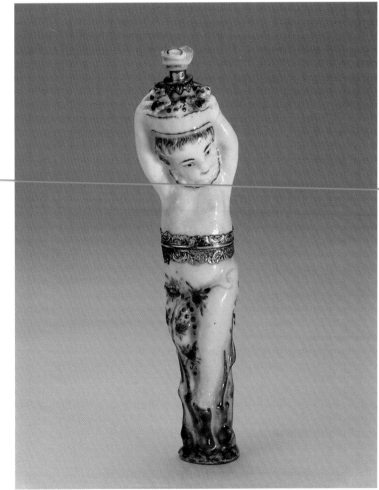

'Girl in a Swing'

SCENT-BOTTLE IN THE FORM OF HARLEQUIN
AND COLOMBINE, late 1750s

Porcelain, overglaze painting, height 3¾ in.
9.5 cm
No mark
Inv. no. 19307

Provenance: collection of the Princes Yusupov,
St Petersburg; entered the Hermitage in
1922–3.

Exhibitions: 1991 Leningrad, no. 26.

Literature: Bryant 1925, pl. 25, no. 4;
Hackenbroch 1957, fig. 162, pl. 73; Foster 1967,
p. 289, no. 27, pl. 213d.

This scent–bottle belongs to the second group
of products made at the Girl in a Swing factory,
which are dated to the end of the 1750s
(Foster 1967). LL

Chelsea

BOTTLE IN THE FORM OF A SMALL BOY ON A
TOY HORSE, 1758–69

Porcelain, overglaze painting, height 2⅞ in. 7.2 cm
No mark. Overglaze inscription on the horse's reins
in red paint (partly erased):
[…] LA PLUS BELLE
Inv. no. 18593

Provenance: collection of the Princes Yusupov,
St Petersburg; entered the Hermitage in 1922–3.

Exhibitions: 1991 Leningrad, no. 75.

Literature: Bryant 1925, pl. 15, no. 3;
Rare Porcelain 1987, p. 22, no. 25, ill. on p. 21.

The model for the bottle is one of the rarer Chelsea
pieces. The only comparable example is in the
British Museum, which until recently had been
considered to be unique (Rare Porcelain 1987). LL

Chelsea

SWEET-JAR WITH THE RAPE OF EUROPA,
early 1770s

Porcelain, overglaze painting, mounted in gold;
lid of moss agate; height 2¹⁄₁₆ in. 5.2 cm
No mark. Overglaze inscription in red paint on
the ribbon: *CAPRICE AMOUREUX*
Inv. no. 19390

Provenance: collection of the Princes Yusupov,
St Petersburg; entered the Hermitage in
1922–3.

Exhibitions: 1991 Leningrad, no. 67.

Literature: Bryant 1925, pl. 45, no. 4; Severne
Mackenna 1952, p. 25; English Art 1979,
no. 117.

This sweet-jar was published in 1979 by K.
Butler and R. Soloveychik, who dated it to
around 1755 (English Art 1979). Bryant
suggested that the examples he knew of that
had been made from the same model could be
dated to *c.* 1760 (Bryant 1925). Severne
Mackenna, however, was of the opinion that
the majority of the Chelsea sweet-jars were
made later, between 1770 and 1784 (the so-
called Duesbury period; Severne Mackenna
1952). The Hermitage piece has those traits
that Severne Mackenna considered to be
characteristic of similar 'porcelain toys': the
internal part of the box is painted with small
sprigs of flowers, and the lid is not of porcelain
but of a different material, in this case moss
agate (in other instances enamel lids were
often used). The Hermitage sweet-jar should
thus be dated to the early 1770s. LL

Wedgwood

VASE, *c.* 1770

black basaltes, with encaustic decoration,
height 8⅝ in. 22 cm
No mark
Inv. no. 19080

Provenance: collection of Arkady K.
Rudanovsky, St Petersburg; entered the
Hermitage in 1919.

Exhibitions: 1995 St Petersburg.

Literature: Macht 1957, p. 45, pl. 20; Honey
1958, p. 13, ill. 45; Chellis 1962, pp. 60–64;
English Art 1979, no. 247; Reilly and Savage
1980, pp. 29, 307; Dawson 1984, p. 34;
Treasure Houses 1985, p. 306, no. 231.

The model for this vase was no. 1 in the first
manuscript 'Shape Number One Book',
probably begun at the end of 1769 and
intended for internal use rather than for
publication. Dawson has noted (1995) that the
form was borrowed from a book of engravings,
the *Suite de vases composée dans le Goût
dell'Antique* (Paris, 1760), made after drawings
by the French artist Joseph-Marie Vien by his
wife Marie-Thérèse Reboul Vien. Dawson also
suggested that the model was originally used
by Wedgwood (around 1769) for a vase of agate
and marbled creamware, and only then in
black basaltes. The 'Shape Book' states that this
piece could be produced in eight sizes, in which
the height of the vase could vary from 6½ to 13
inches (16.5 × 33 cm). Dawson also noted that
a similar black basaltes vase with the addition
of relief garlands was included in George
Stubbs's painting *The Wedgwood Family in the
Grounds of Etruria Hall* (1780; Wedgwood
Museum, Barlaston). In this picture the vase
stands in the centre of the round table on
which the head of the family leans – a symbol
of his working career – and the choice of this
model for inclusion here suggests that it was a
very popular type. There are several variations
on the model – the handles in the form of a
satyr's horns are less twisted and the neck
broader than on the Hermitage piece (Honey
1958).

The painting on the vase involved a matt
technique that Wedgwood described as
'encaustic'. Invented by him for use on
ceramics, it has, in fact, nothing in common
with true encaustic – painting with wax

colours – and the title is purely metaphorical. Wedgwood's use of the term was in a tradition derived from the mistaken theory of an antiquary, the Comte de Caylus, that Antique vessels were decorated with encaustic. Caylus not only studied but also sought to revive the techniques of Antique vase painting, then thought to be lost. We know that Wedgwood made a detailed study of Caylus's experiments, and that in conducting his own he relied on J. H. Muntz's *Encaustics, or Count Caylus's method of painting in the manner of the Ancients* of 1760 (Chellis 1962, pp. 63–4). In naming as 'encaustic' the technique he himself had invented, Wedgwood was encouraging his clients to see his products in the context of a Classical tradition.

This Hermitage vase was discussed by K. Butler and R. Soloveychik in 1979 (English Art 1979), but they did not deal with the history of the model, or the iconographic sources for the painting on it. The motif – a dancing nymph with a tambourine – is nowhere else mentioned or reproduced in the literature on Wedgwood. There are, however, several possible prototypes for the image, one of them the relief on the famous Gaeta Vase, a marble by the Athenian sculptor Salpion, dating to the first century AD. This vase was for many years in the cathedral in Gaeta, where it was used for baptisms. In 1805 it was transferred to the Naples Museum. The relief shows the education of Bacchus: Mercury hands the infant Bacchus to a seated Juno. The main figures are surrounded by Bacchanalian figures, among them a nymph with a tambourine. A reproduction of the relief and a reasonably detailed description of it were included in the second volume of Bernard de Montfaucon's *L'Antiquité expliquée et représentée en figures* (1719, II, p. 230). An English edition (1721–5) of Montfaucon is included in the list of books belonging to Wedgwood and Bentley dated 10 August 1770 (Chellis 1962, p. 60), and we know that Wedgwood often it in his search for sources for relief compositions. Thus in 1776 William Hackwood made a model for a relief of the Birth of Bacchus that reproduced the central scene from the relief on the Gaeta vase. A plaque after a model by Hackwood was also put out by Wedgwood, showing seven figures from the relief decoration of the same vase (Macht 1957). According to Reilly and Savage (1980), Hackwood took as his source in both cases the engraving in Montfaucon's book. In neither case, however, is the dancing Bacchante with her tambourine included.

There is another possible graphic source for the nymph on the Hermitage vase: an engraving published in the Comte de Caylus's *Recueil d'Antiquités Egyptiennes, Etrusques, Grecques et Romaines* (1759, VII, pl. XXXVIII, no. 2). This book is also mentioned in the 1770 list of the Wedgwood and Bentley library (Chellis 1962, pp. 63–4). In Caylus's *Recueil* the figure of the Bacchante (a mirror image of that on the Hermitage vase) is one of the most strongly modelled motifs on the relief.

Another Antique piece, a triangular pedestal, with a relief of a dancing nymph (a Bacchante with a tambourine, with on the other two sides a faun playing a double flute and a faun with a shepherd's crook) is in the collection at Newby Hall, Yorkshire, along with another two pieces of the same type (Treasure Houses 1985, no. 231). Two of Newby's three pedestals (including the one that interests us) were published by the well-known restorer Bartolomeo Cavaceppi in volume III of his *Raccolta d'antiche statue, busti, teste, cognite ed altere sculture antiche* of 1772 (ill. 53). Much earlier, however, they had been illustrated in the *Codex Coburgensis*, which dates from the second half of the 16th century, and in the Dal Pozzo Albani albums, acquired by George III from Cardinal Alessandro Albani in 1762 for the Royal Library at Windsor Castle. The figure of a Bacchante with a tambourine is also to be found on several other pieces of Antique art.

The wealth of possible graphic sources precludes any precise indentification of the prototype for the Hermitage vase. An analysis of the practice at the Etruria manufactory nevertheless tends to support the theory of the use of the engraving in Montfaucon. The very abundance of images bears witness to the fact that Wedgwood sought to reproduce the best-known and most popular iconographic formulae. LL

102

Wedgwood

MEDALLION WITH A PORTRAIT OF WILLIAM SHAKESPEARE, *c.* 1775

Black basaltes; gilded bronze mount, 2³⁄₈ × 1⁹⁄₁₆ in. 6 × 4 cm
Beneath the portrait the stamped inscription: *SHAKESPEARE*; on the back the stamped mark: *WEDGWOOD & BENTLEY*
Inv. no. 19124

Provenance: collection of Louis Ricard-Abenheimer, Frankfurt-am-Main; from 1886 Stieglitz Museum; entered the Hermitage in 1926.

Exhibitions: 1995 St Petersburg.

Literature: Reilly and Savage 1973, p. 303; Reilly and Savage 1980, p. 311.

The celebrated English dramatist, poet and actor William Shakespeare (1564–1616) is shown in four Wedgwood medallions. The Hermitage example is taken from that by William Hackwood of 1744. The medallion was issued in different sizes, from a large oval piece four inches high (10 cm) to a small cameo of seven-eighths of an inch (2.2 cm). LL

Wedgwood

MEDALLION WITH A PORTRAIT OF
CATHERINE II, *c.* 1780

Black basaltes; silver mount, 4½ × 3¾ in.
11.5 × 9.5 cm
Beneath the portrait the stamped inscription:
EMP RUSSIA; on the back the stamped mark:
WEDGWOOD
Inv. no. 19813

Provenance: collection of Princess Maria A.
Shakhovskaya, St Petersburg; from 1918 in the
Shuvalov House Museum; entered the
Hermitage in 1925.

Exhibitions: 1912 St Petersburg; 1995 St
Petersburg.

Literature: Troynitsky 1912, p. 46; Shchukina
1962, p. 86; Reilly and Savage 1973, pp. 84–5.

Born Princess Sophia Frederika Augusta of
Anhalt-Zerbst (1729–96), from 1762 Catherine
II (as she became) ruled as Empress of Russia.
The first mention of a portrait medallion of
her was in the earliest published catalogue of
Wedgwood's decorative products in 1773. This
would seem to have been a small, not very
impressive piece, for on 15 May 1776
Wedgwood informed his partner Bentley that
'We want a good Head of the Empress of
Russia' (cited in Reilly and Savage 1973, p. 85).
Around 1779 Wedgwood produced two versions
of medallions with portraits of Catherine,
based on medals by T. Ivanov made in 1762 and
1774, and they were followed in 1782 by a
medallion with a portrait of the Empress as
Minerva, based on a cameo by Catherine's
daughter-in-law, Grand-Duchess Maria
Fyodorovna.

The piece shown here was taken from
Catherine's coronation medal of 1762. In that
year Ivanov made six stamps for the obverse of
a coronation medal and one stamp for the
reverse (copied from Johann Georg Wechter).
All six obverse designs show one and the same
portrait of the Empress. Shchukina considers
that the portrait may have been taken from one
of the many autograph copies after a painting
by Vergilius Eriksen, in which Catherine is
shown standing before a mirror; the mirror
reflection of her would then have served as the
basis for the medal (Shchukina 1962).

Undoubtedly, this medallion, one of a
number of similar pieces belonging to Princess
M. A. Shakhovskaya, was shown at the
Imperial Academy of Arts in St Petersburg in
1912 as part of an exhibition of Wedgwood
products. The black basaltes medallions with a
portrait of Catherine II from Princess
Shakhovskaya's collection are mentioned by
Troynitsky in the complete list of objects
loaned to the exhibition by private collectors:
'objects of black basalt … very … interesting
also … two busts and a medallion with the
profile of the Empress Catherine II (coll. Pr.
M. A. Shakhovskaya), medallions with the
profile of Empress Catherine II (coll. Pr. M. A.
Shakhovskaya)' (Troynitsky 1912). LL

Wedgwood

MEDALLION WITH A PORTRAIT OF GEORGE
WASHINGTON, c. 1779

Jasper ware; gilded bronze mount, 3⅝ × 3 in.
9.1 × 7.6 cm
Beneath the portrait the stamped inscription:
WASHINGTON; on the back the stamped
mark: *WEDGWOOD & BENTLEY*
Inv. no. 25486

Provenance: Acquired from a private collection
in 1939.

Exhibitions: 1995 St Petersburg.

Literature: Reilly and Savage 1973, p. 332;
Wedgwood Portraits 1976, pp. 82, 94–101;
English Art 1979, no. 245.

The portrait for this medallion was taken from the earliest of five known models made for Wedgwood medallions that depicted George Washington (1732–99). The iconographical source was a medal made to a design by Voltaire that was issued in Paris in 1777.

Wedgwood was initially hesitant about making the Washington medallions. He considered him to be 'at this time more absolute than any Despot in Europe', and asked Bentley 'how then can he be celebrated in such circumstances as the patron of Liberty?' (cited in Reilly and Savage). None the less, in November 1777 the first series of medallions with a portrait of the commander of America's Continental Army (then in winter quarters at Valley Forge) was issued, although the identity of the subject was hidden behind the title 'Grand-Duke of Muscovy'. These were made as pairs to portrait medallions of Benjamin Franklin. Washington's name was only stamped onto the medallions in 1778, and entered the Wedgwood catalogue for 1779. There are also Wedgwood medallions with portraits of Washington taken from the same model as the Hermitage example; the name *CHATHAM* is stamped on them. LL

Wedgwood

MEDALLION WITH A PORTRAIT OF JOSEPH PRIESTLEY, *c.* 1785

Jasper ware, 3⁷/₁₆ × 2³/₄ in. 8.7 × 7 cm
Beneath the portrait the stamped inscription: *PRIESTLEY*; on the back the stamped mark: *WEDGWOOD*
Inv. no. 19804

Provenance: Collection of Prince Alexander S. Dolgoruky, St Petersburg; entered the Hermitage in 1918.

Exhibitions: 1995 St Petersburg.

Literature: Reilly and Savage 1973, pp. 283–4; Arts and Sciences United 1978, pp. 40–44; English Art 1979, no. 246; Reilly and Savage 1980, p. 283.

Joseph Priestley (1733–1804), a chemist, philosopher and theologian, was already a member of both the Royal Society in London and the Académie des Sciences in Paris when, in 1789, he was made an honorary member of the St Petersburg Academy of Sciences.

The model for this medallion was made by William Hackwood in 1779 that copied one by Giuseppe Cerracchi executed earlier the same year, and they are the only known models for Wedgwood medallions of Priestley. The medallion itself forms a pair with one of Isaac Newton.

Wedgwood and Priestley were friends but they also had a business relationship: Priestley conducted his scientific experiments using special faïence vessels ordered from Wedgwood. Following the publication of Priestley's papers, which he had delivered to the Royal Society in 1783 and 1785, Wedgwood received many commissions for vessels for chemical laboratories. LL

106

Wedgwood

PLAQUE WITH BACCHANALIAN FIGURE FROM THE
SERIES 'HERCULANEUM FIGURES OR SUBJECTS',
c. 1785

Jasper ware, diameter 11⁵⁄₁₆ in. 28.7 cm
On the back the stamped mark: *WEDGWOOD*
Inv. no. 19063

Provenance: collection of Prince Alexander S.
Dolgoruky, St Petersburg; entered the
Hermitage in 1918.

Exhibitions: 1912 St Petersburg; 1995
St Petersburg.

Literature: Troynitsky 1912, p. 46; Macht 1957,
pp. 74–80; Kelly 1965, p. 24; English Art 1979,
no. 250; Buten 1980, ill. 83, p. 109; Reilly and
Savage 1980, p. 185; Reilly 1992, p. 89; Reilly
1994, ill. 482, pp. 371, 373; Liackhova 1994,
pp. 15–16; Genius of Wedgwood 1995, p. 18.

This plaque was published in 1979 by
K. Butler and R. Soloveychik under the title
'War' (English Art 1979), forming a pair with
the so-called 'Peace' (in fact a *Dancing Nymph*
from the same series; see cat. 107).

   Two plaques with Bacchanalian figures from
the series Herculaneum Subjects (one of them
of the same type as that in the Hermitage)
formerly decorated the walls of Catherine II's
bedroom in the Great Palace at Tsarskoye Selo.
In Wedgwood's papers (Keele University
archive) there are letters from St Petersburg
relating to the supply of plaques for the
decoration of palace interiors, which were
dispatched by Benjamin Hawksford and Peter
Capper (Blake Roberts 1995, pp. 220–21). The
first of the surviving documents is dated 25
July 1786. Exactly when and through whom
Wedgwood received the order from the
Russian court is, however, unknown. It is
interesting that Wedgwood's idea for the wide
use of ceramic plaques for interior decoration
(expressed in the very first published catalogue
of the firm's decorative wares in 1773) found a
response in Russia.

   This *Bacchanalian Figure* was shown at the
Imperial Academy of Arts in 1912 as part of the
exhibition of the wares of the firm of
Wedgwood. LL

107

Wedgwood

DANCING NYMPH PLAQUE, FROM THE SERIES
'HERCULANEUM FIGURES OR SUBJECTS', *c.* 1785

Jasper ware, diameter 11⅛ in. 28.3 cm
On the back the stamped mark: *WEDGWOOD*
Inv. no. 19067

Provenance: collection of Prince Alexander S.
Dolgoruky, St Petersburg; entered the
Hermitage in 1918.

Exhibitions: 1912 St Petersburg; 1995 St
Petersburg.

Literature: Roux and Barré 1820, IV, pl. 27;
Meteyard 1866, II, pp. 339–40; Troynitsky
1912, p. 46; Macht 1957, pp. 74–80; Kelly 1965,
p. 24; English Art 1979, no. 249; Buten 1980,
ill. 83, p. 109; Reilly and Savage 1980, p. 185;
Reilly 1992, p. 89; Reilly 1994, p. 373;
Liackhova 1994, pp. 15–16; Genius of
Wedgwood 1995, p. 18.

The series of 'Herculaneum Figures or Subjects' appeared in all the published catalogues of the decorative wares of Wedgwood and Bentley. The subjects are listed under 'Class II. Bas-Reliefs, Medallions, Cameo-Medallions, Tablets, &c' as numbers 51 to 65 (number 63 is missing in all the catalogues). The iconographical sources for thirteen of the fourteen pieces in the series were wall paintings discovered in the mid-18th century during excavations at Herculaneum and Pompeii. These paintings were reproduced in volume I of *Le Antichità di Ercolano Esposte* (1757), published in nine volumes between 1757 and 1792 by an anonymous group of scholars for the Spanish King Carlos III. According to Buten (1980), Wedgwood may have been familiar with the publication, which catalogued archaeological finds since 1738, when systematic excavations began. The paintings were also reproduced in *The Antiquities of Herculaneum* by T. Martin and J. Lettice, to which Wedgwood subscribed in 1773 (Genius of Wedgwood 1995). Reilly, however, considers that the Herculaneum Subjects were being produced by Wedgwood as early as June 1769 (Reilly 1994). The models were made from relief copies of the Antique wall paintings commissioned by the Marquess of Lansdowne and brought from Italy by him. Wedgwood received Lansdowne's permission to take casts of them, thanks to which the Marquess received an acknowledgment in the firm's catalogue of decorative wares for 1787.

The series included six compositions of *Dancing Nymphs*, a *Centaur* (with a Bacchante on his back), a *Female Centaur*, a *Centaur Teaching Achilles*, *Polyphemus*, *Marsyas and Young Olympus*, two Bacchanalian figures, plus the composition *Papyrius and his Mother*, the iconographical source for which has not been identified.

The Hermitage's *Dancing Nymph* was published by K. Butler and R. Soloveychik (English Art 1979) under the title 'Peace', as a companion to another plaque entitled 'War' (in fact a Bacchanalian figure from the same series – see cat. 106). The authors were unaware of the fact that the two plaques were not a pair but part of a series, and their error led to the supposition that they may have been modelled by the sculptor John Flaxman. We should note, however, that there has long been a tendency to interpret the *Dancing Nymphs* outside the context of the Wedgwood series. Meteyard called the composition 'Pomona' (the Roman goddess of fruits), and also suggested that Flaxman was involved in its production (Meteyard 1866).

It is interesting to note that one of the publications on the antiquities of Herculaneum and Pompeii also lists the iconographical source for the Hermitage's *Dancing Nymph* as 'Peace' (Roux and Barré 1820). The multiplicity of interpretations of the subjects from the Wedgwood compositions arose from the fact that the plaques were often sold in smaller groups or even singly, and the whole set was rarely to be found with one owner or in one interior. The subjects of the separate compositions were interpreted according to the context in which they were placed.

The Herculaneum Subjects are quite large (the oval plaques are 10 × 7¾ in. (25.4 × 19.7 cm); the round plaques are 11½ inches (29.2 cm) in diameter. These sizeable objects were described in the Wedgwood catalogue for 1881 as 'Very proper and elegant Pictures for the Decoration of large Halls and Stair Cases' (cited in Kelly 1965, p. 25).

The *Dancing Nymph* and *Bacchanalian Figure*, formerly part of the A. S. Dolgoruky collection, were shown at the Imperial Academy of Arts in St Petersburg in 1912 as part of the exhibition of Wedgwood products. Troynitsky's report of the exhibition, which included a full list of pieces provided by private collectors, stated: 'Of the jasper ware objects, we must place first of all: a large vase in the form of a ewer with a Triton seated on the handle and two round medallions belonging to Prince A. S. Dolgoruky' (Troynitsky 1912). LL

Wedgwood

PLAQUE: CATHERINE II REWARDING ART AND PROTECTING COMMERCE, late 1780s

Jasper ware, 16⁷/₁₆ × 12⁷/₁₆ in. 41.8 × 31.6 cm
On the back the stamped mark: *WEDGWOOD*
Inv. no. 23320

Provenance: collection of Baron Alexander L. Stieglitz, St Petersburg; Stieglitz Museum, St Petersburg; entered the Hermitage in 1926.

Exhibitions: 1995 St Petersburg.

Literature: Harriman 1960, p. 51; Reilly and Savage 1980, p. 80.

This plaque is one of the Wedgwood firm's rarest products. Only one other example of this composition is known (Detroit Institute of Arts), a rectangular plaque of black basaltes on the back of which is the stamped inscription *CATHERINE II REWARDING ART AND PROTECTING COMMERCE* plus the mark *WEDGWOOD* (Harriman 1960). Harriman, and later Reilly and Savage (1980), attribute the model to the sculptor John Flaxman, and the latter date it to around 1785. Flaxman's authorship might arguably be supported by the similarity between separate plastic motifs on the Hermitage relief composition and motifs in the sculptor's drawings of a later date.

On the sheet entitled *Athena throwing Nausicae's ball into the sea* from Flaxman's drawings of the second half of 1792 for Homer's *Odyssey*, which were not published as

engravings until 1805 (see Flaxman's *Zeichnungen*, 1910, pl. LXXXVI), there is a depiction of Athena with a shield in her hand, very like the figure of Catherine as Minerva on the Hermitage plaque. The Russian Minerva also holds a shield, albeit in her right hand rather than her left. The similar poses of the two figures, the turn of their heads, the positions of their hands, and particularly the details of the robes are all very similar. The border folds of the drapery on Catherine's breast are treated like a twisting relief ribbon. In the drawing the effect of volume is achieved through the use of a double line: both the outer and inner edge of the border can be seen. This motif is often found in Flaxman's compositions, and it was possibly connected with the artist's experience of working in relief, including the production of the model for the Hermitage plaque. LL

Wedgwood

WATER EWER: SACRED TO NEPTUNE, late 1780s

Jasper ware, height 15 in. 38 cm
On the stand the stamped mark:
WEDGWOOD
Inv. no. 19071

Provenance: collection of Prince Alexander S.
Dolgoruky, St Petersburg; entered the
Hermitage in 1918.

Exhibitions: 1912 St Petersburg; 1995 St
Petersburg.

Literature: Troynitsky 1912, p. 46; Buten 1980,
p. 109, ill. 83; Reilly and Savage 1980, p. 391;
Dawson 1984, pp. 38–40; Blake Roberts 1986,
p. 84; Reilly 1989, I, p. 408; Liackhova 1992,
p. 23; Genius of Wedgwood 1995, B.57, E.31,
E.32.

Sacred to Neptune was issued by Wedgwood as
a companion to a wine ewer, *Sacred to Bacchus*.
Both models were included in Wedgwood's
'Shape Number One Book', under no. 236.
They were made from plastercasts that
Wedgwood acquired in 1775 from John
Flaxman senior, father of the famous sculptor.
These casts, now in the Wedgwood Museum,
Barlaston, were in their turn taken from bronze
ewers. The original models for these vases
would seem to have been exhibited at the Salon
de l'Académie de Saint-Luc in Paris in 1774 by
Sigisbert Michel, nephew of the French
sculptor Claude Michel, known as Clodion
(Genius of Wedgwood 1995, E.31).
     Examples of the Wedgwood *Sacred to
Neptune* and *Sacred to Bacchus* ewers were
acquired in 1786 by Prince Grigory Potemkin
from Benjamin Hawksford, an English
merchant then living in St Petersburg, as we
know from a note in the margin of a letter
from Hawksford dated 11 July 1786 (Blake
Roberts 1986).
     This ewer can be identified as the one that
was shown at the exhibition of Wedgwood
products held at the Imperial Academy of Arts,
St Petersburg, in 1912 (Liackhova 1992). In his
record of the exhibition, Troynitsky wrote: 'Of
the objects of jasper ware, the following must
be given first place: a large vase in the form of
a ewer with a Triton sitting on the handle and
two round medallions, belonging to Prince A.
S. Dolgoruky' (Troynitsky 1912). LL

Wedgwood

TWO CREAM VASES AND COVERS, 1830s–40s

Stoneware, glazed interior, height 12⅜ in.
31.5 cm
On the bottom of each vase the stamped mark:
WEDGWOOD
Inv. nos. 9177, 9178

Provenance: acquired for the Imperial Farm at
Tsarskoye Selo; transferred to the Arsenal at
Tsarskoye Selo; entered the Hermitage in 1912.

Exhibitions: 1995 St Petersburg.

Literature: Mankowitz 1953, pl. 30; Born 1964,
pp. 71, 80; Kelly 1965, pp. 119–24; Reilly and
Savage 1980, p. 113; Stonewares 1982, p. 128,
no. 272; Reilly 1989, I, p. 314, ill. 395; II, p. 113,
ill. 79; Brinding Adams 1992, p. 274, no. 447; p.
275, nos. 451, 452; p. 276, no. 453; Vil'chkovsky
1992, pp. 197, 214–16.

These cream vases formed part of a set of
tableware acquired for the Imperial Farm at
Tsarskoye Selo. According to an inventory of
the property at the farm made in 1860, this set
'of dark-brown English faïence with white
patterns' included four vases in the form of
urns (the cream vases), two 'vases in the form
of chalices', two 'ewers with handles', fourteen
'large long dishes', four 'spoons for milk,
unpatterned', four 'small dishes with strainers,
unpatterned' and two 'unpatterned funnels'
(RGIA Fund 469, op. 15, d. 442, fol. 13).

Judging by the good state of preservation of
the objects now in the Hermitage, they were
rarely, if ever, used, and thus the inventory of
1860 probably gives a good idea of the original
composition of the set.

The Hermitage has seven pieces altogether:
four cream vases (two of which are shown
here) plus one dish, one bowl and one ewer.
The last three objects reached the Museum as
recently as 1934, although the cream vases
came in 1912 from the Arsenal at Tsarskoye
Selo, to which they must have been transferred
with the other pieces from the Imperial Farm.
We should note that the Tsarskoye Selo Arsenal
by this time included not only weapons but also
a collection of porcelain and glass. RGIA has a
1912 'List of porcelain objects selected for the
porcelain gallery of the Imperial Hermitage'
that mentions four 'vases in the shape of urns'
in the museum of the Arsenal at Tsarskoye
Selo, and describes the material of which they

were made: 'English faïence of dark colour with white patterns' (RGIA Fund 472, op. 49, d. 1146, fol. 12).

The Imperial Farm at Tsarskoye Selo also had another similar set of Wedgwood crockery, of Queen's ware, totally without decoration. Three pieces are now in the Hermitage. The set was acquired in 1822 in the 'English shop' of Nichols & Plinke, the first department store to open in St Petersburg (RGIA Fund 487, op. 6, d. 2569, fol. 24). The other Wedgwood service for the Farm may also have been bought at the same shop, where purchases for the court were often made.

The Wedgwood items were kept in the 'crockery room' of the cheese dairy, in one of the Farm's two pavilions. The Farm itself was designed by the architect Adam Menelaws in 1820 in the Gothic Revival style. In Russia this style was associated with England and at the beginning of the 20th century was even called 'Anglo-Gothic' (Vil'chkovsky 1992, p. 214). The acquisition of English ceramics for the Farm was also a tribute to English taste.

The models for the cream vases were no. 1109 in Wedgwood's 'Shape Book' for faïence pieces, a manuscript begun *c.* 1770 and finished *c.* 1815 that appears to have formed the basis for the publication of the first Wedgwood catalogue of faïence, the Queen's ware Catalogue of 1774 (Born 1964).

The relief decoration on the vases is variously described in the literature on Wedgwood ceramics as 'prunus sprays' (Stonewares 1982), 'chrysanthemum and prunus' (Reilly 1989, II) or simply 'prunus' (Brinding Adams 1992). The motif was reproduced in the 1817 catalogue of Wedgwood's decorative objects, in which 'prunus sprays' are used on a teapot listed under no. 148 (Mankowitz 1953). LL

111

Unidentified English master

BERET BUCKLE WITH SUSANNA AND THE
ELDERS, 1510–20

Gold, enamel; chased and engraved,
diameter 1¹⁵⁄₁₆ in. 4.9 cm
Inv. no. 4783

Provenance: from the mid-19th century in the
Gallery of Objets de Vertù of the Hermitage.

Exhibitions: 1986 Lugano, no. 1.

Literature: Liven 1902, p. 108; Hackenbroch
1979, ill. 750; English Art 1979, no. I.

Manuscript inventories of the 19th century list
this buckle as German or Netherlandish work
of the 15th century. Liven attributed it to a
16th-century Italian master, but Hackenbroch
identified it as English work and dated it to
1510–20. Similar pieces are to be found in
London in the British Museum (*Christ and the
Samaritan Woman*) and the Wallace Collection
(*Judith and Holofernes*); these have the same
punched background, the drawing of the
border and the same style for depicting the
faces as the Hermitage buckle. OK

112

Unidentified English master

PENDANT FORMERLY BELONGING TO
SIR FRANCIS DRAKE, late 16th century

Quartz, gold, enamel; polished and painted,
1¹⁄₁₆ × 1¼ in. 2.7 × 3.2 cm
Inscribed on the frame: *Fran. Drackh Jork. A
1590*
Inv. no. 4794

Provenance: in the Winter Palace by 1789;
transferred to the Hermitage in 1807.

Exhibitions: 1991 Boston.

The quartz stone of this pendant, with natural
fractures and scratches, is covered with pink
paint. The gold fitting of the upper part of the
pendant is decorated with an image of the
Earth, the equator marked by a band, and a
ship. This piece probably belonged to the
English navigator Sir Francis Drake (1540–96)
and is linked either with his three-year voyage
around the world (1577–80) or his promotion
to the rank of Vice-Admiral in 1588.

In 1789 a list was made of Catherine II's
valuables 'composing the 'Armitazh' of Her
Majesty'. As well as serving as a catalogue of
the court valuables that were located there at
the end of the 18th century, the list was later
used as an inventory for registering newly
acquired objects. It includes a pendant 'in the
form of an egg of transparent mixed stones of
ruby type'. Against this entry it is noted:
'On the order of his highness Count Nikolai
Alexandrovich Tolstoy, transferred to the
Hermitage 25 November 1807'. OK

113

Hussy & Joyce
(*fl.* first half of the 18th century)

NÉCESSAIRE ON A CHATELAINE WITH ÉTUIS, 1730s

Gold, moss agate, onyx, lapis lazuli, copper, steel; polished, chased and punched. Nécessaire: $3^{9}/_{16} \times 1^{3}/_{16}$ in. 9 × 3 cm; chatelaine: 3 × 1 in. 7.6 × 2.5 cm Inscribed on the hook: *Joyce Hussy* Inv. no. 3013

Provenance: from the middle of the 19th century in the Gallery of Objets de Vertù of the Hermitage.

Literature: Jones 1910, p. 254, pl. 5; Hermitage 1979, ill. 54.

The chatelaine consists of a gilded copper hook, decorated on the front with an image of a helmeted Minerva with a shield and spear. The nécessaire is of lapis lazuli and dendrite in a fluted gold frame, decorated in the centre with ornament in the form of garlands with a basket of flowers. The onyx and lapis-lazuli étuis unscrew. OK

114

Joseph Dudds (*fl.* mid-18th century)

WATCH ON A CHATELAINE WITH A KEY, ADORNED WITH LAPIS LAZULI, *c.* 1750

Gold, silver, lapis lazuli, rock crystal, metal alloys; chased and polished. Watch diameter: $1^{5}/_{8}$ in. 4.2 cm; chatelaine length: $7^{11}/_{16}$ in. 19.5 cm On the mechanism: *Jos Dudds London 3101* Inv. no. 3026

Provenance: at the end of the 18th century in the Winter Palace; from the mid-19th century in the Gallery of Objets de Vertù of the Hermitage.

Exhibitions: 1971 Leningrad, no. 62.

Literature: English Art 1979, no. 66.

The Hermitage has several watches made by the London craftsman Joseph Dudds, who from 1732 was a member of the Clock Company.

The body of this watch and the upper part of the chatelaine are faced with pieces of lapis lazuli, between which are rows of faceted metal beads. This decoration, with beads imitating diamonds, was quite widely used in the mid-18th century. Here it is combined with colourful accents of rock crystal set over red foil. OK

115

Quare & Horseman

GOLD WATCH ON A CHATELAINE, WITH A KEY,
DECORATED WITH DIAMONDS AND SPINEL
RUBIES, 1730s

Gold, silver, diamonds, spinel rubies,
metal alloys; chased, polished, punched. Watch
diameter: 1⅞ in. 4.7 cm; chatelaine length:
5⅝ in. 14.3 cm
On the mechanism: *Quare & Horseman.*
No 1139; on the clockface: *Quare Horseman*
London
Inv. no. 4303

Provenance: acquired by the Empress Elizabeth
Petrovna in the mid-18th century, and kept in
the Winter Palace; at the end of the 19th
century transferred from the Cabinet of
Treasury Diamonds in the Winter Palace to the
Gallery of Objets de Vertù of the Hermitage.

Literature: Jones 1910, p. 254, pl. V; English Art
1979, no. 69.

The firm of Quare & Horseman was
established in 1718 by Daniel Quare
(1649–1724), a renowned English watchmaker
and the inventor of the repeater for clocks, and
Stephen Horseman (from 1702 apprentice,
from 1709 member of the Clock Company).
Despite Quare's death in 1724, it continued for
several more years, but went bankrupt in 1733.
  This watch on a chatelaine in a removable
case is the only extant example of a joint work
by these two craftsmen. The case and the
central links of the chatelaine are decorated
with diamonds in silver settings and large
spinels of a saturated ruby colour in a gold
setting, plus small enamel forget-me-nots.
The clockface is of punched gold with two runs
of numerals: roman for the hours and arabic
for the minutes. OK

116

Robert Hyman
(*fl.* second half of 18th century)

GOLD WATCH ON A CHATELAINE WITH A SEAL,
KEY AND ÉTUI, DECORATED WITH PRECIOUS
STONES AND ENAMEL, 1770s

Gold, silver, diamonds, glass, enamel, metal
alloys; chased. Watch diameter: 1⁵⁄₁₆ in. 3.3 cm;
chatelaine length: 5 in. 12.7 cm
Inscribed on the watch mechanism:
Robt Hyman
Inv. nos. 4289, 4290

Provenance: from the mid-19th century in the
Gallery of Objets de Vertù of the Hermitage.

Exhibitions: 1994 Speyer, p. 212.

Literature: Jones 1910, p. 249, pl. 1.

Robert Hyman emigrated from England to
St Petersburg in 1776, before which he was a
member of the Joiner's Company in London.
The decoration of the watch and the chatelaine
– it is entirely encrusted with diamonds,
which almost totally conceal the surface – is
traditional, and characteristic of the work of
the guild of foreign jewellers in St Petersburg
in the 1770s. The Hermitage has a large
collection of watches on chatelaines, the
greater part of which were acquired in the
mid-18th century by the Empress Elizabeth
Petrovna.
  During the reign of Catherine II there
were several attempts to set up watchmaking
factories in Moscow and St Petersburg, and
Catherine repeatedly commissioned and
acquired watches both abroad and from foreign
craftsmen working in the capital. OK

117

John Ellicott II (1706–1772)

WATCH ON A CHATELAINE
(WITH EMBOSSED DECORATION), 1760

Gold, silver, enamel, glass, diamonds, metal
alloys; chased, engraved and punched,
diameter 2 in. 5.1 cm; chatelaine length:
5¾ in. 14.5 cm
Watch: *Ellicott / London / 4676*; on the
protective lid: *Ellicott / London / 4676*;
on the outer case: *H. Manly*
Marks: on the outer case: *JB* [John Beesly]; on
the chatelaine: sterling standard mark; mark
for London; date letter for 1760–61; maker's
mark *JS – James Smith*
Inv. no. 2056

Provenance: presumed to have been acquired
by the Empress Elizabeth Petrovna in the mid-
18th century; from the mid-19th century in the
Gallery of Objets de Vertù of the Hermitage.

Exhibitions: 1986 Lugano, no. 10; 1992 Tokyo,
no. 8.

Literature: Liven 1902, p. 75; Jones 1910, pl. II;
Yakovleva 1988, pp. 12–14.

The lid of the watch is perforated along the
edge and decorated with engraved *rocaille*
ornament, a chased composition showing
Hannibal's Oath in the centre. The four-part
chatelaine is decorated with chased images of
the allegorical figures of Justice, Wisdom,
Meekness and Strength surrounded by
architectural ornament. The watch is a superb
example of collaboration between several
craftsmen: the watchmaker John Ellicott II,
the embossers and chasers Henry Manly and
John Beesly, and the jeweller James Smith, all
of whom added their signatures or marks to
the object. OK

Charles Cabrier the Elder (d. 1724)

WATCH ON A CHATELAINE, *c.* 1720

Gold, silver, sapphires, enamel, glass, metal
alloys; chased and engraved, diameter 1⅞ in.
4.7 cm; Chatelaine length: 5⅝ in. 14.3 cm
Inscribed on the mechanism:
Cabrier / London; on the face: *London*
Inv. no. 4304

Provenance: acquired by the Empress Elizabeth
Petrovna in the mid-18th century, kept in the
Winter Palace; transferred at the end of the
19th century to the Gallery of Objets de Vertù
of the Hermitage.

Exhibitions: 1991 Boston; 1994 Speyer, p. 184.

There were five watchmakers of French origin
with the name Charles Cabrier at work in
London in the 18th century. This watch was
probably made by Charles Cabrier the Elder,
a member of the Clock Company from 1697 to
1724. It forms part of a superb collection of
English clocks and watches acquired by the
Russian court in the 18th century. It is
decorated with 22 sapphires and 99 diamonds
on the outer case and on the chatelaine. Similar
chatelaine-chains were used to attach watches
to the waist, for in the 18th century watches
were not only functional, they served as a
means of personal adornment. The inner
corpus of the watch is decorated with engraved
rocaille ornament and the British royal coat of
arms. OK

Thomas Thearle (*fl.* mid-18th century)

SET OF A WATCH AND NÉCESSAIRE ON
CHATELAINES, 1752

Gold, agate, silver, diamonds, enamel, onyx,
glass, metal alloys; chased and engraved.
Watch diameter: 1¾ in. 4.5 cm; chatelaine
length: 5 in. 12.7 cm; nécessaire: 4¹¹⁄₁₆ × 1½ in.
11.9 × 3.9 cm; chatelaine length: 3¾ in. 8.2 cm
Marks: on the bottom of the inner corpus of
the watch: *C B 6900*; on the chatelaines:
sterling standard mark; hallmark for London;
date letter for 1752–3; maker's mark *T.T.*
Inscribed on the mechanism and protective lid
of the watch: *C. Cabrier. London 6900*; on the
watchface: *CABRIER London*
Inv. nos. 4310, 4312

Provenance: acquired by the Empress Elizabeth
Petrovna in the mid-18th century, kept in the
Winter Palace; transferred at the end of the
19th century from the Cabinet of Treasury
Diamonds of the Winter Palace to the Gallery
of Objets de Vertù of the Hermitage.

Exhibitions: 1986 Lugano, no. 7; 1994 Speyer,
p. 182.

Literature: Jones 1910, pp. 249, 254; English Art
1979, nos. 68, 107.

The nécessaire and watch are supplied with
chatelaines with which to attach them to the
waist. The decorative style in which this set is
executed – the use of fancy agate plaques, the
embossed trellis ornament and the *rocaille*
pattern of diamonds – is characteristic of
mid-18th-century English jewellers. The
chatelaines bear the mark of the London
master Thomas Thearle. His independent
works began to appear in the 1720s, but his best
pieces are dated to the mid-century. The watch
mechanism is by Charles Cabrier the Younger.
The set is a rare example of the concurrent
production of objects with differing functions
intended to be worn together as personal
adornment. OK

Unidentified London Master

HAND-MIRROR, *c.* 1750

Gold, silver, rubies, garnets, diamonds; chased, engraved, punched, 8⅛ × 15¾ in. 20.7 × 40 cm
Inv. no. 2750

Provenance: kept in the Winter Palace; from the mid-19th century in the Gallery of Objets de Vertù of the Hermitage.

Literature: Benois 1902, p. 313; Ivanov 1904, p. 162.

The frame and handle of this mirror are completely covered with *rocaille* ornament and decorated with lines of diamonds and rubies. On the back is a chased *rocaille* architectural composition with a staircase, columns, a fountain and trees. It is thought that the mirror was presented to the Empress Elizabeth Petrovna on behalf of the Turkish Sultan Osman III, for it is crowned with a sickle moon set with diamonds in silver.

For a long time the mirror was attributed to French masters of the mid-18th century, but the style of chasing, typical of English goldsmiths of the same period, indicates that it is the work of an English craftsman. The absence of any inscription or hallmark suggests that this piece was made to commission. OK

Unidentified London Master

SNUFF BOX WITH A TWO-PART LID, 1740s

Lapis lazuli, gold; carved, polished, engraved
and chased, 1³⁄₈ × 2⁵⁄₈ × 3³⁄₈ in.
3.4 × 6.7 × 8.5 cm
Inv. no. 3911

Provenance: mentioned in the list of *objets de
vertù* of the Empress Elizabeth Petrovna of
1761; from the mid-19th century in the Gallery
of Objets de Vertù of the Hermitage.

This piece, made of lapis lazuli, and a similar
snuffbox of grey agate (inv. no. 3913) were
probably acquired by the Russian court
together with a collection of English watches.
Their mention in documents of the reign of
Elizabeth Petrovna suggests that they entered
the Imperial collection in the mid-18th
century. Traditionally, these two snuffboxes –
'stone lapis lazuli double in a gold frame' and
'stone agate double in a gold frame' – were
dated to the 18th century and attributed to
German jewellers. A study of the *rocaille*
architectural compositions and the work of the
chased outlines, however, suggests that they are
the work of English masters of the mid-18th
century. This is confirmed by a comparison
with similar works in the Louvre (Cardinal
1984, I, pp. 133, 141), the Metropolitan Museum
of Art (London 1984, pp. 141–3) and other
museums and private collections. OK

Unidentified London Master

SNUFFBOX, 1760s–70s

Gold, agate; chased and engraved,
¹⁵⁄₁₆ × 2¹¹⁄₁₆ × 2¹⁄₁₆ in. 2.4 × 6.8 × 5.2 cm
On the edge the hallmark: *E.T.*
Inv. no. 320

Provenance: collection of Grand-Duke Alexei
Alexandrovich; entered the Hermitage in
1908.

Literature: Snowman 1990, pl. 563.

This agate snuffbox with its hinged lid is
decorated with plaques of polished agate in a
chased gold setting. The *rocaille* decoration of
the lid with its image of a Chinese village with
a pagoda, a bridge, trees and figures, is in the
Chinoiserie style. The mark *E.T.* is possibly the
monogram of Elizabeth Tookey, widow of the
London craftsman Thomas Tookey. OK

123

Unidentified London Master

TABLE NÉCESSAIRE OF HELIOTROPE IN A
GOLD FRAME, CONTAINING 12 OBJECTS, *c.* 1760

Gold, silver, mother-of-pearl, glass,
heliotrope, leather; chased and polished,
$2^{11}/_{16} \times 1^{15}/_{16} \times 4^{7}/_{8}$ in. 6.8 × 4.9 × 12.4 cm
Inv. no. 1811

Provenance: from the 18th century in the
Winter Palace; from the mid-19th century
in the Gallery of Objets de Vertù of the
Hermitage.

Exhibitions: 1994 Speyer, p. 196.

Literature: English Art 1979, no. 103.

The Hermitage has a large collection of
nécessaires linked with Russian history.
According to the inscription on the ivory
plaque inserted in this table nécessaire, it was
presented to Catherine II on her name day:
'I congratulate the Most High Merciful
Mother Sovereign on her name day. Almighty
God, multiply the many prosperous years of
the great Imperial Mercy to the least of her
slaves. Both God and Your Highness are most
merciful.'
    Within the nécessaire are tweezers and
a file, a needle, scissors, a pencil, a mirror,
brushes and bottles. The decoration of the
objects, formed of gold *rocaille* bands across
the heliotrope ground, are characteristic of
English craftsmen of the period. OK

124.

James Cox (*fl.* 1749–91)

TABLE CLOCK MOUNTED ON RHINOCEROSES,
WITH A NÉCESSAIRE AND MUSICAL
MECHANISM, 1772

Gold, silver, pink agate, pearls, coloured glass,
metal alloys; chased and engraved,
14½ × 6⅞ × 5¾ in. 36.9 × 17.5 × 14.5 cm
Engraved on the key: *J. Cox. London. 1772;*
on the clockface: *Ja.s Cox 1772*
Inv. no. 2003

Provenance: at the end of the 18th century in
the Winter Palace; from the mid-19th century
in the Gallery of Objets de Vertù of the
Hermitage.

Exhibitions: 1992 Tokyo, no. 1; 1994 Speyer,
p. 214.

Literature: English Art 1979, nos. 208, 209.

James Cox was famous for his clocks set into
table nécessaires of complex form. Works by
him that are analogous to this one in the
Hermitage are to be found in a number of
museums in Europe and the United States.
Similar pieces, made in the characteristic
decorative style of English craftsmen of the
1770s, were quite common in Russia,
particularly in private collections in St
Petersburg. The upper part of this clock is
decorated with sprays of flowers and insects
attached on flexible springs.
   Works by Cox became particularly popular
after Grigorii Potemkin's acquisition of his
large Peacock Clock (fig. 15). It was later
purchased by Catherine II, and in the 19th
century was displayed in the diamond room
of the Hermitage. OK

125

Unidentified London Master

NÉCESSAIRE / INKSTAND WITH CLOCK, *c.* 1750

Gold, heliotrope, mother-of-pearl, enamel, glass; chased and engraved, 4⁵⁄₁₆ × 5 × 4¹¹⁄₈ in.
11 × 12.7 × 10.5 cm
Inscribed on the clock mechanism:
Cabrier London 5231
Inv. no. 2004

Provenance: collection of D. Tatishchev, Russian ambassador to Vienna; entered the Hermitage in 1845.

This rectangular box stands on four legs in the form of sphinxes; the writing set inside is decorated with heliotrope plaques set in a gold *rocaille* frame. On the lid is a gold tripod with a cartouche decorated with architectural ornament, while the clock, by Charles Cabrier the Younger, is set in the centre. OK

Unidentified London Master

CASE OF DRAWING INSTRUMENTS, *c.* 1750

Gold, silver, steel, ivory, diamonds;
chased, polished, engraved and punched,
$3^{13}\!/_{16} \times 1^{7}\!/_{16} \times \sqrt[3]{4}$ in. 9.7 × 3.7 × 1.9 cm
Inv. no. 3004

Provenance: from the mid-19th century in the
Gallery of Objets de Vertù of the Hermitage.

Literature: Benois 1902, pp. 321, 327.

In the mid-18th century, cases containing
miniature instruments were quite common,
and there are numerous nécessaires and cases
of drawing instruments in the Hermitage
collection. This example contains seven
drawing and measuring instruments. The
corpus is decorated with chased architectural
ornament in the form of a round hall with
columns; on the architrave is the figure of a
boy personifying Astronomy and a globe with
a spy-glass. OK

127

Julien de Fontenay (*fl. c.* 1575–1600)

CAMEO: PORTRAIT OF ELIZABETH I, *c.* 1575
Sardonyx; gold frame, 2⁷⁄₁₆ × 1¹³⁄₁₆ in. 6.2 × 4.7 cm
Inv. no. K 1020

Provenance: gem collection of the Duc d'Orléans, Paris; entered the
Hermitage in 1787 as part of that collection.

Exhibitions: 1972, Leningrad, no. 515.

Literature: La Chau and Le Blond 1784, II, pl. 74; Cabinet d'Orléans
1786, no. 1355; King 1866, pp. 175–6; King 1872, p. 431; Fortnum 1874,
XLV, p. 18; O'Donoghue 1894, p. 100, no. 6; Reinach 1895, p. 145, no. 74,
pl. 131; Dalton 1915, p. l; Ilchester 1922, p. 70; Eichler and Kris 1927, p.
175; Strong 1963, p. 131, no. 11; Scott 1973, pp. 18–19 (mistakenly said to
have been acquired by the Duc d'Orléans from the collection of Pierre
Crozat); Kagan 1973a, no. 55; English Art 1979, no. 13; Kagan 1980,
p. 32; Scarisbrick 1986, p. 250; Seidmann 1993, p. 95, fig 6.13.

Of the six carved portraits of Elizabeth I in the Hermitage, this is the
most outstanding in terms of size and quality of carving, and should be
grouped with the most important cameos of the type, in the Cabinet de
Médailles of the Bibliothèque Nationale, Paris (Babelon 1897, no. 967),
the Royal Collection, Windsor Castle (Tonnochy 1935, no. VII), the
Victoria and Albert Museum, London (Davenport 1900, p. 54, pl. VIII),
the collection of the Dukes of Devonshire, Chatsworth (Scarisbrick
1986, no. 57, pl. 89g), and the Kunsthistorisches Museum, Vienna
(Eichler and Kris 1927, p. 175, no. 409, fig. 38). Iconographically it is
closer to the Paris version. Not only do the dress, jewelry and crown
match closely: in both the Queen wears on her breast, on the chain
beneath her ruff, a clearly identifiable cameo with St George – the sign
of the Order of the Garter. Painted portraits of the Queen with this
sign, some with a cameo, dating from *c.* 1575, have been grouped as 'the
Garter Portraits' (Strong 1963, p. 62). Since both are interesting
examples of the depiction of a 'cameo within a cameo', and belong to
the same portrait type, they can be dated to the same time. Individual
details link the Hermitage cameo with other 'cameo' portraits of
Elizabeth – numerous, although not of such high quality – which are in
public and private collections, often with their original settings.
Unfortunately, all the Hermitage examples have lost their settings.

After futile attempts from the 17th century onwards to attribute the
Elizabethan cameos to the leading masters of the Renaissance – Valerio
Belli (see Evelyn 1697, p. 240; Walpole 1862, I, pp. 188, 189), Matteo del
Nassaro and Luca Penny (see King 1872, p. 328) – two theories have
been promoted: one considered the maker to be Richard Atsill (or
Astyll), who began working in England during the reign of Henry VIII
(Fortnum 1874, p. 19; Smith 1903, p. 241; Tonnochy 1935, p. 277); the
second, largely supported by French scholars (Mariette 1750, I, p. 136;
Chabouillet 1858, p. 71; Babelon 1897, p. 140; Lhuillier 1887) and some
of their English colleagues (Davenport 1900, p. 54), attributed them to
the gem-engraver Julien de Fontenay, whom they thought had been
sent specially to Elizabeth's court by the French monarch Henri IV.

Although the second attribution seems more likely in terms of
chronology, neither are confirmed by documentary sources. Master
engravers undoubtedly had large workshops in which cameos were
produced from set models, possibly organized in the same way as the
painting workshops in which portraits of Elizabeth were mass produced
in conditions of secrecy (Strong 1963, pp. 11–12). From the engraving
workshop, cameos then passed to the court jewellers. YU.K

128

Anonymous

CAMEO: ST GEORGE AND THE DRAGON, late 16th century
Sardonyx; gold setting (18th century), 1⁹⁄₁₆ × 1³⁄₁₆ in. 4 × 3 cm
Inv. no. K 652

Provenance: entered the Hermitage at the end of the 18th century.

Literature: English Art 1979, no. 7 (fig. 8); Kagan 1981, p. 189, fig. II.3.

This is one of the earliest examples of a cameo used, along with
enamelled miniatures, for the insignia of the Order of the Garter (the
'Lesser Georges'). Unlike the 'Great Georges' – large pendants of
enamel and precious stones attached to the Order's chain only during
special ceremonies – the 'Lesser Georges' were, from 1522, worn by
Knights of the Order on any and every occasion. In 1715, in *The History
of the ... Order of the Garter*, Ashmole described these decorations:
*divers of them were exquisitely graved in Onix and Agats, and with such a
happy Collection of the Stones, that heightened and received their Beauty
by the Skill of the Artificer, in contriving the Figures and History, the
natural Tincture of the Stones have so Sitted them with Colours for Flesh,
Hair, and everithing else, even to Surprize and Admiration* (Ashmole
1715, pp. 180 –1). The device of the Order was usually fixed in a precious
setting in the form of a medallion. The Hermitage is second probably
only to the Royal Collection at Windsor Castle in terms of the quantity
of such cameos in its possession. As with the portrait cameos of
Elizabeth I, not one of the Hermitage 'Lesser Georges' still has its
original setting. In museum inventories such cameos, including this
one, were usually considered to be the work of Italian masters of the
Renaissance.

Cameo insignia with St George and the Dragon used compositional
schemes established when this subject was developed in Byzantium.
These schemes were repeated on a considerable variety of objects, and
were most perfectly expressed in Raphael's paintings (now in the
Louvre and the NGA, Washington, DC) of the Cappadocian saint. Carvers
tended to treat the depiction of the horseman's pose, his dress and
attributes, as well as the complex foreshortening of horse and dragon,
quite freely. The composition with the Saint thrusting his spear into the
dragon's jaws derives from Raphael's *St George* in Washington, DC,
where he is seen as the patron of the English Order of the Garter.
Presented in 1508 to Henry VII by the Duke of Urbino, Guidobaldo da
Montefeltro, as a sign of gratitude for his elevation to the Order, this
painting was one of the first major works of the Italian Renaissance to
reach England, where it became widely known thanks to engravings by
Luke Vorsterman and painted copies. Another Hermitage cameo
(Kagan 1981, p. 189, fig. II.2), which follows the painting extremely
closely, as well as a 'Lesser George' from the Royal Collection in
Windsor set in a medallion with a miniature after Raphael on the
reverse (Tonnochy 1935, no. 15), indicate that the link between the
painted works of Raphael and cameo insignia was indeed very strong in
England.

In outline and details the closest comparison for this cameo is a work
that has only survived in the form of a cast by Tassie (Raspe 1791, no.
13912). YU.K

129

Anonymous

CAMEO: ST GEORGE AND THE DRAGON
Sardonyx; gold setting (19th century), 1 × ⅞ in. 2.6 × 2.2 cm
Circular legend: *HONY.SOIT.QVI.MAL.Y.PENSE*
Inv. no. K 6348

Provenance: collection of the Yusupov princes, St Petersburg; from 1920
the Yusupov Palace Museum, Petrograd; entered the Hermitage
in 1925.

Literature: English Art 1979, no. 8, fig. 7; Kagan 1981, p. 189, fig. II.1.

Although dated later than the previous example (cat. 128), this cameo
with St George raising his spear above his head and brandishing it at
the dragon, follows Raphael's earlier painted version, *St George* in the
Louvre, which, it is thought, was also linked historically with England
(Linch 1962, pp. 201–2). This cameo is also quite rare in that the device
of the Order is engraved directly onto the cameo's white-bordered
chamfered edge, which is adapted to serve as a garter with a clasp.
A similar example is to be found in the collection of the Duke of
Wellington (Wellington 1953, pl. XIXa). YU.K

130

(?)Thomas Rawlins (*c.* 1620–1670)

CAMEO: PORTRAIT OF CHARLES I, *c.* 1650
Sardonyx: gold setting (18th century), 1 × ⅞ in. 2.5 × 2.2 cm
Inv. no. K 986

Provenance: collection of Pierre Crozat, Paris; from 1741 in the
collection of the Duke of Orléans, Paris; entered the Hermitage in 1787
as part of that collection.

Exhibitions: 1972 Leningrad, no. 519.

Literature: Mariette 1741, p. 60, no. 942; Cabinet d'Orléans 1786, no.
1039; Kagan 1973a, no. 67; English Art 1979, no. 17; Kagan 1981, pp. 183,
185 (drawing 1); Scarisbrick 1986, p. 247.

In iconography and style this cameo is very close to the posthumous
medals and badges of 1649 depicting Charles I, clearly executed under
the influence of Van Dyck's portraits by the court medallist Thomas
Rawlins (Hawkins 1885, nos. 340, 341, 355). Documents and the
literature refer to Rawlins as a gem-carver, and this allows us to link his
name with the Hermitage cameo. When in the collection of Pierre
Crozat this cameo still had its original setting, in the form of a signet
ring with black enamel, possibly similar to that which frames the
cameo with a portrait of Charles I in the British Museum (Dalton 1915,
no. 388). There is a cameo similar to the Hermitage example with a
portrait of Charles I in the collection of the Dukes of Devonshire,
Chatsworth (Scarisbrick 1986, no. 4). YU.K

131

Charles Brown (1749–1795)

INTAGLIO: MARS AND BELLONA, *c.* 1784
Cornelian; gold setting (18th century), 1⅝ × 1⅜ in. 4.1 × 3.5 cm
Signed right: *C. BROWN. INVT*
Inv. no. 3946

Provenance: purchased from Brown through Johann Weitbrecht; entered the Hermitage in 1787.

Exhibitions: 1784 London, RA, no. 289; 1926 Leningrad, Engraved Gems, p. 28; 1976 Leningrad, no. 17.

Archive references: 'Mars & Bellona, monté en or – £150' (from Weitbrecht's bill to the Cabinet of Her Imperial Majesty, October 1787; RGIA Fund 468, op. 1, ch. II, ed. khr. 3902, fol. 73)

Literature: Raspe 1791, no. 7281; Dalton 1915, p. lviii; Forrer 1904–30, VII, p. 126; Etkind 1965a, p. 103; Applied Art 1974, p. 223, no. 127; Industrial Art 1978, no. 85; English Art 1979, no. 221; Saved for Humanity 1985, no. 209; Arts Décoratifs 1986, no. 223.

This intaglio was exhibited at the Royal Academy in 1784 as *Mars and Venus*. Raspe used the same title for this and for a second version of the same subject in the collection of the Prince of Wales (Raspe 1791, no. 7282). This is how it was recorded in the first inventory of the Hermitage's carved gems, and in successive ones. The alternative title *Mars and Venus* was supported by Dalton, Forrer and Maksimova, but in the bill Weitbrecht presented to the Cabinet of Her Imperial Majesty, based on the invoice presented by the Browns themselves, the intaglio is listed as *Mars and Bellona*.

This paired profile, known by the Latin term *capita jugata*, the sources for which go back to the Hellenistic period, is often to be found on coins, gems and medals. In moving away from Antique models, Brown sought to find his own interpretation of the subject, as he noted by adding to his signature the abbreviation INVT (i.e. *invenit*: invented). The composition is filled with numerous freely treated details, moving easily from deep counter-relief to the finest engraving, creating a rich play of light and shade that combines with a remarkable purity of line, making this intaglio one of the best examples of English Neoclassical gem-engraving. Thanks to Tassie's casts it became widely known and was repeated by other carvers both on stone and shell. YU.K

132

William Brown (1748–1825)

INTAGLIO: HEAD OF HYGEIA, *c.* 1785
Cornelian; gold setting (18th century), 1³⁄₁₆ × 1¹⁄₁₆ in. 3 × 2.7 cm
Signed at the bottom: *W. BROWN INVT*
Inv. no. 3698

Provenance: purchased from Brown through Johann Weitbrecht; entered the Hermitage in 1787.

Exhibitions: 1778 London, RA, no. 362; 1976 Leningrad, no. 14.

Archive references: 'La Deesse Hygee, en or & diamans – £120' (from Weitbrecht's bill to the Cabinet of Her Imperial Majesty, October 1787; RGIA Fund 468, op. 1, p. II, ed. khr. 3902, fol. 73).

Literature: Raspe 1791, no. 4116; Dalton 1915, p. lviii; English Art 1979, no. 220.

Gems with the title 'A Head of Hygeia' were shown by Brown at the Royal Academy in London in 1778 (no. 18) and 1785 (no. 362). The classical style of the Hermitage version would seem to be more in keeping with the later date, and indeed the gem with the head of the Goddess of Health entered the Hermitage shortly after this. From the bill presented by Weitbrecht in October 1787 to the Cabinet of Her Imperial Majesty, we learn that it arrived from England in a gold setting decorated with diamonds, but this was soon replaced with a simple, smooth gold frame, as was usual for intaglios in Catherine's collection. A decade later Brown repeated the same head, but this time without the attribute of a snake wound around a staff (Hermitage inv. no. K 1776; 1976 Leningrad, no. 82). YU.K

133

Charles Brown (1749–1795)

INTAGLIO: A HORSE FRIGHTENED BY A LION, before 1790
Cornelian; gold setting (18th century), 1⅛ × 1⅜ in. 2.9 × 3.5 cm
Signed at the bottom: *C.BROWN F.*
Inv. no. 3953

Provenance: purchased from Brown through Johann Weitbrecht; entered the Hermitage in 1791.

Exhibitions: 1926 Leningrad, Engraved Gems, p. 28; 1976 Leningrad, no. 64.

Archive references: 'A yellow Cornelian engraved with a horse frightened by a lion – £45' (from the Browns' bill to Weitbrecht, 28 January 1791; RGIA Fund 468, op. 43, ed. khr. 306, fol. 16).

Literature: Raspe 1791, no. 13234; Etkind 1960, p. 37; Etkind 1965a, p. 101, drawing II.8; Kanter 1968, p. 159; Antonov 1979, p. 842; English Art 1979, no. 225.

This intaglio relates to George Stubbs's *A Horse Frightened by a Lion* (1770, Walker Art Gallery, Liverpool; see fig. 151). Stubbs – the leading horse-painter in England – produced two versions of his composition, which were reproduced in many different media. It gained particular fame through English prints in different techniques. Stubbs himself made a model from it for ceramic plaques to be made at Wedgwood's Etruria manufactory. The first English gem-carver to take up the subject was the Browns' older contemporary, Edward Burch (Raspe 1791, no. 13235).

Charles Brown was also drawn to the subject, repeating it at least twice. The first was an intaglio (Raspe 1791, no. 13233) which he exhibited at the Royal Academy in London in 1774 (no. 17). The Hermitage gem is smaller, more expressive, and sharper in details. The cast from it was not included in Tassie's basic cabinet of casts, but in a small additional set that entered the Hermitage in 1793 (Kagan 1973b, p. 93).

Raspe's statement that Charles Brown used an engraving by William Woollett as a source for the carving (Raspe 1791, p. 701), repeated in later publications on the Hermitage gem, has not been confirmed by recent studies of engravings after Stubbs's work. In terms of similarity, the closest work seems to be a mezzotint by the painter's son, George Townley Stubbs, and it appears that this was Brown's source (Lennox-Boyd 1989, no. 16; see fig. 000). YU.K

Fig. 151: George Townley Stubbs after George Stubbs, *A Horse Frightened by a Lion.* Mezzotint, 17¾ × 21¾ in. (45.1 × 55.3 cm). Published 20 September 1770. Private Collection.

134

Nathaniel Marchant (?1739–1816)

INTAGLIO: BACCHUS AND ARIADNE, *c.* 1783
Sardonyx; gold setting (18th century), diameter 1⅛ in. 2.8 cm
Inv. no. 9333

Provenance: entered the Hermitage before 1794.

Exhibitions: 1926 Leningrad, Engraved Gems, p. 29, fig. II.2.

Literature: Fersman 1961, p. 162, fig. I.12; English Art 1979, no. 238;
Seidmann 1987, p. 45.

Although this intaglio is not signed it is undoubtedly by Marchant,
a replica of an oval intaglio of which Marchant sent a cast in 1783 to
London from Rome, where he was then living, for exhibition at the
Royal Academy (no. 282). The composition derives from a severely
damaged bas-relief from Herculaneum, then in the Palazzo Farnese,
now in the Museo Nationale, Naples (Reinach 1912, II, p. 70, 4). From
the surviving parts of the thyrsus and hands holding the vessel,
Marchant recreated a figure of a standing nymph (or Ariadne),
although it is now thought that the figure in the bas-relief originally
looked rather different. The original gem, so Marchant tells us, was the
property of G. H. Foot (Marchant 1792, no. XXV), and was reproduced
in Tassie's series of casts (Raspe 1791, no. 4349). Rudolf Erich Raspe,
while acknowledging the superb carving, reproached Marchant for his
excessive elongation of the proportions of both figures. Another oval
replica of the same size entered the British Museum in 1799 as part of
the Cracherode Collection (Dalton 1915, no. 700, pl. XXV). The
Hermitage gem differs from the others not just in configuration but
also in some details and in the more precise drawing. YU.K

Fig. 152: *Bacchus,* Engraving after *bas-relief*
from Herculaneum. State Hermitage Museum.

135

Charles Brown (1749–1795)

CAMEO: ALLEGORY OF THE DEFEAT OF THE TURKISH FLEET, 1790
Sardonyx; gold setting (18th century),
2⅛ × 2¹¹⁄₁₆ × 7¹¹⁄₁₆ in. 5.3 × 6.8 cm
Signed at the bottom: *C.BROWN FT*
Inv. no. K 1104

Provenance: purchased from Brown through Johann Weitbrecht;
entered the Hermitage at the beginning of 1791.

Exhibitions: 1926 Leningrad, Engraved Gems, p. 27; 1956 Moscow,
p. 65; 1976 Leningrad, no. 116.

Fig. 153: William Brown, Design in
watercolour for cat. 135. State Hermitage
Museum.

Archive references: 'J'ai eû l'honneur il y a quelque temps de présenter à
Votre Excellence deux dessins de Mrs Brown, qu'ils etoient intentionnés
d'exécuter en camées, et maintenant ils viennent de m'écrire qu'ils les
ont déjà commencés. Ils me disent encore qu'à l'aide d'une empreinte
que je leur ai remise du portrait de Sa Majesté Impériale gravé par Mr
Leberecht, ils se flattent d'attraper la ressemblance dans le numéro 2.
Ils comptent achever l'une et l'autre vers la fin de cette année' (from
Weitbrecht's letter to Khrapovitsky, 15 May 1790; RGADA Fund 1239,
op. 30, ed. khr. 106, fols. 19–21).

'A large-sized agate onyx engraved with an Emblematical subject
representing the conquered Turk resigning his sword to Her Imperial
Majesty – £200' (from the Browns' bill to Weitbrecht, 28 January 1791;
RGIA Fund 468, op. 43, ed. khr. 306, fol. 16).

Literature: Georgi 1794, p. 518; Etkind 1965a, p. 106; Etkind 1965b,
p. 421, fig. 35; Antonov 1979, p. 842; English Art 1979, no. 227, fig. 226.

This cameo was made to commemorate Russia's victory in the war
against Turkey of 1787–91, and forms a pair with the cameo *Catherine
II Instructing her Grandsons* (cat. 136). Like its companion, the image is
an allegory: a kneeling Turk lays down his arms at the foot of a pedestal
supporting a bust of Catherine being crowned with laurels by a figure
of Glory; the eagle hovering in the air on the other side carries in his
beak a palm-branch. The watercolour sketches for both cameos (figs.
153, 154), signed by William, were sent by the Browns to Catherine at
the end of 1789 (RGADA Fund 1239, op. 30, ed. khr. 106, fols. 19–21; the
sketch relating to this cameo is no. 2). From Weitbrecht's letter to
Catherine's secretary, A. Khrapovitsky, of 15 January 1790, it is clear
that work had already begun on the cameos and that he had already
received two sketches from the Browns on the same themes for cameos
that could be produced if the first met with royal approval. He also
stated that, in order to simplify the brothers' work in depicting
Catherine, he had sent them a wax impression of her portrait by the
court medallist and engraver Karl Leberecht. That the Browns had at
their disposal this 'wax medallion' by Leberecht was also mentioned by
Georgi. The Browns, in turn, told Leberecht with satisfaction that they
had been able to achieve an undoubted likeness to the wax version they
had been sent. As promised, the cameo was finished by the end of 1790.
YU.K

136

William Brown (1748–1825) **and Charles Brown** (1749–1795)

CAMEO: CATHERINE II INSTRUCTING HER GRANDSONS, 1791
Agate-onyx; gold setting (18th century), 2⅛ × 2⅝ in. 5.4 × 6.6 cm
Signed at right: *BROWN*
Inv. no. K 1124

Provenance: purchased from the Browns through Johann Weitbrecht; entered the Hermitage in 1791.

Exhibitions: 1926 Leningrad, Engraved Gems, p. 27; 1956 Moscow, p. 65; 1976 Leningrad, no. 119.

Archive references: 'Ils se flattent d'attrapper la ressemblance non seulment dans le numéro 2, mais même dans le numéro 1 ou ce portrait sera très petit. S'ils réussissent à cela, cette pièce déviendra une des plus belles dans son genre' (from Weitbrecht's letter to Khrapovitsky, 15 May 1790; RGADA Fund 1239, op. 30, ed. khr. 106, fols. 19–21). 'Le compagnon de cette pièce sera un très beau groupe, représentant Sa Majesté Impériale en Minerve, les deux jeunes Princes auprès d'Elle avec l'aigle de Russie qui étend ses ailes sur eux. On y travaille depuis deux ans; elle sera achevée au mois de mai' (from Weitbrecht's note regarding the companion cameo, on the Browns' bill of 28 January 1791; RGIA Fund 468, op. 43, ed. khr. 306, fol. 16). On the bill to the Cabinet of Her Imperial Majesty for 1791, which included this cameo, Weitbrecht wrote: '1. L'Education des Princes. Sa Majesté Impériale en Minerve, entourée de divers emblèmes des Sciences […] – 200. NB. Cette belle pièce est encore remarquable par la singulière beauté de l'onyx' (RGIA Fund 468, op. 43, ed. khr. 306, fol. 119).

Literature: Georgi 1794, p. 518; Etkind 1965a, p. 106; Etkind 1965b, p. 422, fig. 34; Antonov 1979, pp. 841–2; English Art 1979, no. 228.

We know that Catherine II herself took the education of Grand-Dukes Alexander and Constantine very seriously. Giving much time to the subject, she drew up a study programme and wrote literary and historical compositions for them. In the Browns' cameo this important side of her life is reflected in allegorical form: the Empress as Minerva, with an open book in her hand, sits before her grandsons (Constantine is closest to her; Alexander is behind him); by her side are various scholarly attributes – a globe, quadrant and telescope; the Grand-Dukes are shielded by the wing of an eagle. Along with the watercolour sketch for the *Allegory of the Defeat of the Turkish Fleet* (cat. 135), at the end of 1789 the Browns sent Catherine (through Weitbrecht) a sketch for this cameo (fig. 154), its companion piece (RGADA Fund 1239, op. 30, ed. khr. 106, fols. 19–21, drawing no. 1). In a letter to Khrapovitsky of 15 January 1790, Weitbrecht informed him that on this occasion the engravers had again managed to produce a good likeness of the Empress, despite the very small size of the image, and promised that he would present the finished work in May. Work dragged on, however, and was only finished in the autumn of 1791. YU.K

Fig. 154: William Brown, *Catherine II Instructing her Grandsons*. Design in watercolour for cat. 136. State Hermitage Museum.

137

Nathaniel Marchant (?1739–1816)

INTAGLIO: HEAD OF ALEXANDER OF MACEDONIA, before 1772,
or early 1780s
Sard onyx; gold setting (18th century), 1³⁄₁₆ × 1 in. 3 × 2.5 cm
Signed at right: *MARCHANT*
Inv. no. 3981

Provenance: collection of Lord Algernon Percy, Alnwick Castle; entered
the Hermitage in 1786.

Exhibitions: 1926 Leningrad, Cameos, p. 29 (as 'A Head of Antinous').

Literature: Marchant 1792, no. LXII; Cades, no. 370 ('copia de medaglia
Greca'); English Art 1979, no. 235 ('Head of Antinous ?'); Seidmann
1987, p. 41, no. 7, fig. 16.

It has been assumed at the Hermitage since the first inventory of gems
was made in 1794 that this intaglio depicts the head of Antinous, and it
was thus that it was included in the exhibition in Moscow in 1926.
It has nothing in common, however, with two versions of Antinous by
Marchant known from casts (Marchant 1792, nos. LXXX, LXXXI), the
first inspired by a bust (now in the Louvre) from the Villa Mondragone
near Frascati, the other by a bas-relief from the Villa Albani (Torlonia)
in Rome. Marchant himself included the intaglio in a series of 100
selected casts from his own works as a *Head of Alexander*, stating that

he carved it for the gem collector Lord Algernon Percy, 1st Earl of
Beverley, basing it on a cornelian fragment in his client's collection.
The small surviving part of the face was insufficient to allow Marchant
to identify the gender of the figure depicted, let alone the subject. In
the catalogue of the Beverley gems the fragment was described as a
'Profile of a Greek Youth or Goddess' (Knight 1921, no. 97). It is difficult
to say if Marchant himself intended an image of Alexander here, or
whether the identification was suggested by the owner. Whichever was
the case, Marchant filled in the missing parts accordingly. In Tommasso
Cades's description of the series of casts, this work was described as a
'Head of Alexander the Great, copy from a Greek medal'.

Gertrud Seidmann, author of the only monograph on Marchant and
compiler of a catalogue of his works, dates the Hermitage gem to
'before 1789', i.e. immediately after Marchant's return to London from
Rome, where he had spent sixteen years, though without taking into
account the fact that the Hermitage's 'Head of Alexander' was in that
part of Algernon Percy's collection acquired by Catherine II in 1786. It
seems more realistic, therefore, to date it either to the first London
period of Marchant's work or to the early 1780s, when Percy himself
was in Rome (Seidmann 1987, p. 51). It is quite possible that it was in
Rome that Percy acquired the fragment that formed the model.

While he was in Rome Marchant produced two more heads of
Alexander from sculptural models (Marchant 1792, nos. LX, LXI). The
Hermitage version was copied by a contemporary, the English carver
William Harris, who roughed his name on the diadem. This gem was
reproduced in Tassie's casts as no. 598 in a small series produced in
addition to the Hermitage set. YU.K

138

William Brown (1748–1825) **and Charles Brown** (1749–1795)

INTAGLIO: THE RAPE OF EUROPA, *c.* 1783
Red cornelian with a white band; gold setting (18th century),
1 × 1⅜ in. 2.6 × 3.5 cm
Signed left: *BROWN INVT*
Inv. no. 3731

Provenance: purchased from the makers through Johann Weitbrecht;
entered the Hermitage before September 1786.

Exhibitions: 1783 London, RA, no. 288; 1926 Leningrad,
Engraved Gems, p. 28; 1976 Leningrad, no. 3.

Literature: Raspe 1791, no. 1170; Etkind 1965a, p. 102; English Art 1979,
no. 224.

The *Rape of Europa* was one of the first works by the Brown brothers to
enter the Hermitage. In this intaglio we can see characteristic features
of their work in the early 1780s, and of particular note is the white-
veined stone, which suggests the watery elements and frothy waves
through which Jupiter, transformed into a bull and accompanied by
Cupid, carries Europa. This work was exhibited at the Royal Academy
in London in 1783. In the 'Accounts of Her Imperial Majesty' we find
bills presented by the court typographer and bookseller Johann Jacob
Weitbrecht, agent and commissioner for the Browns; but this piece is
mentioned neither here, nor in the accounts of the gem-carvers
themselves. Rudolf Erich Raspe, however, in the third part of his
manuscript catalogue of Tassie's casts of gems compiled in 1786,
mentions its location in Catherine II's collection (Hermitage Archives,
Fund 1, op. 6 'c', ed. khr. 32, no. 9497). In the printed catalogue, Raspe
included it in the list of the Browns' works. In both instances it is
described as an outstanding work. In 1794 the Browns returned to the
same subject, depicting on a small, modest octagonal blood-jasper
intaglio (Hermitage inv. no. 3723; 1976 Leningrad, no. 4) the very
moment of abduction, when Europa turns and stretches out her hand,
begging for help from her friends left on the shore. YU.K

Fig. 155: Allegory on the recovery of
George III. 1⅝ × 1⅞ in. (4.2 × 4.7 cm).
State Hermitage Museum.

139

William Brown (1748–1825) **and Charles Brown** (1749–1795)

INTAGLIO: ALLEGORY ON THE RECOVERY OF CATHERINE II, 1789–90
Golden topaz with faceted reverse; gold setting (18th century),
1³⁄₁₆ × 1⁹⁄₁₆ in. 3 × 4 cm
Signed right: *BROWN INVT*
Inv. no. 3680

Provenance: purchased from the Browns through Johann Weitbrecht;
entered the Hermitage in 1790.

Exhibitions: 1926 Leningrad, Engraved Gems, p. 28; 1976 Leningrad,
no. 70.

Archive references: 'A topaz engraved with an allegorical subject: Peace
seated upon riches holding a medallion on which is the portrait of the
Empress. Attended by a figure of Esculapius who holds in his hand an
elevated torch to express Health – £90 (from the Browns' bill to
Weitbrecht, 8 October 1790; RGADA, Fund 1239, op. 30, ed. khr. 107,
fol. 136).

Literature: Etkind 1965b, p. 422, fig. 40; Antonov 1979, p. 841.

In 1789 the Brown brothers made a similar composition from the same
stone with an allegory on the recovery of George III; this in its turn
served as the model for a medal on the same occasion (Raspe 1791, no.
15071). The figure of Aesculapius on the Hermitage gem is unchanged,
but the portrait of the British monarch is here replaced by one of the
Russian empress, and the figure of Britannia holding the medallion is
replaced by the Goddess of Peace with a caduceus in her right hand and
a cornucopia at her feet. Before the discovery of the authors' description
of the intaglio in the archives, the Goddess of Peace was described in
museum inventories as Hygeia, the daughter of Aesculapius. YU.K

140

William Brown (1748–1825) **and Charles Brown** (1749–1795)

INTAGLIO: THE DEATH OF SOCRATES, *c.* 1791
Sapphirine chalcedony; gold setting
(18th century), ⅞ × 1¼ in. 2.3 × 3.1 cm
Signed: *BROWN*
Inv. no. 4072

Provenance: purchased from the Browns through Johann Weitbrecht;
entered the Hermitage in 1791.

Exhibitions: 1926 Leningrad, Engraved Gems, p. 28; 1976 Leningrad,
no. 55.

Archive references: '5. Socrate, il tient le poisson à la main, parlant à ses
amis desolés qui l'entourent – £44' (RGIA Fund 468, op. 43, ed. khr.
306, fol. 119).

Literature: Dalton 1915, p. lviii; Etkind 1965a, pp. 101, 102, drawing 2.5;
Antonov 1979, p. 842; English Art 1979, no. 222.

This is one of a group of three intaglios by the Browns that includes
The Death of Seneca and *The Murder of Archimedes* (1976 Leningrad,
nos. 56, 57). The choice of subjects and their execution are typical of
the brothers' work in the late 1780s and early 1790s. The *Death of
Socrates* was undoubtedly much influenced by paintings on the same
theme by Jean-François Pierre Peyron and Jacques-Louis David that
were exhibited at the Paris Salon of 1787. The Browns may have known
these pictures from their visit to Paris in 1788 or through later
engravings. From David's composition they borrowed the figure of
Socrates making the famous gesture with his left hand, raising a bowl
containing hemlock, with Criton's hand on his knee. But the bed is
taken from Peyron's picture, though here foreshortened, the short end
towards the front of the gem. This allowed the Browns to take an
independent approach and form the group along pyramidal lines.
They were to turn to the image of Socrates once more, in 1794, for the
intaglio *Socrates and Alkibiades* (1976 Leningrad, no. 54). YU.K

141

William Brown (1748–1825) **and Charles Brown** (1749–1795)

CAMEO: CATHERINE II CROWNING PRINCE POTEMKIN WITH LAUREL,
1792
Sardonyx; gold setting (18th century). 1¹⁄₁₆ × 1⅛ in. 2.7 × 2.8 cm
(without the medallion); 2¼ × 2⁵⁄₁₆ in. 5.7 × 5.8 cm (with the
medallion)
Signed at the bottom: *BROWN*; inscription on the shield: *OCZAKOW*
Inv. no. K 1125

Provenance: purchased from the Browns through Johann Weitbrecht;
entered the Hermitage in 1792.

Exhibitions: 1926 Leningrad, Engraved Gems, p. 27, fig. I.8; 1971
Leningrad, drawing 15; 1976 Leningrad, no. 113.

Archive references: '1. Sardonyx à trois couches: Sa Majesté Impériale
recompense le Chef de Ses armées, qui à mis à Ses pieds un sabre et
un croissant' (from Weitbrecht's bill of 15 August 1792; RGIA Fund
468, op. 43, ed. khr. 331, fols. 109–10).

Literature: Georgi 1794, p. 518; Fersman 1961, p. 192, fig. II.8; Etkind
1965a, p. 101, 106, drawing II.6; Etkind 1965b, p. 422, fig. 42; Kagan
1973a, no. 86; Antonov 1979, p. 842; English Art 1979, no. 226, fig. 227;
Henig 1990, p. 120.

This cameo was produced to commemorate the taking of the Ochakov
Fortress on 6 December 1788 by Russian troops under the command of
Field-Marshal General Grigory Potemkin, during the war with Turkey
of 1787–91. Work on the cameo would seem to have begun soon after
the event, but was finished only in 1792, by which time Potemkin, a
favourite of the Empress, was already dead. On arrival the cameo was
given a twisted frame and set under glass in a gold medallion. We do
not know its price as it was included in a general bill for seven pieces
presented by Weitbrecht to the Cabinet of Her Imperial Majesty.

The Browns sent two more pieces to St Petersburg at the same time,
both closely linked to this cameo: one has a winged Victory recording
the success at Ochakov on a shield (1976 Leningrad, no. 112), while the
other, of an attractive whitish-green onyx, has an urn with an emblem
commemorating Potemkin's death (1976 Leningrad, no. 116).
Catherine's secretary, Khrapovitsky, recorded in his diary for 16 August
1792 that the cameos were 'well received, they were admired and the
urn carved on the cameo … was accepted sans aucune sensation'. YU.K

142

William Brown (1748–1825)

CAMEO: TIGER, *c.* 1796
Variegated agate; gold setting (18th century), ¹¹⁄₁₆ × ¹⁵⁄₁₆ in. 1.8 × 2.4 cm
Signed at the bottom: *BROWN*
Inv. no. K 1785

Provenance: purchased from the artist through Johann Weitbrecht;
entered the Hermitage in 1796.

Exhibitions: 1956 Moscow, p. 65; 1976 Leningrad, no. 108.

Archive references: '10. Un tigre – pierre tâchetée. Camée d'après
l'Antique – £30' (from Weitbrecht's bill to the Cabinet of Her Imperial
Majesty, June 1796; RGIA Fund 468, op. 1, ch. II, ed. khr. 4031, fol. 479).

Literature: Etkind 1960, p. 37; Kagan 1973a, no. 88; English Art 1979,
no. 223.

In Weitbrecht's bill to the Cabinet of Her Imperial Majesty for
payment in June 1796, this cameo is included with a group of gems
made after Antique sources. However, it seems that the source for this
gem is James Murphy's engraving after James Northcote's painting
(fig. 156). Without trying to create a naturalistic effect regarding the
tiger's striped skin, the brothers were able to give their slinking beast
an irridescent effect. YU.K

Fig. 156: James Murphy after James Northcote,
A Tiger. Mezzotint. State Hermitage Museum.

143

Unidentified Medallist

MEDAL COMMEMORATING THE PEACE BETWEEN ENGLAND AND SPAIN, 1604

Silver, cast and gilded, diameter 1⅜ in. 34 mm; weight 14.12 g.
Obverse: shoulder-length portrait of James I, three-quarters right, in a crown and plumed hat with a clasp. Circular legend: *IACOBVS.D.G. MAG.BRIT.FRAN.ET.HIBR* [James I by the Grace of God King of England, France and Ireland]
Reverse: two standing female figures face to face, personifying Peace holding a palm-branch and Religion with a cross and beacon-light in her hands, and a cornucopia. To the sides and at the top the legend: *HINC.PAX.COPIA.CLARAQ.RELIGIO* [Hence peace, plenty and pure religion]
Exegue A.1604
Inv. no. 7359

Provenance: collection of Yakov Yakovlevich Reichel (1778–1856), St Petersburg; entered the Hermitage in 1858. (Reichel, a medallist and employee of the Russian Ministry of Finance amassed a collection of over 40,000 coins and medals that was acquired from his heirs for the Hermitage.)

Exhibitions: 1973 Leningrad, no. 2.

Literature: Hawkins 1885, I, p. 193, no. 16; Reichel 1843, p. 65, no. 505; *Pax in nummis* 1912, no. 43; English Art 1979, nos. 14, 15.

Following Elizabeth I's death in 1603, James VI of Scotland (1566–1625) was crowned James I of Great Britain and Ireland. He retreated from England's alliance with France and the United Provinces in favour of a foreign policy of peaceful neutrality, and in 1604 concluded a peace treaty with Spain at Madrid. Ye.shch.

144

Thomas Rawlins (*c.* 1620–1670)

MEDAL COMMEMORATING THE DECLARATION OF PARLIAMENT, 1642

Silver, cast and engraved: 1⁷⁄₁₆ × 1¾ in. 37 × 44 mm (oval); weight 14.36 g.
Obverse: head-and-shoulders portrait of Charles I to right, crowned, with the chain of the Order of the Garter on his chest. Around the image the engraved legend: *SHOVLD HEAR BOTH HOUSES OF PARL [liament] FOR TRUE RELIGION AND SUBIECTS FREDOM STAND*; around the edge a leafy border caught up in a ribbon in four places
Reverse: the two Houses of Parliament assembled under the chairmanship of the King and Speaker; leafy border as on the obverse
Inv. no. 7372

Provenance: collection of Yakov Yakovlevich Reichel, St Petersburg; entered the Hermitage in 1858.

Exhibitions: 1973 Leningrad, no. 6.

Literature: Hawkins 1885, I, p. 292, no. 108; Reichel 1843, p. 70, no. 538; English Art 1979, nos. 18, 19.

Charles I (1600–49) was crowned King of Great Britain and Ireland in 1625, and this medal commemorates an event that directly preceded the start of the Civil Wars in England. By 1642 the confrontation between the King and Parliament had reached its height. After Charles's unsuccessful attempt in January of that year to arrest five Members of Parliament came the declaration to the King of 19 May and then, on 2 June, the 'Nineteen Propositions' in which Parliament put demands to him that in effect sought to nullify the monarch's authority. Charles rejected them, and in a declaration of war a few weeks later raised his royal standard at Nottingham.

Hawkins (1885) correctly noted that despite the presence of the King on this medal, it was most probably issued by Parliament. This is supported by the replacement of the traditional legend with the name and title around the royal portrait by a quotation from the declaration of 19 May 1642, announcing Parliament to be the guarantor of religious and other freedoms. Ye.shch.

145

Thomas Simon (*c.* 1623–1665)

MEDAL ISSUED ON THE DEATH OF ROBERT DEVEREUX,
3RD EARL OF ESSEX, 1646

Gold: ¹¹⁄₁₆ × ¹⁵⁄₁₆ in. 18 × 23 mm (oval), with a loop for suspension;
weight 4.60 g.
Obverse: head-and-shoulders portrait to right, with drapery around the
shoulders; at the bottom: *T.S.F.* [Thomas Simon fecit]; circular legend:
ROB.ESSEX:COM:MIL:PARL:DVX:GEN [Robert Essex, General and
Commander in Chief of the Parliamentary Army]
Reverse: seated figure of a mourner resting on an overturned column,
on the upper part of which are the letters *F.E.R.T.*; at the top, above the
image, the legend: *HINC ILLAE LACRIMAE* [Hence these tears]; at
the bottom: *ABRVP: SEP.14.1646* [Taken away 14 September 1646]
Inv. no. 1710

Provenance: Kunstkamera, St Petersburg; transferred to the Hermitage
in the mid-19th century.

Exhibitions: 1993 St Petersburg, no. 115.

Literature: M.I.P. 1745, II, p. 408; Hawkins 1885, I, p. 327, no. 166.

Robert Devereux (1591–1646), the eldest son of Queen Elizabeth's
favourite, the 2nd Earl, proved himself as a military commander during
his youthful campaigns in the Low Countries. On 6 July 1642 he was
appointed commander of the Parliamentary forces, and won several
battles of the first Civil War. He resigned his command in 1645 when
the New Model Army was formed. Several badges were devoted to
Essex between 1642 and 1646. The Hermitage medal is particularly
rare; indeed, when publishing a similar one (British Museum),
Hawkins had supposed it to be unique. In his publication the letters on
the column depicted on the reverse were deciphered as the first letters
of the device on the chain of the Order of the Annunciation of Savoy,
Fortitudo ejus rempublicam tenuis – His fortitude sustained the
Commonwealth.

   This medal is a brilliant example of miniature portrait sculpture.
It was made when Thomas Simon was at the height of his creative
career and can be compared with other of his works, such as the
portrait of Oliver Cromwell (cat. 146). Ye.shch.

146

Thomas Simon (*c.* 1623–1665)

MEDAL COMMEMORATING THE DECLARATION OF OLIVER CROMWELL
AS LORD PROTECTOR, 1653

Silver; struck and gilded: diameter 1½ in. 38 mm; weight 19.15 g.
Obverse: head-and-shoulders portrait to left in a cuirass, draped with a
cloak; below in two lines: *THO: SIMON:F* [Thomas Simon fecit];
circular legend: *OLIVERVS.DEI.GRA.REIPVB:*
ANGLIÆ.SCO.ET.HIB & PROTECTOR [Oliver by the Grace of God
Protector of the Republic of England, Scotland and Ireland]
Reverse: a lion sejant (sitting upright on its hind legs) supporting the
shield of the Protectorate, a four-part coat of arms (first and second
field with the cross of St George, for England; the second field with the
diagonal cross of St Andrew, for Scotland; the third field with the harp
of Ireland); the central shield has a lion to right, the coat of arms of
Cromwell; the circular legend: *PAX. QUÆRITVR BELLO* [Peace is
sought by war]
Inv. no. 7429

Provenance: collection of Yakov Yakovlevich Reichel, St Petersburg;
entered the Hermitage in 1858.

Exhibitions: 1972 Leningrad, no. 558; 1973 Leningrad, no. 7.

Literature: Reichel 1843, p. 85, no. 685; Hawkins 1885, I, p. 409, no. 45;
Nathanson 1975, pp. 24, 25; English Art 1979, nos. 24, 25.

Oliver Cromwell (1599–1658), the leading figure in the English
Revolution, was elected Lord Protector of England on 16 December
1653. Thomas Simon produced several portraits of Cromwell, using as
his model a miniature by Samuel Cooper. The medal of 1653 occupies
a special place in the iconography of Cromwell, for in comparison
with the medal of 1650 celebrating victory over the Scots at the battle
of Dunbar that September, the sharp features of the sitter have been
noticeably idealized. The heroic image of the Protector is fittingly
complemented on the reverse of the medal by the powerful figure of
the lion supporting the shield with the coat of arms.

   Simon's portrait works undoubtedly impressed Cromwell, for he was
entrusted with the most important commissions to the Mint, and with
commissions that were paid separately. In 1655 he was appointed sole
chief engraver for the Mint and Seals in London.

   Struck examples of this medal are particularly rare, as the stamp
for the reverse was split during striking. In the catalogue of Reichel's
collection the medal is noted to be an extreme rarity and marked with
the symbol *R3*. Ye.shch.

147

(?)Thomas Simon (*c.* 1623–1665)

BADGE FOR SERVICE AGAINST SIX SHIPS (SEA BATTLE OF 1 AUGUST 1650)

Silver; struck: 1⅜ × 1⅞ in. 34 × 47 mm (oval), with a loop for
suspension; weight 21.39 g.
Obverse: an anchor surrounded by a rope, with two oval coats of arms
suspended (on the left the cross of St George for England, on the right
the harp for Ireland); above the image the word *MERUISTI* [Thou hast
merited]
Reverse: a view of a sea battle with three sailing ships in the foreground
and two vessels receding in the distance; above, along the edge, the
legend in two lines: *SERVICE.DON.AGAINST. SIX.SHIPS
IVLY.Y.XXXI.&.AVGVSTY.I 1650*
Inv. no. 7382

Provenance: Kunstkamera, St Petersburg; transferred to the Hermitage
in the mid-19th century.

Exhibitions: 1973 Leningrad, pp. 24–5; 1993 St Petersburg, no. 116.

Literature: M.I.P. 1745, II, p. 127, no. 13; Hawkins 1885, I, p. 390, no. 11;
English Art 1979, nos. 22, 23.

On the night of 31 July 1650, a ship of 22 guns under the command of
Captain Wyard that was convoying merchant vessels from Hull to
London and Rotterdam was attacked by six Irish frigates. The fierce
battle that ensued lasted all night and resulted in total victory for the
English, who forced their opponents to flee.

This badge was acquired for the Kunstkamera and was undoubtedly
the model for several officers' badges in the Russian army, in particular
those issued during the Northern War of 1700–21, for instance for the
battles near Kalisz in 1706 and Lesnaya, 1708. They repeated the oval
form of the English medals and also had chains that allowed them to be
worn around the neck. This medal commemorating the sea battle of
1650 lacks the medallist's signature, but on the obverse of an identical
medal also of 1650 (Hawkins 1885, I, p. 390, no. 12) are the initials of
Thomas Simon. ye.shch.

148

(?)Johann Georg Breuer (d. 1695)

MEDAL COMMEMORATING THE DEFEAT OF THE DUKE OF MONMOUTH IN
1685

Silver; struck: diameter 1¹¹⁄₁₆ in. 43 mm; weight 36.32 g.
Obverse: head-and-shoulders portrait to right, in a wig with long curls,
armour and a lace cravat; at the sides the legend: *IACOBVS.DVX
MONMOVTH* [James, Duke of Monmouth]
Reverse: a column standing amidst trophies of war, topped with three
crowns, with a figure falling halfway down; above the image the legend
PROVIDENTIA. Ex: *IMPROVIDENTIA*
[Prudence. Lack of prudence]
Inv. no. 7394

Provenance: Kunstkamera, St Petersburg; transferred to the Hermitage
in the mid-19th century.

Literature: M.I.P. 1745, II, p. 417, no. 1; Hawkins 1885, I, p. 614, no. 24.

James Scott, Duke of Monmouth (1649–85), was an illegitimate son of
Charles II by his mistress Lucy Walters. He spent his childhood in
France, but after the Restoration of the Stuarts in 1660 returned to
London. He took part in the Third Dutch War (1672–4) and helped to
put down an uprising in Scotland in 1679. As an earnest Protestant,
Monmouth was a popular candidate for the throne, but Charles refused
to legitimize him. Following the accession to the throne of James II in
1685, Monmouth rashly embarked on an uprising. His motley army was
defeated at the Battle of Sedgemoor, while the Duke himself was
captured and taken to London.

An example of this medal in the Royal Collection in Stockholm
bears the date of this event, *1685*, and the month, July, when the Duke
was executed in London. Stylistically the medal commemorating his
defeat is close to the works of the German medallist Johann Georg
Breuer, who worked in Braunschweig. The locks of the luxurious wig
and details of the armour are managed in Breuer's characteristic style
(*c.*f. the medal with a double portrait of dukes Rudolf August and
Anton Ulrich, Brockmann 1985, I, no. 212). There is also close similarity
between the lettering in the legend on the Monmouth medal and those
on works by Breuer, in particular in the form of the letter *T*. The
presence of an example of this rare medal in the Swedish Royal
Collection perhaps supports Breuer's authorship, for in the second half
of the 1680s he made several medals for the King of Sweden. Ye.shch.

149

George Bower (d. 1690)

MEDAL COMMEMORATING THE LANDING OF WILLIAM OF ORANGE AT
TORBAY, 1688

Silver; struck: diameter 1¹⁵⁄₁₆ in. 50 mm; weight 50.56 g.
Obverse: head-and-shoulders portrait to right, in a wig and armour
with a lace cravat; in the truncation of the arm: 1688; below: *C.B.F* [C.
B. fecit]; circular legend:
GVILIELMVS.III.D.G.PRIN.AVR.HOL.ET.WES.GVB [William III,
by the Grace of God Prince of Orange, ruler of Holland and Western
Friesland]
Reverse: bird's-eye view of a seashore and a fleet at sea; on the left in
the foreground William of Orange astride a horse at the head of his
army, to the right William in Antique armour raising from the ground
a fainting figure representing Justice; at the top along the edge the
legend: *TERRAS ASTREA REVISIT* [Justice revisits the earth];
legend on the milling: *NON.RAPIT.IMPERIVM VIS TVA.SED.
RECIPIT* [Your power does not seize the empire, but receives it (by
right)]
Inv. no. 7498

Provenance: entered the Hermitage before 1850.

Exhibitions: 1973 Leningrad, no. 12.

Literature: Hawkins 1885, I, p. 639, no. 64; English Art 1979, nos. 47, 48.

William III (1650–1702), Stadtholder of the Netherlands, became King
of Great Britain and Ireland in 1689, following his landing at Torbay
and the subsequent rout of James II's loyalist forces. William's claim to
the throne was both as grandson of Charles I (through his daughter
Mary) and as husband of James II's elder daughter, also called Mary.
James's unpopularity – much of it due to his increasing enthusiasm for
Catholicism – had led various elite groups to petition the staunchly
Protestant William to seize the British throne. On 5 November 1688
William disembarked on the English shore in Devon at the head of
a 13,000-strong army.

In the legend on the milling, which is a sign of the rarity of the
medal, it is emphasized that William's actions were not simply his own
personal initiative but, above all, an expression of the will of the British
people. At the end of the 17th century and the beginning of the 18th,
there was a tradition of using quotations from classical authors for the
legends on medals, though these quotations were often adjusted to fit
contemporary events. Thus the legend on the reverse commemorating
William's welcome landing at Torbay alludes to Ovid's lines in
Metamorphoses (I.150) describing the moment when Astraea had been
forced to abandon a degenerate world ('terras Astraea reliqvit'). Ye.shch.

150

John Croker (1670–1741)

MEDAL COMMEMORATING THE PEACE OF UTRECHT, 1713

Silver; struck: diameter 1⅜ in. 35 mm; weight 15.9 g.
Obverse: head-and-shoulders portrait of Queen Anne to left, with long curls and a laurel wreath; in the truncation of the shoulder: *I.C.* [John Croker]; circular legend: *ANNA.D.G.MAG.BRI. FR.ET.HIB.REG.* [Anna, by the Grace of God Queen of Great Britain, France and Ireland]
Reverse: standing Britannia with an olive branch in her right hand, the left holding a spear and an oval shield with the arms of Great Britain. In the background to the left is a ship at sea, to the right peasants tilling and sowing. Around the image the legend: *COMPOSITIS. VENERANTVR.ARMIS.* [They honour peace, by laying aside their arms] Ex: *MDCCXIII*
Inv. no. 7468

Provenance: collection of Yakov Yakovlevich Reichel, St Petersburg; entered the Hermitage in 1858.

Exhibitions: 1973 Leningrad, no. 14.

Literature: Reichel 1843, p. 125, no. 938; Hawkins 1885, II, pp. 399, 400, no. 257; *Pax in nummis* 1912, p. 432; English Art 1979, nos. 51, 52.

Anne Stuart (1665–1714), succeeded to the British throne on the death of her brother-in-law William III in 1702. The previous year the War of the Spanish Succession had begun when France invaded the Spanish Netherlands as part of a larger plan to install Louis XIV's grandson as King of Spain. A coalition was formed against France by Britain, the Dutch Republic and other states. The stunning series of military successes achieved against France between 1704 and 1709 by armies led by the Duke of Marlborough and Prince Eugene of Savoy were followed by military deadlock. On 12 April 1713 Britain concluded a peace with France at Utrecht, after which came peace treaties with the Netherlands, Portugal, Spain, Prussia and Savoy.

The crosses of St George and St Andrew seen together on the shield that Britannia holds symbolizes the Act of Union of 1707, which formalized a relationship between England and Scotland that had begun in 1603 when James VI of Scotland was crowned James I of England. This relationship is reflected in the Queen's title on the obverse of the medal. The legend on the reverse is a quotation from Horace (*Odes*, IV.xiv.52), and in combination with the composition emphasizes the significance of peace for the development of trade and the economy. The medal is quite widely found, as it was intended for members of both Houses of Parliament, and was also produced at the Mint for all those wanting a copy. ye.shch.

151

Thomas Hallidey (*c.* 1780–after 1842)

MEDAL COMMEMORATING FIELD-MARSHAL PRINCE MATVEY KUTUZOV
OF SMOLENSK, 1813

Silver; struck; diameter 2⅛ in. 54 mm;
weight 99.66 g.
Obverse: head-and-shoulders portrait to left with an open collar; on the
sitter's neck: *HALLIDEY.F* [ecit]; circular legend: *CASTRENSIS
PRAEFECTVS PRINCEPS SMOLENCI* [Commander-in-Chief
Prince of Smolensk]; beneath the portrait: *MDCCCXIII*
Reverse: in a laurel wreath the two-line legend: *VOTA PVBLICA*
[The will of the people]
Inv. no. 7870

Provenance: collection of K. F. Schroll, St Petersburg; entered the
Hermitage in 1869.

Literature: Iversen 1880–96, II, p. 331; English Art 1979, nos. 313, 314;
Shchukina 1995, p. 59.

Mikhail Illarionovich Kutuzov (1745–1813), a graduate of the Artillery
and Engineering Corps, devoted himself to a military career from the
age of 20. He fought in Poland in 1765 and in the two Russo-Turkish
wars that occurred during Catherine II's reign. At the beginning of the
19th century he came to prominence for his part in the war against
Napoleon, and was appointed to high military posts. In 1811 he made a
brilliant contribution as Commander-in-Chief of the Danube Army in
the war against Turkey, and on 17 August 1812 he took over the
command of Russia's forces. His troops forced the French to retreat
from Russia, and followed it up with a victorious march across Europe.
On 16 April 1813 Kutuzov died in the small Silesian town of Bunzlau;
his remains were returned to St Petersburg and buried in the Kazan
Cathedral. In 1837 a monument to him was set up in front of the
Cathedral.

Early in the 19th century, three medals with a reverse similar
to that of this medal were issued in England. These were marks of
Parliament's gratitude to William Pitt in 1806, and to the Duke of
Wellington in 1807 and 1814 (Brown 1980, nos. 611, 746, 852). Like
these, the Kutuzov medal was made by the firm of Thomasen.

The iconography of Kutuzov on the medal is particular noteworthy.
Using engravings published in London in 1813 (Rovinsky 1886–9, I,
p. 583, nos. 71, 75), the medallist replaced the usual wig with the
hairstyle and open neck fashionable at the beginning of the century.
Iversen's suggestion that the medal was issued during Kutuzov's
lifetime is unlikely, particularly if when we note that Kutuzov died in
April. The medal in honour of Pitt was also issued posthumously.
Ye.shch.

152

Lewis Pingo (1743–1830)

MEDAL GIVEN TO ALEXANDER I BY THE ROYAL HUMANE SOCIETY, 1806

Gold; struck and engraved: diameter 2 1/16 in. 53 mm; weight 92.99 g.
Obverse: the Genius of Life, bearing in his hands a dying torch; legend
at the top: *LATEAT SCINTILLVLA FORSAN* [While there is but the
slightest spark] *Ex: SOC.LOND.IN.RESVSCITAT.
INTERMORTVORVM. INSTIT.MDCCLXXIV* [London Society for
the Resuscitation of the Dying founded 1774]
Reverse: over a depiction of a corona civica (oak wreath) the legend:
HOC PRETIVM CIVE SERVATO TVLIT [Such is the award worn by
those who serve their fellow men]; inside the wreath an engraved
legend: *ALEXANDRO IMPERATORI SOCIETAS REGIA
HUMANA LONDINENSIS HUMILLIME DONAT 1806* [The Royal
London Humane Society humbly presents to Emperor Alexander
1806]; at the bottom around the edge the engraved legend: *HOMO
SUM ET NIHIL HUMANI A ME ALIENUM PUTO* [I am a man
and nothing humane is alien to me]
Inv. no. 371

Provenance: from 1814 in the Winter Palace; transferred to the
Hermitage in 1838.

Literature: Bishop 1974, pp. 4–5; Hawes 1807, pp. 16–21; English Art
1979, nos. 292, 293; Peters 1989, p. 45.

The Royal Humane Society was founded in 1774 by means of private
donations. Its central office was located in Hyde Park near the
Serpentine, on a site donated by George III. The Society subsidized the
publication of instructions for saving the drowning, provided aid to
bathers and those who worked on the river, and gave money prizes and
medals to lifesavers. The Society later extended its activities in order to
mark examples of extreme bravery: the saving of miners in pit
accidents, those suffering from asphyxiation in blast furnaces or in
drainage systems. This Gold Medal was awarded to tsar Alexander I for
his direct involvement in saving a man from drowning in 1806. As he
travelled towards Vilno, Alexander saw on the river-bank a group of
people attempting to revive a man rescued from the water. Springing
from his carriage, Alexander himself applied artificial respiration and
then, when his suite drew up, commanded his physician-in-ordinary,
Y. V. Villie, to continue the necessary measures to save the man's life,
which after much effort was successful. On receiving news of this, the
Society adopted a resolution at its sitting of 29 April 1806 to award its
medal to Alexander (the first foreigner to be given this honour) and also
to request his consent to the receipt of it. It seems extremely likely that
the award of the London Society influenced the founding, on 6 May
1807, and on the tsar's command, of an award 'For saving one's fellow
men', which was given for saving the drowning. Later, during
Alexander's visit to London in 1814, he was elected Vice-President of
the Society.

The image and legend on the obverse of this medal speak eloquently
of the fact that the award was intended for particularly difficult cases
in which a fellow man, literally caught between life and death
(*intermortuorum*), was saved. The oak wreath (*corona civica*) on the
reverse was in ancient Rome reckoned the highest honour for saving
a fellow man. ye.shch.

153

W. Hawes

ANNUAL REPORT OF THE ROYAL HUMANE
SOCIETY FOR 1807

Book, 10⅝ × 5⅛ in. 27 × 13 cm, open at page
15: Engraving of the lid of a snuffbox showing
Alexander I saving a man from drowning and
the medal intended for presentation to him
Leather binding of the first quarter of the 19th
century and gold stamping
Ex-libris Tsarevich, Alexander Nikolaevich
(from 1856 Alexander II).

Held in the Library of the Numismatics
Department of the Hermitage.

154

Monogrammist M.I.

MEDAL COMMEMORATING COUNT MATVEI PLATOV, (?)c. 1814

Silver; struck; length 1⅞ in. 48 mm; weight 80.56 g.
Obverse: head-and-shoulders portrait to right in military uniform with orders and medals – a cross at the neck, a ribbon over the shoulders and a star on his chest; in the truncation of the arm the medallist's monogram: *M.I.*; to the sides of the image the legend: *HETMAN PLATOFF.*
Reverse: four-line legend: *ACRI MILITIA VEXAVIT GALLOS EQUES METUENDUS HASTA* [The zealous warrior baited the Gauls with his terrible spear]
Inv. no. 7703

Provenance: collection of K. F. Schroll, St Petersburg; entered the Hermitage in 1869.

Literature: Iversen 1880–96, II, p. 97; Forrer 1904–30, IV, p. 85; VI, p. 78; English Art 1979, nos. 311, 312; Shchukina 1995, p. 59.

Matvei Ivanovich Platov (1751–1818), son of the leader of the Don Cossack troops, began his military career during the reign of Catherine II, in the two Russo-Turkish wars. In 1801 he became *ataman* (leader) of the Don Cossacks, leading them in the wars against France in 1805 and 1807. Platov made his mark during the war of 1812, and by order of Alexander I he was elevated to the rank of Count. The Cossacks under Platov's command showed their might in the military campaign of 1813–14 in Europe and entered Paris with the Allied troops. In June 1814 Platov visited London as part of Alexander's suite, where he was enthusiastically received. The Prince Regent presented him with his miniature portrait in a precious setting to be worn on the chest, and the City of London with a richly decorated sable. Platov was the subject of several medals made in Russia and abroad, but this is undoubtedly the most successful. This portrait relates to an engraving of 1814 (Rovinsky 1886–9, II, p. 1791, no. 56) and convincingly conveys his noble profile, not least the high forehead and hawklike nose. The legend on the reverse is an abbreviated quotation from Horace (*Odes*, III.ii). The medal, made by the firm of E. Thomasen, Birmingham, is undated. Forrer and Iversen relate it to the work of John Milton, but in that case it would have had to have been made before the beginning of 1805, the year of Milton's death. It is most probably linked to the events of 1812 to 1814, thus excluding the involvement of Milton. ye.shch.

155

Thomas Wyon Jnr (1792–1817)

MEDAL COMMEMORATING THE PEACE OF PARIS, 1814

Gold; struck: diameter 2¹¹⁄₁₆ in. 69 mm; weight 212.21 g.
Obverse: head-and-shoulders portrait of the Prince Regent to right
wearing a laurel wreath. Circular legend: *GEORGIVS PRINCEPS*
WALLIÆ PATRIAM PRO PATRE REGENS MDCCCXIII [George,
Prince of Wales, Regent of the Country for (his) father 1813].
Reverse: depiction of winged Victory placing a laurel wreath on a
standing figure of Britannia with a spear and round shield with the
arms of Great Britain in her left hand. With her right hand Britannia
raises from her knees a female figure in a corona civica, on the edge
of her dress the legend *EUROPA*; to the right beneath the image:
T.WYON.JUN.S. [Thomas Wyon Junior sculpted]; to the sides of the
image the legend: *SEIPSAM CONSTANTIA EVROPAM EXEMPLO*
[(Britannia saved] herself by her fortitude and Europe by her example]
Inv. no. A 1712

Provenance: entered the Hermitage in 1815, among medals sent back
from Vienna by General-Adjutant Prince Pyotr Volkonsky (Hermitage
Archives, Fund I, op. I, d. 4, fol. 3).

Literature: Pax in nummis 1912, no. 783; Forrer 1904–30, I, p. 122; V,
p. 270; Brown 1980, no. 805.

On 30 May 1814 the allies of the anti-Napoleonic coalition – Britain,
Austria, Russia and Prussia – concluded the Peace of Paris, under
which France returned to its borders of 1792. This event was marked by
the issue of many medals. This one shows George, the Prince Regent,
who was crowned King of Great Britain in 1820. Thomas Wyon Jnr, one
in a famous family of medallists, executed it after a sketch by H.
Howard, and it was made by the jewellery firm of Rundell Bridge &
Rundell. Examples of this medal were made in silver and bronze, while
Alexander I was presented with a gold version. Ye.shch.

Attributed to Roach (*fl.* second half of the 18th century) **after Wyatt**

CABINET FOR CASTS OF CARVED GEMS, 1783–8

Carcase of oak, spruce and pine; veneer and engraved marquetry, satinwood, stained maple, ebony, rosewood, thuya. Inside are four rows each of 50 flat drawers, 91⅓ × 40³⁄₁₆ × 14⁹⁄₁₆ in. 232 × 102 × 37 cm
Inv. no. 57

Provenance: commissioned in London by Catherine II, entered the Hermitage between 1783 and 1788.

Exhibitions: 1976 Leningrad.

Literature: English Art, no. 242 (inventory number incorrectly cited).

The Hermitage cabinet is part of a set of furniture made specially for a collection of casts of carved gems from leading 18th-century European collections. The gems were the work of James Tassie, ordered from England by Catherine II in 1781 and made between 1783 and 1790 using a new technique invented by Tassie himself. One condition of the commission was that 'the collection should be fitted in suitable cabinet-cupboards' (Kagan 1973b, p. 87). The first group of casts was delivered to Russia in 1783 and, as we are told by Rudolf Raspe, author of the catalogue of this collection, it was indeed delivered in special cabinets (Raspe 1786, p. 25). He describes them enthusiastically: 'the elegance and simplicity of their forms, the propriety of their external ornaments which were basso relievos in white enamel, with gilt mouldings set on a ground of green satinwood, and the high finishing of the whole, qualified them, at any rate for ornaments in the noble apartments of Her Imperial Majesty's superb Palace at Czarsko Zelo, where they have been placed' (Holloway 1992, p. 14). The collection and the cabinets arrived in several groups between 1783 and 1788 and are now in the Glyptics Cabinet of the Hermitage.

What we have today are thirteen cabinets of various forms and sizes. Five are tall pieces with marquetry, three of which (nos. 57, 344, 345) have on the doors an oval suspended from a ribbon with a chain of octagons along the edges; two of those have inlaid vases on the sides, surrounded with sprays, garlands and ribbons. It is a cabinet of the latter type that is shown here. The four legs of the cabinets rest on a pi-shaped base; the front legs are round, the back legs rectangular and slightly stepped. Two of the five cabinets were reworked in the 19th century (nos. 58, 59).

The group includes cabinets on short bent legs (nos. 343, 346–9) – among them small cupboards with porcelain medallions (no. 482) – and two small single-leaf cupboards decorated with fluted marquetry pilasters (nos. 3147–8).

Another cabinet (no. 342) of slightly different outline and more complex ornament was, as Yulia Kagan has suggested, used to store the collection of carved gems which was given by Catherine II to her favourite Count Lanskoy (English Art 1979, nos. 233–4). All the cabinets use the same kinds of wood both in the construction of the body and in the decoration.

Raspe tells us that the cabinets for the collection of casts were designed by the English architect James Wyatt (Raspe 1786). J. M. Robinson, in his study of the work of the Wyatt family, cites evidence that Catherine II ordered the Russian ambassador in London to offer the architect whatever sum of money he wanted to move to St Petersburg and be court architect (Robinson 1979, p. 59). This was not to be, but he did design the cabinets for her collection, although this is not mentioned by Robinson. We know that Wyatt worked in a similar style to Robert Adam, developing a Neoclassical manner for both architecture and interior design.

The Hermitage cabinets are attributed on the basis of an ivory plaque with the words 'Cabinet-Maker Roach' attached to one of the group (inv. no. 58). Unfortunately there is practically no information about Roach, and he is mentioned by British scholars only as the author of work on Catherine II's cabinets (Edwards and Jourdain 1955, p. 66; Macquoid 1904, p. 220). The only other object that has been linked with his name is a secretaire from Temple Newsam House with similar designs of rectangles and ovals on the veneer ('Bureau-Cabinet', *The Burlington Magazine*, May 1965, p. 285; Gilbert 1978, p. 246, no. 571).

The division of the veneered surface of the furniture into geometrical figures and bands of dark and light grooves is characteristic of the last quarter of the 18th century (Cescinsky 1909–11, pp. 114, 118, 243). We can also find close analogies for the marquetry ornament on the sides (Musgrave 1966, no. 156; Macquoid 1904, no. 30; Cescinsky 1909–11, no. 80).

The German scholar B. Göres rightly noted that the stand and legs of the Hermitage cabinets were reworked, and he linked this with the Russian furniture-maker Christian Mayer, who worked at the Russian court at the end of the 18th century. Indeed, legs of such construction are not be found in English furniture of the late 18th century. The Hermitage cabinets possibly originally had twisted legs. TR

Attributed to John Linnell (1729–1796)

COMMODE, 1750–75

Mahogany veneer, inlaid with lemonwood,
satinwood and maple, 37⅜ × 79⅛ × 28⅜ in.
95 × 201 × 72 cm
Inv. no. 1825

Provenance: entered the Hermitage in 1931
from the association of Detskoye Selo and
Pavlovsk museums.

Literature: Lisenkov 1964, p. 225; Sokolova
1967, p. 97; Biryukova 1972, p. 153; English Art
1979, no. 274; Hayward and Kirkham 1980,
no. 119, pp. 84, 91.

The English cabinet-maker John Linnell was
head of a furniture company in London that
was founded in 1730 and continued in
operation until the early 19th century. Linnell
was head of the company from 1763, taking
over from his father, William. During the
second half of the 18th century it was one of
the leading English furniture manufacturers.

The top of the Hermitage commode is of
'serpentine' shape, while the front is curved.
Similar forms can be found in designs by
Linnell, Thomas Sheraton and James Wyatt
(Ward-Jackson 1958, nos. 248, 239; Fowler and
Cornforth 1978, no. 13). But the closest parallel
is with a drawing by Linnell of 1780 (Victoria
and Albert Museum, London) showing two
commodes, on the basis of which Helena
Hayward has attributed the Hermitage piece
to him (Hayward and Kirkham 1980, p. 58, no.
118). Archive material tells us that John Linnell
did indeed provide furniture for Catherine II.
In letters of 1773–4, mention is made of three
marquetry commodes for the Russian court
(Hayward and Kirkham 1980, p. 184).
Hayward links this order with a French-style
commode in the palace at Peterhof and then at
Tsarskoye Selo, the summer residences of the
Imperial family near St Petersburg, and with
the Hermitage piece. She also considers that
the decoration of the commode with classical
medallions can be linked to Catherine's love for
cameos. There is, however, no concrete
evidence to prove that the letters mentioned
definitely refer to these pieces.

The side doors of the commode have
medallions containing female figures in
classical drapery, based on engravings from the
anthologies containing examples of Antique
painting that were then popular. Medallions
with similar figures also survive on a desk
(Macquoid 1904, no. 13) and clothes press
(Hayward and Kirkham 1980, no. 140) in
British collections. The use of identical
medallions on various pieces leads us to suggest
that they were made in a single workshop,
perhaps that of Christopher Furlogh (a theory
supported by Hayward). Furlogh was a
Swedish master working in England who
specialized in the production of inlay
medallions for furniture. His authorship is
supported not only by the similarity between
the figures and his well-known published
images in medallions, but also by the way they
are attached to the furniture, being set into the
surface of the upper layer of wood. Typical of
the decoration of English furniture of this
time are the inlaid shell in the centre of the
case (Gilbert 1978, no. 465); the segmented
oval on the central doors (Cescinsky 1909–11,
no. 288); and the crossed arrows in the corners
of the panels. Hayward also considers these to
be typical of Linnell's work. TR

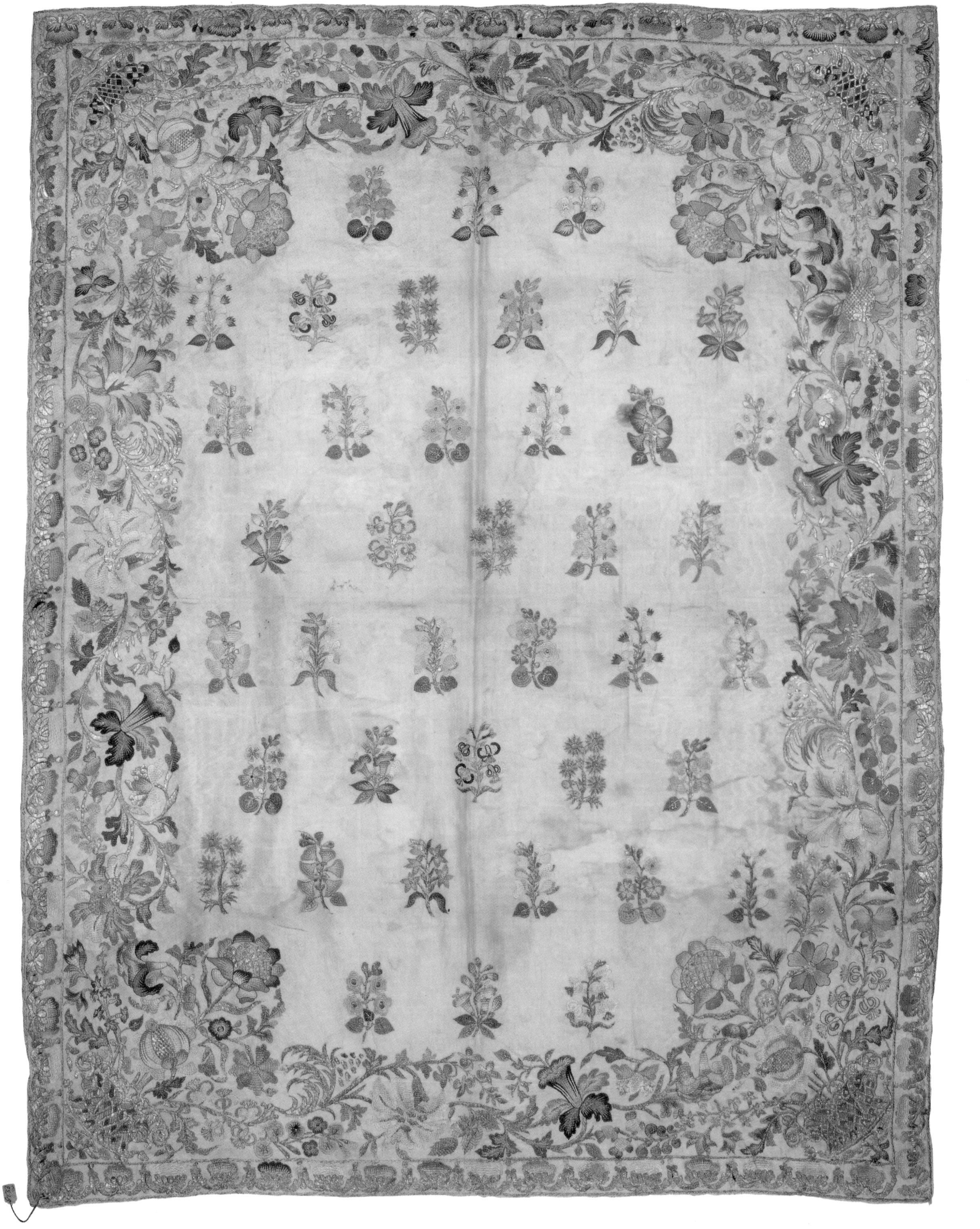

158

Unidentified Embroiderer

TABLECLOTH, *c.* 1700–25

Silk and gold thread; satin stitch, couched work, $38\frac{5}{8} \times 50$ in. 98×127 cm
Inv. no. T–2229

Provenance: collection of J. Kraut, Frankfurt-am-Main; from 1886 in the Stieglitz Museum, St Petersburg; transferred to the Hermitage in the 1920s.

Literature: English Art 1979, no. 79.

The composition of the pattern in this tablecloth, with a broad border of stems and flowers and large details at the corners, the central field being filled with rows of smaller sprigs, is characteristic of English embroideries of the first quarter of the 18th century (King and Levey 1993, pls. 91–95). Similar decorative compositions were used not only in interiors, but also for personal dress, for instance, on aprons (Hackenbroch 1960, fig. 167).

The technique of two-sided embroidery used here allows one to admire the pattern on both sides of the cloth. TK

159

Unidentified Embroiderer

FRAGMENT OF DECORATIVE EMBROIDERY, *c.* 1720–25

Silk and gold threads; satin stitch, laid and couched work, $21\frac{5}{8} \times 22\frac{7}{8}$ in. 55×58 cm
Inv. no. T–3285

Provenance: collection of J. Kraut, Frankfurt-am-Main; from 1886 in the Stieglitz Museum, St Petersburg; transferred to the Hermitage in the 1920s.

Literature: English Art 1979, no. 28.

These curving stems ending in large flowers were a favourite motif in English embroidery during the reign (1558–1603) of Elizabeth I, although their origin is to be found in an earlier age. The means of execution is also traditional: the stems are of gold thread laid in several rows, while the flowers are in silk. This kind of ornament was used not only for the adornment of personal dress and accessories, but also in embroidery intended for the decoration of interiors (Schuette and Muller-Christensen 1963, nos. 389–92; Mayer 1969, pl. 101; Gridgeman and Drury 1978, pl. 13; King and Levey 1993, pl. 46).

By the early 17th century, pattern-books were easily available, for example Thomas Trevelyon's *Commonplace Book* (London, 1608), which contained designs that continued to be advertised in later publications, such as Richard Shorleyker's *A Scholle-house for the Needle* of 1632. TK

Elizabeth Webster Denton

DECORATIVE PANEL WITH A MAP OF ENGLAND
AND WALES, 1701

Canvas and silk thread; cross-stitch,
20⅞ × 18⅛ in. 53 × 46 cm
Inscribed upper right: *A map of England &*
Wales by Elizabeth Webster Denton. September
22 1701
Inv. no. T–16194

Provenance: entered the Hermitage after 1917.

Literature: Kosaurova 1985, pp. 21–3

This embroidery is of very fine execution,
carefully conveying not only all the counties
of England and Wales but also various
geographical features. It is not only a rare
embroidery of the time in that it is signed,
for it is also an interesting example of the
embroidered images that were used for interior
decoration.

The detailed inscription in its medallion
of garlands of flowers suggests that this was
intended as a display of the embroiderer's
skills. Earlier pieces from the end of the 15th
century – a time when there were no printed
pattern-books – were used to record patterns
and technical devices, but by the 18th century
they had become independent artistic works.
King suggests that embroidered maps were
made in England in the 1780s (King 1960, no.
46). The Hermitage panel stands apart in that
it was made much earlier, at the very
beginning of the 18th century, which allows us
to considerably extend the period when maps
of this kind were being produced. TK

EXHIBITIONS

1769/1773 London SA. All references according to A. Graves, *The Society of Artists of Great Britain 1760–1791. The Free Society of Artists 1763–1783. A Complete Dictionary of Contributors and their Works from the Foundation of the Societies to 1791* (London, 1907)

1778/1783/1784 London RA. All references according to A. Graves, *The Royal Academy Exhibitors*, 8 vols (London, 1905)

1779/1789 London RA. All references according to A. Graves, *The Royal Academy of Arts. A Complete Dictionary of Contributors and their Works from First Foundation in 1769 to 1904*, 4 vols (London, 1970)

1870 St Petersburg. *Katalog istoricheskoy vystavki portretov lits XVI–XVIII vv., ustroyennoy Obshchestvom pooshchreniya khudozhnikov* [Catalogue of a Historical Exhibition of Portraits of Figures from the 16th to 18th Centuries, organized by the Society for the Encouragement of Artists], compiled by P. N. Petrov (St Petersburg, 1870)

1902 St Petersburg. *Podrobnyy illyustrirovannyy katalog vystavki russkoy portretnoy zhivopisi za 150 let (1700-1850)* [Detailed Illustrated Catalogue of the Exhibition of Russian Portrait Paintings over 150 years (1700–1850)], compiled by. N. N. Wrangel (St Petersburg, 1902)

1905 St Petersburg. *Katalog [...] istoriko-khudozhestvennoy vystavki russkikh portretov, ustraivayemoy v Tavricheskom dvortse v pol'zu vdov i sirot pavshikh v boyu voinov* [Catalogue ... of a Historical – Artistic Exhibition of Russian Portraits, organized in the Tauride Palace in aid of widows and orphans of those who fell in the War], compiled by S. P. Diaghilev (St Petersburg, 1905), issues 1–8

1909 London. '150th Wedgwood Anniversary Exhibition'

1912 St Petersburg. 'Vystavka starinnogo i sovremennogo farfora i fayansa Vedzhvud' [Exhibition of Wedgwood Ancient and Modern Porcelain and Faïence], no catalogue (Imperial Academy of Arts, St Petersburg)

1926 Leningrad. *Musée de l'Hermitage. Dessins des maîtres anciens. Exposition de 1926*, catalogue by M. Dobroklonsky (Leningrad, 1927)

1926 Leningrad, Engraved Gems. *Gosudarstvennyy Ermitazh. Reznyye kamni XVIII–XIX vekov. Putevoditel' po vystavke* [State Hermitage: Carved Gems of the 18th and 19th Centuries. Guide to the Exhibition], by M. M. Maksimova (Leningrad, 1926)

1937–8 Leningrad. *Gosudarstvennyy Ermitazh. Vystavka portreta* [State Hermitage: Exhibition of Portraits], issues [1]–4 (Leningrad, 1938)

1956 Moscow. *Gosudarstvennyy muzey izobrazitel'nykh iskusstv im. A. S. Pushkina. Vystavka proizvedeniy angliyskogo iskusstva... iz muzeyev SSSR* [Pushkin State Museum of Fine Art: Exhibition of English Works of Art] (Moscow, 1956)

1963 Stockholm. *Masterteckningar fran Eremitaget, Leningrad* (Nationalmuseum, Stockholm 1963)

1967 Glasgow–Edinburgh–London. *Charles Cameron: Architect to the Imperial Russian Court*, cat. by T. T. Rice

1967 London. *Great Britain – USSR: An Historical Exhibition* (The Arts Council, Victoria & Albert Museum, London, 9 February – 2 April 1967)

1968 Leningrad–Moscow. *Ot Dyurera do Pikasso. Pyat'desyat let kollektsionirovaniya i izucheniya zapadnoyevropeyskogo risunka* [From Dürer to Picasso: Fifty Years of the Collecting and Study of Western European Drawings] (Hermitage, Leningrad, 1968)

1968–9 Belgrade. *Stari majstori iz Ermitazha. Dela zapadnoyevropskikh slikara 16–18 veka iz zbirki Drzhavnogo Ermitazha* (Narodni Muzej, Belgrade, 1968)

1969 Leningrad–Moscow. *Izbrannyye risunki iz sobraniya Gosudarstvennogo Ermitazha. K 200-letiyu osnovaniya Otdeleniya Risunkov. Kollektsiya K. Kobentslya* [Selected Drawings from the Collection of the State Hermitage. On the 200th Anniversary of the Foundation of the Department of Drawings] (Hermitage, Leningrad; Pushkin Museum of Fine Arts, Moscow, 1969)

1970 Budapest. *Kiallitas a Leningradi Ermitazs legszebb rajzaibol* (Szépmüveszéti Múzeum, Budapest, 1970)

1971 Leningrad. *Gosudarstvennyy Ermitazh. Zapadnoyevropeyskiye reznyye kamni XIII–XIX vekov. Kratkiy putevoditel' po vystavke* [State Hermitage: Western European Carved Gems of the 13th to 19th Centuries. Short Guide to the Exhibition], by Yu. O. Kagan (Leningrad, 1971)

1972 Leningrad. *Iskusstvo portreta. Katalog vystavki iz sobraniya Gosudarstvennogo Ermitazha* [The Art of the Portrait: Catalogue of the Exhibition, from the Collection of the State Hermitage] (Leningrad, 1972)

1972 Prague. *Kresby evropskych mistru XV–XX stoleti ze sbirek Statni Ermitaze v Leningrad* (Narodni Galerie, Prague, 1972)

1973 Leningrad. *Medal'yernoye iskusstvo Zapadnoy Yevropy XV–XVII vekov. Kratkiy putevoditel' po vystavke iz sobraniya Ermitazha* [The Medallist's Art in Western Europe, 15th–17th Centuries. Short Guide to the Exhibition from the Collection of the Hermitage], compiled by Ye. S. Shchukina (Leningrad, 1978)

1974 London. *Stubbs & Wedgwood*, cat. by B. Tattershall (Tate Gallery, London, 1974)

1974 Manchester. *Drawings by West European and Russian Masters from the Collection of the State Hermitage and the Russian Museum in Leningrad* (Whitworth Art Gallery, Manchester, 1974)

1975 Berlin. *Zeichnungen aus der Ermitage zu Leningrad. Werke des 15 bis 19 Jahrhunderts* (Staatliche Museen zu Berlin; Nationalgalerie, Kupferstichkabinett und Sammlung der Zeichnungen, Berlin, 1975)

1975 Copenhagen–Aarhus. *Tegninger fra det Staslige Eremitage-museum og det Statslige Russiske Museum i Leningrad* (Thorvaldsens Museum, Copenhagen; Kunstmuseum, Aarhus, 1975)

1975–6 Washington – New York – Detroit – Los Angeles –Houston. *Master Paintings from the Hermitage and the State Russian Museum, Leningrad* (National Gallery of Art, Washington, DC; The Detroit Institute of Arts, Detroit, MI; Los Angeles County Museum of Art, CA; The Museum of Fine Arts, Houston, TX)

1976 Leningrad. *Reznyye kamni Yul'yama i Charl'za Braunov* [Carved Gems by William and Charles Brown], compiled by Yu. O. Kagan (Hermitage, Leningrad, 1976)

1976 Mexico. *Pinturas maestras del los Museus estatales del Hermitage y Ruso. Leningrado* (Museo de Arte Moderno losque de Chapultepec Instituto National de Bellas Artes, Mexico City, 1976)

1976 San Francisco. *Master Paintings from the Hermitage and the State Russian Museum, Leningrad* (The Fine Arts Museum of San Francisco, CA. Palace of the Legion of Honor, 27 March–9 May 1976)

1976 Winnipeg–Montreal. *Master Paintings from the Hermitage and the State Russian Museum. Leningrad* (Winnipeg Art Gallery, 13 August – 26 September 1976; Montreal Museum of Fine Arts, 9 October – 14 November 1976)

1980 Moscow. *100 shedevrov zapadnoyevropeyskogo prikladnogo iskusstva iz sobraniya Ermitazha* [100 Masterpieces of Western European Applied Art from the Collection of the Hermitage] (Pushkin Museum of Fine Arts, Moscow, 1980)

1982 London. *Van Dyck in England*, cat. by O. Millar (National Portrait Gallery, London, 1982)

1983 Moscow. 'Gosudarstvennyy muzey izobrazitel'nykh iskusstv im. A. S. Pushkina. Angliyskiy portret XVI–XVIII vekov' [Pushkin State Museum of Fine Arts: English Portraits of the 16th to 18th Centuries], no catalogue

1986 Bogota. *Dibujos de maestros europeos de los siglos XV al XVIII* (Museo de Arte Moderno de Bogota, 1986)

1986 Lugano. *Ori e Argenti dall'Ermitage* (Milan, 1986)

1986 Montevideo–Buenos Aires. *Dibujos de los maestros de Europa occidental de los siglos XV al XVIII. Coleccion del Ermitage de Leningrado* (Museu Nacional de Artes Visuales, Montevideo, 1986)

1987–8 Belgrade–Ljubljana–Zagrab. *Svetski majstori iz riznica Ermitaza od XV– XVIII veka / Hermitage Masterpieces, Paintings and Drawings XV–XVIII Century* (National Museum, Belgrade; National Gallery, Ljubljana; Muzejski Prostor, Zagreb, 1987)

1987 New Delhi. *Masterpieces of Western European Art from the Hermitage, Leningrad* (National Committee Festival of India, The National Museum, New Delhi, 1987)

1987 Sapporo–Fukuoka–Hiroshima. *Works by Western European Masters of the 19th to 20th Centuries from the Hermitage Collection* (Hokkaido Museum of Modern Art, Sapporo; Art Museum of the Hiroshima Prefecture; Fukuoka Prefecture Museum; Sapporo, 1987) [in Japanese]

1990 London. *Paul de Lamerie: An Exhibition of the Work of England's Master Silversmith (1688–1751)*, cat. ed. by S. Hare (Goldsmith's Hall, London, 16 May – 22 June 1990)

1991 Boston. 'Gemstones', no catalogue (Museum of Science, Boston)

1991 Leningrad. *Angliyskaya farforovaya miniatyura XVIII veka* [English 18th-century Porcelain Miniatures] (State Hermitage, Leningrad, 1991)

1992 Tobu. *Dutch and Flemish Art of the 17th century from the State Hermitage Museum* (Tobu Museum of Art, 10 June – 18 August 1992)

1992 Tokyo. *Court Culture of Russia. State Hermitage* (Tokyo, 1992) [in Japanese]

1993 St Petersburg. *Iz kollektsii petrovskoy Kunstkamery*, cat. by O. Ya. Neverov (St Petersburg, 1993)

1994 Kolding. *Zur Tafel im Winterpalast. Russishe und westeuropaishe Porzellan– und Fayencearbeiten aus der Zweiten Halfte des 18. Jahrhunderts* (Museet pa Koldinghus)

1994 Speyer. *Der Zarenschatz der Romanov. Meisterwerke der Eremitage St. Petersburg* (Speyer, 1994)

1995 London. *The Genius of Wedgwood* (Victoria & Albert Museum, London, 1995)

1995 St Petersburg. 'Keramika Dzhozaiyi Vedzhvuda' [The Ceramics of Josiah Wedgwood] (no catalogue)

BIBLIOGRAPHY

Archive, library and publications abbreviations:

RGADA: Russian State Archive of Ancient Deeds
RGIA: Russian State Historical Archive
SbRIO: Sbornik Imperatorskogo Rossiyskogo Istoricheskogo obshchestva
SGE: *Soobshcheniya Gosudarstvennogo Ermitazha* [Bulletin of the Hermitage Museum]
TGE: *Trudy Gosudarstvennogo Ermitazha* (Leningrad)
TOZI: *Trudy Otdela zapadnoyevropeyskogo iskusstva* (Leningrad)

ABBEY 1956 J. R. Abbey, *Travel in Aquatint and Lithography, 1770–1860; From the Library of J. R. Abbey*, 2 vols (London, 1956)

ADAMS 1979 W. H. Adams, *The French Garden, 1500–1800* (New York, 1979)

ADAMS 1987 E. Adams, *Chelsea Porcelain* (London, 1987)

ALEKSEYEV 1982 M. Alekseyev, *Russko-angliyskiye literaturnyye svyazi (XVIII vek - pervaya polovina XIX veka)*, Literaturnoye nasledstvo, 91 (Moscow, 1982)

ALEXANDER 1992 D. Alexander, 'Kauffman and the Print Market in Eighteenth-century Britain', *Angelica Kauffman: A Continental Artist in Georgian Britain*, ed. W. W. Roworth (London, 1992), pp. 141–78

ALEXANDER 1995 D. Alexander, 'James Walker: A British Engraver in Russia', *Print Quarterly*, XII (1995), pp. 412–14

ALLAN 1849 Anon., 'Sir William Allan', *Art Journal* (1849), pp. 108–9

ALLAN 1974 W. Allan, 'Sir William Allan', *The Connoisseur* (June 1974)

ANCKETILL 1978 M. D. Ancketill, 'The Silver Palette', *Lantern* (July 1978), pp. 72–9

ANDERSON 1986 J. Anderson, 'Ten Watercolours by the Derby China Artist: Zachariah Boreman', *National Art Collections Fund Review* (1986)

ANDREEVA 1991 G. Andreeva, 'Ital'ianskie vstrechi: Russkie I britanskie zhivopistsy v Rime vo vtoroi polovine XVIII veka', *Study Group on Eighteenth-century Russia Newsletter*, XIX (1991), pp. 9–12

ANDREEVA 1993 G. Andreeva, 'Portrait of a Painter Remembered', *Country Life* (22 April 1993), pp. 62–4

ANDREYEV 1977 A. K. Andreyev, 'Adam Menelas' [Adam Menelaws], *Problemy sinteza iskusstv i arkhitektury* [Questions of the Synthesis of the Arts and Architecture] (1977), pp. 58–59

ANDREYEV 1991 A. K. Andreyev, *Khudozhnik arkhitektury akademik Ivan Alekseyevich Ivanov i nekotoryye voprosy istorii i teorii russkoy arkhitektury* [The Architectural Artist, Academician Ivan Alexeyevich Ivanov, and Several Questions of the History and Theory of Russian Architecture] (Leningrad, 1991)

ANDREYEVA 1989 G. B. Andreyeva, 'A. S. Pushkin i Dzhordzh Dou. Novyye stranitsy' [A. S. Pushkin and George Dawe: New Pages], *Iskusstvo* [Art], no. 6 (1989), pp. 58–62

ANDREYEVA 1995 G. B. Andreyeva, 'Ob atributsii odnoy kartiny Dzhordzha Doy' [On the Attribution of a Painting by George Dawe], *Soobshcheniya Gosudarstvennoy Tret'yakovskoy galerei* [Bulletin of the State Tretyakov Gallery], Drevnerusskoye iskusstvo. Iskusstvo XVIII – pervoy poloviny XIX veka [Old Russian Art: Art of the 18th and first half of the 19th Century] (Moscow, 1995), pp. 122–32

ANGELO 1904 H. Angelo, *The Reminiscences*, intro. Lord Howard de Walden, 2 vols (London, 1904)

AN IMPERIAL FASCINATION 1991 *An Imperial Fascination: Porcelain. Dining with Czars, Peterhof. An Exhibition of Services from Russian Imperial Palaces*, texts by N. Vernova, V. Znamenov and T. Nosovitch (New York, 1991)

ANTONOV 1979 V. Antonov, 'New Documents about the Browns' Gems', *The Burlington Magazine* (December 1979), pp. 841–2

APPLIED ART 1974 *Prikladnoye iskusstvo Zapadnoy Yevropy XIII–XVIII vv.*, ed. N. Yu. Biryukova (Leningrad, 1974)

ARCHIVE OF PRINCE VORONTSOV 1883, 1891 *Arkhiv knyazya Vorontsova*, XXVIII (Moscow, 1883); XXXVII (Moscow, 1891)

ARMSTRONG 1898 W. Armstrong, *Gainsborough and his Place in English Art* (London, 1898)

ARMSTRONG 1900 W. Armstrong, *Sir Joshua Reynolds* (London, 1900)

ARMSTRONG 1913 W. Armstrong, *Lawrence* (London, 1913)

ARMSTRONG 1962 W. M. Armstrong, 'The Many-sided World of Sir Robert Ker Porter', *The Historian*, XXV (1962), pp. 36–58

ARTS AND SCIENCES UNITED 1978 *Josiah Wedgwood: 'The Arts and Sciences United'*, exh. cat., Science Museum, London (1978)

ARTS DÉCORATIFS 1986 *L'Hermitage. Arts décoratifs* (Leningrad, 1986)

ASHMOLE 1715 E. Ashmole, *The History of the Most Noble Order of the Garter* (London, 1715)

ATKINSON 1986 Beavington Atkinson, *An Art Tour to Russia* (London, 1986)

AUTEROCHE 1770 M. l'Abbé Chappe d'Auteroche, *A Journey into Siberia, Made by Order of the King of France* (London, 1770)

BABELON 1897 E. Babelon: *Catalogue des camees antiques et modernes de la Bibliothèque Nationale* (Paris, 1897)

BALOG 1972 G. P. Balog *et al.*, *Muzei i parki Pushkina* [The Museums and Parks of Pushkin] (Leningrad, 1972)

BARNETT 1972 R. D. Barnett, 'Sir Robert Ker Porter: Regency Artist and Traveller', *Iran*, X (1972)

BARNETT 1996 G. Barnett, *Richard and Maria Cosway* (London, 1996)

BECKETT 1951 R. B. Beckett, *Lely* (London, 1951)

BEMROSE 1885 W. Bemrose, *The Life and Works of Joseph Wright, ARA, commonly called 'Wright of Derby'* (London, 1885)

BENOIS 1902 A. N. Benois, 'Galereya Dragotsennostey Imperatorskogo Ermitazha', *Khudozhestvennyye sokrovishcha Rossii*, XII (St Petersburg, 1902)

BENOIS 1911 A. Benua [Benois], *Putevoditel' po kartinnoy galereye Imperatorskogo Ermitazha* (St Petersburg, [1911])

BENOIS 1921 A. Benua [Benois], 'Dzhozef Rayt' [Joseph Wright of Derby], *Gosudarstvennyy Ermitazh. Sbornik*, issue I (Petersburg 1920/Petrograd 1921)

BERRY AND CRUMMEY 1968 L. E. Berry and R. O. Crummey, eds, *Rude and Barbarous Kingdom: Russia in the Accounts of Sixteenth-century English Voyagers* (Madison, Milwaukee and London, 1968)

BESTERMAN 1953–65 T. Besterman, ed., *Voltaire's Correspondence*, 107 vols (Geneva, 1953–65)

BINYON 1900 L. Binyon, *Catalogue of Drawings by British Artists … in the British Museum*, II (London, 1900)

BIRD 1974 A. Bird, 'British Artists in Russia', *Anglo-Soviet Journal*, XXXV (1974), pp. 17–22

BIRD 1977 A. Bird, 'A Painter of the Russian Aristocracy', *Country Life*, CLVIII (6 January 1977), pp. 32–3

BIRYUKOVA 1972 N. Biryukova, *Zapadnoyevropeyskoye prikladnoye iskusstvo XVII–XVII vekov* [Western European Applied Art of the 17th and 18th Centuries] (Leningrad, 1972)

BIRYUKOVA 1974 *Musée de l'Ermitage. Les arts appliqués de l'Europe Occidentale XIIe–XVIIIe siècle*, ed. N. Birioukova (Leningrad, 1974)

BISHOP 1974 P. J. Bishop, *A Short History of the Royal Humane Society* (London, 1974)

BIVAR 1994 A.D.H. Bivar, 'The Portraits and Career of Mohammed Ali, son of Kazem-Beg: Scottish Missionaries and Russian Orientalism', *Bulletin of the School of Oriental and African Studies, University of London*, LVII (1994)

BLAKE ROBERTS 1986 G. Blake Roberts, 'Wedgwood in Russia', *Ceramics*, no. IV (July–August 1986)

BLAKE ROBERTS 1995 G. Blake Roberts, 'Josiah Wedgwood's Trade with Russia', in *The Genius of Wedgwood* (London, 1995)

BORN 1964 B. A. Born, 'Josiah Wedgwood's First Shape Book', *The Ninth Wedgwood International Seminar, Metropolitan Museum of Art* (New York, 1964)

BRINDING ADAMS 1992 E. Brinding Adams, *The Dwight and Lucille Beeson Wedgwood Collection at the Birmingham Museum of Art* (Birmingham, AL, 1992)

BROCKMANN 1985 G. Brockmann, *Die Medaillen der Welfen, I, Linie Wolfenbuttel* (Cologne, 1985)

BROUGH 1789 A. Brough, *View of the Importance of the Trade between Great Britain and Russia* (London, 1789)

BROWN 1980 L. A. Brown, *British Historical Medals, 1760–1960*, I (London, 1980)

BROWN 1991 C. Brown, *The Drawings of Anthony Van Dyck*, exh. cat., Pierpont Morgan Library, New York (1991)

BRUK 1990 Ya. V. Bruk, *U istokov russkogo zhanra XVIII veka* [At the Sources of Russian 18th-century Genre] (Moscow, 1990)

BRYANT 1925 G. E. Bryant, *The Chelsea Porcelain Toys* (1925)

BUCKLEY 1952 C. E. Buckley, 'Joseph Wright of Derby', *Magazine of Art* (April 1952), pp. 160–67

BURTON 1976 A. Burton, *Josiah Wedgwood* (London, 1976)

BURY 1978 S. Bury, 'A Commesso-cameo of Queen Victoria', *Society of Jewellery Historians Newsletter*, no. 3 (1978), p. 2

BURY 1979 S. Bury, 'A Royal Order of Victoria and Albert', *Society of Jewellery Historians Newsletter*, no. 6 (1979), pp. 8–9

BUTEN 1980 D. Buten, *18th-century Wedgwood: A Guide for Collectors and Connoisseurs* (New York, 1980)

CABINET D'ORLÉANS 1786 *Catalogue des pierres gravées du Cabinet de feu M. le Duc d'Orleans* (Paris, 1786)

CADES [undated] Tommasso Cades, 'Impronte Gemmarie' (MS)

CALL 1827 [Martin Call], 'History of the First Introduction of the Modern Style of Laying Out Grounds in Russia', *The Gardener's Magazine*, II (1827)

CARDINAL 1984 C. Cardinal, *Catalogue des montres du Musée du Louvre* (Paris, 1984)

CARR 1805 J. Carr, *A Northern Summer, or Travels Round [the] Baltic, through Denmark, Sweden, Russia, Prussia, and part of Germany, in the Year 1804* (London, 1805)

CAT. 1773 [E. Munich], *Catalogue raisonné des tableaux qui se trouvent dans les Galleries, Salons et Cabinets du Palais Imperial de Petersbourg*, 3 vols, 1773–85 (Hermitage Archives, op. VI-A, d.85)

CAT. 1797 *Katalog kartinam, khranyashchimsya v imperatorskoy galereye Ermitazha… sochinyonnyy… pri uchastii F. I. Labenskogo v 1797*, Hermitage Archives, Fund I, op. VI-A, d. 87,

CAT. 1958 *Gosudarstvennyy Ermitazh. Otdel zapadnoyevropeyskogo iskusstva. Katalog zhivopisi*, ed. V. F. Levinson-Lessing, 2 vols (Moscow, 1958)

CAT. 1981 *Gosudarstvennyy Ermitazh. Zapadnoyevropeyskaya zhivopis. Katalog, 2. Niderlandy, Flandriya, Bel'giya, Gollandiya, Germaniya, Avstriya, Angliya, Daniya, Norvegiya, Finlyandiya, Shvetsiya, Vengriya, Pol'sha, Rumyniya, Chekhoslovakiya* (Leningrad, 1981)

CESCINSKY 1909–11 H. Cescinsky, *English Furniture of the Eighteenth Century*, 3 vols (London, 1909–11)

CHABOUILLET 1858 A. Chabouillet, *Catalogue général et raisonné des camées et pierres gravées de la Bibliothèque Impériale* (Paris, 1858)

CHAFFERS 1899 W. Chaffers, *Gilda Aurifabrorum* (London, 1899)

CHALONER SMITH 1878–83 J. Chaloner Smith, *English Mezzotinto Portraits*, 4 vols (London, 1878–83)

CHAMBERS 1829 J. Chambers, *A General History of the County of Norfolk, Intended to Convey all the Information of a Norfolk Tour*, 2 vols (Norwich and London, 1829)

CHELLIS 1962 R. D. Chellis, 'Wedgwood and Bentley Source Books', *The Seventh Wedgwood International Seminar, The Art Institute of Chicago* (Chicago, 1962)

CHRISTIE'S, London 1988 *Important European Sculpture and Works of Art*, sale cat., Christie's, London (6 December 1988)

CLARKE 1810 E. D. Clarke, *Travels in Various Countries of Europe, Asia and Africa* (London, 1810)

CLIFFORD ET AL. 1978 T. Clifford, A. Griffiths and M. Royalton-Kisch, *Gainsborough and Reynolds in the British Museum* (London, 1978)

COLLINS 1671 [S. Collins], *The Present State of Russia, in a Letter to a Friend at London* (London, 1671)

COLLINS BAKER 1912 C. H. Collins Baker: *Lely and the Stuart Painters*, 2 vols (London, 1912)

CONWAY 1925 M. Conway, *Art Treasures in Soviet Russia* (London, 1925)

COPELAND 1993 R. Copeland: *Spode and Copeland Marks, and Other Relevant Intelligence* (London, 1993)

CORMACK 1968–70 M. Cormack, 'The Ledgers of Sir Joshua Reynolds', *Walpole Society*, XLII (1968–70), pp. 105–69

COTTON 1856 W. Cotton, *Sir Joshua Reynolds and his Works; Gleanings from his Diary, Unpublished Manuscripts, and from other Sources*, ed. J. Burnet ((London, 1856)

COTTON 1859 W. Cotton, *Sir Joshua Reynolds's Notes and Observations on Pictures, Chiefly of the Venetian School, Being Extracts from his Italian Sketchbooks* (London, 1859)

COXE 1784 W. Coxe, *Travels into Poland, Russia, Sweden and Denmark*, 3 vols (London, 1784)

COXE 1802 W. Coxe, *Travels into Poland, Russia, Sweden and Denmark*, 5 vols, 5th edn (London, 1802)

CRIPPS 1886 W. E. Cripps, *Old English Plate* (London, 1886)

CROFT-MURRAY AND HULTON 1960 E. Croft-Murray and P. Hulton, *Catalogue of British Drawings, I: XVI and XVII Centuries* [in the British Museum], 2 vols (London, 1960)

CROSS 1969a A. G. Cross, 'The Revd William Tooke's Contribution to English Knowledge of Russia at the End of the Eighteenth Century', *Canadian Slavic Studies*, III (1969), pp. 106–15

CROSS 1969b A. G. Cross, 'Arcticus and "The Bee" (1790–4): An Episode in Anglo-Russian Cultural Relations', *Oxford Slavonic Papers*, n.s. IV (1969), pp. 62–76

CROSS 1970 A. G. Cross, 'A Royal Bluestocking: Catherine the Great's Early Reputation in England as an Authoress', *Gorski Vijenats: A Garland of Essays Offered to Professor Elizabeth Mary Hill*, ed. R. Auty *et al.* (Cambridge, 1970), pp. 85–99

CROSS 1971 A. G. Cross, ed., *Russia Under Western Eyes, 1517–1825* (London, 1971)

CROSS 1974 A. G. Cross, 'The English Garden and Russia: An Anonymous Identified', *Study Group on Eighteenth-century Russia Newsletter*, II (1974), pp. 25–9

CROSS 1975a A. G. Cross, 'Early English Specimens of the Russian Poets', *Canadian Slavic Studies*, IX (1975), pp. 449–62

CROSS 1975b A. G. Cross, 'Catherine the Great and an Amusement called Cricket', *The Cricketer*, LVI/11 (1975), p. 60

CROSS 1976 A. G. Cross, 'Mr Fisher's Company of English Actors in Eighteenth-century Petersburg', *Study Group on Eighteenth-century Russia Newsletter*, XXII (1976), pp. 49–56

CROSS 1977 A. G. Cross, *Study Group on Eighteenth-century Russia: Anglo-Russian Relations in the Eighteenth Century*, exh. cat. (Norwich, 1977)

CROSS 1980 A. G. Cross, *'By the Banks of the Thames': Russians in Eighteenth-century Britain* (Newtonville, MA, 1980)

CROSS 1985 A. G. Cross, *The Russian Theme in English Literature from the Sixteenth Century to 1980* (Oxford, 1985)

CROSS 1986 A. G. Cross, 'Richard Paton and the Battle of Chesme', *Study Group on Eighteenth-century Russia Newsletter*, XIV (1986), pp. 31–7

CROSS 1989 A. G. Cross, ed., *An English Lady at the Court of Catherine the Great: The Journal of Baroness Elizabeth Dimsdale, 1781* (Cambridge, 1989)

CROSS 1990 A. G. Cross, 'Catherine the Great and Whately's "Observations on Modern Gardening"', *Study Group on Eighteenth-century Russia Newsletter*, XVIII (1990), pp. 21–9

CROSS 1991a A. G. Cross, 'In Cameron's Shadow: Adam Menelaws, Stonemason turned Architect', *Scottish Studies*, XVII (1991), pp. 7–19

CROSS 1991b A. G. Cross, 'Catherine the Great and the English Garden', *New Directions in Russian and Soviet Art and Culture*, ed. J. Norman (London, 1991)

CROSS 1992 A. G. Cross, *Anglophilia on the Throne: The British and the Russians in the Age of Catherine the Great* (Richmond Press, 1992)

CROSS 1993 A. G. Cross, *Engraved in the Memory: James Walker, Engraver to the Empress Catherine the Great, and his Russian Anecdotes* (Oxford, 1993)

CROSS 1994 A. G. Cross, 'Did Catherine the Great Know English?', *Study Group on Eighteenth-century Russia Newsletter*, XXII (1994), pp. 13–19

CROSS 1996a A. G. Cross, *'By the Banks of the Neva': Chapters from the Lives and Careers of the British in Eighteenth-century Russia* (Cambridge, 1996)

CROSS 1996b A. G. Cross, 'Petrus Britannicus: The Image of Peter the Great in Eighteenth-century Britain', *A Window on Eighteenth-century Russia: Papers from the Fifth International Conference of the Study Group on Eighteenth-century Russia, Gargnano, 1994*, ed. M. Di Salvo and L. Hughes (Rome, 1996)

CUST 1900 L. Cust, *Anthony van Dyck: An Historical Study of his Life and Works* (London, 1900)

DALTON 1915 O. M. Dalton, *Catalogue of Engraved Gems of the Post-classical Period in the British Museum* (London, 1915)

DASHKOVA 1987 Ye. R. Dashkova, *Pis'ma sestyor Vil'mont iz Rossii* [Letters from the Wilmont Sisters from Russia] (Moscow, 1987)

DASHKOVA 1995 Ye. R. Dashkova, 'Le Petit Tour dans les Highland', *XVIII vek*, XIX (1995), pp. 239–53

DAVENPORT 1900 C. Davenport, *Cameos: The Portfolio Monographs* (London, 1900)

DAWSON 1984 A. Dawson, *Masterpieces of Wedgwood in the British Museum* (London, 1984)

DAYDI 1957 M. Olivar Daydi, *Das europäische Porzellan von den Anfängen bix zum Beginn des 19. Jahrhunderts*, I (Bern, 1955); II (Bern and Munich, 1957)

DE LA MOTTRE 1991 A. de la Mottre, 'Iz Puteshestviya...' [From a Journey...], in Yu. N. Bespyatykh, *Peterburg Petra I v inostrannykh opisaniyakh* [Foreign Descriptions of the Petersburg of Peter I] (Leningrad, 1991)

DERWIS 1935 P. Derwis, 'Some English Plate at the Hermitage', *The Burlington Magazine*, LXVII (July 1935), pp. 35–6

DERWIS 1936 P. Derwis, 'More English Plate at the Hermitage', *The Burlington Magazine*, LXIX (July 1936), pp. 25–7

DERZHAVIN 1987 G. R. Derzhavin, *Anakreonticheskiye pesni* [Anachreontic Songs] (Moscow, 1987)

DESCARGUES 1961 P. Descargues, *The Hermitage*, trans. K. Delavenay (London, 1961)

DOBROKLONSKY 1955 *Gosudarstvennyy Ermitazh. Risunki flamandskoy shkoly 17–18 vekov* [State Hermitage: Drawings of the Flemish school, 17th–18th Centuries] (Moscow, 1955)

DRAGESCO 1993 B. Dragesco, *English Ceramics in French Archives* (London, 1993)

DUKELSKAYA 1979 L. A. Dukelskaya, ed., *The Hermitage: English Art, Sixteenth to Nineteenth Centuries* (Leningrad, 1979)

DUKELSKAYA 1983 L. A. Dukelskaya, *Iskusstvo Anglii XVI–XIX vekov: Ocherk-putevoditel'* [English Art, 16th to the 19th Centuries] (Leningrad, 1983)

DUKELSKAYA 1987 L. A. Dukelskaya, 'O portrete Dzhona Lokka, ispolnennym G. Nellerom', *SGE*, LII (1987)

DUKELSKAYA AND RENNE 1990 L. A. Dukelskaya and E. P. Renne, *The Hermitage Catalogue of Western European Painting: British Painting, Sixteenth to Nineteenth Centuries* (Florence and Moscow, 1990)

EDINBURGH–GLASGOW–LONDON 1967–8 *Charles Cameron: Architect to the Imperial Russian Court*, exh. cat. by T. T. Rice; Edinburgh, Glasgow and London (1967)

EDWARDS AND JOURDAIN 1955 R. Edwards and M. Jourdain, *Georgian Cabinet-makers* (London, 1955)

EGERTON 1990 *Wright of Derby*, exh. cat. by J. Egerton; Tate, London; Grand Palais, Paris; Metropolitan Museum of Art, New York (1990)

EICHLER AND KRIS 1927 F. Eichler and E. Kris, *Die Kameen im Kunsthistorischen Museum* (Vienna, 1927)

ENGLISH ART 1979 *The Hermitage: English Art Sixteenth to Nineteenth Century: Paintings, Sculture, Prints and Drawings, Minor Arts* (Leningrad, 1979)

ENGLISH PORCELAIN PAINTERS 1981 *English Porcelain Painters of the 18th Century*, exh. cat., Graham and Oxley (Antiques) Ltd, Fine Ceramics and Works of Art, summer exhibition (1981)

ERFFA AND STALEY 1986 H. von Erffa and A. Staley, *The Paintings of Benjamin West* (New Haven and London, 1986)

ERNST 1965 S. Ernst, 'Portraits by Kneller in Russia', *The Burlington Magazine*, CVII (August 1965), pp. 425–6

ETKIND 1960 Yu. Etkind (Kagan), 'Animalisticheskiye motivy v reznykh kamnyakh V. i. Ch. Braunov', *SGE*, 18 (1960), pp. 35–40

ETKIND 1965a Yu. Etkind (Kagan), 'Reznyye kamni Uil'yama i Charl'za Braunov v Ermitazhe', *TGE*, VIII (Leningrad, 1965), pp. 99–108

ETKIND 1965b Iu. Etkind (Kagan), 'Russian Themes in the Work of the English Gem-cutters William and Charles Brown', *The Burlington Magazine*, CVII (August 1965), pp. 421–5

ETTINGER 1922 P. Ettinger, 'Inostrannye khudozhniki v Rossii: Ye. F. Kanningkhem' [Foreign Artists in Russia: E. F. Cunningham], *Sredi kollektsionerov* [Among Collectors], no. 10 (1922)

ETTINGER 1924 P. Ettinger, 'Portraits of Charles Fox at the Hermitage', *The Burlington Magazine*, XLV (December 1924)

EVANS 1951 J. Evans, *A History of Jewellery, 1100–1870* (London, 1951)

EVANS AND SERJEANSTON 1933 J. Evans and M. S. Serjeanston, *English Medieval Lapidaries* (Oxford, 1933)

EVANS AND STUDER 1924 J. Evans and P. Studer, *Anglo-Norman Lapidaries* (Paris, 1924)

EVELYN 1697 J. Evelyn, *Numismata: A Discourse of Medals, Ancient and Modern* (London, 1697)

EVELYN 1955 J. Evelyn, *The Diary*, ed. E. S. De Beer, 6 vols (Oxford, 1955)

FAGAN 1885 L. Fagan, *A Catalogue Raisonné of the Engraved Works of William Woollett* (London, 1885)

FALCONET 1781 *Oeuvres d'Etienne Falconet, statuaire*, 6 vols (Paris, 1781)

FARÉ 1866 I. de Faré, *Description of the English Pictures* (St Petersburg, 1866)

FARINGTON 1978–84 *The Diary of Joseph Farington*, ed. K. Garlick, A. Macintyre and K. Cave, 16 vols (New Haven and London, 1978–84)

FERSMAN 1961 A. Ye. Fersman, *Ocherki po istorii kamnya*, 2 vols (Moscow, 1961)

FILOSOFOV 1924 M. Filosofov, 'K istorii serviza s zelyonoy lygushkoy', *Sredi kollektsionerov* (May–June 1924)

FINER AND SAVAGE 1965 A. Finer and G. Savage, *The Selected Letters of Josiah Wedgwood* (London, 1965)

FIORILLO 1808 J. D. Fiorillo, *Geschichte der Kunste und Wissenschaften zweyete Ubtheilung Geschichte der eichunden Kunste, Bd. 5: Die Geschichte der Mahlerey in Gross-britannien enthaltend* (Gottingen, 1808)

FITZLYON 1958 *The Memoirs of Princess Dashkov*, trans. K. Fitzlyon (London, 1958)

FLEKEL 1985 M. I. Flekel, *Russkaya gravyura kontsa XVII–XVIII vekov* [Russian Engraving of the 17th and 18th Centuries] (Leningrad, 1985)

FLETCHER 1972 H. Gletcher, 'John Gibson, An English Pupil of Thorvaldsen', *Apollo*, XCVI (October 1972), pp. 336–9

FOELKERSAM 1907 Baron A. Vel'kerzam, *Opisi serebra Dvora Yego Imperatorskogo Velichestva* [Inventories of the Silver of the Court of His Imperial Highness], 2 vols (St Petersburg, 1907)

FOELKERSAM 1913 Baron A. Vel'kerzam, 'Gertsoginya Kingston i yeya prebyvaniya v Rossii' [The Duchess of Kingston and her Time in Russia], *Staryye gody* (June 1913), pp. 3–35

FOMIN 1911 I. I. Fomin, *Istoricheskaya vystavka arkhitektury* [A Historical Examination of Architecture] (St Petersburg, 1911)

FORRER 1904–30 L. Forrer, *Biographical Dictionary of Medallists, Coin, Gem- and Seal-engravers*, 8 vols (London, 1904–30)

FORTNUM 1874 C. D. Fortnum, 'Notes on Some of the Antique and Renaissance Gems and Jewels at Windsor Castle', *Archaeologia*, XIV (1874), pp. 1–28

FOSKETT 1972 D. Foskett, *A Dictionary of British Miniature Painters*, 2 vols (London, 1972)

FOSTER 1967 K. Foster, 'Chelsea Scent Bottles: "Girl in a Swing" and Another Group', *English Ceramic Circle Transactions*, VI/3 (1967)

FOWLER AND CORNFORTH 1978 J. Fowler and J. Cornforth, *English Decoration in the XVIIIth Century* (London, 1978)

FRANKAU 1902 J. Frankau, *John Raphael Smith* (London, 1902)

GAGE 1964 J. Gage, 'Magilphs and Mysteries', *Apollo*, LXXX (July 1964), pp. 38–41

GARLICK 1954 K. Garlick, *Sir Thomas Lawrence* (London, 1954)

GARLICK 1962–4 K. Garlick, 'A Catalogue of the Paintings, Drawings and Pastels of Sir Thomas Lawrence', *Walpole Society*, XXXIX (1962–4), pp. 13–323

GARLICK 1989 K. Garlick, *Sir Thomas Lawrence: A Complete catalogue of the Oil Paintings* (Oxford, 1989)

GATTY 1938–9 H. Gatty, ed., 'Notes by Horace Walpole, Fourth Earl of Orford on the Exhibitions of the Society of Artists and the Free Society of Artists, 1760–1791, *Walpole Society*', XXVII (1938–9), pp. 55–88

GENIUS OF WEDGWOOD 1995 see Exhibitions, 1995 London

GEORGI 1794 I. G. Georgi, *Opisaniye Rossiyskogo imperatorskogo stolichnogo goroda Sankt-Peterburga i dostoprimechatel'nostey v okrestnostyakh onogo*, 3 parts (St Petersburg, 1794)

GERES 1979 B. Geres, *Tvorchestvo Davida Rentgena dlya Rossii i yego svyaz' s russkim mebel'nym iskusstvom kontsa XVIII – nachala XIX vv.* [David Roentgen's Work for Russia and his Link with Russian Furniture at the End of the 18th Century and Beginning of the 19th], thesis summary (Leningrad, 1979), nos. 185, 186

GILBERT 1978 C. Gilbert, *Furniture at Temple Newsam House and Lotherton Hall*, I (London, 1978)

GLANVILLE 1987 P. Glanville, *Silver in England* (London, 1987)

GLEZER 1979 E. N. Glezer, *Arkitekturnyi ansambl' angliiskogo parka* (Leningrad, 1979)

GLINKA AND POMARNATSKY 1963a V. M. Glinka and A. V. Pomarnatsky, *Voyennaya galereya Zimnego dvortsa* (Leningrad, 1963)

GLINKA AND POMARNATSKY 1963b V. M. Glinka and A. V. Pomarnatsky, eds, *Otechestvennaya voyna 1812 v khudozhestvennykh i istoricheskikh pamyatnikakh iz sobraniya Ermitazha* [The Patriotic War of 1812 in Artistic and Historical Monuments from the Collection of the Hermitage] (Leningrad, 1963)

GLINKA AND POMARNATSKY 1981 V. M. Glinka and A. V. Pomarnatsky, *Voyennaya galereya Zimnego dvortsa*, 3rd edn (Leningrad, 1981)

GLÜCK 1931 G. Glück, ed., *Van Dyck. Des Meisters Gemälde in 571 Abbildungen*, Klassiker der Kunst 13 (Stuttgart and Berlin, [1931])

GOLOMBIEVSKIY 1911 A. Golombievskiy, 'Pokinutaya usad'ba. Selo Nadezhdino, byvsheye imeniye knyazey Kurakinykh' [The Abandoned Mansion: The Village of Nadezhdino], *Staryye gody* (January 1911)

GOODISON 1974 N. Goodison, *Ormolu: the Work of Matthew Boulton* (London, 1974)

GORBUNOVA 1974 Xe. Gorbunova, 'Classical Sculpture from the Lyde Browne Collection', *Apollo*, C (December 1974), pp. 460–67

GORYAINOV 1908 S. Goryainov, 'Khudozhestvennyye vpechatleniya korolya Stanislava-Avgusta o svoyom prebyvanii v Sankt-Peterburge v 1797g.', *Staryye gody* (October 1908)

GOWER 1900 R. S. Gower, *The Life of Sir Thomas Lawrence, with a Catalogue of the Artist's Exhibited and Engraved Works, Compiled by A. Graves* (London, 1900)

GOWING 1985 L. Gowing, *The Originality of Thomas Jones* (London, 1985)

GRABAR 1909–16 I. E. Grabar, *Istoriya russkogo iskusstva* [The History of Russian Art], 6 vols (St Petersburg, 1911)

GRAHAM 1927 E. Maxtone Graham, *The Beautiful Mrs Graham and the Cathcart Circle* (London, 1927)

GRANVILLE 1828 A. B. Granville, *St Petersburg: A Journal of Travels to and from that Capital*, 2 vols (London, 1828)

GRAVES 1918–21 A. Graves, *Art Sales from Early in the Eighteenth Century to Early in the Twentieth Century*, 3 vols (London, 1918–21)

GRAVES 1970 A. Graves, *The Royal Academy of Arts: A Complete Dictionary of Contributors and their Work from its Foundation in 1769 to 1904*, 4 vols (reprint, 1970)

GRAVES AND CRONIN 1899–1901 A. Graves and W. Cronin, *A History of the Works of Sir Joshua Reynolds, PRA*, 4 vols (London, 1899–1901)

GREAT ART TREASURES 1994 *The Great Art Treasures of the Hermitage Museum, St Petersburg, foreword by M. B. Piotrovsky*, 2 vols (New York and London, 1994)

GRIDGEMAN AND DRURY 1978 H. Gridgeman and E. Drury, *Needlework: An Illustrated History* (New York and London, 1978)

GRIMWADE 1969 A. G. Grimwade, 'Crespin or Sprimont? An Unsolved Problem of Rococo Silver', *Apollo*, XC (1969)

GRIMWADE 1976 A. G. Grimwade, *London Goldsmiths, 1697–1837* (London, 1976)

GRUNDY 1931 C. Grundy, ed., 'Wright of Derby', *The Connoisseur*, LXXXVI (January 1931)

GUTHRIE 1792 'Arcticus' [Dr Matthew Guthrie], 'On Rearing Timber Trees in Russia', *The Bee*, IX (1792)

HACKENBROCH 1957 Y. Hackenbroch, *Chelsea and other English Porcelain Pottery and Enamel in the Irwin Untermayer Collection* (Cambridge, MA, 1957)

HACKENBROCH 1960 Y. Hackenbroch, *English and other Needlework Tapestries and Textiles in the Irwin Untermayer Collection* (Cambridge, MA, 1960)

HACKENBROCH 1979 Y. Hackenbroch, *Renaissance Jewellery* (London, 1979)

HANOTEAU 1909 J. Hanoteau, ed., *Lettres du prince de Metternich a la comtesse de Lieven* (Paris, 1909)

HARRIMAN 1960 V. Harriman, 'Wedgwood and Royalty', *The Fiftieth Wedgwood International Seminar, Royal Ontario Museum* (Toronto, 1960)

HARRIS 1844 *The Diaries and Correspondence of James Harris, First Earl of Malmesbury*, 4 vols (London, 1844)

HARRISON 1855 R. Harrison, *Notes of a Nine Years' Residence in Russia, from 1844 to 1853, with Notice of the Tsars Nicholas I and Alexander II* (London, 1855)

HARTLEY 1994 J. M. Hartley, 'Crown Jewels and Cameos: Notes from the Irish Archives', *Study Group on Eighteenth-century Russia Newsletter*, XXII (1994), pp. 21–4

HAWES 1807 W. Hawes, *Royal Humane Society, Annual Report* (London, 1807)

HAWKINS 1885 E. Hawkins, *Medallic Illustrations of the History of Great Britain and Ireland to the Death of George II*, ed. A. W. Franks and H. A. Grueber, 2 vols (London 1885)

HAYDEN 1983 P. Hayden, note in *The Garden*, CVIII (1983), p. 78

HAYDEN 1985 P. Hayden, 'British Seats on Imperial Russian Tables', *Garden History*, XIII/1 (1985)

HAYDEN 1991 P. Hayden, 'The Russian Stowe: Benton Seeley's Guidebooks as a Source of Catherine the Great's Park at Tsarskoe Selo', *Garden History*, XIX (1991), pp. 21–7

HAYDON 1960–63 B. R. Haydon, *The Diary*, ed. W. B. Pope, 5 vols (Cambridge, MA, 1960–63)

HAYWARD 1959 J. F. Hayward, *Huguenot Silver in England 1688–1727* (London, 1959)

HAYWARD AND KIRKHAM 1980 H. Hayward and P. Kirkham, *William and John Linnell* (London, 1980)

HENIG 1990 M. Henig, *The Content Family Collection of Ancient Cameos* (Oxford, 1990)

HERBERT 1950 *Pembroke Papers (1780–1794): Letters and Diaries of Henry, Tenth Earl of Pembroke and His Circle*, ed. Lord Herbert (London, 1950)

HERRMANN 1968 L. Herrmann, 'The Drawings by Sir Joshua Reynolds in the Herschel Album', *The Burlington Magazine*, CX (1968), pp. 650–58

HERRMANN 1986 L. Herrmann, *Paul and Thomas Sandby* (London, 1986)

HILL 1744 *The Works of the Late Aaron Hill*, 2nd edn (London, 1744)

HILLES 1929 F. W. Hilles, ed., *Letters of Sir Joshua Reynolds* (Cambridge, 1929)

HILLES 1936 F. W. Hilles, *The Literary Career of Sir Joshua Reynolds* (Cambridge, 1936)

HILLES 1970 F. W. Hilles, 'Sir Joshua and the Empress Catherine', *Eighteenth-century Studies in Honour of Donald F. Hyde*, ed. W. H. Bond (New York, 1970), pp. 267–77

HOARE 1802 P. Hoare, *Extracts of a Correspondence with the Academies of Vienna and St Petersburg* (London, 1802)

HOLLOWAY 1992 J. Holloway, *James Tassie, 1735–1799*, National Galleries of Scotland (Edinburgh, 1992)

HOLMES 1911 M. Holmes, 'Two Recent Additions to the National Portrait Gallery', *The Burlington Magazine*, XIX (1911), p. 163

HONEY 1958 W. B. Honey, *Wedgwood Ware* (London, 1958)

HOUFFE 1989 S. Houffe, 'Portraits from St Petersburg', *Country Life*, CLXXXIII (16 November 1989), pp. 78–81

HOWARD 1903 M. Howard, *Old London Silver: Its History, its Makers and its Marks* (London, 1903)

HOYTE AND PENDRED 1976 D. A. Hoyte and G. L. Pendred, 'The Decoration of Derby Porcelain: Some Interesting Sources of Inspiration', *Antique Dealers Guide* (February 1976)

HUGHES 1988 L. Hughes, 'N. A. L'vov and the Russian Country House', *Russia and the World of the Eighteenth Century*, ed. R. P. Bartlett et al. (Columbus, OH, 1988), pp. 289–300

HULST AND VEY 1960 R.-A. d'Hulst and H. Vey, *Van Dyck. Tekeningen en olieverschetsen*, exh. cat., Amsterdam and Rotterdam (1960)

ILCHESTER 1922 R. Ilchester, 'Cameos of Queen Elizabeth and their Reproduction in Contemporary Portraits', *The Connoisseur*, LXIII (1922), pp. 65–72

ILCHESTER 1937 The Earl of Ilchester, *The Home of the Hollands (1605–1820)* (London, 1937)

INDUSTRIAL ART 1978 *The Hermitage, vol. V: Industrial Art* (Leningrad and Tokyo, 1978)

IRWIN 1975 D. and F. Irwin, *Scottish Painters at Home and Abroad. 1700–1900* (London, 1900)

IVANOV 1904 D. D. Ivanov, *Ob'yasnitel'nyye putevoditel' po khudozhestvennym sobraniyam Peterburg* (St Petersburg, 1904)

IVERSEN 1880–96 Yu. B. Iversen, *Medali v chest' russkikh gosudarstvennykh deyateley i chastnykh lits*, I–III (St Petersburg, 1880–96)

JONES 1909 E. A. Jones, *The Old English Plate of the Emperor of Russia* (London, 1909)

JONES 1910 E. A. Jones, 'The Tsar's Collection of Old English Watches', *The Connoisseur* (August 1910), pp. 249–54

JONES 1946–8 A. P. Oppé, ed., 'Memoirs of Thomas Jones', *Walpole Society*, XXXII (1946–8)

JOUSSOUPOFF 1839 *Musée du Prince Joussoupoff, contenant les tableaux, marbres, ivoires et porcelaines qui se trouvent dans l'hôtel de son Excellence a St Petersburg* (St Petersburg, 1839)

KAGAN 1973a Yu. O. Kagan, *Western European Cameos in the Hermitage Museum* (Leningrad, 1973)

KAGAN 1973b Yu. O. Kagan, 'Kabinet slepkov Dzheymsa Tassi v Ermitazhe. K istorii russo-angliyskikh khudozhest vennykh svyazey v XVIII v.' [James Tassie's Cast Cabinet at the Hermitage. On the History of Russo-English Artistic Links in the 18th Century], *TGE*, XIV (1973), pp. 82–96

KAGAN 1976 Yu. O. Kagan, *Reznye kamni Uil'iama i Charl'za Braunov: katalog vystavki* (Leningrad, 1976)

KAGAN 1980 Yu. O. Kagan, 'Portretnyye kamei epokhi Tyudorov: problemy interpretatsii, datirovki, atributsii', *Muzey I. Khudozhestvennyye sobraniya SSSR* (Moscow, 1980), pp. 23–36

KAGAN 1981 Yu. O. Kagan, 'K istorii gliptiki v Anglii: Semnadtsatyy vek', *Zapadnoyevropeyskoye iskusstvo XVII v.* (Leningrad, 1981), pp. 177–97

KAMER-FUHRER JOURNAL 1777 *Kamer-fur'yerskiy tseremonial'nyy zhurnal 1777 goda* (St Petersburg, 1880)

KAMER-FUHRER JOURNAL 1779 *Kamer-fur'yerskiy tseremonial'nyy zhurnal 1779 goda, c 1-go yanvarya po 1-ye iyulya* (St Petersburg, 1883)

KAMER-FUHRER JOURNAL 1780 *Kamer-fur'yerskiy tseremonial'nyy zhurnal 1780 goda* (St Petersburg, 1888)

KAMER-FUHRER JOURNAL 1781 *Kamer-fur'yerskiy tseremonial'nyy zhurnal 1781 goda* (St Petersburg, 1890)

KAMER-FUHRER JOURNAL 1791 *Kamer-fur'yerskiy tseremonial'nyy zhurnal 1791 goda* (St Petesburg, 1890)

KAMER-FUHRER JOURNAL 1795 *Kamer-fur'yerskiy tseremonial'nyy zhurnal 1795 goda* (St Petersburg, 1894)

KANTER 1968 A. M. Kanter, 'Horses and mainly not-chance', *The XIIIth Wedgwood International Seminar* (1968), pp. 151–63

KANTOR-GUKOVSKAYA 1982 A. S. Kantor-Gukovskaya, 'Aleksandr Kozens i ermitazhnyye risunki, svyazannyye s yego metodom peyzazhnoy kompozitsii', *TGE*, XXII (1982)

KAREV 1989 A. A. Karev, *Miniatyurnyy portret v Rossii XVIII veka* [Miniature Portraits in Russia in the 18th Century] (Moscow, 1989)

KELLY 1965 A. Kelly, *Decorative Wedgwood in Architecture and Furniture* (London, 1965)

KELLY 1980 A. Kelly, 'Wedgwood's Catherine Services', *The Burlington Magazine*, CXXII (August 1980), pp. 554–61

KENDALL 1932–3 G. E. Kendall, 'Notes on the Life of John Wootton with a List of Engravings after his Pictures', *Walpole Society*, XXI (1932–3), pp. 23–52

KETTON-CREMER 1948 R. W. Ketton-Cremer, *A Norfolk Gallery* (London, 1948)

KETTON-CREMER 1964 R. W. Ketton-Cremer, *Horace Walpole: A Biography*, 3rd edn (London, 1964)

KHRAPOVITSKY 1862 A. V. Khrapovitsky, *Pamyatnyye zapiski ...* (1862)

KHRAPOVITSKY 1901 *Dnevnik A. V. Khrapovitskogo (c 18 yanvarya 1782 po 17 sentyabrya 1793 goda* (Moscow, 1901)

KING 1772 J. G. King, *The Rites and Ceremonies of the Greek Church in Russia: Containing an Account of its Doctrine, Worship and Discipline* (London, 1772)

KING 1866 C. W. King, *The Handbook of Engraved Gems* (London, 1866)

KING 1872 C. W. King, *Antique Gems and Rings*, 2 vols (London, 1872)

KING 1960 D. King, *Samplers* (London, 1960)

KING AND LEVEY 1993 D. King and S. Levey, *The Victoria and Albert Museum's Textile Collection: Embroideries in Britain from 1200 to 1750* (London, 1993)

KLINGENDER 1968 F. Klingender, *Art and the Industrial Revolution*, revd edn (London, 1968)

KNIGHT 1921 A. E. Knight, *The Collection of Camei and Intagli at Alnwick Castle, Known as the Beverley Gems* (priv. printed, 1921)

KOHL 1844 J. G. Kohl, *Russia; St Petersburg, Riga, Odessa, the German Provinces on the Baltic, the Steppes, the Crimea and the Interior of the Empire* (London, 1844)

KOMELOVA 1974 G. N. Komelova, 'Russkiy gravyo Gavriil Ivanovich Skorodumov, 1755–1792' [Russian Engraver G. I. Skorodumov], *TGE*, XV (1974), pp. 36–57

KOMELOVA 1978 G. Komelova, G. Printseva and I. Kotet'nikova, eds, *Petersburg v proizvedeniyakh Patersena* [Petersburg in Paterson's Works] (Leningrad, 1978)

KORSHUNOVA 1974 M. F. Korshunova, 'William Hastie in Russia', *Architectural History*, XVII (1974), pp. 14–21

KORSHUNOVA 1976 M. F. Korshunova, 'Graficheskoye naslediye Yu. M. Fel'tena' [The Graphic Legacy of Y. M. Velten], *Pamyatniki kul'tury. Novyye otkrytiya* [Cultural Monuments: New Discoveries], Annual for 1975 (Moscow, 1976)

KORSHUNOVA 1977 M. F. Korshunova, 'Arkhitektor V. Geste' [The Architect W. Hastie], *TGE*, XVII (1977), pp. 132–43

KOSAUROVA 1985 T. Kosaurova, 'Dve angliyskiye vyshivki', *SGE*, L (1985), pp. 21–3

KROLL 1938 A. E. Kroll, *English Portraits of the Eighteenth Century* (1938) [5 n. 50]

KROL' 1939 A. Ye. Krol', *Angliyskiye portrety XVIII veka* [English Portraits of the 18th Century] (Leningrad, 1939)

KROL' 1940 A. Ye. Krol', 'Portrety Tomasa Laurensa v Ermitazhe', *TOZI*, I (1940)

KROL' 1960 A. Ye. Krol', 'Neopublikovannoye pis' mo Dzhoshua Reynoldsa iz arkhiva Vorontsovykh' [An Unpublished Letter from Joshua Reynolds from the Vorontsov Archive], *SGE*, XVIII (1968), pp. 42–4

KROL' 1961a A. Ye. Krol', *Angliyskaya zhivopis' XVI–XIX vv. v Ermitazhe* (Leningrad, 1961)

KROL' 1961b A. Ye. Krol', 'Iz istorii russko-angliyskikh khudozhestvennykh svyazey nachala XIX v. Kartiny angliyskogo romantika na russkiye temy', *TGE*, VI (1961), pp. 389–93

KROL' 1969 A. Ye. Krol', *Gosudarstvennyy Ermitazh. Angliyskaya zhivopis'. Katalog* (Leningrad, 1969)

KUDRIAVTSEVA 1994 Kudriavtseva on Russian porcelain, nos, 94–8; see Exhibitions: 1994 Kolding

KUSHELEV-BEZBORODKO 1863 *Katalog kollektsii khudozhestvennykh proizvedeniy, postupivshikh po zaveshchaniyu grafa N. A. Kusheleva-Bezborodko v sobstvennost' imperatorskoy S. Peterburgskoy Akademii khudozhestv* (St Petersburg, 1863)

LA CHAU AND LE BLOND 1784 De La Chau and Le Blond, *Description de principales pierres gravées du Cabinet de S.A.S. Monseigneur Le Duc d'Orléans*, 2 vols (Paris, 1780–4)

LAMERIE 1990 S. Hare, ed., *Paul de Lamerie: At the Sign of the Golden Ball: An exhibition of the work of England's Master Silversmith (1688–1751)*, exh. cat., Goldsmith's Hall, London (1990)

LANE 1961 A. Lane, *English Porcelain Figures of the 18th Century* (London, 1961)

LANE AND CHARLESTON 1962 A. Lane and R. J. Charleston, 'Girl in a Swing Porcelain and Chelsea', *English Ceramic Circle Transactions*, V/3 (1962)

LANSERE 1924 N. Lansere, 'Arkhitektor Charl'z Kameron' [The Architect Charles Cameron], *Charl'z Kameron* (Moscow and Petrograd, 1924)

LANTSMANIS 1992 I. Lantsmanis, *Ernst Iogann Biron, 1690–1990*, exh. cat., Rundal Palace Museum (1992)

LARSEN 1980 E. Larsen, *L'Opera completa di Van Dyck, classici dell'arte*, 2 vols (Milan, 1980)

LAZAREVA 1965 O. P. Lazareva, *Russkii skul'ptor Fedot Shubin* (Moscow, 1965)

LE BLOND 1912 A. Le Blond, *Charlotte Sophie, Countess Bentinck: Her Life and Times, 1715–1800* (London, 1912)

LENNOX-BOYD 1989 C. Lennox-Boyd, R. Dixon and T. Clayton, *George Stubbs: The Complete Engraved Works* (1989)

LESLIE AND TAYLOR 1865 C. Leslie and T. Taylor, *The Life and Times of Sir Joshua Reynolds, with Notices of Some of his Contemporaries*, 2 vols (London, 1865)

LEVIN 1994a Iu. D. Levin, *The Perception of English Literature in Russia: Investigations and Materials* (Nottingham, 1994)

LEVIN 1994b Iu. D. Levin, 'The English Novel in Eighteenth-century Russia', *Literature, Lives and Legality in Catherine's Russia*, ed. A. G. Cross and G. S. Smith (Nottingham, 1994)

LEVIN 1994c Iu. D. Levin, 'English Literature in Eighteenth-century Russia', *Modern Language Review*, LXXXIX (1994), pp. xxv–xxxix

LEVINSON-LESSING 1986 V. F. Levinson-Lessing, *Istoriya kartinnoy galerey Ermitazha (1764–1917)* [History of the Hermitage Picture Gallery] (Leningrad, 1986)

LHUILLIER 1887 T. Lhuillier, *Julien de Fontenay, graveur en pierres fines du roi Henry IV et ses descendents, graveurs et peintres au château de Fontainbleau* (Paris, 1887)

LIACKHOVA 1992 L. V. Liackhova, 'The Wedgwood Exhibition at the Imperial Academy of Arts (St Petersburg)', *Ars Ceramica*, IX (1992)

LIACKHOVA 1994 L. V. Lyakhova, 'Plaketki Dzh. Vedzhvuda v angliyskom neoklassicheskom inter'yere', *Problemy razvitiya zarubezhnogo iskusstva*, Russian Academy of Arts, pt 2 (St Petersburg, 1994)

LIACKHOVA 1995 L. V. Liackhova, 'The Frog Service in Russia'; see Exhibitions: 1995 London

LIKHACHEV 1982 D. S. Likhachev, *Poeziya sadov: K semantike sadovo-parkovykh stiley* [The Poetry of Gardens: On the Semantics of Garden and Park Styles] (Leningrad, 1982)

LINCH 1962 J. B. Linch, 'The History of Raphael's St George in the Louvre', *Gazette des Beaux-Arts* (April 1962), pp. 201–12

LISENKOV 1964 Ye. Lisenkov, *Angliyskoye iskusstvo XVIII veka* [English Art of the 18th Century] (Leningrad, 1964)

LIST OF PORTRAITS 1904 *Spisok portretov, otobrannykh dlya istoriko-khudozhestvennoy vystavki 1905 goda general'nym komissarom S. P. Dyagilevym v osmotrennykh im v techeniye letnikh mesyatsev 1904 goda 72-kh russkikh imeniyakh* (St Petersburg, 1904)

LIST OF PORTRAITS 1905 *Spisok portretov, otobrannykh dlya istoriko-khudozhestvennoy vystavki 1905 goda v obshchestvennykh i chastnykh sobraniyakh g. S. Peterburg* (St Petersburg, 1905)

LIVEN 1902 G. E. Liven, *Putevoditel' po Kabinety Petra Velikogo i Galereye Dragotsennostey* (St Petersburg, 1902)

LIVRET 1838 *Livret de la Galerie impériale de l'Hermitage de Saint-Petersbourg* (St Petersburg, 1838)

LOCKE 1768 J. Locke, *The Works*, 4 vols (London, 1768)

LOCKE 1927 *The Correspondence of John Locke and Edward Clarke*, ed. B. Rand (Oxford, 1927)

LOCKE 1979–82 J. Locke, *The Correspondence*, ed. E. S. De Beer, 8 vols (Oxford, 1979–82)

LOCKHART 1819 J. G. Lockhart, *Peter's Letters to his Kinsfolk* (Edinburgh, 1819)

LONDON 1984 *Rococo: Art and Design in Hogarth's England*, exh. cat., Victoria and Albert Museum, London (1984)

LONDON 1986 *Reynolds*, exh. cat. ed. N. Penny, Royal Academy, London, Grand Palais, Paris (1986)

LOUDON 1834 J. C. Loudon, *An Encyclopaedia of Gardening* (London, 1834)

LOUKOMSKI 1943 G. Loukomski, *Charles Cameron* (London, 1943)

LUGT 1931 Frits Lugt, 'Beitrage zu dem Katalog der niederlandischen Handzeichnungen in Berlin', *Jahrbuch der preussischen Kunstsammlungen*, 52 (1931)

L'VOV 1994 N. A. L'vov, *Izbrannye sochineniia*, ed. K. Iu. Lappo-Danilevskii (Cologne, Weimar, Vienna and St Petersburg, 1994)

MACHT 1957 C. Macht, *Classical Wedgwood Designs* (New York, 1957)

MACQUOID 1904 P. Macquoid, *A History of English Furniture* (London, 1904)

MAKAROV 1925 V. K. Makarov, 'Risunok tomasa laurensa v Gatchinskom dvortse-muzeye', *Staraya Gatchina*, 4 (1925)

MAKAROV 1940 V. K. Makarov, 'Dzhhorzh Dou v Rossii' [George Dawe in Russia], *TOZI*, I (1940), pp. 175–93

MAKSIMOVA 1976 see Exhibitions: 1976 Leningrad

MALINOVSKII 1990 K. V. Malinovskii, ed., *Zapiski Yakova Shtelina ob izyashchnykh iskusstvakh v Rossii. Sostavleniye, perevod s nemetskogo, vstupitel'naya stat'ya, predisloviya k razdelam i primechaniya K. V. Malinovskogo*, 2 vols (Moscow, 1990)

MALLET 1965 J.V.G. Mallet, 'Chelsea', *English Porcelain 1745–1850*, ed. R. J. Charleston (London, 1965)

MALONE 1819 E. Malone, ed., *The Literary Works of Sir Joshua Reynolds*, 5th edn, 3 vols, (London, 1819)

MANKOWITZ 1953 W. Mankowitz, *Wedgwood* (New York, 1953)

MARCHANT 1792 N. Marchant, *A Catalogue of One Hundred Impressions from Gems* (London, 1792)

MARIETTE 1741 P. J. Mariette, *Descriptions sommaire des pierres gravées du Cabinet de feu M. Crozat* (Paris, 1741)

MARIETTE 1750 P. J. Mariette, *Traité des pierres gravées*, 2 vols (Paris, 1750)

MASKELL 1884 A. Maskell, *Russian Art and Art Objects in Russia* (London, 1884)

MAUQUOY-HENDRICKX 1956 M. Mauquoy-Hendrickx, *L'iconographie d'Antoine Van Dyck*, 2 vols (Brussels, 1956)

MAXTED 1983 I. Maxted, *The British Book Trades, 1701–1777* (Exeter, 1983)

MAYER 1969 C. Mayer, *Masterpieces of Western Textiles from the Art Institute of Chicago* (Chicago, 1969)

MAYER 1984 A. Mayer, *John Wootton, 1682–1764: Landscape and Sporting Art in Early Georgian England*, exh. cat., Kenwood, London (1984)

MCKAY AND ROBERTS 1914 W. McKay and W. Roberts, *Supplement and Index to John Hoppner, RA* (London, 1914)

MEMOIRS 1859 *Memoirs of the Empress Catherine II, Written by Herself* (London, 1859)

METEYARD 1866 E. Meteyard, *The Life of Josiah Wedgwood*, 2 vols (London, 1866)

METEYARD 1875 E. Meteyard, *The Wedgwood Handbook* (London, 1875)

MIKHAILOV 1990 B. B. Mikhailov, 'Sadnovik Frensis Rid v Tsaritsyne i Ostankine' [Gardener Francis Reid at Tsarskoye and Ostankino], *Arkhitektura SSSR*, IV (July–August 1994), pp. 104–9

MIKHAYLOVICH 1912 Grand-Duke Nikolay Mikhaylovich, *Peterburgskiy nekropol* [Petersburg Burial Grounds] (St Petersburg, 1912)

MILLAR 1958–60 O. Millar, ed., 'Abraham Van Der Doort's Catalogue of the Collections of Charles I', *Walpole Society*, XXXVII (1958–60)

MILLAR 1963 O. Millar, *The Tudor, Stuart and Early Georgian Pictures in the Collection of Her Majesty the Queen*, 2 vols (London, 1963)

MILLAR 1978–9 O. Millar, *Sir Peter Lely, 1618–1680*, exh. cat., National Portrait Gallery, London (1978)

MILLAR 1982 see Exhibitions: 1982 London

MILLAR 1994 O. Millar, 'Philip, Lord Wharton, and his Collection of Portraits', *The Burlington Magazine*, CXXXVI (August 1994), pp. 517–30

MILTON 1682 J. Milton, *A Brief History of Muscovia, and of Other Less-known Countries Lying Eastward of Russia as Far as Cathay* (London, 1682)

M.I.P. 1745 *Musei Imperialis Petropolitani*, II, pt 3 (Petropoli, 1745)

MITCHELL 1942 C. Mitchell, 'Three Phases of Reynolds's Method', *The Burlington Magazine* LXXX (April 1942), pp. 35–40

MOORE 1996 A. Moore, ed., *Houghton Hall: The Prime Minister, the Empress and the Heritage* (London, 1996)

MUSGRAVE 1966 C. Musgrave, *Adam and Hepplewhite and other Neoclassical Furniture* (London, 1966)

NATHANSON 1975 A. J. Nathanson, *Thomas Simon: His Life and Work, 1618–1665* (London, 1975)

NEKRASOVA 1954 E. Nekrasova, *Gavrila Ivanovich Skorodumov, 1755–1792* (Moscow, 1954)

NICHOLSON 1818 W. Nicholson, *Portraits of Distinguished Living Characters of Scotland*, V (1818)

NICOLSON 1954 B. Nicolson, 'Joseph Wright's Early Subject Pictures', *The Burlington Magazine* (March 1954)

NICOLSON 1958 B. Nicolson, *Joseph Wright of Derby, 1734–1797*, Tate Gallery, London, and Walker Art Gallery, Liverpool (1958)

NICOLSON 1968 B. Nicolson, *Joseph Wright of Derby: Painter of Light*, 2 vols (New Haven and London, 1968)

NIKOLAY MIKHAILOVICH 1905–9 *Nikolay Mikhaylovich: russkiye portrety XVIII i XIX stoletiy*, 5 vols (St Petersburg, 1905–9)

NORTHCOTE 1813–15 J. Northcote, *Memoirs of Sir Joshua Reynolds, Knt, Late President of the Royal Academy, Comprising Original Anecdotes of Many Distinguished Persons, his Contemporaries and a Brief Analysis of his Discourses*, 2 vols (London, 1813–15)

NORTHCOTE 1818 J. Northcote, *The Life of Sir Joshua Reynolds*, 2 vols (London, 1818)

O'DONOGHUE 1894 F. O'Donoghue, *A Description and Classified Catalogue of Portraits of Queen Elizabeth* (London, 1894)

O'DONOGHUE 1908–25 F. O'Donoghue, *Catalogue of Engraved British Portraits preserved in the Department of Prints and Drawings in the British Museum*, 6 vols (London, 1908–25)

OMAN 1959 C. Oman, 'English Plate at the Hermitage, Leningrad, and the State Historical Museum, Moscow', *The Connoisseur* (August 1959), pp. 14–16

OPPÉ 1927–8 A. P. Oppé, 'A Roman Sketchbook by Alexander Cozens', *Walpole Society*, XVI (1927–8), pp. 81–93

OPPÉ 1952 A. P. Oppé, *Alexander and John Robert Cozens* (London, 1952)

ORLOV-DAVYDOV 1878 V. Orlov-Davydov, *Biograficheskii ocherk grafa Vladimira Grigor'evicha Orlova* (St Petersburg, 1878)

PARKINSON 1971 J. Parkinson, *A Tour of Russia, Siberia and the Crimea, 1792–1794*, ed. W. Collier (London, 1971)

PARSHALL 1993 L. Parshall, 'C.C.L. Hirschfeld's Concept of the Garden in the German Enlightenment', *Journal of Garden History*, XIII (1993), pp. 125–71

PAX IN NUMMIS 1912 J. Schulman: *Pax in nummis. Collection le Maistre* (Amsterdam, 1912)

PEMBROKE 1968 *A Catalogue of the Paintings & Drawings in the Collection at Wilton House, Salisbury, Wiltshire* (London and New York, 1968)

PENZER 1956 N. M. Penzer: 'The Jerningham–Kandler Wine-cooler', Part I, *Apollo*, LXIV (September 1956), pp. 80–82; Part II (October 1956), pp. 111–15

PENZER 1957 N. M. Penzer, 'The Great Wine-coolers', *Apollo*, LXVI (August 1957), pp. 3–7; (September 1957), pp. 39–46

PENZER 1958 N. M. Penzer, 'English Plate at the Hermitage, Part 1', *The Connoisseur*, CXLII (December 1958), pp. 227–32

PERRY 1716 J. Perry, *The State of Russia, Under the Present Czar: In Relation to the Several Great and Remarkable Things he has done, as to his Naval Preparations, the Regulating his Army, the Reforming his People, and Improvement of his Countrey* (London, 1716)

PETERHOF INVENTORY 1885 *Opis' predmetam, imeyushchim preimushchestvenno khudozhestvennoye znacheniye. Peterhof* [Inventory of objects of largely artistic significance. Peterhof] (St Petersburg, 1885)

PETERS 1989 D. I. Peters, *Nagradnyye medali Rossii XIX – nachala XX veka* (Moscow, 1989)

PETROV 1969 A. N. Petrov, *Pushkin: dvortsy i parki* [Pushkin: Palaces and Parks] (Leningrad, 1969)

PIPER 1963 D. Piper, *Catalogue of Seventeenth-century Portraits in the National Portrait Gallery, 1625–1714* (Cambridge, 1963)

PLUMB 1972 J. H. Plumb, *Sir Robert Walpole: The King's Minister*, 2nd edn (London, 1972)

LA PORCELLANE IMPERIALI RUSSE 1993 *Le porcellane Imperiali Russe dal 1744 al 1917*, by N. Vernova, V. Znamenov and T. Nosovic (Faenza, 1993)

POROSHIN 1881 S. Poroshin, *Zapiski* [Notes] (St Petersburg, 1881)

PORTER 1809 R. Ker Porter, *Travelling Sketches in Russia and Sweden during the Years 1805, 1806, 1807, 1808* (London, 1809)

POSTLE 1995 M. Postle, *Sir Joshua Reynolds: The Subject Pictures* (Cambridge, 1995)

POTEMKIN 1891 *Opisi domov i dvozhimogo imushchestva knyazya Potyomkina-Tavricheskogo kuplennykh u naslednikov yego imperatritsey Yekaterinoyu II, Chteniya v imperatorskom obshchestve istorii i drevnostey rossiyskikh*, book 4 (Moscow, 1891)

PRINTSEVA 1988 G. A. Printseva, ed., *Russkaya akvarel' v sobranii gosudarstvennogo Ermitazha, Leningrad* [Russian Watercolours in the Collection of the Hermitage] (Moscow, 1988)

PYLYAYEV 1889 M. I. Pylyayev, *Staryy Peterburg* [Old St Petersburg] (St Petersburg, 1889)

RACKHAM 1928–30 B. Rackham, *Catalogue of the Schreiber Collection*, 2 vols (London, 1928–30)

RADOVSKIY 1961 M. I. Radovskiy, *Iz istorii anglo-russkikh nauchnykh svyazey* [From the History of Anglo-Russian Scientific Links] (Moscow and Leningrad, 1961)

RAE 1971 I. Rae, *Charles Cameron: Architect to the Court of Russia* (London, 1971)

RAEBURN 1990 M. Raeburn, 'Land of the Free: The Views on the Green Frog Service', *35th Annual Wedgwood International Seminar* (Birmingham, 1990)

RAEBURN 1992 M. Raeburn, 'Wedgwood and Bentley's Green Frog Service outside Russia', *Antiques*, CXLI (March 1992)

RAEBURN 1995 M. Raeburn, 'By Imperial Command', *The Genius of Wedgwood* (London, 1995)

RAEBURN, VORONIKHINA AND NURNBERG 1995 M. Raeburn, L. N. Voronikhina and A. Nurnberg, eds, *The Green Frog Service* (London, 1995)

RARE PORCELAIN 1987 *Rare and Documentary 18th-century English Porcelain from the British Museum; The International Ceramics Fair and Seminar, June 1987* (London, 1987)

RASKIN 1981 A. Raskin, *Gorod Lomonosov: Dvortsovo-parkovye ansambli XVIII veka* [The Town of Lomonosov: 18th-century Palace and Park Ensembles] (Leningrad, 1981)

RASPE 1786 R. E. Raspe, *Account of the Present State and Arrangement of Mr James Tassie's Collection of Pastes and Impressions from Ancient and Modern Gems* (London, 1786)

RASPE 1791 R. E. Raspe, *A Descriptive Catalogue of a General Collection of Ancient and Modern Engraved Gems, Cameos as well as Intaglios. Taken from the most celebrated cabinets in Europe, and cast in coloured pastes, white enamel and sulphur by James Tassie, Modeller*, 2 vols (London, 1791)

RÉAU 1932 L. Réau, *Correspondance artistique de Grimm avec Catherine II* (Paris, 1932)

REDGRAVE 1878 S. Redgrave, *Dictionary of Artists of the English School* (London, 1878)

REICHEL 1843 *Die Reichelsche Munzsammlung in St. Petersburg. Sechstes Teil* (St Petersburg, 1843)

REILLY 1989 R. Reilly, *Wedgwood*, 2 vols (London and New York, 1989)

REILLY 1992 R. Reilly, *Josiah Wedgwood, 1730–1795* (London, 1992)

REILLY 1994 R. Reilly, *Wedgwood Jasper* (London, 1994)

REILLY AND SAVAGE 1973 R. Reilly and G. Savage, *Wedgwood: The Portrait Medallions* (London, 1973)

REILLY AND SAVAGE 1980 R. Reilly and G. Savage, *The Dictionary of Wedgwood* (New York, 1980)

REINACH 1895 S. Reinach, *Pierres gravées des collections Marlborough et d'Orléans; des recueils d'Eckhel, Gori, Levesque de Gravelle, Mariette, Millin, Stosch* (Paris, 1895)

REINACH 1912 S. Reinach, *Répertoire des reliefs. Grecs et Romains* (Paris, 1912)

REITLINGER 1962–70 J. Reitlinger, *The Economics of Taste: The Rise and Fall of the Picture Market, 1760–1960* (London, 1962–70)

RENNE 1985 N. Renne, 'Robert Ker Porter v. Rossii' [Robert Ker Porter in Russia], *TGE*, XXV (1985), pp. 105–9

RENNE 1987 Ye. P. Renne, 'Kartiny Bromptona v Ermitazhe' [Brompton's Pictures in the Hermitage], *Zapadnoevropeiskoe iskusstvo XVIII veka: publikatsii i issledovaniia* [Eighteenth-century Western European Art: Publications and Research] (Leningrad, 1987)

RENNE 1990 Ye. P. Renne, 'Voyennaya galereya Zimnego dvortsa' [The Military Gallery in the Winter Palace], in Renne and Dukelskaya 1990

RENNE 1995 E. Renne, 'A British Portraitist in Imperial Russia: Christina Robertson and the Court of Nicholas I', *Apollo*, CXLII (September 1995), pp. 43–5

REYNOLDS 1975 Sir Joshua Reynolds, *Discourses on Art*, ed. R. R. Wark, 2nd edn (New Haven and London, 1975)

RICE 1967 T. T. Rice, 'Charles Cameron, Catherine the Great's British Architect', *The Connoisseur*, CLXV (August 1967), pp. 240–45

RICHARDSON 1784 W. Richardson, *Anecdotes of the Russian Empire, in a Series of Letters Written, a Few Years Ago, from St Petersburg* (London, 1784)

ROBERTS 1834 W. Roberts, *Memoirs of the Life and Correspondence of Hannah More*, 4 vols (London, 1834)

ROBINSON 1979 J. M. Robinson, *The Wyatts: An Architectural Dynasty* (Oxford, 1979)

ROGERS 1983 M. Rogers, *William Dobson. 1611–46*, exh. cat., National Portrait Gallery, London (1983)

ROOSEVELT 1994 P. Roosevelt, 'The Picturesque in the Design of the Late 18th-century Russian Estate', *Literature, Lives and Legality in Catherine's Russia*, ed. A. G. Cross and G. S. Smith (Nottingham, 1994), pp. 79–92

ROOSEVELT 1995 P. Roosevelt, *Life on the Russian Country Estate: A Social and Cultural History* (New Haven and London, 1996)

ROSENBLUM 1986 R. Rosenblum, 'Reynolds in An International Milieu', in London 1986, pp. 43–54

ROTSHTEYN 1910 N. Rotshteyn, 'Serviz s zelyonoy lygushkoy', *Staryye gody* (February 1910)

ROUX AND BARRÉ 1820 H. Roux and M. L. Barré, *Herculaneum et Pompéi*, 8 vols (Paris, 1820)

ROVINSKY 1886–9 D. A. Rovinsky, ed., *Podrobnyy slovar' russikh gravirovannykh portretov*, 4 vols (St Petersburg, 1886–9)

ROVINSKII 1895 D. A. Rovinskii, *Podrbnyi slovar' russkikh graverov XVI–XIX vv.* (St Petersburg, 1895)

RUBINSTEIN 1991 G. Rubinstein, 'Richard Earlom (1743–1822) and Boydell's "Houghton Gallery"', *Print Quarterly*, VIII (1991), pp. 3–27

RUSSELL 1926 C. E. Russell, *English Mezzotint Portraits and their States*, 2 vols (London, 1926)

RUSSIAN ARCHIVE 1907 'Yekaterina Velikaya pro svoikh tsarstvennykh predshestvennikov i sovremennykh yey gosudarey. Chesmenskiy dvorets (Razgovor portretov i medal'yonov)', *Russkiy arkhiv* 1907, II

RUSSIAN PORTRAITS 1905–9 *Russkiye portrety XVIII i XIX stoletiy. Izd. velikiy knyaz' Nikolaya Mikhaylovicha*, 5 vols (St Petersburg, 1905–9)

SALAMAN 1910 M. C. Salaman, *Old English Mezzotints* (London, 1910)

SALMON 1993 F. Salmon, 'Charles Cameron and Nero's Domus Aurea', *Architectural History*, XXXVI (1993), pp. 69–93

SAPRIKINA 1980 N. G. Saprikina, *Kollektsiya portretov sobraniya F. F. Vigel'ya* [Portraits in the Collection of F. F. Vigel] (Moscow, 1980)

SAVAGE 1965 A. and G. Savage, eds, *Selected Letters of Josiah Wedgwood* (London, 1965)

SAVED FOR HUMANITY 1985 *Saved for Humanity: The Hermitage during the Siege of Leningrad. 1941–1944* (Leningrad, 1985)

SBRIO 1874, XIII *Sbornik Imperatorskogo Rossiyskogo Istoricheskogo obshchestva*, XIII (St Petersburg, 1874)

SBRIO 1876, XVII *Sbornik Imperatorskogo Rossiyskogo Istoricheskogo obshchestva*, XVII (St Petersburg, 1876)

SBRIO 1878 XXIII *Sbornik Imperatorskog Rossiyskogo Istoricheskogo obshchestva*, XXIII (St Petersburg, 1878)

SCARISBRICK 1977 D. Scarisbrick, *The Wellington Gems*, cat., S. J. Phillips (London, 1977)

SCARISBRICK 1978 D. Scarisbrick, 'Rings in the Fortnum Collection', *The Connoisseur*, CXCIX (October 1978), pp. 114–20

SCARISBRICK 1979a D. Scarisbrick, 'A. M. Zanetti and the Althorp Leopard', *Apollo*, CX (November 1979), pp. 425–7

SCARISBRICK 1979b D. Scarisbrick, 'The Devonshire Parure', *Society of Jewellery Historians Newsletter*, no. 7 (1979), pp. 4–5

SCARISBRICK 1980 D. Scarisbrick, 'The Ramsden Jewels', *Society of Jewellery Historians Newsletter*, no. 10 (1980), pp. 4–6

SCARISBRICK 1981 D. Scarisbrick, 'Henry Walters and the Marlborough Gems', *Journal of the Walters Art Gallery*, XXXIX (1981), pp. 49–58

SCARISBRICK 1985 D. Scarisbrick, 'The Earl of Arundel's Gem Cabinet', *Patronage and Collecting in the Seventeenth Century: Thomas Howard, Earl of Arundel*, exh. cat., Ashmolean Museum, Oxford (1985)

SCARISBRICK 1986 D. Scarisbrick, 'The Devonshire Parure', *Archaeologica*, CVIII (1986), pp. 240–54

SCARISBRICK 1987 D. Scarisbrick, 'Gem Connoisseurship: The Fourth Earl of Carlisle's Correspondence with Francesco de Ficoroni and Antonio Maria Zanetti', *The Burlington Magazine*, CXXIX (February 1987), pp. 90–104

SCARISBRICK 1994 D. Scarisbrick, 'English Collectors of Engraved Gems: Aristocrats, Antiquaries and Aesthetes', in M. Henig, *Classical Gems: Ancient and Modern Intaglios and Cameos in the Fitzwilliam Museum, Cambridge* (Cambridge, 1994), pp. xiii–xxiii

SCHMIDT 1970 A. J. Schmidt, 'William Hastie, Scottish Planner of Russian Cities', *Proceedings of the American Philosophical Society*, CIV (1970), pp. 226–43

SCHNITZLER 1828 J. H. Schnitzler, *Notice sur les principaux tableaux du musée impérial de l'Hermitage à Saint-Petersbourg* (Berlin, 1828)

SCHRODER 1988 T. Schroder, *English Domestic Silver* (London, 1988)

SCHUETTE AND MULLER-CHRISTENSEN 1963 M. Schuette and S. Muller-Christensen, *La Broderie* (Paris, 1963)

SCOTS MAGAZINE 1817 Anon., 'Scottish Chronicle', *Scots Magazine*, LXXIX (1817)

SCOTT 1973 B. Scott, 'Pierre Crozat: A Maecenas of the Régence', *Apollo*, XCVII (January 1973), pp. 11–19

SEIDMANN 1981 G. Seidmann, 'The Tassie Collection of Casts and Pastes after Engraved Gems at Edinburgh', *Society of Jewellery Historians Newsletter*, no. 11 (1981), pp. 8–10

SEIDMANN 1983–4 G. Seidmann, 'The Taste for Engraved Gems', *The Ashmolean*, no. 4 (1983–4), pp. 14–17

SEIDMANN 1984–5 G. Seidmann, 'A Very Ancient, Useful and Curious Art: The Society of Arts and the Revival of Gem Engraving in Eighteenth-century England', *Journal of the Royal Society of Arts* (November 1984), pp. 811–14; (December 1984), pp. 64–6; (January 1985), pp. 150–53

SEIDMANN 1987 G. Seidmann, 'Nathanial Marchant, Gem-engraver, 1739–1816', *Walpole Society*, LIII (1987), pp. 5–105

SEIDMANN 1993 G. Seidmann: 'Portrait Cameos: Aspects of their History and Function', *Cameos in Context: The Benjamin Zucker Lectures*, 1990 (Oxford, 1993), pp. 85–102

SEMEVSKY 1884 M. I. Semevsky, 'Tsaritsa Katerina Alekseyevna, Anna i Villem Mons 1692–1724' [Empress Catherine Alexeyevna, Anna and Villem Mons 1692–1724], *Ocherki iz russkoy istorii XVIII veka* [Studies in Russian 18th-century History] (St Petersburg, 1884)

SEVERNE MACKENNA 1952 F. Severne Mackenna, *Chelsea Porcelain. The Gold Anchor Wares (with a short account of the Duesbury Period)* (Leigh-on-Sea, 1952)

SHCHERBATOV 1969 M. M. Shcherbatov, *On the Corruption of Morals in Russia*, trans. and ed. A. Lentin (Cambridge, 1969)

SHCHUKINA 1962 Ye. S. Shchukina, *Medal'yernoye iskusstvo v Rossii XVIII veka* (Leningrad, 1962)

SHCHUKINA 1995 Ye. S. Shchukina, 'Medali kollektsii K. F. Shrollya v sobranii Ermitazha', *Mezhdunarodnyy numizmaticheskiy al'manakh 'Moneta'* (Vologda, 1995)

SHMIDT 1908 D. A. Shmidt, 'Svedeniya iz-za granitsy', *Staryye gody* (July 1908)

SHVIDKOVSKY 1986 D. O. Shvidkovsky, 'Tsarskosel'skiy park' [The Park at Tsarskoye Selo]; 'Gorod russkogo Prosveshcheniya [Town of the Russian Enlightenment]; ''I deal'nyy gorod russkogo klassitsizma' [The Ideal Town of Russian Classicism], *Denis Didro i kul'tura yego vremeni* [Denis Diderot and the Culture of his Time] (1986)

SHVIDKOVSKY 1991 D. O. Shvidkovsky, 'Classical Edinburgh and Russian Town Planning of the Late 18th and Early 19th Centuries: The Role of William Hastie (1755–1832)', *Scottish Architects Abroad: Architectural Heritage* (Edinburgh, 1991), pp. 69–78

SHVIDKOVSKY 1992 D. Shvidkovsky, 'Architect to Three Emperors: Adam Menelas in Russia', *Apollo*, CXXXV (January 1992), pp. 36–41

SHVIDKOVSKY 1994a D. O. Shvidkovsky, 'Kameron v Italii' [Cameron in Italy], *Tezisy dokladov na konferentsii v Gosudarstvennom Ermitazhe 'Dzhakomo Kvarengi i neoklassitsizm XVIII v.'* [Outlines of Papers Presented at the Conference in the State Hermitage, 'Giacomo Quarenghi and 18th-century Neoclassicism] (St Petersburg, 1994), pp. 52–4

SHVIDKOVSKY 1994b D. O. Shvidkovsky, *Anglo-russkiye svyazi v arkhitekture vtoroy poloviny XVIII – nachala XIX stoletiya* [Anglo-Russian Links in Architecture of the Second Half of the 18th Century and Early 19th], summary of doctoral thesis (Moscow, 1994)

SHVIDKOVSKY 1996 D. O. Shvidkovsky, *The Empress and the Architect: British Architecture and Gardens at the Court of Catherine the Great* (New Haven and London, 1996)

SIVERS 1927 A. Sivers, 'Medal'er Ben'iamin Skott', *Izvestiia GAIMK*, V (1927), pp. 27–8

SLOAN 1986 K. Sloan, *Alexander and John Robert Cozens: The Poetry of Landscape* (New Haven and London, 1986)

SLOAN 1995 K. Sloan, 'A Cozens Album in the National Library of Wales, Aberystwyth', *Walpole Society*, LVII (1993–4), pp. 79–97

SMITH 1829–42 J. Smith, *A Catalogue raisonné of the Works of the Most Eminent Dutch, Flemish and French Painters* (1829–42)

SMITH 1903 H. C. Smith, 'The King's Gems and Jewels at Windsor Castle, Part III', *The Connoisseur*, nos. 5 and 6 (1903), pp. 238–44

SMITH 1929 J. T. Smith, *Nollekens and his Times*, abridged edn (London, 1929)

SNOWMAN 1990 K. A. Snowman, *Eighteenth-century Gold Boxes of Europe* (London, 1990)

SOMOV 1859 A. Somov, *Kartiny imperatorskogo Ermitazha* [Pictures in the Imperial Hermitage] (St Petersburg, 1859)

SOKOLOVA 1967 T. Sokolova, *Ocherki po istorii khudozhestvennoy mebeli XV–XIX vekov* [Studies in the history of 15th to 19th-century Artistic Furniture] (Leningrad, 1967)

SOMOV 1902 A. Somov, ed., *Imperatorskiy Ermitazh. Katalog kartinnoy galerei*, II: *Niderlandskaya i nemetskaya zhivopis* (St Petersburg, 1902)

SPRIGGE 1968 T.L.S. Sprigge, ed., *The Correspondence of Jeremy Bentham* (London, 1968)

STEPANENKO 1994 I. G. Stepanenko, 'Sadovye mastera logann i Iosif Bushi', *Study Group on Eighteenth-century Russia Newsletter*, XXII (1994)

STEWART 1965 J. D. Stewart, review of D. Green, *Grinling Gibbons* in *The Burlington Magazine*, CVII (1965), pp. 478–9

STEWART 1978 J. D. Stewart: 'New Light on Michael Rysbrack: Augustan England's Classical Baroque Sculptor', *The Burlington Magazine*, CXX (April 1978), pp. 215–22

STEWART 1983 J. D. Stewart: *Sir Godfrey Kneller and the English Baroque Portrait* (Oxford, 1983)

STONEWARES 1982 *Stonewares and Stone Chinas of Northern England to 1851*, exh. cat., City Museum and Art Gallery, Stoke-on-Trent (1982)

STRONG 1963 R. Strong, *Portraits of Queen Elizabeth I* (Oxford, 1963)

STUBBS & WEDGWOOD 1974 *Stubbs & Wedgwood: Unique Alliance between Artist and Potter*, exh. cat., Tate Gallery, London (1974)

STUKELEY 1882–7 W. Stukeley, *The Family Memoirs of the Rev. William Stukeley*, 3 vols (London, 1882–7)

SUNDERLAND 1986 J. Sunderland, 'John Hamilton Mortimer: His Life and Works', *Walpole Society*, XLI (1986), pp. 1–254

SVIN'IN 1821 *Dostopamyatnosti Sankt-Peterburga i yego okrestnostey. Sochineniye Pavla Svin'ina*, IV (St Petersburg, 1821)

SWANN 1968 H. Swann, *Home on the Neva: A Life of a British Family in Tsarist St Petersburg – and after the Revolution* (London, 1968)

SWINTON 1792 A. Swinton, *Travels into Norway, Denmark and Russia in 1788, 1789, 1790, 1791* (London, 1792)

TAIT 1971 A. A. Tait, 'The Picturesque Drawings of Robert Adam', *Master Drawings*, IX (1971), pp. 161–71

TALEPOROVSKY 1939 V. N. Taleporovsky, *Charl'z Kameron* (Moscow, 1939)

TIMOFEYEV 1974 L. N. Timofeyev, 'Romanticheskiye tendentsii v arkhitekture vtoroy poloviny XVIIIv. – pervoy poloviny XIXv.' [Romantic Tendencies in Architecture of the second half of the 19th Century], *Problemy sinteza iskusstv i arkhitektury* [Questions of the Synthesis of the Arts and Architecture], IV (Leningrad, 1974)

TINKER 1938 C. B. Tinker, *Painter and Poet: Studies in the Literary Relations of English Painting* (Cambridge, MA, 1938)

TONNOCHY 1935 A. B. Tonnochy, 'Jewels and Engraved Gems at Windsor Castle', *The Connoisseur* (1935), pp. 275–81

TOOLEY 1935 R. V. Tooley, *English Books with Coloured Plates, 1790–1860* (London, 1935)

TREASURE HOUSES 1985 *The Treasure Houses of Britain: Five Hundred Years of Private Patronage and Art Collecting*, exh. cat. ed. G. Jackson-Stops, National Gallery of Art, Washington, DC (1985)

TROYNITSKY 1912 S. N. Troynitsky, 'Vystavka Yedzhvud', *Staryye gody* (April 1912)

TROYNITSKY 1922 S. Troynitsky, *Kratkiy putevoditel' po galereye serebra* (Petrograd, 1922)

TROYNITSKY 1923a S. Troynitsky, *Angliyskoye serebro* (Petrograd, 1923)

TROYNITSKY 1923b S. Troynitsky, 'Byust Charl'za Foksa raboty Nollekensa v Ermitazhe', *Gosudarstvennyy Ermitazh. Sbornik*, no. 2 (Petrograd, 1923)

TRUBNIKOV 1912 A. A. Trubnikov, 'Popytka Dau vyvezti "Gerkulesa" Reynoldsa' [Dawe's Attempt to Remove Reynolds's 'Hercules'], *Staryye gody* (July–September 1912), pp. 158–60

TRUBNIKOV 1913 A. Trubnikov, 'Materialy po istorii tsarskikh sobraniy' [Materials for the History of the Royal Collection], *Staryye gody* (July–September 1913)

TRUBNIKOV 1914 A. Trubnikov, 'Staryye portrety starogo zamka', *Staryye gody* (July–September 1914)

TRUBNIKOV 1916 A. A. Trubnikov, 'Gravyor Skorodumov pensioner Akademii' [Engraver Skorodumov, Grantee of the Academy], *Russkii bibliofil*, no. 3 (1916)

TWITCHETT 1980 J. Twitchett, *Derby Porcelain* (London, 1980)

VAN DER FELTZ 1982 A.C.A.N. Baron van der Feltz, *Charles Howard Hodges, 1764–1837* (Assen, 1982)

VARSHAVSKAYA 1963 M. Varshavskaya, *Van Deyk. Kartiny v Ermitazhe* (Leningrad and Moscow, 1963)

VASIL'YEVA 1995 N. Ye. Vasil'yeva, 'Al'bom R. Ker Portera s risumkami drevneyshikh pamyatinkov skulptury i arkhitektury' [Porter's Album with Drawings of Ancient Sculptural and Architectural Monuments], *Ermitazhnyye chteniya 1986–94 godov pamyati V. G. Lukonina* [Hermitage Readings 1986–94 in Honour of V. G. Lukonin] (St Petersburg, 1995)

VENABLES 1839 R. Lister Venables, *Domestic Scenes in Russia: In a Series of Letters Describing a Year's Residence in that Country, chiefly in the Interior* (London, 1839)

VERGUNOV AND GOROKOV 1989 A. P. Vergunov and V. A. Gorokov, *Russkie sady i parki* [Russia's gardens and Parks] (Moscow, 1989)

VERIZHNIKOVA 1986 T. F. Verizhnikova, 'Iz istorii russko-angliiskikh zhudozhestvennykh sviazei (pensionerstvo F. I. Iordana v Anglii)', *Problemy razvitiia russkogo iskusstva 18 – pervoi poloviny veka* [Questions in the Development of Russian Art ...] (Leningrad, 1986), pp. 71–86

VERNOVA 1995a N. V. Vernova, *Khask serviz. Pervyy zakaz Yekateriny Velikoy Vedzhvudu*, State Hermitage (St Petersburg, 1995)

VERNOVA 1995b N. V. Vernova, 'Das 'Hask Service'. Die erste Bestellung an Wedgwood durch Katharona die Grosse von Russland', *1795–1995. Wedgwood. Englische Keramik in Worlitz, Staatliche Schlosser und Garten Worlitz* (1995)

VERTUE 1929–50 G. Vertue, 'Notebooks I–VI', *Walpole Society*, XVIII (1929–30) [I]; XX (1931–2) [II]; XXII (1933–4) [III]; XXIV (1935–6) [IV]; XXVI (1937–8) [V]; XXIX (1940–42) [Index to Notebooks I–V]; XXX (1948–50) [VI]

VESELOVSKY 1886 B. Veselovsky, *Kartinnaya galereya Imperatorskoy Akademii khudozhestv, III, Katalog galerei grafa N. A. Kusheleva-Beborodko* (St Petersburg, 1886)

VEY 1962 H. Vey, *Die Zeichnungen Anton van Dycks*, 2 vols (Brussels, 1962)

VIGEL' 1892 *Zapiski Filipa Filipovicha Vigelya* [Notes of Filip Filipovich Vigel'] (Moscow, 1891–2)

VIL'CHKOVSKY 1992 S. N. Vil'chkovsky, *Tsarskoye Selo*, reprint of 1911 publication (St Petersburg, 1992)

VORONIKHINA 1962 L. N. Voronikhina, *Serviz s zelyonoy lyzgushkoy* (Leningrad, 1962)

VORONIKHINA 1988 L. N. Voronikhina, 'O peyzazhakh "Serviza s zelyonoy lyagushkoy"', *Muzey*, no. 9 (1988)

VSEVOLOZHSKAYA 1981 S. Vsevolozhskaya, *Thirteenth to Eighteenth-century Italian Painting from the Hermitage Museum* (New York and Leningrad, 1981)

WAAGEN 1864 G. F. Waagen, *Die Gemaldesammlung in der Kaiserlichen Ermitage in St. Petersburg, nebst Bemerkungen uber andere dortige Kunstsammlungen* (Munich, 1864)

WALISZEWSKL 1894 R. Waliszewskl, *The Romance of an Empress: Catherine II of Russia* (London, 1894)

WALKER 1985 R. Walker, *Regency Portraits*, 2 vols (London, 1985)

WALPOLE 1752 H. Walpole, *Aedes Walpolianae, or a Description of the Collection of Pictures at Houghton Hall in Norfolk, the Seat of the Right Honourable Sir Robert Walpole, Earl of Orford*, 2nd edn (London, 1752)

WALPOLE 1862 H. Walpole: *Anecdotes of Painting in England*, 3 vols (London, 1862)

WALPOLE 1937–83 H. Walpole, *Correspondence*, 48 vols, ed. W. S. Lewis (New Haven and London)

WALTHER 1877 P.A.T. Walther, ed., *Briefweschel der grossen Landgrafin Caroline von Hessen* (Vienna, 1977)

WARD-JACKSON 1958 P. Ward-Jackson, *English Furniture Designs of the Eighteenth Century* (London, 1958)

WATERHOUSE 1941 E. K. Waterhouse, *Reynolds* (London, 1941)

WATERHOUSE 1953 E. K. Waterhouse, 'Preliminary Checklist of Portraits by Thomas Gainsborough', *Walpole Society*, XXXIII (1948–50), pp. 1–130

WATERHOUSE 1958 E. K. Waterhouse, *Gainsborough* (London, 1958)

WATERHOUSE 1981 E. K. Waterhouse, *A Dictionary of British 18th-century Painters in Oils and Crayons* (Woodbridge, 1981)

WATSON 1970 R. Watson, *Joseph Wright of Derby: A Selection of Paintings from the Collection of Mr and Mrs Paul Mellon*, exh. cat., National Gallery of Art, Washington, DC (1970)

WEBER 1723 [F. C. Weber], *The Present State of Russia* (London, 1723)

WEBSTER 1830 J. Webster, *Travels through the Crimea, Turkey and Egypt ... During the Years 1825–8* (London, 1830)

WEDGWOOD PORTRAITS 1976 *Wedgwood Portraits and the American Revolution*, exh. cat., National Portrait Gallery, Smithsonian Institution, Washington, DC (1976)

WEINER 1912 P. Veyner [Weiner], 'Sobraniye Alekseya Zakharovicha Khitrovo', *Staryye gody* (December 1912)

WEINER 1923 P. P. von Weiner, *Meisterwerke der Gemaldesammlung in der Eremitage zu Petrograd* (Munich, 1923)

WELLINGTON 1953 The Duke of Wellington, 'The Scaffold George of Charles I', *The Antiquaries Journal* (1953), pp. 159–68

WESTERN EUROPEAN DRAWING 1981 *The Hermitage Museum: Western European Drawing* (Leningrad, 1981)

WHINNEY 1971 M. D. Whinney, *English Sculpture, 1720–1830 [in the Victoria and Albert Museum]* (London, 1971)

WHITER 1989 L. Whiter, *Spode: A History of the Family Factory and Wares from 1733 to 1833* (London, 1989)

WILLIAMSON 1904 G. Williamson, 'The Collection of Pictures in the Hermitage Palace at St Petersburg', *The Connoisseur* (May 1904)

WILLIAMSON 1909 G. Williamson, *The Imperial Russian Dinner Service* (London, 1909)

WILMOT 1934 The Marchioness of Londonderry and H. M. Hyde, eds, *The Russian Journals of Martha and Catherine Wilmot* (London, 1934)

WILTON 1980 A. Wilton, *The Art of Alexander and John Robert Cozens* (New Haven, 1980)

WORLD OF ART 1902 *Mir iskusstva* [World of Art] (July 1902)

WORTMAN 1995 R. S. Wortman, *Scenarios of Power: Myth and Ceremony in Russian Monarchy* (Princeton, 1995)

WRANGEL 1913 N. Vrangel' [Wrangel], 'Iskusstvo i Imperator Nikolay Pavlovich', *Staryye gody* (June–September 1913)

YAKOVLEVA 1988 L. A. Yakovleva, 'Chasy Dzhon Ellikotta', *SGE*, LIII (1988), pp. 12–14

YOUNG 1898 *The Autobiography of Arthur Young*, ed. M. Betham-Edwards (London, 1898)

YUSUPOV 1920 *Gosudarstvennyy muzeynyy fond. Katalog khudozhestvennykh proizvedeniy byvshey Yusupovskoy galerei* (Petrograd, 1920)

ZARETSKAYA AND KOSAREVA 1960 Z. V. Zaretskaya and N. K. Kosareva, *Gosudarstvennyy Ermitazh. Zapadnoyevropeyskaya skul'ptura XV–XX vv* (Moscow and Leningrad, 1960)

ZARETSKAYA AND KOSAREVA 1970 Z. V. Zaretskaya, N. K. Kosareva, *Zapadnoyevropeyskaya skul'ptura v Ermitazhe* (Leningrad, 1970)

ZEICHNUNGEN 1910 John *Flaxman's Zeichnungen zu Tagen des Klassischen Altertums* (Leipzig, 1910)

ZHIKHAREV 1955 S. P. Zhikharev, *Zapiski sovremennika* [Notes of a Contemporary] (Moscow and Leningrad, 1955)